W9-BHW-023

BARRON'S

COOP/HSPT/ TACHS

COOPERATIVE ADMISSIONS EXAM/ HIGH SCHOOL PLACEMENT TEST/ TEST FOR ADMISSION INTO CATHOLIC HIGH SCHOOLS

4TH EDITION

Kathleen J. Elliott, M.A.
English Department Chair
Lexington Catholic High School,
Lexington, Kentucky

Carmen Geraci, M.A.
Lexington Catholic High School,
Lexington, Kentucky

David Ebner, Ph.D.
Former Mathematics Teacher
High School of Fashion Industries,
  New York, New York
New York University, New York, New York
Touro College, New York, New York

BARRON'S

© Copyright 2017, 2013, 2009 by Barron's Educational Series, Inc.

Previous edition published under the title *How to Prepare for the COOP/HSPT/TACHS,* © Copyright 2005 by Barron's Educational Series, Inc.

All rights reserved.
No part of this book may be reproduced in any form or by any means without the written permission of the copyright owner.

All inquiries should be addressed to:
Barron's Educational Series, Inc.
250 Wireless Boulevard
Hauppauge, New York 11788
www.barronseduc.com

ISBN: 978-1-4380-0867-7

ISSN 2324-7541

PRINTED IN THE UNITED STATES OF AMERICA

9 8 7 6 5 4 3 2 1

10% POST-CONSUMER WASTE
Paper contains a minimum of 10% post-consumer waste (PCW). Paper used in this book was derived from certified, sustainable forestlands.

Contents

PRACTICE EXAMS

Introduction

1

If you are reading this book, then be prepared for the legwork necessary to train yourself to achieve a high score on one of several entrance exams: the Cooperative Admissions Exam (COOP), the High School Placement Test (HSPT), or the Test for Admission into Catholic High Schools (TACHS). On these exams, students need to show their mastery of specific skills, in areas like reading comprehension, language, and mathematics. In order to demonstrate your skills, it's important to keep the following goals related to content review, study time, and test-taking abilities in mind.

First, as you probably know, you've got a mighty task ahead of you: expressing your ability to comprehend what you read, working out mathematical equations correctly, and showing your ability to use inference and deduction are crucial to doing well on the test that you will take. You will have to prepare for these topics through review and plenty of practice. Next, you should know that setting aside time to acquire, review, and practice the skills on which you'll be tested is vital. Between daily life and extracurricular activities, like sports or community service, this can be a lot harder than it sounds. Make sure to give yourself enough time for review and practice. Finally, and perhaps most importantly, it's not just what you know that counts—it's how well you *prove* what you know that is important in these types of exams. Exams like the one facing you evaluate both your intellectual ability *and* your ability to take standardized tests. For this reason, you will also need to learn how to optimize test-taking skills, like pacing and making educated guesses. Overall, while studying for the exam, be prepared to meet these two challenges: proving you've got the intellectual ability and proving you can stand up to the pressure of standardized testing.

We at Barron's have designed this book to accommodate all students who find themselves faced with the trial of standardized exams—students who may have studied for months as well as students who have yet to crack a book. If you have had the foresight and the self-discipline to begin preparations for your high school placement exam well in advance, congratulations! Barron's *COOP/HSPT/TACHS* is designed to reinforce the skills you already possess with plenty of practice sections and thoroughly explained answer keys. If, conversely, you have purchased this book hoping for last minute tips on acing the exam, rest assured! This book comes to you chock full of study tips, elimination strategies, and information about each exam format—information that is sure to help you succeed. Moreover, this book offers numerous and varied practice selections designed to make you comfortable with the testing format, requirements, and pacing.

Now, we know that you want to get right to work. However, we would like to take a minute to thank you for purchasing this book. We strongly believe that our preparation guide to these exams is the best on the market, and we hope that, by the time you finish using this guide, you will feel prepared to succeed when you take the exam. This book offers all the information about the exam you are preparing to take, opportunities for further practice, and thoroughly researched answer key explanations. You have in your hands the best tool for "doing it right."

So let's get started!

COOP VS. HSPT VS. TACHS

The COOP and the HSPT are the main two entrance exams for Catholic high schools. The TACHS is a relatively new arrival to the academic prep scene. By contrast, the ISEE (Independent Schools Entrance Exam) and the SSAT (Secondary Schools Admissions Test) are the main two entrance exams for other private high schools.

The COOP, the HSPT, and the TACHS assess your mastery of essential verbal and analytical skills. You must prove you have a good grounding in vocabulary and an ability to identify main ideas; similarly you must demonstrate prowess in logic and mathematical computation. Regardless of the method used to test or the phrasing of the questions involved, both tests focus on the same skills.

You should be aware, however, that the COOP, the HSPT, and the TACHS vary significantly in their organization and in their phrasing of test questions. Make sure to familiarize yourself with the specific information regarding the exam you will take. The chart on page 3 gives a quick overview of the three exams.

IMPORTANT REMINDER

Be sure to check each test's official website for the most up-to-date information about test dates, testing locations, costs involved, and other specifics.

This book gives you many details regarding these three tests. Naturally, you'll want to investigate in much greater detail before you take any exam. Read the discussion of the testing formats of the COOP (beginning on page 3), the HSPT (beginning on page 4), and the TACHS (beginning on page 5) later in this introduction. We give an overview of each exam and discuss the theory on which the exams are based (especially what they test and how they test it). Also, don't forget the practice tests (two for the COOP, two for the HSPT, and two for the TACHS). Finally, if you have more questions regarding the COOP, the HSPT, or the TACHS, you can contact the companies directly.

COOP
Cooperative Admissions
Examination Office
4603 Middle Country Road
Calverton, NY 11933
(888) 921-COOP (2667)
Email: *support@coopexam.org*
www.coopexam.org

HSPT
Scholastic Testing Service
480 Meyer Road
Bensenville, IL 60106
(800) 642-6STS (6787)
Email: *sts@ststesting.com*
www.ststesting.com

TACHS
Houghton Mifflin Harcourt
Publishing Company
9400 Southpark Center Loop
Orlando, FL 32819
(866) 61T-ACHS (618-2247)
www.tachsinfo.com

Comparison of COOP, HSPT, and TACHS

COOP	
Sequences (see Chapter 2)	20 questions/15 minutes
Analogies (see Chapter 2)	20 questions/7 minutes
Quantitative Reasoning (see Chapter 2)	20 questions/5 minutes
Verbal Reasoning (Words) (see Chapter 3)	20 questions/15 minutes
Verbal Reasoning (Context) (see Chapter 3)	10 questions/7 minutes
Reading and Language Arts (see Chapters 4 and 5)	40 questions/40 minutes
Mathematics (see Chapter 2)	40 questions/35 minutes
HSPT	
Verbal (see Chapter 3)	60 questions/16 minutes
Quantitative (see Chapter 2)	52 questions/30 minutes
Reading (see Chapters 3 and 5)	62 questions/25 minutes
Mathematics (see Chapter 2)	64 questions/45 minutes
Language (see Chapter 4)	60 questions/25 minutes
TACHS	
Reading (see Chapter 5)	50 questions/35 minutes
Written Expression (see Chapter 4)	50 questions/30 minutes
Math (see Chapter 2)	50 questions/40 minutes
Ability (see Chapter 2)	60 questions/32 minutes

THE COOP (COOPERATIVE ADMISSIONS EXAM)

Many dioceses require the COOP exam, which is given only once per year in either October or November. Exam applicants must preregister for the COOP, either through their parochial elementary schools or via applications distributed by parochial high schools. Applicants for the COOP can take the exam only one time. Test takers may list up to three high schools they hope to attend (identified by the appropriate identification codes and numbers) on their COOP testing application.

The COOP, a multiple-choice exam, tests *what you have learned* as well as *how you learn*. The exam consists of testing sessions that last approximately 3 hours including test breaks. Questions are typically arranged in order of difficulty, and the exam does not penalize guessing. You are allowed to write in the test booklet only.

The COOP tests seven basic academic skills: Sequences, Analogies, Quantitative Reasoning, Verbal Reasoning (Words), Verbal Reasoning (Context), Reading and Language Arts, and Mathematics. Different sections test different skills, but the exam follows a clear, theoretical logic. For example, the tests on Sequences, Analogies, and Quantitative Reasoning all focus more on judging how well you process new information and detect patterns; by contrast, the Reading and Language Arts and Mathematics tests both focus more on judging how well you remember information learned in school or from other sources. The Verbal Reasoning tests judge your ability to process new information using previously learned techniques, forming a bridge between the two sections.

Visual learners may find the first three tests particularly manageable; these three tests primarily ask you to locate patterns. The Sequences test, for example, gives sets of figures, numbers, or letters in a pattern; you must identify the pattern and be able to supply the next figure, number, or letter that continues that pattern. Similarly, the Analogies test assesses your ability to locate patterns using pictures. These questions present you with a question grid that is divided into quadrants and into which are set three pictures; your task is to select the picture that best complements the three originally presented pictures. Finally, like the preceding sections, the Quantitative Reasoning section also asks you to detect patterns; you may be given a series of numbers or figures with shaded areas and be asked to locate the pattern within. To find out more specifically how these questions work, check out Chapter 2, which gives examples that you can work through.

As we said before, the Verbal Reasoning sections bridge the gap between your ability to reason and to remember formal classroom instruction. The Verbal Reasoning tests require you to (1) identify essential features of objects, (2) find logical relationships between sets of words, or (3) draw logical conclusions from facts presented. For practice on all the various types of questions that belong in the Verbal Reasoning sections, go to Chapter 3.

The Reading and Language Arts test, conversely, focuses more on determining how well your long-term memory functions than the previous tests do; this test gauges your ability to judge proper English usage as you have learned it in school. Here a large vocabulary—as well as an ability to read quickly and for detail—saves the day. This portion of the COOP also tests many skills through coordinated testing exercises. For starters, you will be given various reading passages and asked to identify elements such as the main idea of the passage or the definition of a word based on its usage in the selection. In addition to being asked to show that you understand what you read, you also may be asked, for example, to show your ability to apply the rules of capitalization and punctuation to standard written English. You should be able to read sentences or entire paragraphs and state whether one or none of the statements have a capitalization or punctuation error. The Reading and Language Arts section of the COOP tests your reading comprehension and language usage skills thoroughly. Be sure to practice. We suggest you test yourself on other practice problems in Chapters 4 and 5.

The exam ends with a Mathematics test. It asks you to compute answers to mathematical questions involving mixed numbers, fractions, decimals, percents, and integers. Go to Chapter 2 for further practice, and remember that, like the reading comprehension sections, the mathematics section requires you to utilize information learned in school and other formal educational sources.

THE HSPT (HIGH SCHOOL PLACEMENT TEST)

The HSPT's testing time and location can be set by individual schools and districts in cooperation with the Scholastic Testing Service; the best way to determine when and where the HSPT will be administered is to check with your guidance counselor or high school admission's office. Check for other application requirements that might apply to your situation; high schools that use the HSPT usually consider HSPT test scores as only part of the requirements for admission.

The HSPT is a multiple-choice exam designed to test what you *have learned* as well as *how you learn*. The exam consists of testing sessions that last approximately 2.5 hours. The exam does not penalize guessing. Test takers are allowed to write in the test booklet and will also be given scratch paper at the testing site. The HSPT often includes optional sections; whether you will have to take any or all of these optional sections will be determined by your desired school; at a minimum, you must take the five required sections of the HSPT.

The HSPT tests academic skills using five different testing sections: Verbal, Quantitative, Reading, Mathematics, and Language. The HSPT alternates between testing your ability to reason out answers and your ability to retain information learned in your classes. The Verbal and Reading sections of the exam, for example, focus more on your ability to react to stimuli presented during the exam (word sequences or on-demand reading passages); conversely, the Quantitative, Mathematics, and Language portions all focus on judging your mastery of skills learned in class.

The Verbal portion of the HSPT focuses on five specific types of questions: (1) synonyms, (2) antonyms, (3) analogies, (4) logic, and (5) verbal classification; this test targets your ability to detect patterns and relationships among elements of speech. While the term "Verbal Classification" sounds tricky, the actual test is not; it merely asks you to determine which word out of a series of four does or does not belong in a given sequence of words. For practice, see Chapter 3.

The HSPT then shifts to assessing your quantitative skills. The Quantitative section of the exam focuses on your ability to work with number series, geometric comparison, nongeometric comparison, and number manipulation. For practice on the kinds of questions you'll encounter, turn to Chapter 2.

The Reading part of the HSPT attempts to judge how well you comprehend what you read and your ability to infer vocabulary meaning. The first part of this section asks you to read and interpret literary passages. While, naturally, you are called upon to use your reading skills, the test assesses how well you understand what you read. The second part of this section tests your knowledge of vocabulary. For practice, see Chapters 3 and 5.

The HSPT then focuses again on Mathematics, in particular concepts and problem solving. This portion of the exam tests your problem-solving abilities and your ability to use previous knowledge of mathematic concepts to solve modern problems. For practice, see Chapter 2.

Finally, the HSPT ends with a test of your Language skills; you will be given questions that test your understanding of writing mechanics, capitalization, punctuation, usage, spelling, thought expression, and sentence order. For practice, see Chapter 4.

THE TACHS (TEST FOR ADMISSION INTO CATHOLIC HIGH SCHOOLS)

TACHS testing occurs only in November of the application school year and only for students interested in attending high schools located in the Diocese of Brooklyn/Queens and Archdiocese of New York. If in doubt or if concerned about unexpected changes to the norm, check the online TACHS handbook (at *www.tachsinfo.com*) or check with your guidance counselor or high school admissions office.

The TACHS is a multiple-choice exam designed to test *what you have learned* as well as *how you learn*. The test runs for an approximate 3-hour testing period including test breaks. Testing does not stop for official breaks and pauses only long enough for new directions to be given. Arrangements can be made for extended testing times for special-needs cases; special requests must be made by October of the testing year, and an IEP must be on hand for such a request to be considered. (For more details, check the online TACHS handbook.) The exam does not penalize guessing. Test takers are not allowed to bring any type of electronic or battery-operated devices, such as calculators, watches, or cell phones. Scratch paper, food, and beverages are also not allowed.

The TACHS tests basic academic skills using four testing rounds: Reading (Vocabulary and Comprehension), Written Expression (Spelling, Capitalization, Punctuation, Usage, and Paragraphs), Math (Concepts, Data Interpretation, and Problem Solving and Estimation), and Ability (Similarities and Changes, and Abstract Reasoning). The TACHS alternates between testing your ability to retain information learned in school and testing your ability to reason out answers spontaneously. The Reading, Written Expression, and Math portions of the exam, for example, generally focus on testing your retained knowledge; the Ability portions generally test your ability to respond to stimuli.

The TACHS begins by evaluating your ability to understand what you read. Part 1 of the Reading portion targets your vocabulary skills. You will be given a phrase in which a word has been highlighted, and you will be asked to define this word on the basis of its context. This part of the exam most commonly asks questions about nouns, verbs, and modifier usage. Part 2 of the Reading section tests your ability to comprehend what you read. The TACHS will offer a wide variety of reading passages, drawn from fiction (such as fables, fairy tales, and poetry) and nonfiction (interviews, diaries, biographies, science, and social studies) sources. Although some questions will involve merely recalling facts from your reading, you will more often be asked to draw inferences and make generalizations based on what you have read. For practice on this part of the TACHS, see Chapter 5.

The Written Expression section of the TACHS, unlike its sister exams, focuses on determining how well you've internalized what you've learned in school. The TACHS prioritizes spelling, capitalization, punctuation, and usage and expression. Moreover, you'll be asked to choose the most logical organization of a paragraph. The TACHS will determine your abilities in these areas through a series of four short tests. These topics are all covered in the Language Arts section (Chapter 4 of this book).

TACHS then assesses your Math skills through two separately timed testing sections. First, you'll be asked to perform short, simple arithmetic calculations, reading problems, and graphs, followed by a section that asks you to do problems in estimation. For practice on this portion, see Chapter 2.

The TACHS concludes with a testing portion on Ability. You'll be asked to show your abstract reasoning ability by determining geometric relationships between figures and manipulating geometric figures mentally. For practice on this portion, see Chapter 2.

COUNTDOWN TO TEST DAY

Now, it's time to face facts. You may be frustrated if you plan to pick up enough of the skills necessary to ace an exam like the COOP, the HSPT, or the TACHS on the fly. Mastering these exams most usually comes as the result of hard, consistent work rather than quick attempts to marshal one's wits. Moreover, the usual method of gauging your progress is not available to you in this case; the COOP, the HSPT, and the TACHS do not publish scores achieved on their exams. Therefore, unlike with other standardized tests, you cannot take a practice exam and expect to rank yourself against other entering high school students across the nation. We've said it before, and we'll say it again: your best method for preparing yourself for the COOP, the HSPT, or the TACHS is a great deal of basic skills preparation.

Simply put, some skills get better through consistent use. Verbal ability is one such skill. The more you read, the more you encounter verbal skills tested on exams such as the COOP, the HSPT, or the TACHS. Analytical ability is another such skill; making comparisons, detecting contrasts, analyzing theme and main idea patterns are all skills that grow sharper with use. The best way to prepare for an exam—and reduce test anxiety—is to cultivate an appreciation for all things intellectual.

This isn't as hard as it sounds; after all, you have been preparing for tests like these for the past eight years in class. Besides, cultivating an appreciation for learning outside of class does not have to be tedious. You can find creative and fun ways to incorporate intellectual activity in your life.

First . . . Read! Read! Read! Both the COOP and the HSPT, for example, use reading passages ranging from four to six paragraphs long; moreover, both use primarily an informative, newsy writing style. Select short passages from weekly news magazines or the topical parts of your local newspapers (e.g., the weekly "science" section or the daily "living and arts" sections), and accustom yourself to identifying the author's intent in writing, the main points of the passage, and the meaning of unfamiliar vocabulary. Also try out the vocabulary-based puzzles commonly found in local newspapers; games like Scrabble or word jumbles are also great for building familiarity with vocabulary while still having fun. Incorporating clever ways to trick yourself into studying verbal skills, therefore, is a snap—you just have to look for them.

For fun yet useful mathematics skills, try working through books of logic puzzles, word problems, brain teasers, and number games either from your local library or local bookstores. The Internet is a good tool, too. Many companies publish free, online IQ assessment tests that are fun to do, quick to assess, and good for limbering up mental muscles.

Probably the second best way to prepare for an exam is to allow yourself sufficient time to sit down and review useful details such as how the exam is designed and topics covered by the exam. Purchasing a preparation guide is a step in a positive direction. We suggest that you maximize your chance of success by following the suggestions we make in the chart entitled "Acing the Exam with 1 Month to Go"; in this chart, we outline a thorough but comfortably paced course of study.

Now, following the "1 Month to Go" chart requires that you devote a month's preparation to your task. It may be that devoting four weeks of preparation to a project is simply not an affordable luxury for you. Relax. Just because it is difficult to master an exam by cramming does not mean that it cannot be done; just because cramming does not provide you with the long-term results that slower paced studying does, does not mean that it should not be done. Look at the chart entitled "Acing the Exam with 1 Week to Go," in which we offer a more streamlined but more challenging "quick study" program. You will need to have both the time and the drive to really focus your studying energies; you will be working "on a deadline." Either chart should assist you greatly in your quest for a high exam score.

4 WEEKS AND COUNTING . . .

☐ **Re-read the introduction:** COOP on page 3, HSPT on page 4, TACHS on page 5. These sections will give you a sense of the kinds of questions you'll face and the strategies you should use.

☐ **Take a practice exam** and score yourself.

☐ **Identify the subjects and types of questions that most troubled you;** refer to the answer explanations as a guide.

☐ **Study the topics that you're unsure of.**

☐ **Work through all the practice sessions.**

☐ **Read the answer explanations;** they'll help you understand the logic behind the questions and their answers.

☐ **English Bonus Tip: Work through the word list provided in Chapter 3.** The best way to learn new words is to think about them, define them, and use them in sentences.

☐ **Ask for help** when you need it.

3 WEEKS TO GO

☐ **Study the chapters that discuss topics that least troubled you. Work through all of the practice sessions.**

☐ **Read the answer explanations;** they'll help you understand the logic behind the questions.

☐ **Review the word list from Chapter 3.** Skip the ones you know well, and focus on the ones you don't.

☐ **Trick yourself into studying**—do crossword puzzles, attempt some riddles, take an IQ test online, try your hand at logical conundrums. Read! Read! Read!

2 WEEKS LEFT

☐ **Review once more the material that really troubled you.**

☐ **Retake your first practice exam,** focusing on the questions you missed.

☐ **Ask for help** when you need it.

1 WEEK

☐ **Take a second practice exam** and compare your results. You will likely see improvement—provided you have stuck to your program!

☐ **Review any areas that remain weak.**

☐ **Read through the answer explanations.**

DAY BEFORE—TIME OUT!

☐ **Give yourself a break.** Do not study. Do something relaxing, like watching a movie or going out with friends.

☐ **Get to bed at a reasonable hour;** no prep can help if you are exhausted and nervous.

7 DAYS

☐ **Re-read the introduction:** COOP on page 3, HSPT on page 4, TACHS on page 5. These sections will give you a sense of the kinds of questions you'll face and the strategies you should use.

☐ **Take a practice exam** and score yourself.

☐ **Note particularly troublesome topics.**

☐ **Consider talking with your teacher(s)** regarding trouble spots. Teachers are your best resource.

6 DAYS

☐ **Identify the types of questions that troubled you the most**; use the answer explanations to help you better understand these questions.

☐ **Study the topics that troubled you the most.**

☐ **Work through all of the practice sessions.**

☐ **Read the answer explanations**; they'll help you understand the logic behind the question.

5 DAYS

☐ **Study the chapters that discuss topics that troubled you.**

☐ **Work through all of the practice sessions.**

☐ **Read the answer explanations.**

4 DAYS

☐ **Talk (again) with your teacher(s) at school** if you still need help; they are your best resource for help. Perhaps they can suggest helpful study tips or mnemonic devices.

3 DAYS

☐ **Review any stubborn trouble spots**; extra work can't hurt.

☐ **English Bonus Tip: study the word list in Chapter 3.** Skip the words you know, but define and think about the ones you don't. The only way to expand your knowledge of words is to incorporate new words into your working vocabulary. Learn—and use—them.

2 DAYS

☐ **Take a second practice exam** and compare your results. You will likely have improved!

☐ **Read the answer explanations.**

☐ **Review any areas that remain weak.**

DAY BEFORE—TIME OUT!

☐ **Give yourself a break.** Do not study. Do something relaxing, like watching a movie or going out with friends and family.

☐ **Get to bed at a reasonable hour**; no prep can help if you are exhausted and nervous.

HELPFUL ADVICE

No matter your level of test preparation, you run a risk of experiencing test-taking anxieties prior to the exam. In this section, we offer a series of anxiety-reducing tips that we hope will help you do your best on the exam. Some of the suggestions require long-term practice before one can see results; however, all are good advice.

GET FIT. People who exercise handle stress better than people who do not. Get in the habit of following a reasonable, sustainable exercise regimen.

GET REST. Recent studies show that people, especially men, who do not get regular, adequate sleep run a greater risk of developing psychoses than those who do. Your brain and body need sleep; give them adequate rest.

GET PACKED. Gather together all the items you will need prior to testing day so that they are ready to bring on testing day. We suggest you bring the following: admission ticket, three or four No. 2 (or equivalent) lead pencils, an eraser, a pen, and a sweater or light jacket (in case of a cold room).

GET FED. Taking tests on an empty stomach—or fueled by the empty carbohydrates in a donut or candy bar—is a sure-fire mistake. Your body needs a constant source of energy—not the roller coaster ride such foods contain. At the very least, drink a big glass of milk.

GET THERE. Make sure that you know where your testing site is and how long it takes to get there. Arrive at your testing site a little early. Late arrivals will not be admitted to the testing site.

GET PSYCHED! Remind yourself that you are prepared for your exam. Relax. Breathe. Concentrate.

GET FOCUSED. Follow the directions exactly as they are asked. Record your answers clearly and accurately, filling in the circles on the answer grid completely. Erase any changes completely (or else the answering machine may score your erasures as answers). Pace yourself. If in doubt, guess because there is no penalty!

IN SUMMARY

You have now finished the introductory section of this study guide. You should have a sense of your task and a sense of how you will master it. Now is the time to begin your study session, probably by taking your first practice exam.

Take a deep breath and plunge in. You'll do fine!

Good luck!

Summary of COOP, HSPT, and TACHS

	COOP	HSPT	TACHS
Type of exam	Multiple-Choice	Multiple-Choice	Multiple-Choice
When should students take the exam?	In the eighth grade	In the eighth grade	In the eighth grade
Who should apply for the exam?	Students seeking admission to Catholic high schools.	Students seeking admission to Catholic high schools.	Students seeking admission to Catholic high schools.
Which subjects are tested?	Language, Reading, Mathematics	Language, Reading, Mathematics	Language, Reading, Mathematics, Ability
When is the exam given?	Once in the Fall	Depends on the school; most schools offer the test in the Fall, but some offer it in early Spring.	November
Where may I obtain forms and register for the exam?	From the parochial high school you are interested in attending or from your own parochial school	From the parochial high school you are interested in attending or from your own parochial school	From the parochial high school you are interested in attending or from your own parochial school
Is the exam the same every year?	No, the exam changes to some extent; however, this book can prepare you for the exam.	No, the exam changes to some extent; however, this book can prepare you for the exam.	No, the exam changes to some extent; however, this book can prepare you for the exam.
What purpose(s) other than admission to Catholic high schools does the exam serve?	The test is used for placing students into specific courses and levels.	The test is used for placing students into specific courses and levels. Each test taker is compared to other students taking the exam, both locally and on a national level.	The test is used for placing students into specific courses and levels.
How often may I take the exam?	Only once.	This is determined by each individual school.	Only once.
Who develops the exam, and where may I obtain further information?	Cooperative Admissions Examination Office 4603 Middle Country Road Calverton, NY 11933 Phone: 888-921-COOP (2667) Email: support@coopexam.org www.coopexam.org	Scholastic Testing Service 480 Meyer Road Bensenville, IL 60106 Phone: 800-642-6STS (6787); Email: sts@ststesting.com www.ststesting.com	Houghton Mifflin Harcourt Publishing Company 9400 Southpark Center Loop Orlando, FL 32819 Phone: 866-61T-ACHS (618-2247) www.tachsinfo.com
What is the registration fee?	$60	This is determined by each individual school.	$63
Should I guess answers or leave blanks?	Your score is based on the number of correct answers, so there is no penalty for incorrect answers. Guess.	Your score is based on the number of correct answers, so there is no penalty for incorrect answers. Guess.	Your score is based on the number of correct answers, so there is no penalty for incorrect answers. Guess.

	COOP	HSPT	TACHS
What are the various sections of the exam?	**Sequences**—Spatial relations, patterns, and sequences of numbers, letters, and figures **Analogies**—Relationships among pictures **Quantitative Reasoning**—Interpretations of pictures into Mathematics **Verbal Reasoning: Words**—Relationships between words and deductive reasoning **Verbal Reasoning: Context**—Deduce meaning from contexts **Reading and Language Arts**—Concepts presented in short selections **Mathematics**—General concepts as well as specific skills in algebra, geometry, arithmetic, and probability	**Verbal**—Antonyms, synonyms, analogies, logic, verbal classification **Quantitative**—Number manipulation, geometric comparisons, nongeometric comparisons, number series **Reading**—Vocabulary, comprehension **Mathematics**—Concepts, problem solving **Language**—Punctuation, capitalization, usage, spelling, composition	**Reading (Vocabulary)**—Identifying vocabulary within the context of sentences and phrases; equal testing of nouns, verbs, modifiers **Reading (Comprehension)**—Understanding what is read, including the ability to draw inferences; texts drawn from biographical sketches, fiction, poetry, social science, sciences, and other nonfiction **Written Expression (Spelling, Capitalization, Punctuation, Usage)**—Showing one has the ability to understand sentence and paragraph structure; specifically tests spelling, capitalization, and punctuation, but also other grammar issues **Written Expression (Paragraphs)**—Tests one's ability to evaluate writing; specifically asks the student to evaluate a text in terms of conciseness, clarity, and organization **Math (Concepts, Data Interpretation, Problem Solving and Estimation)**—Specifically addresses concepts like number relations, problem solving, and data interpretations (e.g., graphs)

Summary of COOP, HSPT, and TACHS (continued)

	COOP	HSPT	TACHS
What are the various sections of the exam? (continued)			**Ability (Similarities and Changes)**—Specifically tests the ability to deal with abstract reasoning, detection of patterns, and visual sequences **Ability (Abstract Reasoning)**—Specifically tests the ability to understand abstract reasoning, patterns, and problem solving; much like the prior section, except without the emphasis on visuals
Are there any optional parts on the exam?	No	Yes. Some high schools may ask you to take one additional test in the Catholic Religion, Mechanical Aptitude, or Science; however, any score on this optional part is not included in the total score on the exam.	No
Is there any passing or failing grade on the exam?	No, each school has its own standards for admission.	No, each school has its own standards for admission.	No, each school has its own standards for admission.
May I use a calculator?	No.	No.	No.

Be sure to check the official test websites for the most up-to-date information regarding fees, addresses, and possible changes to the exams.

Mathematics

2

The mathematics review covers the basic skills necessary for the exams.

INTEGERS

Natural and Whole Numbers

The first numbers developed by primitive peoples were the **natural** or **counting numbers**, such as 1, 2, 3, 4, 5, ...

It's usually more useful to describe a collection of similar items by using "set" notation. In the example, the set of natural or counting numbers may be indicated by {1, 2, 3, 4, 5, . . .}.

A zero was later added to introduce the set of **whole numbers**: {0, 1, 2, 3, 4, 5, . . .}.

This set may be represented on the number line:

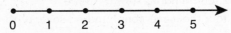

In our number system, the **place** of the digit determines its value. For example, let's take a close look at the following whole number.

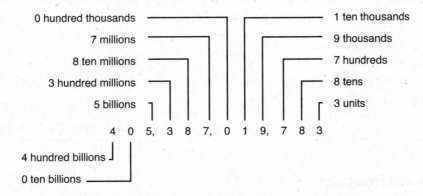

Altogether, the number reads four hundred five billion, three hundred eighty-seven million, nineteen thousand, seven hundred eighty-three.

➡ Example 1 _____

Change 456,372 into words.

Answer: Four hundred fifty-six thousand, three hundred seventy-two.

➡ Example 2 _____

Change "Thirty-six billion, four hundred seventy-nine million, five hundred eighteen thousand, four hundred twenty-six" into numerals.

Answer: 36,479,518,426.

NATURAL AND WHOLE NUMBERS PRACTICE

1. What does the digit 4 represent in the number 456,695,098?

   (A) hundreds
   (B) thousands
   (C) ten thousands
   (D) hundred millions

2. Change 304,473 into words.

   (A) thirty thousand, four hundred seventy-three
   (B) three hundred four thousand, four hundred seventy-three
   (C) thirty four thousand, four hundred seventy-three
   (D) three thousand, four hundred seventy-three

3. Change "Eight hundred fifty-three million, four hundred thirty-two thousand, five hundred sixty-four" into numerals.

   (A) 853,432,000
   (B) 853,564
   (C) 853,432,564
   (D) 8,534,325,640

(See page 100 for answers.)

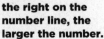

VOCABULARY

Throughout this book, key vocabulary words appear in sidebars. Read the word, its definition, and in some instances a silly sentence that follows. If you write the word in the margin, you'll remember the word more easily.

TIP

The farther to the right on the number line, the larger the number.

Comparing Integers

Negative integers (–1, –2, –3, . . .) were added to the whole numbers, so that we arrived at the set of integers (. . . , –3, –2, –1, 0, 1, 2, 3, . . .)

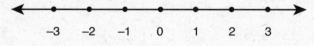

⇒ Example 1 _____

Using the inequality symbol > (greater than), compare 3 and –8.

Answer: 3 > –8

The integer on the left is larger. If necessary, draw the number line.

3 > –8 (3 is greater than –8)

–8   0   3

⇒ Example 2 _____

Use the inequality symbol < (less than) to compare 6 and 0.

Answer: 0 < 6

The integer on the left is the smaller.

0 < 6 (0 is less than 6)

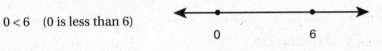

0   6

⇒ Example 3 _____

Order the numbers 5, –1, and –2, from **smallest to largest**.

Answer: –2 < –1 < 5

Draw the number line. The farther to the left, the smaller the number.

–2 < –1 < 5 (–2 is less than –1, which is less than 5)

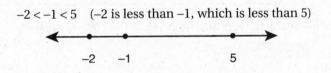

–2   –1   5

COMPARING INTEGERS PRACTICE

1. Use the inequality symbol > to compare 2, 0, and –2.

   (A) –2 > 2 > 0
   (B) 2 > –2 > 0
   (C) 0 > –2 > 2
   (D) 2 > 0 > –2

2. Use the inequality symbol < to compare –5, 3, and –8.

   (A) –8 < –5 < 3
   (B) –8 < 3 < –5
   (C) 3 < –8 < –5
   (D) –5 < –8 < 3

3. Order the numbers 6, –2, and 0, from largest to smallest.

   (A) 0 > –2 > 6
   (B) 6 < –2 < 0
   (C) 6 > –2 > 0
   (D) 6 > 0 > –2

4. Order the numbers –3, 4, and –1, from smallest to largest.

   (A) –1 < 4 < –3
   (B) –3 < –1 < 4
   (C) –1 > 4 > –3
   (D) 4 < –1 < –3

(See page 100 for answers.)

VOCABULARY

The prefix *ex-* means *out* or *from.* The word *expound* literally means "to put outside" (like an exponent), but it more commonly means "to explain."

The successful dieter tastefully expounded the reasons for his ex-pounds.

Exponents

Mathematicians have developed special shorthand notations. One of these very important notations is the exponential notation.

The following products are more conveniently indicated using exponents:

$$6 \cdot 6 = 6^2 \text{ (or 36)}$$
$$5 \cdot 5 \cdot 5 = 5^3 \text{ (or 125)}$$
$$3 \cdot 3 \cdot 3 \cdot 3 = 3^4 \text{ (or 81)}$$
$$a \cdot a = a^2$$
$$b \cdot b \cdot b \cdot b \cdot b = b^5$$

3 is the exponent

Let's get technical: $4^3 = 64$ ◄——— The power is 64

4 is the base

➥ Example 1 _____

What does $5 \cdot 4^3$ simplify to?

Answer: 320

Simplify 4^3 and then multiply by 5.

$$5 \cdot 4^3 = 5 \cdot 4 \cdot 4 \cdot 4 = 5 \cdot 64 = 320$$

➥ Example 2 _____

Simplify the following powers and then select the correct answer.

(*a*) 5^2 (*b*) 2^5 (*c*) 2^3

(A) $a > b$ or $c > a$
(B) $c = a$ or $b < c$
(C) $c > b$ and $a = b$
(D) $b < a$ or $c < b$

Answer: (D)

Simplify each expression and then substitute.

(*a*) $5^2 = 5 \cdot 5 = 25$
(*b*) $2^5 = 2 \cdot 2 \cdot 2 \cdot 2 \cdot 2 = 32$
(*c*) $2^3 = 2 \cdot 2 \cdot 2 = 8$

(D) $b < a$ or $c < b$
$32 < 25$ or $8 < 32$ ✔

➡️ **Example 3**_____

 Simplify $5^2 - 6 \cdot 3^0$.

Answer: 19

Any base raised to a zero exponent is equal to 1.

$$5^2 - 6 \cdot 3^0$$
$$5 \cdot 5 - 6 \cdot 1$$
$$25 - 6$$
$$19$$

EXPONENTS PRACTICE

1. Simplify $2 \cdot 4^3$

    (A) 128
    (B) 64
    (C) 156
    (D) 32

2. What does $5^2 \cdot 2^4$ simplify to?

    (A) 200
    (B) 400
    (C) 80
    (D) 150

3. Simplify the following powers and then select the best answer.

    (a) 6^2 (b) 3^3 (c) 4^3

    (A) $a < c$ and $b > a$
    (B) $c > b$ or $a > b$
    (C) $a > b$ and $b > c$
    (D) $b > c$ or $c < a$

    (See page 100 for answers.)

Order of Operations

Ordinarily, we perform arithmetic operations from **left to right**, with **multiplication and division preceding addition and subtraction**.

 If there are parentheses in an expression, the operations inside the parentheses are performed first.

$$(7 + 5) \cdot 3 = (12) \cdot 3 = 36$$
$$480 \div 6 - 3(4 + 6) = 80 - 3(10) = 80 - 30 = 50$$

➡️ **Example**_____

 Simplify the expression $3 \cdot 4^2 - 48 \div 6 + 2(9 - 4)$.

Answer: 50

Simplify the exponential expression as well as the expression in parentheses first. Then multiply and divide, working from left to right. Finally, add and subtract, working from left to right.

$$3 \cdot 4^2 - 48 \div 6 + 2(9 - 4)$$
$$3 \cdot 16 - (48 \div 6) + 2(5)$$
$$48 - 8 + 10$$
$$40 + 10$$
$$50$$

ORDER OF OPERATIONS PRACTICE

Directions: Simplify the expressions.

1. $5^2 - 4 \cdot 3 + 28 - 4$

    (A) 10
    (B) 40
    (C) 36
    (D) 20

2. $64 - 3^3 + 6 \cdot 2$

    (A) 49
    (B) 38
    (C) 43
    (D) 122

3. $5(-3) + (6 - 1)^2$

    (A) 15
    (B) 40
    (C) 10
    (D) -10

4. $9^1 \cdot (-2)^3$

    (A) -27
    (B) 36
    (C) -72
    (D) 27

(See page 100 for answers.)

Rounding Off Integers

Sometimes we want to get an approximation of a number. In these cases, we don't need an exact answer, so we "round off."

Aunt Rita is the cashier at a local restaurant. At the end of the week, she wants to round off the money in the till to the nearest ten dollars. If $6,384 is in the till, how much is that, to the nearest $10?

When we round off to the nearest ten's place, we look at the units place first. If the units digit is 5 or more, we round the tens digit up one unit. On the other hand, if the units digit is less than 5, we leave the tens digit alone.

$$6 \quad 3 \quad 8 \quad 4$$
$$\uparrow$$

units place: 4 < 5

$6,384 rounds off to $6,380

ROUNDING OFF INTEGERS PRACTICE

1. Round off 456 to the nearest ten.

   (A) 450
   (B) 400
   (C) 500
   (D) 460

2. Round off 5,678 to the nearest hundred.

   (A) 6,000
   (B) 5,600
   (C) 5,700
   (D) 5,800

3. Find the difference between 153 rounded off to the nearest hundred and 153 rounded off to the nearest ten.

   (A) 50
   (B) 40
   (C) 60
   (D) 47

4. What is the sum of 783 rounded off to the nearest 100 and 437 rounded off to the nearest ten?

   (A) 1,240
   (B) 1,140
   (C) 2,350
   (D) 1,400

(See page 100 for answers.)

Prime Numbers

A prime number is a counting number that can only be divided by 1 and itself without resulting in a remainder. The number 1 is excluded from the set of prime numbers.

The prime numbers less than 20 are 2, 3, 5, 7, 11, 13, 17, and 19.

➡ **Example 1** _____

Is 48 a prime number?

Answer: 48 is not a prime number.

If 48 can be divided by any number other than 1, it is not a prime number.

48 may be divided by 6: $48 \div 6 = 8$.

➡ **Example 2** _____

Which of these numbers is prime?

(A) 17
(B) 18
(C) 22
(D) 35

Answer: (A)

A prime number cannot be divided by any number other than 1 and itself.

17 can only be divided by 1 and itself.

PRIME NUMBERS PRACTICE

1. What is the next prime number following 28?

   (A) 30
   (B) 31
   (C) 29
   (D) 37

2. List the prime numbers between 12 and 21.

   (A) 13, 15, 17
   (B) 13, 17, 19
   (C) 13, 17, 19, 21
   (D) 13, 15, 17, 19

3. What are the prime numbers greater than 7 but less than or equal to 13?

   (A) 9, 11
   (B) 11, 13
   (C) 8, 9, 12
   (D) 8, 9, 11

(See page 100 for answers.)

Factors and Multiples

Factors are two or more numbers which, when multiplied together, result in another number called a product.

$$5 \times 3 = 15.$$

If we multiply 5 times 3, the result is 15: $5 \times 3 = 15.$

where the **Factors** are 5 and 3 and the **Product** is 15.

Prime factors are prime numbers that, when multiplied together, result in a product.

$$42 = 21 \times 2 = 7 \times 3 \times 2$$

where 21 and 2 are **Factors** and 7, 3, 2 are **Prime factors**.

Common factors are numbers that are factors of two or more numbers.

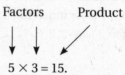

$$\left.\begin{array}{l} 56 = 8 \times \underline{7} \\ 21 = 3 \times \underline{7} \end{array}\right\}$$ The common factor of 56 and 21 is 7.

The **greatest common factor** of two numbers is the common factor with the largest value.

$$54 = \underline{18} \times 3$$
$$72 = \underline{18} \times 4$$

The greatest common factor of 54 and 72 is 18.

A **multiple** of a particular number is the product of that number by other whole numbers.

$$0 \times 3 = 0 \qquad 2 \times 3 = 6 \qquad 4 \times 3 = 12 \qquad 6 \times 3 = 18 \qquad 8 \times 3 = 24$$
$$1 \times 3 = 3 \qquad 3 \times 3 = 9 \qquad 5 \times 3 = 15 \qquad 7 \times 3 = 21 \qquad 9 \times 3 = 27$$

0, 3, 6, 9, 12, 15, 18, 21, 24, 27, . . . are all multiples of 3.

➡ Example _____

Determine a common factor of 15 and 12.

Answer: 3

Find the factors of each number and then find the common factor.

$$15 = \underline{3} \times 5$$
$$12 = \underline{3} \times 4$$

FACTORS AND MULTIPLES PRACTICE

1. Find a common factor of 15 and 55.

   (A) 11
   (B) 3
   (C) 15
   (D) 5

2. What is the greatest common factor of 48 and 54?

   (A) 8
   (B) 3
   (C) 6
   (D) 9

3. 14, 21, 28, and 35 are all multiples of what number?

   (A) 3
   (B) 5
   (C) 2
   (D) 7

4. What are the prime factors of 30?

   (A) 10, 3
   (B) 3, 5, 2
   (C) 15, 2
   (D) 5, 6

   Challenge Question

   Find the greatest common factor of 84 and 28.

   (See page 100 for answers.)

FRACTIONS

numerator
↓

A fraction is a number in the form $\frac{x}{y}$ where y is not 0 or 1 and x and y are whole numbers.

↑
denominator

Definitions	Examples
In a *proper fraction*, the numerator is less than the denominator:	$\frac{2}{5}$, $\frac{4}{9}$, $\frac{12}{45}$
In an *improper fraction*, the numerator is equal to or larger than the denominator:	$\frac{7}{4}$, $\frac{8}{3}$, $\frac{36}{5}$, $\frac{9}{9}$
A *mixed number* is a whole number with a proper fraction remainder:	$8\frac{5}{9}$, $2\frac{3}{4}$, $15\frac{7}{8}$
When we want the *reciprocal* of a fraction, we invert the fraction:	$\frac{5}{3}$ is the reciprocal of $\frac{3}{5}$ $\frac{1}{7}$ is the reciprocal of 7 (or $\frac{7}{1}$)

➡ **Example** _____

Match the items in the two columns:

A		B
1. $\frac{4}{3}$		a. Proper fraction
2. $5\frac{2}{7}$		b. Improper fraction
3. $\frac{8}{9}$		c. Mixed number

Answer: 1b, 2c, 3a

Comparing and Ordering Fractions

If we want to compare fractions, we first have to change all the denominators to the same common denominator.

➡ **Example** _____

Compare $\frac{2}{3}$, $\frac{1}{2}$, and $\frac{3}{4}$ and then determine which of the following statements are true.

(A) $\frac{2}{3} > \frac{3}{4}$

(B) $\frac{1}{2} < \frac{3}{4}$

(C) $\frac{3}{4} < \frac{2}{3}$

(D) $\frac{2}{3} < \frac{1}{2}$

Answer: (B)

In order to compare, let's change all denominators to the same common denominator, 12.

$$\frac{2}{3} = \frac{8}{12}$$ With the same denominators, we can now compare fractions.

$$\frac{1}{2} = \frac{6}{12}$$

$$\frac{3}{4} = \frac{9}{12}$$

$$\frac{6}{12} < \frac{9}{12}$$

(B) $\frac{1}{2} < \frac{3}{4}$

Reducing Fractions

When we reduce a fraction, we keep the numerator and the denominator in the same ratio but with smaller numbers.

➡️ **Example** _____

Reduce $\frac{24}{32}$ to its lowest terms.

Answer: $\frac{3}{4}$

Rewrite the numerator and the denominator as products of factors and then cancel the common factors.

$$\frac{24}{32} = \frac{\overset{1}{\cancel{8}} \times 3}{\underset{1}{\cancel{8}} \times 4} = \frac{3}{4}$$

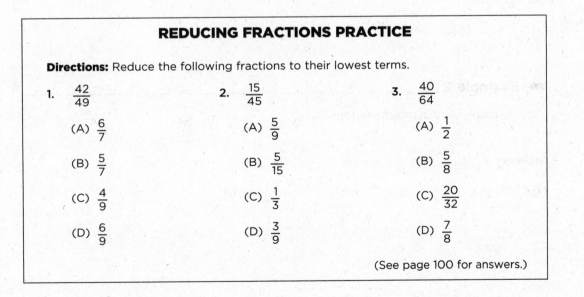

REDUCING FRACTIONS PRACTICE

Directions: Reduce the following fractions to their lowest terms.

1. $\frac{42}{49}$

   (A) $\frac{6}{7}$

   (B) $\frac{5}{7}$

   (C) $\frac{4}{9}$

   (D) $\frac{6}{9}$

2. $\frac{15}{45}$

   (A) $\frac{5}{9}$

   (B) $\frac{5}{15}$

   (C) $\frac{1}{3}$

   (D) $\frac{3}{9}$

3. $\frac{40}{64}$

   (A) $\frac{1}{2}$

   (B) $\frac{5}{8}$

   (C) $\frac{20}{32}$

   (D) $\frac{7}{8}$

(See page 100 for answers.)

DEFINITION

Equivalent
fractions are
fractions that have
the same value.

Equivalent Fractions

For example, let's check whether $\frac{2}{3}$ and $\frac{8}{12}$ are equivalent.

We'll check by multiplying $\frac{2}{3}$ by $\frac{4}{4}$.

$$\frac{2}{3} \times \frac{4}{4} = \frac{8}{12}$$

We can now clearly see that $\frac{2}{3}$ and $\frac{8}{12}$ are equivalent.

As a second example, let's determine whether $\frac{4}{5}$ and $\frac{12}{17}$ are equivalent.

Multiply $\frac{4}{5}$ by $\frac{3}{3}$.

$$\frac{4}{5} \times \frac{3}{3} = \frac{12}{15} \neq \frac{12}{17}$$

The two fractions $\frac{4}{5}$ and $\frac{12}{17}$ are not equivalent.

DEFINITION

An improper
fraction is a
fraction whose
numerator is
larger than its
denominator.

Changing Improper Fractions to Whole or Mixed Numbers

➥ **Example 1**

Change $\frac{14}{7}$ to a whole number.

(A) 4

(B) 1

(C) $2\frac{1}{2}$

(D) 2

Answer: (D)

When converting improper fractions to whole or mixed numbers, divide the denominator into the numerator.

$$\frac{14}{7} = 2$$

➥ **Example 2**

Change $\frac{25}{6}$ to a mixed number.

Answer: $4\frac{1}{6}$

Divide 25 by 6.

$$\frac{25}{6} = 4\frac{1}{6}$$

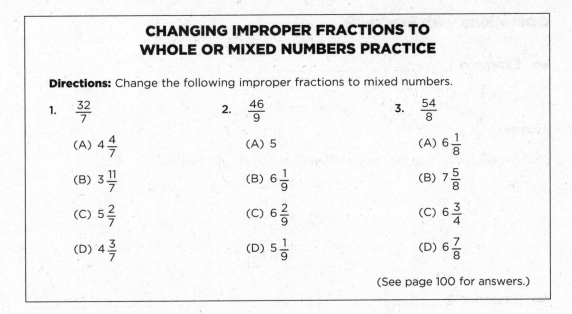

CHANGING IMPROPER FRACTIONS TO WHOLE OR MIXED NUMBERS PRACTICE

Directions: Change the following improper fractions to mixed numbers.

1. $\frac{32}{7}$

   (A) $4\frac{4}{7}$

   (B) $3\frac{11}{7}$

   (C) $5\frac{2}{7}$

   (D) $4\frac{3}{7}$

2. $\frac{46}{9}$

   (A) 5

   (B) $6\frac{1}{9}$

   (C) $6\frac{2}{9}$

   (D) $5\frac{1}{9}$

3. $\frac{54}{8}$

   (A) $6\frac{1}{8}$

   (B) $7\frac{5}{8}$

   (C) $6\frac{3}{4}$

   (D) $6\frac{7}{8}$

(See page 100 for answers.)

Changing Mixed Numbers to Improper Fractions

➡ Example _____

Change $3\frac{5}{8}$ to an improper fraction.

Answer: $\frac{29}{8}$

We want to reverse the previous process, so, in order to change $3\frac{5}{8}$ to an improper fraction, multiply 3 by 8 and add the numerator, 5. Then make this number the numerator and leave 8 the denominator.

$$3\frac{5}{8} = \frac{3 \cdot 8 + 5}{8} = \frac{29}{8}$$

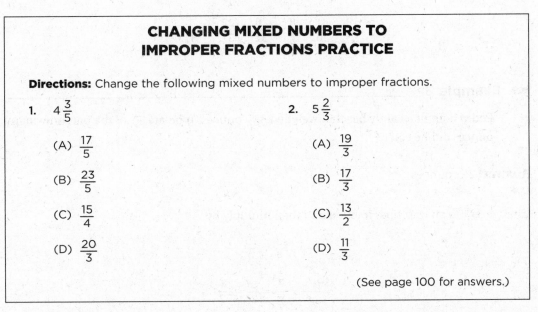

CHANGING MIXED NUMBERS TO IMPROPER FRACTIONS PRACTICE

Directions: Change the following mixed numbers to improper fractions.

1. $4\frac{3}{5}$

   (A) $\frac{17}{5}$

   (B) $\frac{23}{5}$

   (C) $\frac{15}{4}$

   (D) $\frac{20}{3}$

2. $5\frac{2}{3}$

   (A) $\frac{19}{3}$

   (B) $\frac{17}{3}$

   (C) $\frac{13}{2}$

   (D) $\frac{11}{3}$

(See page 100 for answers.)

Operations with Fractions

➡ **Example 1** _____

Add $\frac{2}{3}$ and $\frac{5}{7}$.

Answer: $1\frac{8}{21}$

Change both fractions to the common denominator, 21, and then add.

$$\frac{2}{3} = \frac{14}{21}$$
$$+\frac{5}{7} = \frac{15}{21}$$
$$\overline{\frac{29}{21} = 1\frac{8}{21}}$$

➡ **Example 2** _____

Simplify: $\dfrac{2-\frac{2}{5}}{\frac{3}{4}+\frac{4}{5}}$

Answer: $1\frac{1}{31}$

Simplify the numerator and the denominator and then divide.

$$2 = \frac{10}{5} \qquad\qquad \frac{3}{4} = \frac{15}{20}$$
$$-\frac{2}{5} = \frac{2}{5} \qquad\qquad +\frac{4}{5} = \frac{16}{20}$$
$$\overline{\frac{8}{5}} \qquad\qquad\qquad \overline{\frac{31}{20}}$$

$$\frac{8}{5} \div \frac{31}{20} = \frac{8}{\cancel{5}} \times \frac{\overset{4}{\cancel{20}}}{31} = \frac{32}{31} = 1\frac{1}{31}$$

VOCABULARY

The prefix *multi-* means many. A **multitude** is a large number of something.

The large class contains a multitude of attitudes.

➡ **Example 3** _____

Pedro bought a candy bar that weighed $3\frac{3}{4}$ ounces. If he ate $\frac{2}{3}$ of the bar, how many ounces did he eat?

Answer: $2\frac{1}{2}$ ounces

Change $3\frac{3}{4}$ to an improper fraction and then multiply by $\frac{2}{3}$.

$$3\frac{3}{4} = \frac{15}{4}$$

$$\frac{\overset{5}{\cancel{15}}}{\underset{2}{\cancel{4}}} \times \frac{\overset{1}{\cancel{2}}}{\underset{1}{\cancel{3}}} = \frac{5}{2} = 2\frac{1}{2}$$

➡ **Example 4**_____

Simplify: $\frac{4}{5} \div 2\frac{2}{5}$

Answer: $\frac{1}{3}$

Change $2\frac{2}{5}$ to an improper fraction and invert. Then multiply $\frac{4}{5}$ by the result.

$$2\frac{2}{5} = \frac{12}{5}$$

$$\frac{4}{5} \div \frac{12}{5} = \frac{\overset{1}{\cancel{4}}}{\cancel{5}} \times \frac{\overset{1}{\cancel{5}}}{\underset{3}{\cancel{12}}} = \frac{1}{3}$$

OPERATIONS WITH FRACTIONS PRACTICE

1. Find $\frac{3}{4}$ of $\frac{1}{2}$ of 240.

   (A) 80
   (B) 60
   (C) 110
   (D) 90

2. Add $2\frac{2}{3}$, $3\frac{1}{4}$, and $\frac{5}{6}$.

   (A) $5\frac{1}{2}$
   (B) $4\frac{3}{4}$
   (C) $6\frac{3}{4}$
   (D) $7\frac{2}{3}$

3. A beaker contains $12\frac{5}{8}$ ounces of alcohol. If $2\frac{3}{4}$ ounces is spilled out, how many ounces remain in the beaker?

   (A) $9\frac{7}{8}$
   (B) $8\frac{5}{8}$
   (C) $9\frac{5}{6}$
   (D) $8\frac{1}{2}$

4. Simplify: $\frac{5}{6} \div 2\frac{5}{12}$.

   (A) $\frac{12}{17}$
   (B) $\frac{10}{29}$
   (C) $\frac{11}{19}$
   (D) $\frac{9}{16}$

5. Simplify: $\dfrac{2 + \frac{3}{4}}{1\frac{1}{4} - \frac{3}{8}}$

   (A) $2\frac{3}{5}$
   (B) $3\frac{1}{7}$
   (C) $3\frac{5}{9}$
   (D) $4\frac{2}{5}$

Challenge Question

A large container is being filled with water at the rate of $2\frac{3}{4}$ gallons per minute. If the container leaks at the rate of $\frac{1}{8}$ gallon per minute, how long would it take to fill a 14-gallon container?

(See page 100 for answers.)

DECIMALS

Decimals are another form of fractions. The following list compares decimals with their equivalents in fraction format:

$$0.8 = \frac{8}{10}$$

$$5.06 = 5 + \frac{0}{10} + \frac{6}{100}$$

$$46.348 = 46 + \frac{3}{10} + \frac{4}{100} + \frac{8}{1,000}$$

$$198.7039 = 198 + \frac{7}{10} + \frac{0}{100} + \frac{3}{1,000} + \frac{9}{10,000}$$

Reading Decimals

Number	In Words
16.4	Sixteen and four tenths
234.05	Two hundred thirty-four and five hundredths
6.346	Six and three hundred forty-six thousandths
34.5078	Thirty-four and five thousand seventy-eight ten thousandths

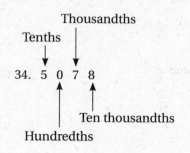

➥ Example

What does the digit 4 represent in the number 563.047?

Answer: Hundredths

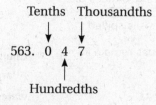

Comparing Decimals and Fractions

 **Example 1**_____

Change $\frac{3}{8}$ to a decimal.

Answer: 0.375

Divide 3 by 8.

$$
\begin{array}{r}
.375 \\
8\overline{\smash{)}3.000} \\
\underline{-24} \\
60 \\
\underline{-56} \\
40 \\
\underline{-40} \\
0
\end{array}
$$

 **Example 2**_____

Change 0.68 to a fraction.

Answer: $\frac{17}{25}$

Rewrite 0.68 as a fraction and reduce to lowest terms.

$$0.68 = \frac{68}{100} = \frac{17}{25}$$

A repeating decimal is indicated by a line over the repeating digits.
For example,

$$0.5555\ldots = 0.\overline{5}$$

$$3.464646\ldots = 3.\overline{46}$$

COMPARING DECIMALS AND FRACTIONS PRACTICE

1. Which decimal is the equivalent of $\frac{5}{8}$?

   (A) 0.655
   (B) 0.700
   (C) 0.625
   (D) 0.850

2. Which fraction is the equivalent of 0.78?

   (A) $\frac{7}{8}$
   (B) $\frac{39}{50}$
   (C) $\frac{7}{100}$
   (D) $\frac{7}{800}$

3. Which decimal is the closest equivalent of $\frac{2}{3}$?

   (A) 0.6
   (B) 0.66
   (C) 6.0
   (D) 0.666

(See page 101 for answers.)

Rounding Off Decimals

➡ **Example** _____

Round off the product of 3.46 and 2.03 to the nearest tenth.

Answer: 7.0

Multiply first. Then look at the hundredths place. If it's 5 or more, round up. If not, drop all the digits beyond the tenth place.

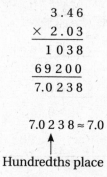

$$7.0\,2\,3\,8 \approx 7.0$$

Hundredths place

ROUNDING OFF DECIMALS PRACTICE

1. Round off the sum of 25.06 and 67.43 to the nearest tenth.

    (A) 92.5
    (B) 92.4
    (C) 92.3
    (D) 92.2

2. Round off the product of 8.53 and 0.9 to the nearest hundredth.

    (A) 7.6
    (B) 7.681
    (C) 7.67
    (D) 7.68

    (See page 101 for answers.)

Operations with Decimals

➡ **Example 1** _____

Add 4.593, 23.08, and 476.

Answer: 503.673

Line up the decimals by adding zeroes as placeholders and then add.

$$
\begin{array}{r}
4.593 \\
23.080 \\
+\ 476.000 \\
\hline
503.673
\end{array}
$$

➥ Example 2

Stephanie weighed a beaker filled with liquid. If the beaker and the liquid weighed 15.478 grams and she spilled out 6.9 grams of liquid, how much did the beaker plus the liquid weigh now?

Answer: 8.578

Line up the decimals and subtract.

$$
\begin{array}{r}
15.478 \\
-\ 6.900 \\
\hline
8.578
\end{array}
$$

➥ Example 3

Multiply 4.56 by 13.7 and round the answer off to the nearest tenth.

Answer: 62.5

Add the number of decimal places in both numbers and then use the result to place the decimal in the answer.

$$
\begin{array}{r}
4.56 \\
\times\ 13.7 \\
\hline
3192 \\
1368 \\
456 \\
\hline
62.472 \approx 62.5
\end{array}
$$

➥ Example 4

Divide 229.862 by 5.26.

Answer: 43.7

$$
\text{Dividend} \longrightarrow \frac{229.862}{5.26} \longleftarrow \text{Divisor} = \text{Answer} \longleftarrow \text{Quotient}
$$

Count the number of decimal places in the divisor. Move the decimal place in the dividend the corresponding number of places and then divide.

$$
\begin{array}{r}
43.7 \\
5\,26.\overline{)229\,86.2} \\
-\ 210\ 4 \\
\hline
1946 \\
-\ 1578 \\
\hline
368\ 2 \\
-\ 368\ 2 \\
\hline
0
\end{array}
$$

$$43.7 \times 5.26 = 229.862 \ ✔$$

OPERATIONS WITH DECIMALS PRACTICE

1. Add 84.29, 234.752, and 45.

   (A) 364.84
   (B) 366.839
   (C) 364.04
   (D) 364.042

2. Jaime packed 12 scales. If each scale weighed 15.73 ounces, what was the total weight of all the scales?

   (A) 188.736 ounces
   (B) 188 ounces
   (C) 188.76 ounces
   (D) 188.754 ounces

3. Multiply 4.58 by 0.7 and round off to the nearest hundredth.

   (A) 3.206
   (B) 3.23
   (C) 3.208
   (D) 3.21

4. Divide 2.0592 by 0.72 and round the answer to the nearest tenth.

   (A) 2.9
   (B) 2.86
   (C) 2.8
   (D) 28.6

(See page 101 for answers.)

(See page 101 for answers.)

DEFINITION

Scientific notation is a compact way of writing a number as the product of another number between 1 and 10 and a power of 10.

Scientific Notation

$$768 = 7.68 \times 100 = 7.68 \times 10^2$$
$$5.04 \times 10^4 = 5.04 \times 10 \times 10 \times 10 \times 10 = 5.04 \times 10,000 = 50,400$$

In the example above, the exponent 4 means that you need to move the decimal 4 places to the right. If the exponent was –4, you would move the exponent 4 places to the left.

➡ **Example** _____

Change 2.35×10^{-2} to its decimal equivalent.

Answer: 0.0235

$$10^{-1} = \frac{1}{10} \quad 10^{-2} = \frac{1}{100} \quad 10^{-3} = \frac{1}{1,000}$$

$$2.35 \times 10^{-2} = 2.35 \times \frac{1}{100} = \frac{2.35}{100} = 0.0235$$

SCIENTIFIC NOTATION PRACTICE

1. Change 4.05×10^3 to a whole number.

   (A) 40.5
   (B) 405
   (C) 4,050
   (D) 40,500

2. Change 6941 to scientific notation.

   (A) 69.41×10^4
   (B) 6.941×10^2
   (C) 69.41×10^3
   (D) 6.941×10^3

(See page 101 for answers.)

(See page 101 for answers.)

PERCENTS

Fractions, decimals, and percents are all different methods of indicating a part of a whole unit.

Changing Fractions and Whole Numbers to Percents

➡ **Example** _____

Change $\frac{4}{9}$ to a two-place percent.

Answer: 44%

Divide 9 into 4.000. Round off to two decimal places. Finally, when changing from a decimal to a percent, multiply by 100 or move the decimal over two places to the right.

$$
\begin{array}{r}
.444 \approx 0.44 = 44\% \\
9\overline{)4.000} \\
-36\downarrow \\
\hline
40 \\
-36\downarrow \\
\hline
40 \\
-36
\end{array}
$$

CHANGING FRACTIONS AND WHOLE NUMBERS TO PERCENTS PRACTICE

1. Change $\frac{6}{7}$ to a two-place decimal.

    (A) 0.86
    (B) 0.87
    (C) 87%
    (D) 0.89

2. Change $\frac{3}{11}$ to a percent. Choose the best answer.

    (A) 28%
    (B) 29%
    (C) 0.27
    (D) 27%

    (See page 101 for answers.)

Changing Percents to Fractions

➡ **Example** _____

Change 45% to a fraction and reduce to lowest terms.

Answer: $\frac{9}{20}$

$$45\% = \frac{45}{100} = \frac{9}{20}$$

CHANGING PERCENTS TO FRACTIONS PRACTICE

1. Change 68% to a fraction and reduce to lowest terms.

    (A) $\frac{17}{25}$

    (B) $\frac{68}{100}$

    (C) $\frac{4}{50}$

    (D) $\frac{19}{100}$

(See page 101 for answer.)

Changing Decimals to Percents

➡ Example

Change 2.33 to a percent.

Answer: 233%

To change from a decimal to a percent, multiply by 100 or move the decimal two places to the right.

$$2.33 = 233\%$$

CHANGING DECIMALS TO PERCENTS PRACTICE

1. Change 68.5 to a percent.

    (A) 0.685%
    (B) 6.85%
    (C) 6850%
    (D) 68.5%

(See page 101 for answer.)

Changing Percents to Decimals

➡ Example

Change 7.32% to a decimal.

Answer: 0.0732

To change from a percent to a decimal, divide by 100 or move the decimal two places to the left.

$$7.32\% = 0.0732$$

CHANGING PERCENTS TO DECIMALS PRACTICE

1. Change 46.3% to a decimal.

    (A) 463
    (B) 4.63
    (C) 46.3
    (D) 0.463

(See page 101 for answer.)

Finding a Percent of a Number

➡ **Example** _____

Find 7% of 430. Round off the answer to the nearest whole number.

Answer: 30

Change 7% to a decimal and multiply.

$$7\% = 0.07$$
$$0.07 \times 430 = 30.1$$
$$30.1 \approx 30$$

Certain percentages easily convert to fractions:

$$12\frac{1}{2}\% = \frac{1}{8}$$

$$16\frac{2}{3}\% = \frac{1}{6}$$

$$33\frac{1}{3}\% = \frac{1}{3}$$

$$66\frac{2}{3}\% = \frac{2}{3}$$

Applications

➡ **Example** _____

If there were 300 people at a dinner and nearly 39% ordered fish, approximately how many ordered fish?

(A) 200
(B) 150
(C) 120
(D) 110

Answer: (C)

Change 39% to a decimal and multiply by 300. Then choose the closest answer.

$$39\% = 0.39$$
$$0.39 \times 300 = 117$$
$$117 \approx 120$$

FINDING A PERCENT OF A NUMBER AND APPLICATIONS PRACTICE

1. Out of a sample of 450 people, 8% were vegetarians. How many were vegetarians?

    (A) 36

    (B) 44

    (C) 28

    (D) 52

(See page 101 for answer.)

DEFINITION

A variable is any letter or symbol used to represent a number and derives its name from the fact that its value may change or vary.

ALGEBRA

Algebra is distinguished from arithmetic in its use of variables.

In the algebraic expression $a + 6$, a is the variable and 6 is the constant.

➡ Example _____

Find the value of the expression $a + 6$ when $a = 8$.

DEFINITION

A constant is a number and derives its name from the fact that its value never changes.

Answer: 14

Substitute 8 for a in the expression $a + 6$.

$$a + 6$$
$$8 + 6$$
$$14$$

ALGEBRA PRACTICE

Directions: Find the value of the following expressions when $b = 5$.

1. $4b - 7$

    (A) 10

    (B) 12

    (C) 13

    (D) 15

2. $2b^3 + 8$

    (A) 198

    (B) 212

    (C) 286

    (D) 258

(See page 101 for answers.)

Arithmetic Operations with Signed Numbers

RULES FOR ADDITION

   i. If the signs of the addends are the same, add the numbers and use that sign.

$$\begin{array}{r} (+3) \\ +\,(+4) \\ \hline +7 \end{array} \qquad\qquad \begin{array}{r} (-2) \\ +\,(-4) \\ \hline -6 \end{array}$$

  ii. If the signs of the addends are different, subtract and use the sign of the larger.

$$\begin{array}{r} +\,(+6) \\ +\,(-3) \\ \hline +3 \end{array} \qquad\qquad \begin{array}{r} (+2) \\ +\,(-4) \\ \hline -2 \end{array}$$

RULES FOR SUBTRACTION

Change the sign of the subtrahend (the quantity to be subtracted) and use the rules of addition:

$$\begin{array}{r} +\,6 \\ - \\ -\,\oplus\,2 \\ \hline +\,4 \end{array} \qquad \begin{array}{r} -\,7 \\ + \\ -\,\ominus\,3 \\ \hline -\,4 \end{array} \qquad \begin{array}{r} +\,3 \\ + \\ -\,\ominus\,4 \\ \hline +\,7 \end{array} \qquad \begin{array}{r} -\,2 \\ - \\ -\,\oplus\,6 \\ \hline -\,8 \end{array}$$

RULES FOR MULTIPLICATION

   i. If the signs of the factors are the same, the product is positive.

$$(+3)(+4) = +12 \qquad\qquad (-2)(-9) = +18$$

  ii. If the signs of the factors are different, the product is negative.

$$(-4)(+6) = -24 \qquad\qquad (+7)(-3) = -21$$

RULES FOR DIVISION

   i. If the signs of the dividend and divisor are the same, the quotient is positive.

$$\frac{+8}{2} = +4 \qquad\qquad \frac{-10}{-5} = +2$$

  ii. If the signs of the dividend and divisor are different, the quotient is negative.

$$\frac{+6}{-2} = -3 \qquad\qquad \frac{-9}{+3} = -3$$

➡ Example 1

The average weight of a student on the soccer team is 159 pounds. Find Ruben's weight if the signed numbers represent pounds above (+) and below (–) the average weight.

Deviation from average weight	+11	–12	+15	–2	+4
Name	Jaime	Ruben	Clotilde	Oscar	Mary

Answer: 147 pounds

Ruben is 12 pounds below the average weight, 159.

$$\begin{array}{r} +159 \\ -\ 12 \\ \hline 147 \end{array}$$

➡ Example 2

Subtract:
$$\begin{array}{r} (+34) \\ -(+89) \\ \hline \end{array}$$

Answer: –55

Change the sign of the subtrahend and use the rules of addition.

$$\left. \begin{array}{r} +\ 34 \\ - \\ -\ \oplus\ 89 \\ \hline -\ 55 \end{array} \right\} +34 - 89 = -55$$

➡ Example 3

Multiply: $(-3)(+4)(-2)(-4)$

Answer: –96

Multiply the integers, and then count the number of negatives. An odd number of negatives will result in a negative answer, while an even number of negatives will result in a positive answer.

$$(-3)(+4)(-2)(-4) =$$
$$(-12)(+8) = -96$$

➡ Example 4

Divide –112 by –8.

Answer: +14

When the signs of both the dividend and divisor are the same, the quotient is positive.

$$\frac{-112}{-8} = +14$$

ARITHMETIC OPERATIONS WITH SIGNED NUMBERS PRACTICE

1. Subtract −47 from +18.

   (A) 65
   (B) 29
   (C) −65
   (D) −29

2. Multiply: (+3)(−2)(−1)(+4).

   (A) −24
   (B) −12
   (C) +24
   (D) +12

3. Divide 1.75 by −0.7.

   (A) 2.5
   (B) −2.5
   (C) 0.25
   (D) −0.25

(See page 101 for answers.)

Formulas

A formula links together variables and constants in some sort of relationship. Given certain information, we can go on to find the value of an unknown quantity in the relationship.

In the United States and in English-speaking countries, temperature is generally measured on the Fahrenheit scale. The rest of the world measures heat in Celsius (or Centigrade). The Swedish astronomer Anders Celsius developed the Celsius scale. It actually makes more sense than the Fahrenheit scale because there are 100 degrees between the freezing point of water (measured at standard atmospheric pressure) at 0° Celsius and its boiling point at 100° Celsius. The German physicist Gabriel Fahrenheit devised the Fahrenheit scale in which the freezing point of water (also at standard atmospheric pressure) is 32° Fahrenheit while its boiling point is 212° Fahrenheit.

We frequently want to convert from one scale to another, so we need a convenient formula to help us with the conversion.

➡ Example

The formula $C = \left(\dfrac{5}{9}\right)(F - 32)$ shows us the relationship between Celsius and Fahrenheit and allows us to change from one scale to another. Change 113° Fahrenheit to Celsius.

Answer: 45° Celsius

Let F = the Fahrenheit temperature.
Let C = the Celsius temperature.
We'll use the formula and simply substitute 113 for F.

$$C = \left(\frac{5}{9}\right)(F - 32)$$

$$C = \left(\frac{5}{9}\right)(113 - 32)$$

$$C = \left(\frac{5}{9}\right)(81)$$

$$C = 45$$

FORMULAS PRACTICE

1. Use the formula $C = \left(\dfrac{5}{9}\right)(F - 32)$ to change 140° Fahrenheit to Celsius.

    (A) 36°C

    (B) 60°C

    (C) 45°C

    (D) 81°C

(See page 101 for answer.)

Equations

➡ Example

Find the value of x in the equation $5x + 12 = 47$.

Answer: 7

Subtract 12 from both sides of the equation and then divide by 5.

$$5x + 12 = 47$$
$$-12 = -12$$
$$5x = 35$$
$$\frac{5x}{5} = \frac{35}{5}$$
$$x = 7$$

EQUATIONS PRACTICE

1. Find the value of x in the equation $3x - 8 = 19$.

    (A) 8

    (B) 9

    (C) 6

    (D) 7

Challenge Question

Find the value of the expression $\dfrac{6xy - 2z}{-4}$ when $x = -1$, $y = 3$, and $z = 5$.

(See page 102 for answers.)

Simplifying Exponential Expressions

Occasionally we can simplify exponential expressions. For example,

$$3^4 \cdot 3^6 = (3 \cdot 3 \cdot 3 \cdot 3)(3 \cdot 3 \cdot 3 \cdot 3 \cdot 3 \cdot 3) = 3 \cdot 3 \cdot 3 \cdot 3 \cdot 3 \cdot 3 \cdot 3 \cdot 3 \cdot 3 \cdot 3 = 3^{10}$$

We can see if we multiply powers with the same base, we simply add the exponents.
What happens when we divide powers with the same base?

$$\frac{7^8}{7^5} = \frac{7 \cdot 7 \cdot 7 \cdot \overset{1}{\cancel{7}} \cdot \overset{1}{\cancel{7}} \cdot \overset{1}{\cancel{7}} \cdot \overset{1}{\cancel{7}} \cdot \overset{1}{\cancel{7}}}{\underset{1}{\cancel{7}} \cdot \underset{1}{\cancel{7}} \cdot \underset{1}{\cancel{7}} \cdot \underset{1}{\cancel{7}} \cdot \underset{1}{\cancel{7}}} = 7^3$$

If we divide powers with the same base, we subtract exponents.
Let's see what happens when we divide a power by itself.

$$\frac{4^{35}}{4^{35}} = 4^{35-35} = 4^0$$

Any time a number is divided by itself, the quotient is 1, so

$$\frac{4^{35}}{4^{35}} = \boxed{4^0 = 1}$$

A base raised to a zero exponent simplifies to 1.

➡ Example _____

Find the value of $\dfrac{8^7 \cdot 6^9 \cdot 5^0}{8^5 \cdot 6^8}$.

Answer: 384

$5^0 = 1$. Whenever we divide powers with the same base, we subtract exponents.

$$\frac{8^7 \cdot 6^9 \cdot 5^0}{8^5 \cdot 6^8} = \frac{\overset{8^2}{\cancel{8^7}} \cdot \overset{6^1}{\cancel{6^9}} \cdot \overset{1}{\cancel{5^0}}}{\underset{1}{\cancel{8^5}} \cdot \underset{1}{\cancel{6^8}}} = 8^2 \cdot 6^1 = 64 \cdot 6 = 384$$

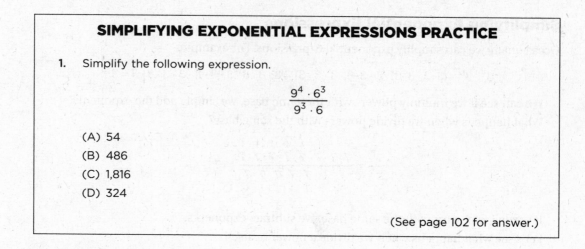

```
┌─────────────────────────────────────────────────────────────────┐
│           SIMPLIFYING EXPONENTIAL EXPRESSIONS PRACTICE            │
│                                                                   │
│   1.   Simplify the following expression.                         │
│                                                                   │
│                            9⁴ · 6³                                │
│                            ─────────                              │
│                             9³ · 6                                │
│                                                                   │
│        (A)  54                                                    │
│        (B)  486                                                   │
│        (C)  1,816                                                 │
│        (D)  324                                                   │
│                                                                   │
│                                       (See page 102 for answer.)  │
└─────────────────────────────────────────────────────────────────┘
```

SIMPLIFYING EXPONENTIAL EXPRESSIONS PRACTICE

1. Simplify the following expression.

$$\frac{9^4 \cdot 6^3}{9^3 \cdot 6}$$

(A) 54
(B) 486
(C) 1,816
(D) 324

(See page 102 for answer.)

Roots and Radicals

Let's find the square root of 25.

$$\sqrt{25} = 5$$

or

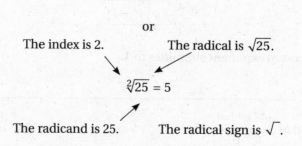

The index is 2.   The radical is $\sqrt{25}$.

$$\sqrt[2]{25} = 5$$

The radicand is 25.   The radical sign is $\sqrt{}$.

When no index appears, 2 is understood to be the index.

There are actually two square roots of 25:

$$(+5)(+5) = 25$$

$$(-5)(-5) = 25$$

We indicate a positive and a negative square root in the following manner:

$$\pm\sqrt{25} = \pm 5$$

When we want the **positive square root** of a number, we call it the **principal square root**:

$$\sqrt{25} = +5$$

The negative square root is indicated by placing a negative sign in front of the radical:

$$-\sqrt{25} = -5$$

Simplifying Radicals

➡ **Example 1** _____

Simplify $\sqrt{b^8}$.

Answer: b^4

We want to find a particular monomial which, when multiplied by itself, results in b^8.

$$\sqrt{b^8} = b^4$$

CHECK: $\quad b^4 \cdot b^4 = b^8$

➡ Example 2

Simplify $\sqrt{50}$.

Try to write 50 as the product of a square and another number and then simplify the result.

$$\sqrt{50} = \sqrt{25 \cdot 2} = \sqrt{25} \cdot \sqrt{2} = 5\sqrt{2}$$

Operations with Radicals

We can perform the basic arithmetic operations of addition, subtraction, multiplication, and division on radicals.

$$13\sqrt{7} - 4\sqrt{7} = 9\sqrt{7}$$
$$12\sqrt{6} - 17\sqrt{6} = -5\sqrt{6}$$
$$5\sqrt{b} \cdot 3\sqrt{c} = 15\sqrt{bc}$$

RADICALS PRACTICE

Directions: Simplify the following radical expressions.

1. $5\sqrt{7} - 2\sqrt{7} + 6\sqrt{7}$

   (A) $11\sqrt{7}$

   (B) $10\sqrt{7}$

   (C) $13\sqrt{7}$

   (D) $9\sqrt{7}$

2. $8\sqrt{2} \cdot 3$

   (A) $24\sqrt{2}$

   (B) $48\sqrt{2}$

   (C) 48

   (D) 4

(See page 102 for answers.)

Inequalities

The following examples illustrate the inequality symbols:

Illustration	Translation
$6 > 3$	6 is greater than 3
$9 < 12$	9 is less than 12
$-3 \geq -4$	−3 is greater than or equal to −4
$0 \leq 0$	0 is less than or equal to 0

INEQUALITIES PRACTICE

1. Which of the following statements is true?

   (A) $4 < -5$ and $9 > 3$
   (B) $7 \geq -2$ and $6 < -5$
   (C) $12 \leq 19$ or $-5 > 0$
   (D) $-9 > -8$ or $7 < 0$

(See page 102 for answer.)

Operations with Monomials and Polynomials

➡ **Example 1** _____

Simplify: $+4t - 5t + 9t - 3t$.

Answer: $+5t$

Perform the additions and subtractions separately and then combine terms.

$$+4t + 9t = +13t$$
$$-5t - 3t = -8t$$
$$+13t - 8t = +5t$$

➡ **Example 2** _____

Subtract $2a - 4$ from $-3a - 6$.

Answer: $-5a - 2$

Change the signs of the subtrahend and then add.

$$
\begin{array}{ccl}
-3a & -6 & \text{(minuend)} \\
- & + & \\
-\oplus 2a & \ominus 4 & \text{(subtrahend)} \\
\hline
-5a & -2 & \text{(difference)}
\end{array}
$$

➡ **Example 3** _____

Find the product of $4t^5$ and $-6t^3$.

Answer: $-24t^8$

Multiply the coefficients and add the exponents.

$$(4t^5) \cdot (-6t^3) = (4)(-6)(t^5)(t^3) = -24t^8$$

➡ **Example 4** _____

Find the quotient of $24g^7 - 18g^5$ and $-6g^4$.

Answer: $-4g^3 + 3g$

Divide the coefficients and subtract the exponents.

$$\frac{24g^7 - 18g^5}{-6g^4} = \frac{24g^7}{-6g^4} - \frac{18g^5}{-6g^4} = -4g^3 + 3g$$

OPERATIONS WITH MONOMIALS AND POLYNOMIALS PRACTICE

1. Simplify: $-3g - 4h + 8g - 3h$

    (A) $4g + 7h$
    (B) $-5g - 11h$
    (C) $5g - 7h$
    (D) $11g + 7h$

2. Subtract $8t - 4z$ from $-5t - 8z$.

    (A) $-13t - 4z$
    (B) $13t + 4z$
    (C) $-3t - 4z$
    (D) $3t - 12z$

3. Find the product of $5a^3$ and $4a^7$.

    (A) $20a^{21}$
    (B) $15a^{10}$
    (C) $20a^{10}$
    (D) $35a^{21}$

4. Find the quotient of $18r^6 - 12r^7$ and $-6r^5$.

    (A) $3r - 2r^2$
    (B) $-3r - 2$
    (C) $3r^2 - 2r$
    (D) $-3r + 2r^2$

    (See page 102 for answers.)

Absolute Value

The absolute value of a number, x, is defined as

$$|x| = \sqrt{x^2}$$

For example,

$$|-3| = \sqrt{(-3)^2} = \sqrt{9} = 3$$

$$|4| = \sqrt{4^2} = \sqrt{16} = 4$$

More practically, the absolute value of any number is its distance from the origin (disregard direction).

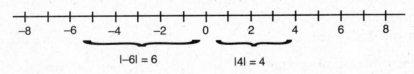

➡ **Example** _____

Simplify $5|-6|$.

Answer: 30

Remove the absolute value sign and multiply by 5.

$$5|-6| = 5(6) = 30$$

ABSOLUTE VALUE PRACTICE

Directions: Simplify the following expressions:

1. $6|-4| + 4|7|$

    (A) -24
    (B) 4
    (C) 52
    (D) -4

2. $7|7| - 3|-2|$

    (A) 55
    (B) 45
    (C) 27
    (D) 43

(See page 102 for answers.)

Ratios and Proportions

The odds of a new business remaining open more than a year are 1 out of 3. What does this mean?

DEFINITION

If two ratios are equal, we have a proportion.

$$\frac{a}{b} = \frac{c}{d}$$

or

$$a : b = c : d$$

It means that only $\frac{1}{3}$ of all new enterprises will remain in business longer than a year, while $\frac{2}{3}$ will close within the year.

$\frac{1}{3}$ is a ratio that also may be expressed as $1 : 3$.

The ratio $a : b$ may be expressed as the fraction $\frac{a}{b}$.

The ratio $9 : 27$ may be reduced:

$$\frac{9}{27} = \frac{1}{3}$$

a, b, c, and d are called the first, second, third, and fourth terms, respectively. The two outer terms are called the extremes, while the two inner terms are called the means.

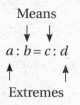

Means
$$a : b = c : d$$
Extremes

➡ **Example 1** _____

Do these ratios form a proportion?

$$\frac{4}{12} \overset{?}{=} \frac{5}{15} \qquad \frac{3a^2}{7a} \overset{?}{=} \frac{6a}{14a^2}$$

$$\frac{1}{3} = \frac{1}{3} \qquad \frac{3a}{7} = \frac{3}{7a}$$

$$\text{Yes!} \qquad\qquad \text{No}$$

In a proportion, the product of the means equals the product of the extremes. In the proportion $a : b = c : d$, $bc = ad$.

➡ Example 2_____

Find the fourth term in the proportion $2 : 7 = 12 : x$.

Answer: 42

The product of the means equals the product of the extremes.

$$2 : 7 = 12 : x$$
$$2x = 84$$
$$x = 42$$

RATIOS AND PROPORTIONS PRACTICE

1. Find the fourth term in the proportion $7 : 9 = 21 : x$.

   (A) 21
   (B) 18
   (C) 27
   (D) 36

(See page 102 for answer.)

Consecutive Integers

Consecutive integers are integers that follow one another:

$$1, 2, 3, \ldots$$
$$22, 23, 24, \ldots$$
$$75, 76, 77, \ldots$$
$$-4, -3, -2, \ldots$$

If we let x represent an integer, $x + 1$ represents the next consecutive integer, $x + 2$ the integer after that, and so forth:

$$x, x + 1, x + 2, \ldots$$

Consecutive even integers are even integers that follow one another:

$$2, 4, 6, \ldots$$
$$18, 20, 22, \ldots$$
$$62, 64, 66, \ldots$$
$$-8, -6, -4, \ldots$$

We have to add 2 to the first even integer to get to the next consecutive even integer.

$$8$$
$$8 + 2 = 10$$
$$10 + 2 = 12$$

If n represents the first even integer, $n + 2$ represents the next consecutive even integer, $n + 4$ the even integer after that, and so forth:

$$n, n + 2, n + 4, \ldots$$

If $n + 1$ represents the first even integer, $(n + 1) + 2$ and $(n + 2) + 4$ represent the next two consecutive even integers.

$$(n + 1), (n + 1) + 2, (n + 1) + 4, \ldots$$

Consecutive odd integers are odd integers that follow one another:

$$5, 7, 9, \ldots$$
$$13, 15, 17, \ldots$$
$$79, 81, 83, \ldots$$
$$-11, -9, -7, \ldots$$

Just as with even integers, we have to add 2 to the first odd integer in order to get to the next consecutive odd integer.

$$5$$
$$5 + 2 = 7$$
$$7 + 2 = 9$$

If $x - 4$ represents the first odd integer, $(x - 4) + 2$ represents the next consecutive odd integer, $(x - 4) + 4$ represents the odd integer after that, and so forth.

$$(x - 4), (x - 4) + 2, (x - 4) + 4, \ldots$$

➡ Example 1

Find two consecutive integers whose sum is 71.

Answer: 35, 36

Let x = the first integer, and let $x + 1$ = the next consecutive integer. The sum is 71.

$$x + (x + 1) = 71$$
$$x + x + 1 = 71$$
$$2x + 1 = 71$$
$$2x = 70$$
$$x = 35$$
$$x + 1 = 36$$
$$35 + 36 = 71 \; ✔$$

➡ Example 2

Find two consecutive even integers whose sum is 86.

Answer: 42, 44

Let x = the first even integer, and let $x + 2$ = the next consecutive even integer. The sum is 86.

$$x + (x + 2) = 86$$
$$2x + 2 = 86$$
$$2x = 84$$
$$x = 42$$
$$x + 2 = 44$$
$$x + (x + 2) = 86$$
$$42 + 44 = 86 \; ✔$$

CONSECUTIVE INTEGERS PRACTICE

1. Find the largest of three consecutive integers whose sum is 231.

   (A) 79
   (B) 83
   (C) 80
   (D) 78

2. What is the smaller of two consecutive even integers that add up to 70?

   (A) 32
   (B) 36
   (C) 34
   (D) 38

3. Find the second of three consecutive odd integers whose sum is 141.

   (A) 45
   (B) 47
   (C) 51
   (D) 49

Challenge Question

The sum of the first and third of three consecutive odd integers is 14. Find the square of the second consecutive odd integer.

(See page 102 for answers.)

PLANE GEOMETRY

Points

Points have no specific size or shape. Points are usually named with capital letters and are used to position objects and lines.

$\bullet$ $\bullet$ $\bullet$
A B   C

Lines

Lines, like points, have no specific width but they extend infinitely in opposite directions.

Line $\overline{AB}$ or $\overline{BA}$

INTERSECTING LINES

Lines $\overleftrightarrow{RS}$ and $\overleftrightarrow{TU}$ intersect at point V. Both lines are in the same plane.

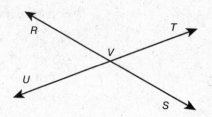

LINE SEGMENTS

Line segments, unlike lines, have a definite length and may be measured.

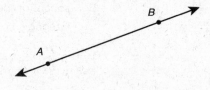

Line segment AB or $\overline{AB}$

RAYS

Rays are parts of lines that extend from one endpoint indefinitely in one direction.

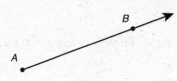

Ray AB or $\overrightarrow{AB}$

Planes

Planes are composed of an infinite set of points on a flat surface. Planes extend infinitely in all directions. The picture below is only a section of the entire plane.

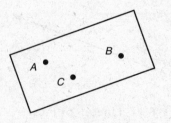

Plane ABC is indicated by three points on the plane. The three points are not located on the same line.

Angles

If two rays meet at a point, they form an **angle** at the point of intersection, called the vertex.

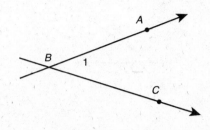

The angle thus formed may be designated in a number of different ways:

    i. ∠ABC

  ii. ∠CBA

 iii. ∠1

PLANE GEOMETRY PRACTICE 1

1. What is another name for ∠DEF?

    (A) ∠D

    (B) ∠DFE

    (C) ∠E

    (D) ∠FDE

(See page 102 for answer.)

A protractor is used to measure the number of degrees in an angle. In the figure below, for example, the protractor measures an angle of 29°.

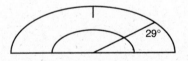

RIGHT ANGLES

Right angles measure 90°. In this case, *AB* is perpendicular to *BC*. Symbolically, $AB \perp BC$.

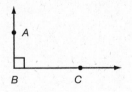

ACUTE ANGLES

Acute angles measure less than 90°.

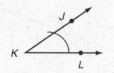

OBTUSE ANGLES

Obtuse angles measure more than 90° but less than 180°.

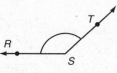

STRAIGHT ANGLES

Straight angles measure 180°. The two adjoining sides, *IH* and *IJ*, extend in opposite directions and form a straight line.

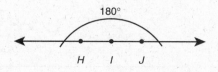

REFLEX ANGLES

Reflex angles measure more than 180° but less than 360°.

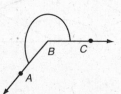

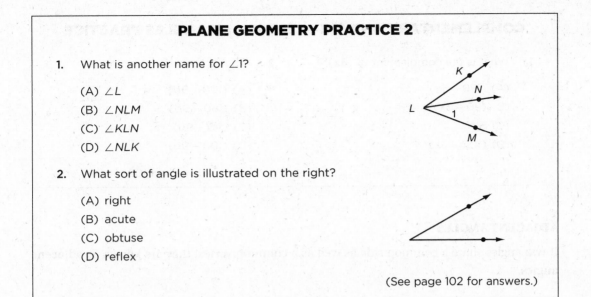

PLANE GEOMETRY PRACTICE 2

1. What is another name for ∠1?

   (A) ∠L
   (B) ∠NLM
   (C) ∠KLN
   (D) ∠NLK

2. What sort of angle is illustrated on the right?

   (A) right
   (B) acute
   (C) obtuse
   (D) reflex

(See page 102 for answers.)

COMPLEMENTARY ANGLES

Two angles are **complementary** if their sum is 90°.
In the diagram at the right, $m\angle a + m\angle b = 90°$.

➡ **Example** _____

Find the complement of 24°.

Answer: 66°
Complementary angles add up to 90°.

$$90 - 24 = 66$$

SUPPLEMENTARY ANGLES

Supplementary angles are two angles that add up to 180°.

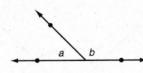

$$m\angle a + m\angle b = 180°$$

➡ **Example** _____

Find the supplement of 47°.

Answer: 133°
Supplementary angles are two angles that add up to 180°.

$$180 - 47 = 133$$

complement/
compliment

**Know the difference
between these two
words. Something**
complementary
**completes
something. (Notice
the spelling with
an e.)**

Something
complimentary
delivers praise.

*The two
45-degree angles
complemented
each other. One
polite angle
complimented the
other: "You're so
acute."*

TIP

**Remember, the
letter "c" comes
before the letter
"s" and 90° comes
before 180°.**

COMPLEMENTARY AND SUPPLEMENTARY ANGLES PRACTICE

1. What is the complement of $(3x)°$?

    (A) $(180 - 3x)°$

    (B) $(90 - 3x)°$

    (C) $5x°$

    (D) $(100 - 3x)°$

2. What is the supplement of $(9b)°$?

    (A) $(100 + 9b)°$

    (B) $(180 - 9b)°$

    (C) $(90 - 9b)°$

    (D) $(100 - 9b)°$

(See page 102 for answers.)

ADJACENT ANGLES

If two angles share a common side as well as a common vertex, they are known as **adjacent angles**.

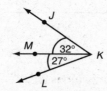

Angle *JKM* and angle *MKL* are adjacent angles because they share a common side, *KM*, and a common vertex, *K*.

➡ **Example**

Add the two adjacent angles.

Answer: 59°

$$
\begin{array}{r}
32° \\
+\,27° \\
\hline
59°
\end{array}
$$

ADJACENT ANGLES PRACTICE

1. Find the measure of $\angle a$.

    (A) 101°

    (B) 47°

    (C) 106°

    (D) 53°

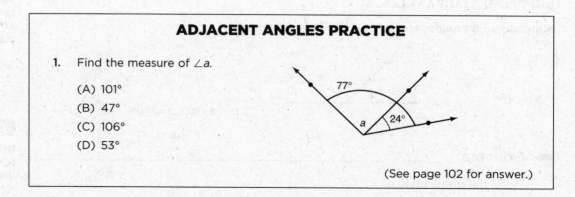

(See page 102 for answer.)

VERTICAL ANGLES

If two straight lines intersect, they form four angles. As we can clearly see, there are a number of adjacent angles:

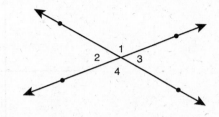

$\angle 1$ and $\angle 3$ are adjacent angles
$\angle 3$ and $\angle 4$ are adjacent angles
$\angle 2$ and $\angle 4$ are adjacent angles
$\angle 1$ and $\angle 2$ are adjacent angles

We also have two sets of angles that are opposite each other, called **vertical angles**, and their measures are equal:

$$m\angle 1 = m\angle 4 \quad \text{and} \quad m\angle 2 = m\angle 3$$

If the measures of two angles are equal, the angles are called congruent.

➡ **Example**

Find the value of x.

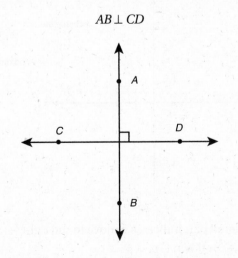

Answer: 46°

Since the angles represented by $2x$ and 92° are vertical angles, their measures are equal.

$$2x = 92$$
$$x = 46$$

Perpendicular Lines

Perpendicular lines intersect in the same plane and form right angles (90°).

$$AB \perp CD$$

Coordinate Geometry

The simplest way to locate points on a plane (flat surface) is to use a graph.

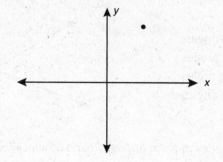

The horizontal axis is called the *x*-axis or abscissa.

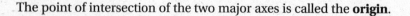

The vertical axis is called the *y*-axis or ordinate.

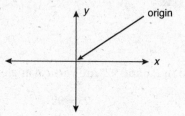

The point of intersection of the two major axes is called the **origin**.

The integers on the major axes locate points on the plane.

For example, the ordered pair (4, 3) is located 4 units to the right and 3 units above the origin.

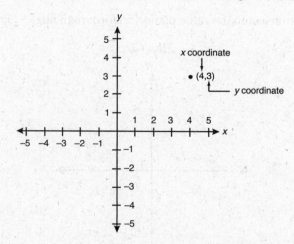

The first digit of the ordered pair indicates a move to the right (+) or left (–) and the second digit indicates a move up (+) or down (–).

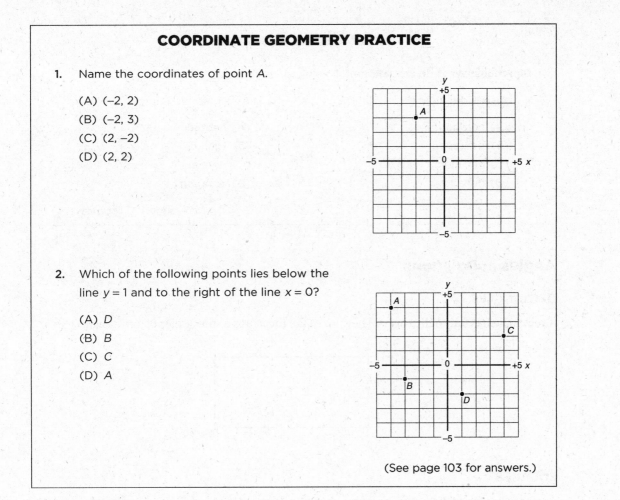

COORDINATE GEOMETRY PRACTICE

1. Name the coordinates of point *A*.

   (A) (–2, 2)
   (B) (–2, 3)
   (C) (2, –2)
   (D) (2, 2)

2. Which of the following points lies below the line *y* = 1 and to the right of the line *x* = 0?

   (A) *D*
   (B) *B*
   (C) *C*
   (D) *A*

   (See page 103 for answers.)

POLYGONS

A **polygon** is a plane (flat) figure totally enclosed by three or more straight lines.

Name of polygon	Number of sides
Triangle	3
Quadrilateral	4
Pentagon	5
Hexagon	6
Heptagon	7
Octagon	8
Nonagon	9
Decagon	10

VOCABULARY

The Greek prefix *poly-*, like the Latin *multi-*, means *many*. A *polygon* has many angles.

My parrot's cage was built as a polygon, but I left the door open. The result? Polly gone.

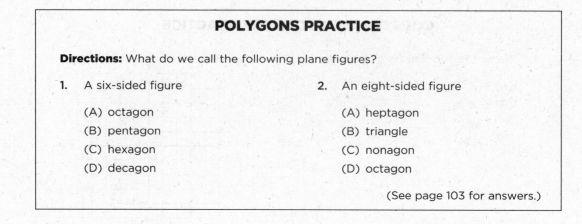

POLYGONS PRACTICE

Directions: What do we call the following plane figures?

1. A six-sided figure

    (A) octagon
    (B) pentagon
    (C) hexagon
    (D) decagon

2. An eight-sided figure

    (A) heptagon
    (B) triangle
    (C) nonagon
    (D) octagon

(See page 103 for answers.)

Angles in Polygons

RECTANGLES

A **rectangle** has four right angles. The sum of the measures of the angles of a rectangle is 360°.

SQUARES

A **square** has four right angles and four congruent sides. The sum of the measures of the angles of a square is 360°.

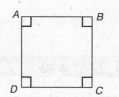

PARALLELOGRAMS

The sum of the measures of the angles of a **parallelogram** is 360°. Opposite angles are congruent: $\angle A \cong \angle C$, $\angle B \cong \angle D$. Two successive angles are supplementary:

$$m\angle A + m\angle B = 180°$$
$$m\angle C + m\angle D = 180°$$

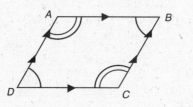

ANGLES IN POLYGONS PRACTICE

1. What is the sum of the angles in a rectangle?

   (A) 180°
   (B) 360°
   (C) 270°
   (D) 90°

2. In parallelogram *ABCD*, if the measure of angle *A* is 123°, find the measure of angle *B*.

   (A) 123°
   (B) 246°
   (C) 57°
   (D) 114°

(See page 103 for answers.)

Triangles

SUM OF THE ANGLES IN A TRIANGLE

The measure of angle *A* + the measure of angle *B* + the measure of angle *C* = 180°.

$$\text{m}\angle A + \text{m}\angle B + \text{m}\angle C = 180°$$

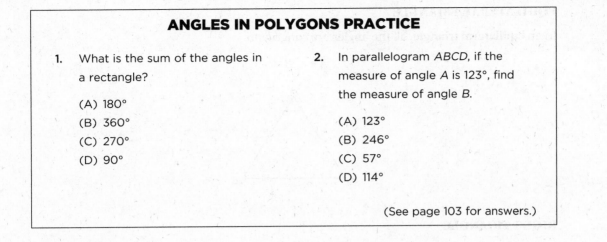

ISOSCELES TRIANGLE

In an **isosceles triangle**, the base angles are congruent.

$$\angle B \cong \angle C$$

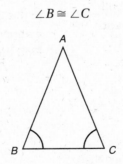

EQUILATERAL TRIANGLE

In an **equilateral triangle**, all the angles are congruent.

$$\angle A \cong \angle B \cong \angle C$$

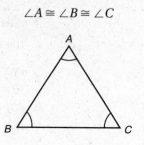

RIGHT TRIANGLE

In a **right triangle**, one angle is a right angle:

$$m\angle C = 90°$$

The other two angles are complementary:

$$m\angle A + m\angle B = 90°$$

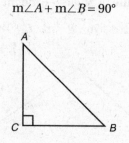

TRIANGLES PRACTICE

1. Select the type of triangle whose base angles are congruent but whose vertex angle is different.

    (A) isosceles
    (B) equilateral
    (C) right

Challenge Question

In this isosceles triangle *ABC*, the exterior angle at C measures 104°. Find the measure of angle *B*.

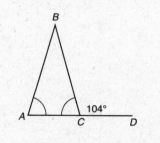

(See page 103 for answers.)

Types of Triangles, Classified by Angles

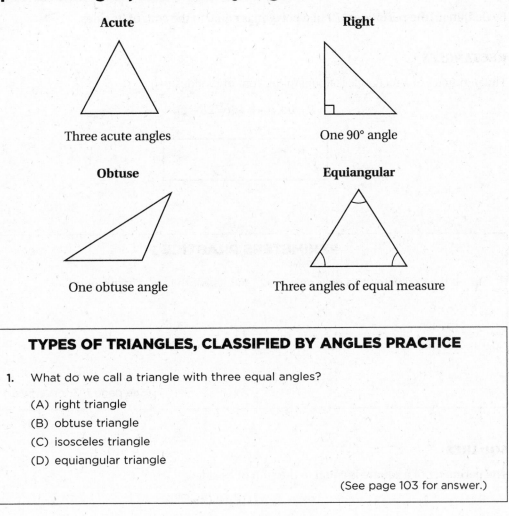

Acute

Three acute angles

Right

One 90° angle

Obtuse

One obtuse angle

Equiangular

Three angles of equal measure

TYPES OF TRIANGLES, CLASSIFIED BY ANGLES PRACTICE

1. What do we call a triangle with three equal angles?

   (A) right triangle
   (B) obtuse triangle
   (C) isosceles triangle
   (D) equiangular triangle

   (See page 103 for answer.)

Types of Triangles, Classified by Sides

Isosceles

Two sides of equal length

Equilateral

Three sides of equal length

Scalene

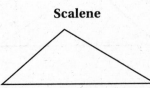

No sides of equal length

Perimeters

By definition, the **perimeter** (P) of a polygon is equal to the sum of its sides.

RECTANGLES

The perimeter of a rectangle is equal to the sum of its sides.

$$P = b + b + h + h = 2b + 2h$$

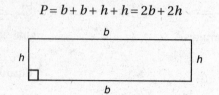

PERIMETERS PRACTICE 1

1. If the perimeter of a rectangle is 42" and its width is 6", find its length.

   (A) 8"
   (B) 12"
   (C) 14"
   (D) 15"

(See page 103 for answer.)

SQUARES

The perimeter of a **square** is equal to the sum of its sides.

$$P = s + s + s + s = 4s$$

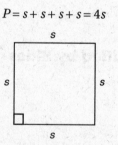

TRIANGLES

The perimeter of a **triangle** is equal to the sum of its sides.

$$P = a + b + c$$

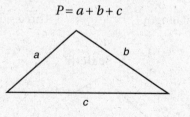

ISOSCELES TRIANGLES

In an **isosceles triangle**, two of the sides are equal.

$$P = a + a + b = 2a + b$$

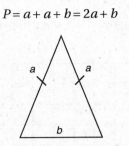

EQUILATERAL TRIANGLES

By definition, an **equilateral triangle** is constructed of three equal sides and the perimeter is the sum of those three sides.

$$P = s + s + s = 3s$$

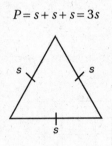

PERIMETERS PRACTICE 2

1. If each of the congruent sides of an isosceles triangle is 11" and the base is 4.6", find the perimeter of the triangle.

   (A) 13.8"
   (B) 37.6"
   (C) 20.2"
   (D) 26.6"

2. If the perimeter of an isosceles triangle is 45.9" and one of the congruent sides is 8.6", find the base of the triangle.

   (A) 37.3"
   (B) 28.7"
   (C) 35.6"
   (D) 27.4"

3. Find one side of an equilateral triangle if its perimeter is 8.

   (A) $2\frac{2}{3}$
   (B) $3\frac{1}{3}$
   (C) 2.5
   (D) 2.45

(See page 103 for answers.)

Areas of Polygons

RECTANGLES

The area (inside space of a rectangle, A) is determined by multiplying its base, b, by its height, h.

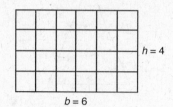

In the diagram, the base is 6, while the height is 4.

$$A = bh$$
$$A = 6 \cdot 4 = 24$$

SQUARES

All the sides of a square are equal, so, to find the area of a square, we multiply side, s, by side, s.
Here, both sides are 5.

$$A = s \cdot s = s^2$$
$$A = 5 \cdot 5 = 25$$

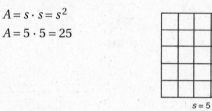

PARALLELOGRAMS

Area = Base × Height

$$A = bh$$
$$A = 5 \cdot 4 = 20$$

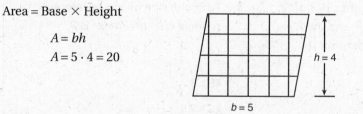

TRIANGLES

Area $= \left(\dfrac{1}{2}\right)$ Base (b) × Height (h)

$$A = \left(\frac{1}{2}\right)bh$$

$$A = \left(\frac{1}{2}\right)(8 \times 4) = \left(\frac{1}{2}\right)32$$

$$A = 16$$

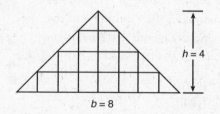

AREAS OF POLYGONS PRACTICE

1. The area of a rectangle is 54. If its length is 12, find its width.

   (A) 3
   (B) 4
   (C) $4\frac{1}{2}$
   (D) $5\frac{1}{2}$

2. If the base of a parallelogram is 24.3 and its height is 8, find the area.

   (A) 194.4
   (B) 188.6
   (C) 203.8
   (D) 200.6

3. If the area of a triangle is 36 square inches and its height is 8 inches, find its base.

   (A) 8 inches
   (B) 9 inches
   (C) 7 inches
   (D) 12 inches

(See page 103 for answers.)

PYTHAGOREAN THEOREM

The ancient Greek mathematician Pythagoras determined a relationship among the sides of a right triangle. He showed that if you erect squares on the sides of a right triangle, the sum of the areas of the two squares on the legs of the right triangle equals the area of the square erected on the hypotenuse of the right triangle.

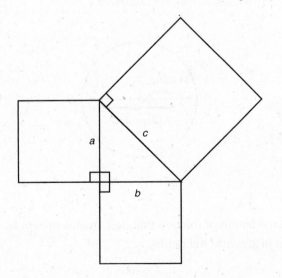

Pythagorean Theorem
$a^2 + b^2 = c^2$, where a and b are the legs, and c is the hypotenuse of the right triangle.

➡️ **Example** _____

Find the hypotenuse of a right triangle whose two legs are 5 and 12.

Answer: 13
Use the Pythagorean Theorem.

$a = 5, b = 12$:

$$a^2 + b^2 = c^2$$
$$5^2 + 12^2 = c^2$$
$$25 + 144 = c^2$$
$$169 = c^2$$
$$13 = c$$

PYTHAGOREAN THEOREM PRACTICE

1. Find the hypotenuse of a right triangle if its two legs are 6 and 8.

   (A) 5
   (B) 12
   (C) 9
   (D) 10

(See page 103 for answer.)

CIRCLES

Radius and Diameter

This is circle O, with center O. AB is the diameter and AO and BO are the two radii. As you can see, the diameter, AB, is twice the size of the radius, AO.

VOCABULARY

The Latin root cir- or circum- means around. (Think of a circle.) To circumscribe (scribe = write) something is to limit it, as if drawing a circle around it.

We circumscribed the scribe by locking him in a round room.

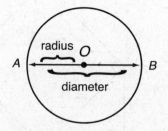

Circumference

The **circumference** is the length of the line that demarcates the circle. The circumference, C, is equal to the product of 2, π, and the radius, r:

$$C = 2\pi r$$

➡ Example _____

Find the circumference of a circle whose diameter is 6. Round the answer to the nearest tenth.

Answer: 18.8

Use the formula $C = 2\pi r$, where $C =$ circumference and $\pi = 3.14$.

The radius is $\frac{1}{2}$ the length of the diameter.

$$r = \frac{1}{2} \cdot d = \frac{1}{2} \cdot 6 = 3$$

$$C = 2\pi r$$
$$C = 2 \times 3.14 \times 3 = 18.84 \approx 18.8$$

CIRCLES PRACTICE

1. If the circumference of a circle is 31.4, find its radius. Use the formula $C = 2\pi r$, where $C =$ circumference, $\pi = 3.14$, and $r =$ radius.

   (A) 4
   (B) 5
   (C) 6
   (D) 9

   (See page 103 for answer.)

Area of a Circle

$A = \pi r^2$, where $\pi = 3.14$ and $r =$ the radius. In this case, $r = 3$, so

$$A = \pi r^2$$
$$A = (3.14)(3)^2 = 3.14\,(9)$$
$$A = 28.26$$

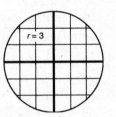

➡ Example _____

If the area of a circle is 154 square inches, find its radius. Let $\pi = \frac{22}{7}$.

Answer: 7

Use the formula $A = \pi r^2$, where $A =$ area and $r =$ radius.

$$A = \pi r^2$$
$$154 = \frac{22r^2}{7}$$
$$1078 = 22r^2$$
$$49 = r^2$$
$$r = 7$$

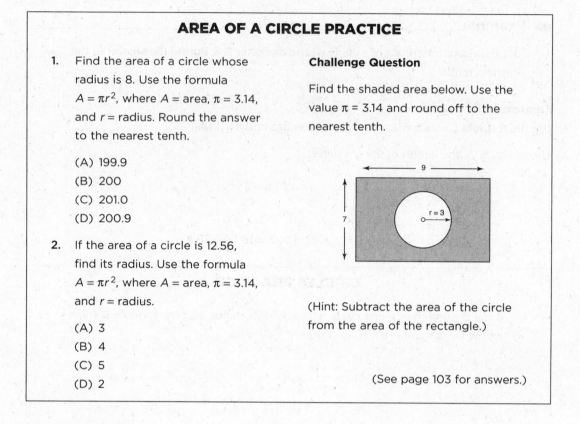

AREA OF A CIRCLE PRACTICE

1. Find the area of a circle whose radius is 8. Use the formula $A = \pi r^2$, where A = area, π = 3.14, and r = radius. Round the answer to the nearest tenth.

    (A) 199.9
    (B) 200
    (C) 201.0
    (D) 200.9

2. If the area of a circle is 12.56, find its radius. Use the formula $A = \pi r^2$, where A = area, π = 3.14, and r = radius.

    (A) 3
    (B) 4
    (C) 5
    (D) 2

Challenge Question

Find the shaded area below. Use the value π = 3.14 and round off to the nearest tenth.

(Hint: Subtract the area of the circle from the area of the rectangle.)

(See page 103 for answers.)

Central Angles

A **central angle** of a circle has its vertex at the center of the circle.

➡ **Example** _____

If two central angles of a triangle are 40° and 80°, find the measure of the third central angle.

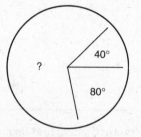

Answer: 240°

All of the central angles add up to 360°, so add up the two given angles and subtract the result from 360°.

$$
\begin{aligned}
x + 40 + 80 &= 360 \\
x + 120 &= 360 \\
-120 \quad &\ -120 \\
\hline
x &= 240
\end{aligned}
$$

CENTRAL ANGLES PRACTICE

1. If three central angles measure 65°, 87°, and 112°, respectively, find the measure of the fourth central angle.

    (A) 96°
    (B) 104°
    (C) 118°
    (D) 76°

    (See page 103 for answer.)

Sectors

➡ **Example** _____

If the radius of the circle below is 4 and the central angle is 60°, find the area of the shaded sector. To simplify matters, let $\pi = 3$.

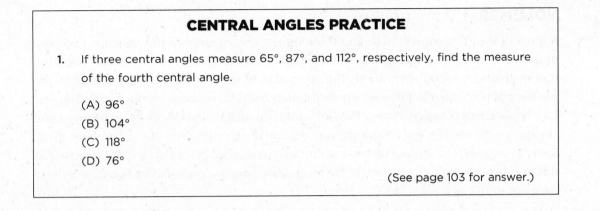

> **DEFINITION**
>
> A **sector** of a circle is an area of the circle determined by the intersection of two radii and the circumference of the circle.

Answer: 8

Find the area of the circle. Then determine the fraction of the entire circle the sector occupies.

Let A = area of the circle, r = radius. $\pi = 3$, $r = 4$:

$$A = \pi r^2$$
$$A = (3)(4)^2$$
$$A = 3(16) = 48$$

There are 360° in the circle. 60° is $\frac{60}{360}$ or $\frac{1}{6}$ of the circle.

$$\frac{1}{6} \times 48 = 8$$

> **TIP**
>
> A central angle delimits an area of the circle in proportion of its ratio to 360°, the number of degrees in an entire circle.

SECTORS PRACTICE

1. If a central angle measures 45° and the radius of its circle is 2, find the area of its sector. Let $\pi = 3$.

    (A) 2
    (B) 1.5
    (C) 3
    (D) 2.5

    (See page 104 for answer.)

VOLUMES

A great deal of present-day two- and three-dimensional geometry still depends upon the propositions developed by the Greek mathematician, Euclid. His most significant contribution to geometry is contained in his thirteen books of the *Elements*. Next to the Bible, the *Elements* is probably the most widely distributed and studied book in the world. The first four books cover plane geometry. The fifth and sixth include the theory of proportions and similarity, while books seven through nine discuss number theory—prime numbers, divisibility of integers, and so on. The last four books discuss solid geometry, and it is precisely in this area that we are going to discuss the formulas originally developed by Euclid, who lived from 306 to 283 B.C.E.

Rectangular Solids

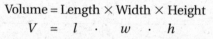

$$V = l \cdot w \cdot h$$

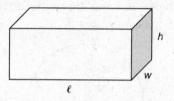

➡ Example

If the length, width, and height of a box are respectively 8″, 7″, and 4.6″, find its volume, correct to the nearest cubic inch.

Answer: 258 cubic inches

Multiply length, width, and height and then round off, correct to the nearest cubic inch. $l = 8$, $w = 7$, $h = 4.6$:

$$V = l \cdot w \cdot h$$
$$V = (8)(7)(4.6) = 257.6 \approx 258$$

VOLUME OF RECTANGULAR SOLIDS PRACTICE

1. Find the volume of a rectangular solid whose length is 6″, width is 8″, and height is 7″.

   (A) 56 in.^{3}
   (B) 336 in.^{3}
   (C) 288 in.^{3}
   (D) 294 in.^{3}

2. We want to construct a box in the shape of a rectangular solid. If its volume is supposed to be 144 cubic inches, its length is 8″, and its width is 3″, find its height.

   (A) 4″
   (B) 6″
   (C) 9″
   (D) 8″

(See page 104 for answers.)

Cubes

A **cube** is a rectangular solid whose sides are equal. If we label each edge e, then the volume, V, is equal to $e \cdot e \cdot e$, or $V = e^3$.

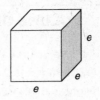

➡ **Example** _____

Find the volume of a cube whose edge is 2.4 meters.

Answer: 13.824 cubic meters

Just use the formula $V = e^3$ and substitute for e. $e = 2.4$:

$$V = e^3$$
$$V = (2.4)^3 = (2.4)(2.4)(2.4) = 13.824$$

VOLUME OF CUBES PRACTICE

1. Find the volume of a cube whose edge is 7 inches.

   (A) 49 in.^{3}
   (B) 343 in.^{3}
   (C) 98 in.^{3}
   (D) 2,401 in.^{3}

2. If the volume of a cube is 216 cubic inches, find one edge.

   (A) 6″
   (B) 8″
   (C) 4″
   (D) 12″

(See page 104 for answers.)

Right Circular Cylinders

Volume = Area of base · Height
Volume = π · Square of the radius · Height
$\qquad V = \pi r^2 h$

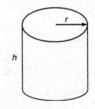

➡ **Example** _____

Find the volume of a cylinder whose diameter is 8 feet and whose height is 5 feet. Let $\pi = 3$.

Answer: 240 ft^3

To find the radius, take half of the diameter. Then just substitute the values into the formula.

$$r = \frac{1}{2}(d) = \frac{1}{2}(8) = 4$$
$$V = \pi r^2 h$$
$$V = (3)(4)^2(5)$$
$$V = 3(16)(5)$$
$$V = 240$$

VOLUME OF RIGHT CIRCULAR CYLINDERS PRACTICE

1. Find the volume of a cylinder whose radius is 2 in. and whose height is 6 in. Use the formula $V = \pi r^2 h$, where V = volume, $\pi = 3$, r = radius, and h = height.

    (A) 72 in.³
    (B) 36 in.³
    (C) 48 in.³
    (D) 40 in.³

Challenge Question

A cylindrical shape is cut out of a cube. To the nearest tenth of an inch, find the volume in the shaded section. Let $\pi = 3.14$.

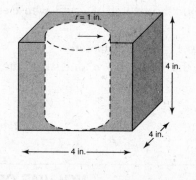

(See page 104 for answers.)

Cones

$$\text{Volume} = \frac{1}{3} \cdot \text{Area of the base} \cdot \text{Height}$$

$$\text{Volume} = \frac{1}{3} \cdot \pi \cdot \text{Square of the radius} \cdot \text{Height}$$

$$V = \frac{1}{3}\pi r^2 h$$

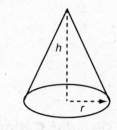

➥ **Example** _____

Find the height of a cone when its radius is 2 millimeters and its volume is 20 cubic millimeters. Let $\pi = 3$.

Answer: 5 millimeters

Substitute the given values into the formula. $V = 20$, $\pi = 3$, $r = 2$:

$$V = \frac{1}{3}\pi r^2 h$$

$$20 = \frac{1}{3} \cdot 3(2)^2 h$$

$$20 = 4h$$

$$5 = h$$

VOLUME OF CONES PRACTICE

1. Find the volume of a cone whose radius is 1" and whose height is 6". Use the formula $V = \frac{1}{3}\pi r^2 h$, where V = volume, $\pi = 3$, r = radius, and h = height.

   (A) 12 in.^{3}

   (B) 8 in.^{3}

   (C) 6 in.^{3}

   (D) 14 in.^{3}

(See page 104 for answer.)

Spheres

Volume = $\frac{4}{3} \cdot \pi \cdot$ Cube of the radius

$V = \frac{4}{3}\pi r^3$

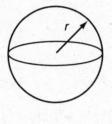

➧ **Example** _____

Find the radius of a sphere whose volume is 256 cubic inches. Let $\pi = 3$.

Answer: 4 inches

$$V = \frac{4}{3}\pi r^3$$

$$256 = \frac{4}{3}(3)r^3$$

$$256 = 4r^3$$

$$64 = r^3$$

$$r = 4$$

VOLUME OF SPHERES PRACTICE

1. Find the volume of a sphere whose radius is 2". Use the formula $V = \frac{4}{3}\pi r^3$, where V = volume, $\pi = 3$, and r = radius.

   (A) 32 in.^{3}

   (B) 48 in.^{3}

   (C) 28 in.^{3}

   (D) 16 in.^{3}

(See page 104 for answer.)

MEASUREMENTS

U.S. Weight Measures

$$1 \text{ pound} = 16 \text{ ounces}$$
$$1 \text{ ton} = 2,000 \text{ pounds}$$

TIP

When converting from larger units to smaller units, divide.

When converting from smaller units to larger units, multiply.

➡ **Example** _____

Change 128,000 ounces to tons.

Answer: 4 tons

There are 32,000 ounces in one ton. Divide 128,000 ounces by 32,000.

$$1 \text{ ton} = 2,000 \text{ pounds} = 16 \text{ ounces} \times 2,000 \text{ pounds} = 32,000 \text{ ounces}$$

$$\frac{128,000 \text{ ounces}}{32,000 \text{ ounces}} = 4 \text{ tons}$$

U.S. WEIGHT MEASURES PRACTICE

1. Change 46 tons to pounds.

    (A) 4,600 lb

    (B) 46,000 lb

    (C) 92,000 lb

    (D) 9,200 lb

(See page 104 for answer.)

U.S. Length Measures

The ancient Romans needed a uniform standard for measuring length. They decided to use the length of the foot of a soldier as this standard measure, the *foot*.

The Romans divided the foot into twelve sections, or *inches*. For longer distances, a mile was the distance marched by 1,000 steps of a Roman soldier, or 5,280 feet. The natives accepted these measurements during the Roman occupation of Britain. In the twelfth century, the king's arm was accepted as a standard measure for a *yard*, or three feet.

1 foot = 12 inches
1 yard = 3 feet
1 yard = 3 feet × 12 inches (per foot) = 36 inches
1 mile = 5,280 feet

Example _____

Jesse can run 44,880 feet per hour. In terms of miles, what is his speed?

Answer: 8.5 miles per hour

To change 44,880 feet to miles, divide by 5,280.

$$
\begin{array}{r}
8.5 \\
5{,}280\overline{)44{,}880.0} \\
-42{,}240 \downarrow \\
\hline
2\,640\,0 \\
-2\,640\,0 \\
\hline
0
\end{array}
$$

U.S. LENGTH MEASURES PRACTICE

1. How many feet are there in 4 miles?

   (A) 23,760 ft
   (B) 21,120 ft
   (C) 22,500 ft
   (D) 20,000 ft

2. Change 216 inches to feet.

   (A) 12 ft
   (B) 4 ft
   (C) 21 ft
   (D) 18 ft

3. How many feet are there in 13 yards?

   (A) 52 ft
   (B) 65 ft
   (C) 78 ft
   (D) 39 ft

(See page 104 for answers.)

U.S. Liquid Measures

1 cup = 8 ounces
1 pint = 2 cups
1 quart = 2 pints
1 gallon = 4 quarts

Example _____

How many pints are there in 16 gallons?

Answer: 128 pints

Change gallons to quarts, then to pints.

16 gallons = 16 × 4 quarts (per gallon) = 64 quarts
64 quarts = 64 × 2 pints (per quart) = 128 pints

U.S. LIQUID MEASURES PRACTICE

1. How many quarts are there in 9 gallons?

    (A) 27 qt
    (B) 36 qt
    (C) 4 qt
    (D) 45 qt

2. Change 24 pints to quarts.

    (A) 8 qt
    (B) 48 qt
    (C) 12 qt
    (D) 6 qt

(See page 104 for answers.)

Metric Length Measures

During the French Revolution, in the last decade of the eighteenth century, French scientists developed a standard unit of measurement, the **meter**. The meter is one ten-millionth of the distance between the North Pole and the Equator.

The system was so rational that most other countries—except for the United States and Great Britain—adopted it.

$$1 \text{ meter} = 100 \text{ centimeters}$$
$$1 \text{ kilometer} = 1,000 \text{ meters}$$

Metric Weight Measures

$$1 \text{ kilogram} = 1,000 \text{ grams}$$

Changing Metric Measures and U.S. Measures

$$1 \text{ meter} = 39.37 \text{ inches}$$
$$1 \text{ kilometer} = 0.62 \text{ mile}$$
$$1 \text{ kilogram} = 2.2 \text{ pounds}$$
$$1 \text{ liter} = 1.06 \text{ quarts}$$
$$1 \text{ mile} = 1.61 \text{ kilometers}$$
$$1 \text{ pound} = 0.45 \text{ kilogram}$$

➡ Example _____

Change 13 kilometers to miles.

Answer: 8.06 miles

One kilometer equals 0.62 mile, so just multiply 13 by 0.62.

$$
\begin{array}{r}
0.62 \\
\times\, 13 \\
\hline
186 \\
620 \\
\hline
8.06
\end{array}
$$

CHANGING METRIC MEASURES AND U.S. MEASURES PRACTICE

1. Change 12 miles to kilometers and round off to the nearest tenth of a kilometer.

    (A) 7.4 kilometers
    (B) 472.8 kilometers
    (C) 19.3 kilometers
    (D) 19.32 kilometers

2. How many pounds are the equivalent of 15.4 kilograms? Round off to the nearest whole pound.

    (A) 34 lb
    (B) 31 lb
    (C) 16 lb
    (D) 45 lb

    (See page 104 for answers.)

GRAPHS AND TABLES

Line Graphs

The average monthly prices for a gallon of regular gasoline are listed below.

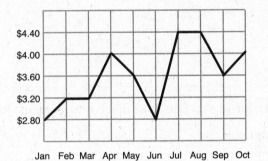

➡ Example

What is the difference in the average price per gallon of gasoline between the months of May and June?

Answer: $0.80

Each horizontal line represents $0.40. Subtract the June price from the May price.

May price – June price: $3.60 – $2.80 = $0.80

LINE GRAPHS PRACTICE

1. Find the average price per gallon of gasoline for the months of February, March, and April and round off to the nearest cent.

   (A) $4.12

   (B) $3.47

   (C) $3.82

   (D) $3.64

(See page 104 for answer.)

Circle Graphs

The **circle graph** below indicates how an average resident of Middletown spends her time in a 24-hour day.

➡ Example

Using the information in the chart, how much time is spent sleeping?

(A) 7 hours, 12 minutes

(B) 7 hours, 14 minutes

(C) 7 hours, 34 minutes

(D) 7 hours, 46 minutes

Answer: 7 hours, 12 minutes

Multiply 24 hours by 30% and then change the decimal part of the answer to minutes.

$$0.30 \times 24 = 7.2 \text{ hours}$$

60 minutes = 1 hour: $\quad 0.2 \times 60 = 12 \text{ minutes}$

$$7.2 \text{ hours} = 7 \text{ hours, 12 minutes}$$

CIRCLE GRAPHS PRACTICE

1. Use the circle graph above to determine, out of a 24-hour day, how much time the average resident of Middletown spends working.

   (A) 7 hours, 12 minutes

   (B) 8 hours, 24 minutes

   (C) 4 hours, 18 minutes

   (D) 9 hours, 8 minutes

(See page 104 for answer.)

Bar Graphs

A bar graph is simply another useful method of pictorially displaying some information.

➡ Example

Using the information in the bar graph below, determine how much sales tax a person would save if she purchased a television set costing $450 in the State of New York rather than in the State of California.

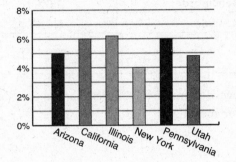

Answer: $9

The state income tax in New York is 4% while it is 6% in California, resulting in a difference of 2%. Multiply $450 by 2% to find the difference in sales tax. Remember to change 2% to 0.02.

$$0.02 \times \$450 = \$9$$

VOCABULARY

The Greek root *graph* (like the Latin *scribe*) means *to write* or *to draw*. When you write your own name, you sign your *autograph*.

I was relieved to find out that geography class did not literally require me to draw a full-scale map of the earth. (That would have taken a lot of graphite!)

BAR GRAPHS PRACTICE

1. Review the graph below and then indicate approximately how many more people reside in Columbus than in Las Vegas.

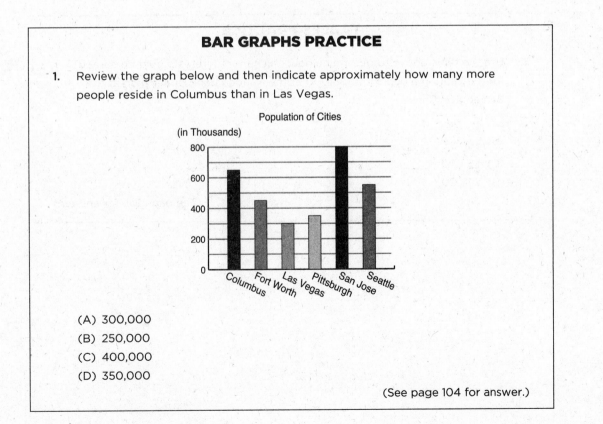

(A) 300,000

(B) 250,000

(C) 400,000

(D) 350,000

(See page 104 for answer.)

Tables

Banks usually change their interest rates monthly. The following table lists the **simple annual interest rates** offered by the indicated banks.

Bank	Annual Interest Rate
Homeland	3.0%
Nautica	2.0%
Bennington	1.0%
Kendale	3.0%

➡ Example

Using the table above, determine the interest earned on a deposit of $5,000 at the Kendale Bank for one month.

Answer: $12.50

If we only want to determine the interest for one month, just divide the given simple annual interest rate by 12.

$$\text{Kendale Bank's interest rate for one month} = \frac{0.03}{12} = 0.0025$$

$$\text{Actual interest for one month} = 0.0025 \times \$5,000 = \$12.50$$

TABLES PRACTICE

1. Use the table above to determine how much more interest could be earned for the year on a deposit of $8,000 at the Nautica Bank rather than at the Bennington Bank.

   (A) $80.00
   (B) $88.00
   (C) $64.00
   (D) $48.00

(See page 105 for answer.)

WORD PROBLEMS

Wage Problems

➡ **Example 1** _____

Kendra is a programmer. She earns $26.50 per hour. How much does she earn in 16 hours?

Answer: $424

Just multiply the wages per hour by the number of hours worked.

$$16 \times \$26.50 = \$424$$

➡ **Example 2** _____

Julio earns $12.54 per hour while Shanequa earns $13.04 per hour. In 12 hours, how much more than Julio does Shanequa earn?

Answer: $6

Multiply the wages per hour by the number of hours worked by each person. Then subtract Julio's total wages from Shanequa's total wages.

Shanequa's wages: $12 \times \$13.04 = \$156.48$
Julio's wages: $- \ 12 \times \$12.54 = \$150.48$
$$\$6.00$$

➡ **Example 3** _____

Mildred earned $22.88 per hour and got paid $1\frac{1}{2}$ times that amount for overtime.

If she worked 44 hours last week and any hours over 40 are considered overtime, how much did she get paid?

Answer: $1,052.48

Multiply 40 hours by the amount she normally gets paid per hour, $22.88. She worked 4 hours overtime, so, for overtime pay, multiply 4 by $1\frac{1}{2}$ by $22.88. Then add the two results together.

Regular pay: $40 \text{ hours} \times \$22.88 = \$915.20$

Overtime pay: $+ \ 4 \text{ hours} \times 1\frac{1}{2} \times \$22.88 = \$137.28$
$$\$1,052.48$$

WAGE PROBLEMS PRACTICE

1. Murray makes $12.74 per hour. How much does he earn in 38 hours?

    (A) $104.12
    (B) $484.12
    (C) $456
    (D) $144.40

2. Hilda earns $14.36 per hour, while her friend, Janice, gets paid $13.37 per hour. If they both work 39 hours, how much more money does Hilda earn?

    (A) $38.61
    (B) $560.04
    (C) $521.43
    (D) $49.30

3. Jules gets paid $12.48 per hour, for his first 40 hours of work per week. He gets paid $15.75 per hour for overtime, which is considered over 40 hours per week. How much does Jules make when he works 47 hours for the week?

    (A) $499.20
    (B) $740.25
    (C) $586.56
    (D) $609.45

Challenge Question

A local supermarket has ten workers and one manager. The manager's yearly salary is $80,000; the average worker, $35,000. If the workers receive an average wage increase of 10% and the manager gets a reduction of 10%, what is the new annual budget for salaries?

(See page 105 for answers.)

TIP

In case we have several investments, total the individual interest payments and set the sum equal to the entire interest.

Investment Problems

➡ **Example** _____

Malcolm has $10,000 to invest. If he invests some money at 4% per year simple interest and the rest at 3% per year simple interest and he derives an income of $385 for the year, how much did he invest at 4%?

Answer: $8,500

Let x = the amount invested at 4%, and let $10,000 - x$ = the amount invested at 3%.

Investment	Percent Interest	Principal ($)	Interest = Percent × Principal ($)
Investment 1	4%	x	4%(x)
Investment 2	3%	$10,000 - x$	3%($10,000 - x$)

The interest from the two investments adds up to $385.

$$4\%(x) + 3\%(10{,}000 - x) = 385$$
$$0.04(x) + 0.03(10{,}000 - x) = 385$$
$$4x + 3(10{,}000 - x) = 38{,}500$$
$$4x + 30{,}000 - 3x = 38{,}500$$
$$x + 30{,}000 = 38{,}500$$
$$x = 8{,}500$$

CHECK

$$0.04(x) + 0.03(10{,}000 - x) = 385$$
$$0.04(8{,}500) + 0.03(10{,}000 - 8{,}500) = 385$$
$$340 + 0.03(1{,}500) = 385$$
$$340 + 45 = 385$$
$$385 = 385 \ \checkmark$$

INVESTMENT PROBLEMS PRACTICE

1. Mrs. Jackson has $7,000 to invest. If she invests part at 6% simple annual interest and part at 8% simple annual interest, she will get an annual return of $520. How much should she invest at 8%?

    (A) $2,500
    (B) $3,000
    (C) $5,000
    (D) $2,000

(See page 105 for answer.)

Age Problems

➡ **Example** _____

Jack is twice as old as Lillian. Six years ago Jack was five times as old as Lillian was then. How old is Lillian now?

Answer:

Let x = Lillian's age now.
Let $2x$ = Jack's age now.
Let $x - 6$ = Lillian's age 6 years ago.
Let $2x - 6$ = Jack's age 6 years ago.

$$2x - 6 = 5(x - 6)$$
$$2x - 6 = 5x - 30$$
$$2x = 5x - 24$$
$$-3x = -24$$
$$x = 8 \text{ years old}$$

AGE PROBLEMS PRACTICE

1. Jenny is now 18 and Carmen is 12. How many years ago was Jenny twice as old as Carmen?

   (A) 3 years ago
   (B) 8 years ago
   (C) 6 years ago
   (D) 4 years ago

2. A father is now 28 years older than his son. Ten years ago the father was 15 times as old as his son. How old is the father now?

   (A) 40 years old
   (B) 28 years old
   (C) 36 years old
   (D) 42 years old

(See page 105 for answers.)

Discounts and Price Increases

➡ **Example** _____

If the city of Pottersville has 8,000 residents now and is projected to lose 8% of its population next year and another 5% the following year, what will be its population at the end of two years?

Answer: 6,992

If Pottersville will lose 8% of its population, it will retain 92%, so take 92% of 8,000. Then, if it loses another 5% of its population, it will retain 95%, so take 95% of the 92% of 8,000.

$$0.92 \times 8,000 = 7,360$$
$$0.95 \times 7,360 = 6,992$$

DISCOUNTS AND PRICE INCREASES PRACTICE

1. The price on a $200 suit was increased by 25%. The merchant was unable to sell the suit, so it was then discounted by 12%. What was the final selling price?

   (A) $225
   (B) $220
   (C) $240
   (D) $210

(See page 105 for answer.)

Percentage Problems

➡ **Example 1** _____

If a suit is reduced by $40 and this represents a 25% discount, what was the original price of the suit?

Answer: $160

Let x = the original price, and set $40 equal to 25% of the original price, x.

$$40 = 0.25x$$
$$100 \times 40 = 0.25x \times 100$$
$$4,000 = 25x$$
$$160 = x$$
$$x = 160$$

➡ **Example 2** _____

What percent of 50 is 90?

Answer: 180%

Let x = the unknown percent. "Of" indicates multiplication, so we have to multiply 50 by a percent in order to arrive at 90.

$$x \cdot 50 = 90$$

Divide by 50:
$$x = \frac{90}{50} = 1.8 = 180\%$$

$$x = 1.80$$

Change to percent:
$$x = 180\%$$

➡ **Example 3** _____

Tiesha works on a base salary of $400 per week plus an 8% commission on sales. If she sold $2,400 worth of items last week, how much was her total salary?

Answer: $592

Find 8% of $2,400, and add to her base salary of $400.

$$0.08 \times \$2,400 = \$192$$
$$+ \$400$$
$$\overline{\$592}$$

PERCENTAGE PROBLEMS PRACTICE

1. An auto dealer increases the price of a used car 15%. If the new price is $6,900, what was the original price of the car?

   (A) $5,000
   (B) $6,200
   (C) $5,900
   (D) $6,000

2. Fifty is what percent of 20?

   (A) 250%
   (B) 40%
   (C) 25%
   (D) 400%

3. Maria is a salesperson. She works on a base salary of $400 per week plus an 8% commission. If she sold $7,000 worth of pharmaceuticals last week, what was her salary?

   (A) $780
   (B) $960
   (C) $840
   (D) $984

(See page 105 for answers.)

Distance Problems

➡ **Example** _____

Glen drove a distance of 182 miles in $3\frac{1}{2}$ hours. What was his average rate of speed?

Answer: 52 mph

Use the distance formula $d = rt$, where d = distance, r = rate, and t = time. $d = 182$, $t = 3\frac{1}{2}$.

$$d = rt$$
$$182 = r\left(3\frac{1}{2}\right)$$
$$182 = \frac{7}{2}r$$
$$\frac{2}{7} \times 182 = \frac{7}{2}r \times \frac{2}{7}$$
$$r = 52$$

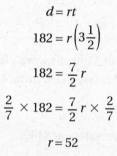

TIP

To determine the total distance traveled, multiply rate times time. Make sure that rate is in the same units as time.

For example, if the rate is 60 miles per hour and the time is 45 minutes, convert 45 minutes to three-quarters of an hour and then multiply.

DISTANCE PROBLEMS PRACTICE

1. Aristide is a train engineer. If the distance between two cities is 350.4 miles, and he wants to make the trip in six hours, what should his average rate of speed be?

   (A) 58.4 mph
   (B) 62.6 mph
   (C) 87.6 mph
   (D) 43.8 mph

(See page 105 for answer.)

STATISTICS

Whenever we're presented with a lot of data, we usually have to sort it out. Statistics helps us make sense of the loads of data we're constantly receiving.

Mean or Average

We are often interested in a typical product, consumer, voter, or the like. When we talk about "typical," we are looking for something representative of an entire group. We are talking about some sort of central tendency.

   We can measure central tendency in three ways:

1. The mean or average
2. The mode
3. The median

➡ **Example** _____

   Julio is on the track team. He recorded the miles he ran each day for the past week: 5.9, 6, 3.7, 6.2, 4.5, 6.1, 3.8. To the nearest tenth of a mile, what was the mean number of miles he ran a day?

Answer: 5.2

Add up all the miles and divide by 7, the number of days Julio ran.

$$\bar{x} = \frac{5.9 + 6 + 3.7 + 6.2 + 4.5 + 6.1 + 3.8}{7} = \frac{36.2}{7} = 5.17\ldots \approx 5.2$$

DEFINITION

The mean or average is simply the sum of the various pieces of data divided by the number of data.

MEAN OR AVERAGE PRACTICE

The Basic Cookware Company has a quality control program. On a weekly basis, inspectors check damages in their manufactured dishes. During the first six weeks of the program, inspectors found the following numbers of dishes damaged, by week: 23, 18, 34, 27, 26, 19.

1. For seven weeks, if management wants to hold the mean number of damaged dishes per week to 24, what is the maximum allowable number of damaged dishes during the seventh week?

   (A) 21
   (B) 24
   (C) 18
   (D) 25

   (See page 105 for answer.)

DEFINITION

The median is the middle number in an ordered set of data.

Median

Sometimes we're not interested in determining the mean. We want to find the middle number.

➡ Example 1 _____

Over the past week, Jose has slept the following numbers of hours per night: 9, 8, 9, 7, 6.5, 7.4, 6.3. Find the median.

Answer: 7.4

In order to determine the median, list the numbers from smallest to largest and then select the middle number.

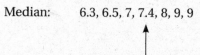

Median: 6.3, 6.5, 7, 7.4, 8, 9, 9

Middle number

➡ Example 2 _____

Find the median of the following numbers: 34, 56, 9, 67, 25, 49.

Answer: 41.5

In this case, we have an even amount of numbers, so we'll first arrange the numbers in ascending order and then we'll add the two middle numbers and divide by 2.

$$9 + 25 + \frac{34 + 49}{2} + 56 + 67$$

$$\frac{34 + 49}{2} = \frac{83}{2} = 41.5$$

MEDIAN PRACTICE

1. Students in the physics class received the following grades on their last exam: 80, 75, 65, 92, 56, 79, 48, 58, 92, 85, 76, 68. Find the median.

   (A) 76
   (B) 74.5
   (C) 75.5
   (D) 74

(See page 105 for answer.)

Mode

The mode is the easiest measure in statistics.

 **Example** _____

Mr. Vargas, the owner of Vargas' Shoe Store, has recorded the daily sales of shoes in his store for the past twelve days: 23, 18, 19, 12, 18, 16, 22, 12, 19, 15, 23, 19. Find the mode and the median and compare the two.

Answer: The mode is 19; the median 18.5.

List the numbers in ascending order. Find the number occurring most often as well as the middle number.

Mode: 12, 12, 15, 16, 18, 18, **19, 19, 19**, 22, 23, 23
         Nineteen occurs most often, so it's the mode.

Median: 12, 12, 15, 16, 18, 18, **19, 19, 19**, 22, 23, 23

$$\frac{18+19}{2} = \frac{37}{2} = 18.5$$

MODE PRACTICE

1. Mr. Hiarnachy, the owner of Howie's Shoes, has recorded the daily sales of shoes for the past twelve days: 35, 19, 23, 32, 19, 28, 35, 31, 23, 18, 17, 19. Find the mode.

    (A) 35
    (B) 23
    (C) 22
    (D) 19

(See page 105 for answer.)

Probability

Probability means the likelihood of a particular event occurring. Probability is a number between and including 0 and 1. A probability of 0 means that the event will absolutely not occur. A probability of 1 means that the event is certain to occur.

Probability is expressed as a percent or a ratio.

$$P(\text{event}) = 25\% \text{ or } 1:4$$

 **Example** _____

A jar contains 6 blue marbles, 7 red marbles, and 2 white marbles. Without looking, find $P(\text{blue})$.

DEFINITION

The mode is the number that occurs most frequently in a given set of data. It's possible to have more than one mode.

TIP

Given the same set of data, we can determine a different mean, mode, or median.

Answer: $\frac{2}{5}$

The probability of selecting a blue marble, $P(b)$, is equal to the number of blue marbles, B, out of the total number of marbles, T.

$$P(b) = \frac{B}{T}$$

$$B = 6, \quad T = 15: \quad P(b) = \frac{6}{15} = \frac{2}{5}$$

PROBABILITY PRACTICE

1. Out of a deck of 52 cards, what is the probability of selecting a king?

   (A) $\frac{1}{13}$

   (B) $\frac{1}{4}$

   (C) $\frac{2}{13}$

   (D) $\frac{3}{52}$

(See page 105 for answer.)

SEQUENCES

In a sequence, we have to determine the pattern.

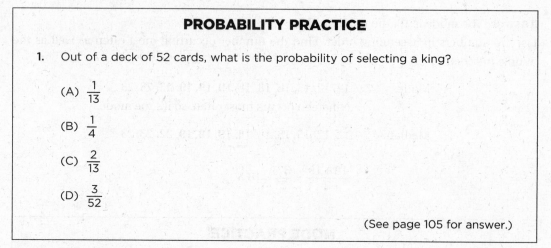

Repeated Patterns in Sequences

Some patterns reappear in the sequences.

➡ Example 1 _____

Find the missing term in the sequence 3, 7, 11, __, 19, 23, ...

Answer: 15

The terms are increasing by 4.

Add 4 to 11: $11 + 4 = 15$

➡ Example 2

Review the sequence: 5, 8, 11, 11, 14, 17, 17, 20, 23, 23, . . . and find the next number.

DEFINITION

In a numeric sequence, find the differences between succeeding numbers to establish a pattern.

Answer: 26

The sequence is divided into groups of three. Within each group, 3 is added to the first and second terms to arrive at the second and third members of the group, respectively. The next group begins with the third member of the previous group, and the pattern is repeated.

5, 8, 11   11, 14, 17   17, 20, 23   23, **26**

➡ Example 3

Review the sequence: VI, 3, IX, 5, _, 7, XV, 9, XVIII, 11, . . . , and find the missing number.

Answer: XII

The Roman numbers are increasing by 3 while the Arabic numbers are increasing by 2.

$$IX + III = XII$$

➡ Example 4

Review the sequence: 32, 33.5, 35, 36.5, 38, 39.5, . . . , and find the next number.

Answer: 41

The sequence is increasing by 1.5.

$$39.5 + 1.5 = 41$$

➡ Example 5

Review the sequence: 86, 15, 81, 15, 76, 15, 71, 15, _, 15, 61, 15, ... What number should fill in the blank space?

Answer: 66

The number 15 repeats alternately and the rest of the sequence reduces by 5.

```
        15,        15,        15,        15,        15,        15,
86,  ^  81,  ^  76,  ^  71,  ^  __,  ^  61,  ^  ...
```

$$71 - 5 = 66$$

➡ Example 6

Find the next two terms in the following sequence:

13, 15, 18, 23, 25, 28, 33, . . .

Answer: 35, 38

In this sequence, the differences between the terms are increasing in a repeating pattern.

Sequence:	13	15	18	23	25	28	33	**35**	**38**
Differences:	+2	+3	+5	+2	+3	+5	+2	+3	+5

The numbers in the sequence are increasing in the pattern 2, 3, 5.

REPEATED PATTERNS IN SEQUENCES PRACTICE

1. Find the missing term in the sequence 8, 13, 18, 23, __, 33, ...

    (A) 25
    (B) 27
    (C) 26
    (D) 28

2. Review the sequence 12, 15, 18, 18, 21, 24, 24, __, 30, ... What number should fill in the blank?

    (A) 27
    (B) 25
    (C) 26
    (D) 24

3. Look at the sequence III, 1, V, 5, VII, 9, IX, 13, ... What number should come next?

    (A) 17
    (B) XI
    (C) XII
    (D) 15

4. Find the missing term in the sequence 33, $31\frac{1}{2}$, 30, $28\frac{1}{2}$, 27, __, 24, $22\frac{1}{2}$.

    (A) 24
    (B) $24\frac{1}{2}$
    (C) $25\frac{1}{2}$
    (D) 25

5. Review the sequence 15, 7, 13, 7, 11, 7, 9, 7, . . . , and find the next term.

    (A) 8
    (B) 7
    (C) 5
    (D) 9

6. Look at the sequence 14, 15, 17, 18, 20, 21, 23, __, 26, . . . , and determine the missing number.

    (A) 23
    (B) 24
    (C) 25
    (D) 22

(See page 105 for answers.)

Squares in Sequences

Some sequences include squares of numbers. Occasionally, constants are embedded in these sequences.

➡ **Example 1** _____

Find the next term in the sequence 4, 9, 16, 10, 9, 16, 25, 10, ...

Answer: 16

There is a constant embedded in a sequence of increasing squares.

				Constant				Constant	
				↓				↓	
Sequence:	4	9	16	10	9	16	25	10	16
Without 10:	4	9	16		9	16	25		16
Power:	2^2	3^2	4^2		3^2	4^2	5^2		4^2

➡ Example 2 _____

Find the next term in the sequence 6, 36, 5, 25, 4, 16, ...

Answer: 3

The sequence is in decreasing order of integers and their squares.

Sequence:	6	36	5	25	4	16	3
Power:	6^1	6^2	5^1	5^2	4^1	4^2	3^1

The next number in the sequence is 3 or 3^1.

SQUARES IN SEQUENCES PRACTICE

Directions: Find the next term in each of the following sequences.

1. 1, 8, 27, 64, 125, . . .

    (A) 250
    (B) 180
    (C) 216
    (D) 256

2. 4, 8, 9, 27, 16, 64, . . .

    (A) 25
    (B) 125
    (C) 128
    (D) 192

(See page 105 for answers.)

Alphabetical Sequences

An alphabetical sequence follows certain patterns, as does a numerical sequence.

➡ Example 1 _____

Find the next letter in the sequence A, C, E, G, I, ...

Answer: K

Let's insert more spaces between the letters. Then we'll attempt to determine some sort of pattern.

Sequence:	A	▼	C	▼	E	▼	G	▼	I	▼	K
Missing letters:		B		D		F		H		J	

The sequence is in ascending alphabetical order, with one letter between each term in the original sequence.

➡ Example 2

Find the next term in the sequence X, U, R, O, L, ...

Answer: I

Leave some space between the letters and then determine which letters are missing.

Sequence:	X	▼	U	▼	R	▼	O	▼	L	▼	I
Missing letters:		W, V		T, S		Q, P		N, M		K, J	

This sequence is in descending alphabetical order, with two letters between each term in the original sequence.

➡ Example 3

Find the next term in the sequence D, F, I, M, R, ...

Answer: X

The sequence is in increasing alphabetical order. Just determine the number of missing letters in the given sequence.

Sequence:	D	▼	F	▼	I	▼	M	▼	R	▼	X
Missing letters:		E		G, H		J, K, L		N, O, P, Q		S, T, U, V, W	
Number of missing letters:		1		2		3		4		5	

The number of missing letters in this sequence is increasing in the pattern 1, 2, 3, 4, 5, ...

➡ Example 4

Find the next letter in the sequence P, P, R, S, P, P, T, U, P, P, V, ...

Answer: W

Here, there's no obvious relationship between individual letters in the sequence. Therefore, let's try another approach. Let's try dividing the sequence into groups of two.

PP RS PP TU PP VW

R, S, T, U are in alphabetical order, with PP in between.

ALPHABETICAL SEQUENCES PRACTICE

Directions: In the following sequences, determine the next letter.

1. J, M, P, S, V, . . .

    (A) Z
    (B) Y
    (C) W
    (D) X

2. X, T, P, L, H, . . .

    (A) F
    (B) G
    (C) D
    (D) E

3. B, D, G, K, P, . . .

    (A) V
    (B) U
    (C) T
    (D) W

(See page 106 for answers.)

Letter/Number Sequences

A3   C6   E9   G12   ?

In this sequence, we have a combination of letters and numbers. The sequence for the letters is independent of the sequence for numbers, so we have to determine each sequence independently.

It is often useful to convert alphabetical letters to their numerical order so that we can spot the pattern. When we take this approach, we should list the letters of the alphabet prior to determining a pattern:

A B C D E F G H I J K L M N O P Q R S T U V W X Y Z
1 2 3 4 5 6 7 8 9 10 11 12 13 14 15 16 17 18 19 20 21 22 23 24 25 26

➡ **Example** _____

Find the next term in the sequence B_9, E^{10}, H_{12}, K^{13}, N_{15}, Q^{16}, ___.

Answer: T_{18}

The subscripts and superscripts alternate. The pattern for subscripts and superscripts is +1, +2.

$$16 + 2 = 18$$

Change the letters to numerical order to determine a pattern.

Alphabetical sequence:	B	E	H	K	N	Q	—
Order of letter in alphabet:	2	5	8	11	14	17	

The letters are increasing by 3.

$$17 + 3 = 20 \ (T)$$

LETTER/NUMBER SEQUENCES PRACTICE

1. Find the next term in the sequence D_1, H^4, L_7, P^{10}, __, ...

   (A) S_{12}

   (B) T^{13}

   (C) S^{12}

   (D) T_{13}

Challenge Question

Find the next term in the sequence

$2A$, D, $\frac{1}{2}I$, $\frac{1}{4}P$, __, ...

(See page 106 for answers.)

ANALOGIES

DEFINITION

An analogy is a comparison between objects.

For example, in the following picture, let's first try to determine what the arch really is. It appears to be a hole in the wall, so let's find the analogy between a mouse and a hole in the wall and a woman and one of the choices offered:

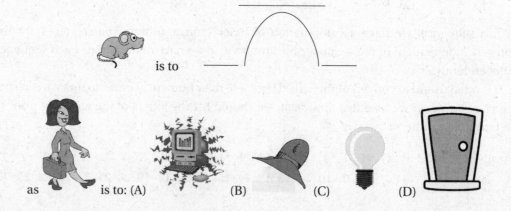

The key to the analogy is the relationship between the mouse and the hole in the wall. One obvious interpretation is that the mouse is going home after a hard day's work chasing that piece of cheese. If we accept that interpretation, the woman is also going home, but she's entering through a door, choice (D).

➡ **Example 1** _____

Here's another analogy problem. In this case, select the picture at the right that will fill the empty box so that the two lower pictures are related to each other in the same manner as the two upper pictures.

TIP
See what relationship the first figure (in the top left corner) has to the second figure (in the top right corner). Then, try to determine a somewhat similar relationship between the third figure (in the bottom left corner) and one of the answer choices.

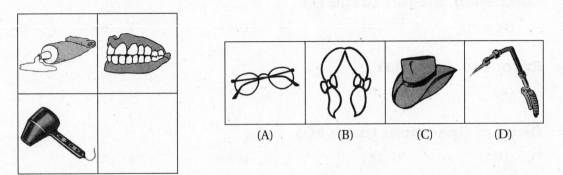

(A)　　　(B)　　　(C)　　　(D)

Answer: (B)

We brush our teeth with toothpaste, and we use a hair dryer on our hair, so (B), hair, is the correct answer.

➡ **Example 2** _____

This last example should "lock in" analogies. Once again, select the picture at the right that will fill the empty box so that the two lower pictures are related to each other in the same manner as the two upper pictures.

(E)　　　(F)　　　(G)　　　(H)

Answer: (E)

A fishing hook is to a fish as a lasso is to a horse. A fishing hook and a lasso are used to, respectively, capture and/or restrain a fish and a horse.

ANSWERS

Natural and Whole Numbers (page 16)

1. **(D)**　　　　2. **(B)**　　　　3. **(C)**

Comparing Integers (page 17)

1. **(D)**　　　2. **(A)**　　　3. **(D)**　　　4. **(B)**

Exponents (page 19)

1. **(A)**　　　2. **(B)**　　　3. **(B)**

Order of Operations (page 20)

1. **(D)**　　　2. **(A)**　　　3. **(C)**　　　4. **(C)**

Rounding Off Integers (page 21)

1. **(D)**　　　2. **(C)**　　　3. **(A)**　　　4. **(A)**

Prime Numbers (page 22)

1. **(C)**　　　2. **(B)**　　　3. **(B)**

Factors and Multiples (page 23)

1. **(D)**　　　2. **(C)**　　　3. **(D)**　　　4. **(B)**

Challenge Question: 28

Reducing Fractions (page 25)

1. **(A)**　　　2. **(C)**　　　3. **(B)**

Changing Improper Fractions to Whole or Mixed Numbers (page 27)

1. **(A)**　　　2. **(D)**　　　3. **(C)**

Changing Mixed Numbers to Improper Fractions (page 27)

1. **(B)**　　　2. **(B)**

Operations with Fractions (page 29)

1. **(D)**　　　3. **(A)**　　　5. **(B)**
2. **(C)**　　　4. **(B)**

Challenge Question: $5\frac{1}{3}$ minutes

Comparing Decimals and Fractions (page 31)

1. **(C)**   2. **(B)**   3. **(D)**

Rounding Off Decimals (page 32)

1. **(A)**   2. **(D)**

Operations with Decimals (page 34)

1. **(D)**   2. **(C)**   3. **(D)**   4. **(A)**

Scientific Notation (page 34)

1. **(C)**   2. **(D)**

Changing Fractions and Whole Numbers to Percents (page 35)

1. **(A)**   2. **(D)**

Changing Percents to Fractions (page 36)

1. **(A)**

Changing Decimals to Percents (page 36)

1. **(C)**

Changing Percents to Decimals (page 37)

1. **(D)**

Finding a Percent of a Number and Applications (page 38)

1. **(A)**

Algebra (page 38)

1. **(C)**   2. **(D)**

Arithmetic Operations with Signed Numbers (page 41)

1. **(A)**   2. **(C)**   3. **(B)**

Formulas (page 42)

1. **(B)**

Equations (page 42)

1. **(B)**

Challenge Question: 7

Simplifying Exponential Expressions (page 44)

1. **(D)**

Radicals (page 45)

1. **(D)**   2. **(A)**

Inequalities (page 46)

1. **(C)**

Operations with Monomials and Polynomials (page 47)

1. **(C)**   2. **(A)**   3. **(C)**   4. **(D)**

Absolute Value (page 48)

1. **(C)**   2. **(D)**

Ratios and Proportions (page 49)

1. **(C)**

Consecutive Integers (page 51)

1. **(D)**   2. **(C)**   3. **(B)**

Challenge Question: 49

Plane Geometry 1 (page 53)

1. **(C)**

Plane Geometry 2 (page 55)

1. **(B)**   2. **(B)**

Complementary and Supplementary Angles (page 56)

1. **(B)**   2. **(B)**

Adjacent Angles (page 56)

1. **(D)**

Coordinate Geometry (page 59)

1. **(B)**   2. **(A)**

Polygons (page 60)

1. **(C)**   2. **(D)**

Angles in Polygons (page 61)

1. **(B)**   2. **(C)**

Triangles (page 62)

1. **(A)**

Challenge Question: 28°

Types of Triangles, Classified by Angles (page 63)

1. **(D)**

Perimeters 1 (page 64)

1. **(D)**

Perimeters 2 (page 65)

1. **(D)**   2. **(B)**   3. **(A)**

Areas of Polygons (page 67)

1. **(C)**   2. **(A)**   3. **(B)**

Pythagorean Theorem (page 68)

1. **(D)**

Circles (page 69)

1. **(B)**

Area of a Circle (page 70)

1. **(C)**   2. **(D)**

Challenge Question: **34.7**

Central Angles (page 71)

1. **(A)**

Sectors (page 71)

1. **(B)**

Volume of Rectangular Solids (page 72)

1. **(B)**   2. **(B)**

Volume of Cubes (page 73)

1. **(B)**   2. **(A)**

Volume of Right Circular Cylinders (page 74)

1. **(A)**

Challenge Question: **51.4 in.^{3}**

Volume of Cones (page 75)

1. **(C)**

Volume of Spheres (page 75)

1. **(A)**

U.S. Weight Measures (page 76)

1. **(C)**

U.S. Length Measures (page 77)

1. **(B)**   2. **(D)**   3. **(D)**

U.S. Liquid Measures (page 78)

1. **(B)**   2. **(C)**

Changing Metric Measures and U.S. Measures (page 79)

1. **(C)**   2. **(A)**

Line Graphs (page 80)

1. **(B)**

Circle Graphs (page 80)

1. **(B)**

Bar Graphs (page 81)

1. **(D)**

Tables (page 82)

1. **(A)**

Wage Problems (page 84)

1. **(B)**   2. **(A)**   3. **(D)**

Challenge Question: $457,000

Investment Problems (page 85)

1. **(C)**

Age Problems (page 86)

1. **(C)**   2. **(A)**

Discounts and Price Increases (page 86)

1. **(B)**

Percentage Problems (page 88)

1. **(D)**   2. **(A)**   3. **(B)**

Distance Problems (page 88)

1. **(A)**

Mean or Average (page 89)

1. **(A)**

Median (page 90)

1. **(C)**

Mode (page 91)

1. **(D)**

Probability (page 92)

1. **(A)**

Repeated Patterns in Sequences (page 94)

1. **(D)**   3. **(B)**   5. **(B)**
2. **(A)**   4. **(C)**   6. **(B)**

Squares in Sequences (page 95)

1. **(C)**   2. **(A)**

Alphabetical Sequences (page 97)

1. **(B)**   2. **(C)**   3. **(A)**

Letter/Number Sequences (page 98)

1. **(D)**

Challenge Question: $\frac{1}{8}$ Y

Verbal Skills

3

The HSPT, the COOP, and the TACHS test verbal skills in different ways. It used to be said that the HSPT focused a bit more on *what* you know, whereas the COOP tested *how* you know something. Changes in the tests and the addition of the TACHS have blurred these differences, so a solid knowledge base *and* strong thinking skills are necessary to do well on all three tests. When possible, we will identify which facts or skills are emphasized on which test, but it would be a good idea to study *all* the material listed here. In fact, it would help you to take all six practice tests in this book. The more practice you get, the better you'll do on any test.

VOCABULARY

Strong vocabulary serves as an essential skill not only for the HSPT and TACHS, but for many of the other standardized tests (SAT, ACT, GRE, LMNOP, TTFN, ASAP, IMHO, and some very difficult blood tests) you will take in your academic career. In fact, some sections of these exams have been accused of being nothing more than complicated vocabulary tests.This is not entirely true, of course, but, obviously, the richer your vocabulary is, the easier it is to solve that portion of the test.

> **PARENTS/TEACHERS**
>
> Building vocabulary will benefit your students in many ways. We make light of standardized tests in the text, but most of the ones students will take in the coming years do include strong vocabulary components. More importantly, though, a rich vocabulary will help students academically through their school years and beyond.

Preparing for the vocabulary section may take the most effort, but the rewards will be great—not only in improving your exam score but also in improving your studies in all other subjects in school. Moreover, a well-spoken person will win respect in life.

The best way to strengthen your vocabulary is to READ. Wow, how old-fashioned! Read what you enjoy. Some students love reading the sports section of the newspaper every day, and that's a great start. Branch out and read some sports magazines. Maybe you enjoy reading the comics section of the paper. You would enjoy checking out some of the many fascinating books on the history of comics.

Many middle school students pride themselves on reading adult best-sellers. However, we should let you in on a terrible secret: Many of these books are actually written **below** your reading level! So if you like Stephen King, you should try Edgar Allan Poe, a horror writer with an incredibly large vocabulary. Perhaps you enjoyed reading young-adult mysteries like those about Nancy Drew or the Hardy Boys. Well, Agatha Christie's novels and the Sherlock Holmes stories by Sir Arthur Conan Doyle contain just as much suspense.

To learn the most vocabulary from these books, you'll have to make yourself a promise to look up unfamiliar words in the dictionary. Any kind will do, but the best dictionary for you will provide pronunciations and word histories (etymologies).

VOCABULARY

Always keep an OPEN dictionary when you read so you can easily look up unfamiliar words.

Oh, it feels like such a chore to get the dictionary off the shelf and then open it up to search for the word. We're tempted to skip learning it.

Those of you with electronic readers can sometimes tap on an unfamiliar word to get the definition. Those of you reading the old-fashioned way have another solution: you should have a dictionary on your desk in front of you whenever you read or do homework.

Electronic books provide us with great conveniences, but research shows that readers retain much more information from physical books. Sometimes you don't have a choice—but if you do, choose a physical book. It employs more of your senses, focuses your eyes more effectively, and improves your memory. Reading with a pencil (for underlining, circling, and writing in the margins) makes an even greater impression.

Just skipping around in the dictionary is a fascinating way to learn, for every word contains a story. For instance, the adjective *maudlin* means "excessively sentimental" or (to use a more casual term) "weepy." *Maudlin* is an alternate version of *Magdalene*. Mary Magdalene was frequently portrayed in art as crying, so something causing this weepy reaction is considered maudlin.

The dictionary is one book that is not going to come out on DVD, so don't wait for the movie. Stop being so slothful/indolent/lazy/idle/lethargic; use the dictionary!

Vocabulary Memory Aids

TIP

Because FLASH CARDS are portable, they are a valuable tool for learning vocabulary.

We can easily read about a word, but remembering the information presents new challenges. One of the best ways to study and remember vocabulary words is by making flash cards. Again, if you have an e-reader or a smartphone, you can download vocabulary applications; however, with flash cards, you can personalize the words with your own sentences and drawings. Have a stack of cards handy, and write down any word that is new to you. Carry them around with you, and study them whenever you have a few minutes to spare—on the bus, before class, after lunch, or in study hall.

To make the words even easier to remember, add some detail to your cards. Write the word on one side and the definition on the other side, of course. Then add a ridiculous **picture** to help you remember it. The more outlandish you make it, the better you'll remember it. Drawing a picture may seem like a pointless step, but we respond strongly to visuals; a picture will further impress the word on your brain.

Finally, write a sentence about the picture. A student once learned the word *sputum* by writing the definition (saliva and mucous spit out of the mouth) on the back of the card and adding a simple picture of a stick person vomiting up some large antacid tablets. The sentence he wrote was "The boy spewed Tums in his sputum." It disgusted us, to be sure, but we never forgot the word.

TIP

Here's an additional way to remember vocabulary: after you find the definition and derivation of a word, do an online image search of the word. What do you see? What picture can help your memory the most?

Try some of these yourself. Draw pictures and compose sentences using the following words.

tedious—tiresome, boring, monotonous
knack—ability, aptitude
panegyric—a speech of high praise
penultimate—next to last
spurious—not genuine; not authentic

Computers

If you use a computer and log onto the Internet, you have access to a myriad (many thousands) of reading sources. The next time you're working online, turn off your Instant Messaging, shut your Facebook, forfeit your games, and quit Twitter. Instead, read an article about something that interests you. If you have trouble getting started, go to a trivia site and get some ideas.

You can also painlessly improve your vocabulary by registering for one of the many organizations that will e-mail you a new word every day. Most of these include sentences, word histories, and interesting information about vocabulary. If you check your e-mail every day, learn the new word, and use it several times that day, the word will become part of your vocabulary.

Several sites also contain word games, such as vocabulary hangman. Do a web search for *SAT* or *ACT* and *hangman* or *vocabulary*, and you'll get many responses. Create Quizlets online for even more interactions. Challenge the machine, and you will emerge victorious!

PARENTS/TEACHERS

Encourage your students to create vocabulary flash cards. In addition to using the cards for review, try placing some of them in different areas of your home.

Crossword Puzzles

Speaking of word games, crossword puzzles provide another fun way to learn vocabulary. They especially help in preparing for vocabulary exams because the writers of these puzzles fill them with tricks in which a word can be used as different parts of speech. For instance, a crossword clue might simply read *test*. You have to read this two ways; it's either a noun (*a test*) or a verb (*to test*). You can fight the good fight, jump the high jump, and land on the land. Some words are pronounced differently and have different definitions. Is *desert* the hot, dry area (DEsert) or is it the verb meaning to leave or abandon (deSERT)? All of the entrance exams contain words like this to test the flexibility of your thinking.

Be aware that if you do the crossword puzzle in the newspaper every day, the editors publish easy clues and puzzles on Monday. Then the puzzles get harder and harder every day. Don't try working your first puzzle on a Friday! By the way, some people think that using a dictionary while you work the crossword puzzle is cheating. We disagree; we call it **learning**.

Word Roots

Knowing the roots of words can also greatly aid you in figuring out definitions. You'll learn a lot of these in the dictionary, but we'll go over some common ones.

TIP

Learning ROOTS can help you define words you've never seen before.

For instance, the root *mor* (or *mort* or *mors*) means *death*. Got it? So if you're reading about some characters named Mordred, Morgan, Voldemort, and Professor Moriarty, and they live in a place called Mordor, you may safely assume **bad** news. Are your parents upset when they make their mortgage payments? Of course they are, because these house payments are named after a "death pledge." Dead bodies are kept in a mortuary. A mortician prepares a body for a funeral. Something immortal cannot die.

Let's try a few more. Take a few minutes to memorize these.

sub—under	*sol*—sun
super—over	*luna*—moon
medi—middle	*terra*—earth (Latin)
extra—beyond	*geo*—earth, ground (Greek)
	mar—sea

VOCABULARY PRACTICE 1

Directions: Define the following words.

1. sublunary
2. Mediterranean
3. subterranean
4. extraterrestrial
5. submarine

VOCABULARY PRACTICE 2

Directions: How did you do on the first practice set? If you feel like you need some more practice, try defining the following words.

1. geocentric
2. extraordinary
3. lunar

(See page 136 for answers.)

TIP

Don't overload your brain by trying to memorize these roots all at one. Learn one section at a time.

Eating

If you've ever studied dinosaurs, you're familiar with the root *vor*, meaning *eat*. Since *carne* means "meat," a *carnivore* is a meat-eater. An *herbivore* is a plant-eater. If *omni* means "all" or "everything," what is an *omnivore*? Well, people are omnivores. We eat pretty much everything, alas. Something with a huge appetite is *voracious*.

Breathing

Something else we do is breathe. The root *anima* means "breath" or "spirit" or "soul." An *animal*, of course, is a living, breathing creature. Someone *animated* is full of life. Animated cartoons move as if alive. Something *inanimate* is lifeless.

Spir also means "breath" or "soul." Your spirit lives. To *inspire* literally means to breathe into, but we use it in its metaphorical sense, to arouse an animated or exalting influence.

Cant means "to sing." We get the word *chant* from this root, as well as *cantor*, the leader of singing, and *incantation*, the chanting of spells.

Dic or *dict* means "to speak." When you *dictate*, you speak aloud. When you *contradict*, you speak against. Your *diction* is your choice of words. Need we mention the word *dictionary*?

Locut or *loqu* also means "to speak" or "talk." Someone who talks a lot is *loquacious*.

Sleeping

Somnus was the Roman god of sleep, so we have the words *somnolent* (sleepy, drowsy, or causing sleep), *somnambulist* (a sleepwalker), and *insomnia* (an inability to sleep).

Before you fall asleep, try to memorize these roots. Then practice.

VOCABULARY PRACTICE 3

Directions: *Bene* means "good" or "well." *Vale* means "goodbye" or "farewell." What do these words mean?

1. What is a *benediction*?
2. What is a *valediction*?
3. What is a *carnival*?

VOCABULARY PRACTICE 4

Directions: Define the following words.

1. voracious
2. inanimate
3. chili con carne
4. contradict
5. loquacious

VOCABULARY PRACTICE 5

Directions: Test yourself even further by seeing if you can define the following five words.

1. prototype
2. century
3. triangle
4. bilingual
5. quadruped

(See page 137 for answers.)

Studying the following lists of roots, prefixes, and suffixes can help you break down many words into understandable sections. For the following roots, can you name some words that use these as prefixes? For instance, for the root *uni*, you could write the word *unicycle*, the one-wheeled vehicle.

Counting

semi/hemi/demi—half

mono—one

uni—one

duo—two

bi—two

tri—three

quad/quat—four

quint—five

pent—five

sext—six

sept—seven (September used to be the seventh month.)

oct—eight (October used to be the eighth month.)

novem—nine (not to be confused with the root *novus*, which means *new*, as in the word *novel*)

dec—ten

cent—hundred

mill—thousand

poly—many

proto—first

Okay, if the Latin root *ped* or *pod* means "foot" (think *pedal* or *pedestrian*), you should know the following words:

biped   *tripod*   *quadruped*   *centipede*

Note: The Greek root *ped* or *pedia* means "child." So a *pediatrician* is a children's doctor; a *podiatrist* is a foot doctor.

Fear

The root *phobia* means "fear" or "dislike." The names of phobias interest some people. Surely you've heard of many of these phobias:

acrophobia—fear of heights

brontophobia—fear of thunder

pedophobia—fear of children

philophobia—fear of love

phonophobia—fear of sound

photophobia—fear of light

pyrophobia—fear of fire

somniphobia—fear of sleep

sophophobia—fear of learning

triskaidekaphobia—fear of the number 13

. . . and the most ironically named one of all:

sesquipedalophobia—fear of long words! (Dare we say *multisyllabic* words?)

Study

The root *logos* literally means "word" (see the earlier root *locut/loqu*), so a *monologue* is a speech for one person. Another form of this root is *ology*, which means "the science" or "study of something."

archaeology—study of ancient history

biology—study of life

cosmology—study of the universe

etymology—study of word origins

genealogy—study of family origins

geology—study of the earth

graphology—study of handwriting

psychology—study of the mind

seismology—study of earthquakes

sociology—study of society

Opposites

Take a look at these opposites. You've probably heard most of these; now you know how they work in words.

cide—kill

viv—live, alive

(If you are full of life, you are

   vivacious.)

micro—small

macro—large

(A *microscope* is an instrument

  you use to see small things.)

hyper—over, above

hypo—under, beneath

endo—within

exo—out of, outside

inter—between

intra—within

homo—alike

hetero—different

belli—war

pace—peace

pre—before

post—after

pro—forward

retro—backward

The following prefixes contain negative and positive feelings.

Negative
a/an—not or without
a/ab—away or from
anti—against, opposite
contra—against
dis—apart, away
dys—bad, ill
mal—bad, ill
mis—hate
in/im—not
non—not
un—not
e/ex—out
ob/op—against

Positive
bene—good
eu—good
philo—love
con/col/com/cor/co—together, with
syn/sym—together, with
pro—forward

Write out some words that contain these prefixes, such as **anti**perspirant or **bene**ficial.

VOCABULARY PRACTICE 6

Directions: Learn the following roots:

auto—self
sophos—wisdom
biblio—book
bio—life

anthropos—people
morph—form
graph—write, draw
potens/potent—power

Now identify the following words. If you can't define them, divide them into their component roots. For instance, for the first one, simply write out *biblio* and *phile*. Does that help you define the word?

1. bibliophile
2. misanthrope
3. philosopher
4. anthropomorphic
5. autograph

6. autobiography
   (You might have to go back earlier in the chapter for the next two.)
7. postmortem
8. omnipotent

(See page 137 for answers.)

Family Roots

pater—father
mater—mother
frat—brother

sor—sister
gen—birth

Progeny means "children" or "offspring." *Genesis* is "the beginning."

Senses and Such

vis/vid—see

tact/tangi—touch

audi—hear

son—sound

patho/pathy—feelings, suffering

corp—body

man—hand

Location

ad—to

ante—before

circum—around

con/com—together, with

de—from, down

in/il/im—in, into, on

inter—between

intro—within

peri—around, about

re—again, back

se—apart

tele—distant

trans—across, beyond

super—over, above

VOCABULARY PRACTICE 7

Directions: Define the following words. If you need to do so, look back through the roots you've learned.

1. supersonic
2. audiophile
3. antebellum
4. telepathic

(See page 137 for answers.)

VOCABULARY PRACTICE 8

Directions: If the root *port* means "to carry," what do the following words mean?

1. transport
2. teleport
3. import
4. report
5. deport

(See page 138 for answers.)

More Movement

tors/tort—twist

flect/flex—bend

fract/frag—break

rupt—break, burst

prehend/prehens—seize, grasp

ject—throw

vers/vert—turn

cur/curr/curs—run

grad— step

Faith

deo/theo—god

cred—believe

fid—faith, trust, loyalty

Did you know that Jupiter (deo-pater) is the father god?

The Apostle's Creed is a prayer listing our beliefs.

Now you know why dogs are named Fido.

Authority

archy—rule   *cracy*—government
vict/vinc—conquer   *mand*—order, command

Try combining and recombining these roots. You'll make up some new words and stumble onto some real ones you may not have heard yet!

VOCABULARY PRACTICE 9

Directions: Define the following words.

1. theocracy   3. anarchy   5. gradual
2. confide   4. credible

(See page 138 for answers.)

Commonly Tested Words

Knowing roots will help you decode the general meaning of many words. However, you'll still need to develop your vocabulary.

This list of commonly tested words will get you started. We've supplied some of the definitions; check others in your dictionary and create your flash cards. It is important to practice using a dictionary and learning how to look up key definitions that you will remember.

Of course you can't learn these all at once; pace yourself and allow the time to go back and "re-remember" the words. **Repetition**, **rest**, and **retrieval** will keep these in your memory. Try to incorporate them into daily conversations, as well.

TIP
Try making flash cards for these common test words. Don't forget to draw a picture and write a sentence.

abate—
abet—to aid
abjure—to renounce, to give something up
abode—
accord—
acrid—
acute—
adamant—hard; stubborn
adept—
adjacent—
advocate—
affable—
affliction—
agile—nimble, quick
akin—
allege—
allot—to distribute (not to be confused with a lot!)
aloof—distant or unsympathetic in attitude

allure—
ambiguous—
amicable—
amiss—
anarchy—
antithesis—the opposite
apathetic—
apex—
apocryphal—doubtful in authenticity
ardor—passion (ardent—passionate)
articulate—
aspire—
assimilate—
assuage—to make easier
astute—
atrocity—
audacious—
augment—
authentic—

avert—

avid—

avuncular—helpful, friendly (like an uncle)

awry—

banter—

barter—

bellicose—warlike

benefactor—

benighted—

benign—good

bigot—

bizarre—

blatant—

bleak—

blithe—happy

boon—a gift

breach—(n) a break; (v) to break

brisk—vigorous, energetic

cache—

callous—

candid—

capacious—

capricious—

capsize—

cascade—

chaff—

chastise—

circumlocution—talking in a roundabout way

citadel—

clad—

clarify—

cogent—

cogitate—

cognizant—

component—

conceited—

concur—to agree

confiscate—

connoisseur—

console—to comfort

conspiracy—

contemporary—

contrive—

copious—

counterfeit—

covet—

credulous—

crucial—

crusade—

culminate—

debut—first appearance

deceptive—

decipher—

decree—

deface—

defer—

deplete—

deplore—

deploy—

deter—

dexterous—

dialect—

diction—

dilapidated—

dilemma—

diminutive—small

dire—

discern—

disclose—

discreet—

discrete—

disdain—

disgruntled—

dismal—

dispatch—

dispensable—

distraught—

docile—

doctrine—belief, creed, dogma

dormant—

dross—

dub—

dubious—

duplicitous—deceitful; double-dealing

durable—

edible—

egress—an exit

elegy—

elite—

embargo—

embark—

encroach—

endeavor—

engender—

enigma—

enmity—

epoch—

equivocate—to lie by using ambiguous
  language

evoke—

facile—easy; superficial

facilitate—

fallacy—

fastidious—

feign—to pretend

flagrant—

flustered—

foreboding—

forfeit—

formidable—

foster—

frivolous—

frugal—thrifty; not costly

fulsome—abundant; offensively insincere

garrulous—excessively talkative

gaudy—

gaunt—thin, bony; emaciated

glut—

grapple—

gregarious—

grueling—

guile—

gullible—

haggard—

hamper—to hinder, to get in the way of, to
  interfere with

harbor—

haughty—

haven—

heinous—

hew—to cut down

hybrid—

ignoble—not noble; common

illiterate—

immaculate—spotlessly clean; pure

impair—

impede—

implore—

inane—

incense—

incite—

incredulous—

in-depth—

indifferent—

indolent—

induct—

inordinate—

invincible—

irascible—

irate—angry

ire—anger

jocular—

jubilant—

languish—

laud—

laudable—

lavish—

lax—

lethargic—

lexicon—

lithe—flexible, supple; graceful

lucid—

lucrative—

luminous—

malcontent—

mar—

martial—

meager—

meander—

mendicant—a beggar

mercenary—

mettle—

millennium—

mimic—

mirth—

modify—

mollify—

monotonous—

morose—

multitude—

mundane—ordinary

municipality—

muse—

nadir—the lowest point (opposite of
  zenith)

negligent—

nimble—

noisome—offensive; foul

nomadic—wandering, roaming

obdurate—stubborn; hard-hearted

oblique—

obstreperous—noisily defiant

odious—offensive, repugnant

opulent—

oration—

ornate—

ostracize—to exclude

ovation—

panegyric—a speech of high praise

paragon—

pathos—

patron—

perfidious—

peripatetic—walking

pernicious—extremely harmful

perturb—

petty—of small importance

pied—multicolored, patchwork

pique—anger

pivotal—

placid—

plausible—

plunder—

potent—powerful

precocious—

prim—excessively proper; prudish

primordial—

principal—

prodigy—

profound—

protean—

prudent—

pseudonym—

pugnacious—inclined to fight, belligerent

pungent—describing a sharp, acrid smell or taste

quench—

query—

rapacious—greedy, grasping

raze—to demolish, to level to the ground

rebuke—

rectify—

redoubtable—intimidating

regicide—

relinquish—

renounce—

renown—

reproach—scold

repugnant—

repulse—

resonant—

robust—

rue—to feel regret

ruminate—to think, to turn over in your mind (literally, to chew cud)

sage—wise

salvage—

sanguine—

serendipity—

serene—

servile—

shackle—

sham—

shrewd—

smite—to strike, to hit

solace—

soporific—something that puts you to sleep

spontaneous—

sporadic—

squalid—

squander—

stamina—

staunch—

stealthy—cautious, quiet; sneaky; furtive

sterile—

stint—

strident—

sublime—

subtle—

succumb—

supplement—

susceptible—

taciturn—untalkative

tedious—

tenacious—persistent, stubborn

tirade—

torpid—

toxic—

transient—

travail—hard work

trepidation—

truculent—fierce, ready to fight, pugnacious

turbulent—

unctuous—oily, slippery; having an insincere charm

ungainly—clumsy

unique—one of a kind

usurp—to seize by force

vain—

valor—

veneer—

veracity—truthfulness

verbose—wordy

vex—to annoy

vilify—to abuse verbally, to malign

visage—a person's face

vivify—to bring to life, animate

vocation—an occupation; a calling

voracious—having great appetite, ravenous

wan—pale

wane—to decrease in size (along with wax, often used when describing the moon)

wary—cautious, on guard

wax—to increase in size

whim—

wince—

wrath—

yearn—

zeal—extreme devotion

zealot—

zenith—

zephyr—the west wind; a gentle breeze

WORD LISTS ON THE HSPT AND COOP

On the HSPT and COOP, you will be shown a list of words and asked which word does not belong. These are not too difficult if you get a lot of simple, concrete nouns. For instance, which of the following words does not belong with the others?

    (A) apple

    (B) orange

    (C) corn

    (D) pear

The words are related to try to confuse you. You can *eat* all of these, and they all grow on *plants*, but apples, oranges, and pears are fruits that grow on trees. The odd one out is C, corn, a vegetable that grows on a stalk.

Oh, if life were always so easy . . . . It gets trickier. Sometimes you will be given three specific nouns and a general one (or vice versa). For instance, which of the following words does not belong?

    (A) novel

    (B) book

    (C) autobiography

    (D) science fiction

Hmmm. You can read all of these, but A, C, and D name specific *kinds* of books, so the answer is B, book. Try another one:

    (A) study guide

    (B) test preparation

    (C) learning aid

    (D) *Barron's COOP/HSPT/TACHS*

This time it's the opposite. We have three general descriptions of a book and one specific one. The correct answer is D (of course).

Often you'll find lists of other parts of speech, such as adjectives and verbs.

- (A) handsome
- (B) comely
- (C) unsightly
- (D) alluring

Perhaps you don't know that *alluring* means attractive. You probably do know that *handsome* and *comely* are positive descriptions. *Unsightly* is negative, so it does not belong.

Here's a trickier one:

- (A) obvious
- (B) obscure
- (C) apparent
- (D) clear

The choice that doesn't belong is B. The test makers tried to trick you by using opposite words that use the same prefix (*obvious* and *obscure*). However, if you **ask yourself what the words have in common**, you'll probably realize that *obvious* means clear and apparent, so B does not belong.

Let's try a list of verbs:

- (A) receive
- (B) refuse
- (C) accept
- (D) obtain

If you have trouble with this one, try picturing yourself performing these verbs. When you *receive, accept,* or *obtain* something, you are **getting** an object—you're opening your hands and taking it. When you *refuse* something, you are holding up your hands and **not** taking it. The answer is B, refuse.

This brings us to the most insidious (treacherous) trick of all: homographs, words that are spelled the same but have different definitions. What part of speech are the following two words?

- (A) refuse
- (B) object

Well, they seem like negative-sounding verbs: to reFUSE and to obJECT. However, look at the next two choices:

- (A) refuse
- (B) object
- (C) scraps
- (D) garbage

C **might** still be a verb, but it is a different form than the others (I object, I refuse, I scraps . . . . Naahh.) *Garbage,* however, is definitely a noun. In fact, pronounced a different way, they are all nouns: REFuse, OBject, scraps, and garbage. The word *object* is the only one that does not necessarily mean trash, so the answer is B.

Lesson: Read ALL of the choices.

Without context, a word might be a different part of speech than you thought. Be flexible in your thinking.

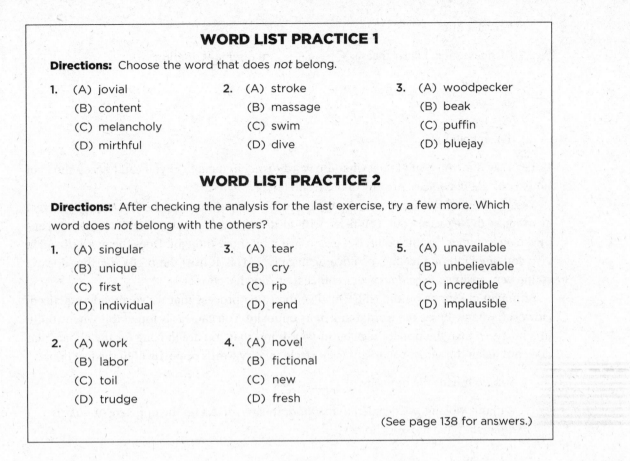

WORD LIST PRACTICE 1

Directions: Choose the word that does *not* belong.

1. (A) jovial
   (B) content
   (C) melancholy
   (D) mirthful

2. (A) stroke
   (B) massage
   (C) swim
   (D) dive

3. (A) woodpecker
   (B) beak
   (C) puffin
   (D) bluejay

WORD LIST PRACTICE 2

Directions: After checking the analysis for the last exercise, try a few more. Which word does *not* belong with the others?

1. (A) singular
   (B) unique
   (C) first
   (D) individual

2. (A) work
   (B) labor
   (C) toil
   (D) trudge

3. (A) tear
   (B) cry
   (C) rip
   (D) rend

4. (A) novel
   (B) fictional
   (C) new
   (D) fresh

5. (A) unavailable
   (B) unbelievable
   (C) incredible
   (D) implausible

(See page 138 for answers.)

SYNONYMS AND ANTONYMS—HSPT AND TACHS

VOCABULARY

If you come up with your own response BEFORE you look at the answer choices, you can sometimes avoid a trick the test makers have planned for you.

Some HSPT and TACHS questions will ask you to identify words that have similar meanings (synonyms). The HSPT will also ask you to identify words that have opposite meanings (antonyms).

Since you are acquiring a large, huge, voluminous, immense, massive, tremendous, enormous, capacious, colossal vocabulary, this will be easy, simple, and facile. Here's a sample question:

HSPT format	**TACHS format**
Similar most nearly means _____.	a <u>similar</u> outlook

Without looking at the answers, how would you fill in the blank or replace the underlined word?

Perhaps you'd use the word *alike*. Now look at the four choices that the test gives you.

(A) alike
(B) merry
(C) identical
(D) different

Ah, your choice is there, so you can be confident that the correct answer is *alike*. Something similar is not really identical; that choice is put there to lead you astray. Guessing ahead of time can sometimes help you to avoid confusion.

Try a harder one:

Dissident most nearly means _____.   a <u>dissident</u> opinion

(A) loyal
(B) weak
(C) feeble
(D) rebellious

Let's say that you don't know what the word *dissident* means, so you can't guess ahead of time. Look at the choices. Are any of them similar?

Yes, *weak* and *feeble* are synonyms. Well, you know you can't mark **both** B and C as correct answers, so those two are out. You're left with *loyal* and *rebellious*, words with opposite meanings. You can guess at this point, but give it just a bit more thought. Does the word *dissident* give you any kind of a feeling, positive or negative? Well, it uses the prefix *dis*; that doesn't sound very positive. *Rebellious* is our choice then, and it's correct.

Antonym questions on the HSPT involve the same process that we've already practiced. However, when you see the word, think of its **opposite**. You can easily forget this when you're in a hurry, so take the time to register in your mind that you are looking for the choice that does **not** mean the same. You might even **circle** the key words **opposite of** in the test book.

Similar means the opposite of _____.

Without looking, we decided that *similar* means *alike*, and the opposite of *alike* is *different*. What are our choices?

(A) alike
(B) merry
(C) identical
(D) different

There it is.

The same guessing and elimination strategies that you practiced for synonyms hold true for antonyms. Try it and see.

Dissident means the opposite of _____.

(A) loyal
(B) weak
(C) feeble
(D) rebellious

You can still eliminate *weak* and *feeble*; and since you're looking for the opposite of the negative-sounding *dissident*, your choice would be A, *loyal*.

SYNONYMS AND ANTONYMS PRACTICE 1

Directions: Choose the word that best fills in the blank.

1. *Diminutive* most nearly means

    _____.

    (A) faded
    (B) small
    (C) dark
    (D) dull

2. *Perilous* means the opposite of

    _____.

    (A) safe
    (B) dangerous
    (C) precarious
    (D) risky

3. *Fray* most nearly means _____.

    (A) attempt
    (B) brawl
    (C) cloth
    (D) sprite

4. *Impudent* means the opposite of

    _____.

    (A) angry
    (B) sullen
    (C) considerate
    (D) disrespectful

SYNONYMS AND ANTONYMS PRACTICE 2

Directions: Choose the word that best fills in the blank.

1. *Shrewd* most nearly means _____.

    (A) lazy
    (B) slothful
    (C) innocent
    (D) cunning

2. *Nadir* means the opposite of _____.

    (A) bottom
    (B) base
    (C) congress
    (D) zenith

3. *Encroach* most nearly means _____.

    (A) intrude
    (B) budget
    (C) divide
    (D) disinfect

4. *Acute* most nearly means _____.

    (A) adorable
    (B) bent
    (C) keen
    (D) crooked

(See page 139 for answers.)

Underlined Synonyms—HSPT and TACHS

Some synonym questions will give you some context—but not much. In the Reading Vocabulary section of the HSPT and the first Reading section of the TACHS, you will be given a phrase that contains an underlined word. For example, the question will look like this:

To <u>circumvent</u> the truth

(A) get around
(B) air out
(C) reveal
(D) speak

If you're familiar with the word, treat it as you would any other synonym question. The context can *sometimes* help you eliminate choices. Choice B, for instance, is awkward if you replace it for the underlined word. Do you ever "air out" the truth? You can eliminate that choice. You can also use the context phrase to check your answer in this way.

If you know that the prefix *circum-* means "around" (as in the word *circumference*), then you know that the answer is A.

UNDERLINED SYNONYMS PRACTICE 1

Directions: Choose the word that has the closest meaning to the underlined word.

1. a thin veneer

    (A) smile
    (B) cloth
    (C) covering
    (D) painting

2. a mature plant

    (A) full grown
    (B) legal
    (C) manly
    (D) serious

3. a vacant stare

    (A) faraway
    (B) blank
    (C) questioning
    (D) funny

4. a benevolent ruler

    (A) angry
    (B) kindly
    (C) dictatorial
    (D) strict

UNDERLINED SYNONYMS PRACTICE 2

Directions: Choose the word that has the closest meaning to the underlined word.

1. a harmless drudge

    (A) investigator
    (B) bore
    (C) journalist
    (D) worker

2. a ramshackle hut

    (A) luxurious
    (B) simple
    (C) straw
    (D) dilapidated

3. a zealous follower

    (A) enthusiastic
    (B) lethargic
    (C) envious
    (D) swift

4. to harbor a criminal

    (A) arrest
    (B) protect
    (C) confine
    (D) capture

(See page 139 for answers.)

ANALOGIES—HSPT

How can you do well on analogies? Of course, the best way is to **know** all of the words! Analogies seem difficult at first, but they are actually the easiest types of questions to figure out.

Analogies are sometimes written like this:

$$A : B :: C : D$$

What it means is this: A is to B as C is to D. Or, A relates to B in the same way that C relates to D.

Okay, now that you know that, you can forget it. The best way to learn analogies is to make your **own** sentence that includes the first pair of words. Try to make the sentence short, and try to use *means* or *is*, if possible. The relationship you're trying to build between these words should be clear, direct, and obvious.

For instance, let's say you get the following sentence.

Food is to pantry as clothes is to _____.

The sentence you create might be *Food goes into a pantry*. Then, use the next word in your sentence: *Clothes* go into a _____.

You may not even have to look at the choices. Fill in the logical word, *closet*. Then look at the choices to see if the word *closet* is there. If so, you've got the answer. If not, you'll need to create another sentence. Yours might not have been specific enough.

Don't go crazy. You can overthink analogies and make them too complicated. *Food is edible and is kept cool and dark in a pantry; clothes are edible and they are kept cool and dark in a . . . .* No, this is **too** specific.

TIP

To solve analogies, create your *own* sentences.

Let's complicate matters. Let's take a look at some possible choices.

(A) closet
(B) hamper
(C) dryer
(D) store

Hmm. Clothes can go into all of these things. What's the relationship?

Well, let's create a new sentence that more specifically defines the relationship. *We put our food into a pantry until we need it.*

Do we put our clothes into the hamper, dryer, or store until we wear them? No, we don't, so *closet* is still correct.

ANALOGIES PRACTICE 1

Directions: Create sentences for the following pairs of words. Try to make each sentence as simple and logical as possible.

1. piece, puzzle

2. grass, green

3. caterpillar, butterfly

4. practice, succeed

5. tree, fruit

(See page 140 for answers.)

PARENTS/TEACHERS

Have your students practice BOTH the HSPT and COOP analogies. It will introduce them to some general thinking skills they'll need for their tests.

If you're stumped by an analogy, try this trick from the last section. Look at the choices. Are any of them synonymous? If so, they can't **both** be correct, so you can eliminate them! So even without looking at the analogy, can you eliminate any of the following choices? (Remember to look for **synonyms**.)

(A) error
(B) guilt
(C) mistake
(D) innocence

An *error* and a *mistake* are the same, aren't they? We can eliminate A and C as choices, as they can't both be the correct answer. This leaves us with *guilt* and *innocence*. We've just doubled our chances of getting the right answer.

Note: If you see two **opposite** choices (such as *guilt* and *innocence*), one of these is very often the correct answer.

Still completely stumped by an analogy? This shouldn't happen too often, since you now know so many vocabulary words and several tricks for solving the questions. However, as a final attempt, you can work backwards. You can make sentences with the answer words. If any of those make a very strong, logical connection, that *could* be the right answer!

[Unknown word] is to [another unknown word] as core is to _____.

(A) apple
(B) tree
(C) squirrel
(D) leaves

The answer is A. The other relationships with *core* make no sense.

ANALOGIES PRACTICE 2

1. Freedom is to independence as purity is to _____.

   (A) error
   (B) guilt
   (C) mistake
   (D) innocence

2. Trust is to doubt as confess is to _____.

   (A) own
   (B) deny
   (C) admit
   (D) deter

3. Empathy is to feeling as comprehension is to _____.

   (A) understanding
   (B) ignorance
   (C) malevolence
   (D) enmity

4. Helmet is to head as glove is to _____.

   (A) leather
   (B) boxing
   (C) cold
   (D) hand

ANALOGIES PRACTICE 3

1. Chair is to sit as bed is to _____.

   (A) lie
   (B) lay
   (C) comfort
   (D) incline

2. Lethargy is to industry as wane is to _____.

   (A) wax
   (B) whim
   (C) wince
   (D) wan

3. Herd is to cow as school is to _____.

   (A) education
   (B) books
   (C) fish
   (D) rock

(See page 140 for answers.)

VERBAL REASONING (ANALOGIES)—COOP

Another type of verbal logic question will ask you to identify relationships among words. It's actually an analogy taken a step further; instead of two words, you have to relate three words.

For instance, what is the relationship between these words?

horse   cow   pig

Again, making a sentence will help you. A *horse*, a *cow*, and a *pig* are all farm animals. Next, the test will ask you to choose a fourth word that belongs in that group.

    (A) chicken
    (B) goat
    (C) barn
    (D) corn

A *chicken* is a farm animal. Yes. A *goat* is a farm animal. Hmmm, yes again. A *barn* is a farm animal. No, it's not. *Corn* is a farm animal. No.

So we've got **two** possible answers. Can we go back and make our sentence more specific? A *horse*, a *cow*, and a *pig* are all four-legged farm animals or A *horse*, a *cow*, and a *pig* are all farm mammals. The answer is B. A goat has four legs; a goat is a mammal.

VERBAL REASONING PRACTICE 1

Directions: Choose the word that is most like the listed words.

1.   Mars   Venus   Jupiter

    (A) moon
    (B) Neptune
    (C) comet
    (D) asteroid

2.   monotonous uniform unvarying

    (F) alone
    (G) unchanging
    (H) variegated
    (J) incongruous

3.   mountain   forest   prairie

    (A) stars
    (B) building
    (C) city
    (D) desert

4.   ire   rage   wrath

    (F) fury
    (G) pathos
    (H) hatred
    (J) jealousy

VERBAL REASONING PRACTICE 2

Directions: After checking the last exercise, try a couple more.

1.   elm   willow   maple

    (A) pinecone
    (B) needle
    (C) leaf
    (D) oak

2.   orate speak talk

    (F) attend
    (G) lecture
    (H) listen
    (J) conceal

(See page 140 for answers.)

You shouldn't have any trouble with these if you've been practicing making sentences, so it would be a good idea to review the last section on analogies and do the exercises.

The COOP isn't willing to leave this alone, however. You'll find additional questions that essentially double this exercise. So now that you've seen analogies and three-part analogies, get ready for double three-part analogies! The problems look like this:

walk	jog	sprint
hour	minute	_____

The words in the top row have a particular relationship, and you are to figure that out and apply it to the bottom row. Let's break it down. Start with the top row only: *walk, jog,* and *sprint*. These are all ways of traveling distance on foot. Furthermore, they increase in speed or intensity. So make a sentence and a mental picture of these words:

> *Walking* is slower than *jogging*, which is slower than *sprinting*.

Now fill in the blank for the related sequence in the bottom row.

> hour   minute   _____

Okay, we'll give you four choices: *race, day, second,* or *clock*.

Did you guess the word *second*? That's correct. The relationship is not exactly the same as the first example, but it is similar enough that you can infer the answer.

Here's another type of relationship. The following words are the top row:

> mammal   feline   tiger

Try to make a sentence using the words. Sometimes it might be easier to use the words in reverse order:

> A *tiger* is a type of *feline*, which is a type of *mammal*.

Now try the bottom row. Using the same kind of sentence, choose the missing word.

> fruit   melon   _____

(A) root
(B) seeds
(C) cantaloupe
(D) vine

The answer is C. A cantaloupe is a type of melon, which is a type of fruit.

TIP

Keep creating your own sentences. You might try using the words in reverse order.

VERBAL REASONING PRACTICE 3

Directions: The words in the top row are related. The words in the bottom row are related in a similar way. Choose the word that completes the sequence in the bottom row.

1. violin   cello   guitar   _____

    trout   salmon   _____

    (A) guppy
    (B) seal
    (C) frog
    (D) fish

2. pamphlet   magazine   book

    hut   _____   mansion

    (F) wood
    (G) skyscraper
    (H) cottage
    (J) room

3. letters   words   sentence   _____

    thread   fabric   _____

    (A) pin
    (B) quilt
    (C) weave
    (D) loom

4. king   knight   pawn

    _____   governor   citizen

    (F) mayor
    (G) deputy
    (H) president
    (J) assistant

(See page 141 for answers.)

On the COOP, you will also be given a word and asked to choose another word that is a necessary part of the first word. This sounds a bit complicated, but it isn't, really. For example, you will be given an underlined word such as this:

staircase

When you look at the choices, ask yourself, "Does a staircase HAVE to have _____?"

(A) wood
(B) bannister
(C) carpet
(D) steps

Does a staircase HAVE to be made of wood? No, it can be made of other materials. *Does it HAVE to have a bannister?* No, it may not be safe, but it's still a staircase. *Does a staircase HAVE to have carpet*? No, it doesn't. *Does a staircase HAVE to have steps*? Yes, it does; those are the stairs, and they're essential. The answer is D.

Another way to approach this type of question is to picture the first word and then read each of the following choices. Take that choice *out* of your picture and see if anything is left.

fortress

(F) roof
(G) moat
(H) tower
(J) walls

Picture a *fortress*. Take away the *roof*. Is it still a fortress? Yes, it still offers protection from attackers, though perhaps not from rain. Take away the *moat*. Is it still a fortress? Yes. Even though many fortresses had moats or ditches, they aren't necessary components. Take away the *tower*. It's still a fortress. Take away the *walls*. In order to provide protection, a fortress has to have walls of some sort. Therefore, the answer is J.

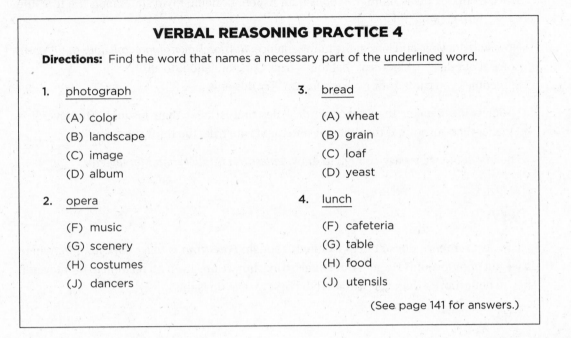

VERBAL REASONING PRACTICE 4

Directions: Find the word that names a necessary part of the underlined word.

1. photograph

   (A) color
   (B) landscape
   (C) image
   (D) album

2. opera

   (F) music
   (G) scenery
   (H) costumes
   (J) dancers

3. bread

   (A) wheat
   (B) grain
   (C) loaf
   (D) yeast

4. lunch

   (F) cafeteria
   (G) table
   (H) food
   (J) utensils

(See page 141 for answers.)

VERBAL LOGIC—HSPT

TIP
Use letters to *diagram* relationships.

The logic questions on the HSPT can give you a headache. You don't have a lot of time, and they're throwing trivial information at you about a bunch of people you don't know.

Picture it. You've got seconds to absorb this information:

> Sierra owns more troll dolls than Aspen. Sierra owns fewer troll dolls than Bismarck. Bismarck owns more troll dolls than Aspen. If the first two statements are true, the third statement is _____.

(A) true
(B) false
(C) uncertain

You will fail the exam if you scream, "Who cares?" So pretend that you care deeply. Sadly, you don't have much time to spend with Sierra and friends.

Fortunately, we have a quick way for you to figure out this problem/dilemma/quandary/puzzle/enigma. Developed by our cave ancestors, it's called *drawing a diagram.*

You don't have to use fancy pictures; letters work best. As soon as you read the first sentence (Sierra owns more troll dolls than Aspen.), write the letter S in the margin—right there in the test booklet. **Below** it, write the letter A, since Sierra owns more troll dolls than Aspen. It will look like this:

 Sierra owns more troll dolls than Aspen. Sierra owns fewer troll dolls than Bismarck. Bismarck owns more troll dolls than Aspen. If the first two statements are true, the third statement is _____.

The next sentence tells us that Sierra owns fewer troll dolls than Bismarck. Since Bismarck has more, place the letter B <u>above</u> the S.

B
S Sierra owns more troll dolls than Aspen. *Sierra owns fewer troll dolls than Bismarck.*
A Bismarck owns more troll dolls than Aspen. If the first two statements are true, the third statement is _____.

Now stop drawing, and look at the third sentence: *Bismarck owns more troll dolls than Aspen.* A glance at our diagram shows us that this is **true**. Congratulations to all.

Sometimes you can't draw a clear diagram. Try this one:

Palestrina is taller than Monteverdi. Palestrina is taller than Josquin. Monteverdi is taller than Josquin. If the first two statements are true, the third statement is _____.

The first sentence is easy enough to draw. *Palestrina is taller than Monteverdi.*

P
M

The next sentence doesn't help us much, though. *Palestrina is taller than Josquin.* Where do we put poor Josquin? He goes under Palestrina, but we are given no relation to Monteverdi. They're both shorter than Palestrina, so the best we can do is this:

P
MJ

Therefore, the third sentence—*Monteverdi is taller than Josquin*—cannot be proven. The answer is C, uncertain.

You may encounter another type of logic question on the HSPT. Rather than greater- or less-than relationships, it may be a connection among parts and a whole. For instance,

No sixth graders take Geography. Beowulf takes Geography during first period. Beowulf is in the sixth grade. If the first two statements are true, the third statement is _____.

(A) true
(B) false
(C) uncertain

This type of question may be easy enough that you don't need a diagram. If you do, though, it might look like this:

STEP 1 The circle is the sixth grade.

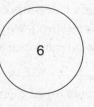

Sixth graders

STEP 2 The square is Geography class. It is outside of the sixth grade, since no sixth graders are scheduled there.

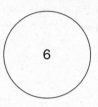

No sixth graders   take   Geography class.

STEP 3 The B is our friend Beowulf, who is in the Geography class.

Beowulf takes Geography during first period.

Obviously, Beowulf is NOT in the sixth grade. The third statement is **false**, choice B.

VERBAL LOGIC—HSPT PRACTICE 1

Directions: Choose the logical answer.

1. All cows eat grass. Ashtabula is a cow. Ashtabula eats grass. If the first two statements are true, the third statement is _____.

   (A) true
   (B) false
   (C) uncertain

2. In choir, Drew can reach a high A, but Strohmann can reach a bit higher—up to a B. Henry sings higher than Drew. Henry sings higher than Strohmann. If the first two statements are true, the third statement is _____.

   (A) true
   (B) false
   (C) uncertain

3. Some seventh graders can take computer class as an elective, but all eighth graders are required to take it. Lavinia is in the seventh grade. Lavinia takes an elective. If the first two statements are true, the third statement is _____.

   (A) true
   (B) false
   (C) uncertain

(See page 141 for answers.)

VERBAL LOGIC—HSPT PRACTICE 2

Directions: Choose the logical answer.

1. All engineers are in the Alpha group. Bernard is an engineer. Bernard is in the Alpha group. If the first two statements are true, the third statement is _____.

    (A) true
    (B) false
    (C) uncertain

2. Grant bowls for six months a year. Charlotte bowls on the same team for seven months. They bowl together at least one month a year. If the first two statements are true, the third statement is _____.

    (A) true
    (B) false
    (C) uncertain

3. Ms. Rush's room has more books than Mr. Howard's room. Mr. Batson's room has more books than Ms. Rush's room. Mr. Batson's room contains more books than Mr. Howard's room. If the first two statements are true, the third statement is _____.

    (A) true
    (B) false
    (C) uncertain

(See page 142 for answers.)

VERBAL LOGIC—COOP

TIP

Ask yourself:

Does this HAVE to be true?

The Verbal Reasoning—Context section of the COOP tests how well you can make inferences given a certain amount of data. You will be given two or three sentences. Based on the information in these sentences, you are to choose a true statement that follows. This is an interesting little challenge; the choices will all be related, but only one can be true. This one is a fact, while the others are simply assumptions.

Read the first three sentences. Then look at each choice, and ask yourself if it MUST be true. Is it NECESSARILY true? Let's try a few.

> Izzy likes to draw with crayons. She has a box containing many colors of crayons. The picture she drew for me is all blue.
>
> (A) I asked Izzy for an all-blue picture.
> (B) Izzy was feeling sad that day.
> (C) I have a blue picture.
> (D) Izzy doesn't like me.

Okay, here's what we know: Izzy has a lot of crayons, but she gave me a picture that was all blue.

Let's go through the choices. *I asked Izzy for an all-blue picture.* This could be true, but our information does not make it necessarily true. *Izzy was feeling sad that day.* We are given no information about whether she was happy or sad, so that is merely an assumption. *I have a blue picture.* This is definitely true. *Izzy doesn't like me.* This is a silly conclusion; does our information make that necessary? No, it does not. Only one choice is obvious: C.

The lesson here is that you should not be afraid to pick the obvious choice. Only one is based on facts. For the rest, you'll be jumping to conclusions.

Try another one:

> Mrs. Gonzales teaches history. She also has a degree in English. She will be teaching at another school next year.

> (F)   Mrs. Gonzales is taking a job teaching English.
> (G)   Mrs. Gonzales is unhappy teaching history.
> (H)   Mrs. Gonzales is still a teacher.
> (J)   Mrs. Gonzales is being transferred.

Mrs. Gonzales is taking a job teaching English. We know she has a degree in English, but we are never told she is going to teach it. *Mrs. Gonzales is unhappy teaching history.* We are never told this, either. It's an unfounded guess. *Mrs. Gonzales is still a teacher.* We are indeed told this. She will be teaching at another school. *Mrs. Gonzales is being transferred.* Again, this is not necessarily true. She could be moving for other reasons; she could have gone to another school by choice, for instance. The answer is obviously H.

> When I was in elementary school, I used to get a new lunch box every year.
> It made going to school more fun. Now I eat in the school cafeteria.

> (A)   School is no longer fun.
> (B)   Cafeteria food is delicious.
> (C)   Our school does not allow students to bring lunch.
> (D)   I don't bring my lunch to school.

School is no longer fun. This is not necessarily logical. Perhaps now that you're older, you don't need a lunch box to make school fun. *Cafeteria food is delicious.* Again, this does not necessarily follow. Maybe it's good on some days, and maybe it's not on others. *Our school does not allow students to bring lunch.* We were never given this information. *I don't bring my lunch to school.* Well, it's not a very interesting answer, but it's the only one we know for certain. The answer is D.

The following logic problem contains a trick.

> A musical instrument that is struck to produce sound is called a percussion instrument. An instrument that produces sound with strings is a stringed instrument. A piano is sounded by striking its strings with hammers.

> (F)   The piano is considered a stringed instrument.
> (G)   The piano is considered a percussion instrument.
> (H)   The piano is difficult to play.
> (J)   The piano has aspects of both a stringed and a percussion instrument.

By the definition listed, we could answer that F is true. However, by the same argument, we could say that G is true. H simply states an opinion that is not stated in the facts. Choice J, however, combines F and G for the most appropriate answer.

It doesn't take a Sherlock Holmes to see that these problems can be solved with little difficulty—as long as you stick to the original facts.

VERBAL LOGIC—COOP PRACTICE

Directions: Choose the statement that must be true.

1. Mr. and Mrs. Larkey have two children. One of them attends St. Paul's School for Boys. The other attends St. Elizabeth's All Girls Academy.

    (A) The Larkeys' youngest child is not in school yet.
    (B) The Larkeys are devout Catholics.
    (C) The Larkeys have a son and a daughter.
    (D) Mrs. Larkey attended parochial school.

2. A huge old Osage Orange tree grows at Fort Harrod. Karen has climbed this tree. Fort Harrod is the oldest settlement in Kentucky.

    (F) Karen likes oranges.
    (G) The Osage Orange is the oldest tree in Kentucky.
    (H) Karen lives in Kentucky.
    (J) The Osage Orange tree grows in Kentucky.

    (See page 143 for answers.)

ANSWERS AND ANALYSES

Vocabulary 1 (page 110)

1. sublunary—under the moon. This refers to earthly things, perhaps worldly or mundane.

2. Mediterranean—middle of the earth. The people who named the Mediterranean Sea obviously thought they were the center of everything!

3. subterranean—under the earth. Your underground hideout is subterranean, Batman.

4. extraterrestrial—beyond earth. UFOs are often thought to originate beyond the limits of Earth.

5. Well, how easy can these get? A submarine travels under the sea.

Vocabulary 2 (page 110)

1. geocentric—earth centered. We once believed that the earth was the center of the universe. (Heliocentric refers to the idea that the sun occupies the center.)

2. extraordinary—beyond the ordinary; remarkable; exceptional

3. lunar—having to do with the moon. A lunar eclipse occurs when the moon moves into the earth's shadow.

Vocabulary 3 (page 111)

1. A *benediction* is a blessing (good speech, good words).

2. A *valediction* is a farewell speech. (A valedictorian delivers one.)

3. A *carnival* is a farewell to meat! You would have a carnival right before Lent.

Vocabulary 4 (page 111)

1. voracious—hungry; craving large quantities of food. It can also mean "extremely eager."

2. inanimate—without life

3. chili con carne—chili with meat

4. contradict—literally, to "speak against," to deny or say the opposite

5. loquacious—talkative, wordy, verbose, garrulous, prolix, voluble, chatty, gabby, etc.

Vocabulary 5 (page 111)

1. prototype—the first of its kind; the original model; a standard example

2. century—a hundred, especially a hundred years

3. triangle—a figure containing three angles

4. bilingual—speaking (or concerning) two languages

5. quadruped—a creature with four feet.

Vocabulary 6 (page 113)

1. *biblio* + *phile* = book lover

2. *mis* + *anthrope* = one who hates people

3. *philo* + *sopher* = lover of wisdom

4. *anthropo* + *morphic* = in the shape of man

5. *auto* + *graph* = self-write, your signature

6. *auto* + *bio* + *graphy* = your self-written story of your life

7. *post* + *mortem* = after death

8. *omni* + *potent* = all powerful

Vocabulary 7 (page 114)

1. supersonic—beyond sound; moving faster than the speed of sound

2. audiophile—someone who loves sound so much that he or she is an expert on music sound systems and sound reproduction (stereos, CDs, LPs, amplifiers, etc.)

3. antebellum—a time period before a war

4. telepathic—literally, to feel from a distance; communicating without visible symbols; mind-reading.

Vocabulary 8 (page 114)

1. transport—to carry across

2. teleport—to carry a long distance

3. import—to carry in

4. report—to carry back

5. deport—to carry away from

Vocabulary 9 (page 115)

1. theocracy— "government by God" or those who represent a god

2. confide—If you confide in someone, you place your trust in him or her.

3. anarchy—without rule

4. credible—believable

5. gradual—moving step by step, by degrees

Word List 1 (page 121)

1. **(C)** *Melancholy* is the only sad word; the others describe happiness.

2. **(B)** This one contains a trick. If you look at the first two words, *stroke* and *massage* seem to be synonyms. However, *swim* and *dive* are associated with water activity. *Stroke* can also be in that category, but *massage* cannot.

3. **(B)** The other choices are birds. This choice, a beak, is a specific **part** of birds.

Word List 2 (page 121)

1. **(C)** *Singular, unique,* and *individual* all refer to something that is *one of a kind.* The word *first* also refers to the number one, but as an ordinal number (a number that denotes *order*).

2. **(D)** When you *trudge*, you *walk* with difficulty. Though it feels laborious, it identifies more specific activity than the general terms *work, labor,* and *toil*.

3. **(B)** The trick here involves the two pronunciations of the word *tear.* Choice B makes us think that the words relate to crying, but choices C and D show us that three of the words involve splitting (*rip, rend, tear*), so *cry* does not belong.

4. **(B)** We encounter the same type of trick here. A *novel* (noun) is *fictional* (adjective). However, the words *new* and *fresh* are both adjectives referring to things just coming into being. Remember that the word *novel* also functions as an adjective, meaning *new. Fictional*, then, is the adjective that differs.

5. **(A)** This one plays with the fact that all of the choices have the *in-*, *im-*, or *un-* prefix, meaning *not*. Choices B, C, and D denote unbelievability. Choice A is the odd one out.

Synonyms and Antonyms 1 (page 123)

1. **(B)** *Diminutive* means *small*. It does not mean dim.

2. **(A)** *Peril* means *danger*, so the only choice that is the opposite of dangerous is *safe*.

3. **(B)** A *fray* is an angry fight, or *brawl*. (It's related to the word *afraid*.) *Fray* can also refer to an unraveling of cloth, but it is not the cloth itself.

4. **(C)** *Impudent* literally means "without shame." If someone acts impudently, he or she is behaving disrespectfully. However, we are looking for the **opposite** here, which is *considerate*. If you didn't know the definition of impudent, you could still guess with some confidence. *Angry*, *sullen*, and *disrespectful* all connote negative feelings, so *considerate* stands out as something different from the rest.

Synonyms and Antonyms 2 (page 123)

1. **(D)** Choices A and B are synonyms, so they can't both be right. *Shrewd* means clever or *cunning*.

2. **(D)** *Nadir* means the lowest point. The **opposite** of that is *zenith*, the highest point.

3. **(A)** To *encroach* is to trespass or to *intrude*. *Encroach* originally meant to seize with a hook, so picture that intrusion!

4. **(C)** An *acute* angle is less than 90 degrees. While that may look cute (or even *bent* or *crooked*), it really means *sharp*. Another word for sharp is *keen*.

Underlined Synonyms 1 (page 124)

1. **(C)** A *veneer* is an outer layer. The word *covering* is closest to that meaning.

2. **(A)** *Full grown* is the only synonym that makes sense in this context.

3. **(B)** *Vacant*, of course, means empty or *blank*.

4. **(B)** Remember the root *bene* means good (*kindly*).

Underlined Synonyms 2 (page 124)

1. **(D)** *Drudge* might be a new word to you, but you've probably heard of *drudgery*, or monotonous work. A *drudge* is a *worker* who performs such tedious labor.

2. **(D)** The word *ramshackle* is almost onomatopoetic, isn't it? You can almost hear the *dilapidated* hut falling apart!

3. **(A)** A *zealous* follower is filled with enthusiasm! We are zealous for exclamation points in this section!

4. **(B)** To *harbor* means to shelter someone or something. A ship is sheltered in a harbor.

Analogies 1 (page 126)

1. A *piece* is part of a *puzzle*.

2. *Grass* is *green*.

3. A *caterpillar* becomes a *butterfly*.

4. If you *practice*, you will *succeed*.

5. A *tree* bears *fruit*.

Analogies 2 (page 127)

1. **(D)** *Freedom* is a part of *independence*. *Purity* is a part of *innocence*.

2. **(B)** *Trust* is used as a verb here. If you *trust* something, you **don't** *doubt* it. If you *confess* something, you **don't** *deny* it.

3. **(A)** *Empathy* is *feeling*. *Comprehension* is *understanding*.

4. **(D)** A *helmet* protects your *head*; a *glove* protects your *hand*.

Analogies 3 (page 127)

1. **(A)** You *lie* in a *bed*. While you can *incline* toward a bed, it's not the same as reclining.

2. **(A)** *Lethargy* and *industry* are opposites. The opposite of *wane* is *wax*. If you don't know these words, look them up and create flash cards.

3. **(C)** A *herd* is a group of *cows*; a *school* is a group of *fish*.

Verbal Reasoning 1 (page 128)

1. **(B)** *Mars*, *Venus*, and *Jupiter* are planets. The *moon* is not a planet. *Neptune* is.

2. **(G)** Something *monotonous* is *uniform* and *unvarying*—and *unchanging*. Because of the prefixes *mono* and *uni*, you might be tricked into thinking that the answer is F, *alone*. Make sure you take **all** of the words into account: *unvarying* does not mean *single* or *alone*. Do you know what *incongruous* means? The prefix *in* means *not*, and *con* means *with* or *together*, so you can already figure out that *not together* isn't a synonym for *uniform* or *unvarying*. (By the way, *incongruous* means *out of place* or *inconsistent*. *Variegated* means varied in *appearance* or *multicolored*.)

3. **(D)** These are all natural landscapes.

4. **(F)** These are all synonyms for *anger*.

Verbal Reasoning 2 (page 128)

1. **(D)** These are all types of trees. The other choices are parts of trees.

2. **(G)** These all involve the use of spoken words.

Verbal Reasoning 3 (page 130)

1. **(A)** The words in the top row are all types of stringed instruments. The words in the bottom row are all types of fish. Choice D, *fish*, is too general; choices B and C are water animals, but they are not fish.

2. **(H)** The fact that a *pamphlet*, a *magazine*, and a *book* are all types of reading material is not specific enough in this case, so you'll have to try another sentence. A *pamphlet* is smaller than a *magazine*, which is smaller than a *book*. A *hut* is smaller than a *cottage*, which is smaller than a *mansion*. The other choices are related to housing, but they do not fit the intermediate size that belongs in the sequence.

3. **(B)** *Letters* create *words*, which create *sentences*. *Thread* creates *fabric*, which creates a *quilt*.

4. **(H)** A *king* holds the highest rank, ruling over a *knight*, who is of higher rank than a *pawn*. The highest rank listed in the second group is the *president*.

Verbal Reasoning 4 (page 131)

1. **(C)** Does a photograph HAVE to have color? Well, it could be a black-and-white photo. Does it HAVE to be a landscape? No, it could be a portrait. Does it HAVE to have an image? Yes, that's what makes it a photograph. Does it HAVE to have an album? No, it's still a photo, whether it's in an album or in a frame. The answer is C.

2. **(F)** An opera requires music—it does not depend on scenery, costumes, or dancers.

3. **(B)** Bread is made of grain—not necessarily wheat (oat, rye, etc.). Unleavened bread uses no yeast.

4. **(H)** Lunch does not have to be served in a cafeteria, nor on a table. Some lunches, such as sandwiches, require no utensils. Lunch does have to include food, however.

Verbal Logic—HSPT 1 (page 133)

1. **(A)** *All cows eat grass.*

   The rectangle indicates the grass-eaters, and all cows are included.

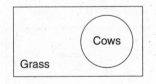

   Ashtabula is a cow.
   Ashtabula goes into the circle of cows.

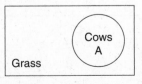

   Ashtabula is in the grass-eating rectangle. Therefore, she eats grass, which means that the third statement is true.

2. **(C)** *Drew can reach a high A, but Strohmann can reach a bit higher.*

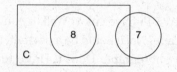

Henry sings higher than Drew.

However, we don't know exactly how much higher. We can draw Henry's range with an arrow.

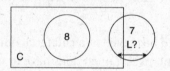

Given this limited information, we don't know whether Henry can sing higher than Strohmann or not so the third statement is uncertain.

3. **(C)** *Some seventh graders can take computer class as an elective, but all eighth graders are required to take it.*

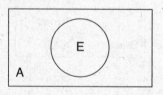

Lavinia is in the seventh grade.

Where in the circle can we put Lavinia, though?

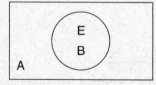

We can't know whether Lavinia is one of the seventh graders in computer class or whether she is in a different elective.

Verbal Logic—HSPT 2 (page 134)

1. **(A)** *All engineers are in the Alpha group.*

Bernard is an engineer.

Therefore, Bernard is in the Alpha group so the third statement is true.

2. **(A)** *Grant bowls for six months a year.*

A year is	12 months.
Grant—6 months	

Charlotte bowls on the same team for seven months.

A year is	12 months.
Grant—6 months	
	Charlotte—7 months

Even if we separate Grant and Charlotte as much as possible, their bowling still overlaps by a month so the third statement is true.

3. **(A)** *Ms. Rush's room has more books than Mr. Howard's room.*

R
H

Mr. Batson's room has more books than Ms. Rush's room.

B
R
H

Yes, Mr. Batson's room contains more books than Mr. Howard's room so the third statement is true.

Verbal Logic—COOP (page 136)

1. **(C)** We are told that Mr. and Mrs. Larkey have two children, and both of them attend school. We are not told of their devotion to their religion, but we do know that one child attends a boy's school and one attends a girl's school. Therefore, the Larkeys have a son and a daughter.

2. **(J)** We know that the tree grows at Fort Harrod and that Fort Harrod is in Kentucky. Therefore, the tree grows in Kentucky. We don't know that Karen likes oranges nor do we know whether Karen lives in Kentucky or just visited there. We also don't know that the Osage Orange tree is the oldest tree at Fort Harrod.

Language Arts 4

PARENTS/TEACHERS

Your child/student should review *all* of this section. Even if some of this material is not specifically tested, the skills are necessary to answer other questions.

The COOP, the HSPT, and the TACHS exams require you to demonstrate your knowledge of English punctuation, usage, and composition. The HSPT and the TACHS both contain entire sections devoted to these skills, while the COOP integrates the Language Arts questions in the Reading Comprehension section.

The types of questions INCLUDE the following:

	COOP	HSPT	TACHS
Identify errors in usage, capitalization, and punctuation	✔	✔	✔
Combine sentences	✔	n/a	n/a
Choose the clearest sentence	✔	✔	✔
Choose the correct word in a sentence	✔	✔	✔
Choose the sentence that does not belong	✔	✔	✔
Choose the sentence that fits a topic or paragraph	✔	✔	✔
Place a sentence logically in a paragraph	✔	✔	✔
Choose an appropriate topic for a paragraph	n/a	✔	✔
Identify spelling errors	n/a	✔	✔

The tests overlap enough that a general review of grammar and composition will help you with all three tests. Furthermore, having a command of what makes a good composition, including grammar, usage, and mechanics, can serve as a tremendous tool for identifying the correct answers.

You should flag any answer choice that contains an error of any kind. If the directions ask you to identify errors, you have found the correct response. In all other cases, that answer can be eliminated. For instance, one section of the test may ask you to choose a sentence that best completes a paragraph. In that case, you can eliminate a sentence that contains a comma error.

Study the following review **in order**; read through all of it, even if you think you already know some sections. You don't need to memorize every label, but you will need to understand a concept in order to master a later one. Relax. Take the time to learn each section thoroughly. Don't try to tackle all of this in one sitting. **Take a break to let each skill sink in, and then go back over it again before moving on.** Brain research shows that this rest and repetition technique improves learning and helps you retain information.

SENTENCES

A **sentence** contains two essential elements.

1. It names something (the subject).

2. That something performs an action (the predicate).

A sentence	states a complete thought.
Subject	*Predicate*

The predicate	contains a verb.
Subject	*Predicate*

The reader	is waking up right about now.
Subject	*Predicate*

But that's not all! The predicate (besides describing a physical action) can also identify a state of being. That is, it can describe or rename the subject using **linking** verbs such as *am, is, are, was, were, be, being, been, has been, might have been, seems,* or *becomes.*

This sentence	is simple.
Subject	*Predicate*

The subject	is always a noun.
Subject	*Predicate*

The reader	was so excited by the grammar chapter.
Subject	*Predicate*

One of the most powerful techniques you can use in Language Arts is to **identify the simple subject and the simple predicate of a sentence**. You can tame the most complicated grammatical construction with this strategy, so let's review. The simple predicate is the **verb**, the action or state of being in the sentence; the **subject** is the actor—the person, place, or thing (noun) performing that action. Can you underline the simple subject and the simple verb in the following sentence? Be warned. The writer of the sentence has tried to make it complicated by widely separating the subject and verb.

> For example, the stalwart student, forced to endure the longest, most tedious, most tortured sentence in the most obscure, archaic, dust-covered book, finds both a simple subject, which will always be a noun, and a simple predicate, which will always be a verb.
>
> This sentence can be broken down to this: Student finds.

That's it. The actor of the sentence is the **student**. The student finds stuff.

In present-day English, we like the subject (S) to appear first, followed by the verb (V). However, this is not always the case. Read the following sentences; in each, the subject is printed in bold and the verb is underlined.

The **dog** chased her tail.
(This is a standard S-V construction: **dog** chased.)

Am **I** calm and confident?
Did **you** remember to bring a pencil?
(Questions mix the usual order: **I** am, **you** did remember.)

On the very top of the hill stands my **house**.
(The subject is delayed for effect: **house** stands.)

There was a young **man** from Peru.
(**Man** was. *There* is not a noun.)

Compound Subjects and Predicates

A sentence can contain more than one subject and verb. They should **not** be separated by commas unless they are part of a series.

My **aunt** and my **uncle** are visiting us. (Compound subject)
They write and edit books for a living. (Compound verb)
Mia, Isabella, and **Josie** are my cousins. (Notice that no comma appears after *Josie*.)

Compound Sentences

A **compound sentence** combines two complete sentences (**subject** and verb + **subject** and verb) with a comma and a conjunction (a connecting word such as *and, or, but, for, nor, so,* and *yet*).

My **cousins** are visiting   , *and*   **they** brought their parents with them.
My **aunt** is a friendly woman   , *but*   my **uncle** only talks to dogs.

Subject-Verb Agreement

Now that you can identify subjects and verbs, you have the skill to answer a common test question: checking subject-verb agreement. The subject and verb of a sentence should agree in number (singular, plural) and person (first, second, or third person). This sounds more complicated than it is. The easiest way to approach this type of question is to **isolate the subject and verb** as we did earlier; then hear if it makes sense. The trick here, of course, is that the subject and verb may be separated in the sentence, so it is important to identify these two elements correctly, even if you must mark them on the exam. Cross out or bracket any phrases that separate the subject and verb; they are there to confuse you.

TIP

To check subject-verb agreement, *isolate* the S and V from the rest of the sentence.

SUBJECT-VERB PRACTICE 1

Directions: Are the following sentences written correctly? Isolate the subjects and verbs to determine the correct answer.

1. Many questions on the test asks you to identify errors in subject-verb agreement.
2. Is the following sentences written correctly?
3. June and July goes by so quickly.

SUBJECT-VERB PRACTICE 2

Directions: Determine whether the following sentences are written correctly.

1. All of the exams require you to demonstrate your verbal skills.
2. Each of the exams require you to demonstrate your verbal skills.
3. One of the exams requires more memorization.

SUBJECT-VERB PRACTICE 3

Directions: Determine whether the following sentences are written correctly.

1. Some of the questions appear difficult, but most students do well.
2. All of the examples except one is easy.
3. All of us have prepared well, so he and I am confident.

(See page 185 for answers.)

Sentence Fragments

TIP

A sentence *must* have a subject *and* a verb. Anything else is a fragment.

Remember, a sentence **must** have a subject and a verb. (This is called a *clause.*)

Santa <u>is</u> a Claus.   A **sentence** <u>is</u> a clause.

Note: Commands have only a verb because the understood subject is *You.*

Remember that.
[You] <u>remember</u> that.

We often speak in fragments, but formal writing on the exams should consist of complete sentences.

No one may write in fragments. Except for me.
                    (*Except for me* is a fragment.)

If you have trouble identifying fragments, try placing the words *I heard that . . .* or *Is it true that . . . ?* in front of the sentence. This often makes the fragment more obvious.

I heard that except for me.
Is it true that except for me?   (These make even less sense.)

A sentence must also make complete sense standing alone. (This is called an *independent* clause.) Be on the lookout for subordinating conjunctions such as *because, since, even though, if, unless,* and *while.* These are called subordinating because they must depend on a complete sentence to make sense.

Because I would not stop for the bus.

This contains a noun and a verb, but it is a *dependent* clause. It cannot stand alone because of the word *because.* Try the test.

I heard that because I would not stop for the bus.

Is it true that because I would not stop for the bus?

This is obviously a fragment. It needs to depend on a sentence to make sense.

Because I would not stop for the bus, <u>it</u>   <u>stopped</u> **for me.**
                                   subject   *verb*

Note: This "I heard that" test only works with a traditional subject-verb sentence. You'll have to add the implied subject in a command.

Keep off the grass.
I heard that keep off the grass. Confusing—add the subject.
I heard that [you] keep off the grass. [Ah. Yes.]

You'll also have to rearrange questions.

<u>Are</u> **you ready?**
I heard that are you ready. Confusing—rearrange the subject and verb.
I heard that you <u>are</u> **ready. [Yes, it's a complete sentence.]**

TIP

When checking to see whether a command (an imperative sentence) is a sentence or a fragment, don't forget to add the implied subject "You."

SENTENCE FRAGMENTS PRACTICE 1

Directions: Determine whether the following examples are written in complete sentences.

1. He has trouble with fragments. Even though he is an excellent reader.
2. Fragment or not a fragment?
3. Look up the answers now.

SENTENCE FRAGMENTS PRACTICE 2

Directions: Determine whether the following examples are written in complete sentences.

1. Sit still!
2. At two o'clock.

(See page 186 for answers.)

SENTENCES REVIEW 1

Directions: Let's see if you can identify these sentence errors before we move on.

1. The word *punctuation* comes from the Latin word *punctus*. Which means "point." Printers call the mark at the end of a sentence a *point*. We call it a *period*. While people in England call it a *full stop*. Nowadays, we even use the word *dot* when we refer to Internet addresses.

2. Repetition, and reinforcement is important in the learning process. Because we retain more when we practice. We should also give the material time to sink in while we rest. Don't this make grammar seem like a sport? Take a break after this exercise.

SENTENCES REVIEW 2

Directions: Have you taken a break? If so, let's review again. Remember, we learn best in short segments, followed by rest and repetition. Correct the following sentences.

1. Carmelo and Cecilia, came to this country in the 1980s.
2. Carmelo trained to be a bicycle racer. Because he likes the exercise.
3. When he enters a race Cecilia cheers him on.
4. Riders in today's contest includes professional racers.
5. He competed in the race, and finished second.

(See page 186 for answers.)

PARTS OF SPEECH

Grammarians generally agree on eight parts of speech: **nouns**, **verbs**, **prepositions**, **pronouns**, **adjectives**, **adverbs**, **conjunctions**, and **interjections**. You can't always tell what part of speech a word is—it depends on its context in the sentence, so now you'll have to read the test sentences carefully in their entirety.

> We **are trying** to win. (*Are trying* is the verb.)
> **Trying** is better than quitting. (*Trying* is a noun in this example.)
> I found it to be a **trying** lesson. (Here it is an adjective.)

The tests will sometimes try to confuse you by playing with the different parts of speech. For instance, can you make sense of the following sentence?

> **Time flies like an arrow; fruit flies like a banana.**

Think about this for a few seconds. Without looking at the answer, can you reword or rewrite the sentence so that the meaning is clearer?

ANSWER

Time <u>flies</u> like an arrow; fruit **flies** <u>like</u> a banana.
  S   V   S   V

Time takes flight as an arrow does, but the insects around fruit enjoy a banana.

Nouns

A **noun**, as you know, *names* a person, place, thing, or idea. You've seen that it can act as the subject of a sentence, but it can also be an object or a complement. For instance, a **direct object** receives the action done by the subject.

The **dog** chased her *tail*.   What did the dog chase? Her tail.
subject *verb*   *object*

A **noun complement** (also called a subjective complement or a predicate noun) renames the subject.

That **dog** is a poodle.   (*Poodle* is a noun telling what kind of dog it is.)
Her **name** is Sophie.   (*Sophie* identifies the subject.)

NOUNS PRACTICE 1

Directions: Identify the part of speech named in the parentheses after each sentence.

1. Finding this subject requires more thinking. (Identify the subject.)
2. Finding this object requires more thinking. (Identify the object.)
3. Actually, these *-ing* nouns are called gerunds. (Identify the noun complement.)
4. Because we have included an introductory clause, this sentence might be a challenge. (Find the main subject.)
5. Running feels strenuous when you're running a fever. (Identify the subject.)

(See page 186 for answers.)

NOUNS PRACTICE 2

Directions: Find these devious nouns.

1. The object of my complaint is the king. (Find the subject.)
2. I am his unwilling subject. (Find the complement.)
3. He gives compliments, but I object. (Find the direct object.)

(See page 187 for answers.)

TIP

A *noun* is a person, place, or thing. Remember, a thing can be something you cannot touch, such as an idea.

Verbs

You should also be able to identify the correct forms and tenses of **verbs**. You don't need to be able to label them (past participle, future perfect, etc.), but you should be able to tell if they are correct or incorrect by the sound of the sentence. Again, read the entire sentence to make sure the verb makes sense in context.

VERBS PRACTICE 1

Directions: Correct the following sentences.

1. I take the test yesterday.
2. I had took the last doughnut.
3. I brung my lunch to school.

VERBS PRACTICE 2

Directions: Correct the following sentences.

1. Who would have thunk of going in there?
2. When the bell had rung, we will go home.
3. I should have did it after we had swum.

(See page 187 for answers.)

Prepositions

TIP

Although *prepositions* are not specifically tested, understanding this part of speech will greatly help you with other types of grammar questions.

A **preposition** is a word that connects a noun to a sentence, usually indicating a relationship in space or time. You probably learned the following mnemonic device (memory aid), in which you can fill a preposition in the blank.

> The mouse ran ___ the house. [in, on, through, around, under, over, to, from, behind, etc.]
> The mouse ran ____ vacation. [during, before, after, etc.]

However, remember that some prepositions don't fit this formula; **the word *of* is a very common preposition**, along with *with, for, due to, except, instead of,* etc. You probably will not be asked to identify prepositions on the exams, but **you will need to understand how they work** in order to identify other sentence errors.

Prepositional phrases consist of the prepositions and the nouns they connect to the sentence. For instance, in the following sentence, we'll put brackets around the prepositional phrases.

> The nouns in brackets are the **objects** of the prepositions.
> The **nouns** [in brackets] <u>are</u> the   objects   [of the **prepositions**].
>   *subject prep. o.p.*   *verb*   *complement*   *prep.*   *o.p. (object of the preposition)*

The basic sentence simply states that **nouns** <u>are</u> *objects*. The prepositional phrases simply add more information.

PREPOSITIONS PRACTICE

Directions: In the following sentences, put brackets around the prepositional phrases (the prepositions and the nouns they connect).

1. Some of the stories in the Bible speak to me on a personal level.
2. On Wednesdays, those of us in the morning section learn Scripture from a teacher of the Jewish faith.
3. At the end of every class, he often teaches us several words in Hebrew.
4. All of us in the class look forward to Wednesday.

(See page 187 for answers.)

PARTS OF SPEECH REVIEW 1

Directions: Identify the nouns, verbs, and prepositional phrases in the following examples. Some are used correctly, while others are not.

1. The number of push-ups increases in gym class yesterday.
2. In the opinion of many doctors, walking is an effective exercise for most people.
3. After exercise, you should rest and recuperate.
4. Rest before the next section.
5. Did you check your answers in the back of the chapter?

(See page 188 for answers.)

Pronouns

Pronouns are words that take the place of nouns. The nouns they replace are called the **antecedents**. For instance, without pronouns, we would write this way:

> Colonel Mustard calmly picked up the piece of paper and put the piece of paper in Colonel Mustard's pocket. Mr. Green saw Colonel Mustard.

Pronouns can simplify the sentence.

> Colonel Mustard calmly picked up the piece of paper and put **it** in **his** pocket.
> Mr. Green saw **him**.

It is the pronoun replacing the antecedent *piece of paper. His* and *him* replace the antecedent *Colonel Mustard.*

PRONOUN-ANTECEDENT AGREEMENT

Pronoun agreement poses a problem for many writers, and it's a tricky construction to identify. Make sure that a pronoun agrees in number with the noun that it replaces. For instance, in the previous example, it would make no sense to write this:

> Colonel Mustard calmly picked up a piece of paper and put it in **their** pocket.

CAUTION

Pronoun-antecedent agreement is a common writing error. Study this section carefully.

PRONOUN-ANTECEDENT AGREEMENT PRACTICE 1

Directions: Are the following sentences written correctly? If not, correct them.

1. The reader is often confused when they encounter disagreement of this sort.
2. Writers have to be very careful when he or she composes a sentence.
3. The sentences should be clear to its readers.

(See page 188 for answers.)

Unfortunately, it gets a bit more complicated when you encounter indefinite pronouns—pronouns that are less specific about what nouns they replace—words such as *anybody, someone, something, all, few,* etc.

Most of them are easy to identify in number. *Each, either, neither, nobody, anyone, someone, everybody,* etc. are obviously singular.

Each of them knows **his** or **her** grammar lessons.
Everybody knows his or her grammar lessons.
No one knows his or her grammar lessons.

Plurals include words such as *many, several, few,* and *both.*

Many of them know **their** grammar lessons.
Several of them know **their** grammar lessons.
Both of them know **their** grammar lessons.

However, some indefinite pronouns can be singular OR plural! Words such as *most, all, none, any, some,* etc. require more information. You will have to look at the **context** to see what noun or nouns the pronoun is replacing. In single sentences, as you'll see on these exams, the context will appear in a **prepositional phrase**.

Most [of the work] was **its** own reward.
(If the noun is uncountable, as in *work*, it counts as singular.)

Most [of the workers] wanted **their** rewards.
(Workers are countable, and there are more than one.)

PRONOUN-ANTECEDENT AGREEMENT PRACTICE 2

Directions: By now you have the tools to identify grammatical errors. Try a few more. Are the following sentences written correctly? If not, revise them.

1. If any one of you needs help, they should raise their hand.
2. Everyone must use a pencil when they take the exam.
3. Everybody must use a pencil when they take the exam.
4. All of that information was kept in its own file.
5. All of them forgot his or her pencils.
6. Jack and Jill made great progress in their climb.
7. If anyone is asleep right now, they should wake up.

(See page 188 for answers.)

PRONOUN CASE

When we talk about pronoun case, we are just pretentiously saying that you should be able to tell whether a pronoun is a **subject** (doing an action) or an **object** (receiving an action). The following chart can help:

Subjects		Objects
(They ACT. They DO things!)		(They RECEIVE action. They just take it.)
I	love	me.
He	loves	him.
She	loves	her.
They	love	them.
We	love	us.
Who	loves	whom?

The object form, therefore, is used after a preposition (the object of the preposition):

Subjects			Objects
I	am talking	to	me.
He	is talking	to	him.
She	is talking	to	her.
They	are talking	to	them.
We	are talking	to	us.
Who	is talking	to	whom?

TIP

The word *who* is a subject; the word *whom* is an object.

If you still have trouble with this, substitute *he* and *him* for *who* and *whom*. They sound similar, and they work exactly the same: He (Who) likes him (whom). Study these sentences, and you should have no trouble with *who* and *whom*. (Owls are supposed to be so smart, but they say "To-who" when they should say "To-whom." An owl has never successfully passed the COOP/HSPT/TACHS.)

Note: On the exams, don't let added words trick you. For example:

> She and me deduced the answers to the COOP questions.

Take out one of the pronouns and see if it still makes sense.

> She deduced the answers. (Okay.)
> Me deduced the answers. (Is Tarzan speaking? Incorrect.)
> She and I deduced the answers. (Correct. They are both SUBJECT pronouns.)

PRONOUN CASE PRACTICE 1

Directions: Correct the following sentences. Why should they be changed?

1. Him and her passed the test.
2. Whomever will help us?
3. These questions don't bother you and I.

PRONOUN CASE PRACTICE 2

Directions: Correct the following sentences.

1. Me and my friends celebrated the birthday of Millard Fillmore.
2. It now makes sense to them and I.
3. To who do I throw the ball?

(See page 189 for answers.)

ANOTHER PRONOUN PROBLEM

Maybe this has happened to you. You answer the telephone and someone, not recognizing your voice, asks to speak with you. You become flustered: "This is me. This is I. Me. I. This is me, I, me. . . . This is—oh, heck! SPEAKING!!!"

Although we rarely use this in conversation, the grammatically elegant way is to say, "This is I."

I KNOW! It sounds wrong! You feel like you're in an old melodramatic movie: "It is I, Mal Dastardly, and I've come for the mortgage money!" (Maniacal laugh)

Or maybe you should think of answering the phone as a Shakespearean character: "'Tis I, m'lord, or m'lady, depending upon whom I am addressing."

Why do we do this? Well, think of linking verbs or being verbs (*am, are, is, was, were,* etc.) as equal signs. The nouns on either side should be exactly the same case so that they are interchangeable.

He is it.	She is this.
he = it	she = this
it = he	this = she
It is he.	This is she.

While understanding linking verbs can help us in our proofreading, we almost never use this formal construction in conversation, so this usage is dying out. Our language is changing, but for the sake of purity, let's understand the logic behind the original construction.

The only exercise for this section is to knock on someone's door. They will ask, "Who is it?" You will reply, in a stentorian voice, "It is I! Zorro!"

PRONOUNS IN COMPARISONS: *THAN* AND *AS*

Another pronoun issue appears when we use the words *than* or *as* to compare things.

He is taller *than* I.	He is taller *than* me.
She is not as friendly *as* he.	She is not as friendly *as* him.

Which is correct? Well, when we use *than* or *as* in a comparison, we often leave words out. In this case, we assume that the verb is implied in the second half of the sentence. (Yes, we're expected to read minds and invisible texts, now. Welcome to English.) Use the subject form.

> **He is taller *than* I (am).**
> **She is not as friendly *as* he (is).**
> **We are as successful *as* they (are).**

POSSESSIVE PRONOUNS

Pronouns have a third case—possessive—and that is often another problem area. Most student writers have difficulty with the words *it's* and *its*. Here is a way to remember the correct usage. The possessive pronouns that end with the letter *s* are *his, hers, theirs, yours,* and *its.* They do **not** use apostrophes. We do not write *her's, hi's, their's,* and *your's,* so we do not use *it's.*

TIP

Confusion between the words *its* and *it's* is another common error.

Its is possessive.

It's is a contraction.

Remember: ***It's*** always **stands for a contraction: *it is* or *it has.***

Likewise, *you're* stands for *you are.* The possessive pronoun is *your.*

> **Your hat belongs to you. You're so attractive in it.**

The contraction *they're* stands for *they are.* The possessive pronoun is *their.*

> **Their shoes have three-inch platforms. They're stuck in the 1970s.**

The contraction *who's* stands for *who is. Whose* is possessive.

> **Whose weasels are those? Who's writing these things, anyway?**

Whenever you see the words *it's, you're, they're,* or *who's,* mentally fill in the words *it is, you are, they are,* or *who is.* Make this a habit.

POSSESSIVE PRONOUNS PRACTICE

Directions: Determine whether these sentences are correct or incorrect.

1. It's a beautiful day in the neighborhood.
2. You're so confident that its scary.
3. The test contains its share of sentences such as this one.
4. Just between you and me, she is much smarter than I.
5. Knock-knock. Whose their? Its me!

(See page 189 for answers.)

PARTS OF SPEECH REVIEW 2

Directions: Practice some of the concepts we've discussed so far by correcting each sentence.

1. Swimming with dolphins appeal to us very much.
2. They and us will enjoy a great time in the water.
3. That dolphin knows it's way around the lagoon.
4. From who did we learn our skills?
5. Each marine biologist has earned their advanced degree.

(See page 189 for answers.)

Adjectives and Adverbs

Adjectives describe (modify) nouns.

> The <u>precarious</u> bridge could not hold us. (*Precarious* describes the noun *bridge*.)

Adverbs describe other parts of speech: verbs, adjectives, and other adverbs.

> The bridge was swinging <u>precariously</u>. (*Precariously* describes how the bridge was swinging.)

Note: Adverbs often end with **-ly**—but not always.

Two common adverbs are *very* and *not*.

> I <u>do</u> **not** <u>run</u> **very** well after a big lunch.

The adverb *not* describes the verb *do run*. The adverb *very* describes the adjective *well*.

Note the usage:

> You write **good**.
> (*Good* is always an adjective. It only describes nouns. Incorrect.)
> You write **well**.
> (*Well* is used as an adverb describing *write*. Correct.)

However, *well* is often used as an adjective when describing health.

> You look **well**. I don't feel **well**. (Correct)

This is a special case where the words *look* and *feel* function as linking verbs. You can replace *look* and *feel* with forms of *to be*.

> You *are* **well**. I *am not* **well**.

You also use this idea when you use the word *bad* concerning health.

> I feel *bad*. (NOT *I feel badly*. The sentence *I am badly* is incorrect.)

COMPARISONS

> He is the best of the pair. (Incorrect—*best* is an adjective used with more than two items.)
> He is the better of the pair. (Correct)

> If you can run a mile in six minutes, you are a **good** runner.
> If you beat your friend in a race, you are the **better** runner of the two of you.
> If you outrun more than one friend, you are the **best** runner in the race.

When comparing with adjectives of one syllable, *-er* and *-est* endings are usually standard:

> big, bigger, biggest   fast, faster, fastest

With adjectives of three or more syllables, it is more common to use the adverbs *more/most* and *less/least*.

> more confident, most confident   less difficult, least difficult

With adjectives of two syllables, the practice varies; however, the use of *more, most, less*, and *least* is more common.

handsomer *or* more handsome   commonest *or* most common

Note: When comparing **adverbs**, we generally use the words *more, most, less*, and *least*.

more quickly   most likely   less elegantly   least willingly

Another note: A very common mistake involves the word **unique**. *Unique*, based on the root *unus* (one), means *the only **one** of its kind*. It makes little sense, then, to use the expression "more" or "most unique." You can't be "the most one and only." You can be the "**most unusual**," but you can only be "**unique**."

ADJECTIVES AND ADVERBS PRACTICE

Directions: Determine whether the following sentences are written correctly.

1. The friendly giant protected the village.
2. Tweedle-Dee was the fattest of the duo.
3. The air is more drier in the desert than in the tropics.
4. I was ill last week, but now I don't feel bad at all!
5. Of all the bears, Yogi is the most unique.

(See page 190 for answers.)

PARTS OF SPEECH REVIEW 3

Directions: Correct the following errors in pronoun use, adjectives, and adverbs.

My cousin and me disagree on an important issue. Whom is the better superhero—Batman or Superman? She likes Superman because he is invincible. I like Batman because he definite is not. He is the most human of the two. A reader is always unsure of the outcome when they read a Batman comic. A story is more exciting when its more suspensfuler.

(See page 190 for answers.)

Conjunctions

Conjunctions are connecting words. **Coordinating conjunctions** connect equal parts of a sentence. The acronym FANBOYS can help you remember these: *for, and, nor, but, or, yet*, and *so*. When two sentences (independent clauses) are joined, they use one of these coordinating conjunctions **and a comma**.

You <u>remember</u> this rule , <u>but</u>   we <u>will repeat</u> it anyway.
subject   *verb*   *, conjunction*   *subject*   *verb*

You *just* <u>read</u> *this rule* , *yet*   we   *<u>repeat</u> it again.*
subject   *verb*   *, conjunction*   *subject*   *verb*

TIP

Pay special
attention to
the neither/nor
construction.
This appears
frequently on
these exams.

Certain conjunctions are used in pairs. Check these **correlative conjunctions** to make sure one of them is not left out of a sentence.

Either _____ or _____   You're either with us or against us.

Neither _____ nor _____   That's neither here nor there.

Whether _____ or _____   I can't tell whether you're happy or sad.

Both _____ and _____   Both Mutt and Jeff arrived early.

We discussed **subordinating conjunctions** (*because, since, even though, if, unless, while,* etc.) under the section entitled "Sentence Fragments" on page 148. If you've forgotten, this would be a good time to go back and review it.

Interjections

Easy! **Interjections** are words that express strong feeling. They usually use an exclamation point, but they can be punctuated with a comma.

Oh! I knew this one!   Oh, I understand.

CONJUNCTIONS AND INTERJECTIONS PRACTICE

Directions: Determine whether the following sentences are written correctly.

1. Neither the wind or the rain bothered the mail carrier.
2. Hiking! I'd love to hike more often, but I'm afraid of the deep woods.
3. We will hold a yard sale whether it rains.

(See page 190 for answers.)

Other Modifiers

DANGLING AND MISPLACED MODIFIERS

A **dangling modifier** is a word, phrase, or clause that is meant to describe a word in a sentence, but that word is missing.

While eating, the radio plays soft music. (Can a radio eat?)
While we're eating, the radio plays soft music. (Better.)

A **misplaced modifier** is placed awkwardly in a sentence so that it seems to describe something else.

Placed in an awkward position, the reader cannot understand the modifier.
   (Why? Is the reader hanging from the ceiling?)
Placed in an awkward position, the modifier confuses the reader.
   (Oh, now I get it.)

MODIFIERS PRACTICE 1

Directions: Are the following sentences clear? If not, correct them.

1. The teacher brought in paper for his students with narrow lines.
2. The fruit was finally served by the waiter, wrapped in pancakes.
3. Walking home from school, the storm drenched me.
4. I noticed fried chicken on the way to lunch.

(See page 190 for answers.)

CONJUNCTIVE ADVERBS

Words such as *however, thus, moreover,* and *furthermore* are useful in transitions, but it is important to remember that these function as adverbs. They **cannot** connect two sentences into one. You **must** use a period or a semicolon before these transitions.

The word *however* cannot connect two sentences.

Consider the use of *however* (*thus, moreover,* etc.) here:

> This is a good transitional word, however it is not a coordinating conjunction.
> (Incorrect)

> This is a good transitional word. However, it is not a coordinating conjunction.
> (Correct)

Conjunctive adverbs *can* also be used as interrupters.

> It is, nevertheless, a good transitional word. It is not, however, one of the FANBOYS.

Note: Interrupters, separated by commas, can be lifted out of a sentence without changing its meaning.

> Interrupters[, moreover,] can be lifted out of a sentence without changing its meaning.

> Interrupters can be lifted out of a sentence without changing its meaning.

DOUBLE NEGATIVES

Double negatives may be proper in other languages, but they are considered incorrect usage in English.

> I don't use no double negatives.   (You just did: *not* and *no.*)

Beware of words such as *hardly, barely,* or *scarcely.* They are considered negative.

> I can't hardly wait. (Incorrect) (I can <u>not hardly</u> wait?)
> I can hardly wait. (Correct)

MODIFIERS PRACTICE 2

Directions: Correct the following sentences.

1. I like old movies, for instance, *The Wizard of Oz* is one of the best.
2. The lion is my favorite character, however, I like almost all of them.
3. I couldn't not care less about those ridiculous monkeys.
4. I'm not afraid of nobody.

(See page 191 for answers.)

PARTS OF SPEECH REVIEW 4

Directions: Correct the following errors. Check conjunctions, dangling and misplaced modifiers, conjunctive adverbs, and double negatives.

1. The Wicked Witch doesn't have no power in Munchkinland, however, she threatens Dorothy during the journey.
2. Neither the Tin Man or the Straw Man is affected by the poppies.
3. Because they are not mammals, the poppies' scent cannot harm them.

(See page 191 for answers.)

PARALLELISM

In clear composition, each item in a series should be written using the same grammatical structure. Now that we've reviewed some grammar, you should be able to spot errors of inconsistency.

Grandmother lives **over the river, through the woods, and extravagantly.**
prep. phrase   prep. phrase   adverb

This is a fun sentence (if that's your idea of fun), but you won't see one like it on the test unless it's an error. It uses two prepositional phrases and an adverb in a series. Detecting errors in parallelism often appears on these exams.

TIP

Errors in parallelism are likely to appear on these tests.

PARALLELISM PRACTICE 1

Directions: Are the following sentences written correctly, using parallelism? If not, correct them.

1. I like walking with the clouds, skipping with the trees, and to run with the badgers.
2. Get fit, get rest, get packed, and you should feed yourself.
3. My emergency plan consists of running, screaming, and waving my hands about.

PARALLELISM PRACTICE 2

Directions: Do the following sentences use parallel structure? If not, correct them.

1. Robert has to take four credits in English, three credits in Latin, and two in Greek.
2. Common literary archetypes include the Hero, Mentor, and the Other.
3. Teachers should strive to educate their students and serving as good role models.

(See page 191 for answers.)

Note: Parallelism is important enough that you should read this section again. Try writing a few parallel sentences of your own. Then get some rest before we go on to a new topic. (We'll let you choose your own resting places from now on.)

SENTENCE COMPLETIONS

Many of the sentence completion (fill in the correct word) questions on the HSPT and COOP involve transition words. The trick here is to make sure you know which words indicate a relationship of **agreement** and which words indicate **disagreement**. You already know the difference between the words *and* and *but*; *and* indicates an agreement or expansion, while *but* signals a disagreement or contrast.

Agreement	Disagreement
and	but
therefore	however
because	nevertheless
furthermore	conversely
for instance	although
for example	though
moreover	while
consequently	instead

SENTENCE COMPLETIONS PRACTICE

Directions: Fill in words that correctly complete the sentences. On the actual exam, you will be given a list of words from which to choose, so feel free to consult the list above.

1. I would go to the movies, _____ I have to work tonight.
2. I have to work _____ I'm saving for college.
3. Chris didn't want to go to the party, so _____, he stayed at home to read.
4. They disagreed on politics; _____, they remained close friends.
5. Dr. Hoffman didn't like my symptoms; _____, he admitted me to the hospital.

(See page 192 for answers.)

COMPOSITION

Coherence and Development

All three exams test elements of good composition. For instance, you will be shown a paragraph and will be asked whether the sentences all fit the topic. You may also be asked to place a sentence logically in a paragraph. Let's prepare with an exercise that combines these tasks.

TIP

Composition is tested on all three exams. Study this *entire* section.

COMPOSITION PRACTICE 1

Directions: Rearrange the following mixed-up sentences to create a coherent paragraph. One of these sentences, however, will not belong! Mark that one out.

(A) The sentences that follow present support for this topic sentence, using examples and explanations of the examples.

(B) Most paragraphs begin with a topic sentence that identifies the main point for the reader.

(C) The paragraph may close with a sentence that restates the topic sentence or sums up the main point.

(D) A paragraph is indented five spaces on a computer.

(E) These sentences can further unify the paragraph by using related ideas, grammatical structures, and words.

(See page 192 for answers.)

By the way, what is the overall point of the paragraph? The COOP will specifically ask you to identify the topic sentence of a paragraph.

COMPOSITION PRACTICE 2

Directions: Which of the following is the topic sentence of the paragraph you just unscrambled in Composition Practice 1? Read it again, in order, and ask yourself what the main point is.

(A) The word *paragraph* derives from the Greek word *paragraphos*.

(B) A paragraph is unified by a single point.

(C) A paragraph should open with an interesting sentence.

(D) Paragraphs are the building blocks of a clear essay.

(See page 192 for answers.)

Sentence Combining and Clear Writing

The COOP will also ask you to combine sentences. The HSPT and TACHS will show you several sentences and ask you to choose which one is most clearly written.

COMPOSITION PRACTICE 3

Directions: Choose the single sentence that most clearly combines the pair of sentences.

1. Good writing is vigorous. Good writing is concise.

   (A) Concise writing is vigorous.
   (B) Vigorous writing is concise.
   (C) Good writing is both vigorous and concise.
   (D) Writing is good when it is vigorous, and it is also good when it is concise.
   (E) Writing, vigorous and concise, is good.

2. My brother is Joseph. He is too young to drive. He rides a bike.

   (A) My brother Joseph is too young to ride a bike, so he drives.
   (B) Because my brother Joseph is too young to drive, he rides a bike.
   (C) My brother Joseph, he's too young to drive, so he rides a bike.
   (D) Joseph, my brother, is too young to drive.
   (E) Brother Joseph, too young, drives a bike.

(See page 193 for answers.)

Guessing

What if you're stumped or can't choose between a couple of choices? When guessing the most clearly written sentence out of a group of choices, **choose the shortest sentence or the next-to-shortest sentence.** This is certainly not always the correct response, but because good writing is concise it's a more likely choice than a longer, wordier sentence. Check the shortest sentence to make sure it's not *too* short; it may be short because it's eliminating necessary material.

Also, a choice containing an active verb is more likely to be the clearest sentence rather than ones written with passive construction or forms of the verbs *have* or *to be*. The subject of a strong sentence should ACT rather than receive action.

> I wrote an active sentence. (The subject *I* acts!)
> A passive sentence was written by me.
>   (The subject *sentence* receives the action.)

Point of View

You may be asked to identify the point of view of a passage.

1ST PERSON

If the narrator is a character in the story and uses the words *I, me, we*, etc., then the story is being told in first person.

> *Some hours ago—never mind how long exactly—having little or no food in my stomach, I thought I would eat some breakfast.*

2ND PERSON

Second person point of view is rarely used in literature. (Advertisements and songs use it more often.) Look for the word *you*. You the reader feel as if you are a character in the story.

> *You are traveling through another dimension, a dimension not only of blighted sound but also of eerie ring tones, whose boundaries are outside your roaming area. There's the tower up ahead! You've just answered the Twilight Phone.*

3RD PERSON

The key words used here are *he, she, them*, etc. In third person point of view, the narrator tells the story but is not a character in it.

An **omniscient** narrator knows everything about the story. A **limited** narrator may know only what the characters know and not any more.

> *It was the worst of times. Farley was dead, to begin with, the buffet lay burning, and it was by far the worst thing that he had ever done when he asked for more crackers. "Please, sir, I want s'mores," he piped, and whether he would turn out to be the hero of this story is anyone's guess.*

PUNCTUATION, CAPITALIZATION, USAGE, AND SPELLING

Punctuation, capitalization, usage, and spelling are specifically tested on the HSPT and TACHS; the COOP does not include specific questions on spelling, but you are expected to know the other skills. Furthermore, remember that identifying grammar errors can help you make a choice among the possible answers. Some questions will ask you to identify an error. Other questions will ask you to choose the best sentence (as we did previously), so you can eliminate choices that contain grammatical errors. Eliminating choices increases your odds of finding the correct answer.

Punctuation

Early writing did not use punctuation all of the writing ran together like this it must have been difficult to tell when a sentence stopped and a new thought began eventually pauses had to be marked. This helped readers and speakers immensely. Later, when books were printed, publishers began developing logical rules for punctuation.

PERIODS

Periods are easy. Use a period at the end of a sentence (unless it's a question or an exclamation). Also use a period for abbreviations.

> **Dr. Smith is engaged to Ms. Mendez.**

QUESTION MARKS

We use a **question mark** after a direct question.

> **Are you serious?**

We do *not* use it after an indirect question.

> **He asked if I was being serious.**
> **I wonder why he asked me that.**

EXCLAMATION POINTS

Exclamation points are not used often. They should be reserved for instances of strong emotion.

> **Help me! I've fallen, and I can't get up!**

COMMAS

Many students use **commas** randomly, but the rules for commas do make sense, and they are well worth learning. Because most punctuation errors involve commas, we'll spend more time looking at these. Strap yourself in! Concentrate!

 TIP

Two *complete* sentences can be joined by using *both* a comma AND a conjunction.

1. Use a comma to separate **two independent clauses** connected by a conjunction (*and, but, or, nor, for, so, yet*).

   A **clause** is a group of words with a subject and a verb. An *independent* clause makes sense standing alone; it's a sentence.

   > **Murray** <u>plays</u> **a red guitar** , **and   Jeff   ** <u>plays</u> **a purple accordion.**
   > *subject   verb   ,   subject   verb*

   Think of the comma as a point of balance; it **must** have a subject and a verb on both sides of it.

   Warning! Many people do this:

   > **Murray plays a red guitar , Jeff plays a purple accordion.**

   The comma is not a strong enough pause to separate two sentences. This is called a **comma splice**. It is the ultimate error in comma usage. Use a period or a comma plus a conjunction instead.

   > **Murray plays a red guitar . Jeff plays a purple accordion.**
   > **Murray plays a red guitar , and Jeff plays a purple accordion.**

   Better yet, if the sentences are closely related, use a semicolon.

   > **Murray plays a red guitar; Jeff plays a purple accordion.**

TIP

A semicolon can also connect two complete sentences.

If you substitute semicolons for comma splices, you will be using a sophisticated style of punctuation. Everyone will assume you are a grammatical genius. **A semicolon is like a period; it ends sentences.** However, it's not as strong as a period, so it shows that the sentences are related.

2. Do not use a comma before a conjunction joining two verbs.

>   Nate visited Russia, and bought a fur hat.   (Incorrect)
>   Nate <u>visited</u> Russia *and* <u>bought</u> a fur hat.   (Correct)
>   (no comma)

Remember that you must have a subject and a verb on both sides of the comma.

| **Jack** | <u>fell</u> down the hill , | *and* | **he** | <u>broke</u> his crown. | | Jack <u>fell</u>, *and* he <u>broke</u>. |
| subject | verb | | subject | verb | | |

| **Jack** | <u>fell</u> down the hill *and* <u>broke</u> his crown. | | Jack <u>fell</u> *and* <u>broke</u>. |
| subject | verb   verb | | |

However, use commas in a **series** of verbs:

>   Nate <u>visited</u> Russia , <u>bought</u> a fur hat , <u>and pretended</u> to be a Wookie.

3. Use commas to separate items in a series of three or more.

>   I brought sandwiches, salad, and cake to the picnic.

4. Separate two or more adjectives before a noun.

>   Matt's filthy , dilapidated bicycle broke down.

Remember this test: In a series of modifiers, use a comma if the word *and* makes sense in its place.

>   Matt's filthy *and* dilapidated bicycle broke down.

COMMA PRACTICE 1

Directions: Are the following sentences punctuated correctly? If not, correct them.

1. The ice, cream truck drove through our neighborhood yesterday.
2. Should I punt, or pass?
3. Semicolons are tricky devices; you should not overuse them.

(See page 193 for answers.)

---

5. In the following examples, commas isolate sections of a sentence that can be **left out**. Try removing these sections to see if the sentences still make sense.

5a. Use commas to set off nonessential phrases and clauses.

What is nonessential? If the sentence doesn't need it to express its meaning, it's non-essential. It's usually just **descriptive**.

>   Morgan, who has red hair, is in our class.

The phrase *who has red hair* is not essential, so we put commas around it. We could take out the section within the commas and it conveys the same message.

> Morgan [, who has red hair,] is in our class.
> Morgan is in our class.

However, what if we said this?

> Morgan is the only person in our class who has red hair.

We don't use a comma in this case; the phrase *who has red hair* is essential. If we took it out, the sentence would **not** mean the same thing!

> Morgan is the only person in our class [who has red hair].
> Morgan is the only person in our class. (Incorrect)

5b. Use commas to separate adjectives that follow a noun.

> Mr. Villanueva, tall, dark, and handsome, was born in Florida.

You can take out *tall, dark, and handsome,* and the sentence still makes sense.

> Mr. Villanueva [, tall, dark, and handsome,] was born in Florida.
> Mr. Villanueva was born in Florida.

5c. Use commas to set off parenthetical phrases (phrases that interrupt a sentence).

> Aubrey can, of course, stand on one hand.
> By the way, you're soaking in it.
> You are, in my opinion, an infectious, beef-witted clotpole.

5d. Use commas to set off an appositive. An appositive renames a noun.

> Ernie, an excellent student, always attended class.
> Ernie always attended class.

However, if we **need** to know the information for the sentence to make sense, don't use a comma. These are called **restrictive phrases or clauses**. This is often the case with proper appositives.

> The novelist Nathaniel Hawthorne is Brandon's favorite author. (Correct)

We lose the meaning if we write the following:

> The novelist, Nathaniel Hawthorne, is Brandon's favorite author.
> The novelist [, Nathaniel Hawthorne,] is Brandon's favorite author.
> The novelist is Brandon's favorite author. (Incorrect)

Compare this to the reverse order:

> Nathaniel Hawthorne, a novelist, is Brandon's favorite author. (Correct)

In this case, *a novelist* is not necessary, so we can separate it with commas.

> Nathaniel Hawthorne [, a novelist,] is Brandon's favorite author.
> Nathaniel Hawthorne is Brandon's favorite author.

COMMA PRACTICE 2

Directions: Are the following sentences punctuated correctly? If not, correct them.

1. Poe's poem, "The Raven," is my favorite.
2. Our test, which falls on a Monday, will not be difficult.
3. I can't stand work, that is scheduled on Mondays.
4. I am of course, an excellent writer.
5. People, who use social media, make me so angry.

(See page 193 for answers.)

6. Use commas to set off nouns of direct address.

   Allison, I just don't know.
   I just don't know, Allison.

   (I am speaking to Allison; I am not saying that I have never met Allison.)

   Honestly, Allison, I just don't know what has become of Sarah.

7. Use a comma after introductory words and mild interjections.

   Why, I do declare!
   Yes, we have no bananas.
   Well, I've never seen anything like it!
   Wow, I do love these comma rules.

8. Use a comma after most introductory clauses and phrases.

   Introductory adverbial clauses:

   While Santa Claus slept, the elf left his presents under the tree.
   (This clause acts as an adverb, telling us when the elf left the presents.)

   More than one introductory prepositional phrase:

   To the students in the far corner, this information will be useless.

   Participial phrases (basically, -*ing* or -*ed* phrases):

   Frothing like a rabid hippopotamus, I opened my grammar book.

9. Use a comma to separate the year when you write a particular date.

   July 4, 1776, is considered our first Independence Day.

10. Use commas after a name with a title such as Jr. or M.D.

    Raymond J. Johnson, Jr.   **Vladimir Acula, Ph.D.**
    Bugs Bunny, Esq.   **Rev. Arthur Fiddle, D.D.**

11. Use commas when you write addresses.

    Every year in Louisville, Kentucky, we attend the Kentucky Derby.
    I lived in an old house at 1985 East 124th Place, Cleveland, Ohio 44106.

12. Use commas to introduce a quote with words such as *says, writes, comments,* and *adds.*

    Dickens writes , "Scrooge was better than his word."

    Do **not** use commas with connecting words such as *that* or *as.*

    Dickens writes that "Scrooge was better than his word."

COMMA PRACTICE 3

Directions: Are the following sentences punctuated correctly? If not, correct them.

1. For most of the students the homework was not difficult.
2. Oh, now the rules get complicated.
3. The author said that, "I never intended to write a fairy tale."
4. I grew up in Bayside, New York during the turn of the century.
5. Didn't I ask you a question Mark?

(See page 194 for answers.)

COLON

The **colon** introduces a list, an example, an explanation, or a quote. If the colon could talk, it would say, "And here they are!" or "And here it is!"

TIP

A colon is like a spokesmodel pointing with her two hands.

> I brought the necessary supplies: bread, peanut butter, and a butter knife.
> The author expressed strong disagreement: "I never intended to write a fairy tale."

Note: *The statement before a colon should be a complete sentence (an independent clause).* A colon is **not** used after a verb or a preposition.

> The necessary supplies were: bread, peanut butter, and a butter knife.
> The colon is unnecessary. Take it out and see. (Incorrect)

> I am afraid of: spiders, quicksand, radioactivity, and dangling modifiers.
> Take out the colon. (Incorrect)

APOSTROPHES

You already know how an apostrophe is used in contractions.

> it's = it is   can't = cannot
> you've = you have   we'll = we will

It gets more complicated when an apostrophe is used for possessives.

Any noun that **does not end with the letter** *s* uses *'s* to form a possessive. It does not matter whether the noun is singular or plural.

> This man's army   The horse's hooves
> The men's locker room   The children's room

Plural nouns that **do** end in *s* form the possessive by simply adding an apostrophe.

> The ladies' invitations   The twins' books
> The horses' stables

Here's where it gets tricky. With singular nouns that end with the sound of *s* or *z*, a single apostrophe usually forms the possessive. This is often the case with ancient or biblical names.

> Moses' importance   Jesus' miracles

However, if the possessive of a single syllable word ending in *s* is pronounced with an extra syllable, many people use *'s*. Either form is acceptable.

> Charles's report   OR   Charles' report
> the class's valedictorian OR   the class' valedictorian

QUOTATION MARKS

1. Use quotation marks for direct quotations.

   > She said, "I can't forget to put a comma after the word *said*."
   > She added that she would "never forget" to omit the comma in a construction such as this.

   Note: In American usage, commas and periods always go *inside* the quotation marks at the end of a quote. **This is a common error**, so be aware of it.

   > "Oh, Todd! You're such a genius," she laughed.

2. Though it seems difficult for many students to remember, you should make sure that the titles of poems and short stories are enclosed in quotation marks.

   > "Miniver Cheevy"   "The Tell-Tale Heart"

   Note: If the poem is book-length, however, the title will be underlined or italicized, as with a book.

   > I shelved my copy of Homer's *Iliad* next to the *Odyssey*.

MORE PARALLELISM

Punctuation also requires a certain degree of parallelism. Make sure that parenthetical, additional, or nonessential material is set off from a sentence with consistent marks of punctuation. That is to say, if you see a comma at the beginning of a sentence interrupter, then you should make sure that interrupter ends with a comma, as well.

> A sentence interrupter, like this one, is set off by commas.

> It can also be set off—in some cases—with dashes.

> Sometimes these are called (obviously enough) parenthetical words or phrases.

> It would be incorrect, not to mention bizarre—to mix the punctuation.
>   (Note that the above uses a comma paired with a dash, which is incorrect.)

PUNCTUATION PRACTICE

Directions: Are the following sentences punctuated correctly? If not, correct them.

1. "I feel I'm forgetting something, she remarked.
2. I really enjoyed Lowry's novel "The Giver."
3. My pet dugong—bizarre as he may seem) amuses my neighbors.
4. My friend, Oliver, completed his homework, plays a video game, and went to bed.
5. I have mastered three marks of punctuation: colons, apostrophes, and quotation marks.

(See page 194 for answers.)

Capitalization

You probably already know the rules of capitalization from everyday use. Here's a quick refresher list to reinforce your knowledge.

1. Capitalize the first letter of the first word of a sentence. That's easy enough. However, make sure you also capitalize the first letter of the first word of a sentence when it is part of a quote.

   > He said, "**The** above example is obvious, isn't it?"
   > "It is," she replied. "**However**, it needs to be said."

   PLEASE NOTE: When a sentence in a quote is interrupted, do NOT capitalize the first letter of the first word of the second half of the sentence.

   > "This sentence," he added, "**is** different because the quote is interrupted."

   Notice the difference:

   > "I promise you," said the teacher. "**This** type of sentence will be on the exam."
   > "I promise you," said the teacher, "**that** this type of sentence will be on the exam."

2. Capitalize proper nouns: the names of particular people, places, organizations, languages, religions, nationalities, products, etc. Also capitalize adjective forms of these words.

   > The Missouri River is the longest river in the United States.
   > (Notice that *river* is not capitalized when used in general.)

Mexico	Kenyan	New Yorker
Greenbriar Drive	Department of Education	Red Rose Tea
John Adams	CIA	Oxford University

3. Capitalize specific regions, but do not capitalize directions.

   > I live in the Deep South.
   > Georgia is located south of Tennessee.

   > We pray for peace in the Middle East.
   > The sun rises in the east and sets in the west.

4. Capitalize titles and words used as parts of *people's names*. Do NOT capitalize them in other cases.

   > My family physician is Dr. Zaius.
   > He is a good doctor.
   > Zaius is a good doctor.

   > Is my father here?
   > Are you here, Father?

   > Have you met Aunt Pina?
   > She is my favorite aunt.
   > Pina is my favorite aunt.

   > Is Dr. Seuss a real doctor?

5. Capitalize the days of the week and months of the year.

   > My father was born on a Friday in September.

6. Capitalize the pronoun *I*. You're important.

   > My mother and I bought him a camera for his birthday.

7. When writing the title of a work, capitalize the first word, important words, and the last word. Do not capitalize articles, short prepositions, and conjunctions unless they are the first or last words.

    Book: *A Tale of Two Cities*   Movie: *Snow White and the*
    Poem: "The Clod and the Pebble"   *Seven Dwarfs*
    Short Story: "A Rose for Emily"   Play: *A Raisin in the Sun*
                                       Painting: *Still Life with Fruit*

Note: Also remember when to use quotation marks and when to italicize (or underline).

8. Capitalize holidays, historical documents, and historical events.

    On Independence Day, we celebrate the signing of the Declaration of Independence, which led to the Revolutionary War.

9. Important religious terms are capitalized (deities, sacred books, religious groups).

Roman Catholic	God (He, His, Him)	Old Testament	Judaism
Bible	Koran	The Book of Job	Jesuits
the Virgin Mary	the Torah	Sisters of Charity	The Book of the Dead

Note, however, that while *Bible* and *Scripture* are capitalized, the words *biblical* and *scriptural* are not.

CAPITALIZATION PRACTICE

Directions: Fix the capitalization errors in the following sentences.

1. I really enjoyed the books in "The lord of the rings" series.
2. "The movies," he explained, "Missed the spirituality of the books."
3. Many of the events of the story have Biblical counterparts.

(See page 194 for answers.)

Usage

We've already covered some common usage errors, such as *it's* and *you're* (contractions) versus *its* and *your* (possessives) and the difference between *well* and *good*. Copy the example sentences in this section for more practice.

    It's well known that **you're** doing **well** in your studies, for knowledge is **its**
    (It is)   (you are)
    own reward.

ACCEPT/EXCEPT

Check these carefully; they are commonly misused.

    Don't **accept** credit cards **except** from people you know.

AFFECT/EFFECT

These are so often misused that you should always check them.

Affect is a verb.	Soft drinks **affect** my system.
Effect is a noun.	They produce a jittery **effect**.

Note: What makes this pair difficult is that the word *effect* can sometimes be used as a verb meaning to cause or to bring about. We wish this weren't the case, but there it is. If you can substitute the words *cause* or *bring about* in its place, *effect* is correct.

The politician thought he could **effect** change.
The politician thought he could **bring about** change. (Correct)

A LOT

Here's another common error. *A lot* consists of **two words**, not one. You don't say *abunch*, *aton*, or *aboatload*. Copy this:

a lot
a   lot
a   lot
a   lot
a   lot of space!

ALL RIGHT

All right consists of two words. All right? All right!

AMONG/BETWEEN

Use *between* when you are talking about two people or items; use *among* with larger numbers.

The thirty students argued **among** themselves, but we had no problems **between** the two of us.

FARTHER, FURTHER

Farther deals with distance. *Further* deals with degree.

The waterfall is **farther** downstream.
Let's discuss this **further**.

FEWER, LESS

Use *fewer* with countable items. *Less* is for noncountable items.

If I use **fewer** ice cubes, I'll have **less** work.

HAVE, OF

These are confused because they sound similar when spoken in sentences. This is a common error on these tests. Remember that *have* is a verb and *of* is a preposition.

I could of sworn this was right.
    (Incorrect) The word *of* does not connect a noun to the sentence.
I could have sworn this was right.
    (Correct) *Could have sworn* is the complete verb.

LAY/LIE, SET/SIT, RAISE/RISE

We **lay** or **set** something down. These require a direct object. (Test: You can replace these words with the word *put*.) We also **raise** something: a thing, a direct object.

We *ourselves* **lie** or **sit** or **rise**.

> I am so tired that I have to **set** down my backpack **and sit**.
> Then I **lay** my head on my pillow and **lie** down.
> I **raise** my arms in a stretch before I **rise** in the morning.

This is simple. The problems occur when we get into tenses.

	Lay	Lie	Raise	Rise
Present Tense	I **lay** it down.	I **lie** down.	I **raise** it up.	I **rise**.
Past	I **laid** it down.	I **lay** down.	I **raised** it up.	I **rose**.
Past Participle	I had **laid** it down.	I had **lain** down.	I had **raised** it up.	I had **risen**.

Look at the past tense of *lie*. That's the problem with the whole business. Conquer that, and you'll lay waste to the test. Chances are, no one will mind if you mix the tenses up in conversation; for the exam, however, you should memorize them.

LOOSE/LOSE

Why is this so difficult? *Lose* is a verb meaning to be without something. *Loose* is an adjective meaning not tight or bound.

> I **lose** pages when writing on **loose**-leaf paper.

Problem: *Loose* is also an old-fashioned verb meaning to loosen or to release something. This sounds too archaic for common use. Save it for poetic writing.

> He **loosed** a barrage of insults.

MYSELF, YOURSELF, HIMSELF, HERSELF, OURSELVES

These words are called intensifiers. They cannot be used alone as a subject or object.

> I **myself** don't make such errors. (Correct)
> Sandy, Ursola, and **myself** worked all day. (Incorrect)
> Sandy, Ursola, and I worked all day. (Correct)

THERE, THEIR, THEY'RE

They're (They are) so unsure of **their** destination that they don't go **there** without a map.

THAT/WHICH

We use the word *that* to connect essential information to a sentence. Remember, too, that we do not use commas when the information is essential.

> The sentence **that** explains this usage contains essential information.

We use the word *which* for nonessential information, and we separate it with commas.

> This sentence, **which** is a lovely sentence, contains nonessential information.

For more review of this, see Rule 5 under Commas on pages 168–169.

TO, TWO, TOO

You know the differences. You've known them for years. *To* is usually a preposition, *two* is a number, and *too* means *also* or *excessive*. Check these when you see them.

To me, two is too many.

UNIQUE

When something is unique, it is one-of-a-kind. Therefore, you cannot say something is **very** unique or **more** or **less** unique or **most** unique. It can **only** be unique. This is a common error, but now you know not to make it! (Does this make you unique?)

OTHER CONFUSED WORDS

In general, beware of similar-sounding words. Other confused pairs include the following:

advice/advise	counsel/council	stationary/stationery
already/all ready	desert/dessert	than/then
cite/site/sight	forth/fourth	weather/whether
capital/capitol	principal/principle	
coarse/course	quiet/quite	

Look these up in a dictionary and read the **entire** definition. Looking them up will cement a stronger connection in your memory.

USAGE PRACTICE 1

Directions: Choose the correct word.

1. She said, "Thank you." I replied, "(Your/You're) welcome."
2. The pungent odor didn't (effect/affect) him at all
3. My grandparents allotted (alot/a lot) for that lot.
4. My teammates and I hold no grudges (among/between) ourselves.
5. I wish a good day to you, (to/too), Brutus!

USAGE PRACTICE 2

Directions: Choose the correct word.

1. Michael is such a sore (looser/loser) in football.
2. I saw (less/fewer) vampires in the daylight.
3. After some thought, she (excepted/accepted) his apology.
4. Just (sit/set) your head on the pillow and (lay/lie) down.
5. What was the (effect/affect) of the gamma rays on the flowers?

USAGE PRACTICE 3

Directions: Choose the correct word.

1. Victor Frankenstein (should of/should have) known better.
2. The campers (rose/raised) at the crack of dawn.
3. Last night, I (lay/laid) awake.
4. I keep a bottle of water (beside/besides) my bed.
5. (All right! Alright!) We're done!

(See page 195 for answers.)

TIP

Spelling
counts—at least
on the HSPT and
TACHS. Oh, it
counts in real
life, too.

Spelling

Spelling? We don't need to know spelling; we've got spell-check, wright?

No, not wright. Nor is it rite. Or write. You see the problems with depending on a program to do our work for us; it doesn't come out quite . . . well, right.

English spelling seems a mess, but there's usually a logical explanation for why a word is spelled a certain way. People throughout history have been trying to organize this huge language that derives from many, many sources. For instance, speakers of Old English didn't write much, so when early Christian writers tried to transcribe these English words into their Roman alphabet, they did their best to write what they heard phonetically. So most of the words that give us trouble today were indeed spelled phonetically at one time. The word *night* was pronounced the way it is spelled—sort of like "nikt." The word *eye* sounded something like "ehyeh." Silent *e* was not always so quiet!

Similarly, many good spellers simultaneously have two pronunciations of a word going on in their heads. We say "vejtabul," but when we write, we silently say to ourselves "ve-ge-table," like the furniture in the dining room. We say "byootiful," but we hear "B-E-A-yoo-tiful" as we write it down. We hear "WED-nes-day," "calen-DAR," "bEEn," "a-GAIN," "temp-er-a-ture," and, of course, "gramm-AR." When you learn a word, try this double pronunciation technique, and see if it works for you. If you mistakenly pronounce the wrong version in public, explain that you speak fluent Middle English. Then ask them how many early languages they know!

You can also use memory aids (often called mnemonic devices). Which is the correct spelling, *tomorrow* or *tommorow*? One way to recall this is to remember that *Tom* is in *tomorrow*: **Tom borrowed** my **barrow** until **tomorrow**.

Do we spell the word *grammar* or *grammer*? If you take the letter *g* from the beginning of the word *grammar* and put it at the end, it will spell *grammar* backwards: *rammarg*. Okay, that's not very exciting, but it reminds us that the word *grammar* contains the letter *a* twice. Maybe it's better to picture your **gramm*a*** studying a **gramm*ar*** book . . . .

Some problem spelling words include the following:

acquire	eighth	mortgage
antique	entrepreneur	necessary
arctic	exercise	nuclear
athletic	February	parallel
bachelor	forehead	parliament
calendar	four, fourteen, forty	popular
column	friend	prejudice
computer	humorous	psychological
conqueror	library	receipt
definite	mischievous	villain

What words give you the most trouble? Make a list and study them. Create your own mnemonics if that helps you.

SPELLING RULES

The history of English is long, complicated, and interesting. Learning the many sources (especially Latin, German, French, and Greek) and the roots, prefixes, and suffixes that make up the language will help your vocabulary and spelling. Having a language with so many sources, though, means that the rules of spelling will have many exceptions.

1. For instance, here's one we've all heard:

    I before E, except after C, or when sounded like "ay" as in *neighbor* and *weigh*.

    This rule often works, but it also has many exceptions. Some words we've adopted from French and German, for instance, don't follow this. You'll just have to learn the exceptions. Here are some of them, Einstein:

    E before I: **Neither** the **sovereign sheik** nor the **counterfeit foreigner** (nor the **feisty heifer**) could **seize** the **heights** of such **weird sleight** of hand without **forfeiting either** work or **leisure** time, and **their heirs** could not drink **caffeine** without **protein.**

    I-E after C: That **ancient species** of omniscient financiers has no **sufficient conscience** when it comes to **science** in **society.**

    Note: Part of the rhyme holds true, though. Words with the "ay" sound will always be spelled E-I after the letter C.

SPELLING PRACTICE 1

Let's solve a problem word. Write the word *receive* ten times right now. As you do so, enunciate it clearly and forcefully at the same time. RECEIVE. Go ahead. Write it in the margins. Rec**ei**ve. You'll now remember how to spell one of the most widely misspelled words.

(See page 195 for more information.)

---

2. Let's look at a rule with no exceptions. When you add a prefix to a word, just add it. You won't have to drop any letters from the root word.

SPELLING PRACTICE 2

Directions: Identify the correct spelling.

1. mispell or misspell
2. extrordinary or extraordinary
3. unatural or unnatural

(See page 195 for answers.)

---

3. When you add a **consonant suffix** (a suffix that begins with a consonant, such as *-less*, *-ful*, or *-ment*) to a word, just add it, unless the root ends with the letter *y*. In that case, change the *y* to *i* and then add the suffix.

harm	pity	neighbor	care
harm**less**	piti**less**	neighbor**ly**	care**ful**
harm**ful**	piti**ful**	neighbor**hood**	care**less**

4. When you add a consonant suffix (-*less, -ful, -ment,* etc.) to a word ending with silent *e,* just add it. (See Rule 3.) When you add a vowel suffix (-*ed, -ing, -er, -al,* etc.) to a word ending with silent *e,* you *usually* drop the silent *e.* The new vowel replaces it.

care	store	captive	love
caring	storing	captivity	loving
cared	storage	captivate	lovable (but *loveable* is also accepted)

5. When do you double letters when adding a suffix? When you add a **vowel suffix** to a word (-*ed, -ing, -er, -al,* etc.), check to see whether the root word ends with a single vowel-consonant combination. Also note which syllable is stressed. Double the root's final consonant if the final syllable is stressed (or is only one syllable).

control	big	occur	refer
controlling	bigger	occurred	referring
controlled	biggest	occurrence	referral

This is a tough rule. Congratulations if you got it before three readings.

SPELLING PRACTICE 3

Directions: Determine the misspelled words in each sentence.

1. The English language contains over fourty sounds.
2. The Roman alphabet, developed for the Latin language, consists of 26 letters.
3. Still, it has proved usful to us until the Internet made it difficult 4 u.

(See page 195 for answers.)

PUNCTUATION, CAPITALIZATION, USAGE, AND SPELLING REVIEW

Directions: Do the following sentences contain spelling errors? If so, correct them.

1. The rising tempretures concerned the meteorologist.
2. Ocasionally, I misspell a word.
3. She had no explaination for it.
4. Who was your sponser at the event?
5. The effects will be irreversible.
6. This property is condemmed.
7. An agrarien society has little time for liesure.
8. The criminal didnt feel well.

(See page 196 for answers.)

TEST FORMATS

The COOP test does not contain a spelling section, but all three exams cover basic language skills such as **capitalization**, **punctuation**, and **usage**. Moreover, you will be asked to choose the **most concise or clear sentence** in a group, and you may be asked to choose the **most logical organization** of a paragraph.

PARENTS

Your child will benefit from completing these questions in *all three* formats. This varied practice will obviously reinforce the skill itself.

However, the formats of the tests differ slightly, so let's examine how the questions are arranged.

The **COOP** (which incorporates the language questions into the Reading section) asks you to identify sentences that *are* well written.

> **Directions:** Choose the sentence that is written correctly.

    A   Floogle Street runs all the way to Niagara falls.
    B   It seems like an ordinary street.
    C   He turned, and moved toward me.
    D   No mistakes.

The **HSPT** reverses the question, asking you to find the sentence that is written *incorrectly*.

> **Directions:** Identify the sentence that contains an error.

    (A)   The Susquehanna Hat Company is located on Floogle Street.
    (B)   I can't find that Street on the map.
    (C)   We enjoy having company over to visit.
    (D)   No mistakes.

The **TACHS** will provide a single sentence, and it tells you what kind of error it contains.

> **Directions:** Identify the line containing an error in <u>**capitalization**</u>.

    A   I have often walked
    B   on this Street before,
    C   but I didn't know its name.
    D   *(No mistakes)*

The correct choice in all three examples is B. The word *street* does not name a particular street, so it is not capitalized.

Try the following sample questions in **all three** formats. You will find that they reinforce your learning, both through practice and by approaching problems in different ways. When you have completed the exercises, check the answers and analyses on page 196.

TEST FORMATS PRACTICE

Directions: For questions 1–4, look for mistakes in **spelling**.

TACHS Format

1
A adjetive
B preposition
C adverb
D conjunction
E (No mistakes)

2
J fellowship
K resolution
L different
M handle
N (No mistakes)

HSPT Format

3. (A) The time is flexible, but the date is definate.
   (B) Lola had a nickel in her pocket.
   (C) What is the origin of that word?
   (D) No mistakes

4. (A) Fumio likes his vegetables steamed.
   (B) Choose one item from the collumn on the right.
   (C) Classic literature will always have something to teach us.
   (D) No mistakes

COOP Format

Directions: For questions 5–7, choose the sentence that is written correctly.

5
A The day Wednesday is named after the Anglo–Saxon god Woden.
B To who am I speaking?
C Saturday is named after a roman god.
D The moon gives its name to monday.

6
F I usually prefer Irish poetry, but I also enjoy the poem *Birches* by Robert Frost.
G "The time has come," the walrus said, "to talk of many things."
H Among the topics on the agenda were: shoes, ships, and sealing wax.
J Have you ever seen a pig fly.

7
A Not all breakfast cereals contain added sugar, but alot do.
B Sometimes it's difficult to accept criticism.
C The movie effected me strongly.
D I tripped because my shoelaces were lose.

HSPT Format

Directions: For questions 8–10, look for errors in capitalization, punctuation, or usage. If you find no mistakes, choose choice (D).

8. (A) My brother's office is located in a town called Mount Washington.
   (B) "I've never seen a mountain there," he admitted.
   (C) My Uncle Angelo owned a beauty salon in Bayside New York.
   (D) No mistakes

9. (A) Whose property is back there?
   (B) The house behind Trinity high school belongs to Dr. Jenny.
   (C) Who's your family dentist?
   (D) No mistakes

10. (A) Churning, thundering, and blowing high winds, Ashford trudged through the storm.
    (B) He is not a mail carrier; he just likes a walk as part of his routine.
    (C) It's been a habit ever since he decided to lose weight.
    (D) No mistakes

TACHS Format

Directions: For questions 11 and 12, look for errors in **capitalization**.

11 A   The train in
    B   Springfield, New Jersey, runs
    C   right by my Aunt's house.
    D   *(No mistakes)*

12 J   Heather and Teresa
    K   brought a lovely
    L   bouquet of Flowers.
    M   *(No mistakes)*

Directions: For questions 13 and 14, look for errors in **punctuation**.

13 A   When you write a sentence,
    B   make sure you don't leave
    C   out essential punctuation
    D   *(No mistakes)*

14 J   Before we eat
    K   the youngest family member
    L   says grace.
    M   *(No mistakes)*

15 **A** When I lay down,

    B I like to lay my head

    C on two soft pillows.

    D *(No mistakes)*

16 **J** Gaetano swam in the ocean;

    K his granddaughters had swum all day in the pool.

    L Alfia did not swim at all.

    M *(No mistakes)*

COOP/HSPT/TACHS Format—Expression

Directions: Questions 17 and 18 are based on the following paragraph.

(1) Early history books are fun to read <u>for the reason that</u> they often contain fantastic stories. (2) For instance, *The Life of St. Columba* includes the very first reference to the Loch Ness monster. (3) It is a fascinating tale. (4) As it is about to devour a swimmer, Columba turns the beast aside with a prayer.

17 Which is the best way to write the underlined part of the first sentence?

    A and

    B because

    C for instance,

    D No change

18 Which sentence could be left out of the paragraph?

    J 1

    K 2

    L 3

    M No change

(See page 196 for answers.)

GUESSING

If you're faced with a question that you simply cannot figure out, skip it and come back to it. When you do, an error might look more obvious the second time. If you still don't know the answer, eliminate the choices you know are wrong; your odds of choosing the correct response will increase. Remember, there are no penalties for guessing incorrectly, so you should always guess.

CONCLUSION

Even if some of the material you've just studied might seem new, realize that you've really been using it every day as you speak, read, and write. Don't be too concerned about fancy grammatical labels; use your common sense—and your ears. You instinctively know what sounds correct or incorrect. After a thorough review of this section, you should be able to trust yourself.

ANSWERS AND ANALYSES

Subject-Verb 1 (page 148)

1. In this sentence, the verb is *asks*. What asks? The test does not ask. The **questions ask**.
    If you marked it, the sentence would look like this:
    Many **questions** [on the test] <u>asks</u> you to identify errors in subject-verb agreement.
    (Questions asks? This sounds wrong. The sentence should read **questions** <u>ask</u>.)

2. In this example, the subject is in the middle of the sentence.
    <u>Is</u> the following **sentences** <u>written</u> correctly?
    (Incorrect. This question should ask "<u>Are</u> the following **sentences** <u>written</u> correctly?")

3. In the third example, the subject is plural.
    June and **July** <u>goes</u> by so quickly. (Incorrect. **June** and **July** <u>go</u>. **They** <u>go</u>.)

Subject-Verb 2 (page 148)

Ignore the prepositional phrase *of the exams*, and identify the subject and verb.

1. **All** [of the exams] <u>require</u>. Correct. *All* is plural.

2. **Each** [of the exams] <u>require</u>. Incorrect. *Each* is singular.
    It should read **Each** <u>requires</u>. (Each one requires.)

3. **One** [of the exams] <u>requires</u>. Correct. One is singular.

Subject-Verb 3 (page 148)

1. This sentence is correct.

2. **All** <u>are</u> easy.

3. The second half of this compound sentence uses a compound subject. **He and I** <u>are</u> confident.

Sentence Fragments 1 (page 149)

1. Perform the sentence test by adding *I heard that* to the examples:
    I heard that he has trouble with fragments. (This sounds fine.)
    I heard that even though he is an excellent reader. (Fragment. Incorrect.)

2. Fragment. (Some of these are just easy!)

3. This is a complete sentence when you remember that the subject is **You**.

Sentence Fragments 2 (page 149)

1. [You] sit still! This command is a sentence.

2. In conversation, this serves as a perfectly reasonable answer to a question. However, in isolation on the test, it fails the sentence test.

Sentences Review 1 (page 150)

1. The word *punctuation* comes from the Latin word *punctus,* which means "point." Printers call the mark at the end of a sentence a *point.* We call it a *period,* while people in England call it a *full stop.* Nowadays, we even use the word *dot* when we refer to Internet addresses.

2. Repetition and reinforcement are important in the learning process because we retain more when we practice. We should also give the material time to sink in while we rest. Doesn't this make grammar seem like a sport? Take a break after this exercise.

Sentences Review 2 (page 150)

1. Do not separate the subject and verb with a comma.
    Carmelo and Cecilia came to this country in the 1980s.

2. Fragment. You can correct this by combining.
    Carmelo trained to be a bicycle racer because he likes the exercise.

3. Place a comma after an introductory element, such as a dependent clause.
    When he enters a race, Cecilia cheers him on.

4. Check subject-verb agreement. Riders *include.*
    Riders in today's contest include professional racers.

5. This is not a compound sentence. This sentence contains a compound verb, so you don't need the comma.

    He competed in the race and finished second.

    You could make the sentence compound by adding a subject after the comma.

    He competed in the race, and he finished second.

Nouns 1 (page 151)

1. Even though we usually think of the word *find* as a verb, some *-ing* forms may act as nouns.
    The subject is *Finding.*

2. Ask yourself: Finding requires what? The direct object is *thinking*, another *-ing* noun.

3. Actually, these *-ing* nouns are called gerunds. (The word *gerunds* is the noun complement because it identifies the subject.)

4. The main subject is the word *sentence*, which is referenced again as the complement *challenge*. (If you want to identify the parts of the dependent clause, you would list *we* as the subject, *have included* as the verb, and *clause* as the direct object.)

5. The noun *running* is the subject in the main part of the sentence, while it functions as a verb in the dependent clause.

Nouns 2 (page 151)

1. The subject is *object*.

2. The complement is *subject*, which renames *I*.

3. The direct object is *compliments*.

Verbs 1 (page 152)

1. The tense here is obviously wrong. I <u>took</u> the test yesterday. *Yesterday* is a key word.

2. The correct form is I <u>had taken</u>.

3. Brung? I <u>brought</u> my lunch to school.

Verbs 2 (page 152)

1. Who <u>would have thought</u> of going in there?

2. When the bell <u>rings</u>, we will go home.

3. I <u>should have done</u> it after we had swum.

Prepositions (page 153)

1. **Some** [of the stories] [in the Bible] <u>speak</u> [to me] [on a personal level]. Again, this will help you with subject-verb agreement. For instance, the verb <u>speaks</u> would be incorrect in this sentence.
   Some <u>speaks</u>. (Incorrect)
   Some <u>speak</u>. (Correct)

2. [On Wednesdays], **those** [of us] [in the morning section] <u>learn</u> Scripture [from a teacher] [of the Jewish faith].

3. [At the end] [of every class], **he** often <u>teaches</u> us several words [in Hebrew].

4. **All** [of us] [in the class] <u>look</u> forward [to Wednesday]. In this sentence, the verb <u>looks</u> would be incorrect.
   All <u>looks</u>.   (Incorrect)
   All <u>look</u>.   (Correct)

Parts of Speech Review 1 (page 153)

1. The **number** [of push-ups] <u>increased</u> [in gym class] yesterday.
       subject   *verb—past tense because it took place yesterday*

2. [In the opinion] [of many doctors], **walking**   <u>is</u> an effective **exercise** [for most people].
                                            subject   *verb*   *noun complement*

3. [After exercise],   **you**   <u>should rest</u> and <u>recuperate</u>.
                       subject   *compound*   *verb*

4. <u>Rest</u> [before the next section].
   *verb (The subject **You** is understood in commands.)*

5. <u>Did</u>   **you**   <u>check</u> your answers [in the back] [of the chapter]?
   verb   subject   verb

Pronoun-Antecedent Agreement 1 (page 154)

1. If we mark the pronoun and its antecedent, it looks like this:
   The <u>reader</u> is often confused when <u>they</u> encounter disagreement of this sort.
   We can see that this is incorrect. *Reader* is singular and *they* is plural.
   We can rewrite the sentence a couple of ways.
   The <u>reader</u> is often confused when <u>he or she</u> encounters disagreement of this sort.
   <u>Readers</u> are often confused when <u>they</u> encounter disagreement of this sort.

2. <u>Writers</u> have to be very careful when <u>he or she</u> composes a sentence.
   Possible corrections: <u>Writers</u> have to be very careful when <u>they</u> compose a sentence.
   A <u>writer</u> has to be very careful when <u>he or she</u> composes a sentence.
   Note that the verbs in the sentence change when the nouns change number.

3. The <u>sentences</u> should be clear to <u>its</u> readers.
   Correction: A <u>sentence</u> should be clear to <u>its</u> readers.

Pronoun-Antecedent Agreement 2 (page 154)

1. This one is easy because it contains the word *one*.
   If any <u>one</u> of you needs help, <u>he or she</u> should raise <u>his or her</u> hand.

2. This still contains the word *one*.
   <u>Everyone</u> must use a pencil when <u>he or she</u> <u>takes</u> the exam.

3. This is the same sentence as in question 2; the singular word *body* just replaces the word *one*.
   <u>Everybody</u> must use a pencil when <u>he or she</u> <u>takes</u> the exam.

4. This sentence is written correctly. Information is uncountable, so we use the singular pronoun.
   <u>All</u> [of that <u>information</u>] was kept in <u>its</u> own file.

5. In this case, the word *them* is obviously plural.
   <u>All</u> [of <u>them</u>] forgot <u>their</u> pencils.

6. This sentence is written correctly. The compound subject makes the pronoun plural.
   Jack and Jill made great progress in **their** climb.

7. Don't let the word *any* fool you. It ends with *-one*. It's singular.
   If **anyone** is asleep right now, **he or she** should wake up.

Pronoun Case 1 (page 156)

1. *Him* and *her* are objects. (He talks to him. She talks to her.)
   Correction: **He** and **she** passed the test.

2. We know that *whom* is an object. (Who talks to whom.)
   Correction: **Whoever** will help us?

3. These questions don't bother **you**. (This sounds fine.)
   These questions don't bother **I**. (Incorrect. *I* is a subject.)
   Correction: These questions don't bother **me**.
   (That's better. The word *me* is an object.
   So: These questions don't bother **you** and **me**.)

Pronoun Case 2 (page 156)

1. We often say this sort of thing in conversation, but please use the subject case in formal writing.
   Correction: **I** celebrated. My **friends** and **I** celebrated.

2. Use the object form.
   Correction: It now makes sense to **me**. It now makes sense to **them** and **me**.

3. The word *to* is a preposition. Use the object pronoun after it.
   Correction: To **whom** do I throw the ball?

Possessive Pronouns (page 157)

1. Correct. Fill in the contraction. *It is* a beautiful day in the neighborhood.

2. Incorrect. *You are so confident* is correct, but *its scary* should be a contraction: *it's (it is) scary*.

3. Correct. If the test were a person, you could say *The test contains his share* or *The test contains her share*. Since the test is an object, it requires a possessive pronoun.

4. Correct. Remember to use the object form in a prepositional phrase (between you and me) and to be aware of the occasional exceptions with than (than I am).

5. Incorrect. So many problems here . . . . *Who's* (*who is*) *there* (*not their*). *It's* (*It is*) *I*. (In conversation, you can get away with saying "It's me.")

Parts of Speech Review 2 (page 157)

1. Check subject-verb agreement.
   <u>Swimming</u> with dolphins <u>appeals</u> to us very much.

2. Use the subject form.
   <u>We will enjoy</u> a great time in the water.

3. Remember that *its* is the possessive pronoun. Get rid of the apostrophe.
   That <u>dolphin</u> knows <u>its</u> way around the lagoon.

4. *Whom* is the object of the preposition *from*. <u>From whom</u> did we learn our skills?

5. The word *each* is singular. <u>Each</u> marine biologist has earned <u>his or her</u> advanced degree.

Adjectives and Adverbs (page 159)

1. Correct. Even though it ends with *-ly*, *friendly* describes the noun *giant*, so it is an adjective.

2. Incorrect. *Fattest* is an adjective used with more than two items. Change it to this: Tweedle-Dee was the *fatter* of the duo.

3. Incorrect. This sentence uses two comparative words in succession. Remove the word *more*. The air is *drier* in the desert than in the tropics.

4. Correct. This is one of those health-related sentences.

5. Incorrect. Remember that the word *unique* means *one-of-a-kind* and cannot be further modified. Of all the bears, Yogi is *unique*.

Parts of Speech Review 3 (page 159)

My cousin and **I** disagree on an important issue. **Who** is the better superhero—Batman or Superman? She likes Superman because he is invincible. I like Batman because he **definitely** is not. He is the **more** human of the two. **Readers are** always unsure of the outcome when they read a Batman comic. A story is more exciting when **it's** [it is] more **suspenseful**.

Conjunctions and Interjections (page 160)

1. Incorrect. *Neither* should be paired with the word *nor*.

2. Correct. Not only is the interjection appropriate, but the comma and conjunction join two independent clauses.

3. Incorrect. Something is missing: We will hold a yard sale whether <u>or not</u> it rains.

Modifiers 1 (page 161)

1. Unclear. Correction: We hope that the writer means *paper with narrow lines*.

2. Unclear. Correction: The waiter finally served the fruit, wrapped in pancakes.

3. Unclear. Correction: Walking home from school, I was drenched by the storm.

4. Unclear. Correction: On the way to lunch, I noticed fried chicken. (The original sentence certainly made a more vivid picture, though!)

Modifiers 2 (page 161)

1. The expression *for instance* cannot connect sentences. Use a period or a semicolon to end the sentence before it.
   I like old movies. For instance, *The Wizard of Oz* is one of the best.

2. The same holds true for the word *however*.
   The lion is my favorite character; however, I like almost all of them.

3. This sentence uses a double negative. Drop one of them.
   I couldn't care less about those ridiculous monkeys.

4. "Not nobody! Not nohow!" Not correct!
   I'm not afraid of anybody.

Parts of Speech Review 4 (page 162)

1. The Wicked Witch doesn't have <u>any</u> power in Munchkinland. <u>H</u>owever, she threatens Dorothy during the journey.

2. Neither the Tin Man <u>nor</u> the Straw Man is affected by the poppies.

3. Because they are not mammals, <u>they cannot be harmed by the poppies' scent</u>. *Or—* <u>The poppies' scent cannot harm</u> them because they are not mammals. [Make it clear that you are saying that the Tin Man and Straw Man are not mammals.]

Parallelism 1 (page 162)

1. Incorrect. You can simplify the sentence by marking out extraneous phrases.
   I like <u>walking</u> [with the clouds], <u>skipping</u> [with the trees], and <u>to run</u> [with the badgers].
   Walking, skipping, and *to run* are not parallel. Correction: I like <u>walking</u> with the clouds, <u>skipping</u> with the trees, and <u>running</u> with the badgers.

2. Incorrect. The repeating verb *get* sets up a pattern, so it is jarring to break the rhythm. Correction: <u>Get</u> fit, <u>get</u> rest, <u>get</u> packed, and <u>get</u> fed.

3. Correct. The words *running, screaming,* and *waving* are parallel.

Parallelism 2 (page 162)

1. Incorrect. Correction: Robert has to take four credits in English, three credits in Latin, and two <u>credits</u> in Greek.

2. Incorrect. Correction: Common literary archetypes include the Hero, <u>the</u> Mentor, and the Other.

3. Incorrect. Correction: Teachers should strive to educate their students and <u>to serve</u> as good role models.

Sentence Completions (page 163)

1. The beginning of the sentence, *I would go*, signals that a contrast will follow. The word *but* fits well. The word *however* can't work here because it would have to start a new sentence.

   I would go to the movies, <u>but</u> I have to work tonight.

   I would go to the movies. <u>However</u>, I have to work tonight.

2. The word *because* indicates a logical relationship between the two clauses.

   I have to work <u>because</u> I'm saving for college.

3. Given the different choices, the word *instead* would fit here.

4. Since they are friends even though they disagree, we could use words such as *however* or *nevertheless*.

5. These cause-and-effect sentences appear very often on these exams. Be familiar with the use of the words *consequently* and *therefore*.

Composition 1 (page 164)

How did you decide on the correct order? You should have looked for clues to show **logical development** in the paragraph.

1. **(B)** Most sentences **begin** with a topic sentence that identifies the main point for the reader.

   The word *begin* tells us that this is chronologically the beginning of the paragraph. It also talks about the *main point*, which is common in the first sentence of a paragraph.

2. **(A)** The sentences that follow present support for **this topic sentence**, using examples and explanations of the examples.

   The word *follow* tells us that something has come before. The words *this topic sentence* show that it refers to sentence B.

3. **(E)** **These** sentences can **further** unify the paragraph by using related ideas, grammatical structures, and words.

   The word *further* tells us that this sentence belongs later in the paragraph.

   The adjective *these* shows that it refers back to the sentences introduced in sentence A.

4. **(C)** The paragraph may **close** with a sentence that restates the topic sentence or sums up the main point.

   This is logically and chronologically the last sentence.

5. **(D)** A paragraph is indented five spaces on a computer.

   This may be true, but it does not fit the overall point of the paragraph. It should be deleted.

Composition 2 (page 164)

(A) This is interesting, perhaps, but it has nothing to do with the other sentences. Incorrect.

(B) The other sentences do all focus on unity. This is a good possibility.

(C) This is good advice, but the overall paragraph does not deal with the opening sentence alone. Incorrect.

(D) Yes, they are, but the sentences do not really discuss essays. Incorrect.

The answer is B. All of the sentences point to this main point of unity.

Composition 3 (page 165)

1. **(C)** The word *both* binds the two adjectives. Choices A and B do not mean the same thing as the original sentences. Choice D is neither vigorous nor concise. If we take out the adjective phrase between the commas in choice E, we get the sentence *Writing is good.* This is not the message of the original sentences.

2. **(B)** This sentence uses an appositive (*my brother Joseph*) and a dependent clause (*Because he is too young*) to combine these sentences. Choices A and D are grammatically correct, but they do not relate the same information as the original sentences. Choice C uses a comma splice to connect a fragment, and choice E is just plain wrong. You get choices like this sometimes.

Comma 1 (page 168)

1. Incorrect. Correction: The <u>ice cream</u> truck drove through our neighborhood yesterday.

2. Incorrect. We do not have a balance on either side of the comma. Corrections:
   <u>Should I punt</u> or pass?
   <u>Should I punt</u>, or <u>should I pass</u>?

3. Correct. If you used a comma instead of a semicolon, you would have a comma splice. A period or a semicolon both work here.

Comma 2 (page 170)

1. Incorrect. Try taking out the words between the commas. Does it still have enough information to make sense? Poe's poem is my favorite. Which poem? The title is essential, so we can't separate it with commas. Correction: Poe's poem "The Raven" is my favorite.

2. Correct. Taking out the words between the commas does not affect the meaning.

3. Incorrect. *I can't stand work.* This is not necessarily true. The speaker is saying that working on Mondays is disagreeable. That part of the sentence is essential, so it should not be set off by a comma. Correction: I can't stand work that is scheduled on Mondays.

4. Incorrect. Set off the interrupter with a pair of commas. Correction: I am, of course, an excellent writer.

5. Incorrect. If we take out the information between the commas, we get this sentence: *People make me so angry.* This is not what the writer means. The information is essential to the meaning, so do not set it off with commas. Correction: People who use social media make me so angry.

Comma 3 (page 171)

1. Incorrect. A comma after the second prepositional phrase would make the sentence clearer. Correction: For most of the students, the homework was not difficult.

2. Correct. *Oh* is used as a mild interjection and uses only a comma.

3. Incorrect. Do not use a comma after a connecting word such as *that*. You may correct this sentence a couple of ways:
The author said, "I never intended to write a fairy tale."
The author said that he "never intended to write a fairy tale."

4. Incorrect. When using an address in a sentence, separate the elements with commas. Correction: I grew up in Bayside, New York, during the turn of the century.

5. Incorrect. We are obviously talking to someone named Mark (direct address), so set his name off with a comma. Correction: Didn't I ask you a question, Mark?

Punctuation (page 172)

1. Incorrect. You have forgotten something (and here it is): the closing quotation mark. Correction: "I feel I'm forgetting something," she remarked.

2. Incorrect. Novel titles are not enclosed by quotation marks. They are underlined or italicized. *The Giver* is a novel. Correction: I really enjoyed Lowry's novel *The Giver.*

3. Incorrect. Either use two dashes or a pair of parentheses; don't mix them.
Correction: My pet dugong—bizarre as he may seem—amuses my neighbors.

4. Incorrect. This sentence contains two errors. The name *Oliver* tells us which friend you are discussing, so the commas are unnecessary. Moreover, his activities should be listed in a parallel manner: in this case, past tense verbs. Correction: My friend Oliver completed his homework, played a video game, and went to bed.

5. Correct. You have mastered them!

Capitalization (page 174)

1. Capitalize the important words in book titles, and make sure they are italicized.
Correction: I really enjoyed the books in *The Lord of the Rings* series.

2. When a sentence in a quote is interrupted, do not capitalize the second part when it resumes. Correction: "The movies," he explained, "missed the spirituality of the books."

3. The word *biblical* should not be capitalized. Correction: Many of the events of the story have biblical counterparts.

Usage 1 (page 177)

1. *You're* (You are) welcome.

2. *Affect* is the verb.

3. The expression *a lot* consists of two words.

4. Use *among* when you're talking about more than two people.

5. Use *too* when you mean *also* or *as well.*

Usage 2 (page 177)

1. A *loser* doesn't win.

2. *Fewer* refers to numbers.

3. She *accepted* the apology. She did not take *exception* to it.

4. Just *set* your head on the pillow and *lie* down. (Remember, your head is an object.)

5. *Effect* is a noun and the subject of the sentence.

Usage 3 (page 177)

1. *Have* is a verb. He *should have known* better.

2. The campers *rose.*

3. In the past, I *lay* awake.

4. The word *beside* refers to close physical proximity (nearness). *Besides* means "in addition to."

5. The expression *all right* consists of two words.

Spelling 1 (page 179)

receive, receive, receive, receive, receive, receive, receive, receive, receive, receive

Spelling 2 (page 179)

1. The prefix *mis-* is added to *spell* to make *mis-spell.* It looks odd, but it's correct.

2. *Extra-ordinary.*

3. The prefix *un-* is added to *natural,* making two "*ns*": *un-natural.*

Spelling 3 (page 180)

1. *Forty* is a problem word for many people because it is spelled differently than *four* or *fourteen.*

2. The word *develop* ends with a single vowel-consonant combination, but it is **not** stressed on the final syllable. Therefore, the final *p* is not doubled (*developed*).

3. The word *use* does not drop the silent *e* when adding a consonant suffix (*useful*). Also, *u* is e-mail spelling, and should not be used when writing formal sentences.

Punctuation, Capitalization, Usage, and Spelling Review (page 180)

1. The word *temperature* contains the word *temper*.

2. *Occasionally*, I miss a letter.

3. We drop the *i* in *explain* when we expand it to *explanation*.

4. Note the ending of the word *sponsor*.

5. These words are spelled correctly. Check them closely.

6. This property is *condemned*. The word *condemned* contains the letter *n* because it is based on the Latin word *condemnare* (to cause loss or damage).

7. Two words are misspelled: *agrarian* and *leisure*. (Look up *agrarian* if you don't know it.)

8. Don't forget the apostrophe in contractions. *The criminal didn't feel well.*

Test Formats (page 182)

1. **(A)** The correct spelling is adjective. If you pronounce it correctly (containing the letter *c*), you will have no problem spelling it.

2. **(N)** No mistakes

3. **(A)** The correct spelling is definite. Remember that it contains the word finite.

4. **(B)** The word column contains only one *l*. You might remember this because the words autumn and hymn contain no double letters, either.

5. **(A)** Choice B should use the object *whom*. Choice C should capitalize Roman, and choice D should capitalize Monday.

6. **(G)** In choice F, the poem should be in quotation marks. A colon is not needed after a verb in choice H. Choice J uses a period rather than a question mark.

7. **(B)** In choice A, a lot should be two words. Choice C should use the verb *affected*, and choice D should use the word *loose*.

8. **(C)** Separate the city and state with a comma: Bayside, New York.

9. **(B)** Because it is the name of a specific school, Trinity High School should be capitalized.

10. **(A)** This sentence contains a misplaced modifier.

11. **(C)** This is not the *name* of your aunt, so it is not capitalized.

12. **(L)** The word *flowers* is a common noun. Do not capitalize it.

13. **(C)** In this case, we've left out the period.

14. **(J)** Use a comma before introductory words, especially when they can cause confusion. It sounds as if you're going to eat your younger brother or sister!

15. **(A)** This is tricky. We *lie* down, but we *lay* our heads down, just as we would lay down any *thing*. You can replace *lay* with the word *put*, as *lay* requires a direct object.

16. **(M)** All of these tenses are correct, and the semicolon is used properly.

17. **(B)** Using a more concise word is usually more effective. The expression "for the reason that" is a longer way to say "because."

18. **(L)** The third sentence is not necessary; the others cannot be removed without making the meaning of the paragraph unclear.

Reading Comprehension

5

The HSPT, COOP, and TACHS require you to demonstrate your ability to understand what you read. You can find examples of the kinds of texts you will be asked to read and interpret in this section as well as in the practice exams.

You can count on the fact that reading passages on the HSPT/COOP/TACHS are not designed to be tricky or confusing in any way; students preparing to enter high school should feel confident that they can understand these passages. Reading carefully and focusing on *identifying the answers to the questions being asked* should allow you to complete this section of the exam you take with confidence.

Make sure you **read the passage from beginning to end** before even looking at the questions. Reading correctly the first time saves you time reading the passage again. Often you will be tempted to guess at the answers without reading the passage, but you must answer the questions based on the information given in the passage, not based on information you already have in your brain. **Read the questions and all the answers** before trying to answer. Finally, **if in doubt, guess**. The HSPT, COOP, and TACHS do not penalize as much for incorrect answers as they do for skipping questions altogether.

Making yourself aware of the types of reading comprehension questions the HSPT, COOP, and TACHS exams typically use is also a good idea. The HSPT, COOP, and TACHS use identifiable phrases and strategies that give clues as to the type of question you are answering. You can read some examples of the methods authors use to call your attention to the types of questions they are asking in the following section.

MAIN-IDEA QUESTIONS (FINDING THE MAIN IDEA)

Main-idea questions ask you to **find the main point** of the passage. They are typically phrased in one of the following ways:

- The passage deals mainly with . . .
- The main idea of this selection may be expressed as . . .
- The title that best expresses the ideas of this passage is . . .
- The writer's main purpose is apparently . . .
- The best name for this story is . . .
- The best title for this passage is . . .

WORD-IN-CONTEXT QUESTIONS (FIGURING OUT MEANING FROM CONTEXT CLUES)

Word-in-context questions want you to **figure out the meaning of words** from the context of other words in the sentence. They typically call your attention to definitions and word context:

- The word ____, as underlined and used in this passage, most nearly means . . .
- Which of the following gives an example of . . .
- Which of the following definitions most closely fits . . .
- Which of the following is an example of ____ . . .

FACT QUESTIONS (DISTINGUISHING FACT FROM OPINION)

Fact questions ask you to **identify facts** in the reading passage. They are typically phrased in a very direct, straightforward manner:

- When did the action described in this passage take place?
- Why did (so-and-so) do (such-and-such)?
- What is the setting of this reading passage?
- What did the protagonist of this passage *not* do?
- All but which of the following facts are true?

INFERENCE QUESTIONS (DRAWING CONCLUSIONS)

Inference questions ask you to **infer information from facts** given in the reading passage. They typically use words that imply judgment or possibility:

- Why do you think that . . .
- What is most likely . . .
- Comparing the two paragraphs in this reading passage, we can say that . . .
- The author implies that . . .
- Based on the information in this passage, the reader can infer that . . .
- Which of the following is most likely true . . .

Each of the upcoming sections in this chapter, therefore, offers (1) discussion of the four types of reading comprehension questions; (2) discussion of useful strategy for answering each type of question; and (3) some opportunities to practice the skill under discussion. We strongly recommend that you work your way through all of the review material before attempting the practice tests included in this book.

MAIN-IDEA QUESTIONS

Strategy for Finding the Main Point

Finding the main point of a reading selection takes some practice, but you can rely on certain hints to help you. After all, authors *want* you to be able to identify their main point. To help you, they either begin or end their passages with a topic sentence that not only introduces their topic but also *summarizes* their main point in writing that passage.

➡ Example _____

Read the following selection and answer the questions that follow.

Shrek, the popular children's movie about an unlikely hero (Shrek the ogre) and an equally unlikely heroine (the lovely Princess Fiona), turns the traditional concept of the fairy tale on its head. Traditional fairy tales present the reader with a passive, innocent, and weak heroine who requires rescuing by her <u>stalwart</u> hero. By contrast, *Shrek* offers a heroine who burps, eats like a horse, and, thanks to her knowledge of martial arts, actually saves her own rescuer at one point. One can only attribute this change in acceptable "heroine" characteristics to social changes affecting women in the U.S. since the 1950s.

The writer's main purpose in writing this passage is _____.

(A) to make the point that *Shrek* was a box office hit

(B) to make the point that traditional fairy tales have a passive heroine and a brave hero

(C) to make the point that changes in social expectations for women have redefined the roles fairy tale heroines can play

(D) to make the point that modern heroines are disgusting creatures who teach modern readers bad behavior

ANALYSIS

How did you do? The correct answer is C. Let's analyze the various answers.

Choice A argues that *Shrek* was a box office hit. While this claim is true, the reading passage does not discuss box office returns at all. The only mention this reading passage makes of *Shrek*'s popularity is one brief descriptive word in the first sentence. One reference is not enough to apply to the whole passage. Therefore the correct answer is not A.

Choice B states that traditional fairy tales typically have a passive heroine and a strong hero; this is true. However, this comment comes as part of a chain of logical statements leading to a larger point. Remember that authors typically put their topic sentence at the beginning or end of reading passages; in this case, the author has put the topic sentence at the end of this passage.

Choice D emphasizes the reader's possible judgmental reaction to Princess Fiona's love of burping and violence. While one might be disgusted at these personal characteristics, nothing about the passage *necessarily* criticizes her actions. The final sentence, crucial to understanding the purpose of the passage, does not pass judgment on the "new heroine," but only makes a guess as to the *inspiration* on which the character is based.

Choice C is the correct answer. This passage argues that fairy tales have changed over time to accommodate the tastes of modern audiences, no more and no less.

WORD-IN-CONTEXT QUESTIONS

Strategy for Determining Hidden Meanings

The word-in-context question asks you to select definitions of words based on the context of the rest of the sentence. Having a big vocabulary helps, but logic and patience do too. After you read the passage, find the word you are being asked to define. Often this word will be brought to your attention in some way (for example, italicized, bolded, or underlined); look for context clues in the surrounding words to help you. Look in particular for **synonyms, a definition, or an example**.

➡ Example _____

The term **stalwart** can be defined as _____.

(A) handsome
(B) foolish
(C) rash
(D) brave

ANALYSIS

The correct answer is D. Did you get it? Let's analyze your options.

Choice A refers to a trait most fairy tale heroes have. However, nothing about the sentence indicates that this hero is necessarily handsome; also, if the reader knows that ogres are ugly, smelly, and misshapen, then one can infer that Shrek (referred to in the first sentence as both a hero and an ogre) is definitely not handsome by human standards.

Choices B and C might be acceptable possibilities, since many fairy tale heroes must perform foolish and dangerous deeds to prove their bravery. However, you should consider two points when selecting your answer. First, the passage is setting up a contrast of the hero-heroine relationship in the traditional fairy tale. The wording of the sentence implies that the hero and the heroine are opposite in personality; typically one does not use the word *foolish* as an antonym for *weak*. Second, your job is to select the **most appropriate** answer, not just an **acceptable** answer. You should force yourself to read and consider all of the possible answers rather than selecting the first possible answer that comes your way.

Choice D is the correct answer. The passage is setting up a contrast of the hero-heroine relationship in traditional fairy tales. The wording of the sentence implies that the hero and the heroine are opposite in personality; therefore, if the heroine is weak, then the hero must be something opposite, like strong or brave. A check in the dictionary proves that one definition for *stalwart* is indeed brave.

FACT QUESTIONS

Strategy for Answering Deceptively Simple Questions

These fact questions seem the easiest to handle, yet they often prove difficult. After all, you are only being asked to pinpoint fact-based statements and use this information in your answers. Too often, however, test takers skim these questions too quickly, hoping to make up time lost on other portions of the exam, and miss obvious answers. Often, too, authors use synonyms in their writing, turning the fact question into a kind of word-in-context question.

What's the bottom line? Don't rush, and pay attention to the actual question being asked of you.

➡ Example _____

Shrek rejects which traditional elements?

(A) a weak heroine and her stalwart hero
(B) an unlikely hero and heroine
(C) a heroine who burps and knows martial arts
(D) a passive heroine and an innocent hero

ANALYSIS

This one should have been a piece of cake. The correct answer is A.

This question asks you to use backwards logic to get the answer. The passage describes details about Shrek that obviously do not fit with traditional fairy tales (burping, etc.); however, the question asks you to identify the elements of traditional fairy tales rather than restate the details that defy tradition. Choices B, C, and D all mention notable words and phrases from the reading passage and hope to catch you incorrectly associating these facts with the purpose of the question. Only choice A relates a description of traditional fairy tale elements.

While this sample question limits itself to questioning factual descriptions in this passage, not all fact questions are set up this way. Often factual questions can include data about science or mathematical topics; equally often, factual questions can require you to **use** the data discussed in the passages, for example, actually reading a series of historical dates and figuring out what century must be involved or subtracting one figure from another to get a difference.

INFERENCE QUESTIONS

Strategy for Drawing Logical Conclusions

Inference questions are by definition trickier and wider ranging than main-idea questions. Inference questions can ask you to detect a hidden meaning in the passage or use the information you read to infer logical conclusions. Moreover, the question can require you to apply the logic of one passage to another, related situation.

The best way to approach an inference question is to make sure you understand the author's *purpose* in writing. Don't allow yourself simply to restate information given in the passage; inference questions ask you to *go beyond* the **superficial** meaning of the sentences you read.

> **VOCABULARY**
>
> The word *superficial* literally means on or near the surface. It can also mean something insubstantial or lacking depth.
>
> *The super official had no real super powers; his superficial power was only in his three-piece suit.*

➡ Example _____

The author implies that _____.

(A) s/he likes fairy tales the way they used to be
(B) s/he thinks the reader will like movies similar to Shrek
(C) s/he thinks the movie Shrek is about an unlikely hero and an equally unlikely heroine
(D) s/he approves of the change in traditional fairy tales

ANALYSIS

The correct answer is D. Ready for the breakdown?

Choice C can be eliminated more quickly than any of the others. Choice C merely restates a factual statement in the passage; since inference questions ask you to draw inferences, a simple restatement of fact is a direct warning. Choice B, on the other hand, is a bit more compelling, since it clearly involves making an inference—that of deciding whether someone will like a movie based on her reaction to a similar one. Unfortunately, choice B demands that you make assumptions that are simply not supported by the question. At no point, for example, does the author imply that s/he has a clue as to the reader's taste in movies, nor does s/he try to match the reader's taste to other movies similar to *Shrek*.

Choice A is the most troubling answer on the list. Authors, unless they are writing editorials or critical reviews, usually strive to be unbiased in their writing; unbiased writing is respected in our culture. Choices A and D require the reader to attempt to figure out the author's approval or disapproval of a topic about which the author is trying to discuss in a disinterested manner. Nevertheless, the author has left clues about her/his opinion on the "new" fairy tale. Words such as *passive* and *weak* have negative connotations, and the author associates them with the traditional heroine; moreover, the author seems to approve of Fiona's martial arts skills ("thanks to her knowledge"). Together these details seem to suggest that the author approves of the changes in fairy tale lore; hence, the best answer for this inference question is choice D.

MAIN-IDEA QUESTIONS PRACTICE

Everyone nowadays feels the pressure to recycle certain products. Communities expend monies to provide recycling bins and other means by which to turn used products back into usable ones. Ad campaigns, from billboards to mail to backs of milk cartons, encourage and even threaten us to recycle. Yet recent scientific investigations present us with startling news: often we pay more to recycle a product than to destroy it and simply make a new one.

1. *The writer's main purpose is apparently _____.*

    (A) to shame people into recycling if they are not already doing so
    (B) to present a point of view opposite from the popular one
    (C) to offer new options for dealing with waste
    (D) to scoff at new scientific theories

Video games have changed substantially since people first conceived them. Gamers today probably do not even remember Pong, a simple hand-eye challenge in which players tried to keep a moving "ball" from bouncing out of bounds—essentially a game of Ping Pong against the computer. Pong, as well as its successors Centipede and PacMan, with their humble graphics and simple sound effects, seem horribly out of date compared to slick modern games such as Halo, or The Sims, and the notorious Grand Theft Auto series.

And yet gamers might notice a disturbing trend—a rejection of actual gaming in favor of glorified fantasy role playing. Today's video games function more like personalized movies. More often than not, players act out variations on preprogrammed scenarios that grant the player an illusion of creativity and personalized entertainment but downplay the dexterity and skill required of the old games.

2. *The writer's main purpose is apparently _____.*

   (A) to give an overview of how video games have changed over the years
   (B) to make the case that video games are unhealthy for gamers
   (C) to make the case that Grand Theft Auto is a particularly bad game, full of flaws
   (D) to assess which games are good and which are bad

Ever notice that children's movies share a common theme? Consider, for example, the writing of Roald Dahl. The protagonist of his stories is typically a smart, good-looking child, who nevertheless suffers great abuse at the hands of the adults surrounding him/her. In *Matilda*, for example, Matilda lives with a despicable father who constantly tells her that she is stupid and denies her access to intellectual activities. Although Matilda manages to escape her family's poisonous grasp, she does so only to fall victim to a second, equally evil force: a stupid, power hungry bureaucrat. Throughout the course of the book, Matilda encounters only one decent adult, Ms. Honey, who has her own difficulties to overcome in the adult world.

Similarly, in *Charlie and the Chocolate Factory*, protagonist Charlie begins the movie in a run down and dejected state due to his long-term exposure to poverty and malnutrition that the adults in his life cannot combat. Charlie wins a once-in-a-million chance to tour a magical chocolate factory, only to meet example after example of despicable adults in the process of recreating themselves through bad parenting of their offspring.

Yet while the children in these movies begin their stories in a powerless state, they end their stories greatly empowered and usually well insulated from harmful adults. The protagonist learns to adapt to his or her situation, maturing until he or she understands his or her place in society. He or she then fights back, willfully yet appropriately, until he or she shapes his/her initially sour situation into a more acceptable one. Matilda, for example, ultimately stands up to Principal Trunchbull and selects for herself the mother of her dreams, represented by Ms. Honey. Similarly, Charlie, through his personal integrity, eventually inherits a surrogate father and a golden kingdom bursting with chocolate and financial security. Essentially, then, these stories warn the reader about possible treachery represented by adults and teach the reader how to find one's place in society through personal endeavor.

3. *The main idea of this selection may be expressed as _____.*

   (A) children's movies are simplistic stories with no deeper meaning other than plot-based amusement
   (B) children's movies show adults depicted in ridiculous, demeaning situations
   (C) children's movies show children how to mature in a confusing, adult-ruled world
   (D) children's movies cost a great deal to produce, especially *Charlie and the Chocolate Factory*

(See page 221 for answers.)

The word "jazz" is another one of those words that have experienced significant change over time. Originally, people used the word "jazz" to refer to activities that took place in the naughtier sections of exciting but dangerous towns like St. Louis and New Orleans, places that prided themselves on their ability to provide immoral yet fun things to do. Later, however, the word came to apply to one activity in particular: the hot music that sprang up from these areas. Musicians like Charlie Parker, Louis Armstrong, and Miles Davis owed their fame (and their livelihood) to jazz. Still later, the word came to be used in such phrases as "All that jazz," meaning "stuff."

4. *Which of the following definitions most closely fits the word "jazz"?*

   (A) The article does not state
   (B) music
   (C) drugs
   (D) violence

Mark Twain, author of such texts as *The Adventures of Tom Sawyer, Life on the Mississippi,* and *The Adventures of Huckleberry Finn*, is himself one of literature's best known creations. The man behind the myth, Samuel Clemens, created an alter ego, Mark Twain, as a way of bridging the gap between two very different personalities. On the one hand, Clemens prided himself on his ability to fulfill the role of Southern Gentleman: the well-mannered, chivalrous, wealthy, and charitable slave owner. Yet, simultaneously, Clemens prided himself on his ability to adopt Yankee behaviors: the educated, principled, industrious abolitionist.

As a result, Twain/Clemens's views strike the reader as both witty and amusing—and often contradictory. Consider, for example, the tone of *The Adventures of Tom Sawyer* with that of *The Adventures of Huckleberry Finn*, written 20 years later. *Tom Sawyer* has a light-hearted tone and focuses on telling an adventure story that honors the glory of the Old South—the South the way Clemens remembers it in the good ol' days. By contrast, *Huck Finn* tells a much darker tale about two people who cannot find peace anywhere in the South due to racial tensions—the New South following the Civil War. Caught somewhere between Clemens and Twain, these literary works grow out of a greatly troubled and inconsistent mind.

5. *The word* contradictory, *as underlined and used in this passage, most nearly means* _____.

   (A) insane
   (B) hateful
   (C) confusing
   (D) evil

You may never have heard of the delightfully noisy little insect known as the cicada before, but if you live in the eastern part of the United States, you are certainly about to. Cicadas live in various parts of the United States year round, but every 17 years, they come out in droves in places like Virginia and Kentucky. The little, red-eyed, singing bugs burrow up out of the ground and spread out in plague-like quantities until you can't walk for crunching them to death with every step. The little guys, however, do no real harm to plant life or anything else; they really only become problematic due to their great numbers. However, like most things

Mother Nature sends our way, the cicadas provide a benefit to humanity—they make quite tasty snacking, as the recipes for Cicada Dumplings attest.

6. *Which of the following gives an example of a definition of the word* droves?

   (A) a word that refers to dogs
   (B) a word that means the past tense of *drives*
   (C) another word for a large collection of trees
   (D) a word that indicates a large number of things

(See page 221 for answers.)

(See page 221 for answers.)

FACT QUESTIONS PRACTICE

Author Stephen King loves to play inside jokes on his readers. From his first short stories to his made-for-TV adaptation of his own novel *The Shining*, this generalization rings true. Take, for example, King's early novel *Christine*, a story about a haunted car who gives her owner popularity and long life in return for souls. The car, a vehicle of death, possesses a radio that only plays the music of dead musicians (like Buddy Holly or the Big Bopper) or musicians whose names mention death (like the Grateful Dead). Later in his miniseries adaptation of *The Shining*, King provides a ghostly band playing mood music for a bunch of revelers; the bandleader is none other than Gage, the little boy killed by a truck in King's *Pet Sematary*, now grown up and evil. These are grisly jokes, indeed, yet amusing for the avid King reader to discover.

7. *Which of the following bands does the car's radio play?*

   (A) Madonna
   (B) Buddy Holly
   (C) The Gyoto Monks
   (D) Rage Against the Machine

Significant events in outer space popularized shirts sporting the phrase, "My other car is on Mars." The quip attempted to remind people that NASA has finally enjoyed a success in its many attempts at space explorations. After "several" fiascos and disasters that claimed the lives of the astronauts aboard exploding rockets, a success is undeniably welcome.

The car to which the T-shirt slogan refers is actually a 400-pound, solar-powered robot, packed with sensors and cameras that allow viewers on Earth a rare glimpse at the red planet. So far the rover has managed to send to earth quite a few photos, including one depicting the Granicus Valles systems, rock formations formed by constant wind patterns. Soon to come will be long-distance testing of soil and rocks in the hopes of sighting evidence of useful and informative minerals on Mars, like iron. The success of the mission thus far has thrilled the scientific community—and the President, who has called for a manned mission to Mars.

8. *To what does the slogan on the T-shirt refer?*

   (A) the wearer's other car, which is in the shop in Memphis
   (B) the wearer's feet; the reference is ironic
   (C) the wearer's pet project, the 400-pound rover now deployed on Mars
   (D) the wearer's candy-apple blue BMW

The art of Shaolin has, as have many other forms of martial arts, suffered at the hands of Americans. You may not know Shaolin by its name, but you have seen it played out, provided you have watched movies such as *Crouching Tiger, Hidden Dragon.* Shaolin ranks among the most dangerous and demanding of the martial arts, but few in America are aware of this fact, blinded as they are by their interest in flashier martial arts forms, like Tae Kwon Do or Karate. Few Masters of Shaolin remain alive in the world; this fact is true only partly because of the great dedication and patience becoming a master requires. It is true in large part because of the simple lack of interest (and attention span) of possible Shaolin apprentices.

9. *How many Masters of Shaolin remain alive today?*

    (A) one
    (B) two
    (C) three
    (D) none

(See page 222 for answers.)

INFERENCE QUESTIONS PRACTICE

I really enjoy the new mystery fiction written by Jonathan Gash. His main character, an odd but captivating antiques dealer, captures the reader with a combination of humor and bravery. The plots are exciting yet believable, things I respect about a good book. I hear that the author will be in town next week for a book signing.

10. *What do you think that the author will do next?*

    (A) Go to the library and check out more Jonathan Gash books.
    (B) Go to the used bookstore and get rid of all his or her Jonathan Gash books.
    (C) Go to the author's book signing next week.
    (D) Go to bed.

One of America's favorite old books remains a favorite today. Although the language is, to put it mildly, rough, and some of the plot elements morally questionable, people find a great deal in J. D. Salinger's *The Catcher in the Rye* to justify the book's existence. The book brings up a serious and important issue—the need for the young to come to terms with the lack of morality in the world that surrounds us.

Readers remain gripped by the existentialist dilemma faced by main character Holden Caulfield. Holden sees those around him losing their integrity as they become older, a process he calls "becoming phony." Holden's fear of becoming phony as he matures into adulthood symbolizes our own as we face what we might call the next evolutionary step in Salinger's projection. We live in an age in which marketing executives pedal thong underwear and tight, saucy T-shirts to 10-year-old girls, and young children everywhere increasingly think high fashion consists of prison-garb-inspired clothing that falls well past the hips. Salinger's concept of phoniness seems to have been superceded with one of moral emptiness. As Yeats once put it, "the center cannot hold . . . mere anarchy is loosed upon the world."

11. *Based on the information in this passage, the reader can infer that _____.*

    (A) the author agrees with J. D. Salinger's worldview

    (B) the author disagrees with J. D. Salinger's worldview

    (C) the author remains neutral regarding J. D. Salinger's worldview

    (D) We cannot answer the question based on the details disclosed in the passage.

School administrations face increasingly tough decisions. Recently, southern schools find it difficult to raise money for needed services; in order to locate that funding, schools have turned to fund-raising in the form of vending machines on school property to get cash.

Students, those with tight schedules that allow for few leisurely meals as well as those who just like junk food—have responded with delight, pouring money hourly into drink and food machines. Teachers have responded with less enthusiasm; while they appreciate the funds generated by student spending, teachers pay a definite cost: shortened attention spans and "juiced up" students too addled with sugar to focus on lessons.

Parents seem to be caught in the middle. On the one hand, they don't like the sinking grades and spiking behavior reports their students receive; on the other, they don't like removing the "free will" represented by allowing maturing students opportunities to manage their money, nutrition, and time.

12. *What subject might the author discuss next?*

    (A) Interviews with local mall merchants regarding how vending machines paid for new football uniforms when they were children

    (B) An alternative plan, generated by students, that the author wants to put before the audience

    (C) SPCA spokespeople weighing in on the debate

    (D) The article will end here.

(See page 222 for answers.)

MORE PRACTICE SESSIONS: A MIXED BAG

Using the theory that practice makes perfect, we offer you now even more opportunities to practice. This section offers several reading passages and questions related to each, much like the last section did. However, we model this series of practice questions on the types of questions (and the format followed) on the actual COOP/HSPT. We suggest you work through these texts and questions; we also suggest you practice identifying the kind of question you are being asked to answer. Therefore, each passage lists reading selections, questions, as well as a space in which to write your guess as to the category of question you are answering. Check your answers at the end. Good luck!

> **Directions:** Questions 1–4 are based on the following passage.

People seem to be the products of their society, upon reflection. U.S. citizens, for example, demand variety and speed above most things; modern marketing strategies seem to focus particularly on getting exactly what one wants with the least degree of inconvenience. It seems unthinkable that something as simple as a postcard can travel from Kentucky to Louisiana within eight hours, a farther distance and a quicker time period than a person could travel less than fifty years ago.

The desire for speed applies to most areas of modern life, including areas of medical treatments. Modern patients seem increasingly interested in quick-fix answers to long-term health problems. Various cities, Lexington, New Orleans, and Atlanta included, have poured vast quantities of money into the prescription drug business, predicting that quick treatments would increase in popularity over time; they were right.

Surprisingly, however, modern studies show that new drugs, ranging from allergy medications to anti-depressants to new treatments for cancer, seem to be increasingly ineffective. Recent clinical studies of patients suffering from depression, for example, studied the effect of new drug therapy. Doctors prescribed actual drugs for some patients, while prescribing placebos for others. Interestingly, patients on placebo-regimens enjoyed improvement at the same rate as patients on real-drug-regimens. Optimists point to these results as proof of the power of positive thinking; critics point to these results as justification for their skepticism.

1. *The best title for this passage would be _____.*

   This question is a/an _____ question.

   (A) Doctor Knows Best
   (B) Placebos: The Miracle Drug
   (C) Go Ask Alice
   (D) Quick Fix Solutions: Not Always What the Doctor Ordered

2. *The author's use of the word* placebo *implies that the word can be defined as _____.*

   This question is a/an _____ question.

   (A) a miracle drug
   (B) a chemical compound that does not actually contain medicine
   (C) a diet aid
   (D) a new treatment for cancer

3. *One city that has poured a great deal of money into drug research is _____.*

   This question is a/an _____ question.

   (A) Louisville
   (B) Lexington
   (C) Savannah
   (D) Shreveport

4. *Which of the following statements is implied by the passage?*

   This question is a/an _____ question.

   (A) People who crave speed and convenience are most likely to be depressed as well.
   (B) Positive attitudes necessarily aid in recuperation.
   (C) Travel has become faster and more common over time.
   (D) Cities like Lexington have actually lost significant amounts of money invested in drug research.

Impressionism, an art form favored by artists such as Camille Pissarro, Pierre Auguste Renoir, and Mary Cassatt, allowed artists a new form of self-expression. Based on the idea that art did not have to be limited to mirror images of real life or to boring pictures of stately historical buildings, Impressionism allowed the imagination more influence. Consequently, Impressionism created enemies for itself almost immediately; indeed Impressionism got its name from a sarcastic comment made by French art critic Louis Leroy about how amateurish he considered the artistic style.

Two very different painters, Claude Monet and Edgar Degas, in particular favored Impressionism. Claude Monet (1840–1926) found great inspiration in nature, and he consistently uses nature in his work. He frequently depicted the interplay of light and shadow in gardens (usually his own). Before his death, Monet managed to complete perhaps his most famous piece, an enormous work of water lilies. Because of his use of nature, some argue, Monet's style is characterized by an ability to express the movement and the joy of life in still life format.

Edgar Degas (1834–1917), by contrast, preferred even more immediate—yet more fleeting—subjects: the swirling mass of humanity surrounding him. He drew inspiration from Japanese art forms and incorporated brilliant hues into his paintings of racetracks, dancers, and café frequenters. His interest in Japanese art also encouraged him to experiment with innovative, asymmetrical angles of observation. Degas' work especially <u>encapsulates</u> a distinctive, sympathetic interest in the struggles and defeats of women; perhaps the work that best shows Degas' sympathy for women is his work entitled *In a Café (The Absinthe Drinker)*.

5. *Which artist discussed in the passage died just before the end of World War I?*

   This question is a/an _____ question.

   (A) Mary Cassat
   (B) Claude Monet
   (C) August Renoir
   (D) Edgar Degas

6. *The author implies that _____.*

   This question is a/an _____ question.

   (A) art created prior to Impressionism was far more realist and conservative
   (B) art created after Impressionism was far more realist and conservative
   (C) without the use of Japanese art forms, Impressionism would not have been created
   (D) Monet only created one piece of art during his career

7. *The use of the word* encapsulates, *as used in this passage, is most likely defined by which of the following?*

   This question is a/an _____ question.

   (A) denies
   (B) leaves behind
   (C) obscures
   (D) shows

8. *This passage's main purpose is most likely _____.*

   This question is a/an _____ question.

   (A) to convince the reader that Impressionist art is somewhat lacking in value
   (B) to introduce some basic principles of Impressionism, as well as some famous examples of Impressionist art and artists, to the reader
   (C) to make the point that Impressionist art is better than modern art
   (D) to encourage the reader to investigate Japanese art forms

---

Directions: Questions 9–12 are based on the following passage.

Ryan and Sue, aged 30, found themselves in the same boat as so many other parents have done: tearing out their hair trying to maintain discipline over their three children. Ryan and Sue's kids behaved relatively well when at home, closely monitored by their parents. However, whenever Ryan and Sue tried to hire a babysitter to watch the children so that they might have a little time away from home all to themselves, their kids acted so badly that they found it difficult to find anyone willing to babysit.

No amount of threatening, punishment, screaming, or cajoling seemed to work against Ryan and Sue's children. Finally, instead of relying on traditional methods, Ryan and Sue sat down to figure out a logical, innovative method for dealing with insubordinate behavior.

Ryan and Sue devised the following plan. First, they called a family meeting. They sat the kids down at their places around the kitchen table. In the center of the table, Ryan and Sue placed the children's allowance for the week. All the crisp, green bills made quite a pretty picture against the wood grain of the table.

Ryan and Sue then informed their children that they were going out to dinner that evening and that Kelly, a local neighbor, would be coming to babysit. Ryan and Sue told the kids that they would leave the weekly allowance on the table, without any explanation to Kelly. However, should Kelly report a single act of disobedience taking place that evening, Ryan and Sue promised to add the weekly allowance to the fee already being paid to Kelly. Should the children behave, they would be allowed to retrieve their allowance the following morning.

When Ryan and Sue returned from dinner, they were pleased to have a glowing report of the children's behavior.

9. *The word* insubordinate *as it is used in the passage most closely means* _____.

   This question is a/an _____ question.

   (A) aggressive
   (B) passive
   (C) unruly
   (D) ridiculous

10. *The main point of this passage is* _____.

    This question is a/an _____ question.

    (A) good babysitters are hard to find
    (B) older parents come up with wiser solutions than younger parents do
    (C) threats are the best means by which to discipline children
    (D) the best means by which to discipline children is to find appropriate motivation, in particular something the children like that they don't want taken away

11. *How many children do Ryan and Kelly have?*

    This question is a/an _____ question.

    (A) none
    (B) one
    (C) two
    (D) three

12. *The event that would most likely take place next would be* _____.

    This question is a/an _____ question.

    (A) Ryan and Sue's children collecting their allowance
    (B) Ryan and Sue's babysitter collecting the children's allowance
    (C) Ryan and Sue going out to dinner again the next evening
    (D) Ryan and Sue giving their babysitter a raise

Directions: Questions 13–16 are based on the following passage.

The popular young readers' books, *A Series of Unfortunate Events*, has generated huge sums since its first installment; indeed the movie alone grossed more than $30 million at the box office its first weekend. The main characters, Violet, Klaus, and Sunny, are enchanting as well as amusing, as they bounce from one <u>dastardly</u> location to another, attempting to escape the bony clutches of their awful Count Olaf. The plots are fun, the details wry, and the puns plentiful.

One reason people find the series so captivating, however, probably remains a mystery: fundamentally, these books situate themselves solidly within the realm of Dark Romanticism.

Dark Romanticism dates back to the 1880s, and those who revel in the trials and tribulations of the Baudelaire children will likely also embrace the sinister stories of such writers as

Edgar Allan Poe, Mary Shelley, and H. P. Lovecraft. These writers tell tales of people buried alive, of horrors in the dark, of people who meet tragic ends tragically. These stories are not without humor, but the laughter is muted and macabre, much like that present when Aunt Josephine's house finally slides pell-mell into Lake Lachrymosa.

Of course, Lemony Snicket is tamed Dark Romanticism. Yet, as readers mature and they leave the Terrible Tales behind them (only thirteen exist, after all), one hopes that such dear readers will strive to pick up where Snicket left off—on the dark shores of Dunwich or just outside the Arkham Asylum.

13. *The author implies that _____.*

   This question is a/an _____ question.

   (A) readers of Lemony Snicket will like the writings of H. G. Wells
   (B) readers of Lemony Snicket will not like the writing of H. P. Lovecraft
   (C) readers of Lemony Snicket will like the movie, *A Series of Unfortunate Events*
   (D) readers of Lemony Snicket will like the writings of Edgar Allan Poe

14. *The word* dastardly *can be defined as _____.*

   This question is a/an _____ question.

   (A) delightful
   (B) wicked
   (C) random
   (D) wonderful

15. *The author's main purpose for writing this passage is _____.*

   This question is a/an _____ question.

   (A) to entice readers of Lemony Snicket into reading other, perhaps more challenging, Dark Romantic texts
   (B) to give an overview of Dark Romanticism since 1880
   (C) to offer readers a chance to try science fiction
   (D) to review the latest Lemony Snicket movie

16. *The author states that which of the following statements is true?*

   This question is a/an _____ question.

   (A) Dark Romanticism is not being written today.
   (B) Dark Romanticism is boring and dull.
   (C) Dark Romanticism dates back to the 1880s.
   (D) Dark Romanticism is necessary to bring about world peace.

Nicholas Johnson makes the case that it is ironic that much of what is praiseworthy about humanity and its accomplishments came about not through thoughtful, preplanned intent, but through accident. Johnson then asks the reader to consider the following cases.

He tells how Ancient Egyptians discovered the fermentation process by accident; a store of grain had been allowed to rot due to an abnormally warm season, and spores, blown in on the wind, settled in the grain and began the chemical reaction now known as the fermentation process. Christopher Columbus' discovery of America came about via a botched attempt to locate a quick trade route to the Indies. The discovery of rubber vulcanization occurred when Charles Goodyear, a man with no formal education, accidentally dropped a piece of sulfur-treated rubber on a hot stove and noticed that the previously brittle substance had acquired significant flexibility. Johnson then makes the claim that many other examples, "too numerous to list here," also exist.

Johnson concludes with a rather pessimistic analysis, namely that, since most innovation comes as the result of accident, there exists no reason for trying to achieve anything on one's own. Such an argument strikes me as overly fatalistic. Indeed, I would suggest turning Johnson's argument on its head; humanity, to me, is worthy of praise for its undeniable ability to turn a negative into a positive, to turn <u>dross</u> into gold. One case in point is the crisis of September 11, 2001.

17. *Based on the author's use of the word* dross *in this passage, which of the following definitions is most appropriate?*

     This question is a/an _____ question.

     (A) something valuable
     (B) something worthless
     (C) something hard
     (D) something heavy

18. *The author attributes the discovery of fermentation to which entity?*

     This question is a/an _____ question.

     (A) Christopher Columbus
     (B) Charles Goodyear
     (C) the Egyptians
     (D) Alexander Dumas

19. *The speaker's main purpose in writing this passage is most likely _____.*

     This question is a/an _____ question.

     (A) to call the reader's attention to the good fortune humanity has enjoyed
     (B) to call the reader's attention to little known facts about fermentation and vulcanization
     (C) to criticize humanity for its failures
     (D) to reassure the reader that something positive can be found in even the most negative of situations

20. The author of this piece will most likely discuss which of the following topics?

This question is a/an _____ question.

(A) A further discussion of inventions that came about by accident
(B) A review of the points already made by the passage
(C) The 2001 Attack on America
(D) A discussion of fatalistic writers, such as Albert Camus

Directions: Questions 21–24 are based on the following passage.

Perhaps one of the most captivating true stories of heroism, daring, and determination comes to us in the form of *Running a Thousand Miles for Freedom: The Story of William and Ellen Craft.* This story, lived and told by ex-slave William Craft, dates back to 1848, when William and his wife Ellen risked everything to gain their freedom. Almost any slave narrative has the ability to capture the attention; the story of the Crafts' escape offers even more drama and sensationalism than most. William and Ellen escaped using trickery: by having Ellen dress as an invalid white slave master, traveling to Philadelphia from Georgia for medical reasons, accompanied by her slave, William.

Why was this story so popular? One reason is because the tale fit so well with the values of its audience. The story pleased Abolitionists and European critics of the American slavery system. Such members of the audience thrilled to hear how two slaves escaped the chains of slavery: outsmarting their masters, finding appropriate and useful loopholes in the South's slavery system, and often traveling disguised in broad daylight under the watchful eyes of their would-be captors. On the other hand, slave owners could not hear the tale often enough, if only due to obsessive self-denigration for having allowed themselves to be tricked.

21. *The story of William and Ellen Craft took place before which of the following?*

This question is a/an _____ question.

(A) The Revolutionary War
(B) The Civil War
(C) World War I
(D) World War II

22. *The word* self-denigration *as used by the author most closely means* _____.

This question is a/an _____ question.

(A) sadness
(B) happiness
(C) anger
(D) self-hatred

23. *This passage most closely resembles which genre of literature?*

    This question is a/an _____ question.

    (A) critical review
    (B) book report
    (C) statistical analysis
    (D) philosophical treatise

24. *The passage deals mainly with _____.*

    This question is a/an _____ question.

    (A) explaining why slave narratives in general are interesting
    (B) explaining why the story of William and Ellen Craft in particular is interesting
    (C) explaining why the South opted for a slave system in the first place
    (D) explaining why the North hated the Craft's story so much

---

Directions: Questions 25–28 are based on the following passage.

Baseball players use hand signals all the time; hand signals are so commonly used during games that observers might be oblivious to their presence in the game. However, hand signals were not always part of baseball.

In the 1880s, pitchers and managers communicated via one-on-one conferences on the pitcher's mound and verbal calls across the diamond. Discussing strategy secretly was crucial; sometimes, teammates covered their mouths and whispered in one another's ears so as to prevent the opposing team from overhearing.

One season, however, William "Dummy" Hoy signed on to play for the Cincinnati Reds. Hoy was an incredible pitcher who ended his career having played for 5 different teams in 15 seasons from 1888 to 1902. He led the National League with 82 stolen bases in his rookie year with the Cincinnati Reds. He stole 30 or more bases in his first 12 years of his career. He scored 100 runs nine times, and his on base average was over .400 four times. Hoy's lifetime batting average was .292, and he had 2,057 hits.

Such a brilliant career began, however, with a rocky start; Hoy was deaf. He couldn't hear verbal signals, nor could he reliably keep up with the game's progress due to his inability to hear team chatter.

In response to this obstacle, however, Hoy's manager showed creativity and innovation. He ordered his entire team to learn the American Universal Sign Language, the language of hand signals created for and used by deaf people. Now, all of Hoy's teammates could communicate with Hoy, and he with them, without the other team being able to <u>infiltrate</u> team strategy.

Other teams, impressed with this silent form of communication, followed the Reds' lead. Now, one cannot attend a baseball game without seeing these familiar hand signals.

25. *The reason why people gave William Hoy the nickname "Dummy" is most likely because _____.*

This question is a/an _____ question.

(A) he had no formal education
(B) he got all C's in school
(C) he was deaf and therefore hard to talk to
(D) he was blind but brilliant at math

26. *The best title for this passage would be _____.*

This question is a/an _____ question.

(A) Three Strikes and You're Out!
(B) Star Struck
(C) From Mouth to Hand
(D) Manners on the Mound

27. *The author uses the word* infiltrate *in this passage to mean _____.*

This question is a/an _____ question.

(A) contaminate
(B) discover
(C) invade
(D) prepare

28. *The use of hand signals in baseball dates back to the _____.*

This question is a/an _____ question.

(A) 1990s
(B) 1890s
(C) 1980s
(D) 1880s

Directions: Questions 29–32 are based on the following passage.

Edgar Allan Poe (1809–1849) is best known for his spooky stories and dark poetry. However, modern literary critics now look to him for his insight into human nature. Despite himself, Poe has gained a reputation as a social commentator.

At first glance, Poe's world view appears to be one of fear and mistrust, especially toward women. Consider a very brief account of Poe's work. His protagonists are almost invariably delicate, highly educated males, who prefer to study in their candle-lit salons rather than interact with other people. They seem fearful of all people, particularly women. Yet despite their apparent fear of women, they nevertheless seek out the secrets women possess. In "Ligea," the protagonist cannot quench his intense desire to look into her eyes, the windows of her soul; in "Berenice," the protagonist obsessively seeks to possess Berenice's teeth.

Hidden beneath these generalizations is a strict division between male and female personality traits. One of Poe's best short stories, "The Fall of the House of Usher," illustrates this relationship between men and women. In this story, Poe's protagonist, Usher, tries to rid himself of his sister. He fails, and his ancestral mansion falls down around him. Modern critics look to this tale as an allegory of the human mind, with Usher representing the male/scientific/left-brained side of the human personality and Usher's sister representing the female/artistic/right-brained side. The inference: Usher tries to bury the half of himself that makes him uncomfortable.

Upon first reading, one might be tempted to infer that Poe advocates such a world view. However, reading between the lines leads to exactly the opposite conclusion. Almost invariably, those of Poe's protagonists who insist upon dividing their personalities between left- and right-brained functions end up mad, incarcerated, or otherwise destroyed.

29. *What is the best concluding sentence for this passage?*

    This question is a/an _____ question.

    (A) Clearly then, Poe is arguing for a strict separation of the male-female impulses.
    (B) Clearly then, Poe is arguing for a balance of the male-female impulses.
    (C) Clearly then, the reader can see that Poe himself feared women.
    (D) Clearly then, one can see that we all share the same world view.

30. *What did the writer not list as one of the characteristics of a Poe protagonist?*

    This question is a/an _____ question.

    (A) Possessing a great degree of education
    (B) Being heavily addicted to opium
    (C) Being obsessive about women
    (D) Possessing a delicate temperament

31. *Which of the following definitions most closely fits the word* invariably?

    This question is a/an _____ question.

    (A) unchangingly
    (B) sporadically
    (C) never
    (D) oddly

32. *The passage mainly discusses _____.*

    This question is a/an _____ question.

    (A) Poe's use of bizarre and strange detail in his work
    (B) the effect of extreme intelligence and intense education on the human personality
    (C) using literature to point out a relationship between human psychology and literature
    (D) a survey of literature typical of the late 19th century

Zelda Fitzgerald, superstar of her generation, set a high standard for madness during an already mad decade. She came from a prominent Alabama family, a fact that became glaringly obvious to those who met her; her wealth and breeding simply radiated from her. Attractive, with red-gold hair, delicate features, and assured body language, she became accustomed to public attention early on.

Eager to maintain her spot in the limelight, she often invented ways of remaining in it. Once, as a young child, she stole away in the family car, enjoying a brief but wild ride before being recaptured. Not much later on a particularly boring day, she phoned the police and alerted them to a young child stranded atop a high rooftop in need of rescue—then she promptly climbed to the roof of her own house to await the excitement.

Her love of chaos continued into her adult life. She intentionally married "beneath her" by accepting the wedding proposal of F. Scott Fitzgerald, a gifted but penniless writer, burned by the amorality of 1920 society. She and Fitzgerald threw wild, lavish, drunken parties, often topping off the evening's revels with a dip in the water fountain or a marital spat or two. Once, jealous that Fitzgerald paid too much attention to a visiting actress, Zelda silently climbed to the top of a stair banister, caught Fitzgerald's attention, and stepped off into the abyss.

Zelda's increasingly dangerous and disturbing <u>antics</u> finally caused people to conclude she was slipping into real insanity. She was institutionalized in 1934 and spent the remainder of her life in and out of asylums. Nevertheless, her beauty, her spirit, and her tragic fall from orbit illustrate perfectly the social culture surrounding her.

33. *Why did Zelda call the police?*

    This question is a/an _____ question.

    (A) She wanted to be rescued from her abusive home life.
    (B) She had gotten stuck accidentally on the roof of her house.
    (C) She wanted to impress her grandmother.
    (D) She was bored and wanted excitement.

34. *When did Zelda get institutionalized?*

    This question is a/an _____ question.

    (A) 1914
    (B) 1924
    (C) 1934
    (D) 1944

35. *Which of the following best defines the word* antics*?*

    This question is a/an _____ question.

    (A) tantrums
    (B) stunts
    (C) confusion
    (D) dementia

36.   *The title that best expresses the ideas of this passage is _____.*

   This question is a/an _____ question.

   (A)   Limelight
   (B)   Once More into the Breach
   (C)   Prohibition and Women
   (D)   Portrait of a Lost Lady

(See page 223 for answers.)

ANSWERS AND ANALYSES

Main-Idea Questions (page 204)

1.   **(B)** This reading selection does not deal with offering new ways to recycle; therefore, rule out choice C. Nor does the article state an opinion on new scientific theories; therefore, you can rule out choice D, since scoffing implies stating an opinion. This passage does seem (superficially) to encourage recycling, so you need to compare choices A and B to find the best answer. The passage begins by stating that society encourages people to recycle. But the passage ends by saying that new scientific evidence states recycling may cause more damage than we originally thought. Since you begin with one idea only to end with its exact opposite, look for an option that shows change. The only option that does so is choice B.

2.   **(A)** The reading does not try to evaluate any type of game, whether that be in terms of programmer skill, gaming skill, or moral correctness. Therefore, you can rule out choices B, C, and D. Only choice A fits the intent of the passage: to give readers a general sense of how video games have changed over time.

3.   **(C)** The reading discusses children's movies and the benefit the author sees in them. Nowhere does the article mention the cost of producing movies, so rule out choice D. While the article briefly cites how adults are depicted in the movies—and while these depictions are not positive ones—this is not the focus of the passage. Rule out choice B. Break down the reading and check:

   Paragraph One: Children's movies show children in bad situations ruled by mean adults.

   Paragraph Three: Children nevertheless deal maturely with their bad luck, and they turn their negative situations into positive ones, gaining personal responsibility, power, and ultimately money.

   The piece clearly moves from one point of view to another: from showing children faced with adversity to showing children triumphing over their situations. You can rule out, therefore, choice A, since the author's message is an optimistic, uplifting one. The correct answer is choice C.

Word-In-Context Questions (page 206)

4.   **(B)** The whole paragraph is written to tell you what *jazz* means, but it does not obviously state the meaning of the word until late in the paragraph; therefore, rule out choice A. The paragraph refers to "naughtier" topics in reference to "jazz," and

although drugs and violence, choices C and D, respectively, are naughty, indeed illegal topics, the article is not referring to them. The final sentences of the passage specifically define the word "jazz" as having something to do with music; your only correct answer is choice B.

5. **(C)** Twain is described in the paragraph as being two sided—on the one hand trying to be a Southerner (and all the things that go along with being a Southerner) and on the other hand trying to be a Northerner (the complete opposite of being a Southerner). Therefore, you are looking for a word that accommodates a person trying to be two conflicting things at once. This is a confusing task; and the word *confusing* is your best choice. The correct answer is choice C.

6. **(D)** You can rule out choice A right off the bat; it is present as an option merely to confuse you into thinking a connection exists between the word *droves* and *Rover*. Ignore it. Choices B and C are more enticing, but they are also wrong. The correlation between *droves* and *drives* is false; the word actually being defined by choice C is *groves*. Ignore these, too. Choice D is the correct answer. Even if you don't know the word *droves*, the piece contains many context clues to help you out—several times the author makes references to quantities of things—phrases like "plague-like quantities" and "great numbers," and the description of someone unable to walk around without stepping on cicadas—a description that implies a *lot* of cicadas. Therefore, you must select choice D as the best answer.

Fact Questions (page 207)

7. **(B)** This question is designed to be a "no-brainer." You check over the reading one last time and notice that nowhere are Madonna, The Gyoto Monks, or Rage Against the Machine mentioned. Your only real option is choice B, Buddy Holly.

8. **(C)** Again, for fact questions, you are simply regurgitating a fact you remember from the reading passage. Here, three of the answers are silly. The only one with any basis in fact is choice C, which refers to the Mars rover, the subject of discussion in the reading passage.

9. **(C)** Careful reading of the passage tells you that only three masters remain alive today.

Inference Questions (page 208)

10. **(C)** While the author of this passage clearly states that he or she likes Jonathan Gash books very much, certain actions presented to you as options simply are not implied by this passage. He or she may certainly go to the library and get more books (choice A) or go to bed (choice D), but nowhere in the selection are you given any reason to think he or she might do so at this particular time. You know that choice B is very unlikely, since the author loves Gash's work so much that he or she would be unlikely to get rid of it. The passage does mention the upcoming book signing; most likely, therefore, given the author's love of Gash, he or she will make definite plans to attend the signing.

11. **(A)** The author seems to take a side in this passage; therefore, you can rule out choices C and D, which state either that you can't tell what the author's point of view is (choice D) or that the author is neutral (choice C). Since the author does not use words that

imply disagreement with Salinger, you can rule out choice B. The best answer is choice A, supported by the fact that the author even brings in an outside author (Yeats) in support of Salinger's point.

12. **(B)** The article seems to present a problem and be all set for discussing it thoroughly. Since only the problem has been discussed, with no mention of possible solutions, it seems very unlikely that the article will end here. Therefore, rule out choice D. Interviews with people seem like a good idea, but why would the author of this piece choose to interview an adult about how vending machines helped his or her school decades before? This choice is simply not the best answer. Rule out choice A. The SPCA is a popular group whose purpose is to protect animals; why they would get to voice an opinion is unclear. Rule out choice C. The best thing, given these options, would be to hear proposed solutions to the problem; choice B offers exactly this logical path.

More Practice Sessions: A Mixed Bag (page 209)

Note: We at Barron's want to help you feel confident that you can identify the type of reading comprehension question that will be asked of you. We, therefore, strongly recommend you verify which type of question is being asked with a quick reference to the information at the beginning of this chapter (page 199). Then check out our explanations of why certain answers are wrong and others are right. Good luck!

1. **(D)** Any time you see a question that asks that you come up with a title for a selection, you are being asked to identify the main idea of that passage; this is a main-idea reading comprehension question. Break down the three-paragraph reading passage by identifying the main idea (or topic sentence) for each paragraph. Your breakdown should read something like the following:

    Paragraph One: Historically, people have desired speed.

    Paragraph Two: People desire speed in many areas of life—whether it be speedy travel or speedy medical recovery.

    Paragraph Three: Quick fixes, in particular placebos, increasingly do not work effectively.

    Now, check out the titles. The title suggestion of "Doctor Knows Best" asks you to think about the patient-doctor relationship but gives no insight into how speed of recovery or effectiveness of certain drugs might come into play. Neither does the title "Go Ask Alice" refer to either of these subjects; the best you can say for it is that it makes a clever reference to a pop song from the sixties ("White Rabbit" by the Jefferson Airplane). Choice B, "Placebos: The Miracle Drug," at least mentions the idea of placebos (as discussed briefly in the third paragraph), so you might be tempted to choose it. But consider choice D, which mentions both a desire for quick solutions to problems as well as disappointment in the result of attempting to use those quick-fix methods. A quick comparison with the paragraph breakdown shows this choice to be the best. **(Main-idea question)**

2. **(B)** The question clearly asks you to define *placebo*; therefore, this is a word-in-context question. The reading passage states that "doctors sometimes prescribe actual drugs for some patients, while prescribing placebos for others." The construction of this phrase implies a contrast with opposites (prescribing one thing for one group and the opposite of that thing for another). The first thing being prescribed is described as

being "actual drugs," which means doctors are giving real medication that will have a documentable effect on the person(s) taking it. Therefore the second thing being described—the placebos—must be something opposite of actual drugs, or something that does not have an effect on the user. In short, you can infer from the use of the word in context that a placebo has no effect on the user. A quick scan of the selections reveals that choice B is the only selection that describes a "drug" that has no effect on the user—because it contains no medicine. **(Word-in-context question)**

3. **(B)** This question is asking that you locate the factual answer to a factual question; therefore, it is a fact question. You need to find out which of the cities on the list is mentioned in the reading passage. Using your memory is best, but if you need to, quickly scan the article again; you discover that Lexington is the only city in the selection list that also appears in the reading passage. **(Fact question)**

4. **(C)** Any time you see the word *implied* in a reading comprehension question, you can be sure that you are being asked an inference question. Using what you have read—and not what you know (or think you know) about the topic—consider your four options. Be careful; you are trying to find the sentence that contains a true implication about *any portion of the reading passage.* Several choices can be ruled out from the first. Rule out, for example, choice A. Nowhere in the paragraph are you given any evidence to believe (or infer) that people who crave speed are more likely to be depressed than anyone else; the only people who you might infer would get depressed more often than others based on this reading passage might be people who keep trying quick-fix drug therapy without results. Choice B also presents a problem: While one might make the case that the use of placebos to treat certain medical conditions successfully is proof that a positive mental attitude is key to recovery, one cannot fully infer this; one might as easily infer that all drug therapy is as likely to work as not to work. You can also reject choice D. Nothing in the paragraph gives any inclination that money is being lost (or gained, for that matter) in the cities attempting experimental drug therapy. In short, choice C is the only sentence that can fully be inferred. Paragraph one states that a postcard sent from Kentucky to Louisiana can travel farther than a human once could; one can definitively infer, therefore, that travel speeds have significantly increased over time; otherwise, people and postcards would still be traveling at the same slow rate. **(Inference question)**

5. **(D)** This question is asking for a fact you recall from your reading the selection in conjunction with a fact you should probably know from your other studies. Comparing the dates tells you that choice D, Edgar Degas who died in 1917, died just before the end of World War I (1918). **(Fact question)**

6. **(A)** Again, notice the key word *implies*; this is an inference question. You can immediately rule out choice D; the reading passage clearly indicates that Monet created more than one work of art (one of gardens, another of water lilies). You can also rule out choice B; the article does not go on long enough for you to make any inferences regarding what the author thinks about post-Impressionist art. Choice C is tempting, since the author seems to think it very important to Degas' work that he was influenced by Japanese art forms, but nowhere does the author imply that all Impressionist artists were influenced by Japanese art—without a "mass movement" in which most Impressionist artists give credit to Japanese art forms for inspiration,

you simply cannot infer that Japanese art forms had that much influence on Impressionism. Your only real inference lies in choice A. Paragraph One indicates by comparison that Impressionism was more exciting and fantastic than the art that came before it; therefore, you can infer that the pre-Impressionist art was more realistic and more "normal" (or conventional) than Impressionist art. **(Inference question)**

7.   **(D)** Since the question asks you to define how a particular word is used in this reading selection, you can easily identify the question as a word-in-context type. Paragraph Three details all of the typical things that Degas' work included; therefore, you can assume that most of the verbs being used in this paragraph will fit the basic definition of *include*. Judging from the list of choices, you can only select choice D as a synonym for *include*. The others simply do not fit (*denies*, *leaves behind*, and *obscures* all basically fit the definition of *excludes*). **(Word-in-context question)**

8.   **(B)** The question's key phrase "main purpose" essentially means main idea. Breaking down the paragraph structure, much as we did in question 1, yields the following result:

   Paragraph One: This paragraph defines Impressionism and gives an impression of popular response to it.

   Paragraph Two: This paragraph introduces Monet and gives examples of his style of Impressionism.

   Paragraph Three: This paragraph introduces a contrasting example of Impressionism, that of the artist Degas.

   All three paragraphs give descriptive, informative, and factual evidence regarding the subject of Impressionism. The piece does not attempt to persuade the reader toward a particular opinion or point of view; therefore, you can rule out choices A, C, and D, which all contain vocabulary that implies an attempt to convince or persuade ("convince" in choice A, "Impressionist art is better than" in choice C, and "encourage the reader" in choice D). **(Main-idea question)**

9.   **(C)** The question asks you to select the best definition for a word used in the passage; this is clearly a word-in-context question. Paragraph One tells the reader that the reason Ryan and Sue cannot find babysitters for their children is because of the bad behavior their kids display; paragraph two shows Ryan and Sue trying to discipline their children. One can infer from the use of the word *insubordinate* that the behavior displayed by Ryan and Sue's children is bad; therefore, *insubordinate* must mean bad. Scanning the list of choices, you notice that choice D is obviously not the answer; ridiculous behavior can be amusing, which might actually work to encourage babysitters to take care of Ryan and Sue's children. Choices A and B are equally unsuitable; neither aggressive (acting out) nor passive (quiet but stubborn resistance) behavior is necessarily bad behavior, and sometimes it is quite necessary—witness the tactics used by Civil Rights activists in the 1960s. However, unruly behavior is by definition bad behavior; therefore choice C is the correct response. **(Word-in-context question)**

10. **(D)** The question uses a glaring hint here—"main point" is basically another way of saying main idea. Break down the reading selection as follows:

   Paragraph One: Ryan and Sue's children act so badly no one will babysit them.

   Paragraph Two: Ryan and Sue are confused about how to get their kids to behave.

   Paragraph Three: Ryan and Sue give the children an allowance.

Paragraph Four: Ryan and Sue tie good behavior with rewards (keeping their allowance) and bad behavior with discipline that the children respect (revoking the allowance).

Paragraph Five: Ryan and Sue are rewarded by well-behaved children (and frequent babysitting).

Essentially, then, the selection outlines the way one set of parents copes with badly behaved children. Nowhere does the article evaluate the quality of babysitters from which Ryan and Sue hired babysitting help; rule out choice A. Nowhere, too, does the selection imply that Ryan and Sue are troubled with badly behaving children or an inability to fix the situation because of their age; rule out choice B. Finally, Paragraph Two clearly states that threats did not work; rule out choice C. The main point of the passage is to persuade parents that the key to good parenting is to find rules and disciplinary action that children respect and respond to; the correct answer is choice D. **(Main-idea question)**

11. **(D)** This question asks for a simple fact recalled from reading; clearly then this is a fact question. Use your short-term memory (or quickly check the passage again); Ryan and Sue have three children. **(Fact question)**

12. **(A)** The phrase "What would most likely take place next" tells you that you must guess (or infer), based on the facts in the selection, what will happen next—this is an inference question. Refer to the paragraph breakdown; if the parents set up a cause-effect relationship with their children in which good behavior gets financial reward, and, upon the completion of the evening, the children behaved well, then we know that the children will receive their reward. Therefore the only correct choice offered is choice A. Choice B must be rejected (unless Ryan and Sue are hypocritical parents). We have no reason to think that Ryan and Sue will test their system again so soon; in fact, they should not, so as to retain the power of their new disciplinary system. Rule out choice C. The skill of the babysitter had nothing to do with the behavior of the children—the power of the situation rested entirely in the power of the children to desire money more than they desire to behave badly; therefore, rule out choice D. **(Inference question)**

13. **(D)** The third paragraph implies a hope that the author seems to have—that readers of Lemony Snicket will go on to read other Dark Romantic writers. Indeed, the final paragraph of the passage hammers the message home. The other options are simply red herrings: the author does not mention H. G. Wells at all and only mentions the Lemony Snicket movie in order to make a point about the series' popularity; moreover, choice B is simply false. **(Inference question)**

14. **(B)** Not only does the word *dastardly* simply sound bad, it is surrounded by negative context, culminating in the mention of the bony-fingered, evil Count Olaf. "Delightful" and "wonderful" are, therefore, right out; and "random" simply makes no sense. The correct answer is B. **(Word-in-context question)**

15. **(A)** Question 15 is much like question 13, just worded differently. However, if you're stuck, you can still use process of elimination to help yourself out. Choice B will not work, as the text only mentions three Dark Romantic writers (four, if you count Lemony Snicket), and many, many more Dark Romantic writers exist. The author does not mention sci fi nor make a plea for the reader to make the attempt to read some;

rule out choice C. Again, the writer only mentions the film to make a point about how popular the books are; rule out choice D. The answer is choice A. (**Main-idea question**)

16. **(C)** Clearly Dark Romantic texts are still being written; the author claims *A Series of Unfortunate Events* is one such text. Rule out choice A. The author also does not feel that Dark Romanticism is dull; he or she says as much in Paragraphs Two and Three; rule out choice B. Nowhere does the author claim that Dark Romanticism will bring world peace; skip choice D. The only remaining answer is choice C. (**Fact question**)

17. **(B)** This question asks you to look at how the author uses a word in the passage; this is a word-in-context question. Rereading the last paragraph of the passage reveals the following phrase: "to turn a negative into a positive, to turn <u>dross</u> into gold." The phrase is based on the principle of the appositive: to give an example of something in close succession to the thing just discussed. You know that gold is a good thing, and you know that "something good" is being discussed; you can equate these two topics. By contrast and by the process of elimination, you can then link up "something bad" with *dross*, even if you don't know what dross is. Finally, you can set up the phrase like an equation:

something negative = dross
something positive = gold

Therefore, if *dross* means something negative, scan the selections to see what matches up. The choice that best fits is choice B. (**Word-in-context question**)

18. **(C)** The question asks you to figure out who the author states is responsible for the discovery of fermentation; this is a fact question. Based on your recollection of the passage—or a quick scan—you discover that the author states the Egyptians discovered the fermentation process; the other names are there as red herrings, to confuse you. Select choice C. (**Fact question**)

19. **(D)** Again, your brain should automatically be signaling that "main purpose" is really code for main idea. Break it down!

    Paragraph One: Johnson (who he really is doesn't matter) talks about how ironic it is that great things come about through accident more often than through intentional human action.

    Paragraph Two: Johnson (by implication) gives an example of the fermentation of alcohol by the Egyptians or the accidental discovery of rubber by Charles Goodyear.

    Paragraph Three: Johnson argues that since good things come about through accident, why attempt to shape the world or the future? The author then starts to give an opposing viewpoint and seems to be about to discuss the crisis of 9/11.

    Choices A, B, and C can all be ruled out; after all, the passage refers to examples of good fortune (choice A) as well as bad (choice C). While the passage makes brief mention of the fermentation process, no careful reader would argue that the entire passage is intended to discuss fermentation. The only possible option is choice D, which says that something positive can come out of bad situations—and all examples supplied by the passage support this view. Alcohol comes from mold; rubber came from accidental burning; and, as the author will now set out to prove, some good came out of the 9/11 attacks. (**Main-idea question**)

20. **(C)** Of the passages we give you for practice, this is an especially tough one; yet challenge is essential to academic success—so stick to it! The phrase "will most likely discuss" should tell you that you are dealing with a possibility, rather than a fact; therefore, this is an inference question. Knowing what the breakdown of the passage is will help; we do this for you in question 19, so we refrain from redoing so here. Check out question 19's explanation if you need to. Essentially, the author is explaining to the reader what someone named Johnson has argued in the past, an argument that the author will then attempt to shoot down. The author ends this passage with the intent of elaborating on his or her opposing argument. The author does not get to explain his or her argument in full. What will he or she argue next? Consider the options. The author has already discussed a series of inventions, and, given the breakdown of the passage, it seems illogical that the reader would consider discussing more inventions at this point. So, rule out choice A. The author clearly seems to be switching topics; therefore, a review or recap of the major points discussed thus far seems to be inappropriate. So, rule out choice B. Nothing about the discussion implies that the next topic would be Albert Camus; rule out choice D. However, the article ends with a brief reference to the infamous 9/11 attacks—attack against the Twin Towers in New York and against the Pentagon in Washington, D.C. Most likely, then, the author will turn to this topic next. The phrase, "one case in point" also implies that the discussion of whatever case is in point will follow. The correct answer is choice C. **(Inference question)**

21. **(B)** The passage asks you to identify a specific fact in the reading passage: when something happened in comparison to when something else happened in history. Knowing your dates helps: the Revolutionary War dates back to the 1770s; the Civil War dates back to the 1860s; and both the First and Second World Wars date back to the 1900s. Paragraph one tells you that William and Ellen Craft's story happens circa 1848; therefore, you can rule out choices C and D. You can also rule out choice A, since the Revolutionary War was long over by 1848. The answer is choice B. **(Fact question)**

22. **(D)** Since the question refers to the definition of a word, you can be sure that this is a words-in-context question. Naturally, it's best for one of these questions that you know the vocabulary from studying in school already. But, check out paragraph two again, if you don't already know the word *self-denigration*. You can tell that the paragraph is setting up a contrast—(1) telling reasons why slaves and abolitionists liked the story of William and Ellen Craft's escape and (2) telling reasons why even slaveholders (who would have been very upset by the tale) listened to the story again and again. The passage states that the slaveholders felt as if they had been tricked—usually something we associate with negative feelings. Scan the list for options that suggest negative feelings. You can rule out choice B, then, since happiness is not a negative feeling. Choice A might work, but slave owners who had been tricked (or imagined themselves being tricked) probably wouldn't be sad—they'd be angry. Narrow your selections to choices C and D. Check out the word *self-denigration* again; the word refers specifically to the self, so select choice D, "self-hatred." (You'll be right!) **(Word-in-context question)**

23. **(A)** This question asks you to compare the reading selection you have just finished to other types of books or reading passages you have read. You are using personal judgment; therefore, you are making an inference. This is an inference question. Scan your options, and rule out obvious wrong answers, like choices C and D. Statistics involves numbers—this passage offers no numbers, aside from the occasional date, at any

point; nor does the author talk about philosophy at any point. Consider choices A and B. Do you see any attempt by the author to *evaluate* how good the book is? Or does the reading selection try to "sell" you interesting aspects of the book and its plot? A quick scan reveals that the passage seems to be trying to make you interested in reading the book but is not trying to evaluate the writing style or the author's intent in writing; therefore, the answer is choice B. **(Inference question)**

24. **(B)** The question uses the word "mainly," which by now should be a strong hint that you are dealing with a main-idea question. You can rule out choices C and D right off. The short reading passage does not even mention reasons why the South decided to build itself on a foundation of slave trade. Additionally, while Southern slave owners may have hated the Crafts for tricking them, according to the passage, the article specifically paints Northern readers as being just as obsessed with the story of William and Ellen Craft as their Southern counterparts (and without discussing motivation for that obsession). So, look again at choices A and B. Clearly the reading passage tells about slave narratives, but does it discuss the 100 or more slave narratives that came out of this time period? Or just the slave narrative telling about William and Ellen Craft? A quick scan again verifies that this passage only discusses the Crafts. Therefore, you must select choice B. **(Main-idea question)**

25. **(C)** This question asks you to make a judgment based on facts in the passage; therefore, it is an inference question. Nowhere in the passage does the author discuss Italy's education; therefore, you can quickly eliminate choices A, B, and D. Your only answer left is choice C. (Sometimes a quick answer like this one can help you catch up on your pacing later.) **(Inference question)**

26. **(C)** Being asked to select the best title is a clue that you are looking for the main idea. Eliminate choice B, since it really is too vague to be the best answer for this question. Eliminate choice A for the same reason; it's clearly appropriate for most baseball-related stories, but we want a title that is appropriate for *this* baseball related story. Choice D just doesn't really fit—manners on the mound could mean a variety of things—and we are not shown people acting rudely and being told to reform their manners (not even in the case where people made up the insensitive nickname of "Dummy" for Hoy). Your best selection is choice C, since the passage talks about how players quit talking with their mouths and started talking with their hands. **(Main-idea question)**

27. **(B)** Since you're being asked to define a word, this is clearly a word-in-context question. Probably you know the word *infiltrate* already, especially if you are at all interested in spy stories, shows, or games. The passage discusses a situation in which two teams use strategy to beat the other, strategy that depends upon each side keeping its plans secret from the "enemy." Words like those in choice A (that deal with contamination) or choice D (that deal with preparation) do not fit the situation, so rule them out. Words like those in choice C also do not really fit, since players are trying to figure out something, not physically invade a territory. Your best selection is choice B, which fits the meaning and the tone of a passage in which trying to figure out secrets is the goal. **(Word-in-context question)**

28. **(D)** This question asks you to identify a fact from the reading; hence, it is a fact question. Based on memory (or a quick glance up) you find out that paragraph two tells you that hand signals date back to the 1880s; you need to select choice D. **(Fact question)**

29. **(B)** The question asks you to read the passage, identify the author's train of thought, and then complete that train of thought by choosing a sentence from the list of options. This is asking you to infer; therefore, this is an inference question. You should break down the passage to make sure you understand the author's train of thought:

    Paragraph One: Poe, usually known for his poetry, also gives great insight into human nature.

    Paragraph Two: Poe creates male characters who fear women, mostly because they desire something the woman possesses.

    Paragraph Three: We can apply this observation to psychology; Poe is saying that some people fear secret, intuitive parts of their own personalities and try to destroy these things they fear.

    Paragraph Four: Poe seems to approve of people who try to bury half of their personalities, but actually he steadfastly disapproves.

    Now that we know the line of thought, finding the correct response shouldn't be too hard. You can rule out choice D, since the author is talking about Poe in particular, not people in general. You can also rule out choice C, since, even though the author does imply that Poe was obsessed by women, this is not the main point of the argument. And, you can rule out choice A, since paragraph four states exactly the opposite view. Your answer should be choice B. **(Inference question)**

30. **(B)** This question is asking you to consider a list of options and figure out which one is inappropriate; you can only do so by remembering the data given to you in the article and making a checklist. Therefore, this is a fact question. You can find choices A, C, and D discussed in paragraph two; therefore, the only characteristic not discussed anywhere in the text is choice B. **(Fact question)**

31. **(A)** This question asks you to define a word; it is a word-in-context question. Knowing some synonyms for the options listed helps here; you can essentially break them down as follows:

unchangingly	=	always
sporadically	=	sometimes
never	=	never
oddly	=	weirdly

    Since the passage, specifically paragraph two, is making a general comment about Poe's writing over time, you are looking for a word that implies something that does not change. The only word in the list that fits this description is choice A. **(Word-in-context question)**

32. **(C)** The key word "mainly" should raise a red flag in your brain; this is a main-idea question. You can rule out choice D, since the passage only discusses Poe's writing; the author makes no attempt to discuss all other Dark Romantic writers of the 19th century, as one might expect in a survey of literature. Choices A and B are equally appealing, since you can point to paragraphs in this passage that do hint at these points. But the best answer is choice C, since the article tries, especially in paragraphs three and

four, to make the point that readers can read literature and gain psychological insight into human nature. (**Main-idea question**)

33. **(D)** This question asks you to consider what you know about Zelda Fitzgerald's personality and make a judgment; this is, therefore, an inference question. Using your memory (or remembering the author's discussion of the event), create a quick character sketch of Zelda. She was highly intelligent and in great need of entertainment; paragraph two states she was extremely bored that day. Therefore, your best choice would be choice D, which fits well with both things we know about Zelda. The other choices simply have no basis in fact that we know; the article does not say whether her early life was abusive (choice A) nor whether she had a need to impress authority figures around her (choice C). And the selection clearly states that she went onto the roof of her own free will. (**Inference question**)

34. **(C)** The question asks you to single out a particular fact; therefore, this is a fact question. Paragraph four clearly states that Zelda was institutionalized in 1934. Therefore, your correct answer is choice C. (**Fact question**)

35. **(B)** Again, the question asks you about a word; this is a word-in-context question. Some of the choices listed are designed to catch sloppy thinkers. Choices C and D, in particular, refer to symptoms a mental patient might exhibit. Just because Zelda eventually became a mental patient does not mean these answers are correct; in fact, they are not correct. Your best answers are choices A and B, since tantrums and antics are superficially very similar; both involve someone trying to get the attention of another person. Knowing the connotations of these words definitely helps. While both definitions are appropriate to this reading passage, tantrums involve inelegant, angry, loud lashing out, usually of two-year-olds against their parents; antics, on the other hand, generally are silly, witty, if occasionally dangerous, and usually only affect the person performing the antic. Since Zelda wanted attention, but usually without causing harm to others, and since she usually showed great wit in her actions, your best choice would be B. (**Word-in-context question**)

36. **(D)** Finding the best title means you are also stating the main idea; this is a main-idea question. You can rule out certain options immediately. While, judging from Zelda's dates, you can clearly see that Prohibition was taking place, the article does not focus on that fact; this passage is clearly written about Zelda, in an almost autobiographical manner. Therefore, choice B simply doesn't make much sense, given what you know about the article. Now, Zelda wanted attention, so you might be drawn to choice A, but the passage talks about more than just her need for attention, so keep looking. The best answer is choice D, since Zelda, for all her wit and wealth, was indeed "lost." (**Main-idea question**)

PRACTICE
EXAMS

ANSWER SHEET
COOP Practice Exam 1

TEST 1   SEQUENCES

1. Ⓐ Ⓑ Ⓒ Ⓓ	6. Ⓕ Ⓖ Ⓗ Ⓙ	11. Ⓐ Ⓑ Ⓒ Ⓓ	16. Ⓕ Ⓖ Ⓗ Ⓙ
2. Ⓕ Ⓖ Ⓗ Ⓙ	7. Ⓐ Ⓑ Ⓒ Ⓓ	12. Ⓕ Ⓖ Ⓗ Ⓙ	17. Ⓐ Ⓑ Ⓒ Ⓓ
3. Ⓐ Ⓑ Ⓒ Ⓓ	8. Ⓕ Ⓖ Ⓗ Ⓙ	13. Ⓐ Ⓑ Ⓒ Ⓓ	18. Ⓕ Ⓖ Ⓗ Ⓙ
4. Ⓕ Ⓖ Ⓗ Ⓙ	9. Ⓐ Ⓑ Ⓒ Ⓓ	14. Ⓕ Ⓖ Ⓗ Ⓙ	19. Ⓐ Ⓑ Ⓒ Ⓓ
5. Ⓐ Ⓑ Ⓒ Ⓓ	10. Ⓕ Ⓖ Ⓗ Ⓙ	15. Ⓐ Ⓑ Ⓒ Ⓓ	20. Ⓕ Ⓖ Ⓗ Ⓙ

TEST 2   ANALOGIES

1. Ⓐ Ⓑ Ⓒ Ⓓ	6. Ⓕ Ⓖ Ⓗ Ⓙ	11. Ⓐ Ⓑ Ⓒ Ⓓ	16. Ⓕ Ⓖ Ⓗ Ⓙ
2. Ⓕ Ⓖ Ⓗ Ⓙ	7. Ⓐ Ⓑ Ⓒ Ⓓ	12. Ⓕ Ⓖ Ⓗ Ⓙ	17. Ⓐ Ⓑ Ⓒ Ⓓ
3. Ⓐ Ⓑ Ⓒ Ⓓ	8. Ⓕ Ⓖ Ⓗ Ⓙ	13. Ⓐ Ⓑ Ⓒ Ⓓ	18. Ⓕ Ⓖ Ⓗ Ⓙ
4. Ⓕ Ⓖ Ⓗ Ⓙ	9. Ⓐ Ⓑ Ⓒ Ⓓ	14. Ⓕ Ⓖ Ⓗ Ⓙ	19. Ⓐ Ⓑ Ⓒ Ⓓ
5. Ⓐ Ⓑ Ⓒ Ⓓ	10. Ⓕ Ⓖ Ⓗ Ⓙ	15. Ⓐ Ⓑ Ⓒ Ⓓ	20. Ⓕ Ⓖ Ⓗ Ⓙ

TEST 3   QUANTITATIVE REASONING

1. Ⓐ Ⓑ Ⓒ Ⓓ	6. Ⓕ Ⓖ Ⓗ Ⓙ	11. Ⓐ Ⓑ Ⓒ Ⓓ	16. Ⓕ Ⓖ Ⓗ Ⓙ
2. Ⓕ Ⓖ Ⓗ Ⓙ	7. Ⓐ Ⓑ Ⓒ Ⓓ	12. Ⓕ Ⓖ Ⓗ Ⓙ	17. Ⓐ Ⓑ Ⓒ Ⓓ
3. Ⓐ Ⓑ Ⓒ Ⓓ	8. Ⓕ Ⓖ Ⓗ Ⓙ	13. Ⓐ Ⓑ Ⓒ Ⓓ	18. Ⓕ Ⓖ Ⓗ Ⓙ
4. Ⓕ Ⓖ Ⓗ Ⓙ	9. Ⓐ Ⓑ Ⓒ Ⓓ	14. Ⓕ Ⓖ Ⓗ Ⓙ	19. Ⓐ Ⓑ Ⓒ Ⓓ
5. Ⓐ Ⓑ Ⓒ Ⓓ	10. Ⓕ Ⓖ Ⓗ Ⓙ	15. Ⓐ Ⓑ Ⓒ Ⓓ	20. Ⓕ Ⓖ Ⓗ Ⓙ

TEST 4   VERBAL REASONING—WORDS

1. Ⓐ Ⓑ Ⓒ Ⓓ	6. Ⓕ Ⓖ Ⓗ Ⓙ	11. Ⓐ Ⓑ Ⓒ Ⓓ	16. Ⓕ Ⓖ Ⓗ Ⓙ
2. Ⓕ Ⓖ Ⓗ Ⓙ	7. Ⓐ Ⓑ Ⓒ Ⓓ	12. Ⓕ Ⓖ Ⓗ Ⓙ	17. Ⓐ Ⓑ Ⓒ Ⓓ
3. Ⓐ Ⓑ Ⓒ Ⓓ	8. Ⓕ Ⓖ Ⓗ Ⓙ	13. Ⓐ Ⓑ Ⓒ Ⓓ	18. Ⓕ Ⓖ Ⓗ Ⓙ
4. Ⓕ Ⓖ Ⓗ Ⓙ	9. Ⓐ Ⓑ Ⓒ Ⓓ	14. Ⓕ Ⓖ Ⓗ Ⓙ	19. Ⓐ Ⓑ Ⓒ Ⓓ
5. Ⓐ Ⓑ Ⓒ Ⓓ	10. Ⓕ Ⓖ Ⓗ Ⓙ	15. Ⓐ Ⓑ Ⓒ Ⓓ	20. Ⓕ Ⓖ Ⓗ Ⓙ

ANSWER SHEET
COOP Practice Exam 1

TEST 5   VERBAL REASONING—CONTEXT

1. Ⓐ Ⓑ Ⓒ Ⓓ   4. Ⓕ Ⓖ Ⓗ Ⓙ   7. Ⓐ Ⓑ Ⓒ Ⓓ   10. Ⓕ Ⓖ Ⓗ Ⓙ
2. Ⓕ Ⓖ Ⓗ Ⓙ   5. Ⓐ Ⓑ Ⓒ Ⓓ   8. Ⓕ Ⓖ Ⓗ Ⓙ
3. Ⓐ Ⓑ Ⓒ Ⓓ   6. Ⓕ Ⓖ Ⓗ Ⓙ   9. Ⓐ Ⓑ Ⓒ Ⓓ

TEST 6   READING AND LANGUAGE ARTS

1. Ⓐ Ⓑ Ⓒ Ⓓ   11. Ⓐ Ⓑ Ⓒ Ⓓ   21. Ⓐ Ⓑ Ⓒ Ⓓ   31. Ⓐ Ⓑ Ⓒ Ⓓ
2. Ⓕ Ⓖ Ⓗ Ⓙ   12. Ⓕ Ⓖ Ⓗ Ⓙ   22. Ⓕ Ⓖ Ⓗ Ⓙ   32. Ⓕ Ⓖ Ⓗ Ⓙ
3. Ⓐ Ⓑ Ⓒ Ⓓ   13. Ⓐ Ⓑ Ⓒ Ⓓ   23. Ⓐ Ⓑ Ⓒ Ⓓ   33. Ⓐ Ⓑ Ⓒ Ⓓ
4. Ⓕ Ⓖ Ⓗ Ⓙ   14. Ⓕ Ⓖ Ⓗ Ⓙ   24. Ⓕ Ⓖ Ⓗ Ⓙ   34. Ⓕ Ⓖ Ⓗ Ⓙ
5. Ⓐ Ⓑ Ⓒ Ⓓ   15. Ⓐ Ⓑ Ⓒ Ⓓ   25. Ⓐ Ⓑ Ⓒ Ⓓ   35. Ⓐ Ⓑ Ⓒ Ⓓ
6. Ⓕ Ⓖ Ⓗ Ⓙ   16. Ⓕ Ⓖ Ⓗ Ⓙ   26. Ⓕ Ⓖ Ⓗ Ⓙ   36. Ⓕ Ⓖ Ⓗ Ⓙ
7. Ⓐ Ⓑ Ⓒ Ⓓ   17. Ⓐ Ⓑ Ⓒ Ⓓ   27. Ⓐ Ⓑ Ⓒ Ⓓ   37. Ⓐ Ⓑ Ⓒ Ⓓ
8. Ⓕ Ⓖ Ⓗ Ⓙ   18. Ⓕ Ⓖ Ⓗ Ⓙ   28. Ⓕ Ⓖ Ⓗ Ⓙ   38. Ⓕ Ⓖ Ⓗ Ⓙ
9. Ⓐ Ⓑ Ⓒ Ⓓ   19. Ⓐ Ⓑ Ⓒ Ⓓ   29. Ⓐ Ⓑ Ⓒ Ⓓ   39. Ⓐ Ⓑ Ⓒ Ⓓ
10. Ⓕ Ⓖ Ⓗ Ⓙ   20. Ⓕ Ⓖ Ⓗ Ⓙ   30. Ⓕ Ⓖ Ⓗ Ⓙ   40. Ⓕ Ⓖ Ⓗ Ⓙ

TEST 7   MATHEMATICS

1. Ⓐ Ⓑ Ⓒ Ⓓ   11. Ⓐ Ⓑ Ⓒ Ⓓ   21. Ⓐ Ⓑ Ⓒ Ⓓ   31. Ⓐ Ⓑ Ⓒ Ⓓ
2. Ⓕ Ⓖ Ⓗ Ⓙ   12. Ⓕ Ⓖ Ⓗ Ⓙ   22. Ⓕ Ⓖ Ⓗ Ⓙ   32. Ⓕ Ⓖ Ⓗ Ⓙ
3. Ⓐ Ⓑ Ⓒ Ⓓ   13. Ⓐ Ⓑ Ⓒ Ⓓ   23. Ⓐ Ⓑ Ⓒ Ⓓ   33. Ⓐ Ⓑ Ⓒ Ⓓ
4. Ⓕ Ⓖ Ⓗ Ⓙ   14. Ⓕ Ⓖ Ⓗ Ⓙ   24. Ⓕ Ⓖ Ⓗ Ⓙ   34. Ⓕ Ⓖ Ⓗ Ⓙ
5. Ⓐ Ⓑ Ⓒ Ⓓ   15. Ⓐ Ⓑ Ⓒ Ⓓ   25. Ⓐ Ⓑ Ⓒ Ⓓ   35. Ⓐ Ⓑ Ⓒ Ⓓ
6. Ⓕ Ⓖ Ⓗ Ⓙ   16. Ⓕ Ⓖ Ⓗ Ⓙ   26. Ⓕ Ⓖ Ⓗ Ⓙ   36. Ⓕ Ⓖ Ⓗ Ⓙ
7. Ⓐ Ⓑ Ⓒ Ⓓ   17. Ⓐ Ⓑ Ⓒ Ⓓ   27. Ⓐ Ⓑ Ⓒ Ⓓ   37. Ⓐ Ⓑ Ⓒ Ⓓ
8. Ⓕ Ⓖ Ⓗ Ⓙ   18. Ⓕ Ⓖ Ⓗ Ⓙ   28. Ⓕ Ⓖ Ⓗ Ⓙ   38. Ⓕ Ⓖ Ⓗ Ⓙ
9. Ⓐ Ⓑ Ⓒ Ⓓ   19. Ⓐ Ⓑ Ⓒ Ⓓ   29. Ⓐ Ⓑ Ⓒ Ⓓ   39. Ⓐ Ⓑ Ⓒ Ⓓ
10. Ⓕ Ⓖ Ⓗ Ⓙ   20. Ⓕ Ⓖ Ⓗ Ⓙ   30. Ⓕ Ⓖ Ⓗ Ⓙ   40. Ⓕ Ⓖ Ⓗ Ⓙ

TEST 1 SEQUENCES

#1-20 15 MINUTES

Directions: Choose the letter that will continue the pattern or sequence.

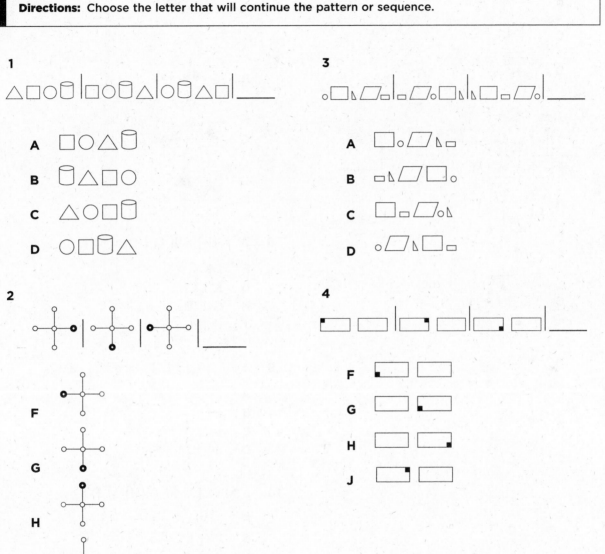

5

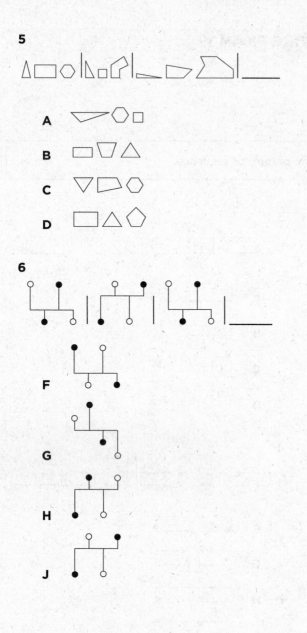

A
B
C
D

6

F

G

H

J

7

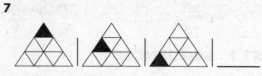

A

B

C

D

8 W V U | S R Q | O N M | _ _ _

   F J K L

   G K J I

   H G F E

   J G L I

9 *a c f | g i l | m o r | s _ x*

   A *t*

   B *u*

   C *v*

   D *w*

10 B M D | C M E | D M F | _ _ _

   F E M G

   G F G I

   H E M F

   J G H J

GO TO NEXT PAGE ➡

11 A C G | B D H | C E I | D F __

A L
B J
C P
D R

12 $A_4B_5C_6$ | $D_6E_7F_8$ | $G_8H_9I_{10}$ | _____ | $M_{12}N_{13}O_{14}$

F $J_{10}K_{11}L_{12}$
G $I_9J_{10}K_{11}$
H $K_{10}L_{11}M_{12}$
J $J_9K_{10}L_{11}$

13 Z Y X | V U T | R Q P | _____ | J I H

A G F E
B N M L
C M N L
D H G F

14 $A_1B_2D_3$ | $F_4G_5I_6$ | $K_7L_8N_9$ | $P_{10}Q_{11}$ —

F S_{12}
G R_{11}
H T_{11}
J S_{11}

15 15 17 20 | 43 45 48 | 9 11 __

A 13
B 14
C 17
D 29

16 XXIV | XXIX | XXXIV | _____ | XLIV

F XXXVII
G XLIV
H KXXXIV
J XXXIX

17 4 7 6 | 8 11 10 | 12 15 14 | 16 __ 18

A 17
B 18
C 15
D 19

18 1 1 1 | 2 4 8 | 3 9 27 | 4 16 __

F 64
G 50
H 100
J 75

19 6 3 1.5 | 8 4 2 | __ 2.5 1.25

A 7
B 9
C 6
D 5

20 21 25 30 | 17 21 26 | 19 __ 28

F 22
G 21
H 23
J 27

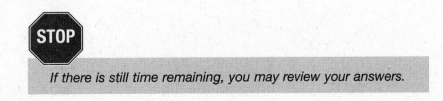

If there is still time remaining, you may review your answers.

TEST 2   ANALOGIES

#1–20   7 MINUTES

> **Directions:** Select the picture that will fill the empty box so that the two lower pictures are related to each other in the same manner as the two upper pictures.

1

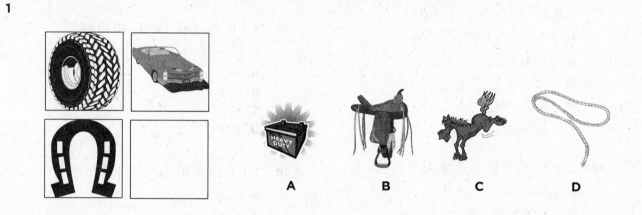

A   B   C   D

2

F   G   H   J

3

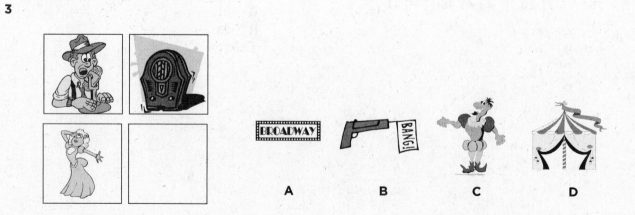

A   B   C   D

GO TO NEXT PAGE ➡

4

F   G   H   J

5

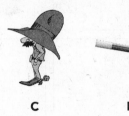  

A   B   C   D

6

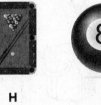

F   G   H   J

7

A   B   C   D

GO TO NEXT PAGE ➡

8

F   G   H   J

9

A   B   C   D

10

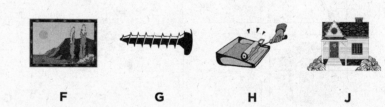

F   G   H   J

11

A   B   C   D

GO TO NEXT PAGE ➡

12

F   G   H   J

13

A   B   C   D

14

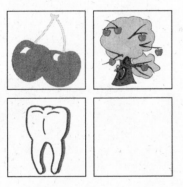

F   G   H   J

15

 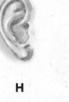 

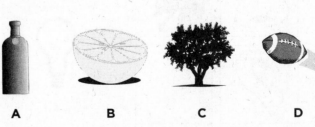

A   B   C   D

GO TO NEXT PAGE ➡

16

17

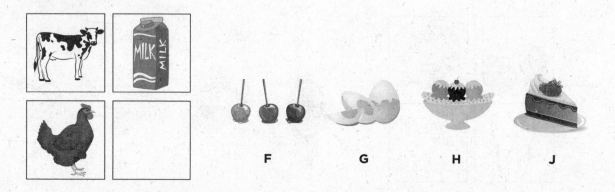

18

19

GO TO NEXT PAGE ➡

F   G   H   J

If there is still time remaining, you may review your answers.

TEST 3 QUANTITATIVE REASONING

#1-20 5 MINUTES

Directions: For questions 1-7, find the mathematical operation that is applied to the first number in each set so as to arrive at the second number. Then apply that operation to find the missing number. Select the correct answer.

1 $2 \rightarrow$ ___ $\rightarrow 4$

$6 \rightarrow$ ___ $\rightarrow 12$

$5 \rightarrow$ ___ $\rightarrow$?

A 12
B 9
C 10
D 18

2 $10 \rightarrow$ ___ $\rightarrow 2$

$15 \rightarrow$ ___ $\rightarrow 3$

$20 \rightarrow$ ___ $\rightarrow$?

F 5
G 10
H 4
J 6

3 $6 \rightarrow$ ___ $\rightarrow 2$

$8 \rightarrow$ ___ $\rightarrow 4$

$5 \rightarrow$ ___ $\rightarrow$?

A 6
B 4
C 2
D 1

4 $\frac{2}{5} \rightarrow$ ___ $\rightarrow 2$

$3 \rightarrow$ ___ $\rightarrow 15$

$\frac{3}{5} \rightarrow$ ___ $\rightarrow$?

F 5
G 4
H 2
J 3

5 $7 \rightarrow$ ___ $\rightarrow 2$

$9 \rightarrow$ ___ $\rightarrow 4$

$4 \rightarrow$ ___ $\rightarrow$?

A −1
B 0
C 3
D 1

6 $\frac{3}{4} \rightarrow$ ___ $\rightarrow \frac{1}{4}$

$1 \rightarrow$ ___ $\rightarrow \frac{1}{2}$

$\frac{3}{2} \rightarrow$ ___ $\rightarrow$?

F $\frac{1}{2}$
G 1
H $\frac{3}{4}$
J $\frac{1}{4}$

7 $24 \rightarrow$ ___ $\rightarrow 6$

$16 \rightarrow$ ___ $\rightarrow 4$

$6 \rightarrow$ ___ $\rightarrow$?

A 2
B 2.5
C 1.5
D 3

GO TO NEXT PAGE ➡

Directions: For questions 8–14, express the part of the grid that is dark.

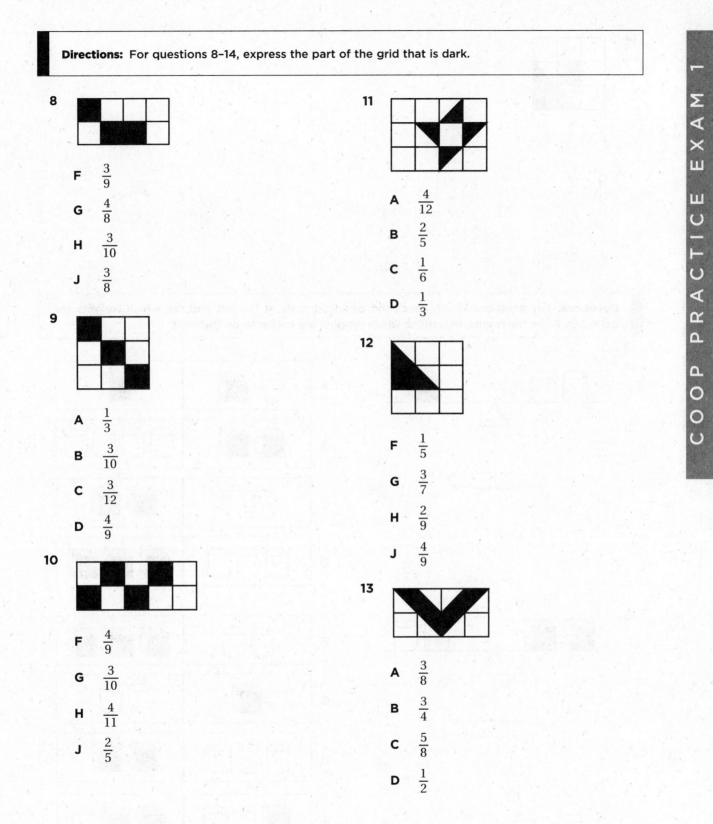

8

F $\dfrac{3}{9}$

G $\dfrac{4}{8}$

H $\dfrac{3}{10}$

J $\dfrac{3}{8}$

9

A $\dfrac{1}{3}$

B $\dfrac{3}{10}$

C $\dfrac{3}{12}$

D $\dfrac{4}{9}$

10

F $\dfrac{4}{9}$

G $\dfrac{3}{10}$

H $\dfrac{4}{11}$

J $\dfrac{2}{5}$

11

A $\dfrac{4}{12}$

B $\dfrac{2}{5}$

C $\dfrac{1}{6}$

D $\dfrac{1}{3}$

12

F $\dfrac{1}{5}$

G $\dfrac{3}{7}$

H $\dfrac{2}{9}$

J $\dfrac{4}{9}$

13

A $\dfrac{3}{8}$

B $\dfrac{3}{4}$

C $\dfrac{5}{8}$

D $\dfrac{1}{2}$

GO TO NEXT PAGE ➡

14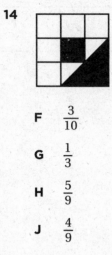

F $\frac{3}{10}$

G $\frac{1}{3}$

H $\frac{5}{9}$

J $\frac{4}{9}$

Directions: For questions 15–20, check the balanced scale at the left and see which weights are balanced. From the results, determine which weights are balanced on the right.

15

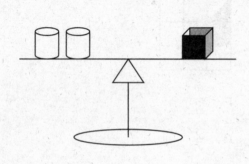

16

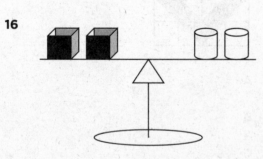

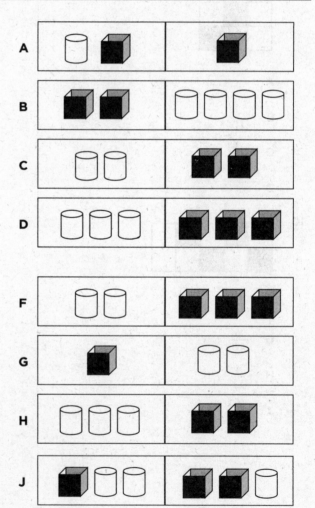

GO TO NEXT PAGE ➡

17

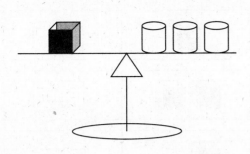

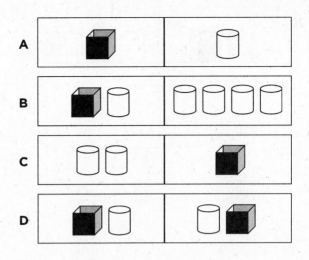

A

B

C

D

18

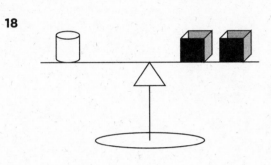

F

G

H

J

19

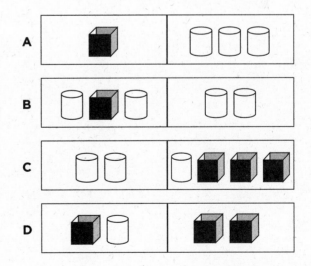

A

B

C

D

GO TO NEXT PAGE ➡

20

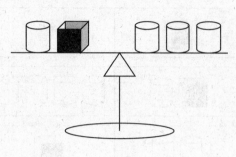

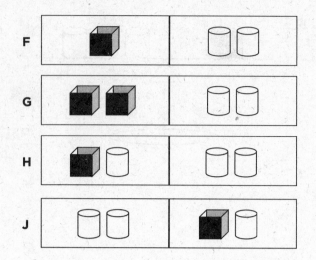

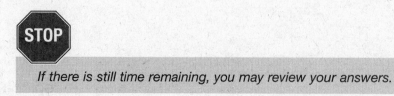

If there is still time remaining, you may review your answers.

#1–20   15 MINUTES

> **Directions:** For questions 1–5, find the word that names a necessary part of the underlined word.

1 <u>painting</u>

    A brush
    B color
    C paint
    D canvas

2 <u>university</u>

    F dormitory
    G students
    H organizations
    J tower

3 <u>tuxedo</u>

    A jacket
    B dance
    C corsage
    D black

4 <u>imagination</u>

    F thought
    G books
    H pictures
    J stories

5 <u>music</u>

    A notation
    B strings
    C song
    D sound

> **Directions:** For questions 6–10, choose the word that is most like the underlined words.

6 <u>telephone</u>   <u>radio</u>   <u>megaphone</u>

    F telegraph
    G microphone
    H fax
    J e-mail

7 <u>physics</u>   <u>chemistry</u>   <u>biology</u>

    A botany
    B plants
    C theory
    D science

8 <u>photograph</u>   <u>painting</u>   <u>movie</u>

    F portrait
    G novel
    H song
    J radio

GO TO NEXT PAGE ➡

9   cream   milk   cheese

A   lemonade
B   butter
C   cow
D   skim

10   address   recite   lecture

F   debate
G   narrate
H   display
J   perform

Directions: For questions 11–15, choose the word that does *not* belong.

---

11   A   foe
     B   rival
     C   enemy
     D   spy

12   F   pigeon
     G   bird
     H   cardinal
     J   dove

13   A   break
     B   fraction
     C   piece
     D   section

14   F   discard
     G   reject
     H   acquire
     J   eliminate

15   A   employ
     B   job
     C   use
     D   hire

Directions: In questions 16–20, the words in the top row are related. The words in the bottom row are related in a similar way. Choose the word that completes the sequence in the bottom row.

16

grizzly	polar	black
orange	lemon	_____

F   panda
G   grapefruit
H   banana
J   apple

17

baseball	bowling ball	basketball
bicycle	truck	_____

A   tricycle
B   bus
C   car
D   taxi cab

GO TO NEXT PAGE ➡

18

rooster	hen	chick
_____	goose	gosling

F   drake
G   gander
H   swan
J   gooster

19

teenager	toddler	infant
delta	beta	_____

A   alpha
B   epsilon
C   pi
D   omega

20

zebra	tiger	skunk
cheetah	leopard	_____

F   dalmatian
G   referee
H   toucan
J   clown fish

STOP

If there is still time remaining, you may review your answers.

#1–10   7 MINUTES

Directions: For these questions, find the statement that is true according to the given information.

---

1 Mrs. Julian listens to country music on her car radio. When Mr. Julian borrowed her car, he switched the radio to a classical station. Mrs. Julian switched it back to country the next day.

A   Mr. Julian's car needed repairs.
B   Mr. and Mrs. Julian have different tastes in music.
C   Mr. Julian is in trouble.
D   Mrs. Julian dislikes having her radio station changed.

2 Mel enjoys watching cartoons in the morning. *The Roadrunner Show* comes on at 8:00 A.M. Mel slept until noon.

F   *The Roadrunner Show* does not run on Saturday.
G   Mel did not feel well that morning.
H   Mel did not watch *The Roadrunner Show* that morning.
J   Mel does not like *The Roadrunner Show*.

3 Tina is writing a book. She is trying to find someone to illustrate it. She has not found an appropriate illustrator yet.

A   Tina is a published author.
B   Tina is writing a children's book.
C   Tina does not consider herself an appropriate illustrator.
D   Tina's book does not require illustrations.

4 Anna takes French, Jeanna takes Spanish, and Nora takes Latin. Their father is a mathematician. Their mother and brother are musicians.

F   Anna, Jeanna, and Nora do not like math or music.
G   Their father is a math teacher.
H   Anna, Nora, and Jeanna are sisters.
J   Their brother is a singer.

5 Mrs. Greene bakes birthday cakes for our staff. Charlie gets his cake from her every September. His favorite is chocolate.

A   Mrs. Greene baked a chocolate cake for Charlie.
B   Charlie's birthday is in September.
C   Mrs. Greene is a professional baker.
D   Only one member of our staff got a cake in September.

6 Michael's favorite book is *Cheaper by the Dozen*. His teacher read it to his class in seventh grade. He did not enjoy the new movie version.

F   The movie version of the book had a sad ending.
G   The movie and the book are different.
H   Michael no longer likes the story.
J   Michael always thinks the book versions are superior.

GO TO NEXT PAGE ➡

7   Mrs. Donne is having a baby. If it's a girl, she's going to name her Emily Elizabeth. If it's a boy, she wants to name him John.

   A   Mrs. Donne is having twins.
   B   Mrs. Donne does not know whether she is having a girl or a boy.
   C   Mrs. Donne prefers to be surprised when her baby is born.
   D   Mrs. Donne is always prepared.

8   All Alphas wear gray clothing all the time. All Deltas wear khaki exclusively. Lenina makes a point to wear green.

   F   Lenina is not an Alpha or a Delta.
   G   Lenina is rebellious.
   H   Lenina looks best in green.
   J   Lenina is a Beta.

9   Barbara and Ernest go for a walk every day at 6:00. We often see them when we walk our dog. Our dog loves to visit Barbara.

   A   Barbara babysits our dog.
   B   Ernest enjoys exercise.
   C   We often walk around 6:00.
   D   We all walk after dinner.

10   Amanda is scheduled to volunteer one day a week at a daycare center. On Wednesday, she and the toddlers played with clay. Exactly one week before, she helped the children paint.

   F   Amanda is an artist.
   G   Amanda's volunteer day is Wednesday.
   H   Amanda has several jobs.
   J   Amanda loves clay and paint.

If there is still time remaining, you may review your answers.

TEST 6 READING AND LANGUAGE ARTS

#1–40   40 MINUTES

> **Directions:** For questions 1–40, read each passage and the questions following that passage. Find the answer.

PASSAGE FOR QUESTIONS 1–6

In 2002, Americans spent a whopping $6.6 billion on kitchen renovations. They also spent a total of $433 million on cookbooks that specialized in making dishes out of specialized items like berries, cherries, and lemons. Increasingly people <u>patronized</u> food stores that offered gourmet items such as cilantro, jicama, chorizo, fresh ginger, and dried chilis. TV networks catered to the new culinary fad by adding cable stations that offered lessons on how to prepare filet mignon and other fancy dishes 24/7.

Yet, despite their purchases and alleged interest in home cooking, America is becoming a "take-out nation." Americans are more likely to read their cookbooks at bedtime than use them to prepare meals. People gaze fondly at the carefully arranged rows of jicama and ginger on their way to the deli counter where they purchase store-brand meals—like fried chicken and mashed potatoes or rotisserie chicken with potato salad. Or, they hop over to a restaurant, or even a fast food joint, and skip the supermarket altogether.

People vigorously defend their paradoxical actions. Some people claim they want to try adventurous foods—like sushi—that they don't trust themselves to prepare at home. Others point to differing gustatory tastes of their family members: mom and dad like it spicy, but the kids like it bland; takeout easily accommodates all diners. Those who are single argue that cooking for themselves is simply not cost-effective. Some simply say despairingly that they don't have the time to do their own cooking. Still others grow defiant; they point out that they can afford to have others prepare food for them.

For whatever reasons, now more than ever, Americans seem to desire the luxury of the home-cooked meal—but not so greatly that they will set aside time to prepare it.

1 Which of the following would publish the above article?

  A the newest edition of Rachel Ray's Cookbook

  B the Leisure and Popular Culture section of weekly news magazines like *Newsweek*

  C *Scientific American Magazine*

  D the *TV Guide*

2 The author of this piece intends _____.

  F to make fun of Americans

  G to praise Americans

  H to reform Americans

  J to point out an ironic paradox about Americans

3 What is the best definition of the word <u>patronized</u>, based on the use of the word in the reading passage?

  A to look down upon the person with whom you are speaking

  B to support a cause, usually with monetary donations

  C to use the services of, usually in connection with acquiring supplies

  D It is impossible to answer this question based on the information in the passage.

GO TO NEXT PAGE ➡

4 What does the author say is ironic about America's recent food purchases?

  F Americans, by and large, support super-sized fast food meals despite the threat to their waistline.

  G Americans like to try different foods— like sushi—but are worried about preparing them at home.

  H Americans have bought supplies that would allow them to prepare nutritious, gourmet meals at home, yet they continue to buy fast food and prepackaged items.

  J Americans keep buying items like jicama without knowing what these items are.

5 Which of the following sentences is written correctly?

  A Many American's get their recipes from the backs of boxes.

  B One of my favorite recipes are the apple pie made without apples.

  C Whom has ever tried this recipe?

  D Someday when I have time, I will make this pie.

Read the following baking directions and answer the question that follows.

  A Bake in a 350-degree oven for 50 minutes.

  B Boil the water and sugar until it forms a syrup.

  C Add this to the crust and crackers, along with butter, cinnamon, and your favorite spices.

  D Break the crackers into the pie crust.

6 What is the best order for these directions?

  F A, B, C, D

  G D, B, C, A

  H B, A, D, C

  J B, C, A, D

GO TO NEXT PAGE ➡

PASSAGE FOR QUESTIONS 7–13

As early as 1786, people set off in search of the great and <u>lucrative</u> Northwest Passage. This fabled water route allegedly connected the Atlantic and Pacific Oceans, and people hoped that such a passage would open up valuable trade markets. A Northwest Passage, after all, would make travel from East to West much easier, safer, and more affordable. Explorers like Christopher Columbus, Ferdinand Magellan, and Ponce de Leon all spent their lives searching fruitlessly for the Northwest Passage, although they did find substitute good stuff along the way—like the rich land west of the Mississippi prime for America settlement. Eventually, people gave up on ever finding a Northwest Passage.

Finally, when people least expected it, Norwegian Roald Mundsen discovered a Northwest Passage. He found it less than a century ago, at about the same time the U.S. government was making plans to dig the Panama Canal. Unfortunately, what Mundsen found was not an answer to travelers'—and merchants'—prayers. The Passage, nestled between Canada's mainland and some of its Arctic islands, still remained inconvenient, and ice often blocked the way. Easy travel remained nearly impossible. Once and for all, therefore, people at last abandoned the idea of using a Northwest Passage. Instead, they chose to create the initially costly, but ultimately practical, water route now known as the Panama Canal.

7 Which of the following sentences is written correctly?

  A Marco Polo brought spices from China to europe in the 13th century, starting a great demand for more.

  B Spices were not simply ingredients for food, they were used for medicine, perfume, and even currency.

  C Finding a quick water route to China, Japan, and India.

  D Christopher Columbus found great inspiration in the writings of Marco Polo.

8 According to the author, which of the following people actually discovered the Northwest Passage?

  F Christopher Columbus
  G Ferdinand Magellan
  H Ponce de Leon
  J Roald Mundsen

9 The author's main purpose in writing is to _____.

  A belittle the contributions of men like Columbus, Magellan, and de Leon

  B illustrate how dangerous and inconvenient travel routes once were

  C explain where the designer label for Northwest Passage clothing came from

  D point out that when we finally found the great Northwest Passage, we no longer wanted it

10 We can infer, based on the passage above, that the author thinks that _____.

  F had people never discovered the Northwest Passage, it would not have greatly affected human activity

  G because we finally discovered the Northwest Passage, we at last became able to realize our highest trade-based hopes

  H using the Panama Canal turned out to be one of the worst decisions ever made by Americans

  J we wasted a great deal of time exploring the Americas for the Northwest Passage

GO TO NEXT PAGE ➡

11 The author's use of the word lucrative is best described as _____.

   A filthy
   B creepy
   C wealthy
   D slow

12 Which sentence is written correctly?

   F Many explorers spent their lives searching fruitlessly for the Northwest Passage.
   G Many explorers spent they're lives searching fruitlessly for the Northwest Passage.
   H Many explorers spend his or her lives searching fruitlessly for the Northwest Passage.
   J Many explorers spend their lives searching fruitless for the Northwest Passage.

13 What is the best way to combine the following two sentences?

The bluish glow of electricity that appears on ships during storms is called Saint Elmo's Fire. Saint Elmo is the patron saint of sailors.

   A Named for the patron saint of sailors, Saint Elmo's Fire is the bluish glow of electricity that appears on ships during storms.
   B The bluish glow that appears on ships during storms is called Saint Elmo's Fire, moreover Saint Elmo is the patron saint of sailors.
   C The patron saint of sailors, St. Elmo, has a fire on ships during storms that is actually an electric bluish glow.
   D The electric bluish glow on ships during storms is called Saint Elmo's Fire, the patron saint of sailors.

GO TO NEXT PAGE ➡

_____. A good example of a palindrome is the following slogan: A man, a plan, a canal—Panama! The very first palindrome is purported to have been uttered by the first man to the first woman: "Madam, I'm Adam."

14 What is the best topic sentence for the above paragraph?

   F Palindromes!

   G What is a palindrome?

   H Sentences that read the same backward and forward are called palindromes.

   J Many people are searching for an example of a palindrome.

15 What is the best way to write the following sentence?

   A The first palindrome is purported to be uttered by the first man to the first woman.

   B The first palindrome was purported to had been uttered by the first man to the first woman.

   C The first palindrome is purportedly uttered by the first man to the first woman.

   D The first palindrome is purported to have been uttered by the first man to the first woman.

16 Which of the following sentences is written correctly?

   F We do not have the original journal of Christopher Columbus; what we do have is a summary made from a copy.

   G Its filled with errors and inconsistencies; some people think Columbus wrote it in code to hide his discoveries.

   H No one seems to consider that the journal could of been a forgery.

   J Regardless, it seems that Columbus was neither saint or villain.

GO TO NEXT PAGE ➡

PASSAGE FOR QUESTIONS 17–21

Current writers of American history seem determined to prove that our Founding Fathers were not as nice as we always thought they were. College freshmen are soon told, for example, that the Pilgrims did more than fight for the right to worship God their way—they also committed fraud and kidnapping to ensure that right. Students convinced of the noble, hard-working nature of early American settlers soon discover that many such colonists came from the <u>dregs</u> of British society (some from prisons, others from brothels), that many came to America merely to find gold, and that some ruthlessly <u>desecrated</u> Native American graves (which often held food offerings) when supplies ran short.

But even young children are getting the harsh news these days. Booksellers report a spike in purchases of children's history books—the type that tell the nitty gritty details. Children as young as 10 and 11 now have access to tales that relate interesting details like the fact that William Howard Taft was so fat that he needed a specially built oversized bathtub or that George Washington was toothless and required ivory dentures. These kids also can easily find out that many American presidents owned slaves (George Washington attempted to avoid the dentures by transplanting nine teeth—extracted from his slaves' mouths—first) and had affairs (like Thomas Jefferson, who somehow produced six kids after the death of his wife).

Some parents support the idea of raising children on fact rather than fantasy. But perhaps the real on-going debate should center around not whether people should know the truth about popular cultural figures—but when they should be told and by whom.

17 Which opinion do you think the author holds?

 A Children need to be sheltered from the truth, even when the truth needs to be told.

 B Children need to be told the truth, at as early an age as possible.

 C Children need to be told the truth, but careful attention should be paid to determining when to tell them.

 D Children can never accept the truth, given their inability to understand deep topics.

18 Based on the context of this passage, to which of the following words is the word <u>dregs</u> similar?

 F upper class
 G middle class
 H lower class
 J criminal class

19 According to the passage, which person removed teeth from slaves in an attempt to make dentures?

 A Taft
 B Washington
 C Jefferson
 D Bush

20 The author most likely intends _____.

 F to challenge children to find out as much as they can about the "dirty" side of history

 G to challenge parents to reevaluate their child-rearing habits

 H to convince people to cover up uncomfortable details about our past

 J to revise current definitions of historical accuracy in research

21 Based on the use of the word in this passage, how would one best define the word desecrated?

 A ransacked
 B opened
 C plowed
 D moved

GO TO NEXT PAGE →

Doctors have frequently enjoyed a reputation of being miracle workers—and no wonder. Their very lives are miraculous, when you consider the hours they work. <u>Residency</u> interns, for example, have historically shouldered a workload averaging 90 hours (or more) per week, a burdensome total by most people's standard. Johns Hopkins Hospital set these expectations back in 1899, although they were not seen as particularly abusive. Back then, after all, the term *residency* meant what it implied—that doctors in training actually lived on hospital premises. But, times have changed. Doctors no longer live at hospitals; they commute, often long distances.

Our exhausted doctors find themselves having to care for increasingly delicate patients. As recently as the 1960s, people visited the hospital and endured long periods of observation and treatment when stricken by illnesses we now consider "out-patient" cases. Newly delivered mothers, for example, stayed in the hospital for a week; now they stay a maximum of two days. Heart attack patients stayed for observation for three weeks; nowadays, they rarely stay three hours. Today, patients who stay in the hospital for long periods of time are far more ill than their counterparts back in the 1960s.

Administrators became concerned that sleep deprivation among the doctors coupled with the more precarious state of the patients themselves was resulting in more, often deadly, mistakes in hospital care. Therefore, the Accreditation Council for Graduate Medical Education has decided medical residents can only work an eighty-hour work-week with no one working more than thirty hours at a stretch. While these hours may still seem abusive, they represent a decided improvement over the past.

22 The word <u>residency</u>, as used in this passage, refers to the fact that _____.

F   doctors have always commuted to work

G   doctors in training traditionally lived at their place of study

H   doctors have always suffered from sleep deprivation

J   doctors need more medical reform to assist them in helping others

23 The main idea of this passage can best be described as _____.

A   sleep deprivation among medical staff has quadrupled since 1910

B   medical training dates back to the 1890s at Johns Hopkins Hospital

C   everyone is concerned that the safety of patients is in the hands of exhausted nursing staff

D   no one is totally satisfied with current medical regulations, but they are an improvement over the past

GO TO NEXT PAGE ➡

24 One can infer from the message of paragraph three that _____.

    F people recover faster from illness

    G people are forced to leave hospitals at a faster rate than at any other time in history

    H people are no longer forced to stay in hospitals longer than advances in treatment require

    J people no longer consider illnesses such as heart attacks deadly

25 According to the passage, the Accreditation Council for Graduate Medical Education requires a(n) __ hour work-week with no one working more than __ hours at a stretch.

    A 90 . . . 36

    B 36 . . . 90

    C 30 . . . 80

    D 80 . . . 30

26 How long, according to the passage, do doctors hold heart attack victims for observation?

    F 3 days

    G 3 hours

    H depends on the seriousness of the case

    J The article does not state.

PASSAGE FOR QUESTIONS 27–32

American parents have grown increasingly anxious to help their kids succeed in life. They provide classical music for the fetus *in utero*, buy specially constructed educational toys for preschool kids, and start working with flashcards as early as age five. Is all the fuss paying off?

Many child experts say no, that there appears to be "no advantage" to pushing kids to achieve ahead of schedule. Despite our best intentions, they say, we are in fact teaching them to be perfectionists focused on the future who lack the ability to enjoy the present.

For those who remain unconvinced, consider the (granted, extreme) case of John Stuart Mill, a child pushed by the age of three to learn to read and speak Latin and Greek and who wrote a compelling dissertation by the age of eight. He won himself a stint in a padded cell before he reached adulthood.

27 The author most likely meant to express which of the following statements?

    A We should push our kids to achieve great things—no matter what the cost.

    B Kids need time to learn, grow, and experience life, without being forced to follow a schedule.

    C While kids need discipline and education, they also need balance with paid, skilled activity.

    D There is no advantage to rush the development of children; indeed there are many severe disadvantages to doing so.

28 What does the phrase *in utero* mean?

    F It refers to an album by the group Nirvana.

    G It refers to the gestational growth required by the human birthing process spent in the human uterus.

    H It refers to the Latin phrase "for the sake of usefulness."

    J We cannot tell from the information given.

GO TO NEXT PAGE ➡

29 Why does the author use the example of John Stuart Mill in the last paragraph?

A as an example of how pushing children too hard can create severe complications in the child

B as an example of how pushing children to achieve can greatly enhance their life experiences

C as an example of how not interfering with the natural course of child-rearing can benefit all involved

D as an example of how waiting until the teen years to begin educating the child is a sensible plan of action

30 By what age did John Stuart Mill learn Greek?

F 2

G 3

H 4

J 5

31 Choose the sentence that is written correctly.

A John Stuart Mill, and Jeremy Bentham devoted their life to social improvement.

B Their philosophy centered on one goal; happiness for the greatest number of people.

C Ironically, Mill found that he himself was not happy.

D Poetry, after having a nervous breakdown, brought him comfort.

32 Choose the best combination of the following sentences.

John Stuart Mill wrote *The Subjection of Women*. In it, he argues passionately for equality for women in all aspects of life.

F In John Stuart Mill's *The Subjection of Women*, he argues passionately for equality for women in all aspects of life.

G John Stuart Mill, author of *The Subjection of Women*, argues passionately in his book for equality for women in all, not just some, aspects of life.

H Equality for women (in all aspects of life) is argued passionately in John Stuart Mill's *The Subjection of Women*.

J In John Stuart Mill's *The Subjection of Women*, he argues passionate that, in all aspects of life, equality is for women.

GO TO NEXT PAGE ➡

By 750 A.D. Muslims had conquered the south and east portions of the Mediterranean area and parts of Spain and had begun pushing north and eastward into Mesopotamia and Persia. Their success can be attributed to various sources. First, the Byzantine and Persian empires had been exhausted by a long period of strife between the Byzantine Emperor Heraclius and the Persian King Chosroes II. Second, the Christian community in the region was divided against itself.

The immediate effect of the Muslim dominance in the Mediterranean was the rise of Western Europe as a distinctive cultural entity. Western Europeans fell back to their own resources and began to develop their own heritage in conjunction with the already existing Germanic and Graeco–Roman cultural foundations. Conversely, cultural centers along the Mediterranean declined, and cities sprang up in direct consequence more toward the interior of the lands lining the sea. Farming became self-reliant and self-regulated, and general exploration in the area ceased. Consequently, the student of history sees a division of culture beginning at this point.

33 In what sort of publication would this text most likely appear?

    A   a literary magazine
    B   a history book
    C   a poetry journal
    D   a science text

34 The word ceased as used in context of this passage most likely means which of the following?

    F   began
    G   continued
    H   waned
    J   ended

35 Which conflict helps account for the rise of Muslim power by 750 A.D.?

    A   the rise of Western Europe and the fall of Eastern Europe
    B   the relationship between Heraclius and Chosroes II
    C   the northward push into Mesopotamia and the southward push into Spain
    D   None of the above.

36 How did farming change during the time period this article discusses?

    F   Farmers began looking to the government for assistance.
    G   Farmers began to rule themselves.
    H   Farmers began exploring in addition to maintaining their agricultural duties.
    J   None of the above.

37 Which of the following careers would *not* be able to use the information presented above?

    A   doctor
    B   teacher
    C   writer
    D   historian

GO TO NEXT PAGE ➡

PASSAGE FOR QUESTIONS 38–40

There's nothing new under the sun. Apparently Shakespeare was right. Again. Some scientists claim, for example, that the West Nile virus, so frightening to so many recently, is no new thing.

Almost 3,000 years ago, Alexander the Great died a feverish death; until now, scientists had put out various theories—that he had died from malaria, from typhoid, or from poisoning. But recent study of the West Nile virus has many scientists putting out the theory that he died from the West Nile virus.

The facts are rather persuasive. Alexander was living in an area <u>plagued</u> by mosquitoes, a common carrier of the West Nile virus. Apparently Alexander witnessed a large number of ravens and "some of them fell dead before him"; we know that the West Nile virus can be fatal to and carried by crows, a relation of ravens. Finally, Alexander the Great was said to have suffered fever and paralysis prior to his death, both symptoms of the West Nile virus.

38 In what sort of publication are you most likely to find this article?

F almanac
G *Guinness Book of World Records*
H the popular science section of your local newspaper
J a journal that publishes articles about Greek and Latin literature

39 The word <u>plagued</u>, based on its use here, is best defined as _____.

A lacking in
B inhabited
C overrun
D made free of

40 Of which of the following have people thought Alexander the Great died?

F malaria
G polio
H strangulation
J AIDS

If there is still time remaining, you may review your answers.

#1–40   35 MINUTES

> **Directions:** Select the best answer from the given choices.

1 Find the value of $\dfrac{3^9}{4 \cdot 3^7}$.

   A 2.25

   B 2.15

   C 3.25

   D 3^2

2 *ABCD* is a parallelogram. The measure of $\angle FAB = 39°$. Find the measure of $\angle BCE$.

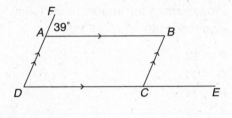

   F 141°

   G 78°

   H 39°

   J 57°

3 Represent the area of a triangle with a base of $2x + y$ and a height of $4z$.

   A $2z(2x + y)$

   B $2x(z + y)$

   C $2xyz$

   D $z(2x + y)$

4 Which number is next in the following series?

1,000, 200, 40, 8, . . .

   F 1.6

   G 2.2

   H 2.6

   J 1.8

5 Dwayne was on a diet. When he weighed himself at the start of his diet, Dwayne weighed 215 pounds. At the end of three months, Dwayne weighed 175 pounds. What fraction of his original weight did he lose? Reduce to lowest terms.

   A $\dfrac{8}{43}$

   B $\dfrac{9}{36}$

   C $\dfrac{7}{29}$

   D $\dfrac{9}{35}$

6 Find the value of *x* in the figure below.

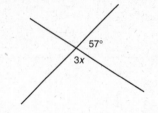

   F 57°

   G 41°

   H 39°

   J 3°

7 $6\dfrac{2}{3} \times 5\dfrac{1}{4} =$

   A $5\dfrac{1}{2}$

   B 16

   C 23

   D 35

GO TO NEXT PAGE ➡

8 The Kanakee Eagles scored 12, 7, 10, 6, and 9 runs in their last 5 games. If they want to maintain an average of 9 runs per game for 6 games, how much do they have to score on their next game?

F 4
G 10
H 8
J 6

9 Which of the the following expressions is the **smallest**?

A $4^2 + 5(9 - 3)$
B $3 \cdot 17 - 4 \cdot 6$
C $7 + 9 \cdot 4 - 6(9 - 7)^3$
D $6 - 2 + \dfrac{48}{6}$

10 Find the shaded area in the figure below.

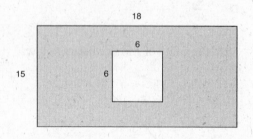

F 234
G 123
H 342
J 188

11 A ticket to the movies is $8 right now. If the price increases 7% this year and 5% the following year, how much will a movie ticket cost at the end of two years? Round off to the nearest cent.

A $10.18
B $10.82
C $9.85
D $8.99

12 Two-fifths of what number subtracted from 18 is equal to 4 more than two-thirds of 6?

F 4
G 12
H 25
J 32

13 Melissa drives from Central City to Marbury, a distance of 154 miles. If she leaves Central City at 8 A.M. and arrives in Marbury at 10:45 A.M., what is her average rate of speed?

A 56 mph
B 39 mph
C 48 mph
D 62 mph

14 Find the missing number in the following expression: $6(? + 5) - 3 = 135$.

F 12
G 23
H 18
J 15

15 Six times a certain number is 24.72. What is the result if we divide that original number by 4?

A 2.4
B 1.03
C 2.35
D 1.8

16 The perimeter of a ranch is 23,760 feet. If Lois walks at the rate of 3 miles per hour, how long will it take for her to walk around the ranch?

F 2 hours
G 2.5 hours
H 1 hour
J 1.5 hours

GO TO NEXT PAGE ➡

17 Hector is putting together a package that weighs 5 pounds 6 ounces. If he removes several items and reduces the weight of the package by 2 pounds 9 ounces, how much does the new package weigh?

   A   3 pounds 4 ounces
   B   2 pounds 13 ounces
   C   3 pounds 8 ounces
   D   4 pounds 7 ounces

18 Solve for the positive value of x in the equation $2x^2 + 4 = 76$.

   F   2
   G   3
   H   5
   J   6

19 Tanika receives a base salary of $300 per week plus an 8% commission on sales over $2,000 for the week. If she sold $3,500 for the week, what was her total salary?

   A $460
   B $560
   C $480
   D $420

20 The average monthly prices for a gallon of regular gasoline are shown in the graph below.

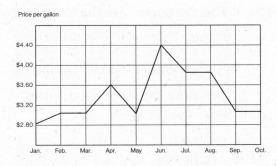

Find the average price of a gallon of gasoline for the months of April and August.

   F $3.90
   G $3.70
   H $4.10
   J $3.60

21 Estimate the product of 34 and 68.

   A   1,800
   B   2,900
   C   3,100
   D   2,100

22 Compare the areas of the following figures.

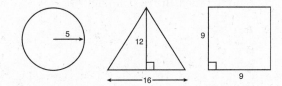

   F   The area of the square is greater than the area of the triangle.
   G   The area of the triangle is less than the area of the circle.
   H   The difference between the area of the triangle and the area of the circle is greater than the area of the square.
   J   The area of the circle is less than the area of the triangle.

23 What number is 6 more than $\frac{1}{8}$ of 40?

   A   15
   B   11
   C   14
   D   13

24 What is the distance from point A (5, 4) to point B (5, –3)?

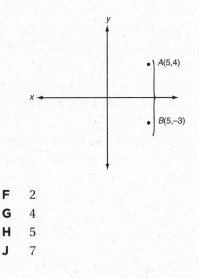

   F   2
   G   4
   H   5
   J   7

GO TO NEXT PAGE ➡

25 In circle O at the right, $CO = 3a$.

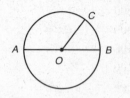

Find the measure of diameter AB.

A $3a$
B a
C $6a$
D $2a$

26 The bar graph summarizes the number of cartoons, dramas, and comedies produced in the United States in the years 2001–2003. Use the information provided in the bar graph to determine which of the following statements is false.

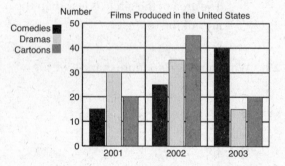

F The number of cartoons in 2003 is fewer than the number of dramas in 2001.
G The number of cartoons in 2001 is fewer than the number of dramas in 2002.
H The number of dramas in 2003 is greater than the number of comedies in 2001.
J The number of comedies in 2002 is greater than the number of cartoons in 2003.

27 Represent the statement "r varies directly as the square of s and inversely as t."

A $rs^2 = kt$
B $rs = kt^2$
C $r = \dfrac{ks^2}{t}$
D $kr = \dfrac{s^2}{t}$

28 What happens to the volume of a cube when each side is doubled?

F multiplied by 8
G doubled
H tripled
J quadrupled

29 Examine these three figures and choose the best answer.

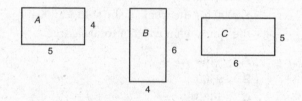

A Area C is smaller than area A.
B Area A is larger than area B.
C Area B is smaller than area C.
D All three areas are the same.

30 Ruben, Shelly, and Malcolm have recorded a hit song. Ruben gets $\frac{2}{5}$ of the income, Shelly gets $\frac{1}{3}$, and Malcolm gets the rest. If they earn $300,000, how much does Malcolm get?

F $80,000
G $250,000
H $210,000
J $90,000

GO TO NEXT PAGE ➡

31 Sides AB and BC in isosceles $\triangle ABC$ are equal in measure. If the exterior angle at C measures 96°, find the measure of angle B.

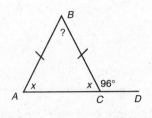

A 18°
B 24°
C 12°
D 16°

32 In the following diagrams, circle O has a radius of 5 and triangle RST has sides of 5 and 12 and a hypotenuse of 13. The circumference of a circle, C, is equal to $2\pi r$ and the area of a circle, A_C, is equal to πr^2. In both of these cases, $\pi = 3.14$ and $r =$ the radius. The area of a triangle, A_T, is equal to $\frac{1}{2} bh$, where $b =$ base and $h =$ height.

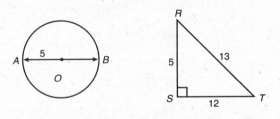

Which of the following statements is true?

F The area of triangle $RST < \frac{1}{2}$ area of circle O.

G The circumference of the circle < the perimeter of triangle RST.

H The area of the circle + the area of the triangle < 100.

J The circumference of the circle – the perimeter of the triangle > 2.

33 If x and y are negative integers and $y > x$, which of the following statements is true?

A $xy < 0$
B $x + y > 0$
C $xy > 0$
D $y - x < 0$

34 What is the least common multiple of 18 and 27?

F 36
G 18
H 9
J 54

35 Find $16\frac{2}{3}\%$ of 360.

A 45
B 60
C 40
D 35

36 The area of a circle inscribed in a square is approximately $\frac{3}{4}$ of the area of the square. Estimate the area of a circle inscribed in a square whose side is 6.2.

F 35
G 27
H 21
J 40

GO TO NEXT PAGE ➡

37 Which one of the following statements is true?

A Nine $0.15 stamps plus six $0.37 stamps cost more than five $0.65 stamps.

B Sixteen $0.15 stamps plus eight $0.37 stamps is less than seven $0.30 stamps plus nine $0.24 stamps.

C Four $0.30 stamps plus five $0.37 stamps cost more than thirteen $0.15 stamps and eight $0.24 stamps.

D Seven $0.24 stamps plus twelve $0.30 stamps cost $0.45 less than four $0.37 stamps

38 Find the total number of interior degrees in the angles of an octagon.

F 540°
G 360°
H 720°
J 1080°

39 From the Venn diagram below, what conclusion can we draw?

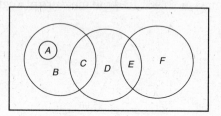

A All members of set *F* are members of set *E*.

B All members of set *C* are members of set *E*.

C Some members of set *D* are members of set *F*.

D Some members of set *B* are members of set *E*.

40 The circle graph indicates how the average high school student spends her/his 24-hour day. How many hours does the average student spend on personal items?

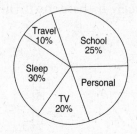

F 4.2 hours
G 2.7 hours
H 1.9 hours
J 3.6 hours

STOP

If there is still time remaining, you may review your answers.

ANSWER KEY
COOP Practice Exam 1

TEST 1   SEQUENCES

1. **B**	6. **J**	11. **B**	16. **J**
2. **H**	7. **B**	12. **F**	17. **D**
3. **D**	8. **G**	13. **B**	18. **F**
4. **F**	9. **B**	14. **F**	19. **D**
5. **C**	10. **F**	15. **B**	20. **H**

TEST 2   ANALOGIES

1. **C**	6. **G**	11. **C**	16. **H**
2. **G**	7. **A**	12. **J**	17. **B**
3. **A**	8. **H**	13. **D**	18. **G**
4. **F**	9. **A**	14. **F**	19. **B**
5. **D**	10. **J**	15. **A**	20. **J**

TEST 3   QUANTITATIVE REASONING

1. **C**	6. **G**	11. **C**	16. **J**
2. **H**	7. **C**	12. **H**	17. **B**
3. **D**	8. **J**	13. **A**	18. **F**
4. **J**	9. **A**	14. **G**	19. **C**
5. **A**	10. **J**	15. **B**	20. **F**

TEST 4   VERBAL REASONING—WORDS

1. **C**	6. **G**	11. **D**	16. **G**
2. **G**	7. **A**	12. **G**	17. **B**
3. **A**	8. **F**	13. **A**	18. **G**
4. **F**	9. **B**	14. **H**	19. **A**
5. **D**	10. **G**	15. **B**	20. **F**

ANSWER KEY
COOP Practice Exam 1

TEST 5   VERBAL REASONING—CONTEXT

1. **B**	4. **H**	7. **B**	10. **G**
2. **H**	5. **B**	8. **F**	
3. **C**	6. **G**	9. **C**	

TEST 6   READING AND LANGUAGE ARTS

1. **B**	11. **C**	21. **A**	31. **C**
2. **J**	12. **F**	22. **G**	32. **F**
3. **C**	13. **A**	23. **D**	33. **B**
4. **H**	14. **H**	24. **H**	34. **J**
5. **D**	15. **D**	25. **D**	35. **B**
6. **G**	16. **F**	26. **G**	36. **G**
7. **D**	17. **C**	27. **D**	37. **A**
8. **J**	18. **J**	28. **G**	38. **H**
9. **D**	19. **B**	29. **A**	39. **C**
10. **F**	20. **G**	30. **G**	40. **F**

TEST 7   MATHEMATICS

1. **A**	11. **D**	21. **D**	31. **C**
2. **H**	12. **H**	22. **J**	32. **F**
3. **A**	13. **A**	23. **B**	33. **C**
4. **F**	14. **H**	24. **J**	34. **J**
5. **A**	15. **B**	25. **C**	35. **B**
6. **G**	16. **J**	26. **H**	36. **G**
7. **D**	17. **B**	27. **C**	37. **A**
8. **G**	18. **J**	28. **F**	38. **J**
9. **C**	19. **D**	29. **C**	39. **C**
10. **F**	20. **G**	30. **F**	40. **J**

ANSWERS EXPLAINED

Test 1   Sequences

1. **(B)** The objects move left, one at a time.

2. **(H)** The dark circle moves clockwise.

3. **(D)** The objects are arranged in size: small, large, small, large, small.

4. **(F)** The small black rectangles move clockwise, only within the large left rectangle.

5. **(C)** The polygons are arranged in order of sides: triangle (three sides), quadrilateral (four sides), hexagon (six sides).

6. **(J)** The open and closed circles reverse after being flipped over the horizontal line.

7. **(B)** The dark triangle moves counterclockwise.

8. **(G)** The letters are listed in backwards alphabetical order, with one letter skipped between groups.

9. **(B)** The letters are listed in alphabetical order. One letter is skipped between the first and second letters of each group and two letters are skipped between the second and third letters in each group.

10. **(F)** M is the middle letter in each group and one letter is skipped between the first and third letters in each group.

11. **(B)** One letter is skipped between the first and second letters. Three letters are skipped between the second and third letters.

12. **(F)** The letters are in alphabetical sequence. The subscripts are increasing and the last subscript in the earlier group is repeated in the following group.

13. **(B)** The letters are listed in backwards alphabetical sequence, and one letter is skipped between each group.

14. **(F)** Skip one letter between groups and one letter between the second and third letters within each group. The subscripts are increasing by one.

15. **(B)** The numerical sequence is $+2, +3$.

16. **(J)** Just add 5 to the preceding Roman numeral.

17. **(D)** The sequence is $+3, -1$.

18. **(F)** The sequence is $1^1, 1^2, 1^3, 2^1, 2^2, 2^3, 3^1, 3^2, 3^3, 4^1, 4^2, 4^3 (=64)$.

19. **(D)** To derive the second and third members of each group, divide the preceding number by 2.

20. **(H)** The sequence in each group is $+4, +5$.

Test 2   Analogies

1. **(C)** Tire is to car as horseshoe is to horse. A car rides along tires, and a horse must be shod.

2. **(G)** Brick is to building as cell is to human. A building is constructed from bricks, and a human is made of cells.

3. **(A)** Announcer is to radio as actress is to the Broadway stage. The announcer is the chief character on the radio, and the actress is the heart of the Broadway stage.

4. **(F)** Chef is to soup as scientist is to chemical experiment. A chef makes soup, and a scientist develops an experiment.

5. **(D)** Dancer is to shoes as magician is to wand. A dancer needs a pair of shoes, and a magician needs a wand.

6. **(G)** Bat is to baseball as basketball is to basket. You score by hitting the baseball and by throwing the basketball into the basket.

7. **(A)** Sun is to sundial as battery is to flashlight. The sundial and the flashlight are dependent upon the sun and a battery, respectively.

8. **(H)** Fork is to cake as spoon is to ice cream. Cake is eaten with a fork. Ice cream is eaten with a spoon.

9. **(A)** Mouse is to cat as worm is to fish. Cats eat mice, and fish eat worms.

10. **(J)** Coat is to woman as paint is to house. A coat covers a woman, and paint covers a house.

11. **(C)** Stamp is to envelope as ticket is to movies. A stamp is the price of mailing an envelope, and a ticket is the price of admission to a movie.

12. **(J)** Horse and buggy is to car as piper cub airplane is to rocket. The horse and buggy preceded the car, and the piper cub airplane preceded the rocket.

13. **(D)** Sail is to sailboat as tire is to car. A wind on the sail drives the boat as the tires move the car.

14. **(F)** Cherries are to trees as tooth is to mouth. Cherries are found on a tree, and teeth are found in a mouth.

15. **(A)** Apples are to pie as grapes are to wine (in a bottle). A pie is made of apples, and wine is made of grapes.

16. **(H)** Napoleon is to the Eiffel Tower as Cleopatra is to the Sphinx. The Eiffel Tower represents France, and Napoleon was the emperor of that country. The Sphinx represents Egypt, and Cleopatra was the queen of that country.

17. **(B)** Computer is to disk as pencil is to notebook. A computer writes on a disk, and a pencil writes on a notebook.

18. **(G)** Cow is to milk as chicken is to egg. A product of the cow is milk. An egg is produced by the chicken.

19. **(B)** Nose is to rose as ear is to violin. A nose can smell a rose, and an ear can hear a violin.

20. **(J)** Mushroom is to pizza as cherry is to ice cream. Mushrooms are toppings for pizza, and cherries are toppings for ice cream.

Test 3   Quantitative Reasoning

1. **(C)** Multiply each given number by 2: $5 \times 2 = 10$.

2. **(H)** Divide each given number by 5: $\frac{20}{5} = 4$.

3. **(D)** Subtract 4 from each given number: $5 - 4 = 1$.

4. **(J)** Multiply each given number by 5: $\left(\frac{3}{5}\right) \times 5 = 3$.

5. **(A)** Subtract 5 from each given number: $4 - 5 = -1$.

6. **(G)** Subtract $\frac{1}{2}$ from each given $\frac{1}{2}$ number: $\left(\frac{3}{2}\right) - \left(\frac{1}{2}\right) = 1\frac{1}{2} - \frac{1}{2} = 1$.

7. **(C)** Divide each given number by 4: $\left(\frac{6}{4}\right) = 1\frac{1}{2} = 1.5$.

8. **(J)** Three out of eight squares are dark: $\frac{3}{8}$.

9. **(A)** Three out of nine squares are dark: $\frac{3}{9} = \frac{1}{3}$.

10. **(J)** Four out of ten squares are dark: $\frac{4}{10} = \frac{2}{5}$.

11. **(C)** Four half squares are shaded: $4 \times \left(\frac{1}{2}\right) = 2$. That makes two out of twelve squares shaded: $\frac{2}{12} = \frac{1}{6}$.

12. **(H)** One square plus two half-squares are shaded: $1 + 2 \times \left(\frac{1}{2}\right) = 1 + 1 = 2$. That makes two out of nine squares shaded: $\frac{2}{9}$.

13. **(A)** Six half-squares are shaded: $6 \times \left(\frac{1}{2}\right) = 3$. That makes three out of eight squares shaded: $\frac{3}{8}$.

14. **(G)** Two squares plus two half-squares are shaded: $2 + 2 \times \left(\frac{1}{2}\right) = 2 + 1 = 3$. That makes three out of nine squares shaded: $\frac{3}{9} = \frac{1}{3}$.

15. **(B)** 1 cube = 2 cylinders. So, 2 cubes = 4 cylinders.

16. **(J)** 2 cubes = 2 cylinders. So, 1 cube = 1 cylinder.

    1 cube + 2 cylinders = 2 cubes + 1 cylinder

17. **(B)** 1 cube = 3 cylinders. Thus, 1 cube + 1 cylinder = 4 cylinders.

18. **(F)** 1 cylinder = 2 cubes. So,

1 cylinder + 2 cubes = 1 cylinder + 1 cylinder or 1 cylinder + 2 cubes = 2 cylinders

19. **(C)** 1 cylinder = 3 cubes. So,

2 cylinders = 1 cylinder + 1 cylinder or 2 cylinders = 3 cubes + 1 cylinder

20. **(F)**

	1 cylinder	+ 1 cube	=	3 cylinders
	− 1 cylinder			− 1 cylinder
		1 cube	=	2 cylinders

Test 4   Verbal Reasoning—Words

1. **(C)** Obviously, paint is necessary for a painting. You don't really need a brush or canvas, and the painting could be all black.

2. **(G)** A university could function without certain buildings and organizations. Students are necessary.

3. **(A)** Picture a tuxedo. Take away the dance, and it's still a tuxedo. Take away the corsage, take away the black, and it's still a tuxedo. Take away the jacket, and it's a pair of pants and a frilly shirt.

4. **(F)** Imagination requires only thought.

5. **(D)** Music does not have to be notated; it does not need strings or song. However, it does need sound.

6. **(G)** All of these require sound, too.

7. **(A)** These are all *specific* sciences.

8. **(F)** A photograph, a painting, a movie, and a portrait are all visual media.

9. **(B)** These are all dairy products.

10. **(G)** These are all verbs relating to speech. Moreover, they are speeches made by a single person, so it cannot be a debate. A performance does not necessarily involve speech.

11. **(D)** A spy is not necessarily an enemy.

12. **(G)** The other choices are specific types of birds.

13. **(A)** The other choices are synonyms for a portion.

14. **(H)** This is the only choice that concerns receiving something rather than throwing it away.

15. **(B)** The word *job* is related to some of the others, but it is a noun. The others are verbs meaning to use.

16. **(G)** Grizzly, polar, and black are types of bear. Orange, lemon, and grapefruit are types of citrus fruit.

17. **(B)** These increase in size.

18. **(G)** The relationship is male, female, and offspring. A male goose is a gander.

19. **(A)** The choices here are in reverse order. Teenager comes after toddler, which comes after infant. The second group is in reverse alphabetical order: delta, beta, alpha.

20. **(F)** Zebras, tigers, and skunks have stripes. Cheetahs, leopards, and dalmatians have spots.

Test 5   Verbal Reasoning—Context

1. **(B)** Mrs. Julian prefers country music, while Mr. Julian prefers classical. We are not told the reasons why Mr. Julian borrowed the car, nor are we told how well they get along otherwise.

2. **(H)** For whatever reason (and on whatever day), Mel did not watch this particular cartoon that morning.

3. **(C)** We don't know if Tina has ever written a book before or what type she is writing now. We do know that she is not considering herself as an illustrator.

4. **(H)** With all the facts about their brother and parents, we know that the girls are sisters.

5. **(B)** Since Charlie got "his" cake in September, that must be his birthday month. We don't know the flavor he got or how many cakes Mrs. Greene baked that month.

6. **(G)** If Michael liked the book but not the movie, they must be different. We don't know how, though.

7. **(B)** Since Mrs. Donne has chosen both male and female names, she does not know if she is having a boy or a girl. We have no facts to back up the other choices. They would be guesses.

8. **(F)** Since we know that "all" Alphas and Deltas wear particular colors all of the time, we can say with certainty that Lenina is not a member of either group.

9. **(C)** We see one another on our walks, so we must all walk at the same time: around 6:00.

10. **(G)** We are told that Amanda volunteers one day a week at the center; we are told that she was there on a Wednesday. This choice simply puts those two facts together.

Test 6   Reading and Language Arts

1. **(B)** The text discusses food, and so one might be tempted to say that a cookbook would be the logical place to find this article; however, the piece also talks about people's buying habits, making it unlikely that a cookbook would print it. So rule out choice A. A science magazine also would not publish such an article (rule out choice C). Choice D might, under certain circumstances, publish such an article, but only on a rare occasion. Choice B is much more likely, for *Newsweek,* like most weekly news magazines, devotes a section of its page count to talking about popular trends. The best answer is choice B.

2. **(J)** The author does not obviously praise Americans for their decisions (since it is illogical—and possibly ridiculous—to buy things for which you have no use); rule out choice G. The author, similarly, does not make fun of Americans for their actions, since were s/he doing so, s/he could have been a lot more biting in her/his comments; rule out choice F. Neither is the author apparently trying to reform anyone, since the article is mostly phrased using neutral language. Your best answer is J; the author does point out a paradox—that Americans routinely spend their money on items they do not intend to use.

3. **(C)** Choice D is not useful to you; if a word is used in a sentence, then you have information at your disposal to help you figure out its meaning. The remaining definitions all apply to the topic, but since the article does not talk about thinking ourselves better than others (choice A) or giving donations to a worthy cause (choice B), rule out choices that deal with these topics. That leaves choice C, and, indeed, the article does discuss buying the services of particular markets to get supplies.

4. **(H)** The author does not discuss whether people are concerned with obesity when they make food-purchasing decisions; rule out choice F. The author does mention that Americans like to try strange new foods but worry about making them themselves (choice G), but this is not the focal point of the piece. The article, moreover, makes it clear that Americans do not purchase strangely named foods often—they will consider doing so but usually do not follow through (paragraph two), so rule out choice J. The whole point of the article revolves around choice H.

5. **(D)** Choice D is written correctly, with no errors in tense. Choice A uses an apostrophe to form the plural of American. (Instead of *American's*, it should be *Americans*). Choice B should read **One** of my favorite recipes *is* the apple pie made without apples. Choice C uses the object form *whom* instead of the subject *who*.

6. **(G)** This is the only logical sequence. You know you will have to end with A (baking), so the other choices can be eliminated. If you go through the other sequences, you will see that they make no sense.

7. **(D)** The word Europe should be capitalized in choice A. Choice B contains a comma splice; the comma can be replaced with a semicolon. Choice C is a fragment.

8. **(J)** The article mentions all of the people listed as options, but only one is defined as the person who actually found the Northwest Passage.

9. **(D)** This question builds on the previous one; the author is bringing new information to light for most readers, the exception being historians who have learned about Roald Mundsen in their studies. But the author shows no inclination to mock early explorers (choice A) or discuss the dangers of early travel (choice B) or explain how the term Northwest Passage became a popular clothing label. The best answer is D.

10. **(F)** The article states that people have accommodated the lack of a Northwest Passage for so long, in part by constructing the Panama Canal, so that by the time the Northwest Passage was discovered, we no longer required it. That implies that we no longer needed an alternate route. So, we can rule out choice G, since no one uses the Northwest Passage for anything lucrative; we can also rule out choice H, since we use

the Panama Canal constantly. One might be tempted to select J, but the article does not dwell on negatives; the best choice is F.

11. **(C)** Lucrative is a word that comes from the Latin *lucre* which refers to money. Most people know this word, and they will select the word automatically. But, when in doubt, substitute. Choice C is the best.

12. **(F)** Choice G uses the contraction *they're* instead of the possessive *their*. Choice H uses incorrect pronoun-antecedent agreement. (Explorers spend *their* lives . . . .) Choice J uses the adjective *fruitless* instead of the adverb *fruitlessly* to describe how they search.

13. **(A)** This is the most accurate and concise combination. Choice B uses a comma splice; the word *moreover* is not a conjunction. Choice C is awkward and wordy, and choice D is inaccurate. (The patron saint's name is not St. Elmo's Fire.)

14. **(H)** This sentence contains essential information. The paragraph doesn't make sense without it.

15. **(D)** The sentence is accurate as it appears in the original essay. It uses the accurate tense (it *is purported to have been uttered*) rather than the construction in choice B (it *was purported to had been uttered*). Choices A and C make little sense in present tense.

16. **(F)** Choice G uses the possessive *Its* rather than the contraction *It's*. Choice H uses the incorrect usage *could of* instead of *could have*. Choice J uses the paired *neither/or* instead of *neither/nor*.

17. **(C)** The author's opinion really seems to come out in the final paragraph of this reading selection. Judging from that paragraph, one would reject choice D, since the author does seem to think that kids can handle tough issues early on. You can also reject choices A and B, since the author refuses to specify exactly when a child "ought" to be informed about life. Your best answer, therefore, is C; here the author makes her/his opinion clear—that kids can handle tough issues—but that the parent has the right—and the responsibility—to disseminate that truth at the appropriate time.

18. **(J)** You may have heard the word dregs used before—the dregs (or bottom leftovers) of a cup of coffee or tea. Generally speaking, dregs means bottom of the barrel. Judging from the list of options, criminal classes would be at the very bottom of most people's social scale.

19. **(B)** Re-reading (or memory) tells you that the author claims it was Washington who tried to use slaves' teeth as replacements for his own.

20. **(G)** You can reject choice F, since this author seems in favor of the *responsible* passing down of information; therefore, this author would likely not favor random dirt-seeking by kids. You can also rule out choice H, since this statement stands diametrically opposed to the author's point of view on the matter. Choice J really has no relevance at all. Your only real choice is G.

21. **(A)** You've probably heard the word *desecrated* before and have a good sense of the meaning; if not, break it down into syllables: *de*, meaning not, and *sacred*, meaning holy. So, if something has been desecrated, it is no longer holy. Now consider the list of choices and the question (which involves graves). All four could take place in

the process of making a grave no longer holy. Rank them in order of seriousness of offense—merely opening a grave seems less offensive than moving a grave; both seem less offensive than plowing under a grave. But probably the worst thing you could do is ransack a grave.

22. **(G)** You have heard the word residency before—every time you move you must establish residency wherever you end up. So residency has something to do with living arrangements. The only option that has anything to do with living arrangements is option G; sure enough, the passage defines the term for you, backing up your guess, in paragraph two.

23. **(D)** The main point of the passage appears in the final paragraph of the piece; the remaining paragraphs merely trace the logical steps the author takes toward this conclusion. Therefore, have a look at the final paragraph and make some connections with the list of options. Nothing in the passage supports choice A. Choice B is true, and even mentioned in the selection, but it is the starting point for the piece, not its ending point. Choice C is true but does not match with the statements of the final paragraph. Your correct answer, therefore, is D.

24. **(H)** Paragraph three talks about how doctors no longer keep heart attack victims in the hospital for long and gives a reason why that is the case: namely that we know more about heart attacks, and, in many cases, we don't require the three-day observation period any longer. Therefore, you can rule out choices F, G, and J, since they give faulty reasons why heart attack victims are released more quickly than they once were.

25. **(D)** Re-reading (or your memory) reveals that new medical legislation demands that doctors only work an 80-hour work-week with no one working more than 30 hours in a shift—an improvement, hard as it may be to realize.

26. **(G)** Again, re-reading (or your memory) reminds you that hospitals tend to keep heart attack patients around for observation for only three hours (or fewer).

27. **(D)** Breaking down the paragraphs to find their logical order helps here. In the first paragraph, you learn that some parents are trying to teach their kids at extremely young ages—even while still in the womb. Paragraph two states that child psychologists claim such tactics are a waste of time, that *in utero* education has no significant effect on developing kids. Finally, paragraph three holds up an example of a child pushed too far. The message is clear: pushing kids to develop according to some sort of predetermined, fast-paced agenda is wrong and ineffective anyway. So, the answer that best matches this stance is D. You might be momentarily attracted to option B, but the phrasing of the answer is too vague to be satisfactory. After all, referring to a schedule can mean many things, and sometimes schedules are good (even necessary) to follow. You are looking for a statement that links the two main points of the article; that would be D.

28. **(G)** Rule out choice J; whenever a word is used, you can figure out the meaning through context—sometimes it's just harder to do so than at other times. The other three options all have some basis in truth, although clearly choice F is out of the question. Since we're talking about children and their development, it's better to choose the option dealing with the uterus rather than any other. The best answer is G.

29. **(A)** The author, as discussed in the last answer explanation, uses Mill as an example of good intentions gone very bad. Choices B, C, and D simply do not address the issue. Your only real option is A.

30. **(G)** Re-reading (or your memory) tells you that Mill learned Greek by the age of three.

31. **(C)** Choice C correctly uses the intensifier *himself*. Choice A uses an unnecessary comma between the subjects *Mill* and *Bentham*. It also refers to *their life* (singular), when it should read *their lives* (plural). Choice B should use a colon rather than a semi-colon to introduce the information. The modifier in choice D is awkwardly placed; the poetry did not have a nervous breakdown. It should read *After a nervous breakdown, he found comfort in poetry.*

32. **(F)** Choice G is wordy. Choice H is passive. Choice J uses the adjective *passionate* rather than the adverb *passionately* to describe how he argues.

33. **(B)** This text discusses a historical event and lists its influences and causes. Therefore, it would not appear in a literary magazine or a poetry journal as these are vehicles for creative writing; nor would it appear in a science text, as it makes no mention of scientific topics, inventions, or mysteries. The best answer is B.

34. **(J)** A good vocabulary or context clues will tell you that <u>ceased</u> generally means "stopped." Rule out choices A and B, for these are opposites. Waned is more tempting but it implies a slow stopping, while <u>ceased</u> means "stopped." J is the only good answer.

35. **(B)** Re-reading or memory tells you that the correct answer is B. The other answers are worded so as to give information opposite to that given in the passage.

36. **(G)** The passage states that farmers grew more independent. Relying on government aid is not taking independence but growing more reliant on others; rule out choice F. Exploring in addition to farming is indeed a form of gaining independence, but it likely takes too much time away from one activity to do the other well, and the article does not support this fact anyway; rule out choice H. J is a misleading, non-answer. The correct answer is G.

37. **(A)** Let us make clear that knowledge is generally a good thing and that it is better to have great knowledge that one does not use than to be ignorant. Knowledge is like sit-ups for the brain. However, some professions use certain types of information more than others. Doctors need medical training more than history; rule out choice A. Teachers and writers might use historical knowledge in their careers, depending on the type of teaching or writing they do. But the only career here mentioned that would absolutely be able to use this historical information would be historian, choice D.

38. **(H)** The article talks about how recent thought about the scary West Nile virus makes people think that disease may have been what struck down Alexander the Great. This is interesting but is hardly "real" science; it's chatty and informational rather than rigorously scientific. Therefore, you must consider these facts when you try to guess which text might publish this piece. Almanacs discuss what the weather will be like on certain days; the *Guinness Book of World Records* documents people doing odd things for extremely long periods of time; neither text seems the appropriate place to read about Alexander the Great or the West Nile virus. On the other hand, a journal that publishes

articles about Greek and Latin literature is likely to have a very different tone from that in the above piece; such articles are rigorous, full of lofty and difficult jargon, and don't usually discuss topical events like the West Nile virus. So, your best option is H.

39. **(C)** A plague is a bad thing, usually a disease, that takes over an area and makes everyone miserable (or kills everything in its path). Therefore, the definition of *overrun* is the best match here. *Inhabited* is too tame a word, and the other two choices both refer to a *lack*, rather than a presence, of plague.

40. **(F)** Re-reading (or memory) tells you that the author lists several possible causes of Alexander the Great's death; of the options listed here, only malaria is one of those enumerated by the author.

Test 7   Mathematics

1. **(A)** Simplify $\dfrac{3^9}{3^7}$ and then divide by 4.

$$\frac{3^9}{4\times 3^7} = \frac{3^{9^{\,3^2}}}{4\times 3^{7}_{\;1}} = \frac{9}{4} = 2\frac{1}{4} = 2.25$$

2. **(H)**

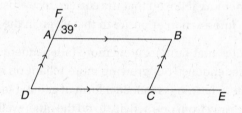

$$m\angle BAD = 180° - 39° = 141°$$
$$m\angle BAD = m\angle DCB = 141°$$
$$m\angle BCE = 180° - 141° = 39°$$

3. **(A)** Use the formula $A = \left(\dfrac{1}{2}\right)bh$, where $A =$ the area, $b =$ the base, and $h =$ the height of the triangle.

$$A = \frac{1}{2}bh$$

$b = 2x + y,$

$h = 4z:$ $\qquad = \dfrac{1}{\cancel{2}}(2x+y)(\cancel{4}^{\,2}z) = 2z(2x+y)$

4. **(F)** Multiply each number by 0.2 to get to the next succeeding number.

$$0.2 \times 8 = 1.6$$

5. **(A)** Determine how much weight Dwayne lost and then let the result be the numerator of a fraction with the original weight the denominator.

Weight Lost:

215 pounds − 175 pounds = 40 pounds

Weight Lost:
Original Weight:
$$\frac{40}{215} = \frac{\cancel{5}\times 8}{\cancel{5}\times 43} = \frac{8}{43}$$

6. **(G)**

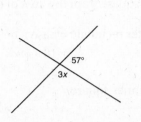

The two angles lie on a straight line, so they add up to 180°.

$$3x + 57 = 180$$
$$\underline{-57 \quad -57}$$
$$\frac{3x}{3} = \frac{123}{3}$$
$$x = 41$$

7. **(D)** Change to improper fractions and multiply.

$$6\frac{2}{3} \times 5\frac{1}{4} = \frac{\overset{5}{\cancel{20}}}{\cancel{3}} \times \frac{\overset{7}{\cancel{21}}}{\cancel{4}} = 35$$

8. **(G)** Let $y =$ the number of runs the team has to score on the last game, and set up an equation to solve for the mean.

$\bar{x} =$ mean: $\quad \bar{x} = \dfrac{12+7+10+6+9+y}{6}$

$\bar{x} = 9$: $\quad 9 = \dfrac{44+y}{6}$

$\quad\quad\quad 54 = 44 + y$

$\quad\quad\quad 10 = y$

9. **(C)**

(A) $4^2 + 5(9-3) = 16 + 5 \cdot 6 = 16 + 30 = 46$

(B) $3 \cdot 17 - 4 \cdot 6 = 51 - 24 = 27$

(C) $7 + 9 \cdot 4 - 6(9-7)^3 = 7 + 36 - 6(2)^3 = 43 - 6(8) = 43 - 48 = -5$

(D) $6 - 2 + \dfrac{48}{6} = 4 + 8 = 12$

10. **(F)**

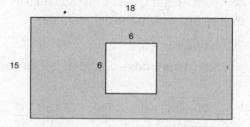

Subtract the area of the inner square from the area of the outer rectangle.

$$\text{Area of outer rectangle} = \text{base} \times \text{height (or } bh\text{)}$$
$$= 18 \times 15$$
$$= 270$$
$$\text{Area of inner square} = s^2$$
$$= 6^2$$
$$= 36$$
$$\text{Area of rectangle} - \text{Area of square} = 270 - 36$$
$$\text{Shaded area} = 234$$

11. **(D)** The price of the ticket at the end of this year will be 107% of the price at the beginning of the year. Then, to find the price at the end of two years, find 105% of the price at the end of this year.

Change 107% to a decimal and multiply:

$$1.07 \times \$8 = \$8.56$$

$$1.05 \times \$8.56 = \$8.988 \approx \$8.99$$

12. **(H)** Let $x =$ the unknown number.

$$18 - \frac{2}{5}x = \frac{2}{3} \cdot 6 + 4$$

$$18 - \frac{2}{5}x = 4 + 4$$

$$5 \times \left(18 - \frac{2}{5}x\right) = (8) \times 5$$

$$90 - 2x = 40$$
$$-2x = -50$$
$$x = 25$$

13. **(A)**

$$\text{Distance } (D) = \text{Rate } (R) \cdot \text{Time } (T)$$
$$D = 154$$

There are 2 hours and 45 minutes $\left(2\frac{45}{60}\right)$ or $2\frac{3}{4}$ hours of time between 8 A.M. and 10:45 A.M.

$$T = 2\frac{45}{60} = 2\frac{3}{4}$$

Divide 154 miles by $2\frac{3}{4}$ in order to obtain the average speed.

$$154 \div 2\frac{3}{4} = 154 \div \frac{11}{4} = 154 \times \frac{4}{11} = \frac{616}{11} = 56$$

14. **(H)**

Let x = the unknown number.

$$6(? + 5) - 3 = 135$$
$$6(x + 5) - 3 = 135$$
$$6x + 30 - 3 = 135$$
$$6x + 27 = 135$$
$$\underline{\quad -27 \quad -27 \quad}$$
$$\frac{6x}{6} = \frac{108}{6}$$
$$x = 18$$

15. **(B)** Let x = the original number. Find that number and then divide by 4.

$$\frac{6x}{6} = \frac{24.72}{6}$$
$$x = 4.12$$
$$4.12 \div 4 = 1.03$$

16. **(J)** There are 5,280 feet in a mile. Change both units of distance to the same measure. In this case, let's just change 3 miles per hour to feet per hour and then divide.

$$3 \text{ miles per hour} = 3 \times 5,280 \text{ feet per hour}$$
$$= 15,840 \text{ feet per hour}$$
$$\frac{23,760}{15,840} = 1.5$$

17. **(B)** Subtract 2 pounds 9 ounces from 5 pounds 6 ounces. Borrow one pound (16 ounces) from 5 pounds and add it to the 6 ounces.

$$\overset{4}{\cancel{5}} \text{ pounds } \overset{16+6=22 \text{ ounces}}{\cancel{6}} \text{ ounces}$$
$$\underline{-2 \text{ pounds } \quad 9 \text{ ounces}}$$
$$2 \text{ pounds } 13 \text{ ounces}$$

18. **(J)**

$$2x^2 + 4 = 76$$
$$\underline{\quad -4 \quad -4 \quad}$$
$$\frac{2x^2}{2} = \frac{72}{2}$$
$$x^2 = 36$$
$$x = \sqrt{36}$$
$$x = \pm 6$$

The positive value of x is +6. The only choice is 6, choice J.

19. **(D)** Find 8% of the excess money over $2,000 and add the result to the $300 base salary.

$$\$3,500 - \$2,000 = \$1,500$$
$$8\% = 0.08$$
$$0.08 \times \$1,500 = \$120$$
$$\$300 + \$120 = \$420$$

20. **(G)**

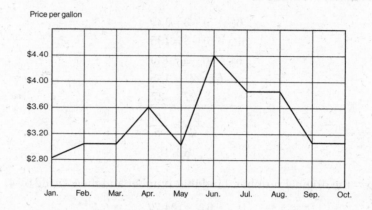

Add the April and August prices and divide by 2.

$$\frac{\$3.60 + \$3.80}{2} = \frac{\$7.40}{2} = \$3.70$$

21. **(D)** To get a rough estimate, let's round off 34 to 30 and 68 to 70.

$$30 \times 70 = 2,100$$

22. **(J)**

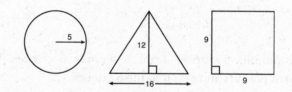

Find the areas of all three figures and then substitute into the given choices.
To simplify calculations, round off π to 3.

$A_C = \pi r^2$, where $A_C =$ area of circle, $r =$ radius

$A_C = (3)(5)^2 = (3)(25) = 75$

$A_T = \left(\dfrac{1}{2}\right)bh$, where $A_T =$ area of triangle, $b =$ base, $h =$ height

$A_T = \left(\dfrac{1}{2}\right)(16)(12) = 96$

$A_S = s^2$, where $A_S =$ area of square, $s =$ side of square

$A_S = (9)^2 = 81$

The area of the circle is less than the area of the triangle.

$$75 < 96 \; ✔$$

23. **(B)**

$$x = \frac{1}{8}(40) + 6$$
$$x = 5 + 6$$
$$x = 11$$

24. **(J)**

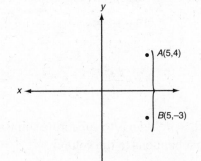

The total distance from –3 to +4 is 7 units.

25. **(C)**

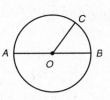

A diameter is equal to twice the measure of its radius.

$$AB = 2 \times CO$$
$$AB = 2 \times 3a = 6a$$

26. **(H)**

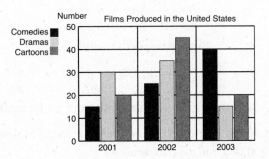

First make a table indicating the number of cartoons, dramas, and comedies produced in each of the indicated years. Then you're in a position to check the given statements for their validity. Each horizontal line represents 10 films.

	2001	2002	2003
Comedies	15	25	40
Dramas	30	35	15
Cartoons	20	45	20

The number of dramas in 2003 is greater than the number of comedies in 2001.

$$15 > 15 \; ✖$$

27. **(C)**

$$r = \frac{ks^2}{t}$$

28. **(F)** The best approach to this problem is to substitute some small positive integers for the side and then to see what happens to the volume.

$$V = s^3 \qquad\qquad V = s^3$$
$$\text{Let } s = 1 \qquad\qquad \text{Let } s = 2$$
$$V = (1)^3 = 1 \qquad\qquad V = (2)^3 = 8$$

The new volume is eight times the measure of the old volume.

29. **(C)**

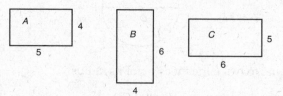

Find all the areas and then substitute the results into the four inequalities.

$$\text{Area } A = bh = 5 \cdot 4 = 20$$
$$\text{Area } B = bh = 4 \cdot 6 = 24$$
$$\text{Area } C = bh = 6 \cdot 5 = 30$$
Area B is less than area C.

$$24 < 30 \; ✔$$

30. **(F)** Add $\frac{2}{5}$ and $\frac{1}{3}$ and then subtract the result from 1 (the total amount).

The answer is Malcolm's portion. Once we determine Malcolm's portion, multiply that fraction by $300,000, the total income.

$$\frac{2}{5} = \frac{6}{15} \qquad 1 = \frac{15}{15}$$
$$+\frac{1}{3} = \frac{5}{15} \qquad -\frac{11}{15} \qquad \frac{4}{15} \times 300{,}000 = 80{,}000$$
$$\frac{11}{15} \qquad\qquad \frac{4}{15}$$

31. **(C)**

STEP 1 The measure of $\angle BCA$ + the measure of $\angle BCD = 180°$ because the angles lie on a straight line and, together, add up to a straight angle. Find m$\angle BCA$.

STEP 2 Since the triangle is isosceles, interior angles A and BCA are the same measure, so let m$\angle A = x$ and let m$\angle BCA = x$. Then add up all three interior angles of $\triangle ABC$, and set the sum equal to $180°$.

STEP 3 Now find the measure of $\angle B$.

STEP 4
$$\text{m}\angle BCA + \text{m}\angle BCD = 180$$
$$x + 96 = 180$$
$$x = 84$$

STEP 5 m$\angle A$ = m$\angle BCA$ = x:
$$\text{m}\angle A + \text{m}\angle B + \text{m}\angle BCA = 180$$
$$x + \text{m}\angle B + x = 180$$
$$2x + \text{m}\angle B = 180$$
$$2(84) + \text{m}\angle B = 180$$
$$168 + \text{m}\angle B = 180$$

STEP 6
$$\text{m}\angle B = 12$$

32. **(F)**

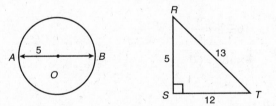

Find the areas and perimeters of the circle and the triangle and then substitute into the preceding statements. Let $\pi = 3.14$.

Circumference of circle O: $C = 2\pi r$
$$= 2(3.14)(5) = 31.4$$

Area of circle O: $A_C = \pi r^2$
$$= (3.14)(5)^2 = 78.5$$

Perimeter of triangle RST: $P = 5 + 12 + 13 = 30$

Area of triangle RST: $A_T = \dfrac{1}{2}bh$
$$= \dfrac{1}{2}(12)(5) = 30$$

$$\text{Area of triangle } RST < \frac{1}{2} \text{ Area of circle } O$$

$$30 < \frac{1}{2}(78.5)$$

$$30 < 39.25 \ ✔$$

33. **(C)** In cases when we are given a generalized statement, make the problem concrete by using actual numbers. The two unknowns, x and y, are negative and $y > x$, so let's try using $x = -2$ and $y = -1$.

$$xy > 0$$
$$(-2)(-1) = +2$$
$$+2 > 0 \ ✔$$

34. **(J)** Which multiples of 18 and 27 are equal?

$$18 \times 3 = 54$$
$$27 \times 2 = 54$$

54 is the least common multiple.

35. **(B)** In a case like this, if we want an exact answer, convert the percentage to a fraction and then multiply.

$$16\frac{2}{3}\% = 16\frac{2}{3} \div 100 = 16\frac{2}{3} \div \frac{100}{1} = \frac{\overset{1}{\cancel{50}}}{3} \times \frac{1}{\underset{2}{\cancel{100}}} = \frac{1}{6}$$

$$16\frac{2}{3}\% = \frac{1}{6}$$

$$\frac{1}{6} \times 360 = 60$$

36. **(G)**

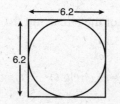

Round off 6.2 to 6. Then find the area of the square and find $\frac{3}{4}$ of the answer.

$$\text{Area of square} = (\text{side})^2 = (6)^2 = 36$$

$$\text{Approximate area of circle} = \frac{3}{4} \times 36 = 27$$

37. **(A)** Nine $0.15 stamps plus six $0.37 stamps cost more than five $0.65 stamps.

$$9 \times \$0.15 + 6 \times \$0.37 > 5 \times \$0.65$$
$$\$1.35 + \$2.22 > \$3.25$$
$$\$3.57 > \$3.25 \checkmark$$

38. **(J)** One method is to first divide the octagon into a number of triangles. Then, since we know that there are 180° in the angles of a triangle, just multiply the number of triangles by 180°.

A second method is to use the formula for determining the number of interior degrees in any polygon: $N_D = (n-2)180$, where $N_D =$ the number of interior degrees and $n =$ the number of sides of the polygon.

Either way, the solution is the same.

Method 1

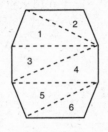

Octagon

6 triangles: $6 \times 180° = 1{,}080°$

$$N_D = 1{,}080°$$

Method 2

$$N_D = (n-2)180$$
$$= (8-2)180$$
$$= 6 \times 180$$
$$= 1{,}080°$$

39. **(C)**

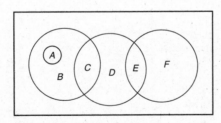

All elements of set A are members of set B. Some elements of set D are in set B, some are in set F, and some are independent of both sets B and F. We'll have to check each statement to determine its truth value.

Some members of set D are members of set F. Set D is represented by the middle circle. Some elements in set D (those elements of set E) are members of set F, so the statement is **true**.

40. **(J)**

To determine the number of hours spent on personal items, add up the various percentages and then subtract from 100%. Then multiply the answer by 24 hours.

$$30\% + 10\% + 25\% + 20\% = 85\%$$
$$100\% - 85\% = 15\%$$
$$0.15 \times 24 = 3.6$$

ANSWER SHEET
COOP Practice Exam 2

TEST 1   SEQUENCES

1. Ⓐ Ⓑ Ⓒ Ⓓ
2. Ⓕ Ⓖ Ⓗ Ⓙ
3. Ⓐ Ⓑ Ⓒ Ⓓ
4. Ⓕ Ⓖ Ⓗ Ⓙ
5. Ⓐ Ⓑ Ⓒ Ⓓ

6. Ⓕ Ⓖ Ⓗ Ⓙ
7. Ⓐ Ⓑ Ⓒ Ⓓ
8. Ⓕ Ⓖ Ⓗ Ⓙ
9. Ⓐ Ⓑ Ⓒ Ⓓ
10. Ⓕ Ⓖ Ⓗ Ⓙ

11. Ⓐ Ⓑ Ⓒ Ⓓ
12. Ⓕ Ⓖ Ⓗ Ⓙ
13. Ⓐ Ⓑ Ⓒ Ⓓ
14. Ⓕ Ⓖ Ⓗ Ⓙ
15. Ⓐ Ⓑ Ⓒ Ⓓ

16. Ⓕ Ⓖ Ⓗ Ⓙ
17. Ⓐ Ⓑ Ⓒ Ⓓ
18. Ⓕ Ⓖ Ⓗ Ⓙ
19. Ⓐ Ⓑ Ⓒ Ⓓ
20. Ⓕ Ⓖ Ⓗ Ⓙ

TEST 2   ANALOGIES

1. Ⓐ Ⓑ Ⓒ Ⓓ
2. Ⓕ Ⓖ Ⓗ Ⓙ
3. Ⓐ Ⓑ Ⓒ Ⓓ
4. Ⓕ Ⓖ Ⓗ Ⓙ
5. Ⓐ Ⓑ Ⓒ Ⓓ

6. Ⓕ Ⓖ Ⓗ Ⓙ
7. Ⓐ Ⓑ Ⓒ Ⓓ
8. Ⓕ Ⓖ Ⓗ Ⓙ
9. Ⓐ Ⓑ Ⓒ Ⓓ
10. Ⓕ Ⓖ Ⓗ Ⓙ

11. Ⓐ Ⓑ Ⓒ Ⓓ
12. Ⓕ Ⓖ Ⓗ Ⓙ
13. Ⓐ Ⓑ Ⓒ Ⓓ
14. Ⓕ Ⓖ Ⓗ Ⓙ
15. Ⓐ Ⓑ Ⓒ Ⓓ

16. Ⓕ Ⓖ Ⓗ Ⓙ
17. Ⓐ Ⓑ Ⓒ Ⓓ
18. Ⓕ Ⓖ Ⓗ Ⓙ
19. Ⓐ Ⓑ Ⓒ Ⓓ
20. Ⓕ Ⓖ Ⓗ Ⓙ

TEST 3   QUANTITATIVE REASONING

1. Ⓐ Ⓑ Ⓒ Ⓓ
2. Ⓕ Ⓖ Ⓗ Ⓙ
3. Ⓐ Ⓑ Ⓒ Ⓓ
4. Ⓕ Ⓖ Ⓗ Ⓙ
5. Ⓐ Ⓑ Ⓒ Ⓓ

6. Ⓕ Ⓖ Ⓗ Ⓙ
7. Ⓐ Ⓑ Ⓒ Ⓓ
8. Ⓕ Ⓖ Ⓗ Ⓙ
9. Ⓐ Ⓑ Ⓒ Ⓓ
10. Ⓕ Ⓖ Ⓗ Ⓙ

11. Ⓐ Ⓑ Ⓒ Ⓓ
12. Ⓕ Ⓖ Ⓗ Ⓙ
13. Ⓐ Ⓑ Ⓒ Ⓓ
14. Ⓕ Ⓖ Ⓗ Ⓙ
15. Ⓐ Ⓑ Ⓒ Ⓓ

16. Ⓕ Ⓖ Ⓗ Ⓙ
17. Ⓐ Ⓑ Ⓒ Ⓓ
18. Ⓕ Ⓖ Ⓗ Ⓙ
19. Ⓐ Ⓑ Ⓒ Ⓓ
20. Ⓕ Ⓖ Ⓗ Ⓙ

TEST 4   VERBAL REASONING—WORDS

1. Ⓐ Ⓑ Ⓒ Ⓓ
2. Ⓕ Ⓖ Ⓗ Ⓙ
3. Ⓐ Ⓑ Ⓒ Ⓓ
4. Ⓕ Ⓖ Ⓗ Ⓙ
5. Ⓐ Ⓑ Ⓒ Ⓓ

6. Ⓕ Ⓖ Ⓗ Ⓙ
7. Ⓐ Ⓑ Ⓒ Ⓓ
8. Ⓕ Ⓖ Ⓗ Ⓙ
9. Ⓐ Ⓑ Ⓒ Ⓓ
10. Ⓕ Ⓖ Ⓗ Ⓙ

11. Ⓐ Ⓑ Ⓒ Ⓓ
12. Ⓕ Ⓖ Ⓗ Ⓙ
13. Ⓐ Ⓑ Ⓒ Ⓓ
14. Ⓕ Ⓖ Ⓗ Ⓙ
15. Ⓐ Ⓑ Ⓒ Ⓓ

16. Ⓕ Ⓖ Ⓗ Ⓙ
17. Ⓐ Ⓑ Ⓒ Ⓓ
18. Ⓕ Ⓖ Ⓗ Ⓙ
19. Ⓐ Ⓑ Ⓒ Ⓓ
20. Ⓕ Ⓖ Ⓗ Ⓙ

ANSWER SHEET
COOP Practice Exam 2

TEST 5   VERBAL REASONING—CONTEXT

1. Ⓐ Ⓑ Ⓒ Ⓓ   4. Ⓕ Ⓖ Ⓗ Ⓙ   7. Ⓐ Ⓑ Ⓒ Ⓓ   10. Ⓕ Ⓖ Ⓗ Ⓙ
2. Ⓕ Ⓖ Ⓗ Ⓙ   5. Ⓐ Ⓑ Ⓒ Ⓓ   8. Ⓕ Ⓖ Ⓗ Ⓙ
3. Ⓐ Ⓑ Ⓒ Ⓓ   6. Ⓕ Ⓖ Ⓗ Ⓙ   9. Ⓐ Ⓑ Ⓒ Ⓓ

TEST 6   READING AND LANGUAGE ARTS

1. Ⓐ Ⓑ Ⓒ Ⓓ   11. Ⓐ Ⓑ Ⓒ Ⓓ   21. Ⓐ Ⓑ Ⓒ Ⓓ   31. Ⓐ Ⓑ Ⓒ Ⓓ
2. Ⓕ Ⓖ Ⓗ Ⓙ   12. Ⓕ Ⓖ Ⓗ Ⓙ   22. Ⓕ Ⓖ Ⓗ Ⓙ   32. Ⓕ Ⓖ Ⓗ Ⓙ
3. Ⓐ Ⓑ Ⓒ Ⓓ   13. Ⓐ Ⓑ Ⓒ Ⓓ   23. Ⓐ Ⓑ Ⓒ Ⓓ   33. Ⓐ Ⓑ Ⓒ Ⓓ
4. Ⓕ Ⓖ Ⓗ Ⓙ   14. Ⓕ Ⓖ Ⓗ Ⓙ   24. Ⓕ Ⓖ Ⓗ Ⓙ   34. Ⓕ Ⓖ Ⓗ Ⓙ
5. Ⓐ Ⓑ Ⓒ Ⓓ   15. Ⓐ Ⓑ Ⓒ Ⓓ   25. Ⓐ Ⓑ Ⓒ Ⓓ   35. Ⓐ Ⓑ Ⓒ Ⓓ
6. Ⓕ Ⓖ Ⓗ Ⓙ   16. Ⓕ Ⓖ Ⓗ Ⓙ   26. Ⓕ Ⓖ Ⓗ Ⓙ   36. Ⓕ Ⓖ Ⓗ Ⓙ
7. Ⓐ Ⓑ Ⓒ Ⓓ   17. Ⓐ Ⓑ Ⓒ Ⓓ   27. Ⓐ Ⓑ Ⓒ Ⓓ   37. Ⓐ Ⓑ Ⓒ Ⓓ
8. Ⓕ Ⓖ Ⓗ Ⓙ   18. Ⓕ Ⓖ Ⓗ Ⓙ   28. Ⓕ Ⓖ Ⓗ Ⓙ   38. Ⓕ Ⓖ Ⓗ Ⓙ
9. Ⓐ Ⓑ Ⓒ Ⓓ   19. Ⓐ Ⓑ Ⓒ Ⓓ   29. Ⓐ Ⓑ Ⓒ Ⓓ   39. Ⓐ Ⓑ Ⓒ Ⓓ
10. Ⓕ Ⓖ Ⓗ Ⓙ   20. Ⓕ Ⓖ Ⓗ Ⓙ   30. Ⓕ Ⓖ Ⓗ Ⓙ   40. Ⓕ Ⓖ Ⓗ Ⓙ

TEST 7   MATHEMATICS

1. Ⓐ Ⓑ Ⓒ Ⓓ   11. Ⓐ Ⓑ Ⓒ Ⓓ   21. Ⓐ Ⓑ Ⓒ Ⓓ   31. Ⓐ Ⓑ Ⓒ Ⓓ
2. Ⓕ Ⓖ Ⓗ Ⓙ   12. Ⓕ Ⓖ Ⓗ Ⓙ   22. Ⓕ Ⓖ Ⓗ Ⓙ   32. Ⓕ Ⓖ Ⓗ Ⓙ
3. Ⓐ Ⓑ Ⓒ Ⓓ   13. Ⓐ Ⓑ Ⓒ Ⓓ   23. Ⓐ Ⓑ Ⓒ Ⓓ   33. Ⓐ Ⓑ Ⓒ Ⓓ
4. Ⓕ Ⓖ Ⓗ Ⓙ   14. Ⓕ Ⓖ Ⓗ Ⓙ   24. Ⓕ Ⓖ Ⓗ Ⓙ   34. Ⓕ Ⓖ Ⓗ Ⓙ
5. Ⓐ Ⓑ Ⓒ Ⓓ   15. Ⓐ Ⓑ Ⓒ Ⓓ   25. Ⓐ Ⓑ Ⓒ Ⓓ   35. Ⓐ Ⓑ Ⓒ Ⓓ
6. Ⓕ Ⓖ Ⓗ Ⓙ   16. Ⓕ Ⓖ Ⓗ Ⓙ   26. Ⓕ Ⓖ Ⓗ Ⓙ   36. Ⓕ Ⓖ Ⓗ Ⓙ
7. Ⓐ Ⓑ Ⓒ Ⓓ   17. Ⓐ Ⓑ Ⓒ Ⓓ   27. Ⓐ Ⓑ Ⓒ Ⓓ   37. Ⓐ Ⓑ Ⓒ Ⓓ
8. Ⓕ Ⓖ Ⓗ Ⓙ   18. Ⓕ Ⓖ Ⓗ Ⓙ   28. Ⓕ Ⓖ Ⓗ Ⓙ   38. Ⓕ Ⓖ Ⓗ Ⓙ
9. Ⓐ Ⓑ Ⓒ Ⓓ   19. Ⓐ Ⓑ Ⓒ Ⓓ   29. Ⓐ Ⓑ Ⓒ Ⓓ   39. Ⓐ Ⓑ Ⓒ Ⓓ
10. Ⓕ Ⓖ Ⓗ Ⓙ   20. Ⓕ Ⓖ Ⓗ Ⓙ   30. Ⓕ Ⓖ Ⓗ Ⓙ   40. Ⓕ Ⓖ Ⓗ Ⓙ

TEST 1 SEQUENCES

#1–20 15 MINUTES

Directions: Choose the letter that will continue the pattern or sequence.

1

^ $ + ! | $ + ! ^ | + ! ^ $ | __

A $ + ! ^

B ! $ + ^

C ! ^ $ +

D ^ $ + !

2

□ ○ ⇨ ⊟ | ○ □ ⊟ ⇨ | □ ○ ⇨ ⊟ | __

F □ ○ ⊟ ⇨

G □ ⊟ ⇨ ○

H ⊟ □ ⇨ ○

J ○ □ ⊟ ⇨

3

% & @ | @ & % # | # % & @ | __

A # % & @

B # & @ %

C % & # @

D @ & % #

4

□ △ ⬠ ⬡ | ⬡ ⬠ ○ □ △ | □ △ ⬠ ⬠ | ____

F ▽ ⬡ ⬠ ⬢

G □ △ ⬠ ⬠

H ▽ ⬢ □ ⬠

J ⬡ ⬠ ○ △

5

⇑ ♡ ◎ ↷ | ◎ ⇑ ♡ ↷ | ♡ ◎ ↑ ↷ | ____

A ◎ ⇑ ↷ ♡

B ♡ ↷ ⇑ ◎

C ◎ ↷ ♡ ⇑

D ⇑ ♡ ◎ ↷

6

✺ □ ☆ ☾ (✺ □ ☆ | ★ ☾ ✺ □ | ____

F ■ ☆ ☾ ✺

G ☾ ✺ ★ □

H ✹ ☆ □ ☆

J □ ☆ ☾ ✺

GO TO NEXT PAGE ➡

7

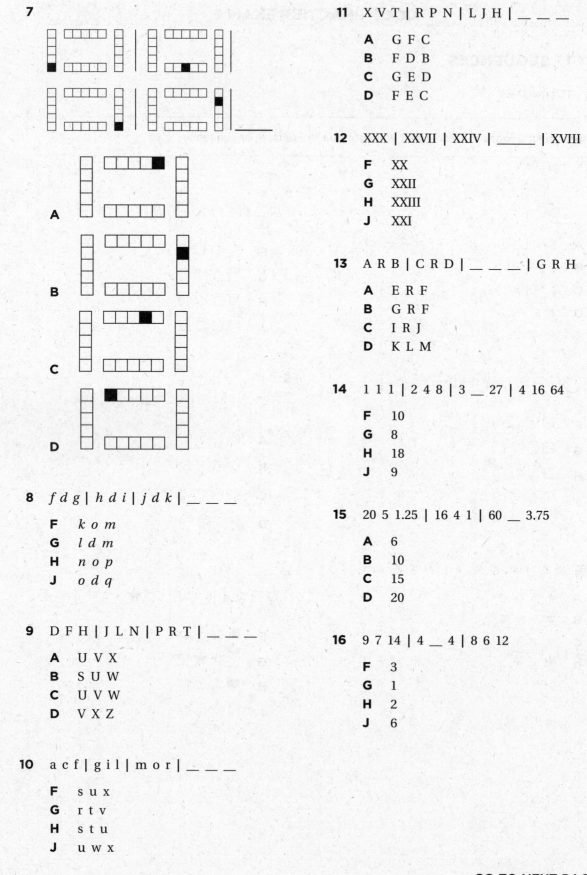

8 *f d g* | *h d i* | *j d k* | _ _ _

    F *k o m*

    G *l d m*

    H *n o p*

    J *o d q*

9 D F H | J L N | P R T | _ _ _

    A U V X

    B S U W

    C U V W

    D V X Z

10 *a c f* | *g i l* | *m o r* | _ _ _

    F *s u x*

    G *r t v*

    H *s t u*

    J *u w x*

11 X V T | R P N | L J H | _ _ _

    A G F C

    B F D B

    C G E D

    D F E C

12 XXX | XXVII | XXIV | _____ | XVIII

    F XX

    G XXII

    H XXIII

    J XXI

13 A R B | C R D | _ _ _ | G R H

    A E R F

    B G R F

    C I R J

    D K L M

14 1 1 1 | 2 4 8 | 3 __ 27 | 4 16 64

    F 10

    G 8

    H 18

    J 9

15 20 5 1.25 | 16 4 1 | 60 __ 3.75

    A 6

    B 10

    C 15

    D 20

16 9 7 14 | 4 __ 4 | 8 6 12

    F 3

    G 1

    H 2

    J 6

GO TO NEXT PAGE ➡

17 1 3 9 | 2 6 __ | 4 12 36

    A 12
    B 18
    C 9
    D 8

18 36 32 28 | 24 20 16 | 12 __ 4

    F 9
    G 5
    H 10
    J 8

19 2 4 3 | 3 5 4 | 7 9 __

    A 8
    B 6
    C 10
    D 11

20 $C_{12} E_{12} H_{12}$ | $I_{10} K_{10} N_{10}$ | $O_8 Q_8 T_8$ | __ __ __

    F $T_6 U_6 W_6$
    G $U_5 W_4 X_2$
    H $U_6 W_6 Z_6$
    J $T_6 V_4 Z_2$

STOP

If there is still time remaining, you may review your answers.

TEST 2 ANALOGIES

#1-20 7 MINUTES

> **Directions:** Select the picture that will fill the empty box so that the two lower pictures are related to each other in the same manner as the two upper pictures.

1

A   B   C   D

2

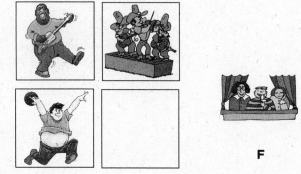

F   G   H   J

3

A   B   C   D

GO TO NEXT PAGE ➡

4

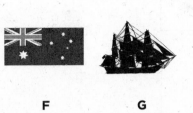

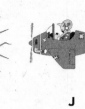

F   G   H   J

5

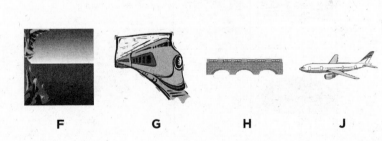

A   B   C   D

6

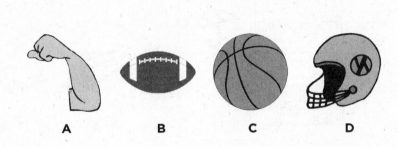

F   G   H   J

7

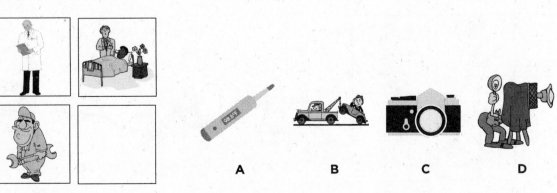

A   B   C   D

GO TO NEXT PAGE ➡

8

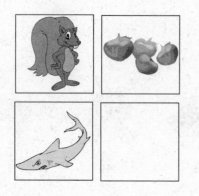

F   G   H   J

9

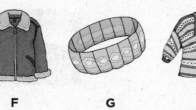 

A   B   C   D

10

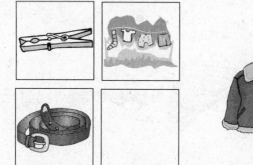

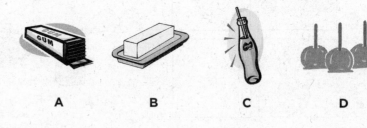

F   G   H   J

11

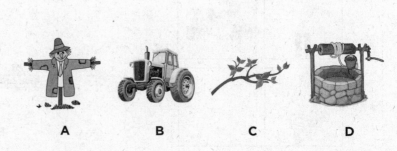

A   B   C   D

GO TO NEXT PAGE ➡

12

F   G   H   J

13

A   B   C   D

14

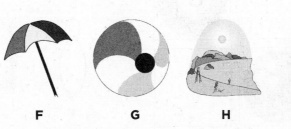

F   G   H   J

15

A   B   C   D

GO TO NEXT PAGE ➡

16

F G H J

17

A B C D

18

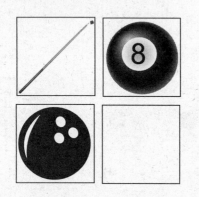

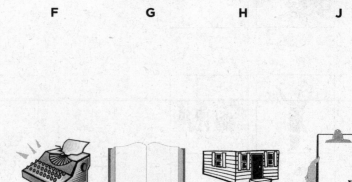

F G H J

19

A B C D

GO TO NEXT PAGE ➡

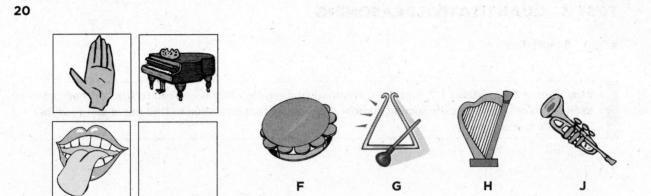

F G H J

STOP

If there is still time remaining, you may review your answers.

> **Directions:** For questions 1–7, find the mathematical operation that is applied to the first number in each set so as to arrive at the second number. Then apply that operation to find the missing number. Select the correct answer.

1 $8 \rightarrow$ ___ $\rightarrow 5$

$9 \rightarrow$ ___ $\rightarrow 6$

$5 \rightarrow$ ___ $\rightarrow ?$

A   0
B   1
C   4
D   2

2 $4 \rightarrow$ ___ $\rightarrow 8$

$3 \rightarrow$ ___ $\rightarrow 6$

$6 \rightarrow$ ___ $\rightarrow ?$

F   12
G   10
H   9
J   6

3 $12 \rightarrow$ ___ $\rightarrow 4$

$9 \rightarrow$ ___ $\rightarrow 3$

$6 \rightarrow$ ___ $\rightarrow ?$

A   1
B   2
C   3
D   4

4 $\frac{4}{9} \rightarrow$ ___ $\rightarrow 4$

$3 \rightarrow$ ___ $\rightarrow 27$

$\frac{2}{3} \rightarrow$ ___ $\rightarrow ?$

F   2
G   6
H   3
J   9

5 $\frac{1}{2} \rightarrow$ ___ $\rightarrow 1$

$2 \rightarrow$ ___ $\rightarrow 2.5$

$1.5 \rightarrow$ ___ $\rightarrow ?$

A   2
B   3.5
C   3
D   2.5

6 $5 \rightarrow$ ___ $\rightarrow 3$

$1 \rightarrow$ ___ $\rightarrow -1$

$4.5 \rightarrow$ ___ $\rightarrow ?$

F   −2.5
G   4
H   2.5
J   4.5

7 $14 \rightarrow$ ___ $\rightarrow 7$

$10 \rightarrow$ ___ $\rightarrow 5$

$8 \rightarrow$ ___ $\rightarrow ?$

A   4
B   16
C   3
D   10

GO TO NEXT PAGE ➡

COOP PRACTICE EXAM 2

Directions: For questions 8–14, express the part of the grid that is dark.

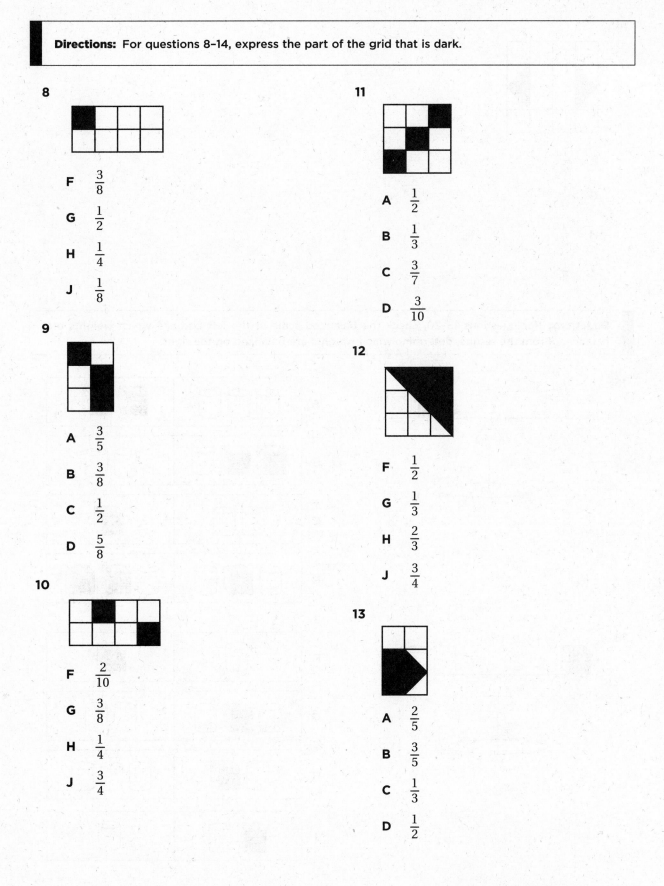

8

F $\frac{3}{8}$

G $\frac{1}{2}$

H $\frac{1}{4}$

J $\frac{1}{8}$

9

A $\frac{3}{5}$

B $\frac{3}{8}$

C $\frac{1}{2}$

D $\frac{5}{8}$

10

F $\frac{2}{10}$

G $\frac{3}{8}$

H $\frac{1}{4}$

J $\frac{3}{4}$

11

A $\frac{1}{2}$

B $\frac{1}{3}$

C $\frac{3}{7}$

D $\frac{3}{10}$

12

F $\frac{1}{2}$

G $\frac{1}{3}$

H $\frac{2}{3}$

J $\frac{3}{4}$

13

A $\frac{2}{5}$

B $\frac{3}{5}$

C $\frac{1}{3}$

D $\frac{1}{2}$

GO TO NEXT PAGE ➡

14

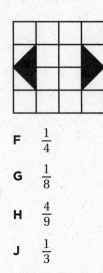

F $\frac{1}{4}$

G $\frac{1}{8}$

H $\frac{4}{9}$

J $\frac{1}{3}$

Directions: For questions 15–20, check the balanced scale at the left and see which weights are balanced. From the results, determine which weights are balanced on the right.

15

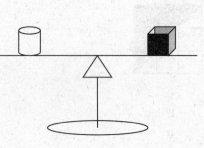

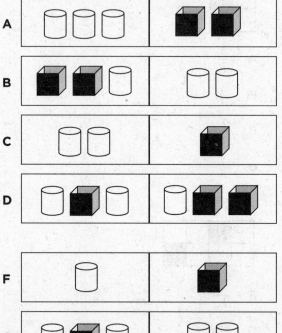

16

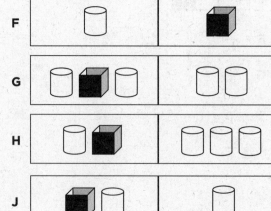

GO TO NEXT PAGE ➡

17

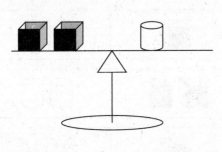

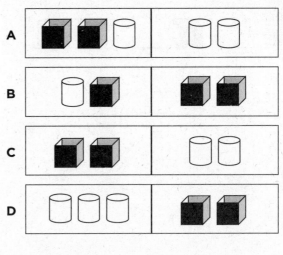

A

B

C

D

18

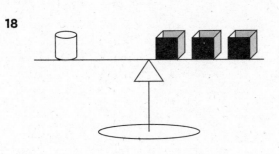

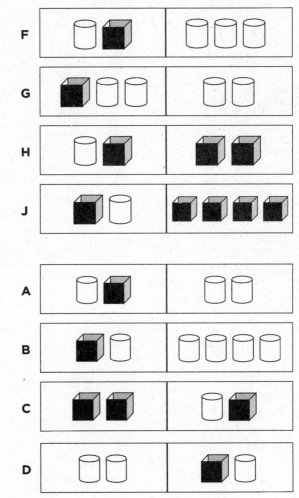

F

G

H

J

19

A

B

C

D

GO TO NEXT PAGE ➡

20

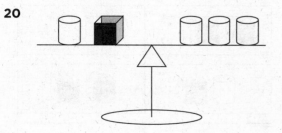

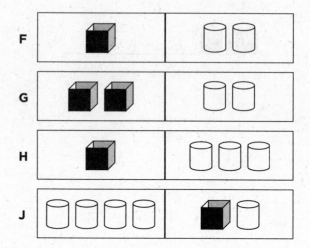

F

G

H

J

STOP

If there is still time remaining, you may review your answers.

TEST 4 VERBAL REASONING—WORDS

#1-20 15 MINUTES

Directions: For questions 1-5, find the word that names a necessary part of the underlined word.

---

1 shoe

- **A** sole
- **B** leather
- **C** laces
- **D** heel

2 bath

- **F** soap
- **G** water
- **H** tub
- **J** towel

3 library

- **A** building
- **B** books
- **C** chairs
- **D** computers

4 movie

- **F** sound
- **G** picture
- **H** popcorn
- **J** theater

5 pencil

- **A** wood
- **B** lead
- **C** paper
- **D** idea

Directions: For questions 6-10, choose the word that is most like the underlined words.

---

6 sport   play   recreation

- **F** tease
- **G** game
- **H** volleyball
- **J** fishing

7 pack   bag   parcel

- **A** suitcase
- **B** sleeper
- **C** bottle
- **D** ice

8 parade   march   pageant

- **F** procession
- **G** circus
- **H** band
- **J** float

9 record   document   transcribe

- **A** manuscript
- **B** chronicle
- **C** history
- **D** inscription

GO TO NEXT PAGE ➡

10 <u>content</u>   <u>pleased</u>   <u>happy</u>

   F   substance
   G   stoic
   H   ambivalent
   J   satisfied

Directions: For questions 11–15, choose the word that does *not* belong.

---

11 **A** music
      B noise
      C sound
      D ear

12 **F** soup
      G milk
      H ice
      J juice

13 **A** balanced
      B fair
      C beautiful
      D pretty

14 **F** shade
      G darken
      H cover
      J discover

15 **A** conflict
      B contrast
      C battle
      D combat

Directions: In questions 16–20, the words in the top row are related. The words in the bottom row are related in a similar way. Choose the word that completes the sequence in the bottom row.

16

influence	power	omnipotence
comma	semicolon	_____

   F quotation
   G period
   H parentheses
   J hyphen

17

valley	hill	mountain
_____	2	5

   A 0
   B 1
   C −1
   D 3

GO TO NEXT PAGE ➡

18

Italy	France	Spain
Panama	Nicaragua	_____

F Canada
G Guatemala
H Russia
J Uganda

19

key	lock	door
_____	field	computer

A password
B file
C website
D menu

20

spaghetti	macaroni	lasagna
maple	oak	_____

F shrub
G cedar
H furniture
J chair

 STOP

If there is still time remaining, you may review your answers.

TEST 5 VERBAL REASONING—CONTEXT

#1–10   7 MINUTES

> **Directions:** For these questions, find the statement that is true according to the given information.

1 Cookies were on sale at the grocery store. Carlo went in to buy cookies, but he came out with fruit, instead.

   A Carlo did not have enough money for cookies.
   B Carlo is on a diet.
   C The store was out of cookies.
   D Carlo changed his mind.

2 David and I shared a locker last year. This year I wanted to share a locker with Steven, but he is not in my homeroom. I ended up sharing a locker with John.

   F David and I no longer get along.
   G David moved away.
   H John is in my homeroom.
   J Steven is sharing a locker with David.

3 Mrs. Stevens hired Mrs. Hall in April. She hired Mrs. Wheat in June. Mrs. Hall and Mrs. Wheat are good friends.

   A Mrs. Hall recommended Mrs. Wheat for a job.
   B Mrs. Hall, Mrs. Wheat, and Mrs. Stevens are very good friends.
   C Mrs. Hall and Mrs. Wheat met on the job.
   D Mrs. Hall, Mrs. Wheat, and Mrs. Stevens all work for the same organization.

4 Brandi has appeared in many plays in many roles. She especially enjoys Shakespeare. Although she prefers comedies, her favorite play is *Romeo and Juliet*.

   F Brandi is an actress.
   G Brandi only likes Shakespearean plays.
   H *Romeo and Juliet* is a comedy.
   J Brandi's favorite role is Juliet.

5 The film crew caught Andy's fancy dribbling on videotape. It played on the eleven o'clock news program. Kristen saw it, but Kelsay couldn't stay awake that late.

   A Kelsay is too young to stay up until 11:00.
   B Kelsay had to watch Andy on tape.
   C Andy is a professional basketball player.
   D Kelsay didn't watch the eleven o'clock news that night.

6 Otto has seven siblings. Three of them are boys, and four of them are girls. He still keeps in touch with all of them, and they all visit their mother and father on holidays.

   F Otto is extremely organized.
   G Otto's family has four sons.
   H All seven children in Otto's family visit their parents.
   J Otto's family is very religious.

GO TO NEXT PAGE ➡

7 Cathy and her husband both speak Latin. They attended the same college and got married while they were in school. Now they write books together.

   A Cathy and her husband have a lot in common.

   B Cathy and her husband write books in Latin.

   C They both received degrees in Latin.

   D Their children speak Latin.

8 Tamara grew up in the eastern part of the state. After a few years in the city, she moved back to the mountains. She missed the country.

   F Tamara does not like cities.

   G The eastern part of Tamara's state has mountains.

   H Tamara's family still lives in the country.

   J The city is located in the mountains.

9 Rhonda and Debbie used to be neighbors and best friends. Rhonda moved to another state when they were in high school. Debbie moved away when she went to nursing school.

   A Rhonda and Debbie live near each other again.

   B Debbie is a registered nurse.

   C Rhonda and Debbie are no longer in contact.

   D Rhonda and Debbie are no longer neighbors.

10 Billy lives on the top floor of his apartment building. When he gets on the elevator on the first floor, he presses the button for the 11th floor. When he arrives, he walks the rest of the way up.

   F Billy is not tall enough to reach the elevator buttons higher than 11.

   G Billy is trying to get more exercise.

   H The elevator in Billy's building does not go past the 11th floor.

   J Billy's building has more than 11 stories.

If there is still time remaining, you may review your answers.

Directions: For questions 1–40, read each passage and the questions following that passage. Find the answer.

PASSAGE FOR QUESTIONS 1–4

The outbreak of World War II brought about changes at all levels of American society. Young men from all over the states, fresh from school and farms, enlisted to serve their country in the war abroad—often losing their lives in the process. Even those not allowed to join the military found ways to contribute to the war effort. Retirees and those unable to serve for a variety of physical reasons manned amateur ham radios, monitoring radio waves for new information. Housewives contributed to the war effort by growing their own food in "victory gardens" and by staining their legs with coffee and tea to mimic the color of nylon stockings—sacrificing the actual nylon to the production of needed war supplies. By 1943, even 16-year-old females got a chance to get involved. Dubbed "gunpowder girls," these young women performed various duties for the military. These jobs ranged from painting aircraft wings with "dope," a thick, noxious liquid that protected them from rain and snow, to tearing apart mangled plane engines.

The demands that World War II made on American society forced young people to grow up fast and to shoulder responsibilities they hadn't thought possible. Returning GIs faced quite a different home front following World War II. Society lacked the luxuries to which the soldiers had been accustomed before the war; women wore rugged clothes and carried themselves with pride, knowing they had helped the military cause in important ways. At first people tried to return to the old behavioral patterns. Fashion catalogs, for example, displayed frilly, feminine clothes for women to wear as they returned to their domestic chores of raising children and cooking hot meals. But Rosie the Riveter, and those like her who had manned the home front, resisted returning to the roles of wife, nursemaid, and cook. Few of those who had experienced the satisfaction of doing a demanding job well and earning a fair wage could peaceably allow themselves to be so <u>constrained</u> again.

1 Which of the following would be the best title for this selection?

A Uncle Sam Wants YOU to Contribute
B 1001 Tips for Old Coffee
C Rosie the Riveter Unriveted by Domestic Duties
D Women: Dutiful in All Ways

2 All but which of the following appears in the reading passage above as an example of a job that nonmilitary people could do to contribute to the World War II cause?

F monitoring radio waves to keep aware of current events
G growing a victory garden to provide cheap but nutritious food
H staining one's legs with coffee to save nylon
J walking instead of driving to save gas

GO TO NEXT PAGE ➡

COOP PRACTICE EXAM 2

3 What kind of publication would print this article?

   A *Good Housekeeping Magazine*
   B *National Geographic*
   C *Slam Magazine*
   D *Highlights Magazine*

4 Based on the use of the word in the passage, what is the best definition of constrained?

   F free
   G imprisoned
   H adventurous
   J angry

PASSAGE FOR QUESTIONS 5–8

American society, hot to try any new method for staying slim (other than a sensible diet and increased exercise), finds itself taken with a new nutritional fad—the low-carb, high-protein diet. But some doctors maintain that such diets are not successful at helping the dieter maintain long-term weight loss. These doctors also point out that such diets are especially dangerous for young kids.

Modern nutritionists debate over what is the cause of American obesity. On the one hand, some claim that genetics are to blame; they say that some people are simply predisposed toward fatness. On the other hand, some claim that individual choice is to blame; they say that if people simply made better nutritional and activity choices, they wouldn't be overweight. Neither choice is entirely satisfying. Focusing on individual responsibility makes it easier to blame people for their own well-being and allows those with self control a certain smug satisfaction. But focusing the debate on genetics brings up uncomfortable implications elsewhere—like whether or not certain populations are genetically more adept at athletics or dancing or intelligence.

The question will probably never be settled until a reliable set of statistics can be generated. So long as we study the question of "nature vs. nurture" by studying children in their domestic situations, being reared by their biological parents, scientists won't be able to distinguish which factors are constant and which are not. Perhaps the best way to answer the question would be to monitor how adoptive children mature and record their level of obesity. Then we could compare the results to the fitness level of the biological parents. Such a study would be expensive—and require scientists to have access to adoptive information (which is currently illegal)—but might finally answer our questions regarding weight.

5 Which of the following statements is true for this author?

   A Problems like obesity clearly stem from lack of self-discipline and issues of free will.
   B Problems like obesity clearly stem from genetic codes that predetermine our lives.
   C Problems like obesity stem from a combination of free will and genetic tendency.
   D We cannot, at this stage of human development, determine exactly whether free will or genetic tendency causes obesity.

6 Why did the author write this piece?

   F to document the history of the debate over whether free will or genetic predetermination rules human behavior
   G to confuse the debate over free will vs. genetics with unnecessary detail
   H to suggest a way that the debate of free will vs. genetics might be resolved
   J to outline several stances by authority figures that contribute to the recurring debate over free will vs. genetic predisposition

GO TO NEXT PAGE ➡

7 Which of the following is the best definition of <u>adoptive</u>?

   A able to adapt well to new situations

   B adults who adopt children into their household

   C children who are adopted into a household

   D being good at a skill

8 Which of the following is a claim made in the course of this paper?

   F People who exercise a lot and eat very little tend to gain the most weight.

   G A high-carb, high-protein diet is fast becoming the diet most recommended by doctors.

   H People who exercise a lot and eat nutritiously always maintain a healthy weight.

   J A low-carb, high-protein diet is dangerous for kids.

PASSAGE FOR QUESTIONS 9–12

For a long time, publishers have tried to provide high-quality reading material for readers aged 13–18. This has proven to be an unsurprisingly difficult task given all the competition for kids' attention, ranging from hula hoops in the 1950s to roller skates in the 1970s and even more recently to the XBOX 360. One option marketers have tried is hiring new authors to create age- and values-appropriate texts that cater to modern tastes; currently such authors as J. K. Rowling, author of the ever popular Harry Potter series, serve up literary works designed to fit this <u>niche</u>.

Nevertheless, marketers have learned that one does not always have to reinvent the wheel. Sometimes one just has to give it a new coat of paint.

Recently the publishers of old favorites like Nancy Drew and the Hardy Boys have <u>gotten out their paint brushes</u>. Originally published by the Edward R. Stratemeyer syndicate, the Nancy Drew and Hardy Boy series have always tried to provide wholesome, PG-rated entertainment that taught good moral values through the actions of admirable and age-appropriate heros. These texts, written since the 1930s by a series of ghost writers, continue to be produced today. Until the 2000s, the main differences among these texts has come in the form of fashion and historical details. Nancy Drew, for example, is still 18, strawberry-blonde, and dating Ned Nickerson—but she now wears designer jeans and cool sweaters rather than neat dresses with white collars, and she volunteers for animal rights rallies rather than running the local Meals-on-Wheels program. Producers of the Hardy Boys, however, have allowed the series to "pump up the excitement" even more. In book one of the updated version, Joe Hardy's girlfriend becomes the victim of a fatal car bombing.

GO TO NEXT PAGE ➡

9 The main idea of this reading passage would be _____ .

   A to show how kids are getting bored with old-fashioned children's books

   B to show how writers, because they recycle old material, are not as clever and creative as they used to be

   C to show how marketers have reacted to changing literary taste by updating old favorites from previous decades

   D to show that people still enjoy pastimes like hula hoops and roller skates despite how long ago they were invented

10 How, according to the reading passage, does Joe Hardy's girlfriend die?

   F strangled at the movie theater

   G blown up at an animal rights rally

   H victim of a car bombing

   J poisoned during her Meals-on-Wheels job

11 What does the author of this piece mean when s/he uses the expression "gotten out their paint brushes"?

   A These old books got new cover art but left the stories the same in order to win over new audiences and keep old fans.

   B The publishers and marketers of the Nancy Drew and Hardy Boys series have begun updating old material in hopes of capturing a new audience.

   C Many publishers and markets have decided to change professions.

   D The publishers and marketers of the Nancy Drew and Hardy Boys series have decided to reject old formulas in favor of concentrated additions of immorality and violence.

12 Based on the use of the word in the passage, which of the following is the best definition of niche?

   F category

   G genre

   H notch

   J philosophy

PASSAGE FOR QUESTIONS 13–17

(1) My father has alot of old Hardy Boys books down in the basement. (2) I like reading them. (3) They represent a more innocent time. (4) The boys don't have to worry about terrorist bombs; their more concerned with finding gold doubloons or following a secret passageway. (5) And you can always tell who the villains are because they always drive black sedans.

13 What is the best way to write the first sentence?

   A My father has a lot of old Hardy Boys books down in the basement.

   B My father has a lot of old, Hardy Boys books down in the basement.

   C My father have a lot of old Hardy Boys books down in the basement.

   D My father he has alot of old Hardy Boys books down in the basement.

14 What is the best way to combine sentences 2 and 3?

   F I like reading them unless they represent a more innocent time.

   G I like reading them, moreover, they represent a more innocent time.

   H I like reading them because they represent a more innocent time.

   J I like reading them, representing a more innocent time than they do.

GO TO NEXT PAGE ➡

15 What is the best way to write this section of sentence 4?

  A Their more concerned, concerning finding gold doubloons and secret passageways.
  B They're more concerned with finding gold doubloons and secret passageways.
  C Finding gold doubloons and secret passageways is something about which they are more concerned.
  D They're most concerned with finding gold doubloons than with secret passageways.

16 What is the best concluding sentence for this paragraph?

  F They seem a bit corny, but I really enjoy them.
  G I don't know why my father kept all of those old books.
  H The Hardy Boys books were published by the Stratemeyer syndicate.
  J My mother has a lot of Nancy Drew books, too.

17 Which of the following sentences is written correctly?

  A Nancy Drew originally drove a red roadster, however, when the book was revised, it was changed into a convertible.
  B The Hardy brothers owned a convertible, of course, as well as twin motorcycles.
  C There friend Chet Morton owned a yellow jalopy that he nicknamed "The Queen."
  D The villains always seemed to drive black sedans; they must of all shopped at the same dealership.

PASSAGE FOR QUESTIONS 18–23

Few would deny that American society craves things that are new, fast, and exciting. One such example is auto racing. But as the media reports increasing numbers of fatalities and injuries due to such activities, the demand for more rigorous safety regulations increases just as fast as public interest in such sports.

NASCAR's research and development facilities in North Carolina are trying to keep up with the safety trend as best they can. They have produced spectacular changes in car safety design just since 2001. Race tracks now provide steel-and-foam cushioning around the track walls that better absorb impact. The cars themselves have benefited from increased Research and Development. Cars now come equipped with escape hatches through which drivers can wriggle if their side exits get blocked or crushed. Air filters that remove carbon monoxide from cockpits are now SOP. Cars also carry black boxes, just like the ones in airplanes, that record crash characteristics—like G-forces that can be studied following impact. And cars use Kevlar straps to keep wheels from flying off and causing collateral damage to other racers during crashes. While racecars can never be 100 percent safe, they can always be a little bit safer than they were last year.

GO TO NEXT PAGE ➡

18 What would be the best title for this reading selection?

   F Relationship between NASCAR and Military Equipment Explored

   G Technology Innovations at NASCAR Move at Sonic Speed

   H The Dangers of Carbon Monoxide

   J Speed First, Safety Second

19 Which of the following relationships is substantiated by the passage?

   A NASCAR vehicles are like airplanes because of the equipment they carry.

   B NASCAR vehicles are like military vehicles because of their bullet-proof armor.

   C NASCAR vehicles are like LA-Z-Boy recliners because of their use of steel-and-foam cushioning at the neck.

   D NASCAR vehicles are like houses because they are both totally safe.

20 What does the author mean by using the acronym SOP?

   F Security Operating Procedures

   G Standard Operating Procedure

   H Safe Operating Practice

   J Scope Of Practice

21 According to the passage, since when have the changes discussed taken place?

   A 2000

   B 2001

   C 2003

   D 2004

22 According to the passage, what is removed from the cockpits of NASCAR vehicles?

   F carbon dioxide

   G oxygen

   H carbon monoxide

   J steel

23 Choose the sentence that is written correctly.

   A After an accident, the black box contained important data.

   B The wheels of a NASCAR vehicle is designed not to fly off.

   C Every design improvement affects the dynamics of racing.

   D Racing fans want innovation, adrenaline, and to feel speed.

GO TO NEXT PAGE ➡

The idea that automobiles were the exclusive playthings of the wealthy ended in 1908. In that year, Henry Ford, the American industrialist and founder of the Ford Motor Company, successfully applied the principles of mass production to the manufacture of automobiles. His Model T car (nicknamed the "Tin Lizzie" or the "Flivver") was the first automobile built on an assembly line with interchangeable parts (available "in any color—so long as it's black").

24 What is the best way to write the opening sentence?

F The idea that automobiles were the exclusive playthings of the wealthy ended in 1908.

G Automobiles, as the exclusive playthings of the wealthy, is an idea that ended in 1908.

H In 1908, the automobile as wealthy plaything ended.

J Before 1908, the automobile was a wealthy plaything; after that date, this ends.

25 What is the best conclusion to this paragraph?

A Henry Ford invented the assembly line.

B This lowered the cost enough to make the car available to the general public.

C This led to the development of NASCAR.

D Black must have been a popular color.

26 Which of the following sentences is written correctly?

F The success of Henry Ford's assembly line delighted many people but it frightened many others.

G Some people feared that growing technology would deprive people of their identities.

H The novel, *Brave New World*, explores the consequences of this technological system.

J In the book, the factories of the future creates people on an assembly line.

GO TO NEXT PAGE ➡

The popular culture produced by a society reflects the fears, passions, and obsessions of that society. In the 1950s, for example, the increase of technology in popular culture, especially the use of <u>standardized</u> procedures like the Xeroxing machine and the assembly line, led to a rise in science fiction that warned against losing one's identity. Stories like *Invasion of the Body Snatchers*, for example, took hold of the nation's imagination; the story tells of people's fear of being replaced with no one noticing the difference or, worse, not caring about the replacement.

Again, in the 1970s, we see pop culture reflecting the values of society. The 1970s encouraged people to find a passion for things that represented the country or, better yet, other cultures. Beads, flowers, face painting, and musical references to setting up a community on a farm where people could share life in peace and communistic harmony abound then. Such references mirror the Hippies' cultural revolt against "<u>straight</u>" society's respect for paying taxes, obeying the rules, going to war, and acting conservatively.

Now, in the 21st century, we can detect the same pattern forming again. Current mass markets show a cultural obsession with reality TV—shows that mirror real life in all its boring realism . . .

27 The author's use of the word <u>standardized</u> can be best defined as meaning _____.

A automated
B streamlined
C fearful
D efficient

28 The author makes the point that popular culture mirrors cultural beliefs. Based on that fact, the author might agree with which of the following statements?

F People in the 1930s, which followed hard on the Great Depression, valued expensive home furnishings.
G People in the 1940s, which were engrossed in the military campaigns of World War II, were not patriotic.
H People in the 1960s, with its fear of prolonged military commitment in Vietnam, respected the government.
J People in the 1980s, with its love of technology, revered jewelry made from used technology (like O-rings and car gaskets).

29 The author's use of the word <u>straight</u> is not typical; which definition fits the author's use of this word?

A legal
B efficient
C normal
D sober

30 Which of the following restates a fact discussed in the reading?

F People in the 1950s watched lots of movies.
G People in the 1970s liked being in nature and wore things to remind them of nature.
H People are always aware of fads and popular trends in their world.
J People currently find themselves obsessed with nature, just like in the 1970s.

GO TO NEXT PAGE ➡

As of 2004, college <u>remediation</u> classes cost the state $15 million; 28 percent of the student body signed up for remedial classes in math, reading, and writing. Why, in this modern era of public education, should this be the case?

Some experts say that the problem is the student, but far more of the experts point the finger at the educational system itself. They call our current K-12 programs old-fashioned, unchallenging, and unable to prepare students for college. The problem is due to not only lack of student performance or lack of teacher expertise but also to an unwillingness to treat high school kids as the adults they are.

Senior year, according to popular wisdom, is <u>going the way of the dinosaur</u>. Finished with the core graduation requirements, struck by senioritis, and demoralized by turning 18 without gaining what they perceive as the proper respect, students lose their motivation to learn. And, perhaps the senior year *should* be sacrificed to social Darwinism. After all, grades earned past the fall semester of the senior year very rarely count toward any concrete goal; GPAs needed for entrance exams or scholarships are typically turned in by November of the fall semester. About the only way that spring semester grades can hurt a graduating senior is by causing them to fail a core requirement class—like English or math.

Whatever the reason, kids aren't paying attention to senior year classes, which severely weakens their academic skills by the time they enter the college scene. But try telling that to a graduating senior. After 11 years of (in some cases) hard work, they feel entitled to a rest—and are willing to risk their initial success at university to do so.

31 What does the author mean by the use of the word <u>remediation</u>?

A redo
B revise
C resubmit
D reevaluate

32 What percentage of the student body enrolled in remedial classes their first year at college?

F 26 percent
G 27 percent
H 28 percent
J 29 percent

33 With which of the following statements would the author most likely agree?

A The education system should remain as it is.
B The education system should be modified.
C The education system should be done away with.
D We cannot tell based on the tone of the passage.

34 What does the author mean when s/he uses the phrase <u>going the way of the dinosaur</u>?

F Something is evolving into a new form.
G Something is becoming extinct.
H Something is becoming a habit.
J Something is being promoted.

35 What would be a good title for this passage?

A Why Johnny Won't Read
B From College to High School: Ten Steps Backwards
C How to Survive in College
D Saving Senior Year

GO TO NEXT PAGE ➡

Jeremy often told his mother about the bad little boy at school. His name was Scott. And was Scott terrible! He ate chalk. He scribbled on other kids' papers. He even hit girls. He spent a long time in the corner or in "time out."

Every day Jeremy came home with a new story about Scott. Today, Scott unrolled all the rolls of toilet paper in the school bathroom. This time, he stepped on the flag. Jeremy's mother came to look forward to the time, every day after school, when Jeremy would tell her the latest bad news. They would laugh together over what Scott had done—and speculate as to what Scott would do next.

One day Jeremy's mother went to the school for a parent-teacher conference. She was surprised when the teacher sat down, a worried look on her face. "I'm a little concerned," said the teacher, "why you haven't answered any of my written notes or telephone messages."

"What notes? What telephone messages?" said Jeremy's mother.

36 Why is the teacher likely having the parent-teacher conference with Jeremy's mother?

F to praise Jeremy for being such a good student

G to ask Jeremy's mother to volunteer for a field trip

H to discuss why Jeremy is acting so terribly at school

J in response to a note Jeremy's mother has sent previously

37 What does the author mean by using the word speculate?

A watch

B argue about

C guess

D list

38 Where might you find this text published?

F an elementary school reader

G a romance novel

H a study guide for *Gone with the Wind*

J the comics section of the newspaper

39 What did Scott do in school?

A flushed the toilet a million times

B stepped on the American flag

C stole money

D pulled Jeremy's hair

40 What can you infer about Jeremy?

F He is afraid of Scott.

G Scott makes Jeremy angry.

H He is Scott.

J He thinks that Scott is funny.

If there is still time remaining, you may review your answers.

> **Directions:** Select the best answer from the given choices.

1 What does the digit 6 represent in the number 346,782?

   A   tens
   B   hundreds
   C   thousands
   D   ten thousands

2 A triangle is inserted into a rectangle as illustrated in the figure below. If the length of the rectangle is 10, the base of the triangle is 6 and the shaded area is 42, find the height of the triangle.

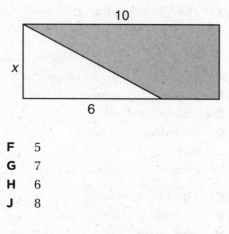

   F   5
   G   7
   H   6
   J   8

3 Simplify the following powers and then select the correct answer.

(a) 5^2 (b) 2^5 (c) 2^3

   A   a > b or c > a
   B   c = a or b < c
   C   c > b and a = b
   D   b < a or c < b

4 If $a = -2$, list the following terms in order, from smallest to largest:

$$a, a^2, a^0, -a$$

   F $a < -a < a^2 < a^0$
   G $a < a^0 < -a < a^2$
   H $a^2 < -a < a^0 < a$
   J $-a < a^0 < a < a^2$

5 The Aztec Chemical Company wants to repackage 1,159 ounces of one of their chemicals into one-pound containers. How many ounces remain after all the chemicals are repackaged?

Sixteen ounces equals one pound.

   A   7 ounces
   B   48 ounces
   C   64 ounces
   D   72 ounces

6 Malcolm filled a bag with some cashew nuts. He then added 2 ounces of cashews and weighed the total, which was 13 ounces. Select the correct answer from the following choices.

   F   The original weight of the cashews was more than 5 times the weight of the added cashews.
   G   The final weight of the cashews was less than 6 times the weight of the added cashews.
   H   The original weight of the cashews was less than 4 times the weight of the added cashews.
   J   The final weight of the cashews was less than 4 times the weight of the added cashews.

GO TO NEXT PAGE ➡

COOP PRACTICE EXAM 2

7 The temperature is 90 degrees at 3 P.M. If it decreases by 40 percent by midnight and then increases by 26 percent by 10 A.M. the next day, what is the temperature at 10:01 A.M.? Round off to the nearest degree.

    A 68
    B 54
    C 66
    D 42

8 What number multiplied by 8 is 18 more than 5 times the number?

    F 3
    G 6
    H 7
    J 8

9 If $x = \dfrac{4}{5}$, $y = \dfrac{2}{3}$, and $z = \sqrt{3}$, find the value of $10x - 9y - 4z^2$.

    A −6
    B −8
    C −10
    D 4

10 If a is a negative integer and b is a positive integer, which of the following statements is true?

    F $a^2 < 0$
    G $b^2 < 0$
    H $a^2 + b^2 > 0$
    J $ab^2 > 0$

11 Simplify $-2|5| \cdot 3\,|{-4}|$.

    A −120
    B 100
    C −80
    D 140

12 The height of the front door in a blueprint of a one-family house measures $\dfrac{3}{4}''$. If the actual door is 8 feet tall, what is the ratio of the blueprint to the actual dimensions of the house?

    F $\dfrac{1}{128}$
    G $\dfrac{2}{5}$
    H $\dfrac{3}{32}$
    J $\dfrac{1}{64}$

13 If a is a positive even integer, and b and c are the following consecutive positive integers, which of the following statements is false?

    A ab is even
    B $a + b$ is odd
    C ac is odd
    D $b + c$ is odd

14 Find the measure of the angle between the hour hand and the minute hand when a clock reads 9:05. Select the best answer.

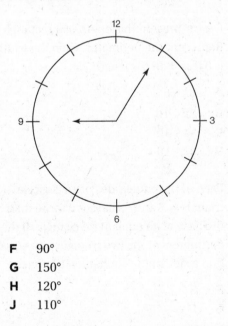

    F 90°
    G 150°
    H 120°
    J 110°

GO TO NEXT PAGE ➡

15 $\overline{AB}$ and $\overline{CD}$ intersect at point E.

If m$\angle DEA = 87°$ and m$\angle CEB = 2y + 19$, find the value of y.

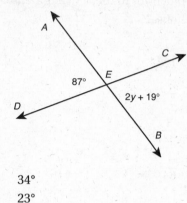

A 34°

B 23°

C 19°

D 65°

16 If $ABCD$ is a square, which statement is false?

F Angle B is a right angle.

G The measure of angle B equals the measure of angle C.

H The measure of angle B plus the measure of angle A equals 180°.

J BC is perpendicular to AD.

17 Let k represent the length of a rectangle. Represent the perimeter when the width is 8 less than the length.

A $6k - 6$

B $2k + 16$

C $4k - 10$

D $4k - 16$

18 Each of the equal sides of an isosceles triangle is 7 and its base is 2 more than the base of an equilateral triangle. If the perimeters of the two triangles are equal, find a side of the equilateral triangle.

F 8

G 5

H 9

J 6

19 The areas of a rectangle and a square are equal. If one side of the square is twice the width of the rectangle and the length of the rectangle is 16, find the width of the rectangle.

A 6

B 10

C 4

D 8

20 The volume of a sphere enclosed in a cube is approximately $\frac{1}{2}$ the volume of the cube. Estimate the volume of a sphere enclosed in a cube, each of whose sides is 10.8.

F 300

G 550

H 800

J 650

21 In the accompanying triangle ABC, the lengths of AC and BC are 5 and 7, respectively. Find the length of the hypotenuse, AB, to the nearest tenth of an inch.

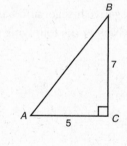

A 7.4

B 4.5

C 8.6

D 5.8

GO TO NEXT PAGE ➡

COOP PRACTICE EXAM 2

22 In a triangle, the sum of any two sides is always greater than the third side. Select the best choice to represent the three sides of a triangle.

F   3, 4, 7

G   4, 5, 8

H   5, 6, 12

J   10, 5, 5

23 Round off 1,147,690 to the nearest thousand.

A   1,147,200

B   1,150,000

C   1,148,000

D   1,149,000

24 Change 0.054% to a decimal.

F   0.0054

G   5.4

H   0.054

J   0.00054

25 Find the value of the expression $3rs - 2t$ when $r = 2$, $s = 3$, and $t = 4$.

A   4

B   6

C   8

D   10

26 Simplify $-4(-2)^3$, and choose the correct answer.

F   +32

G   −32

H   +24

J   −16

27 Of the following expressions, which is the smallest?

A $5 \times 3 - (2 + 7)$

B $5(3) - \dfrac{48}{6}$

C $14 - 5 + \dfrac{30}{6}$

D $\dfrac{18}{2} - 3(4 - 6) + \dfrac{54}{9}$

28 If we let U = the set of all countries of South America, P = {Uruguay, Chile, Brazil}, and Q = {Argentina, Colombia, Paraguay}, find the intersection of P and Q.

F   Paraguay

G   null set

H   Brazil

J   Colombia

29 Simplify $\dfrac{a\sqrt{42}}{b\sqrt{7}}$.

A $\dfrac{a}{b}\sqrt{7}$

B $\sqrt{\dfrac{6a}{7b}}$

C $\dfrac{a}{b}\sqrt{6}$

D $6a\sqrt{b}$

30 If the measures of angles A and C are respectively 32° and 59°, find the measure of exterior angle CBD.

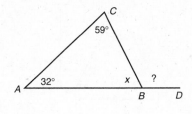

F   59°

G   91°

H   89°

J   98°

GO TO NEXT PAGE ➡

31 *O* is the center of the circle.

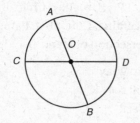

Which of the following statements is true?

A $AB > CD$

B $OC < OB$

C $AB - OB = OD$

D $CD - OB < OD$

32 In the two diagrams, which of the following statements is true?

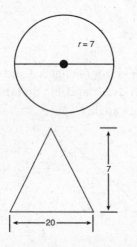

F   Three fifths of the area of the triangle is greater than the area of the circle.

G   The area of the triangle is greater than half the area of the circle.

H   One half the area of the circle is equal to the area of the triangle.

J   The area of the circle is greater than twice the area of the triangle.

33 The circle graph below indicates the types of goods a factory produces. If the factory received $30,000,000 in orders last year, which of the following statements is true?

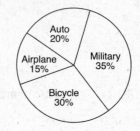

A   The military orders exceeded the airplane orders by less than $5,000,000.

B   The difference between the bicycle and the auto orders was less than $3,000,000.

C   Bicycle and auto orders together were equal to $15,000,000.

D   Airplane orders were $6,000,000 less than bicycle orders.

34 An urn contains 4 blue, 3 green, 5 white, and 6 red marbles. What is the probability of selecting a green marble without looking?

F $\dfrac{2}{9}$

G $\dfrac{5}{18}$

H $\dfrac{1}{6}$

J $\dfrac{1}{3}$

GO TO NEXT PAGE ➡

35 The bar graph represents the average temperature in Alaska during the indicated months. Check the graph and then select the correct answer.

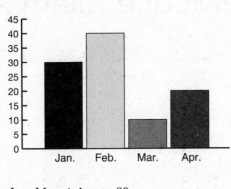

A Mar. + Apr. = 60

B Jan. – Apr. = 20

C Feb. – Mar. > 40

D Apr. + Feb. > 50

36 Michelle spends $t + 4$ hours per day watching television. Carmen spends t hours and Henry watches television $t - 2$ hours per day. Find the average number of hours of TV time for the three students.

F $\dfrac{(3t+2)}{3}$

G $\left(\dfrac{4t}{3}\right)+2$

H $2t + 4$

J $\dfrac{(4t-2)}{3}$

37 Arrange in order, from smallest to largest: 23 ounces, 1.4 pounds, $1\frac{1}{2}$ pounds.

A 23 ounces $< 1\frac{1}{2}$ pounds < 1.4 pounds

B 23 ounces < 1.4 pounds $< 1\frac{1}{2}$ pounds

C $1\frac{1}{2}$ pounds < 23 ounces < 1.4 pounds

D 1.4 pounds < 23 ounces $< 1\frac{1}{2}$ pounds

38 Estimate 8% of 232.

F 50

G 20

H 31

J 47

39 For all integers x and y, $x \# y = \dfrac{x+y}{2}$.

If $5 \# y$ is an integer, what is a possible value for y?

A 2

B 6

C 7

D 4

40 Find the coordinates of the point formed by the intersection of a line parallel to the y-axis and two units to the right of it and a second line parallel to the x-axis and 4 units above it.

F (4, 2)

G (2, 4)

H (0, 4)

J (2, 3)

If there is still time remaining, you may review your answers.

ANSWER KEY
COOP Practice Exam 2

TEST 1 SEQUENCES

1. **C**	6. **F**	11. **B**	16. **H**
2. **J**	7. **C**	12. **J**	17. **B**
3. **D**	8. **G**	13. **A**	18. **J**
4. **J**	9. **D**	14. **J**	19. **A**
5. **D**	10. **F**	15. **C**	20. **H**

TEST 2 ANALOGIES

1. **C**	6. **F**	11. **C**	16. **J**
2. **J**	7. **B**	12. **F**	17. **A**
3. **A**	8. **F**	13. **B**	18. **F**
4. **G**	9. **B**	14. **H**	19. **C**
5. **D**	10. **J**	15. **C**	20. **J**

TEST 3 QUANTITATIVE REASONING

1. **D**	6. **H**	11. **B**	16. **H**
2. **F**	7. **A**	12. **F**	17. **A**
3. **B**	8. **J**	13. **D**	18. **J**
4. **G**	9. **C**	14. **G**	19. **B**
5. **A**	10. **H**	15. **D**	20. **F**

TEST 4 VERBAL REASONING—WORDS

1. **A**	6. **G**	11. **D**	16. **G**
2. **G**	7. **A**	12. **H**	17. **C**
3. **B**	8. **F**	13. **A**	18. **G**
4. **G**	9. **B**	14. **J**	19. **A**
5. **B**	10. **J**	15. **B**	20. **G**

ANSWER KEY
COOP Practice Exam 2

TEST 5 VERBAL REASONING—CONTEXT

1. **D**	4. **F**	7. **A**	10. **J**
2. **H**	5. **D**	8. **G**	
3. **D**	6. **G**	9. **D**	

TEST 6 READING AND LANGUAGE ARTS

1. **C**	11. **B**	21. **B**	31. **A**
2. **J**	12. **F**	22. **H**	32. **H**
3. **B**	13. **A**	23. **C**	33. **D**
4. **G**	14. **H**	24. **F**	34. **G**
5. **D**	15. **B**	25. **B**	35. **A**
6. **H**	16. **F**	26. **G**	36. **H**
7. **C**	17. **B**	27. **A**	37. **C**
8. **J**	18. **G**	28. **J**	38. **F**
9. **C**	19. **A**	29. **C**	39. **B**
10. **H**	20. **G**	30. **G**	40. **H**

TEST 7 MATHEMATICS

1. **C**	11. **A**	21. **C**	31. **C**
2. **H**	12. **F**	22. **G**	32. **J**
3. **D**	13. **C**	23. **C**	33. **C**
4. **G**	14. **H**	24. **J**	34. **H**
5. **A**	15. **A**	25. **D**	35. **D**
6. **F**	16. **J**	26. **F**	36. **F**
7. **A**	17. **D**	27. **A**	37. **D**
8. **G**	18. **F**	28. **G**	38. **G**
9. **C**	19. **C**	29. **C**	39. **C**
10. **H**	20. **J**	30. **G**	40. **G**

ANSWERS EXPLAINED

Test 1   Sequences

1. **(C)** The left figure moves to the right-most place and the other figures move left.

2. **(J)** The first and second figures exchange places, as do the third and fourth figures.

3. **(D)** The first and last figures exchange places, as do the second and third figures.

4. **(J)** The first and third figures exchange places, as do the second and fourth figures.

5. **(D)** The third figure moves to first place and the other figures move to the right.

6. **(F)** The fourth figure moves into first place and changes color. The other figures move to the right.

7. **(C)** In each succeeding diagram, the shaded box moves three units counterclockwise.

8. **(G)** D is always the middle letter. The other letters are in ascending alphabetical order.

9. **(D)** One letter is skipped between each letter in the sequence.

10. **(F)** One letter is skipped between the first and second letters in each group and two letters are skipped between the second and third letters in each group.

11. **(B)** One letter is skipped in backwards alphabetical order.

12. **(J)** The Roman numerals are descending by 3.

13. **(A)** R is the middle letter in each group. The other letters are in alphabetical order.

14. **(J)** The numbers are in the order x, x^2, x^3, where x is a whole number.

15. **(C)** To get to the second number in each group, divide the first number by 4. To get to the third number, divide the second number by 4.

16. **(H)** To find the second number in each group, subtract 2 from the first number. To find the third number, multiply the second number by 2.

17. **(B)** To get to the succeeding number in each group, multiply the preceding number by 3.

18. **(J)** Subtract 4 from each preceding number.

19. **(A)** In order to find the second number in each group, add 2 to the first number. To get to the third number, subtract 1 from the second number.

20. **(H)** One letter is skipped between the first and second letters in each group and two letters are skipped between the second and third letters in each group. The subscripts in each succeeding group are decreased by 2.

Test 2   Analogies

1. **(C)** Scissors is to hair as lawnmower is to grass. Scissors cut hair, and a lawnmower cuts grass.

2. **(J)** Musician is to band as bowler is to bowling team. A musician is a part of a band, and a bowler is part of a team.

3. **(A)** Leash is to dog as ball and chain is to convict. A leash restrains a dog as a ball and chain restrains a convict.

4. **(G)** Stop sign is to car as skull and crossbones are to ship. A stop sign signals stop to a driver, and a skull and crossbones signals a pirate ship to a seaman.

5. **(D)** Foot is to shoe as head is to helmet. A shoe protects the foot, and a helmet protects the head.

6. **(F)** Car is to road as ship is to ocean. A car drives along a road, and a ship sails across the ocean.

7. **(B)** Doctor is to patient as mechanic is to car wreck. A doctor heals a patient, and a mechanic repairs a car.

8. **(F)** Squirrel is to nuts as shark is to fish. Squirrels eat nuts, and sharks eat fish.

9. **(B)** Cloud is to rain as cow is to butter. A cloud produces rain, and a cow produces butter.

10. **(J)** Clothespin is to wash as belt is to jeans. A clothespin holds up clothes, and a belt supports jeans.

11. **(C)** Mother is to baby as tree is to branch. Both a child and a branch derive from a parent.

12. **(F)** Writer is to books as singer is to record. A writer's thoughts are inscribed in a book. A singer's voice is captured in a record.

13. **(B)** Money is to happiness as car collision is to headache. We usually think money brings happiness, and a car collision brings headaches.

14. **(H)** Stool is to kitchen as beach chair is to beach. A stool is found in a kitchen, and a beach chair is found on the beach.

15. **(C)** Maestro is to orchestra as director is to cameraman. A maestro directs musicians. A director directs the men and women operating the cameras.

16. **(J)** Sleeper is to bed as lounger is to lounge chair. Both a sleeper and a lounger rest on their respective pieces of furniture.

17. **(A)** Monkey is to banana as bear is to honey. Monkeys eat bananas, and bears eat honey.

18. **(F)** Cue stick is to billiard ball as bowling ball is to pin. The cue stick hits the billiard ball as the bowling ball knocks over the pin.

19. **(C)** Pot cover is to pot as roof is to house. A pot cover covers a pot, and a roof covers a house.

20. **(J)** Hand is to piano as mouth is to trumpet. A hand plays the piano, and the mouth plays the trumpet.

1. **(D)** Subtract 3 from each given number: $5 - 3 = 2$.

2. **(F)** Multiply each given number by 2: $6 \times 2 = 12$.

3. **(B)** Divide each given number by 3: $\frac{6}{3} = 2$.

4. **(G)** Multiply each given number by 9: $\frac{2}{3} \times 9 = 6$.

5. **(A)** Add $\frac{1}{2}$ to each given number: $1\frac{1}{2} + \frac{1}{2} = 2$.

6. **(H)** Subtract 2 from each given number: $4.5 - 2 = 2.5$.

7. **(A)** Divide each given number by 2: $\frac{8}{2} = 4$.

8. **(J)** One out of eight squares is dark: $\frac{1}{8}$.

9. **(C)** Three out of six squares are dark: $\frac{3}{6} = \frac{1}{2}$.

10. **(H)** Two dark squares out of a total of $8 = \frac{2}{8} = \frac{1}{4}$.

11. **(B)** Three out of nine squares are dark: $\frac{3}{9} = \frac{1}{3}$.

12. **(F)** One half of the entire figure is dark: $\frac{1}{2}$.

13. **(D)** Two full squares plus two half-squares are dark: $2 + 2 \times \frac{1}{2} = 2 + 1 = 3$.

    That makes a total of three out of six dark squares: $\frac{1}{2}$.

14. **(G)** Four half-squares are shaded: $4 \times \frac{1}{2} = 2$. That makes a total of two out of sixteen

    dark squares: $\frac{2}{16} = \frac{1}{8}$.

15. **(D)**

    $$
    \begin{array}{rcl}
    1\ \text{cylinder} & = & 1\ \text{cube} \\
    +\ 1\ \text{cylinder} \quad +1\ \text{cube} & & +\ 1\ \text{cylinder} + 1\ \text{cube} \\
    \hline
    2\ \text{cylinders} \quad +1\ \text{cube} & = & 1\ \text{cylinder} + 2\ \text{cubes}
    \end{array}
    $$

16. **(H)**

    $$
    \begin{array}{rcl}
    1\ \text{cube} & = & 2\ \text{cylinders} \\
    +\ 1\ \text{cylinder} & & +\ 1\ \text{cylinder} \\
    \hline
    1\ \text{cube} \ +1\ \text{cylinder} & = & 3\ \text{cylinders}
    \end{array}
    $$

17. **(A)**

$$2 \text{ cubes} = 1 \text{ cylinder}$$
$$\underline{+ 1 \text{ cylinder} \qquad + 1 \text{ cylinder}}$$
$$2 \text{ cubes } + 1 \text{ cylinder} = 2 \text{ cylinders}$$

18. **(J)**

$$1 \text{ cylinder} = 3 \text{ cubes}$$
$$\underline{+ 1 \text{ cube} \qquad + 1 \text{ cube}}$$
$$1 \text{ cylinder } + 1 \text{ cube} = 4 \text{ cubes}$$

19. **(B)**

$$3 \text{ cylinders} = 1 \text{ cube}$$
$$\underline{+ 1 \text{ cylinder} \qquad\qquad + 1 \text{ cylinder}}$$
$$4 \text{ cylinders} = 1 \text{ cube } + 1 \text{ cylinder}$$
$$\text{or}$$
$$1 \text{ cube} + 1 \text{ cylinder} = 4 \text{ cylinders}$$

20. **(F)**

$$1 \text{ cylinder} + 1 \text{ cube} = 3 \text{ cylinders}$$
$$\underline{- 1 \text{ cylinder} \qquad\qquad - 1 \text{ cylinder}}$$
$$1 \text{ cube} = 2 \text{ cylinders}$$

Test 4   Verbal Reasoning—Words

1. **(A)** A shoe does not *need* to be made of leather, nor does it need a heel or laces. The sole is the essential part of a shoe.

2. **(G)** Water is essential for a bath. You can bathe without soap or a towel, and you can bathe in other places besides a tub.

3. **(B)** A library needs books. A bookmobile does not have a building or chairs, for instance, and libraries have not always had computers.

4. **(G)** Silent movies did not have sound, obviously, and you can watch a movie at home and without popcorn. The picture is essential.

5. **(B)** While ideas are important, the pencil itself needs lead in order to write.

6. **(G)** These are all general words for recreation.

7. **(A)** These are all containers for solid items.

8. **(F)** These are all synonyms. The other choices are related, but they don't mean the same.

9. **(B)** The first three words are verbs meaning "*to* record." Only choice B can be a verb; the other choices are nouns meaning "*a* record."

10. **(J)** *Happy, content, pleased,* and *satisfied* are synonyms for a pleasant feeling. *Stoic* and *ambivalent* do not indicate happiness.

11. **(D)** You hear music, noise, and sound *with* your ear.

12. **(H)** The other choices are all liquids.

13. **(A)** The other choices describe something visually pleasant.

14. **(J)** *Discover* is the opposite of the other words, which indicate covering.

15. **(B)** A contrast does not necessarily indicate fighting or argument.

16. **(G)** Omnipotence is most powerful, while power and influence are less powerful. The strongest stopping point listed is a period.

17. **(C)** A valley is below level ground, a hill is higher than level, and a mountain is highest. The choice below zero is negative one.

18. **(G)** The top row lists countries in Europe. The bottom row lists countries in Central America.

19. **(A)** You use a key in a lock to open a door. You use a password in a field to access a computer.

20. **(G)** The top row lists types of pasta; the bottom row lists types of trees.

Test 5   Verbal Reasoning—Context

1. **(D)** Carlo must have changed his mind. We are not told why.

2. **(H)** We can infer that being in the same homeroom is required in order to share a locker. If John and I share a locker, we must be in the same homeroom.

3. **(D)** If Mrs. Stevens hired Mrs. Hall and Mrs. Wheat, they must all work for the same organization. We don't know how they met, how they were hired, or how they may have become friends.

4. **(F)** If Brandi has appeared in many plays, then she is an actress. We are never told that she *exclusively* likes Shakespeare plays. (She especially enjoys them.) We can easily infer that *Romeo and Juliet* is not a comedy. (Brandi enjoys that play *even though* she prefers comedies.) Furthermore, we are not told that she played Juliet. (That *play* is her favorite.)

5. **(D)** All we know for certain is that Kelsay did not watch the news program that night.

6. **(G)** Otto and his three brothers comprise the four sons in the family. Choice H is incorrect because the family has *eight* siblings in total (including Otto).

7. **(A)** Cathy and her husband have a lot in common. However, we are never specifically told that they share the other choices.

8. **(G)** We are told that Tamara moved *back* to the mountains. Therefore, the eastern part of her state (where she lived before) must be mountainous.

9. **(D)** We are told that these women *used* to be neighbors.

10. **(J)** If Billy must continue walking upstairs after the 11th floor, his building must have more than 11 stories. The rest of the choices *could* be true, but they are not *necessarily* true.

Test 6   Reading and Language Arts

1. **(C)** The article discusses various ways in which World War II affected American society. In particular, however, the piece focuses the reader's attention on the effect the war had on women (see paragraph three). The main point of the article, as described in paragraph three, runs thus: Rosie the Riveter . . . resisted their return to the roles of wife, nursemaid, and cook." Therefore you are looking for a title that communicates this point of view. Choice A can be ruled out because it is too general a call for help, and it addresses no consequences that stem from that help. Choice B is incorrect, simply because the article discusses far more important topics than giving advice on how to use old coffee. And choice D is incorrect, because the women discussed in this piece are not dutiful—even though they love their families, they are nevertheless growing more independent.

2. **(J)** Re-reading (or memory) tells you that the only statement not listed in the article as a fact is J.

3. **(B)** Of the four publications options you are given, only one targets subject matter that might address the issues of the aftereffects of World War II. *Good Housekeeping Magazine* focuses on housekeeping tips, which is the opposite of the article. *Slam Magazine* follows sports news and topics. *Highlights Magazine* is full of games and stories for young children. None of these subjects really fit with the topic of the article; therefore, if only through process of elimination, you can work your way to the correct answer—which is B.

4. **(G)** The final sentence of the piece sets up an opposing situation—women who have enjoyed adventure and freedom will not willingly go back to boredom. So, substitute the words for constrained and see which word fits the tone of the statement best. You will find that choice G is the best fit. (Although you might be briefly tempted by choice J, and even though many women forced to return to the domestic scene after World War II may well have been angry, the word is simply too limited to convey the author's intent.)

5. **(D)** The author strives to keep a neutral balance throughout the presentation of this piece. In fact, s/he offers a solution that s/he feels might settle the issue in a documented, reliable manner in paragraph three. So, you should reject any statements that connote an opinion or biased view of the debate. Therefore, rule out choices A and B. You might be tempted by choice C, but it is really a cop-out. The author makes it very clear that s/he thinks we simply cannot tell whether nature or nurture is stronger; hence s/he offers the solution in paragraph three.

6. **(H)** The author, as discussed in the previous question, seems to be writing primarily to present a new idea regarding how to settle the debate of nature vs. nurture. Check to see whether you can rule out the other options. Choice F is wrong; to discuss an entire history would take considerable space and more fact than this author has chosen to

include. Similarly, choice J is unacceptable, since the author does not reference any claims by authority figures—indeed, the author mentions no one by name, and were s/he attempting to make points by calling our attention to authority figures, surely s/he would have done so. Choice G is wrong, since the author is trying to make things clearer, not more confusing. The only correct answer is H.

7. **(C)** The choices here are intended to make sure you know what you're talking about. Choices A and D, for example, are trying to trick you into thinking you've read the word *adaptive* (able to change) rather than the word *adoptive*. Only choices B and C refer to adoption—the act of parents taking into their family children who are not biologically theirs. But the word *adoptive* in the reading passage is linked to the word children—so you can rule out choice B.

8. **(J)** Re-reading (or memory) proves to you that only J is discussed in the passage.

9. **(C)** Choice D may be true, but the passage does not make this clear; in fact it implies just the opposite. Choice B is not discussed—the creativity of the authors does not come into the discussion except perhaps indirectly in paragraph three when the author questions the bombing of Joe's girlfriend. Choice A is implied in the article, for if kids weren't bored with traditional reading materials, then there would be no need to update or modernize or replace them. But the article does not simply state that kids are bored and gives several examples proving that statement; the article goes on to discuss what people are doing to combat that boredom. The best answer is choice C.

10. **(H)** Re-reading (or memory) proves to you that Joe Hardy's girlfriend was indeed a victim of a car bombing, as ridiculous as that sounds.

11. **(B)** The phrase "gotten out their paint brushes" is indeed meant to convey a message—but not that writers of kids' books are suddenly turning to painting as a profession; rule out choice C. Choices A, B, and D refer to the author's discussion of how writers are adapting to changing kids' tastes. Choice A is clearly wrong, since the piece talks about changes to the plot; naturally, then, the writing has changed in addition to whatever artwork has changed. Choice D might be right, but it is such a biased opinion that we cannot be certain; I certainly feel that blowing up Joe Hardy's girlfriend shows the marketers giving in too much to the 21st-century taste for violence, but you may not—you may think it's just plain exciting, and you were tired of her character anyway. The only legitimate answer, therefore, is B.

12. **(F)** Genre refers to a category of book, but it is not really the same thing as a niche, and giving you notch is just trying to get you to read the question incorrectly. Philosophy as a definition for niche simply doesn't fit, so you are left with choice F.

13. **(A)** This is the most direct way of writing the sentence. Choice B has an unnecessary comma between the words *old* and *Hardy*. Choice C contains an error in subject-verb agreement (My **father** has . . .), and choice D repeats the subject and uses the incorrect usage of *alot* for *a lot*.

14. **(H)** This is the only choice that clearly indicates a reason why the writer enjoys the books.

15. **(B)** This choice is the most concise. Choice A is awkward, and it uses the possessive *Their* instead of the contraction *They're* (They are). Choice C is wordy and passive. Choice D does not convey the original meaning of the sentence.

16. **(F)** This is the only sentence that reinforces the idea that the writer enjoys the books. Choice G hints that the books are not worthy of attention, and choices H and J change the topic with irrelevant information.

17. **(B)** The interrupter (*of course*) is separated correctly with commas. Choice A incorrectly uses the word *however* as a conjunction. Choice C misuses the word *There*, and it places the period outside of the quotation marks. Choice D uses the expression *must of* instead of *must have*.

18. **(G)** While you can find brief mentions of all four subjects in this piece, you must consider the degree to which they are thoroughly discussed in the selection. The author does show a slight connection between NASCAR technology and military innovation (paragraph two), but this connection is not the focus of the passage; rule out F. Clearly people find carbon monoxide a problem in car racing; otherwise, they would not have developed a device to remove it from NASCAR cockpits (paragraph two). But the dangers of CO_2 poisoning are not mentioned often enough to be considered the main point of this article either; rule out H. And the article seems to emphasize safety at all costs, so J doesn't make sense. Your best option is G.

19. **(A)** Remembering basic facts from the article will help you here; NASCAR vehicles don't carry bullet-proof armor, so rule out B; NASCAR vehicles do carry steel-and-foam cushioning at the neck, but the relationship between cars and recliners stops there. No one, even the biggest fans, would make the claim that NASCAR races are safe; rule out C and D. But you might have been interested to find out that NASCAR vehicles, like planes, carry black boxes that help determine causes of wrecks; this is the best connection available to you. The best answer is A.

20. **(G)** We have all heard the term SOP; it may surprise you that the acronym SOP can be comprised of various words. Substitute the various phrases in the sentence; the best fit is G.

21. **(B)** Re-reading (or memory) tells you that safety precautions really took off since 2001.

22. **(H)** Re-reading (or memory) tells you that now devices remove carbon monoxide gas from NASCAR cockpits.

23. **(C)** The verb *affect* is used correctly. Choice A uses a past tense verb (*contained*) after an introduction that places the time in the future. Choice B contains an error in subject-verb agreement. (It should read *The **wheels are designed**.*) Choice D contains a list that is not parallel. (The series should be all nouns: *Racing fans want innovation, adrenaline, and speed.*)

24. **(F)** This is the only sentence without grammatical errors. Choice H sounds as if the car itself is wealthy, and choice J mixes past and present tense.

25. **(B)** The paragraph has been leading to this statement that the general public could then afford to buy cars.

26. **(G)** This sentence contains no errors. Choice F is missing a comma to separate the two independent clauses. Choice H separates a restrictive appositive with commas. (If you took out the title of the novel, the sentence would read as follows: *The novel explores the consequences of this technological system.* We wouldn't know which novel.) Choice J should read **factories** <u>create</u>.

27. **(A)** Looking again at paragraph one, you notice that the paragraph is talking about how people feared losing their jobs—and their identity—to technological advances. Therefore, check out the list of words under consideration. Choice C describes the emotional state of some people, but it does not describe the word *procedures* in the sentence. Choices B and D both describe the term *procedures*, but they do not explain fully why either streamlined or efficient procedures might adversely affect people so badly. Besides, many types of systems can be streamlined and efficient—and not frightening. Only choice A implies precision and lack of humanity, which is the basis of the fear being discussed in paragraph one.

28. **(J)** Choices A, B, C, and D involve the description of a decade and proposed likely inference based on what the author has told you in that description. You are basically reading four cases of cause-effect relationships. However, three of these cause-effect relationships simply don't work. If a decade is forced to save money, they will not value expensive purchases (choice F); if a decade is devoted to a war, they *will* be patriotic (choice G); if a decade is fearful of a long-term military commitment, they will not respect the government forcing them to engage in the long-term military engagement (choice H). The only correct cause-effect relationship listed is in choice J.

29. **(C)** The author's use of quotation marks surrounding the word straight in the sentences gives you a clue that the normal definition of the word does not hold true; rule out option B. Substitute the remaining choices one by one; only choice C makes sense.

30. **(G)** Re-reading (or memory) reminds you that only choice G is stated in the article.

31. **(A)** Most test takers have heard the term *remedial*, which in this case refers to non-credited classes students are forced to take to shore up weaknesses in their basic academic skills. If you are taking a remedial class, you are redoing work you should have mastered earlier. Compare this definition to the list of choices—only choice A fits that context.

32. **(H)** Re-reading (or memory) quickly tells you that you are looking for the figure of 28%.

33. **(D)** This author is striving diligently to maintain a neutral tone for the duration of this piece; however, s/he is not succeeding entirely. Looking carefully, you can identify places where the author seems to agree that something needs to be done to revamp the educational system. Therefore, the best answer is B.

34. **(G)** Dinosaurs are extinct; if something follows the example of the dinosaur ("going the way of the dinosaur"), then it, too, is going extinct. Choose choice G. Choice F talks about something changing (and possibly surviving), and choices H and J definitely refer to something surviving; these options simply do not fit the situation.

35. **(A)** Choice B makes no logical sense—you attend college after high school, so the chronological presentation of movement from college to high school in this proposed title does not make sense. The article does not give tips on how to make it in college; rule out choice C. If the article intended to make suggestions on how to make senior high school year better, the article would contain different facts and a different (persuasive) tone; we have already stated that this selection strives (successfully) for an unbiased tone. Your only option is choice A. And since many students, lately, take remedial classes because they have chosen to be lazy during their senior year, the title makes very good sense—Why Johnny Won't (rather than Can't) Read.

36. **(H)** Paragraph two gives you a clue as to why the teacher and mother are really meeting in conference. Until this point, the reader—and the mother—have been unaware that Jeremy's stories about Scott might be hiding another sort of truth, but the teacher's comment connotes a feeling of foreshadowing that hints trouble might be coming.

37. **(C)** Substitute the words one by one and choose the one that sounds best. Choice A doesn't make much sense; choice B doesn't either—simply because the mother and son seem to be having a good time in their discussion, not arguing. Choice D is tempting—but choice C is better, and your job is to select the best option, not any old option, that works.

38. **(F)** The author gives you a story here, one that strikes you as simplistic; therefore, your best guess as to where it belongs would be in an anthology designed for beginning readers. Choice G is out; there is no mention of romance or dating. Choice H is out; the text never mentions *Gone with the Wind*. Choice J is out—since comics are visual and this story is not.

39. **(B)** Re-reading (or memory) tells you that Scott stepped on the flag, presumably an American flag.

40. **(H)** By the time you reach paragraph three, you have a pretty strong feeling that Jeremy is Scott. The article gives no indication that Jeremy fears Scott (F) or is angered by Scott (G); you might be tempted into choosing choice J—for clearly, Jeremy (and his mother) think Scott is funny in the beginning. But, given the foreshadowing in paragraphs two and three, you must choose H as the best response.

Test 7   Mathematics

1. **(C)**

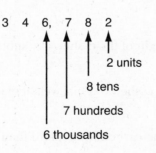

2. **(H)**

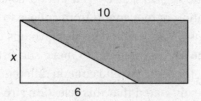

Subtract the area of the triangle from the area of the rectangle, and set the answer equal to 42.

$$10x - \frac{1}{2}(6x) = 42$$

$$10x - 3x = 42$$

$$\frac{7x}{7} = \frac{42}{7}$$

$$x = 6$$

3. **(D)** Simplify each expression and then substitute.

(a) $5^2 = 5 \cdot 5 = 25$
(b) $2^5 = 2 \cdot 2 \cdot 2 \cdot 2 \cdot 2 = 32$
(c) $2^3 = 2 \cdot 2 \cdot 2 = 8$

$$b < a \text{ or } c < b$$
$$32 < 25 \text{ or } 8 < 32 \checkmark$$

4. **(G)** Substitute −2 for a in all of the expressions.

$$a = -2$$
$$a^2 = (-2)(-2) = +4$$
$$a^0 = 1$$
$$-a = -(-2) = +2$$

Therefore, $a < a^0 < -a < a^2$.

5. **(A)** Since one pound equals 16 ounces, divide 1,159 by 16.

$$
\begin{array}{r}
72\text{R}7 \\
16\overline{)\,1{,}159} \\
-112\downarrow \\
\hline
39 \\
-32 \\
\hline
7
\end{array}
$$

6. **(F)** Find the original weight of the cashews by subtracting 2 from 13. Then substitute into the statements.

Original weight of cashews = Final weight of cashews − Added weight
$$11 = 13 - 2$$

The original weight of the cashews was more than 5 times the weight of the added cashews.

$$11 > 5(2)$$
$$11 > 10 \checkmark$$

7. **(A)** On the first day, if the temperature decreases by 40%, it still is at 60% of the original temperature (100% − 40% = 60%). The next day, the temperature increases by 26%, so it is now 126% of the midnight temperature.

$$\left.\begin{array}{l} 60\% = 0.60 \\ 0.60 \times 90 = 54 \end{array}\right\} \text{Midnight temperature}$$

$$126\% = 1.26$$
$$1.26 \times 54 = 68.04$$
$$68.04 \approx 68 \qquad 10 \text{ A.M. temperature}$$

8. **(G)** Let x = the unknown number.

$$\begin{array}{rl} 8x = & 5x + 18 \\ \underline{-5x} & \underline{-5x} \\ \dfrac{3x}{3} = & \dfrac{18}{3} \\ x = & 6 \end{array}$$

9. **(C)** Substitute the values for the variables into the given expression.

$$10x - 9y - 4z^2$$
$$10\left(\frac{4}{5}\right) - 9\left(\frac{2}{3}\right) - 4(\sqrt{3})^2$$
$$8 - 6 - 4(3)$$
$$2 - 12$$
$$-10$$

10. **(H)** Let's substitute −2 for a and 3 for b.

$$a^2 + b^2 > 0$$
$$(-2)^2 + (3)^2 > 0$$
$$4 + 9 > 0 \ ✔$$

11. **(A)** Remove the absolute value signs and then multiply all the numbers.

$$-2|5| \cdot 3\, |-4| = (-2)(5)(3)(4) = -120$$

12. **(F)**

$$\text{Ratio} = \frac{\text{Height of door in blueprint}}{\text{Height of actual door}}$$

Change 8 feet to inches and then simplify the ratio.

$$\text{Ratio} = \frac{\frac{3}{4} \text{ in.}}{8 \text{ ft}}$$

1 foot = 12 in.:

$$\frac{\frac{3}{4} \text{ in.}}{8 \times 12} = \frac{\frac{3}{4}}{96} = \frac{3}{4} \div 96 = \frac{3}{4} \times \frac{1}{96} = \frac{1}{128}$$

13. **(C)** The best way to solve an abstract example like this is to substitute some numbers for a, b, and c. Since a is a positive even integer, let $a = 4$. b and c are the following consecutive positive integers, so let $b = 5$ and $c = 6$. Then see which statement is **false**.

$$ac \text{ is odd}$$
$$4(6) = 24; \ 24 \text{ is not odd.} \ \textbf{✘}$$

14. **(H)**

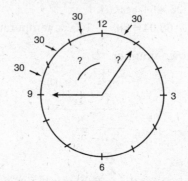

There are 360° in a circle and the numbers 1–12 divide the circle into 12 parts. If we divide 360° by 12, we find that there are 30° between each part. The answer will be approximate since, at 9:05, the hour hand lies a little above the 9. As the diagram clearly shows, there are 4 sections between the hands of the clock at 9:05, so $4 \times 30° = 120°$.

15. **(A)**

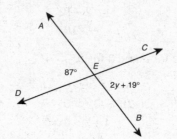

Vertical angles are congruent.

$$
\begin{aligned}
2y + 19 &= 87 \\
-19 \quad &\ -19 \\
\hline
\frac{2y}{2} &= \frac{68}{2} \\
y &= 34
\end{aligned}
$$

16. **(J)**

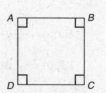

Draw a diagram to help out and remember that all angles in a square are right angles.

(F) Angle B is a right angle. ✔
(G) The measure of angle B equals the measure of angle C. ✔
(H) The measure of angle B plus the measure of angle A equals 180°. ✔
(J) BC is perpendicular to AD. ✘

17. **(D)** Let $P =$ the perimeter. Let $k =$ the length of the rectangle, and let $k - 8 =$ the width of the rectangle.

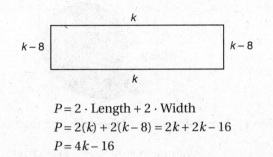

$$P = 2 \cdot \text{Length} + 2 \cdot \text{Width}$$
$$P = 2(k) + 2(k - 8) = 2k + 2k - 16$$
$$P = 4k - 16$$

18. **(F)** Let the base of the equilateral triangle $= x$. Since all the sides of an equilateral triangle are equal, let each side of the equilateral triangle $= x$. Let the base of the isosceles triangle $= x + 2$.

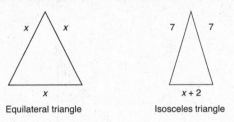

Equilateral triangle   Isosceles triangle

$$x + 2 + 7 + 7 = 3x$$
$$x + 16 = 3x$$
$$\underline{-x \qquad\qquad -x}$$
$$\frac{16}{2} = \frac{2x}{2}$$
$$x = 8$$

19. **(C)** Let $A_S =$ area of the square, and let $A_R =$ area of the rectangle. Let $x =$ the width of the rectangle and $2x =$ one side of the square. Since all sides of a square are equal, all of the sides are equal to $2x$.

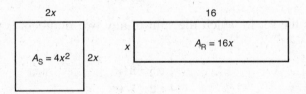

The areas are equal:

$$A_S = A_R$$
$$\frac{4x^2}{4x} = \frac{16x}{4x}$$
$$x = 4 \ (\text{width of the rectangle})$$

20. (J)

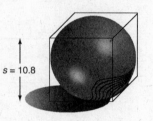

$s = 10.8$

Round off 10.8 to 11. Find the volume of the cube and then take $\frac{1}{2}$ of the answer.

$$\text{Volume of cube} = s^3 = 11^3 = 1331$$

$$\text{Approximate volume of sphere} = \frac{1}{2} \times 1331 = 665.5 \approx 666$$

Since we rounded 10.8 to 11, the final answer should be less than 666.

21. (C)

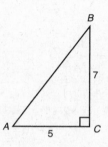

Use the Pythagorean Theorem and let $a = 7$, $b = 5$.

$$a^2 + b^2 = c^2$$
$$7^2 + 5^2 = c^2$$
$$49 + 25 = c^2$$
$$74 = c^2$$
$$c = \sqrt{74}$$
$$c \approx 8.60 \approx 8.6$$

22. (G) Select the set in which the sum of any two numbers is greater than the third number.

$$4 + 5 > 8 \checkmark$$
$$4 + 8 > 5 \checkmark$$
$$5 + 8 > 4 \checkmark$$

23. (C) Look at the hundreds place and then round to the nearest thousand.

hundreds place
↓
1,147,690
↑
add 1 to the thousands place and round off

$$1,147,690 \approx 1,148,000$$

24. **(J)** Move the decimal over two places to the left.

$$0.054\% = 0.00.054 = 0.00054$$

25. **(D)** Substitute the values for r, s, and t in the given expression. When $r = 2$, $s = 3$, $t = 4$:

$$3rs - 2t$$
$$3(2)(3) - 2(4)$$
$$18 - 8$$
$$10$$

26. **(F)** Remember, when we multiply two negatives, the result is a positive, and when we multiply a positive and a negative, the result is a negative.

$$-4(-2)^3 = -4(-2)(-2)(-2) = +8(-2)(-2) = -16(-2) = +32$$

27. **(A)** Simplify expressions within the parentheses and then work from left to right.

(A) $5 \cdot 3 - (2 + 7) = 15 - (9) = 6$

(B) $5(3) - \dfrac{48}{6} = 15 - 8 = 7$

(C) $14 - 5 + \dfrac{30}{6} = 14 - 5 + 5 = 9 + 5 = 14$

(D) $\dfrac{18}{2} - 3(4 - 6) + \dfrac{54}{9} = 9 - 3(-2) + 6 = 9 + 6 + 6 = 21$

28. **(G)** There are no elements in common.

29. **(C)** Divide the letters (representing rational numbers) and the radicals separately.

$$\frac{a\sqrt{42}}{b\sqrt{7}} = \frac{a}{b}\sqrt{\frac{42}{7}} = \frac{a}{b}\sqrt{6}$$

30. **(G)** The sum of the angles of a triangle equals 180º, so, in order to determine the measure of angle ABC, add up the two given angles and subtract from 180°. Then, since the measure of straight angle ABD is 180°, subtract the answer from 180° once again.

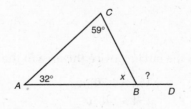

Let $x = \mathrm{m}\angle ABC$:

$$32° + 59° + x = 180°$$
$$91° + x = 180°$$
$$x = 89°$$
$$\mathrm{m}\angle ABC = 89°$$
$$\mathrm{m}\angle ABC + \mathrm{m}\angle CBD = 180°$$
$$89° + \mathrm{m}\angle CBD = 180°$$
$$\mathrm{m}\angle CBD = 91°$$

31. **(C)**

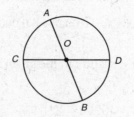

OC, *OD*, *OA*, and *OB* are radii and are therefore equal in length. *AB* and *CD* are diameters and are also equal in length.

diameter *AB* – radius *OB* = radius *OA*

OD and *OA* are radii and are equal in length.

32. **(J)** To determine the area of a circle, use the formula $A_C = \pi r^2$. Let $\pi = \frac{22}{7}$.

A_C = the area, and r is the radius. The area of a triangle, A_T, is equal to $\frac{1}{2}bh$, where b = the base and h = the height.

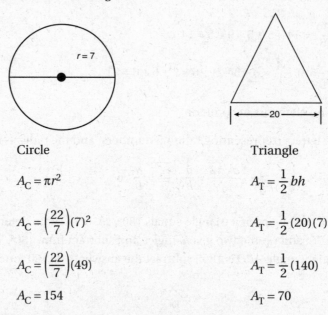

Circle

$$A_C = \pi r^2$$

$$A_C = \left(\frac{22}{7}\right)(7)^2$$

$$A_C = \left(\frac{22}{7}\right)(49)$$

$$A_C = 154$$

Triangle

$$A_T = \frac{1}{2}bh$$

$$A_T = \frac{1}{2}(20)(7)$$

$$A_T = \frac{1}{2}(140)$$

$$A_T = 70$$

Area of the circle > twice the area of the triangle.

$$154 > 2(70)$$
$$154 > 140 \ ✔$$

33. **(C)**

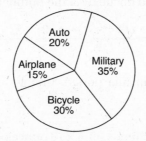

To make life easier, first develop a chart. Change the percentages to dollars and then substitute into the statements.

Order	%	Decimal (d)	$d \times \$30{,}000{,}000$	Final answer
Auto	20%	0.20	$0.20 \times 30{,}000{,}000$	6,000,000
Airplane	15%	0.15	$0.15 \times 30{,}000{,}000$	4,500,000
Bicycle	30%	0.30	$0.30 \times 30{,}000{,}000$	9,000,000
Military	35%	0.35	$0.35 \times 30{,}000{,}000$	10,500,000

Bicycle and auto orders together were equal to $15,000,000.

$$\$9{,}000{,}000 + \$6{,}000{,}000 = \$15{,}000{,}000 \ \checkmark$$

34. **(H)** The probability of selecting a green marble is the ratio of the number of green marbles to the total number of marbles.

$$\frac{\text{Number of green marbles}}{\text{Total number of marbles}} = \frac{3}{18} = \frac{1}{6}$$

35. **(D)**

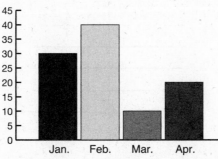

Determine the average temperatures for each month and then do the calculations.

January:	30°
February:	40°
March:	10°
April:	20°

$$\text{Apr.} + \text{Feb.} > 50°$$
$$20° + 40° > 50°$$
$$60° > 50° \ \checkmark$$

36. **(F)** Add up all the hours and divide by 3, the number of students.

$$\bar{x} = \frac{(t+4)+(t)+(t-2)}{3} = \frac{3t+2}{3}$$

37. **(D)** There are 16 ounces in one pound. Change all the measures to the smallest common unit, ounces.

$$1\frac{1}{2} \text{ pounds} = 1.5 \times 16 \text{ ounces} = 24 \text{ ounces}$$

$$1.4 \text{ pounds} = 1.4 \times 16 \text{ ounces} = 22.4 \text{ ounces}$$

$$22.4 \text{ ounces} < 23 \text{ ounces} < 24 \text{ ounces}$$

$$1.4 \text{ pounds} < 23 \text{ ounces} < 1\frac{1}{2} \text{ pounds}$$

38. **(G)** Change 8% to 10% and round 232 to 230.

$$.10 \times 230 = 23 \approx 20$$

39. **(C)** Substitute each possible value into the given expression and then determine which value makes the full expression into an integer.

$$x \# y = \frac{x+y}{2}$$

$$\text{Let } x = 5, y = 7 \quad 5 \# 7 = \frac{5+7}{2} = \frac{12}{2} = 6$$

6 is an integer.

40. **(G)** From the given information, draw a diagram.

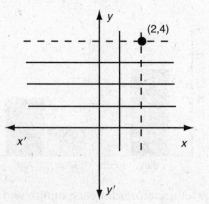

ANSWER SHEET
HSPT Practice Exam 1

SUBTEST 1   VERBAL

1. Ⓐ Ⓑ Ⓒ Ⓓ   16. Ⓐ Ⓑ Ⓒ Ⓓ   31. Ⓐ Ⓑ Ⓒ Ⓓ   46. Ⓐ Ⓑ Ⓒ Ⓓ
2. Ⓐ Ⓑ Ⓒ Ⓓ   17. Ⓐ Ⓑ Ⓒ Ⓓ   32. Ⓐ Ⓑ Ⓒ Ⓓ   47. Ⓐ Ⓑ Ⓒ Ⓓ
3. Ⓐ Ⓑ Ⓒ Ⓓ   18. Ⓐ Ⓑ Ⓒ Ⓓ   33. Ⓐ Ⓑ Ⓒ   48. Ⓐ Ⓑ Ⓒ Ⓓ
4. Ⓐ Ⓑ Ⓒ   19. Ⓐ Ⓑ Ⓒ Ⓓ   34. Ⓐ Ⓑ Ⓒ Ⓓ   49. Ⓐ Ⓑ Ⓒ Ⓓ
5. Ⓐ Ⓑ Ⓒ Ⓓ   20. Ⓐ Ⓑ Ⓒ Ⓓ   35. Ⓐ Ⓑ Ⓒ Ⓓ   50. Ⓐ Ⓑ Ⓒ Ⓓ
6. Ⓐ Ⓑ Ⓒ Ⓓ   21. Ⓐ Ⓑ Ⓒ Ⓓ   36. Ⓐ Ⓑ Ⓒ Ⓓ   51. Ⓐ Ⓑ Ⓒ Ⓓ
7. Ⓐ Ⓑ Ⓒ Ⓓ   22. Ⓐ Ⓑ Ⓒ   37. Ⓐ Ⓑ Ⓒ Ⓓ   52. Ⓐ Ⓑ Ⓒ
8. Ⓐ Ⓑ Ⓒ Ⓓ   23. Ⓐ Ⓑ Ⓒ Ⓓ   38. Ⓐ Ⓑ Ⓒ   53. Ⓐ Ⓑ Ⓒ Ⓓ
9. Ⓐ Ⓑ Ⓒ Ⓓ   24. Ⓐ Ⓑ Ⓒ   39. Ⓐ Ⓑ Ⓒ Ⓓ   54. Ⓐ Ⓑ Ⓒ Ⓓ
10. Ⓐ Ⓑ Ⓒ Ⓓ   25. Ⓐ Ⓑ Ⓒ Ⓓ   40. Ⓐ Ⓑ Ⓒ Ⓓ   55. Ⓐ Ⓑ Ⓒ
11. Ⓐ Ⓑ Ⓒ Ⓓ   26. Ⓐ Ⓑ Ⓒ Ⓓ   41. Ⓐ Ⓑ Ⓒ Ⓓ   56. Ⓐ Ⓑ Ⓒ Ⓓ
12. Ⓐ Ⓑ Ⓒ Ⓓ   27. Ⓐ Ⓑ Ⓒ Ⓓ   42. Ⓐ Ⓑ Ⓒ Ⓓ   57. Ⓐ Ⓑ Ⓒ Ⓓ
13. Ⓐ Ⓑ Ⓒ Ⓓ   28. Ⓐ Ⓑ Ⓒ Ⓓ   43. Ⓐ Ⓑ Ⓒ Ⓓ   58. Ⓐ Ⓑ Ⓒ Ⓓ
14. Ⓐ Ⓑ Ⓒ Ⓓ   29. Ⓐ Ⓑ Ⓒ   44. Ⓐ Ⓑ Ⓒ Ⓓ   59. Ⓐ Ⓑ Ⓒ
15. Ⓐ Ⓑ Ⓒ   30. Ⓐ Ⓑ Ⓒ Ⓓ   45. Ⓐ Ⓑ Ⓒ Ⓓ   60. Ⓐ Ⓑ Ⓒ

SUBTEST 2   QUANTITATIVE

61. Ⓐ Ⓑ Ⓒ Ⓓ   74. Ⓐ Ⓑ Ⓒ Ⓓ   87. Ⓐ Ⓑ Ⓒ Ⓓ   100. Ⓐ Ⓑ Ⓒ Ⓓ
62. Ⓐ Ⓑ Ⓒ Ⓓ   75. Ⓐ Ⓑ Ⓒ Ⓓ   88. Ⓐ Ⓑ Ⓒ Ⓓ   101. Ⓐ Ⓑ Ⓒ Ⓓ
63. Ⓐ Ⓑ Ⓒ Ⓓ   76. Ⓐ Ⓑ Ⓒ Ⓓ   89. Ⓐ Ⓑ Ⓒ Ⓓ   102. Ⓐ Ⓑ Ⓒ Ⓓ
64. Ⓐ Ⓑ Ⓒ Ⓓ   77. Ⓐ Ⓑ Ⓒ Ⓓ   90. Ⓐ Ⓑ Ⓒ Ⓓ   103. Ⓐ Ⓑ Ⓒ Ⓓ
65. Ⓐ Ⓑ Ⓒ Ⓓ   78. Ⓐ Ⓑ Ⓒ Ⓓ   91. Ⓐ Ⓑ Ⓒ Ⓓ   104. Ⓐ Ⓑ Ⓒ Ⓓ
66. Ⓐ Ⓑ Ⓒ Ⓓ   79. Ⓐ Ⓑ Ⓒ Ⓓ   92. Ⓐ Ⓑ Ⓒ Ⓓ   105. Ⓐ Ⓑ Ⓒ Ⓓ
67. Ⓐ Ⓑ Ⓒ Ⓓ   80. Ⓐ Ⓑ Ⓒ Ⓓ   93. Ⓐ Ⓑ Ⓒ Ⓓ   106. Ⓐ Ⓑ Ⓒ Ⓓ
68. Ⓐ Ⓑ Ⓒ Ⓓ   81. Ⓐ Ⓑ Ⓒ Ⓓ   94. Ⓐ Ⓑ Ⓒ Ⓓ   107. Ⓐ Ⓑ Ⓒ Ⓓ
69. Ⓐ Ⓑ Ⓒ Ⓓ   82. Ⓐ Ⓑ Ⓒ Ⓓ   95. Ⓐ Ⓑ Ⓒ Ⓓ   108. Ⓐ Ⓑ Ⓒ Ⓓ
70. Ⓐ Ⓑ Ⓒ Ⓓ   83. Ⓐ Ⓑ Ⓒ Ⓓ   96. Ⓐ Ⓑ Ⓒ Ⓓ   109. Ⓐ Ⓑ Ⓒ Ⓓ
71. Ⓐ Ⓑ Ⓒ Ⓓ   84. Ⓐ Ⓑ Ⓒ Ⓓ   97. Ⓐ Ⓑ Ⓒ Ⓓ   110. Ⓐ Ⓑ Ⓒ Ⓓ
72. Ⓐ Ⓑ Ⓒ Ⓓ   85. Ⓐ Ⓑ Ⓒ Ⓓ   98. Ⓐ Ⓑ Ⓒ Ⓓ   111. Ⓐ Ⓑ Ⓒ Ⓓ
73. Ⓐ Ⓑ Ⓒ Ⓓ   86. Ⓐ Ⓑ Ⓒ Ⓓ   99. Ⓐ Ⓑ Ⓒ Ⓓ   112. Ⓐ Ⓑ Ⓒ Ⓓ

ANSWER SHEET
HSPT Practice Exam 1

SUBTEST 3   READING

113. Ⓐ Ⓑ Ⓒ Ⓓ
114. Ⓐ Ⓑ Ⓒ Ⓓ
115. Ⓐ Ⓑ Ⓒ Ⓓ
116. Ⓐ Ⓑ Ⓒ Ⓓ
117. Ⓐ Ⓑ Ⓒ Ⓓ
118. Ⓐ Ⓑ Ⓒ Ⓓ
119. Ⓐ Ⓑ Ⓒ Ⓓ
120. Ⓐ Ⓑ Ⓒ Ⓓ
121. Ⓐ Ⓑ Ⓒ Ⓓ
122. Ⓐ Ⓑ Ⓒ Ⓓ
123. Ⓐ Ⓑ Ⓒ Ⓓ
124. Ⓐ Ⓑ Ⓒ Ⓓ
125. Ⓐ Ⓑ Ⓒ Ⓓ
126. Ⓐ Ⓑ Ⓒ Ⓓ
127. Ⓐ Ⓑ Ⓒ Ⓓ
128. Ⓐ Ⓑ Ⓒ Ⓓ

129. Ⓐ Ⓑ Ⓒ Ⓓ
130. Ⓐ Ⓑ Ⓒ Ⓓ
131. Ⓐ Ⓑ Ⓒ Ⓓ
132. Ⓐ Ⓑ Ⓒ Ⓓ
133. Ⓐ Ⓑ Ⓒ Ⓓ
134. Ⓐ Ⓑ Ⓒ Ⓓ
135. Ⓐ Ⓑ Ⓒ Ⓓ
136. Ⓐ Ⓑ Ⓒ Ⓓ
137. Ⓐ Ⓑ Ⓒ Ⓓ
138. Ⓐ Ⓑ Ⓒ Ⓓ
139. Ⓐ Ⓑ Ⓒ Ⓓ
140. Ⓐ Ⓑ Ⓒ Ⓓ
141. Ⓐ Ⓑ Ⓒ Ⓓ
142. Ⓐ Ⓑ Ⓒ Ⓓ
143. Ⓐ Ⓑ Ⓒ Ⓓ
144. Ⓐ Ⓑ Ⓒ Ⓓ

145. Ⓐ Ⓑ Ⓒ Ⓓ
146. Ⓐ Ⓑ Ⓒ Ⓓ
147. Ⓐ Ⓑ Ⓒ Ⓓ
148. Ⓐ Ⓑ Ⓒ Ⓓ
149. Ⓐ Ⓑ Ⓒ Ⓓ
150. Ⓐ Ⓑ Ⓒ Ⓓ
151. Ⓐ Ⓑ Ⓒ Ⓓ
152. Ⓐ Ⓑ Ⓒ Ⓓ
153. Ⓐ Ⓑ Ⓒ Ⓓ
154. Ⓐ Ⓑ Ⓒ Ⓓ
155. Ⓐ Ⓑ Ⓒ Ⓓ
156. Ⓐ Ⓑ Ⓒ Ⓓ
157. Ⓐ Ⓑ Ⓒ Ⓓ
158. Ⓐ Ⓑ Ⓒ Ⓓ
159. Ⓐ Ⓑ Ⓒ Ⓓ
160. Ⓐ Ⓑ Ⓒ Ⓓ

161. Ⓐ Ⓑ Ⓒ Ⓓ
162. Ⓐ Ⓑ Ⓒ Ⓓ
163. Ⓐ Ⓑ Ⓒ Ⓓ
164. Ⓐ Ⓑ Ⓒ Ⓓ
165. Ⓐ Ⓑ Ⓒ Ⓓ
166. Ⓐ Ⓑ Ⓒ Ⓓ
167. Ⓐ Ⓑ Ⓒ Ⓓ
168. Ⓐ Ⓑ Ⓒ Ⓓ
169. Ⓐ Ⓑ Ⓒ Ⓓ
170. Ⓐ Ⓑ Ⓒ Ⓓ
171. Ⓐ Ⓑ Ⓒ Ⓓ
172. Ⓐ Ⓑ Ⓒ Ⓓ
173. Ⓐ Ⓑ Ⓒ Ⓓ
174. Ⓐ Ⓑ Ⓒ Ⓓ

ANSWER SHEET
HSPT Practice Exam 1

SUBTEST 4   MATHEMATICS

175. Ⓐ Ⓑ Ⓒ Ⓓ   191. Ⓐ Ⓑ Ⓒ Ⓓ   207. Ⓐ Ⓑ Ⓒ Ⓓ   223. Ⓐ Ⓑ Ⓒ Ⓓ
176. Ⓐ Ⓑ Ⓒ Ⓓ   192. Ⓐ Ⓑ Ⓒ Ⓓ   208. Ⓐ Ⓑ Ⓒ Ⓓ   224. Ⓐ Ⓑ Ⓒ Ⓓ
177. Ⓐ Ⓑ Ⓒ Ⓓ   193. Ⓐ Ⓑ Ⓒ Ⓓ   209. Ⓐ Ⓑ Ⓒ Ⓓ   225. Ⓐ Ⓑ Ⓒ Ⓓ
178. Ⓐ Ⓑ Ⓒ Ⓓ   194. Ⓐ Ⓑ Ⓒ Ⓓ   210. Ⓐ Ⓑ Ⓒ Ⓓ   226. Ⓐ Ⓑ Ⓒ Ⓓ
179. Ⓐ Ⓑ Ⓒ Ⓓ   195. Ⓐ Ⓑ Ⓒ Ⓓ   211. Ⓐ Ⓑ Ⓒ Ⓓ   227. Ⓐ Ⓑ Ⓒ Ⓓ
180. Ⓐ Ⓑ Ⓒ Ⓓ   196. Ⓐ Ⓑ Ⓒ Ⓓ   212. Ⓐ Ⓑ Ⓒ Ⓓ   228. Ⓐ Ⓑ Ⓒ Ⓓ
181. Ⓐ Ⓑ Ⓒ Ⓓ   197. Ⓐ Ⓑ Ⓒ Ⓓ   213. Ⓐ Ⓑ Ⓒ Ⓓ   229. Ⓐ Ⓑ Ⓒ Ⓓ
182. Ⓐ Ⓑ Ⓒ Ⓓ   198. Ⓐ Ⓑ Ⓒ Ⓓ   214. Ⓐ Ⓑ Ⓒ Ⓓ   230. Ⓐ Ⓑ Ⓒ Ⓓ
183. Ⓐ Ⓑ Ⓒ Ⓓ   199. Ⓐ Ⓑ Ⓒ Ⓓ   215. Ⓐ Ⓑ Ⓒ Ⓓ   231. Ⓐ Ⓑ Ⓒ Ⓓ
184. Ⓐ Ⓑ Ⓒ Ⓓ   200. Ⓐ Ⓑ Ⓒ Ⓓ   216. Ⓐ Ⓑ Ⓒ Ⓓ   232. Ⓐ Ⓑ Ⓒ Ⓓ
185. Ⓐ Ⓑ Ⓒ Ⓓ   201. Ⓐ Ⓑ Ⓒ Ⓓ   217. Ⓐ Ⓑ Ⓒ Ⓓ   233. Ⓐ Ⓑ Ⓒ Ⓓ
186. Ⓐ Ⓑ Ⓒ Ⓓ   202. Ⓐ Ⓑ Ⓒ Ⓓ   218. Ⓐ Ⓑ Ⓒ Ⓓ   234. Ⓐ Ⓑ Ⓒ Ⓓ
187. Ⓐ Ⓑ Ⓒ Ⓓ   203. Ⓐ Ⓑ Ⓒ Ⓓ   219. Ⓐ Ⓑ Ⓒ Ⓓ   235. Ⓐ Ⓑ Ⓒ Ⓓ
188. Ⓐ Ⓑ Ⓒ Ⓓ   204. Ⓐ Ⓑ Ⓒ Ⓓ   220. Ⓐ Ⓑ Ⓒ Ⓓ   236. Ⓐ Ⓑ Ⓒ Ⓓ
189. Ⓐ Ⓑ Ⓒ Ⓓ   205. Ⓐ Ⓑ Ⓒ Ⓓ   221. Ⓐ Ⓑ Ⓒ Ⓓ   237. Ⓐ Ⓑ Ⓒ Ⓓ
190. Ⓐ Ⓑ Ⓒ Ⓓ   206. Ⓐ Ⓑ Ⓒ Ⓓ   222. Ⓐ Ⓑ Ⓒ Ⓓ   238. Ⓐ Ⓑ Ⓒ Ⓓ

ANSWER SHEET
HSPT Practice Exam 1

SUBTEST 5 LANGUAGE

239. Ⓐ Ⓑ Ⓒ Ⓓ   254. Ⓐ Ⓑ Ⓒ Ⓓ   269. Ⓐ Ⓑ Ⓒ Ⓓ   284. Ⓐ Ⓑ Ⓒ Ⓓ
240. Ⓐ Ⓑ Ⓒ Ⓓ   255. Ⓐ Ⓑ Ⓒ Ⓓ   270. Ⓐ Ⓑ Ⓒ Ⓓ   285. Ⓐ Ⓑ Ⓒ Ⓓ
241. Ⓐ Ⓑ Ⓒ Ⓓ   256. Ⓐ Ⓑ Ⓒ Ⓓ   271. Ⓐ Ⓑ Ⓒ Ⓓ   286. Ⓐ Ⓑ Ⓒ Ⓓ
242. Ⓐ Ⓑ Ⓒ Ⓓ   257. Ⓐ Ⓑ Ⓒ Ⓓ   272. Ⓐ Ⓑ Ⓒ Ⓓ   287. Ⓐ Ⓑ Ⓒ Ⓓ
243. Ⓐ Ⓑ Ⓒ Ⓓ   258. Ⓐ Ⓑ Ⓒ Ⓓ   273. Ⓐ Ⓑ Ⓒ Ⓓ   288. Ⓐ Ⓑ Ⓒ Ⓓ
244. Ⓐ Ⓑ Ⓒ Ⓓ   259. Ⓐ Ⓑ Ⓒ Ⓓ   274. Ⓐ Ⓑ Ⓒ Ⓓ   289. Ⓐ Ⓑ Ⓒ Ⓓ
245. Ⓐ Ⓑ Ⓒ Ⓓ   260. Ⓐ Ⓑ Ⓒ Ⓓ   275. Ⓐ Ⓑ Ⓒ Ⓓ   290. Ⓐ Ⓑ Ⓒ Ⓓ
246. Ⓐ Ⓑ Ⓒ Ⓓ   261. Ⓐ Ⓑ Ⓒ Ⓓ   276. Ⓐ Ⓑ Ⓒ Ⓓ   291. Ⓐ Ⓑ Ⓒ Ⓓ
247. Ⓐ Ⓑ Ⓒ Ⓓ   262. Ⓐ Ⓑ Ⓒ Ⓓ   277. Ⓐ Ⓑ Ⓒ Ⓓ   292. Ⓐ Ⓑ Ⓒ Ⓓ
248. Ⓐ Ⓑ Ⓒ Ⓓ   263. Ⓐ Ⓑ Ⓒ Ⓓ   278. Ⓐ Ⓑ Ⓒ Ⓓ   293. Ⓐ Ⓑ Ⓒ Ⓓ
249. Ⓐ Ⓑ Ⓒ Ⓓ   264. Ⓐ Ⓑ Ⓒ Ⓓ   279. Ⓐ Ⓑ Ⓒ Ⓓ   294. Ⓐ Ⓑ Ⓒ Ⓓ
250. Ⓐ Ⓑ Ⓒ Ⓓ   265. Ⓐ Ⓑ Ⓒ Ⓓ   280. Ⓐ Ⓑ Ⓒ Ⓓ   295. Ⓐ Ⓑ Ⓒ Ⓓ
251. Ⓐ Ⓑ Ⓒ Ⓓ   266. Ⓐ Ⓑ Ⓒ Ⓓ   281. Ⓐ Ⓑ Ⓒ Ⓓ   296. Ⓐ Ⓑ Ⓒ Ⓓ
252. Ⓐ Ⓑ Ⓒ Ⓓ   267. Ⓐ Ⓑ Ⓒ Ⓓ   282. Ⓐ Ⓑ Ⓒ Ⓓ   297. Ⓐ Ⓑ Ⓒ Ⓓ
253. Ⓐ Ⓑ Ⓒ Ⓓ   268. Ⓐ Ⓑ Ⓒ Ⓓ   283. Ⓐ Ⓑ Ⓒ Ⓓ   298. Ⓐ Ⓑ Ⓒ Ⓓ

SUBTEST 1   VERBAL

#1-60   16 MINUTES

Sample:

Which word does *not* belong with the others?

(A) easy
(B) interesting
(C) simple
(D) facile

Ⓐ ● Ⓒ Ⓓ

1. Which word does *not* belong with the others?

    (A) bicycle
    (B) minivan
    (C) automobile
    (D) motorcycle

2. Which word does *not* belong with the others?

    (A) glum
    (B) pleasant
    (C) kindly
    (D) amiable

3. Which word does *not* belong with the others?

    (A) poodle
    (B) greyhound
    (C) working dog
    (D) collie

4. Payton is taller than Jaylin. Kita is taller than Payton. Kita is taller than Jaylin. If the first two statements are true, the third statement is _____.

    (A) true
    (B) false
    (C) uncertain

5. Prejudice most nearly means _____.

    (A) legality
    (B) bias
    (C) opinion
    (D) decision

6. Dark is to light as clean is to _____.

    (A) heavy
    (B) dirty
    (C) soap
    (D) immaculate

7. Which word does *not* belong with the others?

    (A) maintain
    (B) preserve
    (C) support
    (D) neglect

8. Which word does *not* belong with the others?

    (A) blanket
    (B) quilt
    (C) towel
    (D) bedspread

GO TO NEXT PAGE ➡

9. Which word does *not* belong with the others?

    (A) close
    (B) near
    (C) shut
    (D) seal

10. *Voracious* most nearly means _____.

    (A) hungry
    (B) loud
    (C) foolish
    (D) vast

11. *Malignant* most nearly means _____.

    (A) possessive
    (B) deadly
    (C) positive
    (D) parallel

12. *Liberate* most nearly means _____.

    (A) weigh
    (B) think
    (C) listen
    (D) free

13. Fire is to smoke as lightbulb is to _____.

    (A) brightness
    (B) electricity
    (C) inspiration
    (D) darkness

14. *Reversal* most nearly means _____.

    (A) inversion
    (B) agreement
    (C) indecision
    (D) regret

15. Tim runs faster than Cathy. Cathy runs faster than Nathan. Nathan runs faster than John. If the first two statements are true, the third statement is _____.

    (A) true
    (B) false
    (C) uncertain

16. Which word does *not* belong with the others?

    (A) phrase
    (B) clause
    (C) adverb
    (D) sentence

17. Which word does *not* belong with the others?

    (A) creek
    (B) river
    (C) ocean
    (D) peninsula

18. *Biodegrade* most nearly means _____.

    (A) reminisce
    (B) investigate
    (C) divulge
    (D) decay

19. Car is to key as television is to _____.

    (A) outlet
    (B) sound
    (C) remote control
    (D) cabinet

20. Imprint means the *opposite* of _____.

    (A) stamp
    (B) erase
    (C) read
    (D) steal

GO TO NEXT PAGE ➡

21. Rain is to umbrella as draft is to _____.

  (A) wind
  (B) cold
  (C) thirst
  (D) door

22. All dogs are mammals. The basenji is a breed of dog. The basenji is not a mammal. If the first two statements are true, the third statement is _____.

  (A) true
  (B) false
  (C) uncertain

23. *Sever* most nearly means _____.

  (A) torment
  (B) divide
  (C) repair
  (D) agree

24. Ursola's hair is longer than Jack's. Jack's hair is shorter than Grace's. Grace's hair is longer than Ursola's. If the first two statements are true, the third statement is _____.

  (A) true
  (B) false
  (C) uncertain

25. *Uniformity* most nearly means _____.

  (A) sameness
  (B) stubborness
  (C) diversity
  (D) wardrobe

26. Which word does *not* belong with the others?

  (A) desert
  (B) abandon
  (C) run
  (D) leave

27. A philanthropist is _____.

  (A) greedy
  (B) generous
  (C) wasteful
  (D) anonymous

28. *Congenial* most nearly means _____.

  (A) suitable
  (B) intelligent
  (C) magical
  (D) supernatural

29. The shoes cost more than the skirt. The blouse costs less than the skirt. The shoes cost more than the blouse. If the first two statements are true, the third statement is

  _____.

  (A) true
  (B) false
  (C) uncertain

30. Which word does *not* belong with the others?

  (A) sonnet
  (B) haiku
  (C) limerick
  (D) poem

31. Impressive is to inspiring as derogatory is to

  _____.

  (A) critical
  (B) praiseworthy
  (C) positive
  (D) elevating

32. Which word does *not* belong with the others?

  (A) accept
  (B) command
  (C) decree
  (D) dictate

GO TO NEXT PAGE ➡

33. It's a long way to Tipperary. It's a longer way to Gotham. It is longest to Leicester Square. If the first two statements are true, the third statement is _____.

    (A) true
    (B) false
    (C) uncertain

34. Which word does *not* belong with the others?

    (A) search
    (B) explore
    (C) overlook
    (D) investigate

35. Inequitable is *not* _____.

    (A) fair
    (B) biased
    (C) correct
    (D) worthy

36. Thrifty means the *opposite* of _____.

    (A) expensive
    (B) cheap
    (C) wasteful
    (D) conservative

37. Malfunction is *not* _____.

    (A) failure
    (B) fault
    (C) success
    (D) breakdown

38. Lee weighs 20 more pounds than John. Steven weighs 10 more pounds than Lee. Steven weighs 30 more pounds than John. If the first two statements are true, the third statement is _____.

    (A) true
    (B) false
    (C) uncertain

39. Console means the *opposite* of _____.

    (A) speaker
    (B) comfort
    (C) agitate
    (D) sympathize

40. Roof is to house as head is to _____.

    (A) thought
    (B) body
    (C) brain
    (D) foot

41. Diligence means the *opposite* of _____.

    (A) laziness
    (B) stupidity
    (C) militant
    (D) vigor

42. Moon River is wider than a mile. Pirate Island is less than a mile wide. Pirate Island is narrower than Moon River. If the first two statements are true, the third statement is

    _____.

    (A) true
    (B) false
    (C) uncertain

43. Which word does *not* belong with the others?

    (A) invade
    (B) infiltrate
    (C) trespass
    (D) depart

44. Fork is to eat as pen is to _____.

    (A) paper
    (B) write
    (C) fill
    (D) instruct

GO TO NEXT PAGE ➡

45. *Devise* most nearly means _____.

    (A) startle
    (B) bluff
    (C) create
    (D) outwit

46. Which word does *not* belong with the others?

    (A) engine
    (B) motor
    (C) radio
    (D) mechanism

47. Glorious means the *opposite* of _____.

    (A) esteemed
    (B) serious
    (C) exalted
    (D) unimportant

48. Idle is to employed as graceful is to _____.

    (A) elegant
    (B) clumsy
    (C) petite
    (D) slender

49. The science club has more members than the math club. The math club and the chess club combined have fewer members than the science club. The science club has more members than the chess club. If the first two statements are true, the third statement is _____.

    (A) true
    (B) false
    (C) uncertain

50. Dismay means the *opposite* of _____.

    (A) dread
    (B) dissatisfaction
    (C) courage
    (D) phobia

51. Noise is to irritate as lullaby is to _____.

    (A) sing
    (B) intrude
    (C) soothe
    (D) contemplate

52. My cat is smaller than Ryanne's cat. My cat is not as small as Patsy's cat. Patsy's cat is smaller than Ryanne's cat. If the first two statements are true, the third statement is _____.

    (A) true
    (B) false
    (C) uncertain

53. Which word does *not* belong with the others?

    (A) secret
    (B) mystery
    (C) puzzle
    (D) information

54. Morose means the *opposite* of _____.

    (A) poison
    (B) cheerful
    (C) safe
    (D) seated

GO TO NEXT PAGE →

55. Camellia stayed longer than Kent. Kent stayed longer than Theresa. Theresa stayed longer than Camellia. If the first two statements are true, the third statement is _____.

(A) true
(B) false
(C) uncertain

56. Which word does *not* belong with the others?

(A) vocalize
(B) converse
(C) repress
(D) articulate

57. A *crucial* ingredient is _____.

(A) necessary
(B) extra
(C) optional
(D) rare

58. Bus is to car as whale is to _____.

(A) fish
(B) sea
(C) dolphin
(D) ocean

59. Carol has read 12 books this year. Katie has read 15 books this year. Carol and Katie have read at least 10 of the same books. If the first two statements are true, the third statement is _____.

(A) true
(B) false
(C) uncertain

60. Inga is older than Nicholas. Nicholas is older than Hendrik. Inga is younger than Hendrik. If the first two statements are true, the third statement is _____.

(A) true
(B) false
(C) uncertain

STOP

If there is still time remaining, you may review your answers.

Sample:

What is the sum of 52 and 31?

(A) 21
(B) 83
(C) 84
(D) None of the above   Ⓐ ● Ⓒ Ⓓ

Directions: Select the best answer for each question.

61. Find the next number in the series
    18, 12, 15, 9, 12, 6, 9, ____

    (A) 4
    (B) 5
    (C) 3
    (D) 10

62. The sum of the square of a positive number
    and 3 is equal to the product of 4 and 7.
    What is the number?

    (A) 3
    (B) 6
    (C) 5
    (D) 4

63. Given (a), (b), and (c), select the best answer.

    (a) $7(9 - 3)$

    (b) $2 \times 4 + \dfrac{72}{4}$

    (c) $48 - 3(5 + 6)$

    (A) (a) is less than (b) and less than (c)
    (B) (b) is greater than (c) and less than (a)
    (C) (c) is less than (a) and greater than (b)
    (D) (c) is greater than (a) and greater
         than (b)

64. The quotient of 48 and 6 added to 2 is equal
    to the square root of a number. What is the
    number?

    (A) 5
    (B) 25
    (C) 50
    (D) 100

65. Review the series: 35, 32, 29, 26, ... Find the
    next number.

    (A) 23
    (B) 28
    (C) 27
    (D) 24

66. Find the area of the shaded part in the
    diagram below. The area of a circle is equal
    to πr^2, where $\pi = 3.14$. Round off the answer
    to the nearest tenth.

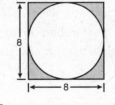

    (A) 12.8
    (B) 13.8
    (C) 13.5
    (D) 12.5

GO TO NEXT PAGE ➡

67. Given (a), (b), and (c), select the best answer.

    (a) 45%
    (b) $\frac{2}{3}$
    (c) 0.45

    (A) (a) is greater than (b) and less than (c)
    (B) (b) is less than (c) and greater than (a)
    (C) (c) is equal to (a) and less than (b)
    (D) (b) is greater than (a) and less than (c)

68. Review the series: 4, 8, 16, 32, ... Find the next number.

    (A) 28
    (B) 36
    (C) 64
    (D) 40

69. What number is equal to 15 more than two thirds of 30?

    (A) 35
    (B) 30
    (C) 25
    (D) 20

70. Given (a), (b), and (c), select the best answer.

    (a) $\frac{3}{7} \times 42$
    (b) $\frac{5}{8} \times 40$
    (c) $\frac{6}{7} \times 35$

    (A) (a) is less than (b) and less than (c)
    (B) (b) is greater than (c) and greater than (a)
    (C) (c) is greater than (b) and less than (a)
    (D) (a) is less than (c) and greater than (b)

71. Determine the value of x in the equation $62 + 2(8 - x) = 72$.

    (A) 2
    (B) 3
    (C) 4
    (D) 5

72. Review the sequence: 51, $49\frac{1}{2}$, 48, $46\frac{1}{2}$, ... Find the next number.

    (A) 44
    (B) 45
    (C) $43\frac{1}{2}$
    (D) $44\frac{1}{2}$

73. Forty-eight divided by what number equals $\frac{2}{3} \times 9$?

    (A) 6
    (B) 12
    (C) 4
    (D) 8

74. The product of what number and 5 is equal to 25% of 80?

    (A) 12
    (B) 8
    (C) 4
    (D) 10

75. Review the series: 2, 15, 6, 13, __, 11, 14, ... What number should fill in the blank?

    (A) 8
    (B) 6
    (C) 10
    (D) 9

GO TO NEXT PAGE ➡

76. Find the first of three consecutive odd integers whose sum is 39.

    (A) 9
    (B) 7
    (C) 13
    (D) 11

77. O is the center of the circle.

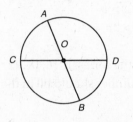

    Which of the following statements is true?

    (A) $AB > CD$
    (B) $CO < OB$
    (C) $AB - OB = DO$
    (D) $CD - OB < OD$

78. A gasoline pump fills an automobile tank at the rate of .7 gallon every 2 seconds. At this rate, how long would it take to fill a 28-gallon tank?

    (A) 1 minute, 20 seconds
    (B) 1 minute, 40 seconds
    (C) 2 minutes, 30 seconds
    (D) 2 minutes, 50 seconds

79. Review the series: $18, 9, 4\frac{1}{2}, 2\frac{1}{4}, \ldots$.
    Find the next number.

    (A) 1
    (B) $1\frac{1}{2}$
    (C) $1\frac{1}{4}$
    (D) $1\frac{1}{8}$

80. Let k represent the length of a rectangle. Represent the perimeter when the width is 8 less than the length.

    (A) $6k - 6$
    (B) $2k + 16$
    (C) $4k - 10$
    (D) $4k - 16$

81. Five times what number equals the difference of 8 squared and 9?

    (A) 8
    (B) 9
    (C) 11
    (D) 12

82. Examine the diagram and select the best choice.

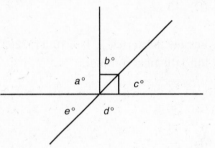

    (A) $a° = d° + e°$
    (B) $a° = b° + c°$
    (C) $c° + d° < a°$
    (D) $c° + e° > a°$

83. What number equals four-fifths of the average of 18 and 42?

    (A) 20
    (B) 15
    (C) 24
    (D) 10

GO TO NEXT PAGE ➡

84. Given (a), (b), and (c), find the best answer.

   (a) 4.06×10^3

   (b) 30×10^2

   (c) 52.4×10^1

   (A) (a) is greater than (b)
   (B) (b) is less than (c)
   (C) (c) is greater than (b)
   (D) (a) is less than (b)

85. Thirty math books were distributed to an algebra class at the beginning of the semester. Four books were lost and the rest were returned. In simplest terms, what is the ratio of returned books to lost books?

   (A) $5 : 4$
   (B) $17 : 9$
   (C) $5 : 13$
   (D) $13 : 2$

86. Review the series: 2, 4, 5, 10, 11, 22, 23, ... Find the next number.

   (A) 34
   (B) 36
   (C) 44
   (D) 46

87. Jocelyn wants to cement the walk to her home. If the walk measures 32 feet by 3.5 feet and costs $12.40 to cement a square foot, what is the total cost of the job?

   (A) $456
   (B) $1,388.80
   (C) $568
   (D) $418

88. Examine the figure in which $a > c > b$. Then select the best answer.

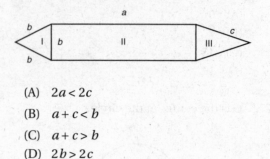

   (A) $2a < 2c$
   (B) $a + c < b$
   (C) $a + c > b$
   (D) $2b > 2c$

89. Review the series: III, 6, IX, 12, __, 18, ... What number should fill in the blank?

   (A) XII
   (B) XV
   (C) 16
   (D) 15

90. In a survey of television watching habits of 8,000 people, it was discovered that 1,600 people watch more than 2 hours a day. What percent of the people questioned watch 2 hours or less a day?

   (A) 80%
   (B) 60%
   (C) 30%
   (D) 70%

91. Examine right triangle *EFG* and square *ABCD* and select the best answer.

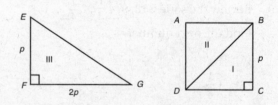

   (A) Area △ I + Area △ II = Area △ III
   (B) Area △ I = Area △ III
   (C) $2 \times$ Area △ II > Area △ III
   (D) Area □ *ABCD* – Area △ I > Area △ III

GO TO NEXT PAGE ➡

92. Review the series: 3.9, 6.1, 8.3, 10.5, ...
Find the next number.

(A) 12.7
(B) 12.1
(C) 11.8
(D) 12.6

93. Keisha purchases 2 books at $9.00 each and 3 books at $15.00 each. What is the mean price for a book?

(A) $11.10
(B) $13.50
(C) $13.90
(D) $12.60

94. Review the series:

2, 1, 3, 2, 6, 5, 15, 14, 42, ...

Find the next number.

(A) 84
(B) 55
(C) 41
(D) 126

95. Find 15% of 20% of 80.

(A) 3
(B) 2.4
(C) 4.6
(D) 3.6

96. Which statement is true?

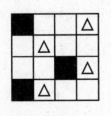

(A) Total ■ > Total △
(B) Total △ + Total ■ > Total □
(C) Total □ − Total △ > Total ■
(D) Total □ − Total ■ < Total △

97. Review the series: X, T, P, L, ...
Find the next letter.

(A) J
(B) I
(C) H
(D) G

98. Examine the rectangle, the triangle, and the following information; then select the best answer.

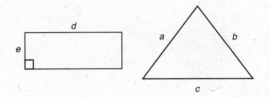

If $a = 2d$ and $b = 2e$, by how much longer is the perimeter of the triangle than the perimeter of the rectangle?

(A) b
(B) c
(C) a
(D) d

99. Review the series: 2, 5, 4, 8, 6, 11, ...
Find the next number.

(A) 8
(B) 7
(C) 10
(D) 11

GO TO NEXT PAGE ➡

100. If you purchase a soup, a burger, French fries, and a soda and hand in a $10 bill, how much change should you receive?

$2.85

$1.89

$1.37

$1.16

(A) $2.75
(B) $2.85
(C) $2.80
(D) $2.73

101. Examine the following figures and choose the best answer.

(a)

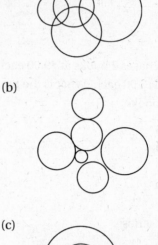

(b)

(c)

(A) Figure (a) includes one less circle than figure (c).
(B) Figure (b) includes two more circles than figure (c).
(C) Figure (c) includes two fewer circles than figure (b).
(D) Figure (b) includes three more circles than figure (c).

102. Review the series:

142, 137, 131, 124, __, 107, ...

What number should fill in the blank?

(A) 118
(B) 116
(C) 109
(D) 111

GO TO NEXT PAGE ➡

103. Examine the chart, and then choose the best answer.

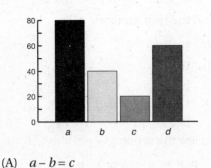

(A) $a - b = c$

(B) $b + c = d$

(C) $b + c > a$

(D) $d - c < b$

104. Look at the series:

$$1, 8, 27, 64, 125, \ldots.$$

Find the next number.

(A) 625

(B) 256

(C) 216

(D) 250

105. Compare (a), (b), and (c).

(a) $\dfrac{4}{100} + \dfrac{5}{10} + 3$

(b) $\dfrac{9}{100} + 3 + \dfrac{3}{10}$

(c) $\dfrac{2}{10} + 3 + \dfrac{3}{100}$

(A) (c) is greater than (b) and less than (a)

(B) (b) is less than (a) and greater than (c)

(C) (a) is less than (b) and less than (c)

(D) (b) is greater than (a) and greater than (c)

106. VR is perpendicular to VT, and VS is perpendicular to VU. Which of the following statements is the best answer?

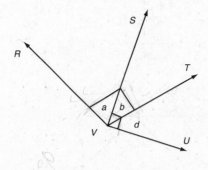

(A) $a + b < b + d$

(B) $d - b = a - b$

(C) $a + b < 90°$

(D) $d > a$

107. Review the series:

$$6, 9, 13, 14, 17, 21, 22, \_\_, 29, 30, \ldots.$$

What number should fill in the blank?

(A) 23

(B) 25

(C) 24

(D) 26

108. Given (a), (b), and (c), select the best answer.

(a) $\dfrac{5}{8} \times 40$

(b) $\dfrac{3}{4} \times 60$

(c) $\dfrac{2}{3} \times 45$

(A) (a) is less than (c) and greater than (b)

(B) (b) is greater than (c) and less than (a)

(C) (c) is less than (b) and greater than (a)

(D) (a) is greater than (b) and greater than (c)

GO TO NEXT PAGE ➡

109.

(a)

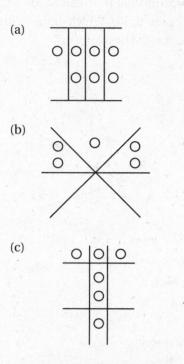

(b)

(c)

Which of the following statements is true?

(A) There is one more circle in (b) than
     lines in (a).
(B) The number of lines in (b) plus the
     number of circles in (a) is equal to the
     number of lines in (c) plus the number
     of circles in (c).
(C) The number of circles in (c) and (a) is
     less than the number of lines in (a)
     and (b).
(D) The number of lines in (a) plus the
     number of circles in (b) is less than the
     number of lines in (b) and (c).

110. Review the series:

                33, 32, 30, 27, 23, ...

      Find the next number.

      (A) 18
      (B) 19
      (C) 17
      (D) 15

111. Review the series:

          P, P, R, S, P, P, T, U, P, P, V, ...

      Find the next letter.

      (A) W
      (B) X
      (C) Y
      (D) Z

112. Review the series:

          128, 125, 120, 113, 104, 93, ...

      Find the next number.

      (A) 77
      (B) 86
      (C) 80
      (D) 78

If there is still time remaining, you may review your answers.

SUBTEST 3 READING

#113–174 25 MINUTES

Sample:

The next test has short reading passages, each one is followed by questions.

Correct marking of the reading passages on the next test will be _____.

(A) all on one page
(B) followed by questions
(C) easy to read
(D) very long   Ⓐ ● Ⓒ Ⓓ

PASSAGE FOR QUESTIONS 113–122

Most students remember learning about the European explorer Marco Polo. Polo, among other things, traveled more than 3,000 miles to reach China where he acted as ambassador and trade merchant between two worlds.

But most students never learn about Rabban Sauma, a Mongolian Christian, who traveled 7,000 miles from Beijing to Rome, Italy. Sauma left China and set out for Baghdad in 1275 A.D., narrowly missing Polo's arrival in Beijing. From Baghdad, Sauma set out for the Vatican, via Paris, where he hoped to arrange a diplomatic relationship that would aid China in its quest to conquer the Middle East. He failed and returned to Baghdad, where he died in 1294 at the age of 75.

Historians claim that had Sauma succeeded in brokering his Mongol-European alliance, his actions would have significantly changed history. Since Jerusalem and Egypt would have fallen into European hands, explorers would not have sailed around looking for a new trade route—and Columbus would never have discovered the Americas.

Sauma's failure to do what Columbus ultimately did strikes modern historians for at least two reasons. First, Sauma wrote memoirs that give us a unique, reliable, and, therefore, valuable account of medieval Europe toward the end of the Crusading period. Second, Sauma's life brings to mind chaos theory and the butterfly effect. Contemporary audiences seem fascinated with alternate realities brought into existence through minute changes in history.

113. What route did Rabban Sauma follow on his journey to Europe?

(A) China to France to Italy
(B) Baghdad to Rome to Paris
(C) Jerusalem to Egypt to America
(D) Beijing to Rome to Versailles

114. In what kind of text would you expect to find this piece?

(A) in a travel guide
(B) in a history book
(C) in a cookbook
(D) in a book of international fairy tales

GO TO NEXT PAGE ➡

115. Which of the following definitions best describes the word quest as used in this selection?

   (A) a dangerous, usually magical, journey upon which a person is forced to go
   (B) an elementary school program designed to stimulate gifted and talented students
   (C) a software program for searching the Internet
   (D) a goal, often long term, to which one is especially dedicated

116. The writer's main purpose in writing this selection is _____.

   (A) to reject the idea that people greatly desired a reliable trade route
   (B) to declare without question that Sauma's diplomatic success would have necessarily changed the course of human history
   (C) to challenge the idea that Marco Polo was the only memorable explorer of the 1200s
   (D) to promote the idea that only Italian explorers accomplished anything of any worth

117. The author of this passage implies that _____.

   (A) had Sauma succeeded in his diplomatic mission, the world would be much the same today
   (B) had Sauma failed in his diplomatic mission, the world would be vastly different
   (C) had Sauma convinced Europe to ally itself with China, many explorers would have been out of a job
   (D) had Sauma won over European allies, World War I would have never taken place

118. What was the likely distance of Sauma's trip?

   (A) 3,000 miles
   (B) 7,000 miles
   (C) 10,000 miles
   (D) 14,000 miles

119. The word brokering as used in this passage is best defined as _____.

   (A) arranging
   (B) defeating
   (C) utilizing
   (D) financing

120. Which of the following titles would best suit this selection?

   (A) Rabban! Sauma!
   (B) There and Back Again
   (C) Arabian Nights
   (D) Around the World in 80 Years

121. The word effect as used in this passage is best defined as _____.

   (A) result
   (B) to impact
   (C) effort
   (D) infect

122. Based on the context of the sentence, what does the word contemporary likely mean?

   (A) outdated
   (B) current
   (C) futuristic
   (D) unreliable

GO TO NEXT PAGE ➡

PASSAGE FOR QUESTIONS 123–132

It's easy to assume that we are all entitled to a childhood; indeed, we feel deprived when we think of various injustices that happen to us during the course of growing up that detract from memories of our "lost innocence."

A popular book, entitled *Centuries of Childhood*, published in 1962 puts such ideas into writing for all to read. The text argues that Victorian culture first began sheltering children from early exposure to the harsh realities of the adult world. This idea of protecting children from the "real world" opposed family practices that took place earlier than the 18th century.

Many writers of other texts pick up where *Centuries of Childhood* leaves off, arguing that 20th century society has extended that period of childhood into longer and longer durations. Consider the hard fact that once a high school graduate could expect to earn a solid living supporting a single-income family; today, it takes a college degree to be a noncommissioned, sales representative at the local mall.

Such authors, like Dr. Benjamin Spock, point to various factors for explanation as to why cultures like ours willingly coddle and handicap their young like this. These authors dispute the wisdom of giving our children a protected childhood. After all, they argue, by encouraging the youth to remain in a state of infancy, we hinder the rate at which they can take over adult responsibilities. We, however, would like to put forth an alternate hypothesis.

123. The word durations as used in this selection refers to the concept of _____.

(A) mass
(B) space
(C) sound
(D) time

124. Based on the information in the selection, what kind of text would include this piece?

(A) a science text
(B) a novel
(C) a sociology article
(D) a biography

125. Which of the following titles would best fit this reading passage?

(A) Rocking the Cradle
(B) The Times, They Are a'Changing
(C) Spare the Rod, Spoil the Child
(D) Spock Speaks

126. Which of the following definitions best suits the word hinder?

(A) damage
(B) slow down
(C) brilliant
(D) advance

127. In which century does the article state that people first began sheltering children from the harsh realities of the world?

(A) 17th century
(B) 18th century
(C) 19th century
(D) 20th century

GO TO NEXT PAGE ➡

128. Based on the information in this selection, what will the author(s) discuss next?

(A) an argument that points out how stupid it is to shelter children from reality

(B) an argument that remains neutral on the topic of sheltering children from reality

(C) an argument that shows the wisdom of sheltering children from reality

(D) We cannot tell from context clues.

129. When does the article state *Centuries of Childhood* was published?

(A) 1920s

(B) 1950s

(C) 1960s

(D) 1980s

130. The author's main purpose in writing this passage is _____.

(A) to discuss the history of child rearing in the United States

(B) to probe psychological reasons behind child rearing in Victorian society

(C) to analyze child-rearing practices of the 17th century

(D) to put forth a theory on the best way to raise children

131. Which of the following would be an example of injustice based on the context at work in paragraph one?

(A) getting a job

(B) having a bratty younger sibling break a favorite possession

(C) losing a tooth and putting it under the pillow for the Tooth Fairy

(D) getting a new pet for Christmas

132. What is the best synonym for the word exposure as it is used in paragraph two?

(A) experience

(B) exile

(C) excitement

(D) extraordinarily cold weather

GO TO NEXT PAGE ➡

So much of the earth surrounding us commands our attention. (1) A great deal of these things are <u>majestic</u>, <u>colossal</u>, and <u>gargantuan</u>. (2) Take, for example, the Grand Canyon, the Great Wall of China, Stonehenge, the giant squid, the Lion's Mane jellyfish, the Giant Isopod, and the Great White shark. (3) Although many enormous miracles exist, it is worth taking a look through the other end of the telescope. (4)

Some of the most fascinating creatures on the planet are the tiny planaria. Planaria are flat worms, about ¼ of an inch long, that have oval-like bodies, triangular heads, and what appear to be crossed eyes (although no evidence exists to suggest that these creatures actually see anything). Planaria feed using a little "nose" tube, usually by vacuuming up nutrients that happen to be in the area; they are especially fond of hard-boiled eggs. Generally, they prefer warm environments; living in petri dishes nestled on the low setting of a heating pad helps approximate their preferred natural habitat.

What is especially fascinating about these little creatures is their ability to regenerate lost body parts. If their bodies are damaged, most of the time they can actually regrow the damaged part. As one might expect, total <u>decapitation</u> will kill planaria, but even significant slices to the head can result in the creation of a two-headed planaria. Scientists like to study these creatures in the hopes that doing so will reveal secrets of <u>regeneration</u>—secrets that may one day be successfully applied to humans.

133. Based on your reading of this passage, what kind of worms are planaria?

    (A) round
    (B) flat
    (C) segmented
    (D) None of the above

134. In what branch of science does this selection belong?

    (A) chemistry
    (B) biology
    (C) astronomy
    (D) physics

135. Which of the following is the best definition of <u>decapitation</u>?

    (A) taking off the cap
    (B) removing the head
    (C) surrender
    (D) seeing things that are not really there

136. Based on your reading of the passage, all but which of the following facts are true?

    (A) Planaria are ¼ of an inch long, on average.
    (B) Planaria like to live in warm environments.
    (C) Planaria absorb nutrients through their nose-tube.
    (D) Planaria like to eat scrambled eggs.

137. Why does the author say it is important to study planaria?

    (A) Studying planaria may allow us to achieve regeneration in humans.
    (B) Planaria are so cute; they are innately fun to study.
    (C) Creation of a two-headed planaria is required for most scientific dissertations.
    (D) Cultivating planaria allows us to test the effectiveness of the new petri dishes.

GO TO NEXT PAGE ➡

138. Based on its usage in the passage, what is the best definition of <u>regeneration</u>?

   (A) new growth of cells
   (B) regrowth of cells
   (C) calculation of cell damage
   (D) documentation of cell division

139. Which of the following is the best title for this reading passage?

   (A) Decapitation in Planaria
   (B) On the Care and Feeding of Planaria
   (C) From Puny to Powerful: The Potential of Planaria
   (D) The Natural Habitat of the Planaria Worm

140. What similar meaning do the words <u>majestic</u>, <u>colossal</u>, and <u>gargantuan</u> have in common, based on your reading of paragraph one?

   (A) limited
   (B) large
   (C) linear
   (D) luminous

141. What does the last sentence in paragraph one (sentence 4) imply will come next?

   (A) the continuation of the ongoing discussion of tiny things
   (B) the start of a discussion on tiny things
   (C) the end of a discussion on tiny things
   (D) the end of the passage

142. In what sort of text would you expect to find this passage?

   (A) a science text
   (B) a history text
   (C) a geography text
   (D) a mathematics text

GO TO NEXT PAGE ➡

Most people don't know it, but Valentine's Day began as an annual <u>pagan</u> marriage rite during which men and women chose marriage partners for the upcoming year. Generally, people made their matches randomly, using a lottery system, but on rare occasions a couple could <u>petition</u> to stay together for longer than the usual year. The Catholic Church, which viewed the Valentine's Day lottery as understandably immoral, soon leveled strong pressure against participants to make marriages permanent. Over time, however, most of the political and religious concerns fell away, and the holiday changed its focus away from arranging marriage contracts to simply expressing one's love for one's spouse, fiancé, or significant other.

Accordingly, the holiday has grown increasingly commercialized—and expensive. Everyone has heard of the traditional costs—a card and candy or a dozen red roses (cost: <u>upwards of $25</u>). But, consider recent romantic options. As of February 2004, for a <u>mere</u> $125,000 you could have arranged for the purchase of his and her Mercedes convertibles (to keep), a candle-lit dinner, and an evening of "stars and s'mores" during which you gazed at constellations; this package came with its very own professional astronomer and a butler to roast your marshmallows. Or, if you were on a more limited budget, you could have made reservations at a wide variety of hotels happy to arrange for fireworks displays, romantic messages laid out in rose-petals, and secluded picnics.

In short, Valentine's Day marketers are <u>upping the ante</u> for everyone. Americans in 2004 spent an average of nearly $100 on Valentine's Day, up from $80 in 2003; unsurprisingly, retailers are out to try to increase that amount.

Why we should feel pressured to express a deep emotion like love using stereotypical and trite methods is a question that should puzzle—and distress—us.

143. One can infer from reading this passage that the author _____.

    (A) approves of the way we celebrate Valentine's Day these days

    (B) puts forth the opinion that the fertility rites originally connected to Valentine's Day were immoral

    (C) thinks that the best Valentine's Day present is a bouquet of flowers and a movie

    (D) disapproves of the way some people celebrate Valentine's Day

144. Which of the following would most likely publish this reading passage?

    (A) an English as a second language linguistics guide

    (B) the "Leisure and Arts" section of the daily newspaper

    (C) a journal that prints the latest research in biological studies

    (D) an encyclopedia

145. What is the best definition of the word <u>petition</u>?

    (A) yell

    (B) protest

    (C) request

    (D) demand

GO TO NEXT PAGE ➡

146. What is likely to come next in this discussion?

 (A) a discussion of St. Valentine's role in the evolution of Valentine's Day
 (B) a discussion of how people in the 1800s celebrated Valentine's Day
 (C) a discussion of how commercialized Valentine's Day has become
 (D) a discussion of how the changes in Valentine's Day celebrations reveals changes in human morals

147. How much does the author say it would cost for a deluxe Valentine package that includes the cars, the astronomy lesson, and the butler-produced s'mores?

 (A) $25
 (B) $80
 (C) $100
 (D) $125,000

148. What does the phrase upping the ante mean, as used in the context of this passage?

 (A) making the playing field equal for those who celebrate Valentine's Day
 (B) increasing the minimum acceptable behavior for celebrating Valentine's Day
 (C) making it more expensive for people to participate in Valentine's Day
 (D) angering those of us who participate in Valentine's Day activities

149. Which of the following words is the best synonym for the word pagan in paragraph one?

 (A) non-Catholic
 (B) wild
 (C) regional
 (D) urban

150. What tone does the word mere take on as it is used in the context of paragraph two?

 (A) It takes on a serious tone. The author truly thinks that $125,000 is a reasonable cost for such a meal.
 (B) It takes on an ironic tone. The author considers the cost of such a meal to be too high.
 (C) It takes on a regretful tone. The author wishes that she could afford such a meal, but she cannot.
 (D) It takes on an angry tone. The author wants to sue the corporation selling such an expensive meal.

151. What does the phrase upwards of $25 mean?

 (A) The cost will be lower than $25.
 (B) The cost will be $25.
 (C) The cost will be at least $25.
 (D) The cost will be more than $25.

152. Who does the article say opposed the early pagan practices of Valentine's Day?

 (A) Valentine's Day marketers
 (B) The Catholic Church
 (C) Americans
 (D) The article isn't clear on that subject.

GO TO NEXT PAGE ➡

153. to <u>peruse</u> a text

    (A) underline
    (B) purchase
    (C) read
    (D) ignore

154. to <u>broach</u> a topic

    (A) disprove
    (B) choose
    (C) mention
    (D) research

155. to <u>amass</u> wealth

    (A) accumulate
    (B) spread
    (C) distribute
    (D) detest

156. an anonymous <u>benefactor</u>

    (A) author
    (B) helper
    (C) request
    (D) worker

157. an <u>irate</u> customer

    (A) angry
    (B) loyal
    (C) calculating
    (D) pleasant

158. rough <u>terrain</u>

    (A) land
    (B) water
    (C) justice
    (D) storm

159. a <u>meticulous</u> worker

    (A) sloppy
    (B) manual
    (C) careful
    (D) ridiculous

160. to <u>condone</u> an action

    (A) disapprove
    (B) pardon
    (C) repeat
    (D) hide

161. a <u>candid</u> response

    (A) misleading
    (B) false
    (C) delayed
    (D) straightforward

162. an <u>edible</u> plant

    (A) poisonous
    (B) eatable
    (C) flowering
    (D) medicinal

163. to <u>revere</u> a hero

    (A) follow
    (B) respect highly
    (C) publicize
    (D) antagonize

164. a <u>vigilant</u> guard

    (A) alert
    (B) violent
    (C) professional
    (D) sleeping

GO TO NEXT PAGE ➡

165. a human <u>foible</u>

(A) weakness
(B) bone
(C) feeling
(D) being

166. an unexpected <u>boon</u>

(A) interruption
(B) explosion
(C) gift
(D) deviation

167. a <u>dubious</u> suggestion

(A) welcome
(B) slow
(C) random
(D) doubtful

168. closest <u>egress</u>

(A) exit
(B) bird
(C) flower
(D) garment

169. to <u>proclaim</u> a belief

(A) support
(B) hear
(C) dismiss
(D) declare

170. a <u>sumptuous</u> banquet

(A) rich
(B) paltry
(C) vegetarian
(D) hypothetical

171. a <u>whimsical</u> poem

(A) adaptable
(B) mechanical
(C) playful
(D) difficult

172. a <u>superfluous</u> part

(A) extra
(B) large
(C) attractive
(D) colorful

173. welcome <u>solace</u>

(A) decoration
(B) relief
(C) anger
(D) speech

174. a <u>sagacious</u> parent

(A) wise
(B) old
(C) feeble
(D) healthy

STOP

If there is still time remaining, you may review your answers.

#175–238   45 MINUTES

Sample:

Round 642 to the nearest hundred.

(A) 650
(B) 600
(C) 700
(D) 640   Ⓐ ● Ⓒ Ⓓ

Directions: Select the best answer for each question.

175.   If the length of a rectangle is 4.2 inches and its width is 3.65 inches, find its perimeter.

   (A)   13.6 inches
   (B)   15.7 inches
   (C)   16.3 inches
   (D)   14.6 inches

176.   Change $5\frac{1}{4}$ % to a fraction.

   (A) $\dfrac{21}{400}$

   (B) $\dfrac{5}{100}$

   (C) $\dfrac{21}{100}$

   (D) $\dfrac{25}{150}$

177.   Which point lies 4 units above the *x*-axis and 2 units to the left of the *y*-axis?

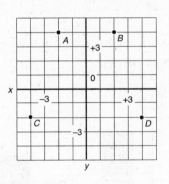

   (A)   *A*
   (B)   *B*
   (C)   *C*
   (D)   *D*

178.   One side of a square is 12. The radius of a circle is 7. Let $\pi = \dfrac{22}{7}$ and choose the best answer.

   (A)   The circumference of the circle is 4 more than the perimeter of the square.
   (B)   The area of the square is 10 more than the area of the circle.
   (C)   The perimeter of the square is 4 more than the circumference of the circle.
   (D)   The area of the circle is 10 less than the area of the square.

GO TO NEXT PAGE ➡

179. In a triangle, the sum of any two sides is always greater than the third side. Select the best choice to represent the three sides of a triangle.

(A) 3, 4, 7
(B) 4, 5, 8
(C) 5, 6, 12
(D) 10, 5, 5

180. Jesse Patterson has a 0.300 batting average (Hits/Times at bat). If he gets a total of 10 more hits the next 10 times at bat, his batting average jumps to 0.400. Determine how many hits he had originally.

(A) 12
(B) 10
(C) 14
(D) 18

181. Examine the bar graph, and select the correct answer.

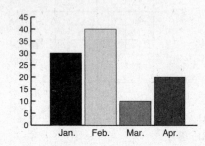

(A) Mar. + Apr. = 60
(B) Jan. – Mar. = 20
(C) Feb. – Mar. > 40
(D) Apr. + Feb. > 100

182. The Gema Corn Flake Company has 2 tons of corn flakes on hand. One ton equals 2,000 pounds and one pound equals 16 ounces. If the company plans to package the corn flakes in 12-ounce boxes, how many boxes will they need? Round the answer to the nearest whole box.

(A) 5,423 boxes
(B) 5,333 boxes
(C) 5,340 boxes
(D) 5,328 boxes

183. Round off 1,147,690 to the nearest thousand.

(A) 1,147,200
(B) 1,150,000
(C) 1,148,000
(D) 1,149,000

184. Find the sum of the squares of the prime factors of 42.

(A) 50
(B) 62
(C) 38
(D) 44

185. Determine the perimeter of the triangle.

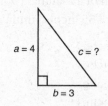

(A) 5
(B) 12
(C) 9
(D) 17

186. The price of a computer dropped from $1,500 to $1,200. What was the percent drop?

(A) 30%
(B) 20%
(C) 38%
(D) 34%

187. Six times a number reduced by 8 is equal to 58. Find the number.

(A) 8
(B) 6
(C) 11
(D) 9

GO TO NEXT PAGE ➡

188. Craymore Electronics sold 81 computers and 52 printers last week. Twenty-five separate customers purchased computers and printers. How many customers purchased only computers?

(A) 39
(B) 42
(C) 49
(D) 56

189. The library has a policy of ordering 5 fiction, 2 historical, 3 biographical, and 3 science books in that order. If 124 books were ordered, what subject was the last book?

(A) fiction
(B) historical
(C) biographical
(D) science

190. Ruben, Shelly, and Malcolm have recorded a hit song. Ruben gets $\frac{2}{5}$ of the income, Shelly gets $\frac{1}{3}$, and Malcolm gets the rest. If they earn $300,000, how much does Malcolm earn?

(A) $80,000
(B) $250,000
(C) $210,000
(D) $90,000

191. What number is 17 more than 5% of 420?

(A) 26
(B) 64
(C) 44
(D) 38

192. Six times a number is 24.72. What is the result if we divide that number by 4?

(A) 2.45
(B) 1.03
(C) 4.34
(D) 3.82

193. Let X represent the set of multiples of 4, and let Y represent the set of multiples of 10. Which of the following statements is true?

(A) $12 \notin X$
(B) $11 \in X$
(C) $40 \in Y$
(D) $8 \notin X$

194. The sum of two consecutive odd integers is 156. What is the larger integer?

(A) 75
(B) 77
(C) 78
(D) 79

195. Add: $-3a + 4b - 6c$ and $7b - 4c - 6a$.

(A) $-9a + 11b - 10c$
(B) $3a + 4b - 10c$
(C) $6a - 2b - 6c$
(D) $-7a - 4b + 8c$

196. Find the value of $\frac{4 \times 5^8}{2 \times 5^6}$.

(A) 50
(B) 40
(C) 25
(D) 100

197. Which of the following choices will satisfy the inequality $-2 < x < 2.3$?

(A) -5
(B) 3.2
(C) 0
(D) 2.4

198. What percent of 80 is 17.6?

(A) 22%
(B) 79%
(C) 82%
(D) 46%

GO TO NEXT PAGE ➡

199. Add: $(-4) + (+9) + (-6) + (+3)$

 (A) −4
 (B) +3
 (C) −6
 (D) +2

200. If x and y are negative integers and $y > x$, which of the following statements is true?

 (A) $xy < 0$
 (B) $x + y > 0$
 (C) $xy > 0$
 (D) $y - x < 0$

201. If the perimeter of a rectangle is 44 feet and its width is 7 feet, what is its length?

 (A) 12
 (B) 11
 (C) 15
 (D) 14

202. If two interior angles of a triangle are 47° and 58°, select the third angle.

 (A) 75°
 (B) 43°
 (C) 59°
 (D) 36°

203. Select the greatest prime factor of 42.

 (A) 7
 (B) 6
 (C) 3
 (D) 14

204. The rectangle measures 16 units long and 14 units wide. If each square on the edges of the rectangle measures 3 by 3 units, find the shaded area in the figure below.

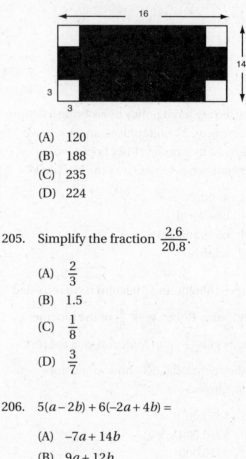

 (A) 120
 (B) 188
 (C) 235
 (D) 224

205. Simplify the fraction $\dfrac{2.6}{20.8}$.

 (A) $\dfrac{2}{3}$
 (B) 1.5
 (C) $\dfrac{1}{8}$
 (D) $\dfrac{3}{7}$

206. $5(a - 2b) + 6(-2a + 4b) =$

 (A) $-7a + 14b$
 (B) $9a + 12b$
 (C) $33b - 5a$
 (D) $-6a - 15b$

207. Change the expression

 $$7 \times 10^3 + 5 \times 10^2 + 2 \times 10^1 + 6 \times 10^0$$

 to a four-digit number.

 (A) 7,345
 (B) 7,890
 (C) 7,738
 (D) 7,526

GO TO NEXT PAGE ➡

208. What happens to the area of a triangle when its height is doubled and its base remains the same?

    (A) remains the same
    (B) is doubled
    (C) is tripled
    (D) is multiplied by 2.5

209. Find the mean of the following weights. Round off your answer to the nearest pound.

# of persons	4	3	1	2
weights	138	145	121	154

    (A) 145
    (B) 142
    (C) 136
    (D) 139

210. Simplify $\sqrt[3]{64a^3b^9}$.

    (A) $8ab^3$
    (B) $4a^3b^3$
    (C) $4a^3b$
    (D) $4ab^3$

211. The letters a, b, and c are consecutive odd integers in the given order. If $c = 11$, what is the product of a and b?

    (A) 55
    (B) 63
    (C) 72
    (D) 87

212. In an auto manufacturing plant, the ratio of executives to assembly line workers is 1 : 15. If there are 480 employees altogether, how many assembly line workers are there?

    (A) 450
    (B) 800
    (C) 250
    (D) 600

213. Simplify $\dfrac{4\frac{2}{3}}{5\frac{1}{4}}$.

    (A) $\dfrac{5}{8}$
    (B) $\dfrac{3}{5}$
    (C) $\dfrac{8}{9}$
    (D) $\dfrac{5}{7}$

214. BA is perpendicular to BD. Angle ABE measures 17°, and angle DBC measures 54°. Find the measure of angle EBC.

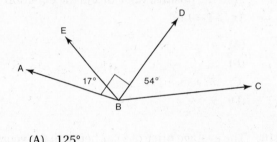

    (A) 125°
    (B) 71°
    (C) 127°
    (D) 144°

215. In the parallelogram below, which two sides are parallel?

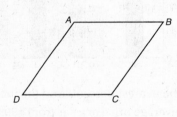

    (A) AB and BC
    (B) BC and CD
    (C) CD and AD
    (D) AD and BC

GO TO NEXT PAGE ➡

216. If the two central angles of the adjoining circle are 55° and 115°, find the average of all three central angles.

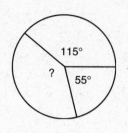

(A) 55°
(B) 85°
(C) 120°
(D) 60°

217. Find the positive value of x in the equation $3x^2 + 2 = 149$.

(A) 4
(B) 5
(C) 7
(D) 6

218. The average price of a car between the years 1998 and 2005 is given in the chart below.

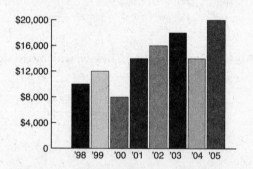

To the nearest percent, find the increase in the average price of a car from 1999 to 2005. Disregard the intervening years.

(A) 67%
(B) 35%
(C) 44%
(D) 66%

219. The following table represents the frequency distribution of students' weights. Find the mean weight and round to the nearest tenth.

Pounds, p_i	Frequency, f_i	$p_i f_i$
98	2	
105	1	
109	1	
120	3	
126	2	
132	4	

(A) 119.3
(B) 119.7
(C) 119.0
(D) 119.2

220. Simplify $\dfrac{7}{17\frac{1}{2}}$.

(A) $\dfrac{3}{7}$

(B) $\dfrac{2}{5}$

(C) $\dfrac{5}{9}$

(D) $\dfrac{7}{8}$

221. Find the value of x in the adjoining diagram.

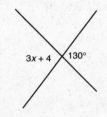

(A) 54°
(B) 38°
(C) 46°
(D) 42°

GO TO NEXT PAGE ➡

222. If the Big Peach Supermarket is selling raisins at $0.20 per ounce, how much would 8 pounds cost?

(A) $18.40
(B) $24.60
(C) $25.60
(D) $32.20

223. Madison High School held a junior prom. The total receipts amounted to $3,070. Members of the Student Organization paid $5, while non-members paid $11. If 170 tickets were sold to non-members, how many tickets were sold to Student Organization members?

(A) 244
(B) 240
(C) 285
(D) 482

224. Malika wants to build a fence in the shape of a hexagon around her property. The sides of the fence are 49.4 feet, 34.9 feet, 53.6 feet, 65.8 feet, 72.6 feet, and 48.7 feet. If fencing costs $5.30 per foot, find the cost for the complete fence.

(A) $2,340.60
(B) $1,893.60
(C) $2,342.80
(D) $1,722.50

225. The sides of a pentagon are represented by x, $x+2$, $x+5$, $2x+2$, and $3x-1$. If the perimeter is 56, find the length of the longest side.

(A) 18
(B) 19
(C) 17
(D) 14

226. The area of a square is represented by $4x+20$. If each side is 8, find x.

(A) 9
(B) 11
(C) 8
(D) 10

227. Latisha is 5 years older than Wanda. Three years ago Wanda was $8a$ years old. How old is Latisha now?

(A) $8a+5$
(B) $8a-3$
(C) $8a+8$
(D) $8a+3$

228. In a two-digit number, the sum of the digits is 11. Three times the tens digit is 5 more than the units digit. Find the number.

(A) 47
(B) 16
(C) 53
(D) 39

229. ABC is an isosceles triangle with side AB congruent to side BC. If the exterior angle at C measures 105°, what is the measure of angle B?

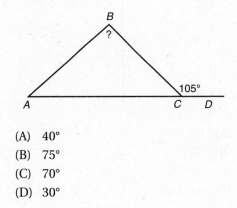

(A) 40°
(B) 75°
(C) 70°
(D) 30°

GO TO NEXT PAGE ➡

230. Find side *BC* of the adjoining right angle.

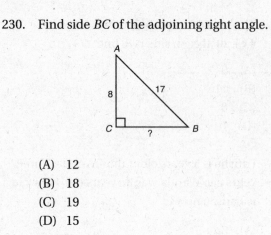

(A) 12
(B) 18
(C) 19
(D) 15

231. Of the following expressions, which is the largest?

(A) $2 \times 5^2 - 9 \div 3$
(B) $3^3 - (18 \div 2) + 7$
(C) $5(8 - 3)^2$
(D) $4 \times 9 + 3(6 - 2)$

232. If $6(a + 2) - 2c = 6$ and $a = 4$, find c.

(A) 15
(B) 18
(C) 12
(D) 17

233. Find the measure of $\angle a$.

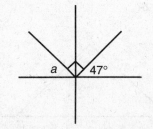

(A) 54°
(B) 23°
(C) 43°
(D) 47°

234. Which of the following numbers is 8 less than two-thirds of 27?

(A) 10
(B) 8
(C) 6
(D) 4

235. 5 feet 7 inches – 2 feet 9 inches =

(A) 2 feet 2 inches
(B) 3 feet 1 inch
(C) 3 feet 5 inches
(D) 2 feet 10 inches

236. Jack collects tolls. On average, he collects $5.25 per minute. How much does he collect in two hours?

(A) $460
(B) $540
(C) $400
(D) $630

237. Find the shaded area if the radius of the outer circle is 8 inches and the radius of the inner circle is 5 inches. Let $\pi = 3.14$.

(A) 198.44
(B) 234.82
(C) 122.46
(D) 202.56

238. $5\sqrt{2} \times 3\sqrt{8} =$

(A) $10\sqrt{24}$
(B) $\sqrt{10}\sqrt{16}$
(C) 60
(D) 40

If there is still time remaining, you may review your answers.

Sample:

Which sentence below contains an error?

(A) Andrew and he were leaving.
(B) We was going to the store.
(C) Josh and Sarah will buy food for us.   Correct marking of samples
(D) No mistakes.   Ⓐ ● Ⓒ Ⓓ

(A) Work on the car in here.
(B) Where will we end up?
(C) Enter through the front door, please.   Correct marking of samples
(D) No mistakes.   Ⓐ Ⓑ Ⓒ ●

Directions: For questions 239–278, choose the sentence in each group that contains an error in capitalization, punctuation, or usage. If you find no mistakes, select D on your answer sheet.

239. (A) Alfia and I started our own business.
      (B) Paul can you tell Lisa to come to the party?
      (C) I can hardly contain my enthusiasm.
      (D) No mistakes.

240. (A) I attended the St Andrew parish school when I was younger.
      (B) Many of his books are set in New Mexico.
      (C) Although the course was difficult, we stayed with it.
      (D) No mistakes.

241. (A) Shannon and Ben make a good couple.
      (B) The ingredients include salt, pepper, and nutmeg.
      (C) Merry and Pippin are the taller hobbits in all of the Shire.
      (D) No mistakes.

242. (A) Mother sent my sister and me to the store.
      (B) Avery wrote an excellent paper on theology.
      (C) Morgan hardly ever misses class.
      (D) No mistakes.

243. (A) One of the men on the team have dropped out of the game.
      (B) Ms. Johns and Mr. Schneider have done a lot of volunteer work.
      (C) Phillip's brother's name is Adrian.
      (D) No mistakes.

244. (A) Francisco chose the saxophone; David chose the trumpet.
      (B) Would you mind stirring the kettle.
      (C) My friends and I play chess during lunch.
      (D) No mistakes.

GO TO NEXT PAGE ➡

245. (A) Tom, Guy, Sandy, and me, went to the game together.
     (B) Vince and Nella walked to the corner and bought some lemon ice.
     (C) Gulliver visited many lands during his travels.
     (D) No mistakes.

246. (A) Could you set the package on the chair?
     (B) I vowed, therefore, that I would never shop there again.
     (C) She returned the textbook to myself.
     (D) No mistakes.

247. (A) What's the frequency, Kenneth?
     (B) "I never make exceptions," warned the professor.
     (C) Its a difficult problem, but we can handle it.
     (D) No mistakes.

248. (A) The cold medicine had some unpleasant side effects.
     (B) Whom is speaking?
     (C) For further information on pronunciation, consult your dictionary.
     (D) No mistakes.

249. (A) Its bark is worse than its bite.
     (B) In this election, the voter doesn't have enough information to know if they should support the tax.
     (C) Sherri, my next door neighbor, volunteered to baby-sit.
     (D) No mistakes.

250. (A) Bobby studies silent in his seat most of the time.
     (B) Outside of class, he is very talkative.
     (C) In fact, he talks too much.
     (D) No mistakes.

251. (A) Our oldest teacher was born on September, 23, 1960.
     (B) No, the color of an airplane's black box is actually orange.
     (C) Give the directions to Joseph, Jenny, and me.
     (D) No mistakes.

252. (A) The theme of the story concerned the destructive greed for powerfulness.
     (B) Sinon convinced the Trojans to accept the horse.
     (C) The revolving door is an efficient way to conserve energy.
     (D) No mistakes.

253. (A) Kat was the meanest manager at the store.
     (B) It's hard to believe, but it's true.
     (C) Bring the following to class, pen, pencil, paper, and books.
     (D) No mistakes.

254. (A) Theo bought a blanket for his baby sister.
     (B) Is Trish getting married in December or in June?
     (C) Jake is the truthfullest person I have ever met.
     (D) No mistakes.

255. (A) It is further to Cleveland than to Philadelphia.
     (B) Did you hear Isaac and me come in?
     (C) Amanda sings beautifully.
     (D) No mistakes.

256. (A) Meredith was always on time, but John was usually late.
     (B) Several of the guests have arrived.
     (C) I don't have a lot of free time, nevertheless, I would like the job.
     (D) No mistakes.

GO TO NEXT PAGE ➡

257. (A) No I have never seen a live rhinoceros.
(B) Our zoo is the smallest in the state.
(C) I still enjoy visiting, however.
(D) No mistakes.

258. (A) I concluded, therefore, that I'd like to attend the university.
(B) It's expensive, but I am saving my money.
(C) Moreover, I plan on earning a scholarship.
(D) No mistakes.

259. (A) You won't have to look for Joe and I.
(B) We'll be wearing green jackets.
(C) It's a daring fashion choice, but we're willing to risk it.
(D) No mistakes.

260. (A) Since you're so smart, you won't mind answering a few questions.
(B) Can you bake some cookies for our sale?
(C) I realized I had been mistook.
(D) No mistakes.

261. (A) I studied for hours, but the test was still difficult.
(B) He had already gone before we arrived at the dance.
(C) One of the teachers had volunteered to coach the bowling team.
(D) No mistakes.

262. (A) I enjoy walking on the beach and to run in the surf.
(B) Josiah, by the way, is living in Boston now.
(C) He used to wear a black hat and a long coat.
(D) No mistakes.

263. (A) Really, you're living in a golden age.
(B) If you arrive late, just blend into the crowd.
(C) I only have time to eat drink and sleep.
(D) No mistakes.

264. (A) Did you enjoy the skating program?
(B) Dennis performed good on the ice.
(C) The music was carefully chosen.
(D) No mistakes.

265. (A) Aunt Wendy often takes Al and I to lunch.
(B) John Heywood collected and published many famous proverbs; you've probably never heard of him, though.
(C) Mr. Meyers said—and rightly so—that the rules should apply to all.
(D) No mistakes.

266. (A) The book on the top shelf is too high to reach.
(B) The deer reared up on it's hind legs.
(C) You're a mean one, Mr. Grinch.
(D) No mistakes.

267. (A) Derrick listed *The Hobbit* as his favorite book.
(B) I chose *The Adventures of Sherlock Holmes.*
(C) I read my first mystery when I was in the third grade.
(D) No mistakes.

268. (A) My favorite Aunt is visiting with my cousin.
(B) Her sister, an immigrant from Ethiopia, arrived later.
(C) They enjoy singing, reading, and cooking.
(D) No mistakes.

GO TO NEXT PAGE ➡

HSPT PRACTICE EXAM 1

269. (A) Everett hardly ever has time for small talk.
(B) Our school finished first, his school placed second.
(C) Neither Shannon nor Melissa missed a shot in that game.
(D) No mistakes.

270. (A) Incidentally, amateurs are encouraged to apply.
(B) My parents are immigrants; they came from Sicily.
(C) Is that why you named your daughter Cicely?
(D) No mistakes.

271. (A) Shakespeare wrote, "To thine own self be true".
(B) Lucy received her degree three years ago.
(C) Mr. White said, "Keep it simple."
(D) No mistakes.

272. (A) Don't loose your tickets, or you won't be able to get in.
(B) Mrs. Brown kindly offered me a seat.
(C) The fruit salad consists of the following: cherries, grapes, and peaches.
(D) No mistakes.

273. (A) Neither Jimmy or Tommy has ever been to Canada.
(B) Fiona is more timid than Martha.
(C) You'll feel better if you lie down, Griffin.
(D) No mistakes.

274. (A) Larry has always been an excellent pianist.
(B) He enjoys singing, dancing, and telling jokes.
(C) I just want to set on my porch and swing.
(D) No mistakes.

275. (A) Is the soup ready yet?
(B) My least favorite flavor is vanilla.
(C) Gus transferred here from another school.
(D) No mistakes.

276. (A) I wish I could visit Avonlea.
(B) You and me are best friends, aren't we?
(C) Most people are basically kind, aren't they?
(D) No mistakes.

277. (A) Solomon lives across town; nevertheless, we are best friends.
(B) My neighbors own a german shepherd.
(C) My leisure time is spent reading classic novels.
(D) No mistakes.

278. (A) Since he started walking.
(B) Holden has been playing baseball.
(C) He plays catcher for a team in Rye, New York.
(D) No mistakes.

279. (A) Autumn is the loveliest season of the year.
   (B) I doubt we'll ever know the answer to that puzzle.
   (C) We rode thorough the tunnel on the way to the shore.
   (D) No mistakes.

280. (A) The monster was portrayed as a mishapen creature.
   (B) In the book, he is described as an eloquent man.
   (C) We have to ask which character is more monstrous.
   (D) No mistakes.

281. (A) He carfully unwrapped his gifts.
   (B) Listen to the surgeon when he speaks.
   (C) Matt's techniques are unique in his profession.
   (D) No mistakes.

282. (A) Imagine what the chief could do with that new machine.
   (B) Don't interrupt your professor.
   (C) Where did you aquire that artifact?
   (D) No mistakes.

283. (A) The first volume is truly useful.
   (B) Even though the role was foolish, the actor was not embarassed.
   (C) Chris intends to pursue a career in management.
   (D) No mistakes.

284. (A) Gomer was surprised to find himself in that situation.
   (B) The warranty on the toaster oven expired long ago.
   (C) The hospital discourages visitors after dark.
   (D) No mistakes.

285. (A) She has always been greatly concerned about the enviroment.
   (B) Whether or not you attend, I will be there.
   (C) The government's foreign policy is flexible.
   (D) No mistakes.

286. (A) Freddy immediately ran to the grocery.
   (B) I always go to my science teacher for advise before a new experiment.
   (C) Henry's interests are in fantasy books.
   (D) No mistakes.

287. (A) Do you believe in guardian angels?
   (B) Too many people use apostrophes to write plurals.
   (C) I'll bet I saw that forty times last month.
   (D) No mistakes.

288. (A) Lightining and thunder can be terrifying experiences.
   (B) Grammar is an indispensable part of my knowledge.
   (C) The bookkeeper resigned from the committee.
   (D) No mistakes.

GO TO NEXT PAGE ➡

289. I couldn't sing in the choir last week _____ I had lost my voice.

(A) furthermore
(B) for example
(C) because
(D) and

290. Bess wears slippers to bed in the winter; _____, her feet are warm.

(A) because
(B) consequently
(C) nevertheless
(D) none of these

291. Choose the group of words that best completes this sentence:

After clearing the dishes, _____.

(A) a nap can be taken by all
(B) we can, all of us, take a nap
(C) we can all take a nap
(D) a nap will feel good

292. Which of the following expresses the idea most clearly?

(A) Many stories of the supernatural were written by Nathaniel Hawthorne, the 19th-century American novelist; this is forgotten a lot today.
(B) Though it is forgotten today, the 19th-century American novelist Nathaniel Hawthorne wrote many stories of the supernatural.
(C) Hawthorne, a forgotten novelist, wrote supernatural stories, in 19th-century america.
(D) It is forgotten that Nathaniel Hawthorne, the American novelist who lived in the 19th century, wrote many stories about the supernatural.

293. Which of the following expresses the idea most clearly?

(A) Since he would not apologize to me, I apologized to him.
(B) He would not apologize to me. So, therefore, I apologized to him.
(C) I apologized to him, because no apology was forthcoming from him first.
(D) I felt that I would apologize to him, after realizing that I would get no apology from him.

294. Which of the following sentences best fits under the topic "Medical Benefits of Garlic"?

(A) Garlic can give you bad breath, but it tastes good.
(B) Garlic can lower the risks of some cancers.
(C) Chicago was named after a strong variety of garlic.
(D) None of these

295. Which topic is most appropriate for a one-paragraph essay?

(A) origins of language
(B) the history of the English dictionary
(C) the derivation of the word *etymology*
(D) None of these

GO TO NEXT PAGE ➡

296. Which sentence does NOT belong in the following paragraph?

(1) Stonehenge was built around 5,000 years ago. (2) The monument predates the Celts and the Romans in England. (3) The Irish are descendants of the Celts. (4) No one really knows why Stonehenge was built.

(A) Sentence 1
(B) Sentence 2
(C) Sentence 3
(D) Sentence 4

297. Which sentence does NOT belong in the following paragraph?

(1) Blowing air over hot soup dissipates the moist vapor over the surface. (2) This allows the soup to cool faster. (3) Putting a lid on soup preserves the vapor, keeping it hot. (4) Some soups, such as gazpacho, are served cold.

(A) Sentence 1
(B) Sentence 2
(C) Sentence 3
(D) Sentence 4

298. Where should the sentence "Medieval Germany had many forests" be placed in the following selection?

(1) In the Middle Ages, many people observed a holiday called Adam and Eve day. (2) On December 24, a tree was displayed, representing the tree of knowledge from the Garden of Eden. (3) This eventually led to the custom of having a Christmas tree in the house.

(A) Between sentences 1 and 2
(B) Between sentences 2 and 3
(C) After sentence 3
(D) The sentence does not fit in this paragraph.

STOP

If there is still time remaining, you may review your answers.

ANSWER KEY
HSPT Practice Exam 1

SUBTEST 1   VERBAL

1. A	16. C	31. A	46. D
2. A	17. D	32. A	47. D
3. C	18. D	33. C	48. B
4. A	19. C	34. C	49. A
5. B	20. B	35. A	50. C
6. B	21. D	36. C	51. C
7. D	22. B	37. C	52. A
8. C	23. B	38. A	53. D
9. B	24. C	39. C	54. B
10. A	25. A	40. B	55. B
11. B	26. C	41. A	56. C
12. D	27. B	42. A	57. A
13. A	28. A	43. D	58. C
14. A	29. A	44. B	59. C
15. C	30. D	45. C	60. B

SUBTEST 2   QUANTITATIVE

61. C	74. C	87. B	100. D
62. C	75. C	88. C	101. D
63. B	76. D	89. B	102. B
64. D	77. C	90. A	103. B
65. A	78. A	91. A	104. C
66. B	79. D	92. A	105. B
67. C	80. D	93. D	106. B
68. C	81. C	94. C	107. B
69. A	82. B	95. B	108. C
70. A	83. C	96. C	109. B
71. B	84. A	97. C	110. A
72. B	85. D	98. B	111. A
73. D	86. D	99. A	112. C

ANSWER KEY
HSPT Practice Exam 1

SUBTEST 3 READING

113.	**A**	129.	**C**	145.	**C**	161.	**D**
114.	**B**	130.	**D**	146.	**D**	162.	**B**
115.	**D**	131.	**B**	147.	**D**	163.	**B**
116.	**C**	132.	**A**	148.	**B**	164.	**A**
117.	**C**	133.	**B**	149.	**A**	165.	**A**
118.	**D**	134.	**B**	150.	**B**	166.	**C**
119.	**A**	135.	**B**	151.	**D**	167.	**D**
120.	**A**	136.	**D**	152.	**B**	168.	**A**
121.	**A**	137.	**A**	153.	**C**	169.	**D**
122.	**B**	138.	**B**	154.	**C**	170.	**A**
123.	**D**	139.	**C**	155.	**A**	171.	**C**
124.	**C**	140.	**B**	156.	**B**	172.	**A**
125.	**A**	141.	**B**	157.	**A**	173.	**B**
126.	**B**	142.	**A**	158.	**A**	174.	**A**
127.	**B**	143.	**D**	159.	**C**		
128.	**C**	144.	**B**	160.	**B**		

SUBTEST 4 MATHEMATICS

175.	**B**	191.	**D**	207.	**D**	223.	**B**
176.	**A**	192.	**B**	208.	**B**	224.	**D**
177.	**A**	193.	**C**	209.	**B**	225.	**C**
178.	**C**	194.	**D**	210.	**D**	226.	**B**
179.	**B**	195.	**A**	211.	**B**	227.	**C**
180.	**D**	196.	**A**	212.	**A**	228.	**A**
181.	**B**	197.	**C**	213.	**C**	229.	**D**
182.	**B**	198.	**A**	214.	**C**	230.	**D**
183.	**C**	199.	**D**	215.	**D**	231.	**C**
184.	**B**	200.	**C**	216.	**C**	232.	**A**
185.	**B**	201.	**C**	217.	**C**	233.	**C**
186.	**B**	202.	**A**	218.	**A**	234.	**A**
187.	**C**	203.	**A**	219.	**D**	235.	**D**
188.	**D**	204.	**B**	220.	**B**	236.	**D**
189.	**B**	205.	**C**	221.	**D**	237.	**C**
190.	**A**	206.	**A**	222.	**C**	238.	**C**

SUBTEST 5   LANGUAGE

239. **B**	254. **C**	269. **B**	284. **D**
240. **A**	255. **A**	270. **D**	285. **A**
241. **C**	256. **C**	271. **A**	286. **B**
242. **D**	257. **A**	272. **A**	287. **D**
243. **A**	258. **D**	273. **A**	288. **A**
244. **B**	259. **A**	274. **C**	289. **C**
245. **A**	260. **C**	275. **D**	290. **B**
246. **C**	261. **D**	276. **B**	291. **C**
247. **C**	262. **A**	277. **B**	292. **B**
248. **B**	263. **C**	278. **A**	293. **A**
249. **B**	264. **B**	279. **C**	294. **B**
250. **A**	265. **A**	280. **A**	295. **C**
251. **A**	266. **B**	281. **A**	296. **C**
252. **A**	267. **D**	282. **C**	297. **D**
253. **C**	268. **A**	283. **B**	298. **D**

ANSWERS EXPLAINED

Subtest 1 Verbal

1. **(A)** A *bicycle* is the only vehicle listed without a mechanical engine.

2. **(A)** *Glum* means *sad*. The others are happy, friendly words. If you don't know the word *amiable*, think of the French word for friend—*ami*. Doesn't that sound happy?

3. **(C)** The other words are **specific** breeds of dog.

4. **(A)** True. If you draw the relationship, it should look like this:
   K
   P
   J

5. **(B)** A *prejudice* is a *bias*. It can be an opinion (C), but *bias* is closer to the negative connotation of *prejudice*.

6. **(B)** *Dirty* is the opposite of *clean*, as **light** is the opposite of *dark*.

7. **(D)** *Neglect* is the opposite of all the supportive words.

8. **(C)** These are all similar items, but you don't usually use a *towel* to keep warm in bed.

9. **(B)** It's getting a bit trickier. The first word *close* has two meanings and two pronunciations. The pronunciation /*cloze*/ means to shut or seal, so the remaining word, *near*, does not belong.

10. **(A)** If you don't know the word *voracious*, perhaps you can figure out the root *vor* from *carnivore* or *herbivore*. It means to eat.

11. **(B)** *Mal* is one of those "bad" prefixes.

12. **(D)** *Liberate* means to free. Think of the Statue of *Liberty*.

13. **(A)** *Fire* causes *smoke*; a *lightbulb* causes *brightness*.

14. **(A)** *Reversal* and *inversion* both involve backward movement.

15. **(C)** This one is tricky. We don't hear about John until the last sentence, so we don't know anything about his relationship to the first two.
   T
   C
   N

16. **(C)** *Phrases*, *clauses*, and *sentences* refer to groups of words. An *adverb* is often a single word.

17. **(D)** *Peninsula* is the only land mass listed.

18. **(D)** *Bio* means life, and the degradation of life would be *decay*.

19. **(C)** A *car* is started by a *key*. A *television* is started by a *remote control*. *Outlet* is not quite right, as you are not looking for the power source, but rather the instrument that turns it on.

20. **(B)** If you *imprint* something, you put a mark on it. The opposite is to *erase*.

21. **(D)** An *umbrella* keeps out *rain*. A *door* keeps out a *draft*.

22. **(B)** You might draw a box for mammals and put a circle D for dogs inside of that box. A b for basenji would be inside of the circle. Therefore, the third statement is false.

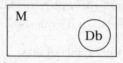

23. **(B)** *Sever* means to cut or separate, which is closest to *divide*.

24. **(C)** We don't know how long Ursola's hair is compared to Grace's. Our diagram might look like this:
U G?
J

25. **(A)** You might be tricked into guessing *wardrobe* (D), but remember that *uni-* means one. *One form* means *sameness*.

26. **(C)** *Run* does not necessarily mean to run *away*, which the other words express.

27. **(B)** *Philo* means *love*, so it's a positive word. Only (B) is positive. A philanthropist is a person who loves people (*anthropos*) and often donates to charitable organizations.

28. **(A)** *Magic* and *supernatural* are similar, so you can eliminate them; they can't both be the correct choice. *Con* means with or together. Things that go together are *suitable* for one another.

29. **(A)** Shoes
Skirt
Blouse

30. **(D)** The other choices are specific kinds of poems.

31. **(A)** Something *impressive* is *inspiring*, so you're looking for a synonym for *derogatory*. If you don't know the meaning of *derogatory*, see if you can eliminate some of the choices. The other choices are all positive synonyms, so they can't all be correct. That leaves only the word *critical*, which is a synonym for *derogatory*.

32. **(A)** The other choices are all commands.

33. **(C)** We are not given enough information.

34. **(C)** The other words denote active searching.

35. **(A)** *Not equal* is not fair.

36. **(C)** *Thrifty* people save their money. They are *not wasteful*.

37. **(C)** *Mal* is one of those negative prefixes, so it is not a success.

38. **(A)** S + 10
L + 20
J

39. **(C)** *Console* (pronounced conSOLE) means to comfort. The opposite is to *agitate*.

40. **(B)** A *roof* is the top of a *house*. A *head* is the top of the *body*. You wouldn't choose *brain* (top of the attic) or *foot* (top of the foundation).

41. **(A)** *Diligence* means hard work. The opposite is *laziness*.

42. **(A)** Moon River
    mile
    Pirate Island

43. **(D)** The other choices are forward moving.

44. **(B)** Use a *fork* to *eat*. Use a *pen* to *write*.

45. **(C)** This is not the noun *device*, but the verb *devise*, which means to make or *create*.

46. **(D)** The other choices are specific types of machines.

47. **(D)** Glory is important; its opposite is unimportant.

48. **(B)** Someone *idle* is not *employed*. Someone *graceful* is not *clumsy*.

49. **(A)** S
    M + C

50. **(C)** The other choices are all negative.

51. **(C)** *Noise* irritates you. A *lullaby soothes* you.

52. **(A)** R
    cat
    P

53. **(D)** The other choices indicate a *lack* of information.

54. **(B)** *Morose* is the opposite of *cheerful*.

55. **(B)** C
    K
    T

56. **(C)** The other words deal with speaking aloud. *Repress* means to hold back.

57. **(A)** *Crucial* means *necessary*.

58. **(C)** A *bus* is like a large *car*. A *whale* is a large <u>sea</u> mammal, such as a *dolphin*.

59. **(C)** K-15 C-12   We are given no indication that these books overlap.

60. **(B)** Inga
    Nicholas
    Hendrik

61. **(C)**

$$\begin{array}{ccccccc} -6 & +3 & -6 & +3 & -6 & +3 & -6 \\ \end{array}$$

18,   12,   15,   9,   12,   6,   9,   <u>3</u>

62. **(C)** Let $x =$ the number.

$$x^2 + 3 = 4 \times 7$$
$$x^2 + 3 = 28$$
$$\underline{-3 \quad -3}$$
$$x^2 = 25$$
$$x = \sqrt{25}$$
$$x = 5$$

63. **(B)** Simplify (a), (b), and (c) and then substitute the results into (A), (B), (C), and (D).

   (a) $7(9 - 3) = 7(6) = 42$

   (b) $2 \times 4 + \dfrac{72}{4} = 8 + 18 = 26$

   (c) $48 - 3(5 + 6) = 48 - 3(11) = 48 - 33 = 15$

   (A) (a) is less than (b) and less than (c): $42 < 26$ and $42 < 15$ ✖

   (B) (b) is greater than (c) and less than (a): $26 > 15$ and $26 < 42$ ✔

   (C) (c) is less than (a) and greater than (b): $15 < 42$ and $15 > 26$ ✖

   (D) (c) is greater than (a) and greater than (b): $15 > 42$ and $15 > 26$ ✖

64. **(D)** "Quotient" indicates division. Let $x =$ the unknown number.

$$\frac{48}{6} + 2 = \sqrt{x}$$
$$8 + 2 = \sqrt{x}$$
$$10 = \sqrt{x}$$

Square both sides: $100 = x$

65. **(A)** Subtract 3 from each preceding number.

$$26 - 3 = 23$$

66. **(B)** Find the areas of the square and the circle and subtract the two. The diameter of the circle is 8, so the radius is 4.

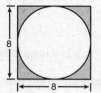

Area of square, A_S: $A_S = s^2$

$s = 8$: $= 8^2 = 64$

Area of circle, A_C: $A_C = \pi r^2$

$\pi = 3.14$, $r = 4$: $= 3.14(4)^2$

                            $= 3.14(16)$

                            $= 50.24$

$A_S - A_C = 64 - 50.24 = 13.76 \approx 13.8$

67. **(C)** Change (a), (b), and (c) to decimals and then substitute into (A), (B), (C), and (D).

(a) $45\% = 0.45$

(b) $\dfrac{2}{3} = 0.66\ldots$

(c) $0.45 = 0.45$

(A) (a) is greater than (b) and less than (c): $0.45 > 0.66$ and $0.45 < 0.45$ ✖

(B) (b) is less than (c) and greater than (a): $0.66 < 0.45$ and $0.66\ldots > 0.45$ ✖

(C) (c) is equal to (a) and less than (b): $0.45 = 0.45$ and $0.45 < 0.66\ldots$ ✔

(D) (b) is greater than (a) and less than (c): $0.66 > 0.45$ and $0.66\ldots < 0.45$ ✖

68. **(C)** Double each preceding number.

$$2 \times 32 = 64$$

69. **(A)** Let $x =$ the unknown number.

$$x = \frac{2}{3} \times 30 + 15$$

$$x = 20 + 15$$

$$x = 35$$

70. **(A)** Simplify (a), (b), and (c), and substitute into (A), (B), (C), and (D).

(a) $\dfrac{3}{7} \times 42 = 18$

(b) $\dfrac{5}{8} \times 40 = 25$

(c) $\dfrac{6}{7} \times 35 = 30$

(A) (a) is less than (b) and less than (c): $18 < 25$ and $18 < 30$ ✔

(B) (b) is greater than (c) and greater than (a): $25 > 30$ and $25 > 18$ ✖

(C) (c) is greater than (b) and less than (a): $30 > 25$ and $30 < 18$ ✖

(D) (a) is less than (c) and greater than (b): $18 < 30$ and $18 > 25$ ✖

71. **(B)** First multiply the expression inside the parentheses by 2. Then subtract 78 from both sides of the equation and, finally divide by -2.

$$62 + 2(8 - x) = 72$$
$$62 + 16 - 2x = 72$$
$$78 - 2x = 72$$
$$\underline{-78\qquad\quad = -78}$$
$$-2x = -6$$
$$\frac{-2x}{-2} = \frac{-6}{-2}$$
$$x = 3$$

72. **(B)** Subtract $1\frac{1}{2}$ from each preceding number.

$$46\frac{1}{2} - 1\frac{1}{2} = 45$$

73. **(D)** Let $y =$ the unknown number.

$$\frac{48}{y} = \frac{2}{3} \times 9$$

$$\frac{48}{y} = 6$$

$$y\left(\frac{48}{y}\right) = (6)y$$

$$48 = 6y$$

$$\frac{48}{6} = \frac{6y}{6}$$

$$8 = y$$

74. **(C)** Let $y =$ the unknown number and let $25\% = 0.25$.

$$5y = 0.25 \times 80$$
$$5y = 20$$
$$y = 4$$

75. **(C)** There are two series here in alternate positions. The first series begins with 2 and increases by 4. The second series begins with 15 and decreases by 2. The missing number is a member of the first series and is thus 4 more than 6.

$$6 + 4 = 10$$

76. **(D)** Let $x =$ the first of the three consecutive odd integers. Let $x + 2$ equal the second of the three consecutive odd integers. Let $x + 4$ equal the third of the three consecutive odd integers.

$$x + (x + 2) + (x + 4) = 39$$
$$3x + 6 = 39$$
$$\underline{ -6 \quad -6}$$
$$\frac{3x}{3} = \frac{33}{3}$$
$$x = 11$$

77. **(C)**

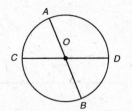

CO, OD, AO, and *OB* are radii and are therefore equal in length. *AB* and *CD* are diameters and are also equal in length.

$$AB - OB = DO$$
$$\text{diameter } AB - \text{radius } OB = \text{radius } DO$$

DO is a radius, and all radii in the same circle are equal in length.

78. **(A)** First determine the number of .7 gallons there are in 28 gallons. Then multiply your answer by 2 seconds.

$$\frac{28}{.7} = 40$$

$$40 \times 2 \text{ seconds} = 80 \text{ seconds} = 1 \text{ minute, } 20 \text{ seconds}$$

79. **(D)** Take half of the previous number.

$$\frac{1}{2} \times 2\frac{1}{4} = 1\frac{1}{8}$$

80. **(D)** Let P = the perimeter. Let k = the length of the rectangle and let $k - 8$ = the width of the rectangle.

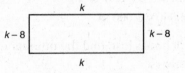

$$P = 2 \cdot \text{length} + 2 \cdot \text{width}$$
$$P = 2(k) + 2(k - 8) = 2k + 2k - 16$$
$$P = 4k - 16$$

81. **(C)** Let y = the unknown number.

$$5y = 8^2 - 9$$
$$5y = 64 - 9$$
$$\frac{5y}{5} = \frac{55}{5}$$
$$y = 11$$

82. **(B)**

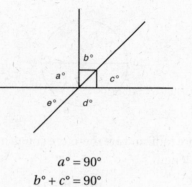

$$a° = 90°$$
$$b° + c° = 90°$$
$$a° = b° + c°$$

83. **(C)** Let x = the unknown number.

$$x = \frac{4}{5} \frac{(18+42)}{2}$$
$$x = \frac{4}{5}(30)$$
$$x = 24$$

84. **(A)** Simplify (a), (b), and (c) and substitute into (A), (B), (C), and (D).

(a) $4.06 \times 10^3 = 4.06 \times 1{,}000 = 4{,}060$
(b) $30 \times 10^2 = 30 \times 100 = 3{,}000$
(c) $52.4 \times 10^1 = 52.4 \times 10 = 524$

(A) (a) is greater than (b): $4{,}060 > 3{,}000$ ✔
(B) (b) is less than (c): $3{,}000 < 524$ ✘
(C) (c) is greater than (b): $524 > 3{,}000$ ✘
(D) (a) is less than (b): $4{,}060 < 3{,}000$ ✘

85. **(D)** Using the number of books lost, find the number of books returned. Then compare both numbers.

Original Number of Books:	30
– Number of Books Lost:	4
Number of Books Returned:	26

Ratio of returned books to lost books: $\dfrac{26}{4} = \dfrac{13}{2}$

86. **(D)** To determine the pattern, double the first number. Then add 1 to the next number.

$$2 \times 23 = 46$$

87. **(B)** To determine the area of the walk, multiply 32 by 3.5. Then, to find the total cost, multiply the answer by $12.40, the cost of cementing a square foot.

$$32 \text{ ft} \times 3.5 \text{ ft} = 112 \text{ sq ft}$$
$$112 \text{ sq ft} \times \$12.40 \text{ per sq ft} = \$1{,}388.80$$

88. **(C)**

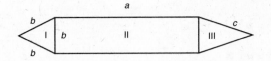

Substitute sample lengths into (A), (B), (C), and (D). $a = 6$, $b = 2$, and $c = 3$.

(A) $2a < 2c = 2(6) < 2(3) = 12 < 6$. (Incorrect)
(B) $a + c < b = 6 + 3 < 2 = 9 < 2$. (Incorrect)
(C) $a + c > b = 6 + 3 > 2 = 9 > 2$. (Correct)
(D) $2b > 2c = 2(2) > 2(3) = 4 > 6$. (Incorrect)

89. **(B)** The series is increasing by 3 and is written in alternate Arabic and Roman numerals.

15 is the missing number, or, in Roman numerals, XV.

90. **(A)**

$$8,000 - 1,600 = 6,400$$

$$\frac{6,400}{8,000} = .80 = 80\%$$

91. **(A)**

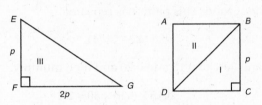

The area of a triangle is equal to $\frac{1}{2}$ the product of the base (b) and the height (h).

Since $ABCD$ is a square, all the sides are of equal length and $AB = BC = CD = p$.

$$\text{Area} \triangle \text{I} = \frac{1}{2} bh = \frac{1}{2} p \cdot p = \frac{1}{2} p^2$$

$$\text{Area} \triangle \text{II} = \frac{1}{2} bh = \frac{1}{2} p \cdot p = \frac{1}{2} p^2$$

$$\text{Area} \triangle \text{III} = \frac{1}{2} bh = \frac{1}{2}(2p)(p) = p \cdot p = p^2$$

(A) Area $\triangle$ I + Area $\triangle$ II = Area $\triangle$ III

$$\frac{1}{2} p^2 + \frac{1}{2} p^2 = p^2 \ ✔$$

(B) Area $\triangle$ I = Area $\triangle$ III

$$\frac{1}{2} p^2 = p^2 \ ✘$$

(C) $2 \times$ Area $\triangle$ II $>$ Area $\triangle$ III

$$2 \times \frac{1}{2}p^2 > p^2$$

$$p^2 > p^2 \; \bm{\times}$$

(D) Area $\square ABCD -$ Area $\triangle$ I $>$ Area $\triangle$ III

$$p^2 - \frac{1}{2}p^2 > p^2$$

$$\frac{1}{2}p^2 > p^2 \; \bm{\times}$$

92. **(A)** The series is increasing by 2.2.

$$10.5 + 2.2 = 12.7$$

93. **(D)**

$$(2 \times 9) + (3 \times 15) = 18 + 45 = \frac{63}{5} = 12.60$$

94. **(C)** The second number in the series is one less than the first number. The third number is triple the second. This pattern is repeated.

$$42 - 1 = 41$$

95. **(B)** Change 15% and 20% to 0.15 and 0.20 and then multiply.

$$0.15 \times 0.20 \times 80 = 2.4$$

96. **(C)**

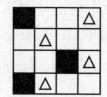

Find the totals of ■, □, and △; substitute into (A), (B), (C), and (D).

Totals: 3 ■, 9 □, 4 △

(A) Total ■ $>$ Total △
$3 > 4$ ✖

(B) Total △ $+$ Total ■ $>$ Total □
$4 + 3 > 9$ ✖

(C) Total □ $-$ Total △ $>$ Total ■
$9 - 4 > 3$ ✔

(D) Total □ $-$ Total ■ $<$ Total △
$9 - 3 < 4$ ✖

97. **(C)** The series is listed in backwards alphabetical order, with three letters in between each of the given terms.

L, K, J, I, **H**

98. **(B)**

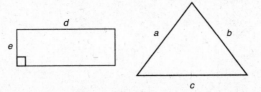

Find the perimeters of the triangle and the rectangle, substitute $2d$ for a and $2e$ for b in the perimeter of the triangle, and then compare the two figures.

$$\text{Perimeter of the triangle} = 2d + 2e + c$$

$$\text{Perimeter of the rectangle} = 2d + 2e$$

Subtract the perimeter of the rectangle from the perimeter of the triangle:

$$(2d + 2e + c) - (2d + 2e)$$
$$2d + 2e + c - 2d - 2e$$
$$c$$

99. **(A)** There are two alternating series here: 2, 4, 6, . . . and 5, 8, 11 . . . .

The next number $= 6 + 2 = 8$.

100. **(D)**

$2.85

$1.89

$1.37

$1.16

Find the total bill and subtract from $10.

$$
\begin{array}{ll}
\$2.85 & \$10.00 \\
1.89 & -\ 7.27 \\
1.37 & \overline{\$2.73} \\
+\ 1.16 & \\
\overline{\$7.27} &
\end{array}
$$

101. **(D)**

(a)

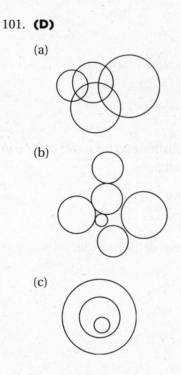

(b)

(c)

Determine the number of circles in (a), (b), and (c) and then substitute into (A), (B), (C), and (D).

Circles in (a): 4
Circles in (b): 6
Circles in (c): 3

(A) Figure (a) includes one less circle than figure (c): $4 = 3 - 1$ ✖
(B) Figure (b) includes two more circles than figure (c): $6 = 3 + 2$ ✖
(C) Figure (c) includes two fewer circles than figure (b): $3 = 6 - 2$ ✖
(D) Figure (b) includes three more circles than figure (c): $6 = 3 + 3$ ✔

102. **(B)** Find the differences between the numbers and look for a pattern.

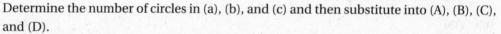

$\leftarrow -5 \rightarrow$ $\leftarrow -6 \rightarrow$ $\leftarrow -7 \rightarrow$ $\leftarrow -8 \rightarrow$ $\leftarrow -9 \rightarrow$

142   137   131   124   **116**   107

103. **(B)**

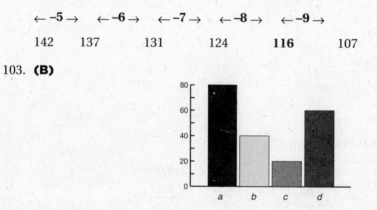

Determine a, b, c, and d and then substitute into (A), (B), (C), and (D).

$a = 80$
$b = 40$
$c = 20$
$d = 60$

(A) $a - b = c$: $80 - 40 = 20$ ✘
(B) $b + c = d$: $40 + 20 = 60$ ✔
(C) $b + c > a$: $40 + 20 > 80$ ✘
(D) $d - c < b$: $60 - 20 < 40$ ✘

104. **(C)** The series is in the form $1^3, 2^3, 3^3, 4^3, 5^3, \ldots$.

$$6^3 = 6 \times 6 \times 6 = 216$$

105. **(B)** Solve (a), (b), and (c) and substitute into (A), (B), (C), and (D).

(a) $\dfrac{4}{100} + \dfrac{5}{10} + 3 = 0.04 + 0.5 + 3 = 3.54$

(b) $\dfrac{9}{100} + 3 + \dfrac{3}{10} = 0.09 + 3 + 0.3 = 3.39$

(c) $\dfrac{2}{10} + 3 + \dfrac{3}{100} = 0.2 + 3 + 0.03 = 3.23$

(A) (c) is greater than (b) and less than (a): $3.23 > 3.39$ and $3.23 < 3.54$ ✘
(B) (b) is less than (a) and greater than (c): $3.39 < 3.54$ and $3.39 > 3.23$ ✔
(C) (a) is less than (b) and less than (c): $3.54 < 3.39$ and $3.54 < 3.23$ ✘
(D) (b) is greater than (a) and greater than (c): $3.39 > 3.54$ and $3.39 > 3.23$ ✘

106. **(B)**

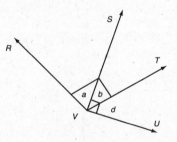

Perpendicular lines form right angles.

$$a + b = 90°, \ b + d = 90°$$

Therefore:

$$a + b = b + d$$
$$a = d$$

(A) $a + b < b + d$: $90° < 90°$ ✘
(B) $d - b = a - b$: Since $d = a$: $a - b = a - b$ ✔
(C) $a + b < 90°$: $90° < 90°$ ✘
(D) $d > a$: Since $d = a$: $d > a$ ✘

107. **(B)** The series is increasing by 3, 4, and 1 units.

$$22 + 3 = 25$$

108. **(C)** Solve for (a), (b), and (c) and substitute into (A), (B), (C), and (D).

(a) $\frac{5}{8} \times 40 = 25$

(b) $\frac{3}{4} \times 60 = 45$

(c) $\frac{2}{3} \times 45 = 30$

(A) (a) is less than (c) and greater than (b): $25 < 30$ and $25 > 45$ ✘
(B) (b) is greater than (c) and less than (a): $45 > 30$ and $45 < 25$ ✘
(C) (c) is less than (b) and greater than (a): $30 < 45$ and $30 > 25$ ✔
(D) (a) is greater than (b) and greater than (c): $25 > 45$ and $25 > 30$ ✘

109. **(B)**

(a)

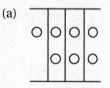

(b)

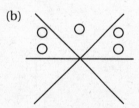

(c)

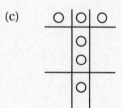

Determine the number of circles and straight lines in (a), (b) and (c) and substitute.

(a) 7 circles, 5 straight lines
(b) 5 circles, 3 straight lines
(c) 6 circles, 4 straight lines

(A) There is one more circle in (b) than lines in (a).

$$5 = 5 + 1 \ \text{✖}$$

(B) The number of lines in (b) plus the number of circles in (a) is equal to the number of lines in (c) plus the number of circles in (c).

$$3 + 7 = 4 + 6 \ \text{✔}$$

(C) The number of circles in (c) and (a) is less than the number of lines in (a) and (b).

$$6 + 7 < 5 + 3 \ \text{✖}$$

(D) The number of lines in (a) plus the number of circles in (b) is less than the number of lines in (b) and (c).

$$5 + 5 < 3 + 4 \ \text{✖}$$

110. **(A)** The series is decreasing by 1, 2, 3, 4, ...

$$23 - 5 = 18$$

111. **(A)** The letters PP reappear after every two intervening letters. The other letters in the series are increasing in alphabetical order.

V, **W**

112. **(C)** The numbers in the series are decreasing in the order –3, –5, –7, –9, –11, ...

$$93 - 13 = 80$$

Subtest 3 Reading

113. **(A)** This question requires you to identify a fact from the reading—simply Sauma's itinerary. While Sauma indeed traveled through all of the locations in choice B, he did not do so in the order it lists. Choice D is wrong because Sauma never visited Versailles, according to the reading. The correct answer is A.

114. **(B)** This question asks you to guess which kind of book would publish this kind of information and presumes that you are aware of certain genres (or types) of books. The information in the passage makes sense for either choice A or B, since the text talks about geographical locations and travel. The information does not make sense in terms of choices C or D; no mention is made of recipes or ingredients nor typical fairy tale creatures. But your job is to make the *best* choice; while you might find such a chatty piece in a travel guide, you are more likely to find it in a history book. The correct answer is B.

115. **(D)** All the definitions presented are viable ones for the word *quest*, but only one is appropriate in the context of the sentence. Paragraph two discusses China's long-term intent (another word for goal) to expand its territory. Therefore only choice D is appropriate.

116. **(C)** This question asks you to locate a fact—to identify the main idea in a piece; there-fore, you should look for factual information. Choice A is simply wrong; paragraph two states as much. Choice B is also wrong since it uses the phrase "declare without question"; nowhere in the piece does the author definitively state that if X happened (Sauma's treaty) then Y would necessarily follow (a necessary change in world events). Instead, the piece is laced with words that connote hesitation or lack of assurance (claim, may have, would have). Choice D singles out Italian explorers for no apparent reason, despite the fact that the article mentions explorers from several nationalities; choice D essentially makes no sense. The only correct answer is C; the author is trying to bring to light a little known but interesting fact about early human exploration.

117. **(C)** This question is very similar to the previous one, except that it asks you to infer what the author thinks *is likely to have happened* had Sauma got his treaty; asking for inference gives you a great deal more flexibility in your answer. The author seems to attempt being unbiased, but still seems to lean toward a particular opinion on the topic of Sauma's explorations. You can rule out choice D, since the piece does not address the topic of World War II nor does it give you any reason to think that an event taking place in the 1200s could clearly affect an event taking place in the 1940s. Choices A and B give you no help; the article refuses to commit itself to either position. The only answer left to you is choice C, since, whether or not Sauma's treaty would have had any long-term effects, it would clearly have had a short-term effect—that of shifting the type of explorer likely to go traveling.

118. **(D)** This question asks for a factual answer, although you have to do a little math to get the answer. Just add the distance of Sauma's trip to the Vatican (7,000 miles) to the distance of the trip back home (7,000). The answer is 14,000 or choice D.

119. **(A)** The term *brokering* usually applies to finances, but using that definition in this context does not make sense; rule out choice D. Choices B and C also do not make sense; substitute the words and you will agree. Your only real choice is A.

120. **(A)** This question is meant rather playfully and takes a bit of subtlety on your part. You can rule out C or D; nowhere does the piece specifically refer to Arabia, nor does Sauma attempt to travel the world. Choice B is more compelling and does fit the con-text. However choice A is best. Think back to your childhood, of your days of playing Marco! Polo! in the pool. Had Marco Polo not gotten all the historical attention, Sauma may well have—we may have been playing Rabban! Sauma! in our pools instead.

121. **(A)** The word *effect* relates to a development or *result* of a specific action or set of actions. Be careful not to confuse *effect* (a *result*) with affect (*to impact*) as in choice B. Choices C and D may sound like the word *effect* but they do not share similar definitions.

122. **(B)** The word *contemporary* simply means *current* and cannot mean past (*outdated*), future (*futuristic*), or a word that has no time connection (*unreliable*).

123. **(D)** From your schooling (especially in science and math) you should be able to recall that *duration* is a word we associate with *time*, not *mass*, *space*, or *sound*.

124. **(C)** The article discusses human behavior. That kind of writing tends to appear in many forms. Most often it tends to appear in nonfiction forms—either in history texts (because they document human action) or sociology texts (because they discuss how

and *why* people perform actions); therefore, you can rule out choices A (because this article is clearly not a scientific discussion), B (since novels, while they can discuss why and how people behave, discuss such topics through fictional means), and D (since biographies usually deal with a single person rather than a class of people).

125. **(A)** Of the title choices offered to you, choices C and D make the least sense. Dr. Spock (yes, a real person) is mentioned only once throughout the course of the article, and you really are not given enough information about him to justify naming an entire writing sample for him. Choice C seems just too broad for the topic at hand; anything can be discussed under this title. You want something tailor-made for *this* topic. Choices A and B are more persuasive, but arguably choice A is best; rocking has a double meaning here—both rocking (lulling) a child to sleep (which fits with the idea of keeping kids sheltered) and rocking (challenging) society's views (which fits well with the idea of refusing to shelter kids any longer).

126. **(B)** Traditionally the word *hinder* means either to hold back or slow down. No one argues that the word *hinder* means the definitions in choices C or D. Given that the use of the word in the sentence implies a slowing down of progress, your only real option is choice B.

127. **(B)** Re-reading (or your memory) brings up the correct fact that historians point to the 18th century for the time when people began sheltering their children (see paragraph two).

128. **(C)** The last sentence of paragraph four gives the answer away: The author clearly states a position in opposition to the statement immediately preceding it. Essentially, then, the author thinks that there are some circumstances in which it is okay to shelter a child from reality. The answer is choice C.

129. **(C)** Re-reading (or your memory) brings up the correct date—1962.

130. **(D)** The main idea behind this article is to advise parents on the issues of child rearing—specifically how to manage the information flow between reality and home. Choices A, B, and C are all briefly mentioned throughout the article, but never to such a degree that you should feel comfortable selecting them as the main idea.

131. **(B)** The article talks briefly about how we all have memories of bad events happening to us. Therefore, look for the option that discusses bad events. Of the four options listed, three are good events—getting a job, trying to get money from the Tooth Fairy, and getting a pet. Therefore, the only option remaining is choice B.

132. **(A)** Here you are looking for a word that means the same thing as the word *exposure*. *Exposure* means to be revealed or made available to something. The word *exile* means banishment, while the word *excitement* describes an emotion; neither has a direct connection to the word exposure. *Exposure* can have a connection to weather—being in direct contact with harsh weather conditions—but, in the context of the passage, that definition of *exposure* simply doesn't make sense. The only option is choice A.

133. **(B)** Re-reading (or memory) will help you identify the planaria as belonging to the flat worm family.

134. **(B)** Remembering what you have learned about the various branches of science, you can make a good inference here. Chemistry studies the chemical bonds and structure of

the world; astronomy studies planets and stars; and physics studies how things move. None of these are appropriate answers. Biology, however, studies various life forms, and planaria are indeed one version of a life form; therefore, choice B is your best answer.

135. **(B)** Choices C and D are present to distract you; choice C really has nothing to do with decapitation, and choice D is there in case you mistake it for the word *delusion.* Choices A and B are closer to the mark, but the correct answer is choice B, removing the head.

136. **(D)** This is a typical fact question that reverses the way it asks for information. Three of the four answers are actual facts from the text; you are looking for the single incorrect fact listed. While planaria do indeed like eggs, the article specifies hard-boiled rather than scrambled eggs. The correct answer is choice D.

137. **(A)** While the author might agree with the opinions expressed by choices B and D, they are not the main point of the passage. The production of a scientific dissertation is full of quite difficult requirements. Creating a two-headed planaria is not difficult; therefore, you can rule out choice C. The best answer is choice A, in large part because the author practically spells it out for you in paragraph three.

138. **(B)** Break down the word *regeneration* into parts—notice the *re-generation. Generation* means birth/growth. *Re* means again. Therefore the best definition is growth again or regrowth. Your best answer is choice B.

139. **(C)** Questions asking you to pick a title are always a way of asking what the main idea of the passage is. While the passage touches briefly on choices A, B, and D, they do not constitute the main purpose of the article and, therefore, cannot be considered the main idea of the selection. Your only logical answer is choice C; the word *potential* is particularly appropriate, since the article states that we study planaria hoping that by doing so we can create potential hope for humanity.

140. **(B)** Again, a *colossal* vocabulary comes to your rescue. All three words in the question are variations on the idea of *large.* The other words are simply words that being with *l,* designed to make you question your choice before making a final selection.

141. **(B)** The passage begins with a look at large, amazing things and progresses toward a discussion of a single, fascinating, small thing. Choice D is ridiculous; you would have noticed if the passage simply ended. Choices C and A are factually untrue when you consider the order in which the passage is organized. The only legitimate answer is choice B.

142. **(A)** While the author briefly mentions geography, the degree to which he or she focuses our attention on a small living organism suggests that the proper source for the article is in a science text.

143. **(D)** Since the article ends with a dismal assessment on the way Valentine's Day has turned out, you can infer that the author does not approve.

144. **(B)** A journal on biological subjects would have no interest in publishing a text like the one you have just read. Choices A, B, and D are more compelling, but only choice B is the best. Encyclopedias generally do not express opinions, nor do linguistics guides; rule out choices A and D. The best answer is choice B—newspapers routinely publish this sort of historical trivia-based story that amuses and informs.

145. **(C)** To make a petition is to make a request. The only definition appropriate to this would be choice C.

146. **(D)** The last paragraph in the selection is intended to form a bridge from this topic to another. You can rule out choices A and B since they discuss subjects that the author has already discussed; there is no need to revisit them. Given the tone of the final paragraph, you can assume a criticism of some sort is forthcoming. The author has essentially covered choice C. Choice D is the only option that matches the tone and likely topic the author will touch on next.

147. **(D)** Re-reading tells you that the cost of the cars, and other items as revealed by the passage, is $125,000.

148. **(B)** The phrase "upping the ante" comes from poker, in which you add to the requirements imposed on people who want to keep playing the game. Therefore, you are not making it easier for people to play (choice A). You may be angering people by raising the ante, but not necessarily. You can rule out choice D. Choices B and C are more tricky. By raising the ante for participation in Valentine's Day, you may or may not be raising the amount of money required—you are certainly raising the level of participation required. Therefore, go with choice B rather than any other choice.

149. **(A)** The choices of *wild* or *regional* might have been valid options if the author had not given more specific context clues. Since the author discusses the Catholic Church's reaction to the early dating rituals, select the answer most associated with the Catholic Church. In this case, the answer is the term non-Catholic, choice A.

150. **(B)** The author's words imply that she does not approve of spending such a huge sum of money on such a frivolous thing; therefore, choices A and C can be eliminated. The author's choice of linking the word *mere* (a diminishing word) and $125,000 (a very large sum of money) is intended to communicate a disconnect. $125,000 is NOT a small sum, despite the author's description of it as such. This is, therefore, ironic. Irony usually contains two other emotions: mockery and irritation. Irritation is a mild form of anger; choosing choice D would be taking the author's tone a little too far. The only really good choice here is choice B.

151. **(D)** The word *upwards* means to go *up from*. Therefore, this idiom is intended to describe a sum greater than the starting amount stated.

152. **(B)** Re-reading the passage indicates pretty clearly that the Catholic Church was opposed to early pagan practices and did its best to change them. Reject the other options as being factually incorrect and not present in the passage .

153. **(C)** To *peruse* a text is to *read* or look at it carefully. The prefix *per-* usually means very or thoroughly (as in *permanent* or *perfect*).

154. **(C)** To *broach* a topic is to bring it up for the first time. (A brooch is a decorative pin. *I was afraid to broach the subject of her brooch because it was so ugly.*)

155. **(A)** Choices B and C are similar, so they cannot both be correct. To *accumulate* or *amass* is to collect something into a mass or pile.

156. **(B)** Remember that the prefix *bene-* means *good*. A *helper* is the most positive choice.

157. **(A)** *Irate* means *angry*.

158. **(A)** The root *terra* means *land*.

159. **(C)** Choices A and C are opposites, so the answer is likely one of these. A *meticulous* worker cares for detail.

160. **(B)** Since the prefix *con-* means *together*, we'll choose a positive word. To *condone* something is to overlook or forgive it.

161. **(D)** Choices A and B are synonyms, so we can eliminate those. A candid *response* is frank, sincere, and *straightforward*.

162. **(B)** You can eat something safely if it is *edible*.

163. **(B)** If you *revere* someone, you look on him or her with awe.

164. **(A)** Choices A and D are opposites, so look closely at these. A *vigilant* guard keeps a *vigil*; he is awake and *alert*. (Have you ever attended "midnight" mass for Easter or Christmas Vigil?)

165. **(A)** The word *foible* is related to the word *feeble*. It's a small defect or *weakness*.

166. **(C)** A *boon* is a *gift*, a benefit, or a blessing.

167. **(D)** *Doubtful* and *dubious* share the same root.

168. **(A)** An *egress* is an *exit*. You might be able to guess this from the context. You wouldn't ordinarily have much reason to refer to the closest bird, flower, or garment.

169. **(D)** This one isn't too difficult. If you *proclaim* something, you *declare* or announce it.

170. **(A)** You can eliminate choice D, as it doesn't make sense in this context. *Sumptuous* means *expensive*, and choice A is the closest match.

171. **(C)** Whimsy is something humorous or fanciful.

172. **(A)** Since we know the prefix *super-* means *over*, we can narrow our choices to A (*extra*) or B (*large*). Something *superfluous* is unnecessary—more than sufficient.

173. **(B)** *Solace* is a word worth knowing. It means *relief*, comfort, or consolation.

174. **(A)** If someone is *sage*, he or she is *wise*. This one is tricky because the choices contain a pair of opposites, *feeble* and *healthy*. These choices really don't make much sense in context however.

Subtest 4 Mathematics

175. **(B)** Add up all four sides of the rectangle.

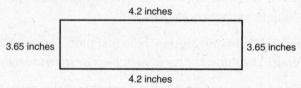

Perimeter = 4.2 inches + 4.2 inches + 3.65 inches + 3.65 inches = 15.7 inches

176. **(A)**

$$5\frac{1}{4}\% = \frac{5\frac{1}{4}}{100}$$

$$\frac{5\frac{1}{4}}{100} = \frac{\frac{21}{4}}{100} = \frac{21}{4} \div \frac{100}{1} = \frac{21}{4} \cdot \frac{1}{100} = \frac{21}{400}$$

177. **(A)**

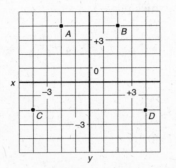

The points above the x-axis have positive y values, while the points below the x-axis have negative y values. The points to the left of the y-axis have negative x values, while the points to the right of the y-axis have positive x values.

Points A and B are both 4 units above the y-axis. Point A is also 2 units to the left of the y-axis.

178. **(C)**

12 · 12 · 12 · 12 (square)

Perimeter $= 4 \times 12 = 48$

$r = 7$ (circle)

Circumference $= 2\pi r$

$$= 2 \times \frac{22}{7} \times 7$$

$$= 44$$

Area $= s^2$

$$= 12^2$$

$$= 144$$

Area $= \pi r^2$

$$= \frac{22}{7} \times 7 \times 7$$

$$= 154$$

(A) $C_\bigcirc \overset{?}{=} P_\square + 4$

    $44 \neq 48 + 4$ ✖

(B) $A_\square \overset{?}{=} A_\bigcirc + 10$

    $144 \neq 154 + 10$ ✖

(C) $P_\square \overset{?}{=} C_\bigcirc + 4$

    $48 = 44 + 4$ ✔

(D) $A_\bigcirc \overset{?}{=} A_\square - 10$

    $154 \neq 144 - 10$ ✖

179. **(B)** Select the set in which the sum of any two numbers is greater than the third number.

$$4 + 5 > 8 \text{ ✔}$$
$$4 + 8 > 5 \text{ ✔}$$
$$5 + 8 > 4 \text{ ✔}$$

180. **(D)** Let BA_O = original batting average, H = the number of original hits, and G = the total number of original games played.

$$BA_O = \frac{H}{G}$$

Original Batting Average

$BA_O = 0.300$: $0.300 = \dfrac{H}{G}$

$$H = 0.3G$$

New Batting Average = $BA_N = 0.400$:

$$0.400 = \frac{H + 10 \text{ (10 more hits)}}{G + 10 \text{ (10 more games played)}}$$

$$0.4(G + 10) = H + 10$$
$$0.4G + 4 = 0.3G + 10$$
$$0.1G = 6$$
$$G = 60$$
$$H = 0.3G = .3(60) = 18$$

181. **(B)**

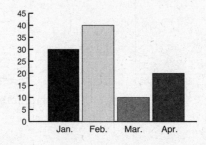

Construct a table and select the values for each month. Then substitute into each of the choices.

Months

Jan.	Feb.	Mar.	Apr.
30	40	10	20

(B) Jan. – Mar. = 20

   $30 - 10 = 20 \text{ ✔}$

182. **(B)** Change 2 tons to pounds and then pounds to ounces. Then divide the answer by 12.

$$2 \text{ tons} = 2 \times 2{,}000 \text{ pounds} = 2 \times 2{,}000 \times 16 \text{ ounces} = 64{,}000 \text{ ounces}$$

$$\frac{64{,}000}{12} = 5333.3333\ldots \approx 5333$$

183. **(C)** Find the hundreds place and then round off to the nearest thousand. If the digit in the hundreds place is 5 or greater, increase the thousands place by 1. Otherwise, leave the thousands place alone.

$$1{,}147{,}690 \approx 1{,}148{,}000$$

↑

hundreds place

184. **(B)** Determine the prime factors of 42. Then add their squares.

$$42 = 7 \cdot 6 = 7 \cdot 3 \cdot 2$$

Sum of the squares: $7^2 + 3^2 + 2^2 = 49 + 9 + 4 = 62$

185. **(B)**

Use the Pythagorean Theorem to find the hypotenuse. Then add up all the sides of the triangle.

$$a^2 + b^2 = c^2$$
$$4^2 + 3^2 = c^2$$
$$16 + 9 = c^2$$
$$25 = c^2$$
$$c = 5$$

$$\text{Perimeter} = 4 + 3 + 5 = 12$$

186. **(B)** The price dropped $300. $300 is what percent of the original price, $1,500?

$$\frac{300}{1500} = \frac{1}{5} = 0.20 = 20\%$$

187. **(C)** Let $x =$ the unknown number.

$$6x - 8 = 58$$
$$\underline{+8 = +8}$$
$$6x = 66$$
$$\frac{6x}{6} = \frac{66}{6}$$
$$x = 11$$

188. **(D)** If 25 customers purchased computers and printers, subtract 25 from 81 to determine how many customers remained who purchased only computers.

$$81 - 25 = 56$$

189. **(B)** Add up all the ratios and divide into 124. Find the remainder and then check to see which is the last book in the remainder.

$$5+2+3+3=13$$
$$\frac{124}{13}=9\frac{7}{13}$$

There is a remainder of 7. In order, we can purchase 5 fiction and 2 historical books. The historical book is the last book we can order.

190. **(A)** Add $\frac{2}{5}$ and $\frac{1}{3}$ and then subtract the result from 1 (the total amount). The answer is Malcolm's portion. After we determine Malcolm's portion, multiply that fraction by $300,000, the total income.

$$\frac{2}{5}=\frac{6}{15} \qquad 1=\frac{15}{15}$$
$$+\frac{1}{3}=\frac{5}{15} \qquad -\frac{11}{15}$$
$$\frac{11}{15} \qquad \frac{4}{15}$$

$$\frac{4}{15}\times\$300,000=\$80,000$$

191. **(D)** Let x = the unknown number. Then find 5% of 420 and add 17.

$5\% = 0.05$:
$$x=5\% \cdot 420 + 17$$
$$x=0.05(420)+17$$
$$x=21+17$$
$$x=38$$

192. **(B)** Set up an equation. Find the number and then divide by 4.

Let x = the unknown number.
$$6x=24.72$$
$$x=4.12$$

Divide the number by 4.

$$\frac{4.12}{4}=1.03$$

193. **(C)** Check each statement. There will be more than one statement that is false.

$$X = \{4, 8, 12, 16, \ldots\}$$
$$Y = \{10, 20, 30, 40, \ldots\}$$

$$10\in Y$$
$$40\in \{10, 20, 30, 40, \ldots\} \checkmark$$

194. **(D)** Let x = the first consecutive odd integer and let $x + 2$ = the next consecutive odd integer.

$$x + (x + 2) = 156$$
$$2x + 2 = 156$$
$$\underline{\quad -2 \qquad -2 \quad}$$
$$\frac{2x}{2} = \frac{154}{2}$$
$$x = 77$$

$$x + 2 = \underline{\;\;79\;} \text{ (larger integer)}$$
$$156$$

195. **(A)** Line up the as, bs, and cs and then add.

$$-3a + \;\;4b - \;\;6c$$
$$\underline{+ \;-6a + \;\;7b - \;\;4c}$$
$$-9a + 11b - 10c$$

196. **(A)** Divide 5^8 by 5^6 and then simplify.

$$\frac{\overset{2}{\cancel{4}} \times \overset{5^2}{\cancel{5^8}}}{\underset{1}{\cancel{2}} \times \underset{1}{\cancel{5^6}}} = 2 \times 25 = 50$$

197. **(C)** Which of the given numbers is greater than -2 but less than 2.3?

$$-2 < 0 < 2.3$$

198. **(A)** It's sometimes easier to understand this type of problem if we make it into an equation, so let's represent the answer by the letter x.

$$x \cdot 80 = 17.6$$
$$x = \frac{17.6}{80}$$
$$x = 0.22$$
$$x = 22\%$$

199. **(D)** Add the negative and positive numbers separately and then combine the two answers.

$$(-4) + (-6) = -10$$
$$\underline{(+9) + (+3) = +12}$$
$$+2$$

200. **(C)** In cases when we are given a generalized statement, make the problem concrete by using actual numbers fitting the description. The two unknowns, x and y, are negative and $y > x$, so let's try using $x = -2$ and $y = -1$.

$$xy > 0$$
$$(-2)(-1) = +2$$
$$+2 > 0$$

201. **(C)** Draw a diagram and label the width. Then length = l, perimeter = P = 44 feet, and width = 7 feet.

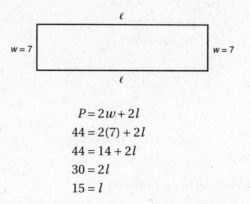

$$P = 2w + 2l$$
$$44 = 2(7) + 2l$$
$$44 = 14 + 2l$$
$$30 = 2l$$
$$15 = l$$

202. **(A)** The sum of the angles of a triangle equals 180°, so add up the two angles and subtract from 180°.

$$47 + 58 = 105$$
$$180 - 105 = 75$$

203. **(A)** Determine all the prime factors of 42. Then select the greatest prime factor.

$$42 = 2 \times 3 \times 7$$

204. **(B)** Find the area of the outer rectangle. Then calculate the total areas of the smaller rectangles and subtract.

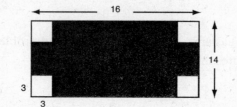

Area of the larger rectangle $\qquad = 16 \times 14 = 224$
$-$ Total areas of the smaller squares $\qquad = 4 \times 3 \times 3 = -36$
$$\overline{188}$$

205. **(C)** Reduce to simplest terms.

$$\frac{2.6}{20.8} = \frac{\overset{1}{2} \times \overset{1}{\cancel{1.3}}}{\underset{2}{4} \times \underset{4}{\cancel{5.2}}} = \frac{1}{8}$$

206. **(A)** Multiply and then combine like terms.

$$5(a - 2b) + 6(-2a + 4b) = 5a - 10b - 12a + 24b$$
$$= -7a + 14b$$

207. **(D)** Simplify and then combine terms.

$$7 \times 10^3 = 7 \times 10 \times 10 \times 10 \qquad = 7 \times 1{,}000 \qquad = \qquad 7{,}000$$
$$5 \times 10^2 = 5 \times 10 \times 10 \qquad\quad = 5 \times 100 \qquad = \qquad 500$$
$$2 \times 10^1 = 2 \times 10 \qquad\qquad\qquad\qquad\qquad = \qquad 20$$
$$+ \quad 6 \times 10^0 = 6 \times 1 \qquad\qquad\qquad\qquad\qquad = \qquad 6$$
$$\overline{\qquad\qquad\qquad\qquad\qquad\qquad\qquad\qquad\qquad 7{,}526}$$

208. **(B)** Use the formula for the area of a triangle, $A = bh$, where A = area, b = base, and h = height.

Area of original triangle, A_O: $\qquad\qquad A_O = \frac{1}{2}bh$

Area of new triangle,
$\quad A_N$, when the height is doubled: $\qquad A_N = \frac{1}{2}(b)(2h) = bh$

The area is doubled.

209. **(B)**

# of persons	4	3	1	2
weights	138	145	121	154

$$\frac{(4 \times 138) + (3 \times 145) + (1 \times 121) + (2 \times 154)}{10} = \frac{552 + 435 + 121 + 308}{10} = \frac{1416}{10} = 141.6 \approx 142$$

210. **(D)** We want to find a monomial that, when multiplied by itself 3 times, is equal to $64a^3b^9$.

$$\sqrt[3]{64a^3b^9} = 4ab^3$$
$$\text{Check:} \quad 4ab^3 \cdot 4ab^3 \cdot 4ab^3 = 64a^3b^9 \quad \checkmark$$

211. **(B)** The letter c is the last odd integer in the series. Find the two preceding odd integers and multiply.

$$c = 11, b = 9, a = 7$$
$$a \cdot b = (7)(9) = 63$$

212. **(A)** Let x = the number of executives, and let $15x$ = the number of assembly line workers. The total number of employees is 480, so let $15x + x = 480$.

$$15x + x = 480$$
$$16x = 480$$
$$x = 30$$
$$15x = 15(30) = 450$$

213. **(C)** Divide $4\frac{2}{3}$ by $5\frac{1}{4}$.

$$4\frac{2}{3} \div 5\frac{1}{4}$$
$$\frac{14}{3} \div \frac{21}{4}$$
$$\frac{\overset{2}{\cancel{14}}}{3} \times \frac{4}{\underset{3}{\cancel{21}}} = \frac{8}{9}$$

214. **(C)** First, find the measure of angle *EBD*. Then add the result to 54° (measure of angle *DBC*) to find the measure of angle *EBC*.

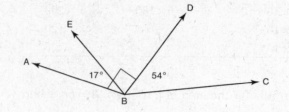

$$m(\angle DBE) = 90° - 17° = 73°$$
$$m(\angle EBC) = 73° + 54° = 127°$$

215. **(D)** In a parallelogram, the opposite sides are parallel.

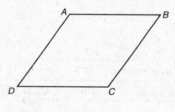

AD is parallel to *BC*.

216. **(C)** All the central angles add up to 360°, so find the missing third angle (call it *x*) and then find the average of all three angles.

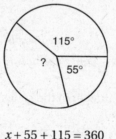

$$x + 55 + 115 = 360$$
$$x + 170 = 360$$
$$x = 190$$

Find the average of the three central angles:

$$\frac{(55+115+190)}{3} = \frac{360}{3} = 120$$

217. **(C)**

$$3x^2 + 2 = 149$$
$$\underline{-2 = -2}$$
$$3x^2 = 147$$
$$x^2 = 49$$
$$x = 7$$

218. **(A)**

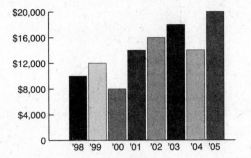

Find the increase in price between 1999 and 2005 and then divide that increase by the base price in 1998.

$$
\begin{array}{lr}
\text{Price in 2005:} & \$20,000 \\
-\text{Price in 1999:} & \$12,000 \\
\hline
\text{Price increase:} & \$8,000
\end{array}
$$

$$
\frac{\text{Price increase:}}{\text{Price in 1999:}} = \frac{\$8,000}{\$12,000} = .6666\ldots \approx .67 = 67\%
$$

219. **(D)** Multiply the pounds, p_i, by the frequencies, f_i, and then divide by the total frequencies.

Pounds, p_i	Frequency, f_i	$p_i f_i$
98	2	$2 \times 98 = 196$
105	1	$1 \times 105 = 105$
109	1	$1 \times 109 = 109$
120	3	$3 \times 120 = 360$
126	2	$2 \times 126 = 252$
132	4	$4 \times 132 = 528$
Totals	13	1,550

$$
\frac{p_i f_i}{f_i} = \frac{1,550}{13} = 119.23 \approx 119.2
$$

220. **(B)** Divide 7 by $17\frac{1}{2}$.

$$
7 \div 17\frac{1}{2}
$$

$$
\frac{7}{1} \div \frac{35}{2}
$$

$$
\frac{\overset{1}{\cancel{7}}}{1} \times \frac{2}{\underset{5}{\cancel{35}}} = \frac{2}{5}
$$

221. **(D)**

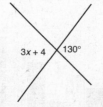

$3x + 4$ $130°$

Vertical angles are of the same measure, so set $3x + 4$ equal to $130°$.

$$3x + 4 = 130$$
$$3x = 126$$
$$x = 42$$

222. **(C)** One pound is equivalent to 16 ounces, so first change 8 pounds to ounces. Then multiply by \$0.20, the price per ounce of raisins.

$$8 \text{ pounds} = 8 \times 16 \text{ ounces} = 128 \text{ ounces}$$
$$128 \text{ ounces} \times \$0.20 \text{ (per ounce)} = \$25.60$$

223. **(B)** Let $x =$ the number of tickets sold to S.O. members.

	Number (n)	Price per ticket, (p)	Total price, np
S.O. members	x	\$5	$5x$
Nonmembers	170	\$11	11(170)

The total revenue from members and nonmembers is \$3,070:

$$5x + 11(170) = 3,070$$
$$5x + 1,870 = 3,070$$
$$5x = 1,200$$
$$x = 240$$

224. **(D)** A hexagon is a six-sided figure, so, to find the cost of the fence, add up all the sides and multiply by \$5.30, the cost per foot of fence.

$$49.4 + 34.9 + 53.6 + 65.8 + 72.6 + 48.7 = 325$$

$$325 \times \$5.30 = \$1,722.50$$

225. **(C)** A pentagon is a five-sided figure, so add up all the sides and set the sum equal to the perimeter, 56. Find x and then substitute the value of x into the five terms to determine the longest side.

$$x + (x + 2) + (x + 5) + (2x + 2) + (3x - 1) = 56$$
$$8x + 8 = 56$$
$$8x = 48$$
$$x = 6$$

Check:

$$x + 2 = 8$$
$$x + 5 = 11$$
$$2x + 2 = 14$$
$$\underline{+ \ 3x - 1 = 17 \text{ (longest side)}}$$
$$56$$

226. **(B)** To determine the area of a square, multiply two adjacent sides. Then, to determine x, set the result of the multiplication equal to $4x + 20$.

Area of a square = side × side:

$$8 \times 8 = 4x + 20$$
$$64 = 4x + 20$$
$$44 = 4x$$
$$11 = x$$

227. **(C)** Let x = Wanda's age now and then develop a table.

Name	Age now	Age 3 years ago
Latisha	$x + 5$	$x + 5 - 3$
Wanda	x	$x - 3$

Three years ago Wanda was $8a$ years old.

$$x - 3 = 8a$$
$$x = 8a + 3$$

Latisha's age now = $x + 5 = (8a + 3) + 5 = 8a + 8$.

228. **(A)** Let t = the tens digit, and let u = the units digit.

The sum of the digits is 11:	(i)	$t + u = 11$
Three times the tens digit is 5 more than the units digit:	(ii)	$3t = u + 5$
In equation (i), find t alone:	(i)	$t = 11 - u$
Substitute the value for t $(11 - u)$ into equation (ii):	(ii)	$3(11 - u) = u + 5$
	(ii)	$33 - 3u = u + 5$
Add $3u$:	(ii)	$33 = 4u + 5$
Subtract 5:	(ii)	$28 = 4u$
Divide by 4:	(ii)	$7 = u$
	(i)	$t + u = 11$
$u = 7$:	(i)	$t + 7 = 11$
Subtract 7:	(i)	$t = 4$

The original number:

$$10t + u = 10(4) + 7 = 40 + 7 = 47$$

229. **(D)** If the triangle is isosceles, the base angles are congruent. Angle ACB is supplementary to angle BCD.

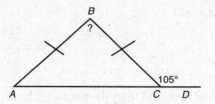

$$m\angle ACB + 105° = 180°$$
$$m\angle ACB = 75°$$
$$m\angle A = m\angle ACB = 75°$$
$$m\angle A + m\angle ACB + m\angle B = 180°$$
$$75° + 75° + m\angle B = 180°$$
$$150° + m\angle B = 180°$$
$$m\angle B = 30°$$

230. **(D)**

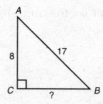

Use the Pythagorean Theorem, $a^2 + b^2 = c^2$, where a and b are two legs of a right triangle and c is the hypotenuse.

$$a^2 + b^2 = c^2$$
$$a^2 + 8^2 = 17^2$$
$$a^2 + 64 = 289$$
$$a^2 = 225$$
$$a = 15$$

231. **(C)** Simplify expressions within the parentheses and then work from left to right.

(A) $2 \times 5^2 - 9 \div 3 = 2 \times 25 - 3 = 50 - 3 = 47$
(B) $3^3 - (18 \div 2) + 7 = 27 - 9 + 7 = 18 + 7 = 25$
(C) $5(8 - 3)^2 = 5(5)^2 = 5(25) = 125$
(D) $4 \times 9 + 3(6 - 2) = 36 + 3(4) = 36 + 12 = 48$

232. **(A)** Substitute 4 for a in the given expression.

$$6(a + 2) - 2c = 6$$
$$6a + 12 - 2c = 6$$
$$6(4) + 12 - 2c = 6$$
$$24 + 12 - 2c = 6$$
$$36 - 2c = 6$$
$$-2c = -30$$
$$c = 15$$

233. **(C)**

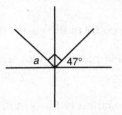

$$m\angle a + 90° + 47° = 180°$$
$$m\angle a + 137° = 180°$$
$$m\angle a \quad = 43°$$

234. **(A)** Subtract 8 from the product of $\frac{2}{3}$ and 27.

$$\frac{2}{3} \times 27 - 8 = 18 - 8 = 10$$

235. **(D)** 1 foot = 12 inches

$$\overset{4}{\cancel{5}} \text{ feet } \overset{12+7=19}{\cancel{7}} \text{ inches}$$
$$\underline{-2 \text{ feet } 9 \text{ inches}}$$
$$2 \text{ feet } 10 \text{ inches}$$

236. **(D)** Change 2 hours to minutes and multiply by \$5.25 per minute.

$$2 \text{ hours} = 120 \text{ minutes}$$
$$\$5.25 \times 120 = \$630$$

237. **(C)**

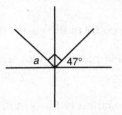

Subtract the area of the inner circle from the area of the outer circle.

$$A = \pi r^2$$

A_O, $r = 8$: $\quad A_O = 3.14 \cdot 8^2 = 3.14 \cdot 64 = 200.96$

A_I, $r = 5$: $\quad -A_I = 3.14 \cdot 5^2 = 3.14 \cdot 25 = \underline{78.50}$

Shaded area: $ 122.46$

238. **(C)** Multiply the whole numbers and the radicals separately and then simplify.

$$5\sqrt{2} \times 3\sqrt{8} = 15\sqrt{16} = 15 \times 4 = 60$$

239. **(B)** Paul, can you tell Lisa to come to the party? Use a comma after direct address.

240. **(A)** I attended the St. Andrew parish school when I was younger. Use a period for abbreviations.

241. **(C)** Merry and Pippin are the tallest hobbits in *all* of the Shire. Use *-est* when comparing more than two.

242. **(D)** No mistakes.

243. **(A)** **One** [of the men on the team] has dropped out of the game. Subject-verb agreement.

244. **(B)** Would you mind stirring the kettle? This is a question.

245. **(A)** Tom, Guy, Sandy, and I went to the game together. No comma between subject and verb. *I* is the subject form.

246. **(C)** She returned the textbook to me. Use the object pronoun *me* instead of the reflexive pronoun *myself.*

247. **(C)** It's a difficult problem, but we can handle it. *It's* is the contraction for *It is.*

248. **(B)** Who is speaking? *Who* is the subject form; *whom* is the object form.

249. **(B)** In this election, the voters don't have enough information to know if they should support the tax. Pronoun-antecedent agreement. *They* refers to more than one voter.

250. **(A)** Bobby studies silently in his seat most of the time. The adverb form is silent**ly**.

251. **(A)** Our oldest teacher was born on September 23, 1960. Do not use a comma between the month and day.

252. **(A)** The theme of the story concerned the destructive greed for power. Use *power* instead of the awkward *powerfulness.*

253. **(C)** Bring the following to class: pen, pencil, paper, and books. Use a colon before a list.

254. **(C)** Jake is the most truthful person I have ever met. Use *most truthful* rather than *truthfullest.*

255. **(A)** It is farther to Cleveland than to Philadelphia. *Farther* refers to distance. *Further* refers to degree.

256. **(C)** I don't have a lot of free time; nevertheless, I would like the job. *Nevertheless* is an adverb, not a coordinating conjunction. Use a period or semicolon instead of a comma.

257. **(A)** No, I have never seen a live rhinoceros. Use a comma after a mild interjection.

258. **(D)** No mistakes.

259. **(A)** You won't have to look for Joe and me. The object form is *me*. You won't have to look for me.

260. **(C)** I realized I <u>had been mistaken</u>. The correct past participle is *had been mistaken*, not *had been mistook*.

261. **(D)** No mistakes.

262. **(A)** I enjoy <u>walking</u> on the beach and <u>running</u> in the surf. Use parallel forms of the verb.

263. **(C)** I only have time to eat, drink, and sleep. Use commas in a series.

264. **(B)** Dennis performed well on the ice. *Well* is an adverb.

265. **(A)** Aunt Wendy often takes Al and <u>me</u> to lunch. Use the object form: She often takes <u>me</u>.

266. **(B)** The deer reared up on <u>its</u> hind legs. The possessive form of *it* is *its*. *It's* is the contraction of *it is*.

267. **(D)** No mistakes.

268. **(A)** My favorite <u>aunt</u> is visiting with my cousin. The word *aunt* is not capitalized because it is not part of a specific person's name (such as Aunt Itoro).

269. **(B)** Our school finished first<u>;</u> his school placed second. Use a period or semicolon between sentences. Using a comma here is called a comma splice.

270. **(D)** No mistakes.

271. **(A)** Shakespeare wrote, "To thine own self be true." Periods should go <u>inside</u> quotation marks.

272. **(A)** Don't <u>lose</u> your tickets, or you won't be able to get in. Be careful not to confuse the words *lose* and *loose*.

273. **(A)** Neither Jimmy <u>nor</u> Tommy has ever been to Canada. Use *nor* with *neither*.

274. **(C)** I just want to <u>sit</u> on my porch and swing. A person sits.

275. **(D)** No mistakes.

276. **(B)** You and <u>I</u> are best friends, aren't we? *I* is the subject form.

277. **(B)** My neighbors own a German shepherd. Capitalize names of countries.

278. **(A)** Fragment. *Since he started walking* is not a complete sentence.

279. **(C)** *Thorough* should be *through*.

280. **(A)** When you add a prefix, just add it: *mis-shapen* has two *s*'s.

281. **(A)** He <u>carefully</u> unwrapped his gifts.

282. **(C)** Where did you <u>acquire</u> that artifact?

283. **(B)** Even though the role was foolish, the actor was not <u>embarrassed</u>.

284. **(D)** No mistakes.

285. **(A)** She has always been greatly concerned about the <u>environment</u>. This word is a problem if you don't pronounce it correctly.

286. **(B)** I always go to my science teacher for <u>advice</u> before a new experiment. *Advice* is a noun; *advise* is a verb.

287. **(D)** No mistakes.

288. **(A)** <u>Lightning</u> and thunder can be terrifying experiences.

289. **(C)** I couldn't sing in the choir last week <u>because</u> I had lost my voice. Choices A and B are incorrect because they would begin a new sentence. Choice C, *because*, is the only word that indicates a cause/effect relationship.

290. **(B)** Bess wears slippers to bed in the winter; <u>consequently</u>, her feet are warm. The word *consequently* indicates a result.

291. **(C)** After clearing the dishes, we can all take a nap. Choice C is the most concise. Choice A is passive, choice B is wordy, and choice D would result in an awkward modifier.

292. **(B)** This is the only choice that contains all of the information most concisely. Choice C is the shortest, but it contains erroneous information and a capitalization error.

293. **(A)** This is the most direct statement.

294. **(B)** This is the only sentence that deals with medical matters.

295. **(C)** A paragraph should focus on a single idea. The other topics are far too broad.

296. **(C)** All of the sentences except this one are about Stonehenge.

297. **(D)** This sentence is not about how the temperature of soup is regulated.

298. **(D)** The paragraph focuses on the holiday tradition rather than the location of the trees.

ANSWER SHEET
HSPT Practice Exam 2

SUBTEST 1 VERBAL

1. Ⓐ Ⓑ Ⓒ Ⓓ
2. Ⓐ Ⓑ Ⓒ Ⓓ
3. Ⓐ Ⓑ Ⓒ Ⓓ
4. Ⓐ Ⓑ Ⓒ Ⓓ
5. Ⓐ Ⓑ Ⓒ
6. Ⓐ Ⓑ Ⓒ Ⓓ
7. Ⓐ Ⓑ Ⓒ Ⓓ
8. Ⓐ Ⓑ Ⓒ Ⓓ
9. Ⓐ Ⓑ Ⓒ Ⓓ
10. Ⓐ Ⓑ Ⓒ Ⓓ
11. Ⓐ Ⓑ Ⓒ Ⓓ
12. Ⓐ Ⓑ Ⓒ Ⓓ
13. Ⓐ Ⓑ Ⓒ Ⓓ
14. Ⓐ Ⓑ Ⓒ
15. Ⓐ Ⓑ Ⓒ Ⓓ

16. Ⓐ Ⓑ Ⓒ Ⓓ
17. Ⓐ Ⓑ Ⓒ Ⓓ
18. Ⓐ Ⓑ Ⓒ Ⓓ
19. Ⓐ Ⓑ Ⓒ Ⓓ
20. Ⓐ Ⓑ Ⓒ Ⓓ
21. Ⓐ Ⓑ Ⓒ Ⓓ
22. Ⓐ Ⓑ Ⓒ
23. Ⓐ Ⓑ Ⓒ Ⓓ
24. Ⓐ Ⓑ Ⓒ
25. Ⓐ Ⓑ Ⓒ Ⓓ
26. Ⓐ Ⓑ Ⓒ Ⓓ
27. Ⓐ Ⓑ Ⓒ Ⓓ
28. Ⓐ Ⓑ Ⓒ Ⓓ
29. Ⓐ Ⓑ Ⓒ
30. Ⓐ Ⓑ Ⓒ Ⓓ

31. Ⓐ Ⓑ Ⓒ Ⓓ
32. Ⓐ Ⓑ Ⓒ Ⓓ
33. Ⓐ Ⓑ Ⓒ
34. Ⓐ Ⓑ Ⓒ Ⓓ
35. Ⓐ Ⓑ Ⓒ Ⓓ
36. Ⓐ Ⓑ Ⓒ Ⓓ
37. Ⓐ Ⓑ Ⓒ Ⓓ
38. Ⓐ Ⓑ Ⓒ
39. Ⓐ Ⓑ Ⓒ Ⓓ
40. Ⓐ Ⓑ Ⓒ Ⓓ
41. Ⓐ Ⓑ Ⓒ Ⓓ
42. Ⓐ Ⓑ Ⓒ Ⓓ
43. Ⓐ Ⓑ Ⓒ Ⓓ
44. Ⓐ Ⓑ Ⓒ Ⓓ
45. Ⓐ Ⓑ Ⓒ Ⓓ

46. Ⓐ Ⓑ Ⓒ Ⓓ
47. Ⓐ Ⓑ Ⓒ Ⓓ
48. Ⓐ Ⓑ Ⓒ Ⓓ
49. Ⓐ Ⓑ Ⓒ
50. Ⓐ Ⓑ Ⓒ Ⓓ
51. Ⓐ Ⓑ Ⓒ Ⓓ
52. Ⓐ Ⓑ Ⓒ
53. Ⓐ Ⓑ Ⓒ Ⓓ
54. Ⓐ Ⓑ Ⓒ Ⓓ
55. Ⓐ Ⓑ Ⓒ
56. Ⓐ Ⓑ Ⓒ Ⓓ
57. Ⓐ Ⓑ Ⓒ Ⓓ
58. Ⓐ Ⓑ Ⓒ
59. Ⓐ Ⓑ Ⓒ Ⓓ
60. Ⓐ Ⓑ Ⓒ

SUBTEST 2 QUANTITATIVE

61. Ⓐ Ⓑ Ⓒ Ⓓ
62. Ⓐ Ⓑ Ⓒ Ⓓ
63. Ⓐ Ⓑ Ⓒ Ⓓ
64. Ⓐ Ⓑ Ⓒ Ⓓ
65. Ⓐ Ⓑ Ⓒ Ⓓ
66. Ⓐ Ⓑ Ⓒ Ⓓ
67. Ⓐ Ⓑ Ⓒ Ⓓ
68. Ⓐ Ⓑ Ⓒ Ⓓ
69. Ⓐ Ⓑ Ⓒ Ⓓ
70. Ⓐ Ⓑ Ⓒ Ⓓ
71. Ⓐ Ⓑ Ⓒ Ⓓ
72. Ⓐ Ⓑ Ⓒ Ⓓ
73. Ⓐ Ⓑ Ⓒ Ⓓ

74. Ⓐ Ⓑ Ⓒ Ⓓ
75. Ⓐ Ⓑ Ⓒ Ⓓ
76. Ⓐ Ⓑ Ⓒ Ⓓ
77. Ⓐ Ⓑ Ⓒ Ⓓ
78. Ⓐ Ⓑ Ⓒ Ⓓ
79. Ⓐ Ⓑ Ⓒ Ⓓ
80. Ⓐ Ⓑ Ⓒ Ⓓ
81. Ⓐ Ⓑ Ⓒ Ⓓ
82. Ⓐ Ⓑ Ⓒ Ⓓ
83. Ⓐ Ⓑ Ⓒ Ⓓ
84. Ⓐ Ⓑ Ⓒ Ⓓ
85. Ⓐ Ⓑ Ⓒ Ⓓ
86. Ⓐ Ⓑ Ⓒ Ⓓ

87. Ⓐ Ⓑ Ⓒ Ⓓ
88. Ⓐ Ⓑ Ⓒ Ⓓ
89. Ⓐ Ⓑ Ⓒ Ⓓ
90. Ⓐ Ⓑ Ⓒ Ⓓ
91. Ⓐ Ⓑ Ⓒ Ⓓ
92. Ⓐ Ⓑ Ⓒ Ⓓ
93. Ⓐ Ⓑ Ⓒ Ⓓ
94. Ⓐ Ⓑ Ⓒ Ⓓ
95. Ⓐ Ⓑ Ⓒ Ⓓ
96. Ⓐ Ⓑ Ⓒ Ⓓ
97. Ⓐ Ⓑ Ⓒ Ⓓ
98. Ⓐ Ⓑ Ⓒ Ⓓ
99. Ⓐ Ⓑ Ⓒ Ⓓ

100. Ⓐ Ⓑ Ⓒ Ⓓ
101. Ⓐ Ⓑ Ⓒ Ⓓ
102. Ⓐ Ⓑ Ⓒ Ⓓ
103. Ⓐ Ⓑ Ⓒ Ⓓ
104. Ⓐ Ⓑ Ⓒ Ⓓ
105. Ⓐ Ⓑ Ⓒ Ⓓ
106. Ⓐ Ⓑ Ⓒ Ⓓ
107. Ⓐ Ⓑ Ⓒ Ⓓ
108. Ⓐ Ⓑ Ⓒ Ⓓ
109. Ⓐ Ⓑ Ⓒ Ⓓ
110. Ⓐ Ⓑ Ⓒ Ⓓ
111. Ⓐ Ⓑ Ⓒ Ⓓ
112. Ⓐ Ⓑ Ⓒ Ⓓ

ANSWER SHEET
HSPT Practice Exam 2

SUBTEST 3 READING

113. Ⓐ Ⓑ Ⓒ Ⓓ	129. Ⓐ Ⓑ Ⓒ Ⓓ	145. Ⓐ Ⓑ Ⓒ Ⓓ	161. Ⓐ Ⓑ Ⓒ Ⓓ
114. Ⓐ Ⓑ Ⓒ Ⓓ	130. Ⓐ Ⓑ Ⓒ Ⓓ	146. Ⓐ Ⓑ Ⓒ Ⓓ	162. Ⓐ Ⓑ Ⓒ Ⓓ
115. Ⓐ Ⓑ Ⓒ Ⓓ	131. Ⓐ Ⓑ Ⓒ Ⓓ	147. Ⓐ Ⓑ Ⓒ Ⓓ	163. Ⓐ Ⓑ Ⓒ Ⓓ
116. Ⓐ Ⓑ Ⓒ Ⓓ	132. Ⓐ Ⓑ Ⓒ Ⓓ	148. Ⓐ Ⓑ Ⓒ Ⓓ	164. Ⓐ Ⓑ Ⓒ Ⓓ
117. Ⓐ Ⓑ Ⓒ Ⓓ	133. Ⓐ Ⓑ Ⓒ Ⓓ	149. Ⓐ Ⓑ Ⓒ Ⓓ	165. Ⓐ Ⓑ Ⓒ Ⓓ
118. Ⓐ Ⓑ Ⓒ Ⓓ	134. Ⓐ Ⓑ Ⓒ Ⓓ	150. Ⓐ Ⓑ Ⓒ Ⓓ	166. Ⓐ Ⓑ Ⓒ Ⓓ
119. Ⓐ Ⓑ Ⓒ Ⓓ	135. Ⓐ Ⓑ Ⓒ Ⓓ	151. Ⓐ Ⓑ Ⓒ Ⓓ	167. Ⓐ Ⓑ Ⓒ Ⓓ
120. Ⓐ Ⓑ Ⓒ Ⓓ	136. Ⓐ Ⓑ Ⓒ Ⓓ	152. Ⓐ Ⓑ Ⓒ Ⓓ	168. Ⓐ Ⓑ Ⓒ Ⓓ
121. Ⓐ Ⓑ Ⓒ Ⓓ	137. Ⓐ Ⓑ Ⓒ Ⓓ	153. Ⓐ Ⓑ Ⓒ Ⓓ	169. Ⓐ Ⓑ Ⓒ Ⓓ
122. Ⓐ Ⓑ Ⓒ Ⓓ	138. Ⓐ Ⓑ Ⓒ Ⓓ	154. Ⓐ Ⓑ Ⓒ Ⓓ	170. Ⓐ Ⓑ Ⓒ Ⓓ
123. Ⓐ Ⓑ Ⓒ Ⓓ	139. Ⓐ Ⓑ Ⓒ Ⓓ	155. Ⓐ Ⓑ Ⓒ Ⓓ	171. Ⓐ Ⓑ Ⓒ Ⓓ
124. Ⓐ Ⓑ Ⓒ Ⓓ	140. Ⓐ Ⓑ Ⓒ Ⓓ	156. Ⓐ Ⓑ Ⓒ Ⓓ	172. Ⓐ Ⓑ Ⓒ Ⓓ
125. Ⓐ Ⓑ Ⓒ Ⓓ	141. Ⓐ Ⓑ Ⓒ Ⓓ	157. Ⓐ Ⓑ Ⓒ Ⓓ	173. Ⓐ Ⓑ Ⓒ Ⓓ
126. Ⓐ Ⓑ Ⓒ Ⓓ	142. Ⓐ Ⓑ Ⓒ Ⓓ	158. Ⓐ Ⓑ Ⓒ Ⓓ	174. Ⓐ Ⓑ Ⓒ Ⓓ
127. Ⓐ Ⓑ Ⓒ Ⓓ	143. Ⓐ Ⓑ Ⓒ Ⓓ	159. Ⓐ Ⓑ Ⓒ Ⓓ	
128. Ⓐ Ⓑ Ⓒ Ⓓ	144. Ⓐ Ⓑ Ⓒ Ⓓ	160. Ⓐ Ⓑ Ⓒ Ⓓ	

ANSWER SHEET
HSPT Practice Exam 2

SUBTEST 4   MATHEMATICS

175. Ⓐ Ⓑ Ⓒ Ⓓ	191. Ⓐ Ⓑ Ⓒ Ⓓ	207. Ⓐ Ⓑ Ⓒ Ⓓ	223. Ⓐ Ⓑ Ⓒ Ⓓ
176. Ⓐ Ⓑ Ⓒ Ⓓ	192. Ⓐ Ⓑ Ⓒ Ⓓ	208. Ⓐ Ⓑ Ⓒ Ⓓ	224. Ⓐ Ⓑ Ⓒ Ⓓ
177. Ⓐ Ⓑ Ⓒ Ⓓ	193. Ⓐ Ⓑ Ⓒ Ⓓ	209. Ⓐ Ⓑ Ⓒ Ⓓ	225. Ⓐ Ⓑ Ⓒ Ⓓ
178. Ⓐ Ⓑ Ⓒ Ⓓ	194. Ⓐ Ⓑ Ⓒ Ⓓ	210. Ⓐ Ⓑ Ⓒ Ⓓ	226. Ⓐ Ⓑ Ⓒ Ⓓ
179. Ⓐ Ⓑ Ⓒ Ⓓ	195. Ⓐ Ⓑ Ⓒ Ⓓ	211. Ⓐ Ⓑ Ⓒ Ⓓ	227. Ⓐ Ⓑ Ⓒ Ⓓ
180. Ⓐ Ⓑ Ⓒ Ⓓ	196. Ⓐ Ⓑ Ⓒ Ⓓ	212. Ⓐ Ⓑ Ⓒ Ⓓ	228. Ⓐ Ⓑ Ⓒ Ⓓ
181. Ⓐ Ⓑ Ⓒ Ⓓ	197. Ⓐ Ⓑ Ⓒ Ⓓ	213. Ⓐ Ⓑ Ⓒ Ⓓ	229. Ⓐ Ⓑ Ⓒ Ⓓ
182. Ⓐ Ⓑ Ⓒ Ⓓ	198. Ⓐ Ⓑ Ⓒ Ⓓ	214. Ⓐ Ⓑ Ⓒ Ⓓ	230. Ⓐ Ⓑ Ⓒ Ⓓ
183. Ⓐ Ⓑ Ⓒ Ⓓ	199. Ⓐ Ⓑ Ⓒ Ⓓ	215. Ⓐ Ⓑ Ⓒ Ⓓ	231. Ⓐ Ⓑ Ⓒ Ⓓ
184. Ⓐ Ⓑ Ⓒ Ⓓ	200. Ⓐ Ⓑ Ⓒ Ⓓ	216. Ⓐ Ⓑ Ⓒ Ⓓ	232. Ⓐ Ⓑ Ⓒ Ⓓ
185. Ⓐ Ⓑ Ⓒ Ⓓ	201. Ⓐ Ⓑ Ⓒ Ⓓ	217. Ⓐ Ⓑ Ⓒ Ⓓ	233. Ⓐ Ⓑ Ⓒ Ⓓ
186. Ⓐ Ⓑ Ⓒ Ⓓ	202. Ⓐ Ⓑ Ⓒ Ⓓ	218. Ⓐ Ⓑ Ⓒ Ⓓ	234. Ⓐ Ⓑ Ⓒ Ⓓ
187. Ⓐ Ⓑ Ⓒ Ⓓ	203. Ⓐ Ⓑ Ⓒ Ⓓ	219. Ⓐ Ⓑ Ⓒ Ⓓ	235. Ⓐ Ⓑ Ⓒ Ⓓ
188. Ⓐ Ⓑ Ⓒ Ⓓ	204. Ⓐ Ⓑ Ⓒ Ⓓ	220. Ⓐ Ⓑ Ⓒ Ⓓ	236. Ⓐ Ⓑ Ⓒ Ⓓ
189. Ⓐ Ⓑ Ⓒ Ⓓ	205. Ⓐ Ⓑ Ⓒ Ⓓ	221. Ⓐ Ⓑ Ⓒ Ⓓ	237. Ⓐ Ⓑ Ⓒ Ⓓ
190. Ⓐ Ⓑ Ⓒ Ⓓ	206. Ⓐ Ⓑ Ⓒ Ⓓ	222. Ⓐ Ⓑ Ⓒ Ⓓ	238. Ⓐ Ⓑ Ⓒ Ⓓ

ANSWER SHEET
HSPT Practice Exam 2

SUBTEST 5   LANGUAGE

239. Ⓐ Ⓑ Ⓒ Ⓓ   254. Ⓐ Ⓑ Ⓒ Ⓓ   269. Ⓐ Ⓑ Ⓒ Ⓓ   284. Ⓐ Ⓑ Ⓒ Ⓓ
240. Ⓐ Ⓑ Ⓒ Ⓓ   255. Ⓐ Ⓑ Ⓒ Ⓓ   270. Ⓐ Ⓑ Ⓒ Ⓓ   285. Ⓐ Ⓑ Ⓒ Ⓓ
241. Ⓐ Ⓑ Ⓒ Ⓓ   256. Ⓐ Ⓑ Ⓒ Ⓓ   271. Ⓐ Ⓑ Ⓒ Ⓓ   286. Ⓐ Ⓑ Ⓒ Ⓓ
242. Ⓐ Ⓑ Ⓒ Ⓓ   257. Ⓐ Ⓑ Ⓒ Ⓓ   272. Ⓐ Ⓑ Ⓒ Ⓓ   287. Ⓐ Ⓑ Ⓒ Ⓓ
243. Ⓐ Ⓑ Ⓒ Ⓓ   258. Ⓐ Ⓑ Ⓒ Ⓓ   273. Ⓐ Ⓑ Ⓒ Ⓓ   288. Ⓐ Ⓑ Ⓒ Ⓓ
244. Ⓐ Ⓑ Ⓒ Ⓓ   259. Ⓐ Ⓑ Ⓒ Ⓓ   274. Ⓐ Ⓑ Ⓒ Ⓓ   289. Ⓐ Ⓑ Ⓒ Ⓓ
245. Ⓐ Ⓑ Ⓒ Ⓓ   260. Ⓐ Ⓑ Ⓒ Ⓓ   275. Ⓐ Ⓑ Ⓒ Ⓓ   290. Ⓐ Ⓑ Ⓒ Ⓓ
246. Ⓐ Ⓑ Ⓒ Ⓓ   261. Ⓐ Ⓑ Ⓒ Ⓓ   276. Ⓐ Ⓑ Ⓒ Ⓓ   291. Ⓐ Ⓑ Ⓒ Ⓓ
247. Ⓐ Ⓑ Ⓒ Ⓓ   262. Ⓐ Ⓑ Ⓒ Ⓓ   277. Ⓐ Ⓑ Ⓒ Ⓓ   292. Ⓐ Ⓑ Ⓒ Ⓓ
248. Ⓐ Ⓑ Ⓒ Ⓓ   263. Ⓐ Ⓑ Ⓒ Ⓓ   278. Ⓐ Ⓑ Ⓒ Ⓓ   293. Ⓐ Ⓑ Ⓒ Ⓓ
249. Ⓐ Ⓑ Ⓒ Ⓓ   264. Ⓐ Ⓑ Ⓒ Ⓓ   279. Ⓐ Ⓑ Ⓒ Ⓓ   294. Ⓐ Ⓑ Ⓒ Ⓓ
250. Ⓐ Ⓑ Ⓒ Ⓓ   265. Ⓐ Ⓑ Ⓒ Ⓓ   280. Ⓐ Ⓑ Ⓒ Ⓓ   295. Ⓐ Ⓑ Ⓒ Ⓓ
251. Ⓐ Ⓑ Ⓒ Ⓓ   266. Ⓐ Ⓑ Ⓒ Ⓓ   281. Ⓐ Ⓑ Ⓒ Ⓓ   296. Ⓐ Ⓑ Ⓒ Ⓓ
252. Ⓐ Ⓑ Ⓒ Ⓓ   267. Ⓐ Ⓑ Ⓒ Ⓓ   282. Ⓐ Ⓑ Ⓒ Ⓓ   297. Ⓐ Ⓑ Ⓒ Ⓓ
253. Ⓐ Ⓑ Ⓒ Ⓓ   268. Ⓐ Ⓑ Ⓒ Ⓓ   283. Ⓐ Ⓑ Ⓒ Ⓓ   298. Ⓐ Ⓑ Ⓒ Ⓓ

SUBTEST 1   VERBAL

#1–60   16 MINUTES

Sample:

Which word does *not* belong with the others?

(A) easy
(B) interesting
(C) simple
(D) facile

Ⓐ ● Ⓒ Ⓓ

---

1. Which word does *not* belong with the others?

   (A) shoes
   (B) socks
   (C) boots
   (D) laces

2. Which word does *not* belong with the others?

   (A) increase
   (B) enlarge
   (C) dilute
   (D) magnify

3. Hero is to villain as antagonist is to _____.

   (A) character
   (B) protagonist
   (C) mentor
   (D) companion

4. Stationary most nearly means _____.

   (A) unmoving
   (B) writing
   (C) guarding
   (D) driving

5. Last week, Dr. Zorba saw more patients than Dr. Kildare. Dr. Kildare did not see as many patients as Dr. Casey. Dr. Casey saw more patients than Dr. Zorba. If the first two statements are true, the third statement is _____.

   (A) true
   (B) false
   (C) uncertain

6. Which word does *not* belong with the others?

   (A) toys
   (B) blocks
   (C) doll
   (D) yo-yo

7. Which word does *not* belong with the others?

   (A) furniture
   (B) chair
   (C) table
   (D) couch

GO TO NEXT PAGE ➡

8. Which word does *not* belong with the others?

   (A) display
   (B) uncover
   (C) presentation
   (D) exhibition

9. Resilient most nearly means _____.

   (A) flexible
   (B) rigid
   (C) unmoving
   (D) serene

10. Which word does *not* belong with the others?

    (A) fool
    (B) clown
    (C) deceive
    (D) mislead

11. Donor most nearly means _____.

    (A) hermit
    (B) doctor
    (C) contributor
    (D) misanthrope

12. Shrill most nearly means _____.

    (A) piercing
    (B) melodious
    (C) low
    (D) rumbling

13. Drill is to hole as blender is to _____.

    (A) flour
    (B) batter
    (C) eggs
    (D) milk

14. Mr. Quigley has one daughter. Mr. Zuniga has one daughter. The members of the coaching staff have a total of two daughters. If the first two statements are true, the third statement is _____.

    (A) true
    (B) false
    (C) uncertain

15. Lethargy most nearly means _____.

    (A) inactivity
    (B) speed
    (C) efficiency
    (D) poison

16. Which word does *not* belong with the others?

    (A) philosopher
    (B) sage
    (C) scholar
    (D) solicitor

17. Which word does *not* belong with the others?

    (A) hospital
    (B) schoolhouse
    (C) office tower
    (D) government

18. Scrutiny most nearly means _____.

    (A) revision
    (B) ignorance
    (C) examination
    (D) liability

19. Plunder means the *opposite* of _____.

    (A) rest
    (B) restore
    (C) raid
    (D) steal

GO TO NEXT PAGE ➡

20. Coat is to jacket as chair is to _____.

   (A) stool
   (B) table
   (C) couch
   (D) counter

21. Financial is to money as psychological is to
   _____.

   (A) mind
   (B) spirit
   (C) body
   (D) academic

22. Jack is three years older than Ralph. Peterkin
   is two years younger than Ralph. Jack is five
   years older than Peterkin. If the first two
   statements are true, the third statement is
   _____.

   (A) true
   (B) false
   (C) uncertain

23. Punctual most nearly means _____.

   (A) prompt
   (B) late
   (C) rude
   (D) careless

24. Jimmy is younger than Tommy. Maria is
   older than Tommy. Maria is older than
   Jimmy. If the first two statements are true,
   the third statement is _____.

   (A) true
   (B) false
   (C) uncertain

25. Notorious most nearly means _____.

   (A) infamous
   (B) honorable
   (C) hopeful
   (D) fast

26. Obscure most nearly means _____.

   (A) vague
   (B) transparent
   (C) clear
   (D) perfect

27. Which word does *not* belong with the
   others?

   (A) period
   (B) question mark
   (C) comma
   (D) exclamation point

28. A counterfeit is _____.

   (A) imaginary
   (B) opposite
   (C) false
   (D) ambiguous

29. Perry is a stronger swimmer than Ashton.
   Perry does not swim as well as Joey. Joey is
   a stronger swimmer than Ashton. If the first
   two statements are true, the third statement
   is _____.

   (A) true
   (B) false
   (C) uncertain

30. Which word does *not* belong with the
   others?

   (A) biology
   (B) chemistry
   (C) astronomy
   (D) science

31. Cap is to baseball as helmet is to
   _____.

   (A) soccer
   (B) tennis
   (C) cycling
   (D) golf

GO TO NEXT PAGE ➡

32. Which word does *not* belong with the others?

    (A) scent
    (B) fragrance
    (C) aroma
    (D) atmosphere

33. Holmes is taller than Watson. Watson is taller than Lestrade. Lestrade is taller than Holmes. If the first two statements are true, the third statement is _____.

    (A) true
    (B) false
    (C) uncertain

34. Which word does *not* belong with the others?

    (A) record
    (B) list
    (C) tabulate
    (D) repress

35. Rampant is not _____.

    (A) controlled
    (B) dominant
    (C) common
    (D) difficult

36. Affluent means the *opposite* of _____.

    (A) destitute
    (B) quiet
    (C) speechless
    (D) constructive

37. Earnest is not _____.

    (A) serious
    (B) important
    (C) solemn
    (D) ridiculous

38. Cicely had the highest score in our math class. Luke is in our math class. Cicely scored higher than Luke. If the first two statements are true, the third statement is _____.

    (A) true
    (B) false
    (C) uncertain

39. Meager means the *opposite* of _____.

    (A) abundant
    (B) skinny
    (C) rare
    (D) sympathetic

40. Puppy is to paw as colt is to _____.

    (A) horse
    (B) hoof
    (C) pony
    (D) run

41. Maladroit means the *opposite* of _____.

    (A) clumsy
    (B) skillful
    (C) inept
    (D) cruel

42. Loren sings lower than Claire. Sarah sings higher than Claire. Sarah sings higher than Loren. If the first two statements are true, the third statement is _____.

    (A) true
    (B) false
    (C) uncertain

43. Which word does *not* belong with the others?

    (A) room
    (B) den
    (C) kitchen
    (D) office

GO TO NEXT PAGE ➡

44. Nose is to face as finger is to _____.

   (A) foot
   (B) hand
   (C) ear
   (D) head

45. Jeopardy most nearly means _____.

   (A) game
   (B) peril
   (C) twice
   (D) knowledge

46. Which word does *not* belong with the others?

   (A) depot
   (B) station
   (C) terminal
   (D) vehicle

47. Meticulous means the *opposite* of _____.

   (A) haphazard
   (B) careful
   (C) precise
   (D) lethargic

48. Modest is to vanity as innocent is to _____.

   (A) happiness
   (B) reason
   (C) fear
   (D) guilt

49. The *Herald* contains fewer stories than the *Leader*. The *Courier* has more stories than the *Leader*. The *Courier* contains more stories than the *Herald*. If the first two statements are true, the third statement is _____.

   (A) true
   (B) false
   (C) uncertain

50. Decrepit means the *opposite* of _____.

   (A) weak
   (B) feeble
   (C) slow
   (D) robust

51. Recess is to play as breakfast is to _____.

   (A) dress
   (B) pancakes
   (C) juice
   (D) eat

52. Faust is older than Prospero. Merlin is older than Prospero. Merlin is older than Faust. If the first two statements are true, the third statement is _____.

   (A) true
   (B) false
   (C) uncertain

53. Which word does *not* belong with the others?

   (A) calculator
   (B) keyboard
   (C) telephone
   (D) DVD

54. Hygienic means the *opposite* of _____.

   (A) contaminated
   (B) clean
   (C) safe
   (D) sanitary

55. Bach is more complicated than Vivaldi. Handel is simpler than Vivaldi. Bach is more complicated than Handel. If the first two statements are true, the third statement is _____.

   (A) true
   (B) false
   (C) uncertain

GO TO NEXT PAGE →

56. Which word does *not* belong with the others?

(A) excuse
(B) pardon
(C) forgive
(D) accuse

57. A pernicious rumor is _____.

(A) harmful
(B) false
(C) entertaining
(D) harmless

58. Willow Court is shorter than Greenbriar Drive. Greenbriar Drive is not as long as Lexington Street. Lexington Street is longer than Willow Court. If the first two statements are true, the third statement is _____.

(A) true
(B) false
(C) uncertain

59. Desert is to arid as rain forest is to _____.

(A) humid
(B) dessicated
(C) dry
(D) unexplored

60. Corbo's Bakery has a larger selection than Presti's. Presti's carries more varieties than Spalding's. Spalding's has fewer varieties than Corbo's. If the first two statements are true, the third statement is _____.

(A) true
(B) false
(C) uncertain

If there is still time remaining, you may review your answers.

SUBTEST 2 QUANTITATIVE

#61–112   30 MINUTES

Sample:

What is the sum of 52 and 31?

(A) 21
(B) 83
(C) 84
(D) None of the above   Ⓐ ● Ⓒ Ⓓ

Directions: Select the best answer for each question.

61. Examine the rectangle and the equilateral triangle, and then select the best answer.

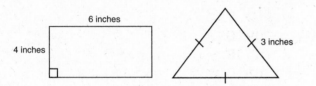

6 inches

4 inches

3 inches

(A) The perimeter of the rectangle is 10 inches more than the perimeter of the equilateral triangle.
(B) The perimeter of the equilateral triangle is 8 inches less than the perimeter of the rectangle.
(C) The perimeter of the rectangle is 11 inches more than the perimeter of the equilateral triangle.
(D) The perimeter of the equilateral triangle is 12 inches less than the perimeter of the rectangle.

62. Find the next term in the series
21, 18, 18.9, 18, 16.8, 18, 14.7, 18, _____.

(A) 13.5
(B) 12.8
(C) 13.1
(D) 12.6

63. Forty percent of what number is equal to 2 more than the product of $\frac{1}{2}$ and 60?

(A) 24
(B) 80
(C) 32
(D) 60

64. Examine the line graph, and then select the best answer.

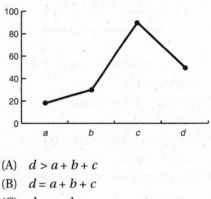

(A) $d > a + b + c$
(B) $d = a + b + c$
(C) $d = a + b$
(D) $a + d = 90$

GO TO NEXT PAGE ➡

65. Review the series: 18, 6, 2, $\frac{2}{3}$, ... Find the next number.

   (A) $\frac{2}{9}$

   (B) $\frac{1}{3}$

   (C) $\frac{1}{6}$

   (D) $\frac{3}{8}$

66. Two-thirds of what number is equal to 18 plus 60% of 40?

   (A) 27
   (B) 33
   (C) 36
   (D) 63

67. Examine the table, and select the best answer.

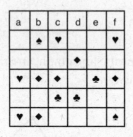

   (A) Column a has one more ♥ than column f.
   (B) Column b has two more ♦ than column d.
   (C) Column c has one less ♣ than column e.
   (D) Column d has one more ♦ than column c.

68. O and O′ are the centers of their respective circles.

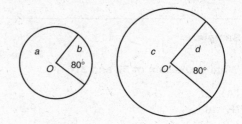

   Choose the best answer.

   (A) Area c > Area a
   (B) Area a + Area b > Area c + Area d
   (C) Area c – Area a > Area a + Area d
   (D) Area c – Area b = Area d + Area a

69. Review the series: A, E, I, M, ... Find the next letter.

   (A) P
   (B) Q
   (C) R
   (D) O

70. What number is 8 more than two-thirds of 60?

   (A) 68
   (B) 48
   (C) 40
   (D) 52

71. Review the series: 92, 17, 96, 15, 100, 13, ... Find the next number.

   (A) 98
   (B) 11
   (C) 17
   (D) 104

GO TO NEXT PAGE ➡

72. Michelle spends $t + 4$ hours per day watching television. Carmen spends t hours and Henry watches television $t - 2$ hours per day. Find the average number of hours of TV time for the three students.

(A) $\dfrac{(3t + 2)}{3}$

(B) $\left(\dfrac{4t}{3}\right) + 2$

(C) $2t + 4$

(D) $\dfrac{(4t - 2)}{3}$

73. Fill in the blank in the series
9.6, 11.9, 14.2, 16.5, ___, 21.1.

(A) 9.6
(B) 11.2
(C) 18.8
(D) 13.4

74. What number is 12 less than $\dfrac{3}{4}$ of 24?

(A) 10
(B) 8
(C) 14
(D) 6

75. Review the series: 7, 11, 10, 14, 13, 17, ...
Find the next number.

(A) 21
(B) 16
(C) 19
(D) 22

76. Examine the diagram, and then choose the best answer.

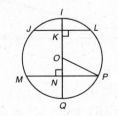

(A) $JL > MP$
(B) $OQ < OK$
(C) $NQ > JL$
(D) $OP > ON$

77. Based on the information in the diagram below, select the best answer.

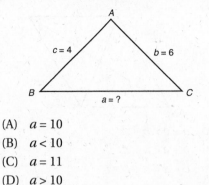

(A) $a = 10$
(B) $a < 10$
(C) $a = 11$
(D) $a > 10$

78. The formula for the volume of a cylinder is given by the formula $V = \pi r^2 h$, where
V = volume, $\pi = \dfrac{22}{7}$, and h = height.
Find the volume of a cylinder whose radius is 7 ft and whose height is 6 ft.

(A) 586 cu ft
(B) 924 cu ft
(C) 726 cu ft
(D) 838 cu ft

79. Review the series: 4, 8, 9, 27, 16, 64, ...
Find the next two numbers.

(A) 96, 192
(B) 32, 96
(C) 81, 243
(D) 25, 125

80. The difference of what number and 54 is equal to four-fifths of the product of 12 and 5?

(A) 80
(B) 102
(C) 94
(D) 86

81. Review the series: 24, 9, 21, 9, 18, 9, 15, ...
Find the next two numbers.

(A) 9, 12
(B) 7, 9
(C) 9, 10
(D) 9, 11

GO TO NEXT PAGE ➡

82. Given that $c < d$ in the parallelogram, select the best answer.

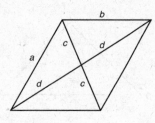

(A) $a + c > b + d$

(B) $a + c < a + d$

(C) $c + d = a + b$

(D) $b - c = a + d$

83. What number is 9 more than three-fifths of 40?

(A) 33

(B) 24

(C) 37

(D) 49

84. Review the series: 38, 40, 43, 47, 52, 58, ... Find the next number.

(A) 59

(B) 65

(C) 55

(D) 61

85. Find side BC of the right triangle below.

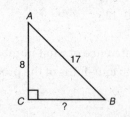

(A) 12

(B) 18

(C) 19

(D) 15

86. Examine the diagram below, and then select the best answer.

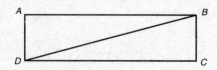

(a)   (b)   (c)

(A) There are 2 more ●s in (b) than □s in (c).

(B) There are 2 fewer □s in (b) than ●s in (a).

(C) There is 1 less ○ in (c) than □s in (a).

(D) There are 2 more □s in (a) than ●s in (b).

87. Five-eighths of what number is equal to the product of $\frac{1}{3}$ and 60?

(A) 20

(B) 18

(C) 28

(D) 32

88. Review the series: 65, 63, 64, 62, 63, 61, ... Find the next number.

(A) 62

(B) 69

(C) 63

(D) 60

89. Examine the rectangle, and then select the best answer.

(A) $BD = BC$

(B) $AB > BD$

(C) $BD = AB$

(D) $BD > AB$

GO TO NEXT PAGE ➡

HSPT PRACTICE EXAM 2

90. Review the series: B, E, H, K, N, ... Find the next letter.

(A) O
(B) P
(C) Q
(D) R

91. If ■ = 4, □ = 3 , * = 2, · = multiplication, + = addition, and – = subtraction, find the value of 5 · ■ + 3 · □ − 4 · *.

(A) 23
(B) 34
(C) 21
(D) 18

92. Review the series: 4, 8, 9, 18, 19, 38, 39, ... Find the next number.

(A) 40
(B) 41
(C) 78
(D) 48

93. Twenty-five subtracted from two-thirds of what number is equal to 5 more than 3 times 12?

(A) 99
(B) 100
(C) 98
(D) 96

94. Review the following diagram and information, and then select the best answer.

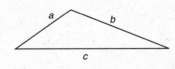

Side c is twice as long as side a, which is 3 inches less than side b.

(A) $c = 2(b − 3)$
(B) $a = b + 3$
(C) $c > a + b$
(D) $b < a − 3$

95. Boxes A, B, D, E, F, and G are of equal size. Box C is twice the size of Box A. What is the sum of the areas of Boxes B, C, and F?

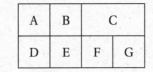

(A) A + D + E
(B) D + E + G
(C) A + B
(D) A + D + E + G

96. The quotient of 36 and a number is equal to the product of five-eighths and 80 reduced by 41. Find the number.

(A) 6
(B) 4
(C) 8
(D) 12

97. Review the diagram, and then select the best answer. The squares indicate right angles.

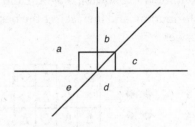

(A) $m\angle a = m\angle b$
(B) $m\angle a + m\angle d < 90°$
(C) $m\angle c = m\angle d$
(D) $m\angle b + m\angle c = 90°$

98. Review the series: 1, 4, 9, 16, ... Find the next number.

(A) 10
(B) 20
(C) 36
(D) 25

GO TO NEXT PAGE ➡

99. Simplify $-4(-2)^3$ and choose the correct answer.

   (A) −16
   (B) −32
   (C) +24
   (D) +32

100. Examine the diagram, and then select the best answer. $m\angle 1 = m\angle 4$, $m\angle 2 = m\angle 6$, and $m\angle 3 = m\angle 5$. Circle O' > Circle O.

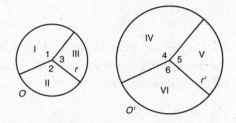

   (A) Area I + Area II > Area IV
   (B) Area I + Area IV = Area II + Area V
   (C) Area IV + Area V > Area I + Area III
   (D) Area VI > Area I + Area III

101. Examine the following diagram and information, and then select the best answer.

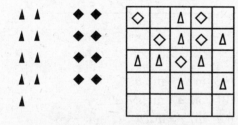

   The hollow figures in the table, △ and ◊, have to be filled in with the dark figures, ▲ and ♦. If all the hollow figures are filled in, how many dark figures remain?

   (A) 3 ▲ and 2 ♦
   (B) 1 ♦ and 1 ▲
   (C) 2 ▲ and 1 ♦
   (D) 3 ♦ and 1 ▲

102. Review the series: 2, 3, 6, __, 3, 6, 2, 3, 6, ... What number should fill in the blank?

   (A) 6
   (B) 2
   (C) 8
   (D) 3

103. If the product of 8 and a number is reduced by two-thirds of 48, the result is equal to the quotient of 160 and 4. Find the number.

   (A) 9
   (B) 7
   (C) 12
   (D) 8

104. Review the given information, and then choose the best answer.

   (a) 5^2
   (b) 3^4
   (c) 2^5

   (A) (b) < (a) and (c) > (b)
   (B) (a) < (b) < (c)
   (C) (c) < (a) and (c) > (b)
   (D) (b) > (c) and (b) > (a)

GO TO NEXT PAGE ➡

105. Examine the diagram and then select the best answer.

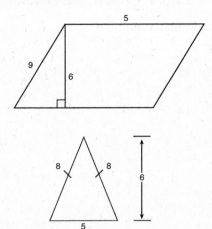

(A) Area of the parallelogram > 2 · Area of the triangle

(B) Area of triangle > $\frac{1}{2}$ · Area of parallelogram

(C) Perimeter of triangle < $\frac{1}{2}$ · Perimeter of parallelogram

(D) Perimeter of parallelogram > Perimeter of triangle + 5

106. Review the series:

$$24\frac{1}{2}, 22, 19\frac{1}{2}, 17, 14\frac{1}{2}, 12, \ldots.$$

Find the next number.

(A) 10

(B) $10\frac{1}{2}$

(C) 9

(D) $9\frac{1}{2}$

107. Examine the trapezoid, and then select the best answer.

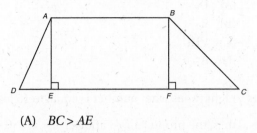

(A) $BC > AE$

(B) $AD = FC$

(C) $DE > FC$

(D) $FC > AB$

108. Examine the diagram, and then select the best answer. Lines a and b are congruent and O is the center of the circle.

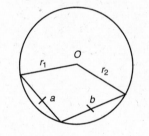

(A) $r_1 + b = a + r_2$

(B) $r_1 + r_2 = a + b$

(C) $r_1 + b < a + r_2$

(D) $r_1 + r_2 < a + b$

109. What number squared is equal to 8 more than the product of 7 and 8?

(A) 7

(B) 8

(C) 9

(D) 10

GO TO NEXT PAGE ➡

110. Review the series: XVIII, 3, XV, 5, XII, 7, ...
Find the next number.

(A) IX
(B) 9
(C) VIII
(D) 8

111. Eight times what number is equal to 15 less
than the product of $\frac{7}{9}$ and 81?

(A) 6
(B) 4
(C) 9
(D) 11

112. Review the series:

3, 5, 7, 5, 7, 9, 7, 9, 11, 9, 11, 13, ...

Find the next number.

(A) 11
(B) 13
(C) 9
(D) 15

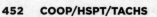

STOP

If there is still time remaining, you may review your answers.

SUBTEST 3   READING

#113–174   25 MINUTES

> **Sample:**
>
> The next test has short reading passages, each one is followed by questions.
>
> Correct marking of the reading passages on the next test will be _____.
>
> (A) all on one page
> (B) followed by questions
> (C) easy to read
> (D) very long   Ⓐ ● Ⓒ Ⓓ

PASSAGE FOR QUESTIONS 113–122

One of the literary texts best known to mankind began as a contest. On a dark and stormy evening, Mary and Percy Bysshe Shelley and their friend Lord Byron, bored with the usual evening entertainments, decided upon a creative challenge. They would each separate and invent a story, then share that story with the others. Dr. Polidori would judge who had made up the best tale.

The result of this literary playtime was *Frankenstein*, a story known by nearly the entire world in one form or another. Numerous versions abound, including one of the most recent retellings produced and directed by Kenneth Branagh, with Robert De Niro as the creature himself.

Frankenstein tells of a war being waged between man and God. Victor Frankenstein <u>glories</u> in his intellectual achievements to the extent that he <u>equates</u> himself with God, the creator of man. In his delusion, Frankenstein attempts to create life, but what he ends up creating is both less and more than a man.

The text cleverly calls Frankenstein's creation a monster, but few realize how appropriate the term is. "Monster" comes from the Latin term *monstra*—which literally means only "result," something brought about by a human; but since results can vary, we get multiple words from this term. We get, for example, both the word "demonstration" and the word "monster." The people in the story who surround Frankenstein do not recognize the significance of the *monstra* (a creation intended to astound them); they only see the monster (a menacing creature that frightens them). Ultimately, feared and rejected by society, hunted like a beast, the creature retreats to an icy, watery grave—taking Frankenstein, his creator, with him.

Shelley warns us through her novel that playing with science, toying with knowledge we hardly understand or control, is a dangerous activity. Frankenstein represents that part of humanity that struggles to create and to conquer even those things over which we have (and should have) no control. We should acknowledge her warning—especially when it comes to modern day experimentation with modern day Frankensteins.

GO TO NEXT PAGE ➡

113. What will likely follow paragraph five?

    (A) a discussion of the novel *Dracula*
    (B) an analysis of the term Polydor (which translates into the phrase "many gifts")
    (C) a section of text outlining what is meant by the term "Frankensteins"
    (D) a review of the Kenneth Branagh–Robert De Niro version of *Frankenstein*

114. The use of the word equates, as used in this passage, most closely means _____.

    (A) be superior to
    (B) be equal with
    (C) be inferior to
    (D) be indecisive about

115. How do you think the author likely feels about the question of cloning, based on your reading of this passage?

    (A) S/he thinks it a worthwhile endeavor that deserves funding and resources.
    (B) S/he remains neutral on the topic, refusing to take a side.
    (C) S/he thinks it a dangerous idea because we know so little about what we're doing and the long-term results of practicing it.
    (D) We cannot tell from the passage.

116. According to the passage, the word "monster" comes from _____.

    (A) the word *monstra*
    (B) the word *remonstrate*
    (C) the word *demonstrate*
    (D) the word *monstrosity*

117. Because Frankenstein considers himself equal to God, we can best compare him to which of the following?

    (A) Lucifer
    (B) Dr. Polidori
    (C) Percy Bysshe Shelley
    (D) Thomas Edison

118. How does Frankenstein end his existence, according to this passage?

    (A) by fire
    (B) by suffocation
    (C) by drowning
    (D) by starvation

119. Why does the author write this piece?

    (A) to stoke dialog over feminist rights
    (B) to encourage us to write
    (C) to get us to read *Frankenstein*
    (D) to warn us against engaging in activities we may not be able to control

120. Which of the following would be the best title for this article?

    (A) Playing with Fire
    (B) It Was a Dark and Stormy Night
    (C) Monster Mash
    (D) Capturing Our Inner Monster

121. What does the word glories mean in the context of paragraph three?

    (A) victories
    (B) flags
    (C) triumphs
    (D) flowers

122. Which of the following people plays the creature in a film version of the novel *Frankenstein*?

    (A) Victor Frankenstein
    (B) Robert De Niro
    (C) Percy Bysshe Shelley
    (D) Kenneth Branagh

GO TO NEXT PAGE ➡

In World War II the Japanese hatched a <u>nefarious</u> plan. They had already planned uses for the military personnel, the planes, and the troops. However, they found a use for nonmilitary personnel as well, especially the women.

Japanese officials commissioned women to create balloons. The women created 9,000 of these balloons, all of them from white paper or rubberized silk. Into each balloon the women then carefully placed a bomb, primed for destruction.

Periodically, weather permitting, the women launched the balloons putting them into the jet stream of air that would allow the deadly "<u>white birds</u>" to sift toward their targets.

As one might have guessed, the target was the United States.

The attack did not come off as well as the Japanese had hoped, however. Many of the bombs drifted astray, eventually landing in the ocean and sinking harmlessly below the waves. Others indeed landed on U.S. soil, carrying duds rather than live bombs. Of all of the potential deathtraps that landed in the United States, few exploded, and fewer hit human targets. Japanese officials stopped launching the balloons at the end of the war, in June 1945, having tallied only six victims.

Perhaps the plan was foolhardy from the beginning. After all, the odds of finding a way to bring together all the necessary parts required to direct such a fragile attack force are <u>infinitesimal</u>. Maybe it was fate that that destructive plan eventually transformed into something more positive. Japanese custom now holds a great reverence for white, paper-folded cranes as a symbol of peace. Indeed, the story goes that the person who folds 1,000 origami cranes will be blessed with health and a long life.

123. What does the word <u>nefarious</u> mean, according to the passage?

   (A) neat
   (B) clever
   (C) efficient
   (D) treacherous

124. Why is the author telling you this story?

   (A) to belittle Japanese culture for such a stupid idea
   (B) to tell you of a creative and successful mission
   (C) to relate an interesting but little known true story that took place during World War II
   (D) to illustrate how brave Americans were in the face of danger

125. To what, based on the reading passage, does the term <u>white birds</u> most likely refer?

   (A) the white balloons
   (B) the white herons popular in the region
   (C) the white clouds that provided camouflage
   (D) the white stone that flanked the northern shores of Japan

126. Who made the white balloons for the attack, according to the article?

   (A) kamikaze pilots
   (B) nonmilitary women
   (C) children
   (D) soldiers

GO TO NEXT PAGE ➡

127. What does the word <u>infinitesimal</u> mean based on the context of paragraph six?

(A) infinite
(B) normal
(C) large
(D) tiny

128. According to the article, what was NOT a reason why the "white bird" attack failed?

(A) Many of the bombs drifted away.
(B) The workers purposely made the bombs incorrectly.
(C) Many of the bombs turned out to be duds.
(D) Some sank harmlessly into the ocean.

129. Which of the following statements illustrates the main point of paragraph six?

(A) Putting faith and money into such a fragile plan was certainly foolhardy.
(B) The odds of the "white bird" plan working were good.
(C) Origami was a cost-effective way of creating another attack on the U.S.
(D) It is fitting that, since Japanese culture considers the "white bird" a symbol of peace, the plan using the white bird to promote war failed.

130. Select the pair of words that best fits the following analogy: <u>duds</u> are to <u>live bombs</u> as _____.

(A) Christmas is to Easter
(B) black is to white
(C) swimming is to playing tennis
(D) love is to like

131. According to the article, who was the intended target of the "white birds"?

(A) Japan
(B) United States
(C) women
(D) "white birds"

132. According to the passage, how many of the bombs successfully detonated?

(A) 6
(B) 600
(C) 6,000
(D) 9,000

GO TO NEXT PAGE ➡

PASSAGE FOR QUESTIONS 133–142

African culture <u>reveres</u> many ideas that seem foreign to American cultural habits and values. One such idea involves the concept of the "spirit spouse." According to Baule tribal tradition, life is balanced between two worlds: a spirit world from which the soul comes and the "real world" into which everyone is physically born. Everyone in the real world has a spirit spouse whom they have left behind in the spirit world. The spirit spouse awaits the eventual return of the real world spouse to the spirit world after death.

However, sometimes the spirit spouse misses the real world spouse. When this happens, the spirit spouse may become <u>jealous</u>, <u>irritable</u>, and <u>neglected</u>; the spirit spouse may then disrupt the real world life of the real world spouse. As a sign of respect for this spirit spouse, a person will then construct a statue that represents that spirit spouse and keep the sculpture in their home, paying it special attention on a daily basis. However, if the spirit spouse is not <u>placated</u>, then the real world spouse will dedicate one night a week to living with and paying special attention to the spirit spouse. The real world spouse will give the spirit spouse gifts of clothing or jewelry; in return the spirit spouse is supposed to send dream visits from the other world.

Before concluding that African culture is "unusual," however, it ought to be mentioned that nearly every other culture worldwide has its own version of the spirit spouse. Anthropologists have found evidence of belief in the spirit spouse in, among other places, Chile, China, France, Guatemala, and Siberia. Even in America we find <u>remnants</u> of the belief, which makes sense given the high degree of immigration from the outside world.

133. What is the author's purpose in writing this piece?

   (A) to suggest that we adopt the practice of spirit spouses in America
   (B) to explain the concept of the spirit spouse
   (C) to make fun of African tradition
   (D) to discuss idolatry in foreign countries

134. Based on the author's use of the term, you can tell that *Baule* refers to _____.

   (A) a round object used in games of sport
   (B) an arid geographical region near India
   (C) an African tribe
   (D) a fancy dress party

135. Which of the following is an example of the kind of thing a real world spouse would present a spirit spouse?

   (A) gifts of food
   (B) gifts of incense
   (C) gifts of clothing
   (D) gifts of money

136. Based on the author's use of the word <u>placated</u>, you can tell that it means _____.

   (A) appeased
   (B) offended
   (C) obliterated
   (D) angered

GO TO NEXT PAGE ➡

137. The practice of giving gifts to the spirit spouse as a way to make it happy is most like which of the following?

(A) a tax
(B) a bribe
(C) a tip
(D) a law

138. Based on the context of paragraph three, what does the word <u>remnants</u> mean?

(A) traces
(B) witnesses
(C) reminders
(D) cloth

139. Based on its use in paragraph one, what does the word <u>reveres</u> mean?

(A) relishes
(B) reviews
(C) respects
(D) rejects

140. What is likely the author's opinion on the concept of a "spirit spouse"?

(A) It is important given how many cultures believe in it; it deserves some respect.
(B) It is a dangerous belief; it ought to be censored.
(C) It is a rumor; no one believes in the spirit spouse.
(D) It is a weird idea; people who believe in the spirit spouse ought to be mocked.

141. Which of the following countries is NOT listed as believing in the spirit spouse?

(A) America
(B) China
(C) Guatemale
(D) Guam

142. Which of the following observations best connects the words <u>jealous</u>, <u>irritable</u>, and <u>neglected</u>?

(A) They are all positive emotions.
(B) They are all words that describe negative traits.
(C) They are all feelings that animals simply can't feel.
(D) They are listed in alphabetical order.

GO TO NEXT PAGE ➡

Have you ever been in a multiple-choice test-taking situation? Most people have at some time or other in their lives. By now, you know the routine: read all the choices through, and make your selection. Then work your way through the test, and, if you have time, check through as many answers as you can before time runs out and tests are collected. The question I have always pondered, as you probably have, is this: What if I think I've made an incorrect answer selection? Should I change my answer? Or should I go with my original impulse?

Well, today is your lucky day. Today you find out what the experts advise on this topic.

Psychologists at King's College in Ontario have studied this problem for the past few years and have come up with some surprising <u>results</u>. First, females are more likely than males to change their answers. While this may indicate more flexibility and willingness to admit mistakes on the part of females than males, unfortunately, females are also more likely to make changes from the right answer to the wrong answer. Researchers <u>attribute</u> this discovery to the well-documented lower levels of self-esteem under which women seem to labor.

But, you began reading this article because you wanted to know about those changes over which you have been agonizing. Here's the scoop: Of all changes people make to multiple-choice test questions, 50% go from wrong to right, 25% go from right to wrong, and 25% go from wrong to wrong. So, bottom line? Go ahead and make those changes; your first instinct may well have been wrong.

143. Based on the information in this passage, it is better _____.

(A) to resist the temptation to change your first answer on a multiple-choice test
(B) to give in to the temptation to change your first answer on a multiple-choice test
(C) to change both your first and second answers to multiple-choice test questions
(D) the article does not give clear enough advice to make a decision

144. Why does the article state that women are more likely than men to change their answers?

(A) Women are more likely to admit they are wrong and accept new instruction.
(B) Men are more stubborn.
(C) Women are more likely to second-guess themselves, talking themselves into getting answers wrong.
(D) Men are more likely to cheat.

145. What percentage of multiple-choice test takers are likely to change an answer from wrong to wrong?

(A) 100%
(B) 50%
(C) 25%
(D) 0%

146. Where are you most likely to read this kind of article?

(A) guidance counselor's office
(B) psychology journal
(C) Teen Beat magazine
(D) *Reader's Digest*

147. Based on the author's use of the word <u>attribute</u>, which of the following is the best definition?

(A) blame
(B) describe
(C) associate
(D) refer to

GO TO NEXT PAGE ➡

148. Where are the researchers responsible for this human behavior study based?

(A) Quebec
(B) Canada
(C) Ontario
(D) Newfoundland

149. What would be the best title for this piece?

(A) Cheating: An Increasing Problem for 21st-Century Students
(B) Overcoming Indecision
(C) To Change or Not to Change
(D) The Times They Are A'changing

150. What percentage of people tend to change their answers from wrong to right?

(A) 100%
(B) 50%
(C) 25%
(D) 0%

151. Which of the following words would be the best synonym for the word results as it is used in this passage?

(A) observations
(B) reviews
(C) hypotheses
(D) questions

152. Which of the following statements best summarizes the observation about women made in paragraph three?

(A) Scientists don't really know why men are more likely than women to change their first guess.
(B) Men might be less likely to change their first guess because of low self-esteem.
(C) Men and women are equally unlikely to change their first guess.
(D) Women might be more likely to change their first guess due to low self-esteem.

GO TO NEXT PAGE ➡

153. an odious task

    (A) hateful
    (B) attractive
    (C) smelly
    (D) easy

154. a petty disagreement

    (A) loving
    (B) serious
    (C) violent
    (D) unimportant

155. a strict agenda

    (A) code
    (B) personality
    (C) classroom
    (D) plan

156. a lucid argument

    (A) confusing
    (B) clear
    (C) weak
    (D) irrelevant

157. a gentle zephyr

    (A) breeze
    (B) caress
    (C) whisper
    (D) animal

158. to enumerate the reasons

    (A) eliminate
    (B) list
    (C) assign
    (D) argue

159. an inopportune moment

    (A) untimely
    (B) convenient
    (C) quick
    (D) inconclusive

160. a pungent aroma

    (A) sweet
    (B) fresh
    (C) sharp
    (D) subtle

161. to shirk responsibilities

    (A) evade
    (B) destroy
    (C) assume
    (D) delegate

162. a credible witness

    (A) first-hand
    (B) believable
    (C) expert
    (D) unreliable

163. to feign interest

    (A) pretend
    (B) encourage
    (C) slow
    (D) stimulate

164. a thin veneer

    (A) liquid
    (B) expression
    (C) surface
    (D) volume

GO TO NEXT PAGE ➡

165. <u>lax</u> discipline

(A) loose
(B) strict
(C) oppressive
(D) fair

166. total <u>anarchy</u>

(A) dictatorship
(B) monarchy
(C) democracy
(D) disorder

167. <u>tangible</u> evidence

(A) admissible
(B) irrelevant
(C) physical
(D) eyewitness

168. an interesting <u>lecture</u>

(A) book
(B) stand
(C) reader
(D) speech

169. to <u>impede</u> progress

(A) quicken
(B) race
(C) hinder
(D) support

170. a strong <u>antipathy</u>

(A) sympathy
(B) aversion
(C) chemical
(D) opinion

171. a dedicated <u>pacifist</u>

(A) swimmer
(B) soldier
(C) sports fan
(D) one opposed to war

172. published <u>posthumously</u>

(A) anonymously
(B) after death
(C) before midnight
(D) in a series

173. the <u>penultimate</u> question

(A) most difficult
(B) final
(C) second to last
(D) first

174. <u>verbose</u> directions

(A) laconic
(B) specific
(C) incorrect
(D) wordy

STOP

If there is still time remaining, you may review your answers.

SUBTEST 4   MATHEMATICS

#175–238   45 MINUTES

Sample:

Round 642 to the nearest hundred.

(A) 650
(B) 600
(C) 700
(D) 640   Ⓐ ● Ⓒ Ⓓ

Directions: Select the best answer for each question.

---

175. Review statements (a), (b), and (c), and then select the true statement.

   (a) $\dfrac{(24 \cdot 2)}{6}$

   (b) $\left(\dfrac{24}{6}\right) \cdot 2$

   (c) $\left(\dfrac{24}{2}\right) + 6$

   (A) (a) < (b) and (a) < (c)
   (B) (c) > (a) and (a) = (b)
   (C) (b) > (a) and (c) > (b)
   (D) (b) < (a) and (a) > (c)

176. If b is a negative number, which of the following terms is the smallest?

   (A) b^2
   (B) $-b$
   (C) b^0
   (D) b^3

177. Simplify the following powers, and then select the correct answer.

   (a) 5^2
   (b) 2^5
   (c) 2^3

   (A) (a) > (b) or (c) > (a)
   (B) (c) = (a) or (b) < (c)
   (C) (c) > (b) and (a) = (b)
   (D) (b) < (a) or (c) < (b)

178. Find the value of $\dfrac{3^9}{4 \times 3^7}$.

   (A) 3
   (B) $3\dfrac{1}{2}$
   (C) $2\dfrac{1}{4}$
   (D) $2\dfrac{3}{4}$

179. Arrange the following expressions in descending order. Use the letters to represent the expressions.

   (a) $4^2 + 5(9 - 3)$
   (b) $3 \cdot 17 - 4 \times 6$
   (c) $7 + 9 \cdot 4 - 6(9 - 7)^3$
   (d) $6 + 2 + \dfrac{48}{8} - 2(3 - 1)^2$

   Select the correct answer.

   (A) (a) > (b) > (d) > (c)
   (B) (b) > (a) > (d) > (c)
   (C) (d) > (a) > (c) > (b)
   (D) (a) > (d) > (c) > (b)

GO TO NEXT PAGE ➡

180. Round off 1,742,143 to the nearest hundred.

    (A) 1,742,200
    (B) 1,742,100
    (C) 1,742,000
    (D) 1,740,000

181. Malcolm and Dwayne start off running around the track at the same time. If Malcolm can run around the track in 5 minutes and Dwayne can cover the same distance in 3 minutes, when will they again meet at the start of the track?

    (A) 12 minutes
    (B) 15 minutes
    (C) 16 minutes
    (D) 18 minutes

182. Perform the indicated operations, and select the correct answer.

    (a) $1\frac{1}{2} \cdot 2\frac{3}{4}$

    (b) $\frac{3}{4} \cdot 4\frac{1}{2}$

    (c) $3\frac{1}{2} \cdot \frac{3}{4}$

    (d) $\frac{1}{2} \cdot 3\frac{1}{4}$

    (A) (c) < (d) or (c) < (a)
    (B) (d) < (c) and (d) > (a)
    (C) (b) > (a) and (b) < (c)
    (D) (a) > (d) and (a) < (b)

183. Henry drives from Middletown to Rockville, a distance of 206.5 miles. If he leaves Middletown at 2:30 P.M. and drives at the rate of 59 mph, what time will he arrive in Rockville?

    (A) 4:30 P.M.
    (B) 5 P.M.
    (C) 5:30 P.M.
    (D) 6 P.M.

184. A car uses 12.4 gallons of gasoline in 236.5 miles. To the nearest tenth, how many miles per gallon does the car use?

    (A) 13.8
    (B) 23.7
    (C) 32.4
    (D) 19.1

185. Twenty-four students in a class are right-handed and 6 are left-handed. If these figures represent the entire class, what percent is left-handed?

    (A) 15%
    (B) 25%
    (C) 20%
    (D) 30%

186. Which of the following numbers is greater than .77 but less than $\frac{7}{8}$?

    (A) $\frac{2}{3}$

    (B) $\frac{3}{4}$

    (C) .82
    (D) .913

187. What number is 14 less than two-thirds of 54?

    (A) 22
    (B) 42
    (C) 38
    (D) 36

188. Find the cube root of –0.027.

    (A) –0.2
    (B) 0.2
    (C) –0.3
    (D) 0.3

GO TO NEXT PAGE ➡

189. Select a value for x that satisfies the condition $-3 \leq |2x + 1| < 2$.

    (A) -4

    (B) 0

    (C) 3

    (D) 2

190. A jar contains 3 blue marbles, 4 red marbles, and 2 yellow marbles. Without looking, what is the probability of selecting either a blue or a yellow marble?

    (A) $\dfrac{2}{3}$

    (B) $\dfrac{4}{7}$

    (C) $\dfrac{5}{9}$

    (D) $\dfrac{2}{7}$

191. Mildred weighs $x - 3$ pounds. Her brother Hector weighs 8 pounds more than Mildred, while her sister Stacey weighs 12 pounds less than Hector. Find their total weight.

    (A) $4x - 5$

    (B) $5x + 3$

    (C) $x + 12$

    (D) $3x - 5$

192. Simplify $45|-63| \div 5|9|$.

    (A) 63

    (B) -12

    (C) 9

    (D) -14

193. The ratio of a drawing on a blueprint to an actual object is 1 : 100. If a building is 90 feet high, how long would its image be on the blueprint, in inches?

    (A) 12.4 inches

    (B) 16.8 inches

    (C) 13.6 inches

    (D) 10.8 inches

194. The sum of two consecutive integers is 51. Select the larger integer.

    (A) 19

    (B) 21

    (C) 25

    (D) 26

195. In the diagram below, a right angle is formed by the intersection of the vertical and horizontal lines. Determine the value of x.

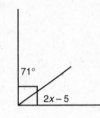

    (A) $12°$

    (B) $18°$

    (C) $24°$

    (D) $32°$

196. What is the complement of $a°$?

    (A) $(180 - a)°$

    (B) $(90 + a)°$

    (C) $(90 - a)°$

    (D) $(180 + a)°$

197. Find the measure of angle a.

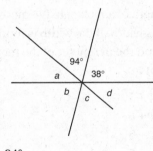

    (A) $94°$

    (B) $48°$

    (C) $132°$

    (D) $58°$

GO TO NEXT PAGE ➡

198. At how many points do the sides of a septagon intersect?

(A) 8
(B) 6
(C) 5
(D) 7

199. Which of the following is an obtuse triangle?

(A)

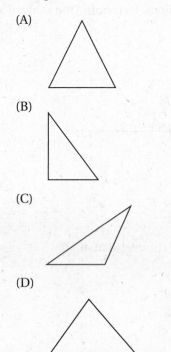

(B)

(C)

(D)

200. The length of a rectangle is 4 more than twice its width. If the width is represented by w, find the perimeter of the rectangle in terms of w.

(A) $6w + 12$
(B) $4w + 8$
(C) $6w - 6$
(D) $6w + 8$

201. *ABCD* is a rectangle with length 12 and width 4. *RSTU* is a square, with *V* and *W* the midpoints of *RS* and *TU*, respectively. *RU* is 8.

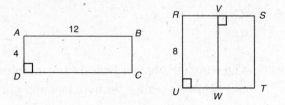

Select the correct statement.

(A) The perimeter of *ABCD* is greater than the perimeter of *RSTU*.
(B) The perimeter of *ABCD* is less than the perimeter of *RVWU*.
(C) One-half of the perimeter of *ABCD* is equal to the perimeter of *RVWU*.
(D) One-half the perimeter of *ABCD* is less than the perimeter of *RSTU*.

202. The area of a parallelogram is 114. If its base is 12, find its height.

(A) 9.5
(B) 8
(C) 11
(D) 10.5

203. The measure of the vertex angle of an isosceles triangle is 50°. Find the measure of an exterior angle to one of the base angles of the triangle.

(A) 65°
(B) 125°
(C) 115°
(D) 80°

GO TO NEXT PAGE ➡

204. Substitute 2 for r and 5 for s in (a), (b), and (c). Then simplify the following expressions and select the TRUE statement below.

(a) $(r + 4)^2$
(b) $9(s - 3)^2$
(c) $2r^2s$

(A) (a) < (b) and (c) > (b)
(B) (a) = (b) or (c) > (a)
(C) (b) < (a) and (c) > (b)
(D) (c) < (a) and (a) < (b)

205. Simplify the ratio of 6 ounces to 3 pounds.

(A) $\dfrac{1}{2}$

(B) $\dfrac{2}{5}$

(C) $\dfrac{1}{8}$

(D) $\dfrac{3}{8}$

206. Determine the value of x in the equation $62 + 2(8 - x) = 72$.

(A) 9
(B) 8
(C) 4
(D) 3

207. The distance between cities A and B is 45 miles. On a map, if $\dfrac{1}{2}$ inch represents 9 miles, how many inches represent the distance between the two cities?

(A) 2 inches
(B) $3\dfrac{1}{2}$ inches
(C) 3 inches
(D) $2\dfrac{1}{2}$ inches

208. If the circumference of a circle is 62.8, find its radius. Let $\pi = 3.14$.

(A) 6
(B) 10
(C) 7
(D) 4

209. In the following diagrams, circle O has a radius of 5, and triangle RST has sides of 5 and 12 and a hypotenuse of 13. The circumference of a circle, C, is equal to $2\pi r$, and the area of a circle, A_C, is equal to πr^2. In both of these cases, $\pi = 3.14$ and $r =$ the radius.

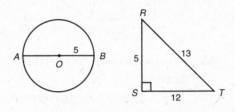

Which of the following statements is true?

(A) Area of triangle $RST < \dfrac{1}{2}$ Area of circle O
(B) Circumference of circle < perimeter of triangle RST
(C) Area of circle + Area of triangle < 100
(D) Circumference of circle – perimeter of triangle > 2

210. Larisa is pumping oxygen into an emergency room at the rate of 3 cubic meters per minute. If the room is 9 meters long by 6 meters wide by 4 meters high, how long will it take for the room to be filled with oxygen?

(A) 64 minutes
(B) 72 minutes
(C) 86 minutes
(D) 44 minutes

GO TO NEXT PAGE ➡

211. Simplify $\dfrac{56\sqrt{b^3c^4}}{7\sqrt{bc^3}}$.

(A) $8bc$

(B) $8\sqrt{bc}$

(C) $8b^2\sqrt{c}$

(D) $8b\sqrt{c}$

212. Select the best answer.

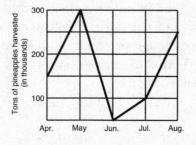

(A) August harvest + July harvest = June harvest

(B) May harvest – April harvest > July harvest

(C) April harvest < August harvest – July harvest

(D) July harvest – June harvest = May harvest

213. If 16 people, with a total weight of 2,560 pounds, are standing on a floor measuring 20 feet by 32 feet, what is the average weight each square foot of the floor is supporting?

(A) 4 lb per sq ft

(B) 2 lb per sq ft

(C) 3 lb per sq ft

(D) 5 lb per sq ft

214. Change $4\dfrac{3}{4}$ to a percent.

(A) 4.75%

(B) 47.5%

(C) 434%

(D) 475%

215. The formula $d = 16t^2$ represents the distance, d, an object falls in t seconds, where d is in feet. Find the distance an object drops in 3 seconds.

(A) 144 ft

(B) 96 ft

(C) 166 ft

(D) 128 ft

216. Julio earns $13.54 per hour while Shanequa earns $15.93 per hour. In 12 hours, how much more than Julio does Shanequa earn?

(A) $27.26

(B) $191.16

(C) $28.68

(D) $43.36

217. Find the measure of angle 2.

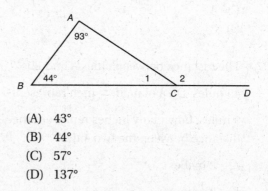

(A) 43°

(B) 44°

(C) 57°

(D) 137°

GO TO NEXT PAGE ➡

218. Find the area of the entire figure.

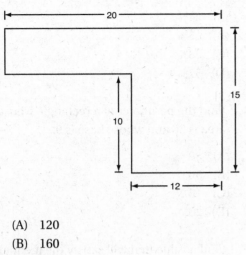

(A) 120
(B) 160
(C) 220
(D) 240

219. What are the coordinates of point *A*?

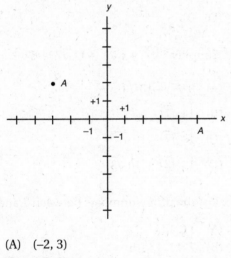

(A) (–2, 3)
(B) (–3, 2)
(C) (–1, 4)
(D) (4, –1)

220. Simplify the ratio 15 seconds to 3 minutes.

(A) $\dfrac{1}{12}$

(B) $\dfrac{2}{5}$

(C) $\dfrac{1}{4}$

(D) $\dfrac{3}{7}$

221. Find the value of the expression $5x^2 + 2yz$ when $x = 3$, $y = -2$, and $z = 4$.

(A) 32
(B) 29
(C) 18
(D) 37

222. What is the greatest common factor of 36 and 54?

(A) 9
(B) 6
(C) 8
(D) 18

223. Find the value of *x* in the following figure.

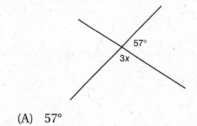

(A) 57°
(B) 41°
(C) 39°
(D) 3°

224. $6\dfrac{2}{3} \times 5\dfrac{1}{4} =$

(A) $5\dfrac{1}{2}$

(B) 16

(C) 23

(D) 35

GO TO NEXT PAGE ➡

225. The Buffalo Jaguars scored 12, 7, 10, 6, and 9 runs in their last five games. If they want to maintain an average of 9 runs per game for six games, how much do they have to score in their next game?

(A) 4
(B) 10
(C) 8
(D) 6

226. The sum of the first and second of four consecutive even integers is 8 more than the fourth. Find the smallest integer.

(A) 12
(B) 14
(C) 16
(D) 10

227. A magazine costs $6.60 right now. If the price increased 10% two years ago and 20% six months ago, how much did the magazine cost before the first increase two years ago?

(A) $4.50
(B) $5.00
(C) $5.50
(D) $6.00

228. Two centimeters are what part of a meter?

(A) 3%
(B) 2%
(C) $\frac{1}{500}$
(D) $\frac{1}{25}$

229. If $\frac{a^2}{b} + c = 3\frac{1}{2}$ and $a = 3$, $b = 6$, find c.

(A) 5
(B) 2
(C) 8
(D) 7

230. What percent of 120 is 45? Round off to the nearest percent.

(A) 24%
(B) 25%
(C) 38%
(D) 37%

231. Find the perimeter of a rectangle whose area is 36 and whose base is 9.

(A) 30
(B) 36
(C) 18
(D) 26

232. Find a value that will satisfy the inequality $-3.2 < a - 4 < 3.1$.

(A) 9
(B) −2
(C) 7
(D) 0

233. Simplify $3\sqrt{7} - 4\sqrt{3} + 11\sqrt{7} - 6\sqrt{3}$.

(A) $9\sqrt{7} - 10\sqrt{3}$
(B) $14\sqrt{7} + 7\sqrt{3}$
(C) $14\sqrt{7} - 10\sqrt{3}$
(D) $14\sqrt{21} - 10\sqrt{3}$

234. List the prime numbers between 7 and 15.

(A) 11, 13
(B) 7, 11, 13, 15
(C) 11, 13, 15
(D) 7, 11, 13

235. Which of the following angles can represent the three angles of a triangle?

(A) 43°, 56°, 47°
(B) 58°, 29°, 68°
(C) 56°, 72°, 38°
(D) 59°, 53°, 68°

GO TO NEXT PAGE ➡

236. The library has a policy of ordering
4 fiction, 6 historical, 1 biographical, and
2 science books in that order. If 200 books
were ordered, what subject was the last
book?

(A) fiction
(B) historical
(C) biographical
(D) science

237. A 25-foot tree casts a shadow of 15 feet.
How long is the shadow of a nearby
300-foot building if the tree and its shadow
are in the same ratio as the building and
its shadow?

(A) 180 ft
(B) 120 ft
(C) 200 ft
(D) 140 ft

238. This graph represents the percentage of
federal income tax based upon annual
income.

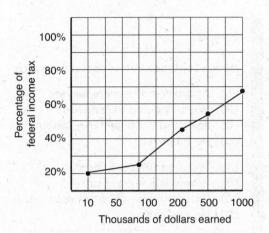

What is the best estimate of the income tax
of someone earning $90,000 per year?

(A) $52,000
(B) $27,000
(C) $9,000
(D) $62,000

If there is still time remaining, you may review your answers.

Sample:

Which sentence below contains an error?

(A) Andrew and he were leaving.
(B) We was going to the store.
(C) Josh and Sarah will buy food for us.   Correct marking of samples
(D) No mistakes.   Ⓐ ● Ⓒ Ⓓ

(A) Work on the car in here.
(B) Where will we end up?
(C) Enter through the front door, please.   Correct marking of samples
(D) No mistakes.   Ⓐ Ⓑ Ⓒ ●

Directions: For questions 239–278, choose the sentence in each group that contains an error in capitalization, punctuation, or usage. If you find no mistakes, select D on your answer sheet.

---

239. (A) Genny and Rhodes make a cute couple.
     (B) Brigid, Becky, and I are inseparable.
     (C) Dan and Nazee ate cake, and played at the birthday party.
     (D) No mistakes.

240. (A) Dr. Garcia gave them and me high recommendations.
     (B) I don't have problems reading the book but I don't have a lot of time tonight.
     (C) Mollie, I'd like you to meet one of my favorite people.
     (D) No mistakes.

241. (A) Patrick knew that Liz wasn't feeling well.
     (B) Either Dr. Avery or Dr. Thomas will be on call.
     (C) She and i are best friends, and we chat on the Internet often.
     (D) No mistakes.

242. (A) I really enjoyed the first two volumes of *The Lord of the Rings.*
     (B) However, I cannot finish the trilogy.
     (C) Because the last volume is checked out of the library.
     (D) No mistakes.

243. (A) I could of listened to them sing all day.
     (B) Keep off the playground until the mud dries.
     (C) We (the students in Lauren's class) all chipped in for a get-well gift.
     (D) No mistakes.

244. (A) I've known Anne's mother, Myra, for many years.
     (B) I didn't fall asleep until after he had began speaking.
     (C) Let's face the music and dance.
     (D) No mistakes.

GO TO NEXT PAGE ➡

245. (A) With an outline, an author knows what they are going to write next.
(B) The purple ribbons in Sadie's hair match her dress beautifully.
(C) Which of the jackets is mine?
(D) No mistakes.

246. (A) To who shall I address this letter?
(B) I'd like to see these people: Susan, Laura, Chuck, and Ingrid.
(C) Augie is gracious, intelligent, and moral.
(D) No mistakes.

247. (A) Tell us all about it, Leo.
(B) Oh my goodness I almost forgot the cake.
(C) It's never too late to begin studying.
(D) No mistakes.

248. (A) Which of the twins can swim fastest?
(B) She ran quickly across the court.
(C) Pass the potatoes, please.
(D) No mistakes.

249. (A) Can you run an errand for Mother?
(B) Nick is always drumming the desk, tapping his feet, or he bobs his head.
(C) Jordan, have you met Lydia?
(D) No mistakes.

250. (A) April is the cruelest month.
(B) The falling leaves of October fill the yard with color.
(C) Its the humidity that really makes us feel the heat.
(D) No mistakes.

251. (A) I can't tell the difference between oranges and tangerines.
(B) Sandy taught me to ride without training wheels.
(C) Dr. Daniel easily recognized her photos.
(D) No mistakes.

252. (A) After the rainstorm, our neighbor washed his car again.
(B) Daphne doesn't like alot of fuss.
(C) The colors of the rainbow are red, orange, yellow, green, blue, indigo, and violet.
(D) No mistakes.

253. (A) Your job pays more than Carrie's job.
(B) My discount card expired last month.
(C) The groundhog didn't see it's shadow this year.
(D) No mistakes.

254. (A) Eric plays the tuba, and Nora plays the trombone.
(B) I can't believe I misplaced my keys again.
(C) The stories of sea adventure always gives me a thrill.
(D) No mistakes.

255. (A) The bus had already departed.
(B) Neither she or I have missed a day of school this year.
(C) They're going to be surprised next fall.
(D) No mistakes.

256. (A) After Anastasia left, the party was over.
(B) "Look out!" cried Sonya.
(C) Boris accepted the award graciously.
(D) No mistakes.

257. (A) I want to see you rested, relaxed, and tomorrow.
(B) Do you recall where you were last Saturday afternoon?
(C) Amy and Lolita are moving to California.
(D) No mistakes.

GO TO NEXT PAGE ➡

258. (A) Kelsey sat beside me during the flight.
(B) Girl Scouts sell cookies; Boy Scouts sell popcorn.
(C) Sam said, "I know I have something to do.
(D) No mistakes.

259. (A) The director of the play was born in St. Louis.
(B) Will you call the restaurant for me.
(C) Branan makes me laugh, but Aaron makes me cry.
(D) No mistakes.

260. (A) The clock in the old, red, tower chimes at noon.
(B) Calculating the costs will not be difficult.
(C) We three always travel together.
(D) No mistakes.

261. (A) Doug, our church organist, is the most talented musician I know.
(B) Include the following in your paragraph, a topic sentence, supporting details, and a closing statement.
(C) Tom and Joanne walked home together.
(D) No mistakes.

262. (A) I was amazed, and delighted by the music.
(B) With such talent, the band will go far.
(C) The rates at the bank change monthly.
(D) No mistakes.

263. (A) Amy had taken piano lessons when she was a child.
(B) Joe and Joan are happy with they're new business.
(C) The book that I borrowed is on the third shelf.
(D) No mistakes.

264. (A) Jorge thought about it and said, "I don't recall sugar as one of the ingredients".
(B) Cameron lives a mile farther down the road.
(C) When the patrons departed, they left their programs in their seats.
(D) No mistakes.

265. (A) Coach Thacker my social studies teacher is a big movie fan.
(B) Is Charlie always so friendly?
(C) We had to memorize the poem "Kubla Khan."
(D) No mistakes.

266. (A) Did you receive any exotic gifts, Mrs. Noel?
(B) On the forth day, he sent me some birds.
(C) The absentee list (which includes tardies) is distributed before lunch.
(D) No mistakes.

267. (A) Harris told us about the funniest book he has ever read.
(B) Everyone begged to watch the game, but the teacher went on with class.
(C) I still enjoy reading childrens' books.
(D) No mistakes.

268. (A) Mary Shelley was a teenager when she wrote her novel "Frankenstein."
(B) The members of the club talked among themselves until the meeting started.
(C) After the encounter with the skunk, our yard smelled bad for days.
(D) No mistakes.

269. (A) The fog was so thick that we could hardly see.
(B) I ordered the buffet: pizza, pasta, breadsticks, and salad.
(C) Several empty desks stand between you and me.
(D) No mistakes.

GO TO NEXT PAGE ➡

270. (A) Spring vacation usually takes place during April.
(B) Which Doctor did you see?
(C) How, in your opinion, can we avoid such problems?
(D) No mistakes.

271. (A) I was excepted into the club last year.
(B) Please sit down and tell me your story.
(C) My grandmother set up a bank account for me when I was born.
(D) No mistakes.

272. (A) Does anyone collect box tops anymore?
(B) When I was a little boy, I used to wait patiently for the mailman.
(C) If Mr. Cerulean would assign less homework, he would have less papers to grade.
(D) No mistakes.

273. (A) Rachel has been planning a trip to Italy.
(B) The woman who designed the building also has a degree in history.
(C) The river flowed over the rocks and under the bridge.
(D) No mistakes.

274. (A) Their truck can pull a lot of weight.
(B) Many members of my family are allergic to milk.
(C) The special affects in the movie were amazing.
(D) No mistakes.

275. (A) Leah and Jeff were both in my class.
(B) Amber, Sumi, and me formed a jazz band.
(C) Which of these cartons is on sale?
(D) No mistakes.

276. (A) The movie, by the way, was too long.
(B) She felt sick, so she went to lay down.
(C) Michael can bowl well when he practices.
(D) No mistakes.

277. (A) For example, most people choose their own screen names.
(B) "Have you eaten?" asked Richard.
(C) Lie your head on the pillow and sleep.
(D) No mistakes.

278. (A) Emily is exceptionally polite.
(B) Of course, we always love to see Julian.
(C) Both of them are always welcome.
(D) No mistakes.

GO TO NEXT PAGE ➡

279. (A) On July 4th, we celebrate Independence Day.
   (B) He was to popular to be defeated in the election.
   (C) She wore the most exquisite jewelry to the wedding.
   (D) No mistakes.

280. (A) I declined the roll of Hamlet, considering it too demanding on my memory.
   (B) The eighth grade is a difficult one, filled with transition.
   (C) He used to write a humorous column for the newspaper.
   (D) No mistakes.

281. (A) I don't recall ever having a president who could pronounce the word "nuclear."
   (B) The ceiling appeared too low in the apartment.
   (C) I never realized how many nickels I had acquired in change.
   (D) No mistakes.

282. (A) His forehead was definitely at least four inches in height.
   (B) I hope I'm not mistaken, but aren't you the famous psychologist on television?
   (C) I get weary of the cold weather during Febuary, March, and April.
   (D) No mistakes.

283. (A) I try not to be illegible, so people won't think I'm illiterate.
   (B) Due to the sheriff's couragous efforts, no one was hurt.
   (C) Save your receipts; you can redeem them at school.
   (D) No mistakes.

284. (A) Should we view King Richard as a villain or a conqueror?
   (B) Pam said she'd meet me at the libary, but she must have been detained elsewhere.
   (C) He viewed computers as unnecessarily complicated.
   (D) No mistakes.

285. (A) The classes joked that the temperature in the room was positively freezing.
   (B) We have a lot of athletes attending our school.
   (C) We occasionally have to write summaries of certain books of literature.
   (D) No mistakes.

286. (A) Although I felt confident, I was not arrogant.
   (B) The genuine article felt heavier in my grasp.
   (C) We can consider the whole controversy as an educational experience.
   (D) No mistakes.

287. (A) I assumed a long speech was unnesessary for this occasion.
   (B) Bowing to the sheik was a respectful gesture.
   (C) Aren't you curious about what's in the shipment?
   (D) No mistakes.

288. (A) Oh, she can be mischevious when she's in a spunky mood.
   (B) The banquet included some of my favorite vegetables.
   (C) I predict great success on my exams.
   (D) No mistakes.

GO TO NEXT PAGE ➡

289. Graymalkin hates to be bathed, _____ she doesn't like to be dirty, either.

    (A) because
    (B) yet
    (C) for instance
    (D) however

290. Sheila wanted to watch the end of the awards program, _____ it was past her bedtime.

    (A) however
    (B) but
    (C) because
    (D) thus

291. Which of the following expresses the idea most clearly?

    (A) She brought brevity, she brought wit, and she brought style to the broadcast.
    (B) Brevity, wit, and style were brought by her to the broadcast.
    (C) To the broadcast she brought brevity, wit, as well as style.
    (D) She brought brevity, wit, and style to the broadcast.

292. Which of the following expresses the idea most clearly?

    (A) Erasmus Darwin was Charles Darwin's grandfather; he excelled in many areas. Some of them were science, philosophy, and poetry.
    (B) Erasmus Darwin, who was the grandfather of Charles Darwin, excelled in many areas: science, philosophy, and poetry.
    (C) Charles Darwin's grandfather, Erasmus Darwin, excelled in many areas, including science, philosophy, and poetry.
    (D) Erasmus Darwin, Charles Darwin's grandfather, excelled in many areas; these included science and philosophy and poetry.

293. Choose the group of words that best completes this sentence:

    According to legend, _____ .

    (A) the Grand Canyon was created by the ax dragging of Paul Bunyan
    (B) Paul Bunyan created the Grand Canyon by dragging his ax
    (C) Paul Bunyan dragged his ax, thereby creating what is called the Grand Canyon
    (D) the Grand Canyon was created by Paul Bunyan, who dragged his ax

GO TO NEXT PAGE ➡

294. Which of the following sentences best fits under the topic "Horse Mythology"?

(A) Horses are related to the hippopotamus.
(B) Pegasus is the famed winged horse in Greek legend.
(C) The Kentucky Derby is the most famous horse race in the United States.
(D) None of these.

295. Which topic is best suited for a one-paragraph essay?

(A) Shakespeare and King James
(B) Neanderthal Man
(C) World War II
(D) None of these.

296. Which sentence does NOT belong in the following paragraph?

(1) After a rainfall, we often see earthworms on the sidewalk. (2) This is because worms, like us, have to breathe, and the ground is saturated with water when it rains. (3) In order to survive, the worms have to temporarily leave their homes until some of the water evaporates. (4) Earthworms are also called Night Crawlers or Angleworms.

(A) Sentence 1
(B) Sentence 2
(C) Sentence 3
(D) Sentence 4

297. Where should the sentence "We know it today as the pretzel" fit into this paragraph?

(1) In the Middle Ages, monks would give rewards to children who learned their lessons and prayers. (2) One of these prizes was a snack called a pretiola, which is Latin for "little reward." (3) This snack was made of strips of dough, looped around to look like a pair of arms folded in prayer.

(A) between 1 and 2
(B) between 2 and 3
(C) after 3
(D) The sentence does not fit in this paragraph.

298. Where should the sentence "To throw a curve, the pitcher twists his wrist during the throw" fit into this paragraph?

(1) Curve balls are difficult for batters to hit. (2) This spin on the ball creates less air pressure under the ball than on the top. (3) This, in turn, causes the ball to drop faster than it ordinarily would, confusing the batter.

(A) between 1 and 2
(B) between 2 and 3
(C) after 3
(D) The sentence does not fit in this paragraph.

STOP

If there is still time remaining, you may review your answers.

ANSWER KEY
HSPT Practice Exam 2

SUBTEST 1 VERBAL

1. **D**	16. **D**	31. **C**	46. **D**
2. **C**	17. **D**	32. **D**	47. **A**
3. **B**	18. **C**	33. **B**	48. **D**
4. **A**	19. **B**	34. **D**	49. **A**
5. **C**	20. **A**	35. **A**	50. **D**
6. **A**	21. **A**	36. **A**	51. **D**
7. **A**	22. **A**	37. **D**	52. **C**
8. **B**	23. **A**	38. **A**	53. **D**
9. **A**	24. **A**	39. **A**	54. **A**
10. **B**	25. **A**	40. **B**	55. **A**
11. **C**	26. **A**	41. **B**	56. **D**
12. **A**	27. **C**	42. **A**	57. **A**
13. **B**	28. **C**	43. **A**	58. **A**
14. **C**	29. **A**	44. **B**	59. **A**
15. **A**	30. **D**	45. **B**	60. **A**

SUBTEST 2 QUANTITATIVE

61. **C**	74. **D**	87. **D**	100. **C**
62. **D**	75. **B**	88. **A**	101. **D**
63. **B**	76. **D**	89. **D**	102. **B**
64. **C**	77. **B**	90. **C**	103. **A**
65. **A**	78. **B**	91. **C**	104. **D**
66. **D**	79. **D**	92. **C**	105. **D**
67. **A**	80. **B**	93. **A**	106. **D**
68. **A**	81. **A**	94. **A**	107. **A**
69. **B**	82. **B**	95. **D**	108. **A**
70. **B**	83. **A**	96. **B**	109. **B**
71. **D**	84. **B**	97. **D**	110. **A**
72. **A**	85. **D**	98. **D**	111. **A**
73. **C**	86. **A**	99. **D**	112. **A**

ANSWER KEY
HSPT Practice Exam 2

SUBTEST 3 READING

113. **C**	129. **D**	145. **C**	161. **A**
114. **B**	130. **B**	146. **A**	162. **B**
115. **C**	131. **B**	147. **C**	163. **A**
116. **A**	132. **A**	148. **C**	164. **C**
117. **A**	133. **B**	149. **C**	165. **A**
118. **C**	134. **C**	150. **B**	166. **D**
119. **D**	135. **C**	151. **A**	167. **C**
120. **A**	136. **A**	152. **D**	168. **D**
121. **C**	137. **B**	153. **A**	169. **C**
122. **B**	138. **A**	154. **D**	170. **B**
123. **D**	139. **C**	155. **D**	171. **D**
124. **C**	140. **A**	156. **B**	172. **B**
125. **A**	141. **D**	157. **A**	173. **C**
126. **B**	142. **B**	158. **B**	174. **D**
127. **D**	143. **B**	159. **A**	
128. **B**	144. **C**	160. **C**	

SUBTEST 4 MATHEMATICS

175. **B**	191. **D**	207. **D**	223. **B**
176. **D**	192. **A**	208. **B**	224. **D**
177. **D**	193. **D**	209. **A**	225. **B**
178. **C**	194. **D**	210. **B**	226. **A**
179. **A**	195. **A**	211. **D**	227. **B**
180. **B**	196. **C**	212. **B**	228. **B**
181. **B**	197. **B**	213. **A**	229. **B**
182. **A**	198. **D**	214. **D**	230. **C**
183. **D**	199. **C**	215. **A**	231. **D**
184. **D**	200. **D**	216. **C**	232. **C**
185. **C**	201. **D**	217. **D**	233. **C**
186. **C**	202. **A**	218. **C**	234. **A**
187. **A**	203. **C**	219. **B**	235. **D**
188. **C**	204. **B**	220. **A**	236. **B**
189. **B**	205. **C**	221. **B**	237. **A**
190. **C**	206. **D**	222. **D**	238. **B**

ANSWER KEY
HSPT Practice Exam 2

SUBTEST 5   LANGUAGE

239. **C**	254. **C**	269. **D**	284. **B**
240. **B**	255. **B**	270. **B**	285. **B**
241. **C**	256. **D**	271. **A**	286. **D**
242. **C**	257. **A**	272. **C**	287. **A**
243. **A**	258. **C**	273. **D**	288. **A**
244. **B**	259. **B**	274. **C**	289. **B**
245. **A**	260. **A**	275. **B**	290. **B**
246. **A**	261. **B**	276. **B**	291. **D**
247. **B**	262. **A**	277. **C**	292. **C**
248. **A**	263. **B**	278. **D**	293. **B**
249. **B**	264. **A**	279. **B**	294. **B**
250. **C**	265. **A**	280. **A**	295. **D**
251. **D**	266. **B**	281. **D**	296. **D**
252. **B**	267. **C**	282. **C**	297. **C**
253. **C**	268. **A**	283. **B**	298. **A**

Subtest 1   Verbal

1. **(D)** The other choices *cover* your foot.

2. **(C)** The other words deal with increasing the size or strength. To *dilute* something is to weaken it.

3. **(B)** A *hero* is the opposite of a *villain*; an *antagonist* is the opposite of a *protagonist*.

4. **(A)** *Stationary* is *unmoving*.

5. **(C)** Uncertain. Drs. Casey and Zorba are not compared in the first two statements.
Z C
K

6. **(A)** The other choices are specific types of toys.

7. **(A)** The other choices are specific types of furniture.

8. **(B)** *Uncover* is a verb. The others are nouns meaning a type of show.

9. **(A)** Something *resilient* springs back. Choices B and C mean the opposite of this. Choice D means calm.

10. **(B)** The other choices involve deception.

11. **(C)** A *donor* is a *contributor*—one who donates.

12. **(A)** A *shrill* sound is a high-pitched, *piercing* one.

13. **(B)** A *drill* makes a *hole*. A *blender* makes *batter*. (It does not *make* flour, eggs, or milk.)

14. **(C)** We are not told that these men are on the coaching staff.

15. **(A)** Something lethargic is slow and drowsy.

16. **(D)** A *solicitor* is not necessarily a scholar or wise person.

17. **(D)** The *government* is not a building.

18. **(C)** To scrutinize something is to look closely at it.

19. **(B)** To *plunder* means to steal; its opposite is to *restore*.

20. **(A)** A *coat* is a larger version of a *jacket*; a *chair* is a larger version of a *stool*.

21. **(A)** A *financial* profile examines *money*, while a *psychological* profile examines the *mind*.

22. **(A)** This is trickier. Your chart may look like this: Jack is three years older than Ralph. Peterkin is two years younger than Ralph.
J + 3
R
P – 2

This can be rewritten showing Ralph as two years older than Peterkin.

J + 3
R + 2

23. **(A)** *Punctual* means on time—*prompt*.

24. **(A)** M
T
J

25. **(A)** *Notorious* and *infamous* both mean well known for something bad.

26. **(A)** Choices B and C are synonyms, so they can't both be correct. *Obscure* means unclear.

27. **(C)** A *comma* cannot end sentences.

28. **(C)** A *counterfeit* bill is a copy. It is *false*.

29. **(A)** J
P
A

30. **(D)** Choices A, B, and C are *specific* sciences.

31. **(C)** A *baseball* player wears a *cap*; a *cyclist* wears a *helmet*.

32. **(D)** The other choices are smells.

33. **(B)** H
W
L

34. **(D)** The other choices are synonyms for counting or checking.

35. **(A)** Something *rampant* is out of control.

36. **(A)** *Affluent* means wealthy; its opposite is *destitute*.

37. **(D)** *Earnest* means serious. It is not *ridiculous*.

38. **(A)**

39. **(A)** *Meager* means poor. Its opposite is *abundant*.

40. **(B)** A *puppy's* foot is a *paw*; a *colt's* foot is a *hoof*.

41. **(B)** *Mal* is one of those negative prefixes. A *maladroit* person is not *skillful* (not adroit).

42. **(A)** S
C
L

43. **(A)** The other choices are *specific* rooms.

44. **(B)** Your *nose* is part of your *face*; your *finger* is part of your *hand*.

45. **(B)** *Jeopardy* is danger.

46. **(D)** The other choices are places.

47. **(A)** *Meticulous* means careful or precise. Its opposite is *haphazard*.

48. **(D)** Someone who is *modest* has no *vanity*; someone who is *innocent* has no *guilt*.

49. **(A)** C
    L
    H

50. **(D)** *Decrepit* means weak or feeble. Its opposite is *robust* or *healthy*.

51. **(D)** You *play* at *recess*; you *eat* at *breakfast*.

52. **(C)** Uncertain. The best we can say is this:
    F M
    P

53. **(D)** A *DVD* does not have a keypad.

54. **(A)** *Hygienic* means clean or sanitary. Think of good hygiene.

55. **(A)** B
    V
    H

56. **(D)** Choices A, B, and C are synonyms.

57. **(A)** *Pernicious* means *harmful*. You might have narrowed this down to choices A and D, since they are opposites.

58. **(A)** L
    G
    W

59. **(A)** A *desert* is *arid*; a *rain forest* is *humid*.

60. **(A)** C
    P
    S

Subtest 2 Quantitative

61. **(C)**

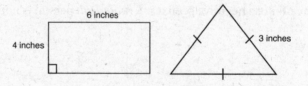

All sides of the equilateral triangle are 3 inches. The opposite sides of the rectangle are congruent. Find both perimeters and substitute into the choices.

Perimeter of the rectangle = 6 inches + 6 inches + 4 inches + 4 inches = 20 inches

Perimeter of the triangle = 3 inches + 3 inches + 3 inches = 9 inches

The perimeter of the rectangle is 11 inches more than the perimeter of the equilateral triangle.

$$20 \text{ inches} = 9 \text{ inches} + 11 \text{ inches} \ \checkmark$$

62. **(D)** Each term is decreased by 2.1 with the number 18 as the alternating term in between.

$$21 - 2.1 = 18.9$$
$$18.9 - 2.1 = 16.8$$
$$16.8 - 2.1 = 14.7$$
$$14.7 - 2.1 = 12.6$$

63. **(B)** Let x = the unknown number and change 40% to 0.40.

$$0.40x = \frac{1}{2} \cdot 60 + 2$$

$$0.40x = 30 + 2$$
$$0.40x = 32$$
$$100(0.40x) = 100(32)$$
$$\frac{40x}{40} = \frac{3,200}{40}$$
$$x = 80$$

64. **(C)**

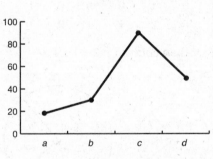

Determine the values of a, b, c, and d, and then substitute into (A), (B), (C), and (D).

$$a \approx 20$$
$$b \approx 30$$
$$c \approx 90$$
$$d \approx 50$$

$$d = a + b$$
$$50 = 20 + 30$$
$$50 = 50$$

65. **(A)** Each succeeding number in the series is one-third the previous number.

$$\frac{1}{3} \cdot \frac{2}{3} = \frac{2}{9}$$

66. **(D)** Let x = the unknown number, and change 60% to 0.60.

$$\frac{2}{3}x = 0.60 \cdot 40 + 18$$

$$\frac{2}{3}x = 24 + 18$$

$$3\left(\frac{2}{3}x\right) = (42)3$$

$$\frac{2x}{2} = \frac{126}{2}$$

$$x = 63$$

67. **(A)**

a	b	c	d	e	f
	♠	♥			♥
			♦		
♥	♦	♦		♣	♦
		♣	♣		
♥	♦				♠

Count the number of ♥s, ♠s, ♦s, and ♣s in each column and substitute.

	a	b	c	d	e	f
♥	2	0	1	0	0	1
♣	0	0	1	1	1	0
♠	0	1	0	0	0	1
♦	0	2	1	1	0	1

Column a has one more ♥ than column f: $2 = 1 + 1$ ✔

68. **(A)**

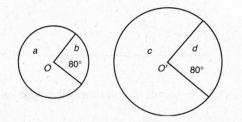

Since circle O' is larger than circle O and the central angles are congruent, Area d > Area b and Area c > Area a.

Area c > Area a ✔

69. **(B)** There are three letters between each two given letters in the series.

M, N̲, O̲, P̲, **Q**

70. **(B)** Let x = the unknown number.

$$x = \frac{2}{3} \cdot 60 + 8$$

$$x = 40 + 8$$

$$x = 48$$

71. **(D)** There are two series here: 92, 96, 100, . . . , which increases by 4, and 17, 15, 13, . . . , which decreases by 2.

$$100 + 4 = 104$$

72. **(A)** Add up all the hours and divide by 3, the number of students.

$$\bar{x} = \frac{(t+4)+(t)+(t-2)}{3} = \frac{3t+2}{3}$$

73. **(C)** The difference between any terms is 2.3 (i.e., 11.9 − 9.6 = 2.3). So, we'll add:

$$16.5 + 2.3 = 18.8$$

74. **(D)** Let x = the unknown number.

$$x = \frac{3}{4} \cdot 24 - 12$$
$$x = 18 - 12$$
$$x = 6$$

75. **(B)** The series increases by four units and then decreases by one unit.

$$17 - 1 = 16$$

76. **(D)**

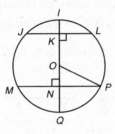

OQ, OP, and OI are all radii and are congruent.

$OP > ON$: OP is a radius, while ON is only a part of radius OQ. Therefore, the statement is true. ✔

77. **(B)**

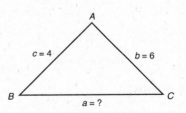

The sum of two sides of a triangle is always larger than the third side.

(A) $a = 10$: If $a = 10$, then $6 + 4$ will form a straight line and will coincide with side a. No triangle will be formed.

(B) $a < 10$: If $a < 10$, then sides 6 and 4 will form a triangle. ✔

(C) $a = 11$: If $a = 11$, then sides 4 and 6 will never meet and no triangle will be formed.

(D) $a > 10$: If $a > 10$, then sides 4 and 6 will never meet and no triangle will be formed.

78. **(B)**

$$\pi = \frac{22}{7}, \, r = 7, \, h = 6$$

$$V = \pi r^2 h$$

$$V = \left(\frac{22}{7}\right)(7)(7)(6)$$

$$V = 924 \text{ cu ft}$$

79. **(D)** The series forms the pattern $2^2, 2^3, 3^2, 3^3, 4^2, 4^3, \ldots$

$$5^2, \, 5^3 \text{ or } 25, \, 125$$

80. **(B)** Let x = the unknown number.

$$x - 54 = \frac{4}{5} \cdot 12 \cdot 5$$

$$x - 54 = 48$$

$$x = 102$$

81. **(A)** The number 9 is inserted into alternate positions in the series $24, 21, 18, 15, \ldots$ Each successive number in the series is reduced by 3.

$$24, 9, 21, 9, 18, 9, 15, \underline{9}, \underline{12}, \ldots$$

82. **(B)**

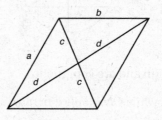

The only information we are certain about is that $c < d$.

$$c < d$$
$$\underline{+\,a = +\,a}$$
$$a + c < a + d$$

83. **(A)** Let x = the unknown number.

$$x = \frac{3}{5} \cdot 40 + 9$$

$$x = 24 + 9$$

$$x = 33$$

84. **(B)** The numbers are increasing in the pattern $+2, +3, +4, +5, +6, \ldots$

$$58 + 7 = 65$$

85. **(D)**

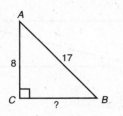

Use the Pythagorean Theorem.

$$a^2 + b^2 = c^2$$
$$a^2 + 8^2 = 17^2$$
$$a^2 + 64 = 289$$
$$\underline{\ -64\quad -64}$$
$$a^2 = 225$$
$$a = \sqrt{225}$$
$$a = 15$$

86. **(A)**

	a	b	c
●	4	5	3
□	4	3	3
○	2	2	4

There are 2 more ●s in (b) than □s in (c).

$$5 = 3 + 2 \ ✔$$

87. **(D)** Let x = the unknown number.

$$\frac{5}{8}x = \frac{1}{3} \cdot 60$$

$$8\left(\frac{5}{8}x\right) = (20)8$$

$$\frac{5x}{5} = \frac{160}{5}$$

$$x = 32$$

88. **(A)** The numbers are increasing and decreasing in the pattern –2, +1, –2, +1, –2, ...

$$61 + 1 = 62$$

89. (D)

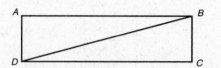

The longest side is *BD*, the diagonal.

$$BD > AB$$

90. (C) There are two missing letters between each term of the series.

<u>B</u>, C, D, <u>E</u>, F, G, <u>H</u>, I, J, <u>K</u>, L, M, <u>N</u>, O, P, **<u>Q</u>**

91. (C) Just substitute the given numbers for the symbols in the algebraic expression.

$$5 \cdot \blacksquare + 3 \cdot \square - 4 \cdot *$$
$$5 \cdot 4 + 3 \cdot 3 - 4 \cdot 2$$
$$20 + 9 - 8$$
$$21$$

92. (C) The pattern is to double and then increase by one.

$$2 \times 39 = 78$$

93. (A) Let x = the unknown number.

$$\frac{2}{3}x - 25 = 3 \cdot 12 + 5$$

$$\frac{2}{3}x - 25 = 36 + 5$$

$$\frac{2}{3}x - 25 = 41$$

$$3\left(\frac{2}{3}x\right) = (66)3$$

$$\frac{2x}{2} = \frac{198}{2}$$

$$x = 99$$

94. (A)

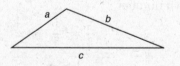

Change the words into algebraic form.

$$c = 2a$$
$$a = b - 3$$

Therefore,
$$c = 2a = 2(b - 3).$$

95. **(D)** Box C is double the size of any of the smaller boxes, so we can just add any other four boxes to equal the area of B + C + F.

$$B + C + F = A + D + E + G$$

96. **(B)** Let x = the unknown number.

$$\frac{36}{x} = \frac{5}{8} \cdot 80 - 41$$

$$\frac{36}{x} = 50 - 41$$

$$\frac{36}{x} = 9$$

$$36 = 9x$$

$$4 = x$$

97. **(D)**

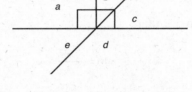

From the diagram, m$\angle a° = 90°$ and m$\angle b$ + m$\angle c = 90°$.

$$m\angle b + m\angle c = 90°$$

98. **(D)** The numbers are increasing in squares.

$$1^2, 2^2, 3^2, 4^2, \underline{5^2}, \ldots$$

99. **(D)** Remember, when we multiply two negatives, the result is a positive and when we multiply a positive and a negative, the result is a negative.

$$-4(-2)^3 = -4(-2)(-2)(-2) = +8(-2)(-2) = -16(-2) = +32$$

100. **(C)**

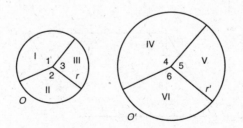

Let's eliminate the possible answers, and just select the answer we're certain about.

Since Circle O' > Circle O, the corresponding sectors are unequal in the same order.

$$\text{Area IV + Area V > Area I + Area III}$$

101. **(D)**

Count the number of dark and hollow figures and subtract.

$$8\,\blacklozenge \qquad 9\,\blacktriangle$$
$$\underline{-\;5\,\lozenge \qquad 8\,\triangle}$$
$$3\,\blacklozenge \qquad 1\,\blacktriangle$$

102. **(B)** The series repeats.

$$2, 3, 6, \underline{\mathbf{2}}, 3, 6, 2, 3, 6, \ldots$$

103. **(A)** Let x = the unknown number.

$$8x - \frac{2}{3} \cdot 48 = \frac{160}{4}$$
$$8x - 32 = 40$$
$$8x = 72$$
$$x = 9$$

104. **(D)** Simplify (a), (b), and (c), and substitute into (A), (B), (C), and (D).

(a) $5^2 = 5 \cdot 5 = 25$

(b) $3^4 = 3 \cdot 3 \cdot 3 \cdot 3 = 81$

(c) $2^5 = 2 \cdot 2 \cdot 2 \cdot 2 \cdot 2 = 32$

(D) (b) > (c) and (b) > (a)
   81 > 32 and 81 > 25 ✔

105. **(D)**

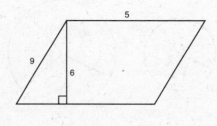

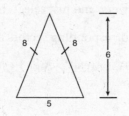

Area (parallelogram) $= b \cdot h$
$$= 5 \cdot 6 = 30$$

Area (triangle) $= \frac{1}{2} b \cdot h$

$$= \frac{1}{2}(5)(6) = 15$$

Perimeter (parallelogram) $= 5 + 9 + 5 + 9 = 28$

Perimeter (triangle) $= 5 + 8 + 8 = 21$

Perimeter of parallelogram > Perimeter of triangle + 5

$$5 + 5 + 9 + 9 > 21 + 5$$
$$28 > 26 \; ✔$$

106. **(D)** The series is decreasing by $2\frac{1}{2}$.

$$24\frac{1}{2},\, 22,\, 19\frac{1}{2},\, 17,\, 14\frac{1}{2},\, 12,\, 9\frac{1}{2},\, \ldots$$

107. **(A)**

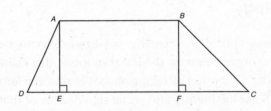

From all of the possible answers, select the best answer.

$$BC > AE$$

108. **(A)**

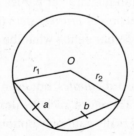

All radii in the same circle are congruent. Lines a and b are congruent. Select the best possible answer from the given choices.

The two radii are congruent, as are lines a and b, so $r_1 + b = a + r_2$.

109. **(B)** Let $x =$ the unknown number.

$$x^2 = 7 \cdot 8 + 8$$
$$x^2 = 56 + 8$$
$$x^2 = 64$$
$$x = \pm 8$$

110. **(A)** The Roman numbers are decreasing by 3, while the Arabic numbers are increasing by 2.

$$XII - III = IX$$

111. **(A)** Let x = the unknown number.

$$8x = \frac{7}{9} \cdot 81 - 15$$
$$8x = 63 - 15$$
$$8x = 48$$
$$x = 6$$

112. **(A)** The series is divided into groups of three. Within each group, 2 is added to the first and second terms to arrive at the second and third members of the group, respectively. The next group begins with the second member of the previous group and the pattern is repeated.

$$3, 5, 7, \quad 5, 7, 9, \quad 7, 9, 11,$$
$$9, 11, 13, \quad \underline{\mathbf{11, 13, 15, \ldots}}$$

Subtest 3 Reading

113. **(C)** The final paragraph of the reading passage seems to be a transitional piece. Breaking down the organization of the piece supports this claim. Paragraphs one and two catch the reader's attention by telling about the plot of a famous novel. Paragraphs three and four discuss the literary and social significance of that novel. Paragraph five then relates the underlying message of the novel—a warning against engaging in activities we don't really understand. The paragraph ends with a sentence that bridges the discussion from one of the novel to a subsequent discussion of examples against which the author will warn us. Therefore, it is unlikely that the author will discuss yet another novel (choice A), analyze random character names (choice B), or return to the (very) brief mention of the movie version of *Frankenstein* (choice D). More likely, the discussion will turn to modern topics that define what the author means by "Frankensteins" (choice C).

114. **(B)** You probably know the word *equates*, but even if you don't, you can identify the root word for *equal* within it. Therefore, pick the definition that best matches with the meaning of equal. Choice B is really your only option.

115. **(C)** Since the author never specifically states his/her opinion on cloning, you do have to make an educated guess. However, since the author seems to agree with Mary Shelley regarding the foolishness of engaging in activity we understand little and control less, it is likely that the author will not be liberal in supporting many controversial topics. Cloning currently raises a great deal of debate, nor do we know much about the repercussions that will stem from experimenting with it. Therefore, choice C is your best answer.

116. **(A)** Re-reading (or memory) will help you remember that the text specifically traces back the word "monster" from the Latin term *monstra*.

117. **(A)** The question is asking you to make a connection between the actions of Dr. Frankenstein and that of one of the individuals listed. All four of the individuals are well known for various reasons, some positive, others negative. However, only one presumed to put himself on par with God, and that is Lucifer.

118. **(C)** Re-reading (or memory) clearly states that Frankenstein dies an "icy, watery" death—in other words drowning.

119. **(D)** The author does not mention feminism (aside from the slight hint, perhaps, by stressing slightly the revelation that the author of *Frankenstein* was a woman), nor does the author say anything overtly to get us to read or write (although s/he does try to interest us in the text, generally speaking). The author *does* in the final paragraph attempt to get us to use good judgment when deciding how to live our lives and explore various new fields. Therefore, choice D is the correct response.

120. **(A)** Choices C and D are intended to distract you simply by incorporating the word *monster* into the title. Reject them. Choice B is a little more compelling because the passage discusses story tellers, and the suggested title is a common opening to a scary story. The best choice, however, is choice A. The passage talks a great deal about how doing things before we've properly prepared to do them is a bad idea. Playing with fire is also a bad idea. Therefore, Playing with Fire is the best selection for a title.

121. **(C)** The word *glories* can be tricky since it can either be the plural of the word *glory* or the present tense form of the verb *glory*. Choices A and D, therefore, are present to trick you; they are plural forms of nouns. Choice D, indeed, is tempting since you may know that a flower named the Morning Glory (often shortened to "glories") exists. Choices B and C are even more tempting since either can be the plural of a noun or the present tense of a verb. The best choice, however, is choice C since the definition of *flag* means to *falter*, while the definition of *triumph* means *to take pride in*. Taking pride in something is the best synonym available here for the word *glories*.

122. **(B)** While all the names appear in the text, a quick rescan of the material—or your memory—will reveal that the answer is Robert De Niro, choice B

123. **(D)** You can tell from the context that nefarious is meant to be a negative word; of the four definitional choices, only choice D can be construed as negative.

124. **(C)** You can rule out choice B, since, by anyone's standards, the balloon bombs were unsuccessful (a dud, if you will). Similarly, you can omit choice D because we Americans didn't get much opportunity to be brave because the mission was not successful. Choice A is not an option because the idea seems clever, resourceful, and cheap—just unlucky. Therefore, the best answer is choice C.

125. **(A)** The article makes no mention of herons, clouds, or stones; by process of elimination, you can select choice A.

126. **(B)** Re-reading (or memory) helps you pick out the only true fact in the piece—the fact that women made the bombs.

127. **(D)** With any luck, your vocabulary study allows you to recall that the definition of *infinitesimal* is *small*. The other words available mean huge (choices A and C) or have no relation at all to the word *infinitesimal* (choice B).

128. **(B)** A quick fact check of the text reassures you that the only reason that does not appear in the text is choice B.

129. **(D)** Choices A, B, and C are wrong. First, the author does say that the plan seemed foolhardy, but that was not the main point of that paragraph. Choice B contradicts what the author says; reject it. Choice C is your second best option, but don't select second-best. The best option is choice D; why else would the author, who could have ended the piece with simply a discussion of a failed terrorist attack, instead bring into the discussion the cultural—and symbolically opposed—superstition about how making paper cranes can bring peace (not war) to the world?

130. **(B)** A *dud* is something that doesn't work. A *live bomb*, on the other hand, does work. Therefore the two words are opposites. Choices A and C both offer you two of the same types of things (holidays and sports). Choice D gives you a single emotion just at different degrees of intensity (love is a much stronger version of like). The only real option is choice B.

131. **(B)** A quick re-reading (or your memory) proves to you that the answer is choice B.

132. **(A)** Again, a quick re-reading (or your memory) proves to you that the answer is choice A.

133. **(B)** The article is mostly informational, sincerely interested, and unbiased (not mocking—choice C—or patronizing—choice D—or persuasive—choice A); therefore, you can rule out all choices but choice B.

134. **(C)** The writers of the test are trying to make sure you do not confuse *Baule* with homonyms (choices A or D). The writers are also testing your knowledge of basic geography (choice B). The only choice backed up by reading the passage is choice C.

135. **(C)** Re-reading (or memory) helps you pick out the correct statement that it is appropriate to give gifts of clothing to the sculpture of the spirit spouse. The other objects may also be appropriate, but the article does not specifically state as much.

136. **(A)** Scanning the word *placated*, you notice a significant similarity to the word *please*. Therefore, compare the word *pleased* to the remaining definitions; only choice A comes close to matching in meaning.

137. **(B)** The idea of giving the spirit spouse a gift does not, according to the article, occur unless the spirit spouse is bothering the living person. The person is giving the gift in order to appease the spirit spouse. This is, put another way, a bribe.

138. **(A)** The only option here, as your vocab study will support, is choice A. The word *witnesses* really has no connection to the discussion at all. Choices C and D are there to confuse you. *Reminders* looks a little like *remainders*, so, if you are moving too quickly through the test, you might get tripped up here. Furthermore, a *remainder* can be scraps of *cloth* sold by stores at reduced prices. However, as stated in the first sentence, choice A is the only correct choice.

139. **(C)** The definition of the word *revere* is *respect*. The other words are simply words that start with the same original sound.

140. **(A)** Nothing in the article gives any indication that the author has strong negative feelings on the topic; rule out choice B. The author states that we have facts gathered by anthropologists who recorded beliefs in spirit spouses; therefore, rule out choice C since facts cancel out rumors. The author rejects choice D. We know this because she debunks the idea that a spirit spouse is "unusual," coming down firmly on the side of giving the spirit spouse concept the benefit of the doubt. The only correct answer is choice A.

141. **(D)** A quick scan of the passage reveals that the country not listed is Guam.

142. **(B)** None of the emotions listed are positive; rule out choice A. We don't know what animals can or cannot feel, although we can certainly speculate; rule out choice C. The words are clearly not listed in alphabetical order; rule out choice D. You are left with the correct answer, choice B.

143. **(B)** Re-reading the text (or memory) tells you that the article advises you to go ahead and change your first answer on a multiple-choice test since, statistically speaking, you are probably doing the right thing.

144. **(C)** Re-reading the text (or memory) tells you that the article thinks that because women suffer more than men from low self-esteem, they are more likely to change a right answer to a wrong answer through second-guessing themselves.

145. **(C)** Re-reading the text (or memory) of the article tells you that people change from a wrong answer to a wrong answer 25% of the time.

146. **(A)** The article gives advice on acing multiple-choice tests, and the people most likely to desire such advice are students. Therefore, of the options, students might be most likely to find this information from their school guidance offices. Choices C (teen mag) and D (pop culture mag) are close runners up (because they make their living doling out snippets of wisdom), but they are not as reliable. Choice B would be the least likely place to find this article.

147. **(C)** You can rule out choice A since attribute has nothing to do with placing blame on anyone. You might consider choice B, since we all have attributes (characteristics by which we can be described), and that fact might make us think of the word *describe*. The two best answers are choices C and D. Nevertheless, you are looking for a word that means something like *links with* or *looks to*; choice C is your best answer.

148. **(C)** Re-reading the text (or memory) tells you that these researchers are based in Ontario.

149. **(C)** The article discusses the topic of whether or not to change your answers on a multiple-choice test. It does not discuss cheating (rule out choice A) or people's behavior in society (rule out choice D). Choice B is more compelling, but indecision is a broad term that can apply to any aspect of life; choice C is better because it clearly narrows the discussion down to a more manageable level.

150. **(B)** Re-reading the text (or memory) tells you that the article states that 50% of the time people change their first answer on a multiple-choice exam from wrong to right.

151. **(A)** Reject choices C and D; these are words that describe *inquiries*, and the author is discussing something more certain than a question. You can also reject choice B; a *review* is biased and opinion-based, but the passage discusses scientists bent on finding facts. The best answer is choice A. The scientists are reporting their *results* or what they *observed* while experimenting.

152. **(D)** A quick re-reading of the passage reveals that the only viable answer is choice D.

153. **(A)** This is a word you need to know because it can trick you. It doesn't mean what you might think. (It has nothing to do with odor.) Something *odious* is detestable, repugnant, and loathsome.

154. **(D)** Something *petty* is small (think *petite*) and insignificant, so the word *unimportant* is the closest choice.

155. **(D)** An *agenda* is a *plan* or a list of things to do. It is related to the words *agent* (a doer) and *agency* (an organization to do something).

156. **(B)** The root *luc* or *luce* means light. Something *lucid* is bright, light, or *clear*.

157. **(A)** The ancient Greeks called the west wind *Zephyr*. It can now refer to any gentle *breeze*.

158. **(B)** If you thought that *enumerate* has to do with numbers or counting (as in *numerals*), you're correct. The closest word to counting is to *list*.

159. **(A)** The negative prefix *in-* leads us to choices A and D. Something not appropriate or not convenient or not a good opportunity is not at a good time (*untimely*) rather than not with a conclusion (*inconclusive*).

160. **(C)** A *pungent* aroma is a *sharp* smell. Pungent is related to *puncture*, *point*, and *punctual* (on time to a point)!

161. **(A)** If you *shirk* doing your laundry, your shirt may shrink. (Or you can just picture a lazy shark.)

162. **(B)** Remember that the root *cred* means *believe* (as in the Apostle's Creed: "I believe . . ."). Something incredible is unbelievable.

163. **(A)** To *feign* is to simulate or imitate. *Pretend* is the best choice.

164. **(C)** A *veneer* is a thin face or covering. It's literally the thin wood that covers the *surface* of some furniture.

165. **(A)** If you think of the word *relax*, you'll choose the correct answer, *loose*. (You can easily eliminate *strict* and *oppressive*.)

166. **(D)** You learned that the suffix *-archy* means rule. *Anarchy* is without rule. *Disorder* is the closest choice.

167. **(C)** *Tangible* means touchable. Something *physical* is touchable.

168. **(D)** A lectern is a reading stand or desk, and a lector is a reader or lecturer.

169. **(C)** Though it seems strange, you can actually use etymology to figure this one out. *Im-pede* means not foot, right? That would eliminate choices A (*quicken*) and B (*race*). Moreover, because it's negative, it would eliminate D (*support*). If your feet are blocked, you are definitely hindered.

170. **(B)** Etymology works again! *Anti-pathy* means against feeling. It's the opposite of *sym-pathy* (with feeling).

171. **(D)** *Pace* means peace.

172. **(B)** This one is tricky. *Post-humous* literally means after earth/dirt or after burial!

173. **(C)** If the ultimate is the final, the *penultimate* is the *second to last*. The ultimate pen was too expensive, so I bought the next best writing utensil, the penultimate pen.

174. **(D)** *Verb* means word. (By the way, *noun* or *nom* means name.)

Subtest 4 Mathematics

175. **(B)** Simplify statements (a), (b), and (c), and then substitute into (A), (B), (C), and (D).

(a) $\dfrac{(24\cdot 2)}{6} = \dfrac{48}{6} = 8$

(b) $\left(\dfrac{24}{6}\right) \cdot 2 = 4 \cdot 2 = 8$

(c) $\left(\dfrac{24}{2}\right) + 6 = 12 + 6 = 18$

$$(c) > (a) \text{ and } (a) = (b)$$
$$18 > 8 \text{ and } 8 = 8 \ ✔$$

176. **(D)** Let $b = -1$ and substitute into the given terms.

(A) $b^2 = (-1)^2 = +1$
(B) $-b = -(-1) = +1$
(C) $b^0 = (-1)^0 = +1$
(D) $b^3 = (-1)^3 = (-1)(-1)(-1) = -1$

177. **(D)** Simplify each expression, and then substitute.

(a) $5^2 = 5 \cdot 5 = 25$
(b) $2^5 = 2 \cdot 2 \cdot 2 \cdot 2 \cdot 2 = 32$
(c) $2^3 = 2 \cdot 2 \cdot 2 = 8$

$$(b) < (a) \text{ or } (c) < (b)$$
$$32 < 25 \text{ or } 8 < 32 \ ✔$$

178. **(C)** Divide 3^9 by 3^7, and then simplify.

$$\frac{\overset{3^2}{\cancel{3^9}}}{4 \times \underset{1}{\cancel{3^7}}} = \frac{9}{4} = 2\frac{1}{4}$$

179. **(A)** Simplify all the expressions, and then arrange from the largest to the smallest.

(a) $4^2 + 5(9 - 3) = 16 + 5 \cdot 6 = 16 + 30 = 46$

(b) $3 \cdot 17 - 4 \cdot 6 = 51 - 24 = 27$

(c) $7 + 9 \cdot 4 - 6(9 - 7)^3 = 7 + 36 - 6(2)^3 = 43 - 6(8) = 43 - 48 = -5$

(d) $6 + 2 + \dfrac{48}{8} - 2(3 - 1)^2 = 8 + 6 - 2(2)^2 = 14 - 8 = 6$

$$46 > 27 > 6 > -5$$
$$(a) > (b) > (d) > (c)$$

180. **(B)** Look at the tens place. If the tens digit is five or more, round the hundreds digit one unit higher. If the tens place is less than five, let the hundreds digits stand.

$$1{,}742{,}143 \qquad \approx 1{,}742{,}100$$

the tens digit < 5

181. **(B)** They'll meet again at the start of the track whenever 3 and 5 share a common multiple.

Dwayne

Minutes per track	×	Turns around track	=	Total minutes
3	×	1	=	3
3	×	2	=	6
3	×	3	=	9
3	×	4	=	12
3	×	**5**	=	**15**

Malcolm

Minutes per track	×	Turns around track	=	Total minutes
5	×	1	=	5
5	×	2	=	10
5	×	**3**	=	**15**
5	×	4	=	20
5	×	5	=	25

Dwayne and Malcolm will meet in 15 minutes.

182. **(A)** Multiply the mixed numbers and then substitute into the inequalities.

(a) $1\frac{1}{2} \cdot 2\frac{3}{4} = \frac{3}{2} \cdot \frac{11}{4} = \frac{33}{8} = 4\frac{1}{8}$

(b) $\frac{3}{4} \cdot 4\frac{1}{2} = \frac{3}{4} \cdot \frac{9}{2} = \frac{27}{8} = 3\frac{3}{8}$

(c) $3\frac{1}{2} \cdot \frac{3}{4} = \frac{7}{2} \cdot \frac{3}{4} = \frac{21}{8} = 2\frac{5}{8}$

(d) $\frac{1}{2} \cdot 3\frac{1}{4} = \frac{1}{2} \cdot \frac{13}{4} = \frac{13}{8} = 1\frac{5}{8}$

$$(c) < (d) \quad or \quad (c) < (a)$$
$$2\frac{5}{8} < 1\frac{5}{8} \quad or \quad 2\frac{5}{8} < 4\frac{1}{8} \quad \checkmark$$

183. **(D)** Divide the distance, 206.5 miles, by the rate of speed, 59 mph, in order to determine the time it takes to drive from Middletown to Rockville. Then add the number of hours to 2:30 P.M., the starting time.

$$\begin{array}{r} 3.5 \\ 59\overline{)206.5} \\ \underline{177}\downarrow \\ 29\ 5 \\ \underline{29\ 5} \\ 0 \end{array}$$

2:30 P.M. + 3.5 hours = 6 P.M.

184. **(D)** Divide 236.5 by 12.4 and round off to the nearest tenth.

185. **(C)** Add the right- and left-handed numbers of students to obtain the total number. Then divide the total into the number of left-handed students.

Total number of students: $\qquad 6 + 24 = 30$

Left-handed students/total: $\qquad \frac{6}{30} = 0.20$

$$0.20 = 20\%$$

186. **(C)** Change all the numbers to decimals and then compare them.

$$.77 = .770$$
$$\frac{7}{8} = .875$$
$$\frac{2}{3} = .666\ldots$$
$$\frac{3}{4} = .750$$
$$.82 = .820$$
$$.913 = .913$$

$$.7700 < .820 < .875$$

187. **(A)** Let x = the unknown number.

$$x = \frac{2}{3} \times 54 - 14$$
$$x = 36 - 14$$
$$x = 22$$

188. **(C)** Determine which number, when multiplied by itself three times, is equal to –0.027.

$$\sqrt[3]{-0.027} = -0.3$$

Check: $\qquad (-0.3)(-0.3)(-0.3) = -0.027$

189. **(B)** Test out all the possibilities.

$$-3 \leq \qquad |2x + 1| < 2$$
$$-3 \leq \qquad |2(0) + 1| < 2$$
$$-3 \leq \qquad |1| \quad < 2$$
$$-3 \leq \qquad 1 \quad < 2 \ ✔$$

190. **(C)** Add the number of blue and yellow marbles, and use the result as the numerator. Then, add all the marbles total, and use the result as the denominator.

$$\text{blue marbles} = 3$$
$$\text{red marbles} = 4$$
$$\text{yellow marbles} = 2$$

$$\frac{\text{blue marbles + yellow marbles}}{\text{total number of marbles}} = \frac{3+2}{3+4+2} = \frac{5}{9}$$

191. **(D)** Develop a chart for all the given information, and then add all their weights.

Mildred's weight:	$x - 3$
Hector's weight:	$(x - 3) + 8 = x - 3 + 8 = x + 5$
Stacey's weight:	$(x + 5) - 12 = x + 5 - 12 = x - 7$
Total weights:	$3x - 5$

192. **(A)** Remove the absolute value signs and then divide all the numbers.

$$\frac{45|-63|}{5|9|} = \frac{\overset{9 \times 7}{\cancel{45} \times \cancel{63}}}{\underset{1 \times 1}{\cancel{5} \times \cancel{9}}} = 63$$

193. **(D)** Find $\frac{1}{100}$ of 90. The answer is in feet. Then convert feet into inches.

$$\frac{1}{100} \times 90 = 0.90 \text{ feet} \qquad 0.9 \times 12 = 10.8$$

194. **(D)** Let x = the first integer, and let $x + 1$ = the next consecutive integer.

$$x + (x + 1) = 51$$
$$2x + 1 = 51$$
$$2x = 50$$
$$x = 25$$
$$x + 1 = 26$$

195. **(A)**

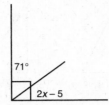

The two angles add up to a right angle.

$$(2x - 5) + 71 = 90$$
$$2x + 66 = 90$$
$$2x = 24$$
$$x = 12$$

196. **(C)** Two angles are complementary when they add up to 90°. Let x = the unknown angle.

$$x + a = 90$$
$$x = 90 - a$$

197. **(B)**

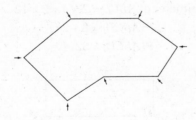

Together, $m\angle a + 94° + 38° = 180°$.

$$m\angle a + 94° + 38° = 180°$$
$$m\angle a + 132° = 180°$$
$$m\angle a = 48°$$

198. **(D)** A septagon is a seven-sided figure, so simply draw any seven-sided figure and count the points of intersection.

7 points of intersection

199. **(C)**

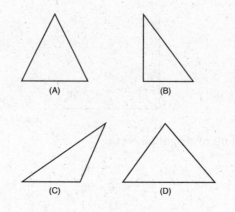

(A)   (B)
(C)   (D)

An obtuse triangle has one obtuse angle (an angle > 90°).

(C) is the only triangle with an angle greater than 180°.

200. **(D)** Let w = width, and let $2w + 4$ = length.

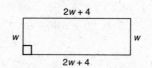

Perimeter $= (2w + 4) + (2w + 4) + w + w$
                    $= 2w + 4 + 2w + 4 + w + w$
                    $= 6w + 8$

201. **(D)**

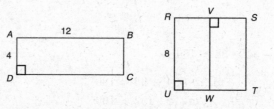

Find the perimeters of *ABCD*, *RSTU*, *RVWU*, and *VSTW*. Since *RSTU* is a square and *RU* = 8, all the sides are equal to 8. The midpoints, *V* and *W*, divide *RS* and *TU* in half, respectively.

Perimeter of $ABCD = 2 \times 4 + 2 \times 12$

$P(ABCD) = 8 + 24$

$P(ABCD) = 32$

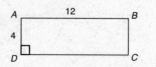

HSPT PRACTICE EXAM 2

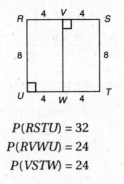

$$P(RSTU) = 32$$
$$P(RVWU) = 24$$
$$P(VSTW) = 24$$

One-half the perimeter of *ABCD* is less than the perimeter of *RSTU*.

$$\left(\frac{1}{2}\right)32 < 32$$
$$16 < 32 \ ✔$$

202. **(A)** Let h = the height. Use the formula for the area of a parallelogram, $A = bh$.

$$A = bh$$
$$114 = 12h$$
$$9.5 = h$$

203. **(C)** Draw a diagram of an isosceles triangle. Let x = each of the base angles. Then set the sum of the measures of all three angles equal to 180°.

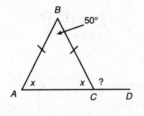

$$(x) + (x) + (50) = 180$$
$$2x + 50 = 180$$
$$2x = 130$$
$$x = 65$$

$\angle BCD$ and $\angle BCA$ are supplementary:

$$m\angle BCA + m\angle BCD = 180$$
$$65 + m\angle BCD = 180$$
$$m\angle BCD = 115$$

204. **(B)** Simplify each expression and then substitute.

(a) $(r + 4)^2 = (2 + 4)^2 = 6^2 = 36$
(b) $9(s - 3)^2 = 9(5 - 3)^2 = 9(2)^2 = 9(4) = 36$
(c) $2r^2s = 2(2)^2(5) = 2(4)(5) = 40$

$$(a) = (b) \ or \ (c) > (a)$$
$$36 = 36 \ or \ 40 > 36$$

205. **(C)** 1 pound = 16 ounces.

$$\frac{6 \text{ ounces}}{3 \text{ pounds}} = \frac{6 \text{ ounces}}{3 \times 16 \text{ ounces}} = \frac{6}{48} = \frac{1}{8}$$

206. **(D)** Multiply the expression inside the parentheses by 2.

$$62 + 2(8 - x) = 72$$
$$62 + 16 - 2x = 72$$
$$78 - 2x = 72$$
$$-2x = -6$$
$$x = 3$$

207. **(D)** Divide 9 into 45 in order to determine how many $\frac{1}{2}$ inches are needed to display a distance of 45 miles. Then multiply the answer by $\frac{1}{2}$.

$$\frac{45}{9} = 5$$
$$5 \times \frac{1}{2} = \frac{5}{2} = 2\frac{1}{2} \text{ inches}$$

208. **(B)** Use the formula $C = 2\pi r$, and substitute 62.8 for C and 3.14 for π.

$$C = 2\pi r$$
$$62.8 = 2(3.14)r$$
$$62.8 = 6.28r$$
$$10 = r$$

209. **(A)**

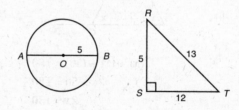

Find the areas and perimeters of the circle and the triangle and then substitute into the statements below.

Circumference of Circle O:

$$C = 2\pi r$$
$$= 2(3.14)(5) = 31.4$$

Area of Circle O:

$$A_C = \pi r^2$$
$$= (3.14)(5)^2 = (3.14)(25) = 78.5$$

Perimeter of Triangle RST:

$$P = 5 + 12 + 13 = 30$$

Area of Triangle *RST*:

$$A_T = \frac{1}{2}bh$$

$$= \frac{1}{2}(12)(5) = 30$$

The Area of triangle *RST* < $\frac{1}{2}$ Area of circle *O*.

$$30 < \frac{1}{2}(78.5)$$

$$30 < 39.25 \checkmark$$

210. **(B)** Find the volume of the room and then divide by the rate of the flow of oxygen, 3 cubic meters per minute.

$$V = l \cdot w \cdot h$$
$$= (9)(6)(4) = 216 \text{ cu m}$$
$$\frac{216}{3} = 72 \text{ minutes}$$

211. **(D)** Divide whole numbers and radical expressions separately and then simplify the result.

$$\frac{56\sqrt{b^3c^4}}{7\sqrt{bc^3}} = \frac{\overset{8}{\cancel{56}}}{\cancel{7}}\sqrt{\frac{\cancel{b^3}\,\overset{b^2c}{\cancel{c^4}}}{\cancel{bc^3}}} = 8\sqrt{b^2c} = 8b\sqrt{c}$$

212. **(B)**

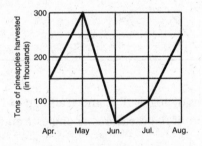

Determine the number of tons of pineapples harvested in each month. Then substitute into (A), (B), (C), and (D).

$$\text{April} = 150,000 \text{ tons}$$
$$\text{May} = 300,000 \text{ tons}$$
$$\text{June} = 50,000 \text{ tons}$$
$$\text{July} = 100,000 \text{ tons}$$
$$\text{August} = 250,000 \text{ tons}$$

$$\text{May harvest} - \text{April harvest} > \text{July harvest}$$
$$300,000 - 150,000 > 100,000$$
$$150,000 > 100,000 \checkmark$$

213. **(A)** Find the area of the floor (20 × 32) and then divide the total weight (2,560) by the area.

$$20 \times 32 = 640$$

$$\frac{2,560}{640} = 4 \text{ lb per sq ft}$$

214. **(D)** First change $\frac{3}{4}$ to a decimal. Then add the result to 4.

$$\frac{3}{4} = 0.75$$

$$4\frac{3}{4} = 4.75 = 475\%$$

215. **(A)** Substitute 3 for t in the given formula ($t = 3$).

$$d = 16t^2$$
$$= 16(3)^2$$
$$= 16(9)$$
$$= 144$$

216. **(C)** Determine both wages and then subtract.

$$
\begin{array}{r}
\text{Shanequa's wages: } 12 \times \$15.93 = \$191.16 \\
- \text{ Julio's wages: } 12 \times \$13.54 = \$162.48 \\
\hline
\$28.68
\end{array}
$$

217. **(D)**

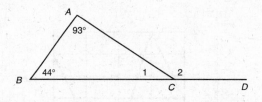

The sum of the measures of angles A, B, and C add up to 180°, so first find the measure of angle 1. Then the sum of the measures of angles 1 and 2 add up to a straight angle or 180°.

Find m∠1:
$$m\angle A + m\angle B + m\angle 1 = 180°$$
$$93° + 44° + m\angle 1 = 180°$$
$$137° + m\angle 1 = 180°$$
$$m\angle 1 = 43°$$

Find m∠2:
$$m\angle 1 + m\angle 2 = 180°$$
$$43° + m\angle 2 = 180°$$
$$m\angle 2 = 137°$$

218. **(C)**

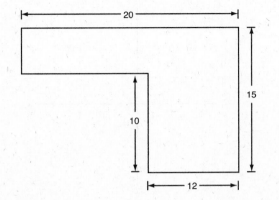

Divide the large figure into two rectangles, A and B, and then use the formula $A = bh$, where A = the area of a rectangle, b = the base, and h = the height. Finally, add the areas of the two rectangles together.

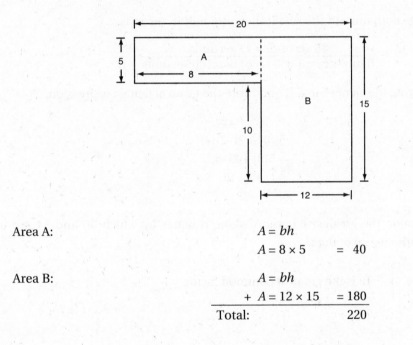

Area A:
$$A = bh$$
$$A = 8 \times 5 \quad = \quad 40$$

Area B:
$$A = bh$$
$$+ \; A = 12 \times 15 \quad = 180$$

Total: 220

219. **(B)**

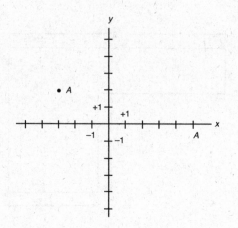

The *x*-coordinates of points to the left of the *y*-axis are negative. The *y*-coordinates of points above the *x*-axis are positive.

3 units to the left and 2 units up: (–3, 2)

220. **(A)** Change both units to the smallest common unit, seconds.

$$\frac{15 \text{ seconds} = 15 \text{ seconds}}{3 \text{ minutes} = 3 \times 60 \text{ seconds} = 180 \text{ seconds}} = \frac{1}{12}$$

221. **(B)** Substitute the values for *x*, *y*, and *z* into the given algebraic expression.

$$5x^2 + 2yz$$
$$5(3)^2 + 2(-2)(4)$$
$$5(9) + 2(-8)$$
$$45 - 16$$
$$29$$

222. **(D)** Determine the greatest common whole number by which 36 and 54 are both divisible without remainders.

$$\left.\begin{array}{l} 36 = 18 \times 2 \\ 54 = 18 \times 3 \end{array}\right\}$$ 18 is the greatest common factor

223. **(B)**

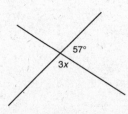

The two angles lie on a straight line, so they are supplementary and add up to 180°.

$$3x + 57 = 180$$
$$3x = 123$$
$$x = 41$$

224. **(D)** Change to improper fractions and multiply.

$$6\frac{2}{3} \times 5\frac{1}{4} = \frac{\overset{5}{\cancel{20}}}{\underset{1}{\cancel{3}}} \times \frac{\overset{7}{\cancel{21}}}{\underset{1}{\cancel{4}}} = 35$$

225. **(B)** Let y = the number of runs the team has to score in the last game, and set up an equation to solve for the mean.

$\bar{x}$ = mean: $\bar{x} = \dfrac{12+7+10+6+9+y}{6}$

$\bar{x} = 9$: $9 = \dfrac{44+y}{6}$

Multiply by 6: $54 = 44 + y$
Subtract 44: $10 = y$

226. **(A)**

Let x = the first even integer.
Let $x + 2$ = the second even integer.
Let $x + 4$ = the third even integer.
Let $x + 6$ = the fourth even integer.

The sum of the first and second of four consecutive even integers is 8 more than the fourth:

$$(x) + (x + 2) = (x + 6) + 8$$
$$2x + 2 = x + 14$$
$$2x = x + 12$$
$$x = 12$$

227. **(B)** Let x = the original price before the increase two years ago. 110%x or $1.10x$ = the price after the first increase. 120%$(1.10x)$ or $1.20(1.10x)$ = the price after the second increase. Set the price after the second increase equal to $6.60.

$$1.20(1.10x) = \$6.60$$
$$1.32x = \$6.60$$
$$x = \$5$$

228. **(B)** There are 100 centimeters in one meter.

$$1 \text{ centimeter} = \frac{1}{100} \text{ of a meter}$$

$$2 \text{ centimeters} = \frac{2}{100} = \frac{1}{50} \text{ of a meter}$$

$$\frac{1}{50} = 0.02 = 2\%$$

229. **(B)** Substitute the given values for a and b into the given expression.

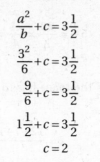

$$\frac{a^2}{b} + c = 3\frac{1}{2}$$

$$\frac{3^2}{6} + c = 3\frac{1}{2}$$

$$\frac{9}{6} + c = 3\frac{1}{2}$$

$$1\frac{1}{2} + c = 3\frac{1}{2}$$

$$c = 2$$

230. **(C)** Let x = the unknown percent, and translate the information into an equation.

$$x \cdot 120 = 45$$

$$x = \frac{45}{120} = \frac{9}{24} = 0.375$$

$$= 37.5\% \approx 38\%$$

231. **(D)** Use the formula $P = 2b + 2h$ for the perimeter, P, of a rectangle with base b and height h. For the area of a rectangle, use the formula $A = bh$, where A = area and b and h represent base and height, respectively.

Area of rectangle:

$$A = bh$$
$$36 = 9 \cdot h$$
$$4 = h$$

Perimeter of rectangle:

$$P = 2b + 2h$$
$$P = 2 \cdot 9 + 2 \cdot 4$$
$$= 18 + 8 = 26$$

232. **(C)**

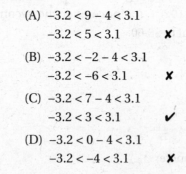

(A) $-3.2 < 9 - 4 < 3.1$
  $-3.2 < 5 < 3.1$ ✗

(B) $-3.2 < -2 - 4 < 3.1$
  $-3.2 < -6 < 3.1$ ✗

(C) $-3.2 < 7 - 4 < 3.1$
  $-3.2 < 3 < 3.1$ ✔

(D) $-3.2 < 0 - 4 < 3.1$
  $-3.2 < -4 < 3.1$ ✗

233. **(C)** Combine similar terms.

$$3\sqrt{7} + 11\sqrt{7} = 14\sqrt{7}$$
$$\underline{-4\sqrt{3} - 6\sqrt{3} = -10\sqrt{3}}$$
$$14\sqrt{7} - 10\sqrt{3}$$

234. **(A)** A prime number has only two factors, itself and 1.

$$11, 13$$

235. **(D)** The measures of the three angles of a triangle add up to 180°.

$$59 + 53 + 68 = 180$$

236. **(B)** Add up all the ratios and divide into 200. Find the remainder and then check to see which is the last book in the remainder.

$$4 + 6 + 1 + 2 = 13$$
$$\frac{200}{13} = 15\frac{5}{13}$$

There is a remainder of 5. In order, we can purchase 4 fiction books and 1 historical book. The historical book is the last book we can order.

237. **(A)** If we set up two similar triangles, their corresponding sides are in proportion.

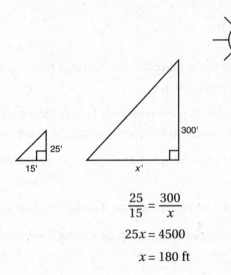

$$\frac{25}{15} = \frac{300}{x}$$
$$25x = 4500$$
$$x = 180 \text{ ft}$$

238. **(B)**

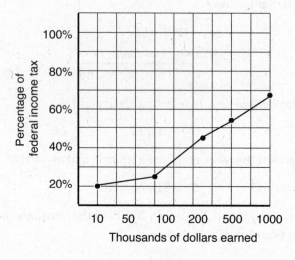

The horizontal axis represents income in thousands of dollars, while the vertical axis represents the percent income tax. Find the percent income tax on $90,000, change the percent to a decimal, and multiply times $90,000.

According to the graph, it looks like the percent income tax on $90,000 is about 30%.

$$30\% = 0.30$$
$$0.30 \times \$90,000 = \$27,000$$

Subtest 5 Language

239. **(C)** Dan and Nazee <u>ate</u> cake and <u>played</u> at the birthday party. This is not a compound sentence, so a comma is unnecessary.

240. **(B)** I don't have problems reading the book<u>,</u> but I don't have a lot of time tonight. This is a compound sentence, so use a comma to separate the two parts.

241. **(C)** She and <u>I</u> are best friends, and we chat on the Internet often. Capitalize the pronoun I.

242. **(C)** Because the last volume is checked out of the library. This is a fragment.

243. **(A)** I could <u>have</u> listened to them sing all day. Be careful not to confuse the preposition *of* with the helping verb *have*.

244. **(B)** I didn't fall asleep until after he <u>had begun</u> speaking. The past participle is *had begun*, not *had began*.

245. **(A)** With an outline, <u>authors</u> know what <u>they</u> are going to write next. Check pronoun-antecedent agreement. *Authors* and *they* should both be plural.

246. **(A)** To <u>whom</u> shall I address this letter? *Whom* is the object form.

247. **(B)** Oh my goodness<u>,</u> I almost forgot the cake. Use a comma or exclamation point after an interjection.

248. **(A)** Which of the twins can swim <u>faster</u>? The suffix *-er* is used when comparing two people or items.

HSPT PRACTICE EXAM 2

249. **(B)** Nick is always <u>drumming</u> the desk, <u>tapping</u> his feet, or <u>bobbing</u> his head. Keep words in parallel form in a series.

250. **(C)** <u>It's</u> the humidity that really makes us feel the heat. *It's* is the contraction for *It is.*

251. **(D)** No mistakes.

252. **(B)** Daphne doesn't like <u>a lot</u> of fuss. *A lot* is two words.

253. **(C)** The groundhog didn't see <u>its</u> shadow this year. The possessive form of *it* is *its.*

254. **(C)** The **stories** [of sea adventure] always <u>give</u> me a thrill. Check subject-verb agreement, disregarding any words in between.

255. **(B)** Neither she <u>nor</u> I have missed a day of school this year. Use *neither* and *nor* together.

256. **(D)** No mistakes.

257. **(A)** I want to see you <u>rested and relaxed,</u> tomorrow. Keep the words in a series parallel.

258. **(C)** Sam said, "I know I have something to do<u>."</u> When you open a quote, be sure to close it.

259. **(B)** Will you call the restaurant for me? This is a question.

260. **(A)** The clock in the old, <u>red tower</u> chimes at noon. Remove the comma between *red* and *tower.* You do not use a comma between the last adjective and the modified noun; you would not call it *the old <u>and</u> red <u>and</u> tower.*

261. **(B)** Include the following in your paragraph: a topic sentence, supporting details, and a closing statement. Use a colon before a list.

262. **(A)** I was <u>amazed and</u> delighted by the music. Do not use a comma to separate a compound verb.

263. **(B)** Joe and Joan are happy with <u>their</u> new business. Check the use of *there, their,* and *they're.*

264. **(A)** Jorge thought about it and said, "I don't recall sugar as one of the ingredients<u>."</u> A period goes inside quotation marks.

265. **(A)** Coach Thacker, my social studies teacher, is a big movie fan. Use commas to set off nonessential information. We don't need to be told that the coach teaches social studies.

266. **(B)** On the <u>fourth</u> day, he sent me some birds. The correct spelling is *fourth.*

267. **(C)** I still enjoy reading <u>children's</u> books. The word *children* is already plural and does not need an *s* to make it so.

268. **(A)** Mary Shelley was a teenager when she wrote her novel *Frankenstein.* Novels are italicized or underlined.

269. **(D)** No mistakes.

270. **(B)** Which doctor did you see? The word *doctor* is not capitalized unless you refer to a specific doctor.

271. **(A)** I was accepted into the club last year. Be careful not to confuse the words *accept* and *except.*

272. **(C)** If Mr. Cerulean would assign less homework, he would have fewer papers to grade. Use the word *less* with noncountable items; use *fewer* with countable items.

273. **(D)** No mistakes.

274. **(C)** The special effects in the movie were amazing. Be careful not to confuse the words *effect* and *affect.*

275. **(B)** Amber, Sumi, and I formed a jazz band. The word *I* is a subject; the word *me* is an object.

276. **(B)** She felt sick, so she went to lie down. You *lie yourself* down. You *lay* down something else.

277. **(C)** Lay your head on the pillow and sleep. You *lie yourself* down. You *lay* down something else—even if it's your head.

278. **(D)** No mistakes.

279. **(B)** He was too popular to be defeated in the election. Always double-check *to, two,* and *too.*

280. **(A)** I declined the role of Hamlet, considering it too demanding on my memory.

281. **(D)** No mistakes, but it would be nice if educated people could pronounce *nuclear.*

282. **(C)** I get weary of the cold weather during February, March, and April.

283. **(B)** Due to the sheriff's courageous efforts, no one was hurt.

284. **(B)** Pam said she'd meet me at the library, but she must have been detained elsewhere.

285. **(B)** We have a lot of athletes attending our school.

286. **(D)** No mistakes.

287. **(A)** I assumed a long speech was unnecessary for this occasion.

288. **(A)** Oh, she can be mischievous when she's in a spunky mood. *Mischievous* is another word most people misspell and mispronounce.

289. **(B)** The conjunction *yet* is the only one that logically connects these contrasting sentences. The word *however* cannot be a conjunction.

290. **(B)** The conjunction *but* indicates a contrast.

291. **(D)** This sentence is most concise. The other choices are neither brief, witty, nor stylish.

292. **(C)** This sentence includes all of the information in the most efficient way.

293. **(B)** This is the clearest choice. Choice A is passive, choice C is wordy, and choice D is awkward.

294. **(B)** This is the only sentence that deals with legend or mythology.

295. **(D)** None of these topics focuses on a single, brief idea.

296. **(D)** This sentence is not about how rainwater affects worms.

297. **(C)** This sentence concludes the paragraph.

298. **(A)** The sentence fits logically between the first and second sentences. The words "This spin" in the second sentence must refer to the "twist" in the added sentence.

ANSWER SHEET
TACHS Practice Exam 1

READING—PART 1

1. Ⓐ Ⓑ Ⓒ Ⓓ 6. Ⓙ Ⓚ Ⓛ Ⓜ 11. Ⓐ Ⓑ Ⓒ Ⓓ 16. Ⓙ Ⓚ Ⓛ Ⓜ
2. Ⓙ Ⓚ Ⓛ Ⓜ 7. Ⓐ Ⓑ Ⓒ Ⓓ 12. Ⓙ Ⓚ Ⓛ Ⓜ 17. Ⓐ Ⓑ Ⓒ Ⓓ
3. Ⓐ Ⓑ Ⓒ Ⓓ 8. Ⓙ Ⓚ Ⓛ Ⓜ 13. Ⓐ Ⓑ Ⓒ Ⓓ 18. Ⓙ Ⓚ Ⓛ Ⓜ
4. Ⓙ Ⓚ Ⓛ Ⓜ 9. Ⓐ Ⓑ Ⓒ Ⓓ 14. Ⓙ Ⓚ Ⓛ Ⓜ 19. Ⓐ Ⓑ Ⓒ Ⓓ
5. Ⓐ Ⓑ Ⓒ Ⓓ 10. Ⓙ Ⓚ Ⓛ Ⓜ 15. Ⓐ Ⓑ Ⓒ Ⓓ 20. Ⓙ Ⓚ Ⓛ Ⓜ

READING—PART 2

21. Ⓐ Ⓑ Ⓒ Ⓓ 29. Ⓐ Ⓑ Ⓒ Ⓓ 37. Ⓐ Ⓑ Ⓒ Ⓓ 45. Ⓐ Ⓑ Ⓒ Ⓓ
22. Ⓙ Ⓚ Ⓛ Ⓜ 30. Ⓙ Ⓚ Ⓛ Ⓜ 38. Ⓙ Ⓚ Ⓛ Ⓜ 46. Ⓙ Ⓚ Ⓛ Ⓜ
23. Ⓐ Ⓑ Ⓒ Ⓓ 31. Ⓐ Ⓑ Ⓒ Ⓓ 39. Ⓐ Ⓑ Ⓒ Ⓓ 47. Ⓐ Ⓑ Ⓒ Ⓓ
24. Ⓙ Ⓚ Ⓛ Ⓜ 32. Ⓙ Ⓚ Ⓛ Ⓜ 40. Ⓙ Ⓚ Ⓛ Ⓜ 48. Ⓙ Ⓚ Ⓛ Ⓜ
25. Ⓐ Ⓑ Ⓒ Ⓓ 33. Ⓐ Ⓑ Ⓒ Ⓓ 41. Ⓐ Ⓑ Ⓒ Ⓓ 49. Ⓐ Ⓑ Ⓒ Ⓓ
26. Ⓙ Ⓚ Ⓛ Ⓜ 34. Ⓙ Ⓚ Ⓛ Ⓜ 42. Ⓙ Ⓚ Ⓛ Ⓜ 50. Ⓙ Ⓚ Ⓛ Ⓜ
27. Ⓐ Ⓑ Ⓒ Ⓓ 35. Ⓐ Ⓑ Ⓒ Ⓓ 43. Ⓐ Ⓑ Ⓒ Ⓓ
28. Ⓙ Ⓚ Ⓛ Ⓜ 36. Ⓙ Ⓚ Ⓛ Ⓜ 44. Ⓙ Ⓚ Ⓛ Ⓜ

WRITTEN EXPRESSION—PART 1—ENGLISH

1. Ⓐ Ⓑ Ⓒ Ⓓ Ⓔ 11. Ⓐ Ⓑ Ⓒ Ⓓ 21. Ⓐ Ⓑ Ⓒ Ⓓ 31. Ⓐ Ⓑ Ⓒ Ⓓ
2. Ⓙ Ⓚ Ⓛ Ⓜ Ⓝ 12. Ⓙ Ⓚ Ⓛ Ⓜ 22. Ⓙ Ⓚ Ⓛ Ⓜ 32. Ⓙ Ⓚ Ⓛ Ⓜ
3. Ⓐ Ⓑ Ⓒ Ⓓ Ⓔ 13. Ⓐ Ⓑ Ⓒ Ⓓ 23. Ⓐ Ⓑ Ⓒ Ⓓ 33. Ⓐ Ⓑ Ⓒ Ⓓ
4. Ⓙ Ⓚ Ⓛ Ⓜ Ⓝ 14. Ⓙ Ⓚ Ⓛ Ⓜ 24. Ⓙ Ⓚ Ⓛ Ⓜ 34. Ⓙ Ⓚ Ⓛ Ⓜ
5. Ⓐ Ⓑ Ⓒ Ⓓ Ⓔ 15. Ⓐ Ⓑ Ⓒ Ⓓ 25. Ⓐ Ⓑ Ⓒ Ⓓ 35. Ⓐ Ⓑ Ⓒ Ⓓ
6. Ⓙ Ⓚ Ⓛ Ⓜ Ⓝ 16. Ⓙ Ⓚ Ⓛ Ⓜ 26. Ⓙ Ⓚ Ⓛ Ⓜ 36. Ⓙ Ⓚ Ⓛ Ⓜ
7. Ⓐ Ⓑ Ⓒ Ⓓ Ⓔ 17. Ⓐ Ⓑ Ⓒ Ⓓ 27. Ⓐ Ⓑ Ⓒ Ⓓ 37. Ⓐ Ⓑ Ⓒ Ⓓ
8. Ⓙ Ⓚ Ⓛ Ⓜ Ⓝ 18. Ⓙ Ⓚ Ⓛ Ⓜ 28. Ⓙ Ⓚ Ⓛ Ⓜ 38. Ⓙ Ⓚ Ⓛ Ⓜ
9. Ⓐ Ⓑ Ⓒ Ⓓ Ⓔ 19. Ⓐ Ⓑ Ⓒ Ⓓ 29. Ⓐ Ⓑ Ⓒ Ⓓ 39. Ⓐ Ⓑ Ⓒ Ⓓ
10. Ⓙ Ⓚ Ⓛ Ⓜ Ⓝ 20. Ⓙ Ⓚ Ⓛ Ⓜ 30. Ⓙ Ⓚ Ⓛ Ⓜ 40. Ⓙ Ⓚ Ⓛ Ⓜ

ANSWER SHEET
TACHS Practice Exam 1

WRITTEN EXPRESSION—PART 2—PARAGRAPHS

41. Ⓐ Ⓑ Ⓒ Ⓓ   44. Ⓙ Ⓚ Ⓛ Ⓜ   47. Ⓐ Ⓑ Ⓒ Ⓓ   50. Ⓙ Ⓚ Ⓛ Ⓜ
42. Ⓙ Ⓚ Ⓛ Ⓜ   45. Ⓐ Ⓑ Ⓒ Ⓓ   48. Ⓙ Ⓚ Ⓛ Ⓜ
43. Ⓐ Ⓑ Ⓒ Ⓓ   46. Ⓙ Ⓚ Ⓛ Ⓜ   49. Ⓐ Ⓑ Ⓒ Ⓓ

MATH—PART 1

1. Ⓐ Ⓑ Ⓒ Ⓓ   9. Ⓐ Ⓑ Ⓒ Ⓓ   17. Ⓐ Ⓑ Ⓒ Ⓓ   25. Ⓐ Ⓑ Ⓒ Ⓓ
2. Ⓙ Ⓚ Ⓛ Ⓜ   10. Ⓙ Ⓚ Ⓛ Ⓜ   18. Ⓙ Ⓚ Ⓛ Ⓜ   26. Ⓙ Ⓚ Ⓛ Ⓜ
3. Ⓐ Ⓑ Ⓒ Ⓓ   11. Ⓐ Ⓑ Ⓒ Ⓓ   19. Ⓐ Ⓑ Ⓒ Ⓓ   27. Ⓐ Ⓑ Ⓒ Ⓓ
4. Ⓙ Ⓚ Ⓛ Ⓜ   12. Ⓙ Ⓚ Ⓛ Ⓜ   20. Ⓙ Ⓚ Ⓛ Ⓜ   28. Ⓙ Ⓚ Ⓛ Ⓜ
5. Ⓐ Ⓑ Ⓒ Ⓓ   13. Ⓐ Ⓑ Ⓒ Ⓓ   21. Ⓐ Ⓑ Ⓒ Ⓓ   29. Ⓐ Ⓑ Ⓒ Ⓓ
6. Ⓙ Ⓚ Ⓛ Ⓜ   14. Ⓙ Ⓚ Ⓛ Ⓜ   22. Ⓙ Ⓚ Ⓛ Ⓜ   30. Ⓙ Ⓚ Ⓛ Ⓜ
7. Ⓐ Ⓑ Ⓒ Ⓓ   15. Ⓐ Ⓑ Ⓒ Ⓓ   23. Ⓐ Ⓑ Ⓒ Ⓓ   31. Ⓐ Ⓑ Ⓒ Ⓓ
8. Ⓙ Ⓚ Ⓛ Ⓜ   16. Ⓙ Ⓚ Ⓛ Ⓜ   24. Ⓙ Ⓚ Ⓛ Ⓜ   32. Ⓙ Ⓚ Ⓛ Ⓜ

MATH—PART 2

33. Ⓐ Ⓑ Ⓒ Ⓓ   38. Ⓙ Ⓚ Ⓛ Ⓜ   43. Ⓐ Ⓑ Ⓒ Ⓓ   48. Ⓙ Ⓚ Ⓛ Ⓜ
34. Ⓙ Ⓚ Ⓛ Ⓜ   39. Ⓐ Ⓑ Ⓒ Ⓓ   44. Ⓙ Ⓚ Ⓛ Ⓜ   49. Ⓐ Ⓑ Ⓒ Ⓓ
35. Ⓐ Ⓑ Ⓒ Ⓓ   40. Ⓙ Ⓚ Ⓛ Ⓜ   45. Ⓐ Ⓑ Ⓒ Ⓓ   50. Ⓙ Ⓚ Ⓛ Ⓜ
36. Ⓙ Ⓚ Ⓛ Ⓜ   41. Ⓐ Ⓑ Ⓒ Ⓓ   46. Ⓙ Ⓚ Ⓛ Ⓜ
37. Ⓐ Ⓑ Ⓒ Ⓓ   42. Ⓙ Ⓚ Ⓛ Ⓜ   47. Ⓐ Ⓑ Ⓒ Ⓓ

ABILITY

1. Ⓐ Ⓑ Ⓒ Ⓓ Ⓔ   4. Ⓙ Ⓚ Ⓛ Ⓜ Ⓝ   7. Ⓐ Ⓑ Ⓒ Ⓓ Ⓔ   10. Ⓙ Ⓚ Ⓛ Ⓜ Ⓝ
2. Ⓙ Ⓚ Ⓛ Ⓜ Ⓝ   5. Ⓐ Ⓑ Ⓒ Ⓓ Ⓔ   8. Ⓙ Ⓚ Ⓛ Ⓜ Ⓝ
3. Ⓐ Ⓑ Ⓒ Ⓓ Ⓔ   6. Ⓙ Ⓚ Ⓛ Ⓜ Ⓝ   9. Ⓐ Ⓑ Ⓒ Ⓓ Ⓔ

*This TACHS test is a representative example of what you will find on the actual exam. Although it illustrates the types of problems you can expect, the number of questions may vary.

READING—PART 1

20 QUESTIONS   10 MINUTES

> **Directions:** This is a test about words and their meanings.
>
> • For each question, you are to decide which one of the four answers has most nearly the same meaning as the underlined word(s) above it.

1   a unanimous decision

- **A**   inactive
- **B**   hasty
- **C**   agreeing completely
- **D**   unsound

2   contemporary art

- **J**   anti-establishment
- **K**   rare
- **L**   washable
- **M**   modern

3   to disregard the evidence

- **A**   disrespect
- **B**   weigh
- **C**   ignore
- **D**   discuss

4   a boisterous gathering

- **J**   exuberant
- **K**   solemn
- **L**   violent
- **M**   formidable

5   a fine lithograph

- **A**   signature
- **B**   printed picture
- **C**   physique
- **D**   spiral design

6   to succumb to temptation

- **J**   flirt with
- **K**   give in to
- **L**   move toward
- **M**   resist

7   a venomous snake

- **A**   poisonous
- **B**   harmless
- **C**   huge
- **D**   recently fed

8   synchronized watches

- **J**   similarly engraved
- **K**   of the same material
- **L**   at the same time
- **M**   identical in shape

9   a hypodermic needle

- **A**   sharp
- **B**   under the skin
- **C**   sewing
- **D**   dry grass

10   an indefatigable hero

- **J**   invincible
- **K**   muscular
- **L**   overweight
- **M**   untiring

GO TO NEXT PAGE ➡

11 posthumous fame

- **A** premature
- **B** hidden
- **C** buried
- **D** after death

12 a chronic disease

- **J** long lasting
- **K** contagious
- **L** curable
- **M** infectious

13 the multitudinous seas

- **A** deep
- **B** many
- **C** green
- **D** living

14 to circumvent the obstacles

- **J** get around
- **K** run over
- **L** ignore
- **M** air out

15 Roman centurion

- **A** senator
- **B** senior citizen
- **C** commander
- **D** banker

16 to feel no remorse

- **J** guilt
- **K** sympathy
- **L** pain
- **M** sensation

17 an amorphous terror

- **A** without shape
- **B** huge
- **C** harmless
- **D** wingless

18 a utilitarian function

- **J** fanciful
- **K** religious
- **L** dishonest
- **M** useful

19 a heartless automaton

- **A** car
- **B** dictator
- **C** man
- **D** robot

20 to plummet rapidly

- **J** run
- **K** fall
- **L** decay
- **M** rise

GO TO NEXT PAGE ➡

READING—PART 2

30 QUESTIONS 25 MINUTES

Directions: This part has short reading passages, each one followed by questions. Choose the best answer to each question.

Correct marking of sample   Ⓐ ● Ⓒ Ⓓ

Example

The reading passages on the next part will be _____.

A all on one page
B followed by questions
C easy to read
D very long

PASSAGE FOR QUESTIONS 21–26

Mankind has created a number of dastardly devices that plague him and his enemy. In particular, clever innovations, such as the atomic bomb, the iron maiden, the Spanish Inquisition, and bureaucratic "red tape" come to mind. However, little of what human creations torture us can compare to the foul play wreaked upon us by Nature herself. What forms of pain and suffering come to us in the fair guise of the great outdoors! The flesh-eating bite of a brown recluse, the maliciousness of the horsefly, and the deceptively inedible wild potato make it clear how outgunned by Nature we are.

Take for example the luxuriant, deceptively inviting plant, poison ivy. This tri-partite, gorgeously green, leafy plant exudes an oily sap called *urushiol* that irritates the skin for up to two weeks. It begins innocently enough; the unwary gardener might at first believe that he or she has escaped being exposed. However, within two days of exposure, the sap raises itchy, bumpy welts that range in color from normal skin color to pink to blood colored. Although one can relatively quickly rid themselves of surface traces of the sap using special poison ivy soap, vodka, or gasoline, the venom spreads through the blood stream, popping up in places sometimes surprisingly far away from the initial site.

Urushiol is potent and long lasting. Even having uprooted the plant does not necessarily render it powerless. Researchers experimented by leaving lengths of poison ivy atop a metal roof. Lacking soil and water (aside from rain and snow), these cuttings were exposed to unmitigated weather conditions for a year, and even then the plants were able to pass along rashes to any who touched them.

GO TO NEXT PAGE ➡

21 Based on the author's use of the word in this passage, what is a good definition of <u>exudes</u>?

A   inhales
B   leaks
C   calls out
D   leaves

22 How does the author of this passage most likely feel regarding poison ivy?

J   That this is an underestimated plant that needs to be incorporated into domestic gardening.
K   That the plant is relatively unremarkable, a casual irritant at best.
L   That this strain of ivy needs to be eliminated from the face of the earth.
M   That the best way to treat poison ivy is to take oatmeal colloid baths.

23 Through what range of colors might the welts caused by poison ivy appear?

A   deep red to crimson
B   flesh colored to blood red
C   brown to black
D   beige to pink to blood red

24 What is the scientific name for the sap poison ivy oozes that causes welts?

J   urine
K   urail
L   ukelele
M   urushiol

25 Select the best title for this article from the following options.

A   Poison Ivy: No Walk in the Park
B   Poison Ivy: Creepin' Your Way!
C   Poison Ivy: Go Green!
D   Poison Ivy: Man's Best Friend

26 You can tell from context that _____.

J   most people have been exposed to poison ivy already
K   long after one expects poison ivy to be inert, it can still cause pain
L   poison ivy is a topic worthy of study
M   most people do not find poison ivy a problem

GO TO NEXT PAGE ➡

Those who adore vintage posters might be familiar with such artists as Van Gogh, Salvador Dalí, and M. C. Escher. In their searches for this kind of art, such <u>aficionados</u> may have, perhaps unknowingly, come across works by Henri Toulouse-Lautrec emblazoned with the words *chat noir*. The term literally means "black cat," but in the context of French history, the phrase takes on a much deeper meaning.

The French often take some ribbing for their inability to prevent a German takeover of Paris during World War II; however, while it is easy to <u>chide</u> them for allowing their city to be overrun, it is only fair to acknowledge some of the ways in which Parisians resisted Nazi occupation. Historians point to the strategic use of underground cemeteries called *catacombs* that the French used to hide resistors and move about unnoticed; they also revere the playwright Jean-Paul Sartre, who so cleverly revised certain Greek myths so that Nazi audiences applauded and cheered for more, unaware that the plays embodied vicious anti-Germany propaganda.

<u>*Chat noir*</u> represents yet another form of French resistance. This art form grew out of a satirical and fatalistic cabaret scene; much like Punch and Judy shows, a *chat noir* theatre used thin metal cutouts of shapes to create silhouettes on a wall that were then used to tell a silly story—usually lambasting allegedly fictitious people (whom the audience knew were really a mockery of real-life political figures and sometimes of Hitler himself).

27 *Chat noir* became noteworthy during which era, according to this article?

   A   World War I
   B   World War II
   C   The Crimean War
   D   The War to End All Wars

28 What does the word <u>chide</u> mean in the context of this passage?

   J   praise
   K   anger
   L   criticize
   M   feel apathy for

29 Who, based on what you read in the article, would the *chat noir* artists most likely satirize if they still existed today?

   A   Hillary Clinton
   B   Barack Obama
   C   George W. Bush
   D   All of the above.

30 The author wrote this passage in order to _____.

   J   tell the reader about an old format of *The Daily Show*
   K   tell the reader about Latin vocabulary studies
   L   tell the reader about the French Resistance during World War II
   M   tell the reader about the final days of Mussolini

31 The phrase *chat noir* literally means _____.

   A   black hat
   B   useless chatter
   C   hot air
   D   black cat

GO TO NEXT PAGE ➡

32 Based upon your reading of this passage, the word <u>aficionado</u> most likely means _____.

   J   someone who is an expert at something

   K   someone who is unskilled at something

   L   someone with affection or passion for something

   M   someone with a distaste or hatred for something

33 Which of the following artists do not appear in this article?

   A   Henri Toulouse-Lautrec

   B   Salvador Dalí

   C   Vincent Van Gogh

   D   Claude Monet

GO TO NEXT PAGE ➡

Mauritis Cornelius Escher (better known as M. C. Escher) came into this world in 1909 and did not leave it until 1972. He became intrigued at an early age with graphic arts, and he spent much of his life experimenting with the use of pen and ink, pencil work, and printing techniques. Born in Holland, Escher spent most of his early years in Rome, absorbing the culture and learning new methods.

Escher's experimentation with art led him to explore the scientific laws around him. He became fascinated with enigma, with conundrum, and with "possible impossibilities" of illusion. Hence, Escher is best known for fantastic yet beautiful pieces of hands drawing hands, birds that merge subtly into fish, mobius strips, and castles that rest on impossible struts and foundations.

Ironically, the artist who so successfully called into focus the relationship of art and mathematics held no mathematics degree. Escher's juxtaposition of two quite different theories isolated him significantly from his fellow artists; few of his peers could follow in his artistic footsteps (either in skill or in vision), and he could not discuss his ideas with mathematicians, due to his ignorance of current math theory. Luckily his work captivated the post-war audience, especially the Americans, so significantly that he never lacked for funding, and he was supported by the International Union of Crystallography in 1965, an event that finally validated his life's work in his own eyes.

34 Based on the use of the word juxtaposition in this passage, what does this word mean?

- **J** division of
- **K** combination of
- **L** attitude toward
- **M** hatred toward

35 Based on the context as appears in this passage, what does enigma most likely mean?

- **A** a secret puzzle
- **B** an obvious answer
- **C** a puzzling fact
- **D** an egregious error

36 What finally justified the artist's work in his own eyes?

- **J** support by the Association of International Artists
- **K** informal conversations with mathematicians
- **L** formal publication in a journal put forth by the International Union of Crystallography
- **M** experimenting with the use of pen and ink in Holland

37 Why do you think that Escher chose printing techniques as an art form?

- **A** because making prints is easier than drawing art
- **B** because printing allows for crisp lines and repetition necessary for Escher's favorite subjects
- **C** because he had a friend in the wood trade that made getting supplies easier
- **D** because his father had always loved printing and lithographs

38 Based on the context of the article, what does "graphic arts" mean?

- **J** oil paint
- **K** pencil
- **L** permanent marker
- **M** watercolor

39 Which of the following titles best fits the passage?

- **A** M. C. Escher: Mystery Unto Himself
- **B** M. C. Escher: Clear Cut Mind
- **C** M. C. Escher: Mixture of Art and Pain
- **D** M. C. Escher: Clarity Through Mystery

GO TO NEXT PAGE ➡

Morning

1 Will there really be a morning?

2   Is there such a thing as day?

3 Could I see it from the mountains

4   If I were as tall as <u>they</u>?

5 Has it feet like water lilies?

6   Has it feathers like a bird?

7 Is it brought from famous countries

8   Of which I've never heard?

9 Oh, some scholar! Oh, some sailor!

10   Oh, some wise man from the skies!

11 Please to tell <u>a little pilgrim</u>

12   Where the place called *morning* lies?

Emily Dickinson

40 To which noun does the pronoun <u>they</u> refer in line 4?

J mountains
K lilies
L countries
M skies

41 To whom does <u>a little pilgrim</u> in line 11 refer?

A the day referenced in line 2
B the bird referenced in line 6
C the sailor referenced in line 9
D the author who wrote the piece

42 What is the main point of this text?

J the author questions where morning comes from
K the author questions the wisdom of mankind
L the author questions the meaning of life
M the author questions the existence of evil

43 What mood pervades this text?

A joy
B fear
C anger
D innocence

GO TO NEXT PAGE ➡

44 Of the following words, which would be an appropriate synonym for the word <u>pilgrim</u> as used in line 11?

J one of the people who sailed on the Mayflower in 1692

K a line from virtually any John Wayne movie

L a reference to someone who goes on a religious journey

M an allusion to one of Juliet's lines from Shakespeare's *Romeo and Juliet*

45 Which of the following titles would you choose if you were going to rename this poem?

A Question

B Evening

C Summer

D Why?

GO TO NEXT PAGE ➡

J.C.: Greetings! J.C. here, with today's guest, Matt Crafton. How are you doing, Matt?

M.C. Great. Glad to be here.

J.C.: For those of you who don't know, as if any of those people exist! Matt here is a race car driver. He's driven in NASCAR races for the past seven years and raced in more than 177 races. But, it's been a rocky seven years, right, Matt?

M.C.: You're right. By race 177, I hadn't won a race. There wasn't a day that went by that I didn't think about that first win or am I ever going to get my first win.

J.C.: But May 16, 2008, changed all that, didn't it, Matt?

M.C.: You betcha. That's the day I won the NASCAR Craftsman Truck Series at Lowe's Motor Speedway. Race 178. Maybe that'll be my new lucky number!

J. C.: Things are looking up, I'll bet.

M.C.: You'd better believe it. To break the longest first series win drought in NASCAR history—that's a big deal. My crew and I had been joking about how we were getting a monkey off our backs, and I said it wasn't a monkey, it was a gorilla! It was just a ton of weight off my shoulders. Once I got that win, it made me a different person. It made me a happier person to be around.

J.C.: So, how do you feel about the upcoming Kentucky Speedway?

M.C.: Great. I've got the win, and that's awesome, but at the same time we have to keep putting ourself in position to win. If we can consistently be in a position to win then we'll have a chance to run for a championship.

J.C.: Great! That's just great! What an attitude! Well, good luck, and we'll be rooting for you! This is J.C., signing off, saying, "Get 'er done!"

46 Which race in Matt Crafton's career marked his first career win?

J 176
K 177
L 178
M 179

47 What emotion was Matt Crafton likely feeling prior to winning?

A elation
B confusion
C frustration
D fear

48 How many years has Matt Crafton driven for NASCAR, according to this text?

J six
K seven
L eight
M nine

49 Matt Crafton refers to his consistent losing as a "monkey on his back." This is known as which of the following grammatical constructions?

A simile
B metaphor
C analogy
D ellipses

GO TO NEXT PAGE ➡

50 Which of the following grammatical errors
appear in the passage?

J I've got the win, and that's awesome.

K We have to keep putting ourself in
position to win.

L It made me a happier person to be
around.

M This article has no grammatical errors.

STOP

If there is still time remaining, you may review your answers.

WRITTEN EXPRESSION

Part 1—English

40 QUESTIONS   23 MINUTES

> **Directions:** This is a test of how well you can find mistakes in writing. The directions below tell what type of mistake to look for.
>
> • On the questions with mistakes in spelling, capitalization, punctuation, and usage, choose the answer with the same letter as the line containing the mistake. When there is no mistake or no change needed, choose the last answer.
> • On the questions about expression, follow the specific directions for each question.

> **Directions:** Look for mistakes in **spelling**.

1
- **A** outgoing
- **B** unoticed
- **C** ragged
- **D** selfless
- **E** *(No mistakes)*

2
- **J** galaxie
- **K** crisis
- **L** bonus
- **M** devour
- **N** *(No mistakes)*

3
- **A** steal
- **B** iron
- **C** copper
- **D** brass
- **E** *(No mistakes)*

4
- **J** ardor
- **K** concise
- **L** equasion
- **M** zenith
- **N** *(No mistakes)*

5
- **A** discreet
- **B** discrete
- **C** odious
- **D** edible
- **E** *(No mistakes)*

6
- **J** tommorrow
- **K** accommodate
- **L** committee
- **M** occurrence
- **N** *(No mistakes)*

7
- **A** frugle
- **B** counterfeit
- **C** breach
- **D** astute
- **E** *(No mistakes)*

8
- **J** mortgage
- **K** nucular
- **L** pitiful
- **M** harmful
- **N** *(No mistakes)*

9
- **A** tripod
- **B** triumph
- **C** tripel
- **D** trivia
- **E** *(No mistakes)*

10
- **J** aquire
- **K** parallel
- **L** receipt
- **M** library
- **N** *(No mistakes)*

GO TO NEXT PAGE ➡

Directions: Look for mistakes in **capitalization**.

11 A Because of its climate,
    B Canada is sometimes called
    C the Great White North.
    D *(No mistakes)*

12 J My brother's friend
    K studies English at
    L Rutgers university.
    M *(No mistakes)*

13 A I've often wondered
    B if Italics were invented
    C in Italy.
    D *(No mistakes)*

14 J Ask your Mother
    K if you can drive her Honda
    L when we go to Boston.
    M *(No mistakes)*

15 A do you enjoy
    B modern poetry as much
    C as I do?
    D *(No mistakes)*

16 J The spelling rule
    K concerning "i before e"
    L is one i can never remember.
    M *(No mistakes)*

17 A In the play *King Lear*,
    B Shakespeare writes that the Gods
    C "kill us for their sport."
    D *(No mistakes)*

18 J My aunt in New Jersey
    K was always a supporter
    L of governor Whitman.
    M *(No mistakes)*

19 A My Doctor recommends
    B that I exercise on Mondays,
    C Wednesdays, and Fridays.
    D *(No mistakes)*

20 J The text of the prayer
    K Hail Mary can be found
    L in the Gospel of Luke.
    M *(No mistakes)*

Directions: Look for mistakes in **punctuation**.

21 A The character named
    B Hannah Montana does not live
    C in a town called Hannah Montana.
    D *(No mistakes)*

22 J The Great Sabbatini
    K was an accomplished escape artist,
    L and a skillful card manipulator.
    M *(No mistakes)*

23 A In the play, *King Lear*,
    B Shakespeare writes that the gods
    C "kill us for their sport."
    D *(No mistakes)*

24 J Although, he was
    K only 12 years old,
    L Oliver entered high school last year.
    M *(No mistakes)*

25 A Track athletes
    B require; speed,
    C agility, and endurance.
    D *(No mistakes)*

26 J Track athletes
    K require: speed,
    L agility, and endurance.
    M *(No mistakes)*

GO TO NEXT PAGE ➡

27
A My brothers
B new house in the suburbs
C is bigger than his old house in the city.
D *(No mistakes)*

28
J Newer house's tend to have
K much more closet space than older ones;
L perhaps we buy more clothes now.
M *(No mistakes)*

29
A "Isn't it one's duty
B to use one's mind
C to the utmost?" she asked.
D *(No mistakes)*

30
J After the recital
K we decided
L to get some ice cream.
M *(No mistakes)*

Directions: Look for mistakes in **usage and expression**.

31
A It's difficult to memorize
B all the rules, it's easier
C to experience them.
D *(No mistakes)*

32
J There's a robot
K that's got a clock
L for it's heart.
M *(No mistakes)*

33
A In order to succeed at this game,
B you have to be
C as quite as a mouse.
D *(No mistakes)*

34
J Me and my friends
K used to make up secret codes
L to use in our club.
M *(No mistakes)*

35
A The sounds of fifes and drums
B were an exciting part
C of the lifes of our colonial ancestors.
D *(No mistakes)*

36
J Immigrants from
K Latin America has contributed
L greatly to our society.
M *(No mistakes)*

37
A It may seem odd,
B but I enjoy working math problems.
C Because they exercise my mind.
D *(No mistakes)*

38 Choose the clearest sentence.

J I was surprised to see a bear, driving my car through the mountains.
K Driving my car through the mountains, I was surprised to see a bear.
L Surprisingly, I saw a bear driving my car, through the mountains.
M Through the mountains, I surprised a bear, while driving my car.

GO TO NEXT PAGE ➡

Directions: For questions 39 and 40, choose the best answer based on the following letter.

TACHS PRACTICE EXAM 1

Dear Students,

Due to the fact that so many of you hold the belief that your writing skills are adequate enough at the present time, I will postpone until later my lessons on the basic fundamentals of composition.

Perhaps in the near future, we may give consideration to the value of simplicity.

Sincerely,

Mr. Jarczewski

---

39 Choose the words that best replace the underlined expressions in the first sentence of the letter.

  A Since, hold, enough, presently, stretch, complexities

  B Because, believe, adequate, now, postpone, basics

  C Even though, have beliefs, fine, now, postpone, grammatical structures

  D Therefore, hold beliefs, inadequate, at present, delay, fundamental foundations

40 Choose the sentence that best replaces the second sentence in the letter.

  J Perhaps soon, we may consider the value of simplicity.

  K Maybe later I may provide guidance for simplicity in compositional studies.

  L Perhaps in the future, we possibly might discuss this in an effort to simplify.

  M Perhaps in the near future, we may give consideration to the value of simplicity.

Part 2—Paragraphs

10 QUESTIONS   7 MINUTES

PASSAGE FOR QUESTIONS 41–47

Dr. Polidori

Poor Polidori. (1)

If anyone has ever heard of John William Polidori, it is probably with this adjective attached. (2) Not that the hapless Dr. Polidori was lacking in money or intelligence during most of his short life. (3) He was a brilliant student and considered entering the priesthood. (4) However, his father pushed him toward medicine, and John William never dared to defy the elder Polidori, a strong personality who emigrated from Italy to England in 1790. (5)

Young Polidori received his medical degree from the prestigious University of Edinburgh (just as Arthur Conan Doyle did years later) at the age of nineteen. (6) But after fulfilling his father's plans for him, he had to decide what he really wanted to do, and that was to become a writer (as Doyle did, as well). (7)

He got his opportunity when the famous Romantic poet Lord Byron needed a doctor to accompany him during his travels throughout Europe. (8) Polidori spoke Italian and French and was eager to learn from the great writer. (9) Unfortunately, the two men did not get along. (10) Polidori, so eager to please Byron just as he was with his own father, became the butt of Byron's cruel wit. (11) Byron started calling him "Polly Dolly" and even ridiculed his medical talent: "The doctor has no more patience—because his patience are no more." (12)

One night in Geneva, Byron, Polidori, Percy Shelley, and Mary Shelley decided to write scary stories. (13) Percy Shelley and Byron never completed theirs, but they achieved lasting fame with their poetry. (14) Mary Shelley became famous for writing the novel Frankenstein as her entry in their contest. (15) They all ridiculed Polidori's contribution. (16) Mary wrote in her diary, "Poor Polidori had some terrible idea about a skull-headed lady . . . He did not know what to do with her . . ." (17)

Polidori later reworked his short story, basing its main character, a sophisticated count, on Byron, and called it "The Vampyre." (18) Somehow, it was published in a magazine without his permission—and worse yet, the author was listed as Lord Byron! (19) It became a famous and influential tale, but despite his and Byron's protests, no one quite believed that Polidori was the author. (20)

Poor Polidori. (21)

GO TO NEXT PAGE ➡

41 Which adjective in the passage is referenced in sentence 2?

  A brilliant
  B poor
  C young
  D elder

42 Which sentence is a fragment?

  J sentence 2
  K sentence 3
  L sentence 4
  M sentence 5

43 What change would you make to keep the main focus of the third paragraph?

  A remove the references to Doyle
  B remove the name of the university
  C remove the type of degree that Polidori earned
  D remove sentence 7

44 How should you rewrite the quote in sentence 12?

  J No change is necessary.
  K "The doctor has no more patients—because his patience are no more".
  L "The doctor has no more patients—because his patients are no more".
  M "The doctor has no more patience—because his patients are no more."

45 How would you rewrite sentence 15?

  A Mary Shelley became famous for writing the novel "Frankenstein" as her entry in their contest.
  B Mary Shelley became famous for writing the novel 'Frankenstein' as her entry in their contest.
  C Mary Shelley became famous for writing the novel, *Frankenstein,* as her entry in their contest.
  D Mary Shelley became famous for writing the novel *Frankenstein* as her entry in their contest.

46 How would you rewrite sentence 18?

  J No change is necessary.
  K Polidori later reworked his short story, basing it's main character, a sophisticated count, on Byron, and called it "The Vampyre."
  L Polidori later reworked his short story, basing its' main character, a sophisticated count, on Byron, and called it "The Vampyre."
  M Polidori later reworked his short story, basing its main character, a sophisticated count, on Byron, and called it *The Vampyre.*

47 What does the word *hapless* mean in sentence 3?

  A unhappy
  B wealthy
  C unlucky
  D depressed

GO TO NEXT PAGE ➡

A Short History of Ketchup

How would you feel if you ordered ketchup for your fries and you were served brown sauce? (1) Actually, you would be eating the most authentic version of ketchup, which originally included fish as its main ingredient. (2)

For centuries, the Chinese had been enjoying a paste of fermented anchovies and salt; they called it ketsiap—or at least, that's what it sounded like to British sailors trading in Southeast China and Vietnam. (3) They brought it to England, and it became a popular condiment and ingredient in recipes. (4) The British experimented with different bases, especially mushrooms and walnuts. (5) It remained a savory brown sauce for many years until someone thought to use tomatoes. (6)

Even then, the mixture of red, green, and yellow tomatoes yielded a brown sauce, but it tended to spoil easily. (7) Henry Heinz, a Pittsburgh ketchup manufacturer, decided to use red tomatoes, which contain more of the natural preservative pectin. (8) He also added more vinegar, another preservative, and sugar, for taste. (9) This proved to be the most popular version of ketchup (sometimes spelled catsup) by far, so you are unlikely to get a packet of anchovy paste at your next trip to the hot dog stand. (10)

48 How could you improve sentence 8?

J Henry Heinz, a Pittsburgh ketchup manufacturer decided to use red tomatoes, which contain more of the natural preservative pectin.

K Henry Heinz, a Pittsburgh ketchup manufacturer, decided to use only red tomatoes, which contain more of the natural preservative pectin.

L Henry Heinz, a Pittsburgh ketchup manufacturer, decided to use only red tomatoes, that contain more of the natural preservative pectin.

M Henry Heinz, a Pittsburgh ketchup manufacturer, decided to use red tomatoes, which contain more of the natural preservative.

49 How could you improve the focus of the last paragraph?

A remove the transitional phrase "Even then"

B add more information about the thickness of the sauce

C add some information about mustard as an additional condiment

D remove the reference to "catsup"

50 In context, what does the word *savory* mean in sentence 6?

J economical

K brown

L flavorful without sugar

M disagreeable

STOP

If there is still time remaining, you may review your answers.

MATH—PART 1

32 QUESTIONS   30 MINUTES

Directions: Select the best answer out of the four choices.

1 Change 2.36 to a mixed number and reduce to lowest terms.

   A $2\frac{36}{100}$

   B $2\frac{18}{50}$

   C $2\frac{3}{8}$

   D $2\frac{9}{25}$

2 Add $3\frac{3}{4}$, $2\frac{1}{3}$, and $5\frac{1}{2}$.

   J $10\frac{7}{9}$

   K $10\frac{5}{9}$

   L $11\frac{7}{12}$

   M $9\frac{7}{11}$

3 Which of the following numbers is a multiple of 7?

   A   56

   B   36

   C   48

   D   72

4 Change $\frac{5}{8}$ to a decimal and round off to the nearest hundredth.

   J   0.63

   K   0.56

   L   0.64

   M   0.57

5 Find the value of $9r^2 - 2s + 3t$ when $r = -2$, $s = 4$, and $t = -3$.

   A   12

   B   19

   C   −3

   D   −9

6 Which of these numbers is the equivalent of 9^3?

   J   512

   K   729

   L   392

   M   649

7 Simplify $3(7 - 3)^2 - 4(6 + 2)$.

   A   18

   B   16

   C   17

   D   20

8 Which of the following is a prime number?

   J   7

   K   9

   L   12

   M   15

9 Find the product of $\frac{3}{4}$ and $\frac{2}{5}$. Reduce to lowest terms.

   A $\frac{6}{20}$

   B $\frac{5}{8}$

   C $\frac{3}{10}$

   D $\frac{4}{9}$

GO TO NEXT PAGE →

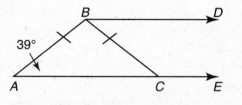

10 *ABC* above is an isosceles triangle. *BD* is parallel to *ACE* and angle *A* measures 39°. Find the measure of angle *DBC*.

J   39°
K   78°
L   64°
M   46°

11 Kelly weighs 119 pounds. Her brother, Hector, weighs 12 pounds more than Kelly while her sister, Jasmine, weighs 17 pounds less than Hector. Find their total weight.

A   364 pounds
B   356 pounds
C   354 pounds
D   350 pounds

12 Mario is on the track team. He ran the following number of miles each day for three meets: 5.9, 6, 3.7. What was the average number of miles Mario ran at a meet?

J   4.5 miles
K   6.2 miles
L   5.1 miles
M   5.2 miles

13 Each of five cabbies drive an average of 453 miles a day. Six other cabbies each drive an average of 487 miles a day. How many miles do all eleven cabbies drive per day?

A   5,585 miles
B   5,387 miles
C   5,187 miles
D   5,516 miles

14 A flat piece of metal weighs 2.4 grams per square centimeter. Find the weight of a 7-centimeter by 12-centimeter piece of metal.

J   201.6 grams
K   204.7 grams
L   203.5 grams
M   209.8 grams

15 Carter was on a diet. When he weighed himself at the start of his diet, he weighed 220 pounds. At the end of six months, Carter weighed 180 pounds. What fraction of his original weight did he lose?

A $\dfrac{1}{8}$

B $\dfrac{4}{13}$

C $\dfrac{3}{16}$

D $\dfrac{2}{11}$

16 If $900 is to be divided equally among a group of people, how many persons are in the group?

J   17
K   19
L   21
M   15

17 Roger has a 0.250 batting average. If he went up to bat 240 times, how many times did he fail to get any hits? (A 0.250 batting average means that he got hits 0.250 times at bat.)

A   170 times
B   180 times
C   190 times
D   200 times

GO TO NEXT PAGE ➡

18 The Maxim Movie Theater collected $1,314 yesterday. If the adults paid $1,050 and each child's admission was $5.50, how many children were admitted?

J 48
K 52
L 46
M 51

19 Carmen wants to paint a wall 12 feet high by 32 feet long. If 1 quart of paint covers 24 square feet of wall space, how many quarts of paint does Carmen need to cover the entire wall?

A 16 quarts
B 14 quarts
C 15 quarts
D 13 quarts

20 A cargo ship has a capacity of 4,000 tons. If it sails from Los Angeles to Singapore carrying $\frac{2}{5}$ of its capacity and returns carrying $\frac{4}{5}$ of its capacity, how many tons did it carry round-trip?

J 3,800 tons
K 4,600 tons
L 4,700 tons
M 4,800 tons

Directions: Use the graph below to answer questions 21 and 22.

= 4,000 people

	Residents in 2009
Barstow	(3 figures)
Silverton	(1 figure)
Castle City	(4 figures)
Newton	(5 figures)
Hillsborough	(4 figures)

21 How many people lived in Barstow in 2009?

A 16,000
B 8,000
C 20,000
D 12,000

22 How many more people lived in Newton than in Silverton in 2009?

J 14,000
K 8,000
L 16,000
M 12,000

GO TO NEXT PAGE ➡

GO TO NEXT PAGE ➡

Directions: Use the table below to answer questions 23 and 24.

Major Network Television Shows

	2006	2007	2008	2009	Summary
Reality	2	3	12	14	31
Comedy	7	9	8	7	31
Law	3	6	7	5	21
Detective	7	7	6	10	30
Cartoons	10	12	12	16	50
News	20	24	15	15	74
Summary	49	61	60	67	237

23 In 2008, what percent of all television shows were detective stories?

A   25%
B   18%
C   30%
D   10%

24 How many more news programs were there in 2006 than in 2009?

J   6
K   7
L   5
M   4

Directions: Use the chart below to answer questions 25 and 26.

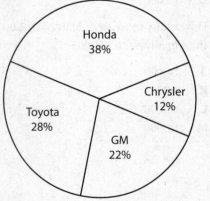

2,600 Cars Sold by Zany Dealers

Honda 38%
Chrysler 12%
Toyota 28%
GM 22%

25 According to the chart, how many Chryslers did the dealership sell?

A   298
B   312
C   324
D   402

26 How many more Toyotas than GM cars did Zany Dealers sell?

J   156
K   312
L   728
M   208

Directions: Use the table below to answer questions 27 and 28.

The table below lists weights of a group of six persons.

Pounds	# of persons
118	2
132	3
163	1

27 Find the average weight, correct to the nearest pound.

    A 133
    B 143
    C 145
    D 139

28 If we drop the two persons weighing 118 pounds, what is the average weight of the remaining persons, correct to the nearest tenth of a pound?

    J 154.6
    K 152.3
    L 141.4
    M 139.8

Directions: Use the graph below to answer questions 29 and 30.

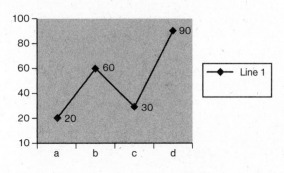

29 Which statement is true?

    A $a + b > d$
    B $b + c < d$
    C $b + c = d$
    D $a + c = d$

30 Which is the correct statement?

    J c is greater than b
    K d is less than a
    L a is 10 less than c
    M d is 20 more than b

GO TO NEXT PAGE ➡

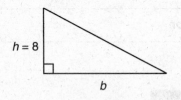

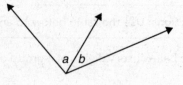

31 The area of the triangle above is 56, and its height is 8. Find its base.

A 12
B 16
C 10
D 14

32 Find the measure of angle *a* above if angle *b* equals 27° and the combined measure of both angle *a* and angle *b* is 104°.

J 77°
K 56°
L 43°
M 63°

GO TO NEXT PAGE ➡

MATH—PART 2

> **Directions:** Estimate the answer in your head. No writing is permitted. An exact answer is not expected.

33   Estimate $6 \times 4.95 - 1.8$.

   A   34
   B   30
   C   28
   D   29.3

34   On average, there are approximately 2 left-handed people out of every 11. About how many persons in a sample population of 2,250 would you expect to be left-handed?

   J   600
   K   400
   L   800
   M   300

35   Estimate the difference of 8,786 and 5,579.

   A   2,900
   B   4,000
   C   3,000
   D   3,200

36   What is the closest estimate of the sum of $45\frac{3}{4}$, $16\frac{2}{3}$, and $34\frac{1}{2}$?

   J   106
   K   97
   L   88
   M   101

37   Karl can paint a wall at the rate of 78 square feet per hour. At this rate, about how many hours would he need to paint a wall 920 square feet?

   A   12 hours
   B   18 hours
   C   8 hours
   D   10 hours

38   In a study, it was discovered that 2% of the television sets manufactured by the Roric Corporation were defective. Out of 121,345 sets, approximately how many would you expect to be defective?

   J   2,000
   K   2,400
   L   1,900
   M   1,800

39   Select the closest estimate of $3(8.3 + 3.8) - 2(9.6 - 2.7)$.

   A   19
   B   27
   C   29
   D   22

40   Select the closest estimate of $(5.62)^2$.

   J   38
   K   40
   L   45
   M   32

GO TO NEXT PAGE ➡

Directions: Use the graph below to answer questions 41 and 42.

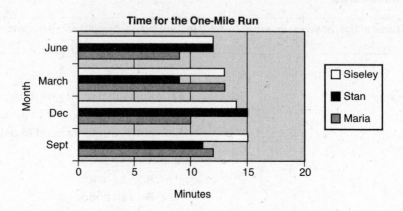

Time for the One-Mile Run

41 Check the chart above and estimate how many minutes it took Siseley to jog 1 mile in March.

   A   10 minutes
   B   11 minutes
   C   9 minutes
   D   13 minutes

42 About how many minutes faster did Stan jog one mile in March than it took for Maria to jog 1 mile in September?

   J   5 minutes
   K   6 minutes
   L   3 minutes
   M   7 minutes

GO TO NEXT PAGE ➡

43 The height of a tree is 12 feet. If the height is represented on a blueprint as $\frac{1}{2}$ inch, what is the ratio of the blueprint diagram to the actual height of the tree?

A　1 : 110
B　2 : 85
C　3 : 97
D　1 : 288

44 Jackie weighs $x + 2$ pounds. Her brother, Manuel, weighs 12 pounds more than Jackie and her sister, Elaine, weighs 6 pounds less than Jackie. What is the average weight of all three siblings?

J　$\dfrac{2x - 4}{3}$
K　$x + 4$
L　$x - 6$
M　$\dfrac{2x + 4}{3}$

45 On the real number line, if the distance between two numbers is 6.9, which of the following sets represents the two numbers?

A　11.2 and 19.4
B　5.7 and 12.6
C　3.7 and 11.8
D　4.9 and 13.8

46 Find the largest of three consecutive odd integers whose sum is 39.

J　11
K　13
L　15
M　19

47 Find the difference of 2|–3| minus 4|5|.

A　12
B　–6
C　18
D　–14

48 The price of a television set dropped 10% and then an additional 30% of the original price. What percent of the original price was the selling price after the second drop?

J　48%
K　56%
L　63%
M　72%

49 Simplify $\sqrt[3]{27x^3y^9}$.

A　$3xy$
B　$3xy^3$
C　$3xy^2$
D　$3x^2y^3$

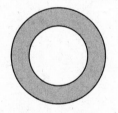

50 In the figure above, the inner circle has a radius of 6 while the outer circle has a radius of 9. Find the shaded area. Leave your answer in terms of π.

J　36π
K　54π
L　45π
M　39π

If there is still time remaining, you may review your answers.

ABILITY

10 QUESTIONS   5 MINUTES

> **Directions:** For questions 1–3, the top three figures are similar in certain ways. Try to determine the similarity and then select the figure that continues the similarity.

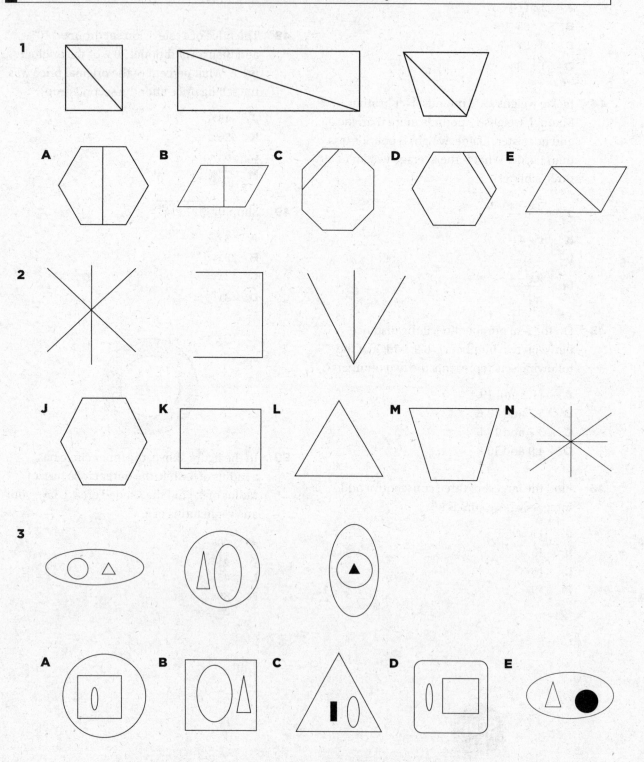

GO TO NEXT PAGE ➡

Directions: For questions 4–7, in the illustrative example, the first figure is linked to the second figure. Using the same principle, select the form that is linked to the third figure.

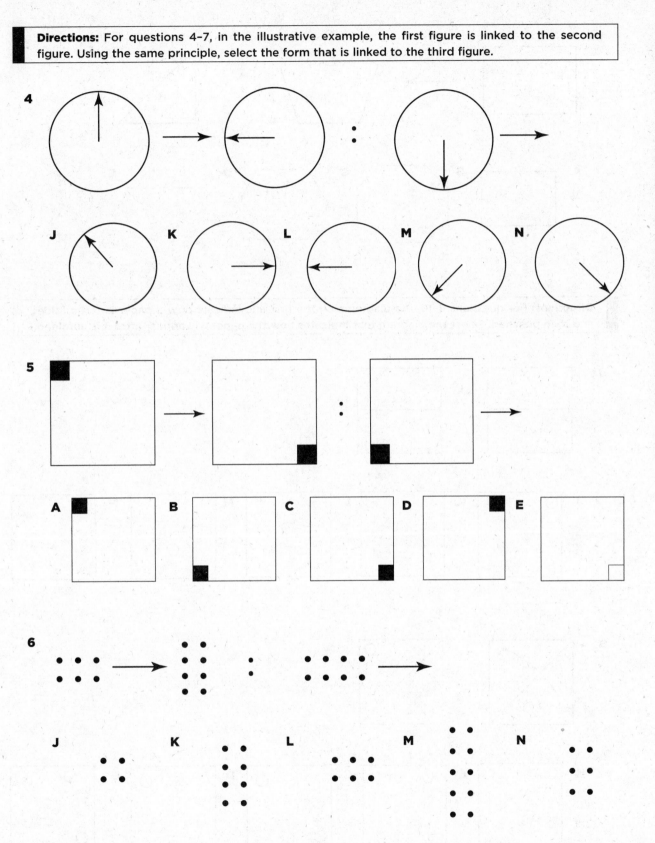

GO TO NEXT PAGE ➡

7

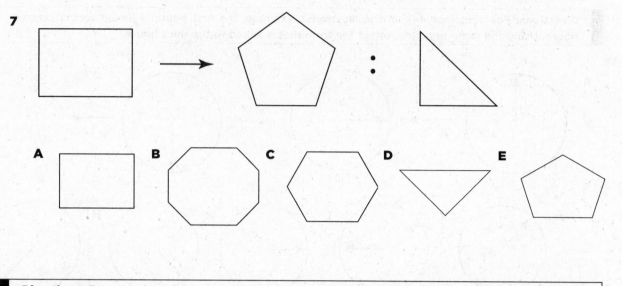

Directions: For questions 8–10, the diagrams on the first line indicate how a paper is to be folded and then punched. Select the diagram that indicates how the paper will appear after it is unfolded.

8

9

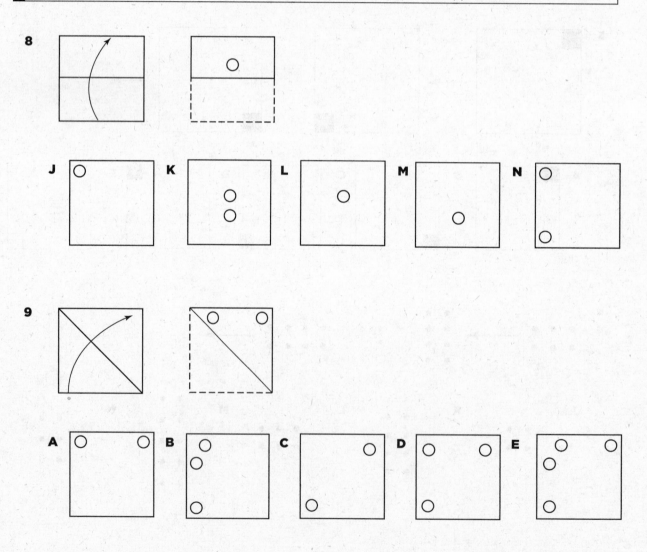

GO TO NEXT PAGE ➡

10

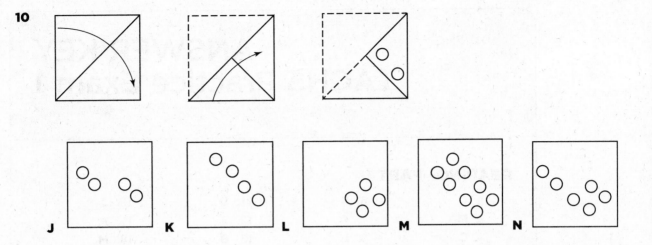

If there is still time remaining, you may review your answers.

ANSWER KEY
TACHS Practice Exam 1

READING—PART 1

1. **C**	6. **K**	11. **D**	16. **J**
2. **M**	7. **A**	12. **J**	17. **A**
3. **C**	8. **L**	13. **B**	18. **M**
4. **J**	9. **B**	14. **J**	19. **D**
5. **B**	10. **M**	15. **C**	20. **K**

READING—PART 2

21. **B**	29. **D**	37. **B**	45. **A**
22. **L**	30. **L**	38. **K**	46. **L**
23. **B**	31. **D**	39. **D**	47. **C**
24. **M**	32. **L**	40. **J**	48. **K**
25. **A**	33. **D**	41. **D**	49. **B**
26. **K**	34. **K**	42. **J**	50. **K**
27. **B**	35. **C**	43. **D**	
28. **L**	36. **L**	44. **L**	

WRITTEN EXPRESSION—PART 1—ENGLISH

1. **B**	11. **D**	21. **C**	31. **B**
2. **J**	12. **L**	22. **K**	32. **L**
3. **E**	13. **B**	23. **A**	33. **C**
4. **L**	14. **J**	24. **J**	34. **J**
5. **E**	15. **A**	25. **B**	35. **C**
6. **J**	16. **L**	26. **K**	36. **K**
7. **A**	17. **B**	27. **A**	37. **C**
8. **K**	18. **L**	28. **J**	38. **K**
9. **C**	19. **A**	29. **D**	39. **B**
10. **J**	20. **M**	30. **J**	40. **J**

WRITTEN EXPRESSION—PART 2—PARAGRAPHS

41. **B**	44. **M**	47. **C**	50. **L**
42. **K**	45. **D**	48. **K**	
43. **A**	46. **J**	49. **D**	

ANSWER KEY
TACHS Practice Exam 1

MATH—PART 1

1. **D**	9. **C**	17. **B**	25. **B**
2. **L**	10. **J**	18. **J**	26. **J**
3. **A**	11. **A**	19. **A**	27. **A**
4. **J**	12. **M**	20. **M**	28. **M**
5. **B**	13. **C**	21. **D**	29. **C**
6. **K**	14. **J**	22. **L**	30. **L**
7. **B**	15. **D**	23. **D**	31. **D**
8. **J**	16. **M**	24. **L**	32. **J**

MATH—PART 2

33. **C**	38. **K**	43. **D**	48. **L**
34. **K**	39. **D**	44. **K**	49. **B**
35. **D**	40. **M**	45. **B**	50. **L**
36. **K**	41. **D**	46. **L**	
37. **A**	42. **L**	47. **D**	

ABILITY

1. **E**	4. **K**	7. **A**	10. **M**
2. **L**	5. **D**	8. **K**	
3. **E**	6. **M**	9. **E**	

ANSWERS EXPLAINED

Reading—Part 1

1. **(C)** *Unanimous* means "united in one mind."

2. **(M)** *Con* (with) + *tempus* (time) = with the times, up-to-date, *modern*.

3. **(C)** *Dis* is a negative prefix. To disregard literally means to look away or *ignore*.

4. **(J)** *Boisterous* means noisy or rowdy. Boys will be boisterous when boiled.

5. **(B)** Remember that the root *graph* means to write or draw.

6. **(K)** To *succumb* is to *give in to*. She succumbed to sucking her thumb.

7. **(A)** A snake's *poison* is called *venom*.

8. **(L)** *Syn* (together) + *chronos* (time) = together in time.

9. **(B)** *Hypo* (beneath) + *derma* (skin) = *under the skin*.

10. **(M)** *Indefatigable* = not fatigable (if that's a word), *untiring*.

11. **(D)** A *posthumous* award is given after someone's *death*.

12. **(J)** Remember that *chronos* has to do with time.

13. **(B)** *Multi*, of course, means *many*.

14. **(J)** *Circum* means *around*.

15. **(C)** A *centurion commanded* a troop of 100 soldiers.

16. **(J)** *Remorse* originally meant "to bite again (*re*—again + *mordere*—bite)!" That's some conscience!

17. **(A)** *Morph* = shape; *amorphous* = *without shape*.

18. **(M)** If you *utilize* something, you use it.

19. **(D)** An *automaton* is a machine, especially a *robot*.

20. **(K)** Sailors use a plumb line—a string with a lead weight attached to it—to measure depth. It **plunges** straight down; it *plummets*. The closest meaning here is *to fall*.

Reading—Part 2

21. **(B)** Of course, knowing vocabulary helps here. However, you can likely exclude some answers right off the bat. Apply logic. If the liquid *inside* the plant is the thing that catalyzes irritation on human skin, it has to get out before it can cause harm. Write off choices A, C, and D.

22. **(L)** The passage drips with sarcasm and otherwise scathing remarks about the terrible things that poison ivy can do; additionally, it talks about how poison ivy, even when left alone for years, can still cause welts in a victim. Therefore, one can only conclude that the author hates poison ivy (indeed, one can surmise that the author has fallen prey

to poison ivy's terrors previous to writing this article), and wants it wiped out. Choose answer L.

23. **(B)** The article clearly states that the welts caused by poison ivy can range in color from the color of "normal flesh" to blood red. One can rule out, therefore, choices A and C. However, one must be careful regarding choices B and D. One might be tempted to choose choice D. However, not all human skin is beige; human skin ranges from pale white to beige to tan to deep black. Choosing D is incorrect. The only correct answer is choice B, in which the non-color-specific choice of "flesh colored" provides a broad enough range of skin color to be accurate.

24. **(M)** Based on the article, the answer is choice M. The other answers are designed to distract you from the right answer, based on the fact that they all start with the letter "u" and are actual words (albeit words that do not appear anywhere in this passage).

25. **(A)** Given that the author does not like poison ivy, indeed that he or she hates poison ivy, select a title that implies antagonism. Choices B, C, and D all imply friendliness; go for choice A, which implies criticism.

26. **(K)** This article does not support the idea that most people have contracted poison ivy; skip choice J. This article does not address the idea that people do or do not find poison ivy a problem; skip choice M. Choice L is implied by the mere fact that someone decided that poison ivy was a topic about which is worth writing. However, the best answer, far and away, is choice K, which relates a topic verified by the passage.

27. **(B)** The passage states in paragraph two that the French were occupied by the Germans. The only time that this happened was in the context of World War II.

28. **(L)** Imagine yourself in the following position. You have caught your friend in an embarrassing position and you want to make a point. You would remind him or her of what mistake he or she made and laugh, yes? However, since you like this person, and value his or her friendship, you would not want to be too cruel. You therefore, *chide* this person for his or her mistake. That means not outright praising him or her (choice J) or being angry (choice K) or even feel nothing (apathy) for (choice M). The correct choice is therefore L, a gentle criticism.

29. **(D)** The article tells you that *chat noir* is a form of satire; satire is a literary genre devoted to poking fun. Choices A, B, and C are all political candidates, equally worthy of satirical comment. Since the author gives you the option of "All of the above," this is the best answer.

30. **(L)** The article does not mention *The Daily Show*, even though it is indeed a modern form of satiric commentary. Although the term *chat noir* is from another language, it is a French, not a Latin, phrase. The passage is not about Latin vocabulary. The article does mention World War II and some related topics, but it does not dwell on Mussolini or his final days. The best answer is choice L.

31. **(D)** Re-reading (or memory) tells you that paragraph one defined *chat noir* for you: black cat.

32. **(L)** The author uses the word *adore* in conjunction with the term *aficionado* implying a link between the two; use this information to help you narrow your choices. Consider

the answers. Whether someone is skilled or unskilled at something has little to do with liking something, although it can have a connection. Rule out choices J and K. The author's context tells you that the link between adoring something and being an aficionado is a positive one; rule out choice M.

33. **(D)** Re-reading verifies that the only artist in this list not mentioned in the passage is Claude Monet.

34. **(K)** The use of the word juxtaposition in this article implies a connection or combination. Rule out answers that do not fulfill this context. The best answer is choice K.

35. **(C)** The article implies that an enigma is something not known, or not completely understood. Therefore, rule out choice B. There is nothing in the article to suggest that something is incorrect; therefore rule out choice D. Choices A and C are more difficult, but you can rule out choice A, since context tells you that an enigma is based in truth (the reference to law), albeit not immediately recognized truth.

36. **(L)** Re-reading the passage, or memory, tells you that Escher considered his publication in the International Union of Crystallography as his crowning achievement.

37. **(B)** This question asks you to make an inference. You can tell from the passage that Escher was captivated by scientific law and art; his was a mind drawn to clarity, rhythm, system, and order. Choose the answer that fits these parameters—logic, clarity, order. Choices A, C, and D are irrational and nonfactual (at least according to this passage), and so your best choice is B.

38. **(K)** Paragraph 1 links graphic arts with pencil, ink, and printing techniques. Of those three options, the answer that most closely links up is choice K. (By the way, permanent marker did not exist back then.)

39. **(D)** The passage keeps making the point that Escher looked for clear answers through investigating mysteries. He did possess a clear cut mind, but the article discusses more than this, so rule out choice B. While Escher struggled for his art, the article does not imply undue degrees of pain, so rule out choice C. Choice A is tempting, but the best answer is choice D.

40. **(J)** To answer the question one must isolate the sentence in question. Grammatically, the pronoun "they" refers to the nearest noun previous to it. In this case the nearest noun is "mountains."

41. **(D)** The poem is delivered from a personal perspective, from a wondering "I." Therefore, choose the answer that best fits a first-person perspective. Choices A, B, and C do not match up with this perspective; choice D is the answer.

42. **(J)** The main point of this poem is to convey a questioning attitude. While one might read into the poem deeper ideas—like the meaning of life or the existence of evil—these are not concretely found. The only concretely found unifying form to the poem is the idea of whence morning comes. Choice J is the answer.

43. **(D)** The tone of the poem does not convey fear or anger. It may convey joy, but it definitely conveys innocence. Choice D is the answer.

44. **(L)** Interestingly, all four of these definitions for pilgrim are correct. We need, however, to pick the one best suited for this poem. This poem refers to someone who is wandering, in need of answers, with a reverential yet innocent attitude. The poem does not refer to things like Massachusetts (choice J), movies (choice K), or ill-fated loves (choice M). Therefore, the best answer is choice L.

45. **(A)** This is a rather opinionated question, as inference questions sometimes are, but you can get it right. Renaming the poem Evening does not work; nothing about the poem implies the end of the day. Renaming the poem Summer does not work; nothing about the poem implies a season. Question and Why are both tempting, but the title Why narrows the scope of the poem too much; the best answer is Question.

46. **(L)** The author has chosen a series of similar numbers to test your reading skills. The correct answer is L (see paragraph 6).

47. **(C)** Matt speaks about his time prior to his win in a way that implies frustration. He does not seem confused, happy, or fearful, so the best answer is choice C.

48. **(K)** Again, check the passage or check your memory. The answer is choice K.

49. **(B)** Matt implicitly states that his inability to win a race weighed heavily upon him. However, he uses no "like" or "as"; therefore, rule out choices A and C. An ellipses is an omission, as when one quotes someone in a paper; rule out choice D. Matt is using a metaphor. Choice B is correct.

50. **(K)** Choice K should read, "We have to keep putting ourselves in position to win" and therefore, choice K is the right answer.

Written Expression—Part 1—English

1. **(B)** *Unoticed* is misspelled. Remember that when you add a prefix to a word, the original word remains unchanged. So just add it: *un + noticed = unnoticed*. (*Misspelled* is another example of this.)

2. **(J)** The correct spelling is *galaxy*.

3. **(E)** *(No mistakes)* Did you fall for this trick? No, *steal* is not a metal (that's *steel*), but *steal* is still a word (to take without permission). It's spelled correctly, even though it doesn't belong in the same category. The TACHS exam questions probably won't be this tricky, but this keeps you focused on spelling. (You'll thank us later.)

4. **(L)** *Equasion* should be spelled *equation*.

5. **(E)** *(No mistakes)* This was another trick. *Discreet* and *discrete* are both correctly spelled words. Look them up in a dictionary if you don't know the different meanings.

6. **(J)** *Tommorrow* should be spelled *tomorrow*. This is sometimes a troublesome spelling word, so memorize it.

7. **(A)** *Frugle* should be spelled *frugal*.

8. **(K)** *Nucular* should be spelled *nuclear*.

9. **(C)** The correct spelling is *triple*.

10. **(J)** The correct spelling is *acquire*.

11. **(D)** *(No mistakes)* Specific regions are capitalized.

12. **(L)** Specific universities are capitalized: Rutgers University.

13. **(B)** The word italics does not refer to a specific country, so it is not capitalized.

14. **(J)** The word *mother* is only capitalized when it is used as a name. Note the difference between *Ask Mother* [your name for her) and *Ask your mother*.

15. **(A)** Don't forget to capitalize the first word in a sentence.

16. **(L)** Always capitalize the pronoun *I*.

17. **(B)** Shakespeare does not refer to a specific deity, so the word *gods* is not capitalized.

18. **(L)** The title *governor* is associated with a specific name, so it is capitalized: Governor Whitman.

19. **(A)** The title *doctor* is not associated with a specific name here.

20. **(M)** *(No mistakes)*

21. **(C)** Use a comma between a city and state: Hannah, Montana.

22. **(K)** No comma is needed here, as it does not separate two independent clauses.

23. **(A)** You've seen this sentence before, but this time it's punctuated incorrectly. The play *King Lear* cannot be taken out of the sentence without losing essential information, so it cannot be separated by commas.

24. **(J)** No comma is needed after the word *although*, as the introductory element is not yet completed. It should read as follows: *Although he was only 12 years old, Oliver entered high school last year.*

25. **(B)** A semicolon cannot be used to introduce a list. A semicolon primarily separates two independent clauses.

26. **(K)** Yes, a colon introduces a list; however, it is not necessary after a verb or a preposition. Remove the semicolon and see that the sentence makes perfect sense. *Track athletes require speed, agility, and endurance.*

27. **(A)** This possessive requires an apostrophe: *my brother's house.*

28. **(J)** The apostrophe is not necessary to create a plural. The plural of *house* is *houses.*

29. **(D)** *(No mistakes)*

30. **(J)** Use a comma after an introductory element: *After the recital, we decided to get some ice cream.*

31. **(B)** This error is called a comma splice. A comma cannot separate sentences; use a period or a semicolon, instead.

32. **(L)** The possessive form of *it* is *its*. No apostrophe is needed. (Remember: *his, hers, theirs, yours, ours,* and *its* do not require apostrophes.)

33. **(C)** You have to be as *quiet* as a mouse.

34. **(J)** The subjective form of the first person pronoun is *I: My friends and* I *made up secret codes.*

35. **(C)** The plural of *life* is *lives.*

36. **(K)** Watch for subject-verb agreement: **Immigrants** *[from Latin America]* **have contributed** greatly.

37. **(C)** This choice is a fragment.

38. **(K)** Look out for misplaced modifiers, and stay away from bears. Bears are very dangerous. Don't feed them. I'm not kidding.

39. **(B)** If you replace the underlined sections with these words, the meaning of the sentence becomes clear.

40. **(J)** Keep it simple. Keep it clear.

Written Expression—Part 2—Paragraphs

41. **(B)** The second sentence refers to the adjective *poor* in the previous sentence.

42. **(K)** Although it is effective in context, sentence 3 is a fragment.

43. **(A)** Referring to a future author adds nothing to a paragraph about a different author earning a difficult degree at such a young age.

44. **(M)** Byron's joke only makes sense if it refers to people, or *patients*. Further, the period must be enclosed in the punctuation marks.

45. **(D)** The title of a novel should be italicized, not placed in quotes. Also, in this sentence, the title of the novel is necessary in order for the sentence to make sense, so you should not separate it with commas. A good way to test this is to remove the words in parentheses and see if the sentence still makes sense.

    Mary Shelley became famous for writing the novel as her entry in their contest.

    Mary Shelley became famous for writing the novel *Frankenstein* as her entry in their contest.

    The first of these sample sentences lacks necessary information. The second is correct.

46. **(J)** No change is necessary. Remember that the word *its* functions as a possessive pronoun. *It's* contracts *it is* or *it was*. Also, short stories use quotation marks rather than italics.

47. **(C)** The word *hapless* means *unlucky*, which the passage illustrates. You might have been tempted to guess *unhappy*, but there is also the synonymous choice *depressed*, and they can't both be correct.

48. **(K)** Red tomatoes were already in use, so we need the distinction *only* before "red tomatoes." Sentences J and L misuse commas, and sentence M leaves out an important detail about what preservative red tomatoes contain.

49. **(D)** The reference to "catsup" is unnecessary since it's described as "ketchup" throughout the passage. This paragraph brings the history of ketchup to a close by showing how it got to be the sweet/sour red condiment we know today. We don't need information about spelling, the thickness of the sauce, or mustard. The transitional phrase in choice A lead us into our final paragraph so it should stay as is.

50. **(L)** Savory means flavorful, but not necessarily sweet. If it meant *brown*, that would be redundant since it is already described as brown in the sentence. The paragraph talks about ketchup's popularity so it can't mean *disagreeable*. The word *economical* tries to trick you because the word *savory* sounds like *save*.

Math—Part 1

1. **(D)** Let's first write 2.36 as a mixed number. Then we can reduce the fraction part.

$$2.36 = 2\frac{36}{100} = 2\frac{9}{25}$$

2. **(L)** Find a common denominator and then add.

$$3\frac{3}{4} = \frac{9}{12}$$
$$2\frac{1}{3} = \frac{4}{12}$$
$$+ \quad 5\frac{1}{2} = \frac{6}{12}$$
$$\overline{10\frac{19}{12} = 10 + 1\frac{7}{12} = 11\frac{7}{12}}$$

3. **(A)** Find the product of 7 and some whole number that will result in one of the given numbers.

$$7 \times 8 = 56$$

4. **(J)** Divide the denominator 8 into the numerator 5, and then round off to the nearest hundredth.

$$
\begin{array}{r}
.625 \\
8\overline{)5.000} \\
-48\downarrow \\
\hline
20 \\
-16\downarrow \\
\hline
40 \\
-40 \\
\hline
0
\end{array}
$$

To the nearest hundredth, $.625 \approx .63$.

5. **(B)**
$$9(-2)^2 - 2(4) + 3(-3) =$$
$$9(4) - 8 - 9 =$$
$$36 - 17 = 19$$

6. **(K)** Expand 9^3.
$$9^3 = 9 \times 9 \times 9 = 729$$

7. **(B)** Complete the work in the parentheses first.
$$3(7-3)^2 - 4(6+2) = 3(4)^2 - 4(8)$$
$$= 3(16) - 32$$
$$= 48 - 32$$
$$= 16$$

8. **(J)** A prime number has no other factors than 1 and itself.

   (J) $7 = 7 \times 1$
   (K) $9 = 3 \times 3$
   (L) $12 = 4 \times 3$ and $12 = 6 \times 2$
   (M) $15 = 5 \times 3$

9. **(C)** Multiply numerators and denominators separately and then reduce.
$$\frac{3}{4} \times \frac{2}{5} = \frac{6}{20} = \frac{3}{10}$$

10. **(J)**

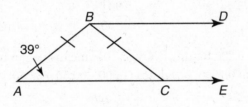

Since $\triangle ABC$ is isosceles, m $\angle A$ = m $\angle ACB$ = 39°. *BD* and *ACE* are parallel lines, so their alternate interior angles are equal: m $\angle DBC$ = m $\angle ACB$ = 39°.

11. **(A)** First, determine each person's weight. Then add them all.

Kelly =	119 pounds
Hector = 119 + 12 =	131 pounds
+ Jasmine = 131 − 17 =	114 pounds
	364 pounds

12. **(M)** Add up the figures and divide by three.

$$
\begin{array}{r}
5.9 \\
6.0 \\
\underline{+\ 3.7} \\
15.6
\end{array}
\qquad
\begin{array}{r}
5.2 \\
3\overline{)15.6} \\
-15 \downarrow \\
\overline{0\,6} \\
-6 \\
\overline{0}
\end{array}
$$

13. **(C)** Multiply 453 by 5 and 487 by 6 and add the two totals.

$$
\begin{array}{ccc}
453 & 487 & 2265 \\
\underline{\times 5} & \underline{\times 6} & \underline{+2922} \\
2265 & 2922 & 5187
\end{array}
$$

14. **(J)** Find the area of the metal and then multiply by 2.4, the gram weight of one centimeter of metal.

$$7 \times 12 = 84 \text{ square centimeters}$$

$$
\begin{array}{l}
8\ 4 \text{ square centimeters} \\
\underline{\times\, 2.4} \text{ grams per square centimeter} \\
336 \\
\underline{+\, 1680} \\
201.6 \text{ grams}
\end{array}
$$

15. **(D)** Find the difference in Carter's weight and then divide by 220, his original weight.

$$220 - 180 = 40$$

$$\frac{40}{220} = \frac{2}{11}$$

16. **(M)** Determine which number divides into 900 without a remainder that continues indefinitely.

17. **(B)** If Roger has a 0.250 batting average, that means he got hits 0.250×240 times. But he failed to get a hit 0.750×240 times $(1.000 - 0.250 = 0.750)$.

$$
\begin{array}{r}
240 \\
\underline{\times\, 0.750} \\
12000 \\
\underline{+\, 168000} \\
180.000
\end{array}
$$

18. **(J)** Subtract the adult admissions from the total money collected. Then, divide the result by $5.50, the price of a single child's admission.

$$
\begin{array}{r}
48 \\
5.50\,)\overline{264.00} \\
\underline{-\,2200}\downarrow \\
4400 \\
\underline{-\,4400} \\
0
\end{array}
$$

$$
\begin{array}{r}
\$1314 \\
\underline{-\ \ 1050} \\
\$\ 264
\end{array}
$$

19. **(A)** First, find the area of the wall. Then, divide by 24, the number of square feet that 1 gallon of paint covers.

$$
\begin{array}{r}
32 \\
\times\,12 \\
\hline
64 \\
+\,320 \\
\hline
384
\end{array}
\qquad
\begin{array}{r}
16 \\
24\overline{)384} \\
-\,24\downarrow \\
\hline
144 \\
-\,144 \\
\hline
0
\end{array}
$$

20. **(M)** For the weight carried from Los Angeles to Singapore, multiply $\frac{2}{5}$ by 4,000.

For the return weight, from Singapore back to Los Angeles, multiply $\frac{4}{5}$ by 4,000. Then, add the two results.

$$\frac{2}{\cancel{5}} \times \overset{800}{\cancel{4,000}} = 1,600$$

$$+\;\frac{4}{\cancel{5}} \times \overset{800}{\cancel{4,000}} = 3,200$$

$$\overline{}$$

4,800 tons

21. **(D)** Each figure represents 4,000 inhabitants. Just count the number of figures and multiply by 4,000.

$$3 \times 4,000 = 12,000$$

22. **(L)** Determine the number of inhabitants of Newton and Silverton in 2009 and subtract.

$$
\begin{array}{l}
\text{Newton} = 5 \times 4,000 = 20,000 \\
-\;\text{Silverton} = 1 \times 4,000 = 4,000 \\
\hline
\phantom{-\;\text{Silverton} = 1 \times 4,000 = }16,000
\end{array}
$$

23. **(D)** In 2008, there were 6 detective stories out of a total of 60 shows.

$$
\frac{6}{60} = \quad
\begin{array}{r}
.10 \\
60\overline{)6.00} \\
-\,6\,0\downarrow \\
\hline
00
\end{array}
= 10\%
$$

24. **(L)** Subtract the number of news programs in 2009 from the news programs in 2006.

$$
\begin{array}{l}
\text{News Programs in } 2006 = 20 \\
-\,\text{News Programs in } 2009 = 15 \\
\hline
\phantom{-\,\text{News Programs in } 2009 = }5
\end{array}
$$

25. **(B)** Change the percentage of Chrysler cars sold to a decimal and multiply by the total number of cars sold.

Chrysler: 12% = .12

$$
\begin{array}{r}
2600 \\
\times\,.12 \\
\hline
5200 \\
+26000 \\
\hline
312.00
\end{array}
$$

26. **(J)** Change percentages to decimals, multiply by the total number of cars sold, and subtract.

Toyota: 28% = .28   Toyota:
GM: 22% = .22

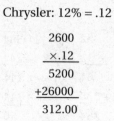

$$
\begin{array}{r}
2600 \\
\times\,.28 \\
\hline
20800 \\
+52000 \\
\hline
728.00
\end{array}
\qquad
\begin{array}{r}
\text{GM:}\ 2600 \\
\times\,.22 \\
\hline
5200 \\
+52000 \\
\hline
572.00
\end{array}
$$

$$
\begin{array}{r}
\text{Toyota:}\quad 728 \text{ cars sold} \\
-\ \ \text{GM:}\quad 572 \text{ cars sold} \\
\hline
156
\end{array}
$$

27. **(A)** Multiply 118 by 2 and 132 by 3. Get their sum, add 163, and divide by 6. Round off to the nearest whole number.

$$
\begin{array}{r}
2\times118 = 236 \\
3\times132 = 396 \\
+163 \\
\hline
795
\end{array}
$$

$$
\begin{array}{r}
132.5 \approx 133 \\
6\overline{)795.0} \\
-\,6\ \ \ \ \ \\
\hline
19 \\
-\,18 \\
\hline
15 \\
-\,12 \\
\hline
3\,0 \\
-\,3\,0 \\
\hline
0
\end{array}
$$

28. **(M)** Add 163 to the product of 3 and 132. Divide by 4 and round off to the nearest tenth of a pound.

$$
\begin{array}{r}
3\times132 = 396 \\
+163 \\
\hline
559
\end{array}
$$

$$
\begin{array}{r}
139.75 \approx 139.8 \\
4\overline{)559.00} \\
-\,4\ \ \ \ \ \\
\hline
15 \\
-\,12 \\
\hline
39 \\
-\,36 \\
\hline
3\,0 \\
-\,2\,8 \\
\hline
20 \\
-\,20 \\
\hline
0
\end{array}
$$

29. **(C)** Determine the values of a, b, c, and d and then substitute into (A), (B), (C), and (D).

$$a = 20$$
$$b = 60$$
$$c = 30$$
$$d = 90$$

$$\text{(C)} \quad b + c = d$$
$$60 + 30 = 90 \ \checkmark$$

30. **(L)** Use the given values for a, b, c, and d and substitute into the choices.

(J) c is greater than b
$$30 > 60 \ \times$$

(L) a is 10 less than c
$$20 = 30 - 10 = 20 \ \checkmark$$

(K) d is less than a
$$90 < 20 \ \times$$

(M) d is 20 more than b
$$90 = 60 + 20 \ \times$$

31. **(D)**

$$\text{Area of a triangle } (A) = \left(\frac{1}{2}\right) \text{base } (b) \times \text{height } (h)$$

$$56 = \left(\frac{1}{2}\right) b \times 8$$

$$56 = 4b$$
$$14 = b$$

32. **(J)** If two angles share a common side as well as a common vertex with no common interior points, they are adjacent angles, and the two angles add up to the measure of the inclusive angle.

$$\text{Total} - b = a$$
$$104° - 27° = 77°$$

Math—Part 2

33. **(C)** Round off 4.95 to 5 and 1.8 to 2.

$$6 \times 5 - 2 = 30 - 2 = 28$$

34. **(K)** Round off 2,250 to 2,200, mentally divide 11 into 2,200, and then multiply by 2.

$$\frac{2}{\cancel{11}_{1}} \times \overset{200}{\cancel{2200}} = 400$$

35. **(D)** Round off 8,786 to 8,800 and 5,579 to 5,600 and subtract.

$$8,800 - 5,600 = 3,200$$

36. **(K)** Mentally add 45, 16, and 34. Then find the sum of $\frac{3}{4}$ and $\frac{1}{2}$ and add $\frac{2}{3}$, which is a bit more than $1\frac{3}{4}$.

$$45 + 16 + 34 = 95$$

$$\frac{1}{2} + \frac{3}{4} = 1\frac{1}{4}$$
$$1\frac{1}{4} + \frac{2}{3} > 1\frac{3}{4}$$

Total: $> 96\frac{3}{4}$

The best choice is 97.

37. **(A)** Round off 78 to 80 and mentally divide 80 into 920.

$$\frac{920}{80} \approx 11+$$

The closest choice is 12 hours.

38. **(K)** Round off 121,345 to 120,000 and then multiply by .02.

$$.02 \times 120,000 = 2,400$$

39. **(D)** Round off the sum of 8.3 and 3.8 to 12 and round off the difference of 9.6 and 2.7 to 7.

$$3(8.3+3.8)-2(9.6-2.7) \approx 3(12)-2(7)$$
$$36-14$$
$$22$$

40. **(M)** The square of 5.62 is between 5 squared and 6 squared.

$$5^2 = 25 \quad 5.62^2 = ? \quad 6^2 = 36$$

The best choice is 32.

41. **(D)** Siseley's bar looks a bit longer than halfway between 10 and 15 minutes; perhaps 13 or 14 minutes.

The closest choice is 13 minutes.

42. **(L)** Stan took 8 or 9 minutes to jog a mile in March.

Maria took about 11 or 12 minutes to jog a mile in September.

$$12 - 8 = 4 \qquad 11 - 8 = 3$$
$$12 - 9 = 3 \qquad 11 - 9 = 2$$

Of the choices given, the best choice is 3 minutes.

43. **(D)** Change 12 feet to inches.

$$12 \text{ ft.} \times 12 \text{ in.} = 144 \text{ in.}$$

$$\frac{1}{2} : 144 = \frac{1}{2} \times \frac{1}{144} = \frac{1}{288}$$

44. **(K)** Add all the weights, and divide by 3.

$$
\begin{array}{r}
\text{Jackie} = x + 2 \\
\text{Manuel: } (x + 2) + 12 = x + 14 \\
+ \quad \text{Elaine: } (x + 2) - 6 = x - 4 \\
\hline
= 3x + 12
\end{array}
$$

$$\text{Average weight} = \frac{3x+12}{3} = x + 4$$

45. **(B)** Test each answer choice:

Choice A: $19.4 - 11.2 = 8.2 \neq 6.9$ ✗

Choice B: $12.6 - 5.7 = 6.9 = 6.9$ ✔

Choice C: $11.8 - 3.7 = 8.1 \neq 6.9$ ✗

Choice D: $13.8 - 4.9 = 8.9 \neq 6.9$ ✗

Therefore, choice B is the correct answer.

46. **(L)** Let x equal the first integer, let $x + 2$ equal the second integer, and let $x + 4$ equal the third integer.

$$
\begin{aligned}
x + x + 2 + x + 4 &= 39 \\
3x + 6 &= 39 \\
3x &= 33 \\
x &= 11
\end{aligned}
$$

If x equals 11, then $x + 2$ equals 13 and $x + 4$ equals 15. The largest of these three numbers is 15.

47. **(D)** The absolute value of any number is its positive value.

$$
\begin{aligned}
2|{-3}| - 4|5| &= \\
2(3) - 4(5) &= \\
6 - 20 &= -14
\end{aligned}
$$

48. **(L)** Let x equal the original price. Then, $.90x$ equals the price after the first drop. Finally, $.70(.90x) = .63x$ equals the price after the second drop.

49. **(B)**

$$\sqrt[3]{27x^3y^9} =$$
$$\sqrt[3]{27} = 3$$
$$\sqrt[3]{x^3} = x$$
$$\sqrt[3]{y^9} = y^3$$
$$\sqrt[3]{27x^3y^9} = 3xy^3$$

50. **(L)**

A = area; r = radius; the formula for the area of a circle is $A = \pi r^2$

Shaded area = Area of the larger circle – Area of the smaller circle

$$= (\pi \times 9^2) - (\pi \times 6^2)$$
$$= 81\pi - 36\pi$$
$$= 45\pi$$

Ability

1. **(E)** In each of the sample cases, there is a diagonal across the figure. The only diagonal appears in choice E.

2. **(L)** There are three lines in each of the sample pictures. The only diagram with three lines is the triangle.

3. **(E)** The three original pictures include a triangle, a circle, and an oval.

4. **(K)** In each case, the arrow rotates 90° counterclockwise, so just rotate the last arrow the same way.

5. **(D)** The black square moves across diagonally. Just move the last black square diagonally across to the upper right corner of the larger square.

6. **(M)** In the first figure, 6 dots are changed into 8 dots and the figure is changed from horizontal to vertical, so let's add 2 dots to the last figure and rearrange it vertically.

7. **(A)** A four-sided figure is changed into a five-sided figure, so let's just add one side to the triangle.

8. **(K)** If we fold over the square paper and punch one hole near the middle, we have a paper with two holes on both sides of the diagonal when we unfold it.

9. **(E)** When we punch one hole in the corner and another hole near the diagonal of a folded paper, we finish with a piece of paper with a third hole diagonally across from the hole in the corner and a fourth hole on the other side of the diagonal.

10. **(M)** We fold the square paper twice, each time along the diagonal. Thus, when we punch two holes near the last diagonal, we finish with a paper with eight holes, all along the diagonal.

ANSWER SHEET
TACHS Practice Exam 2

READING—PART 1

1. Ⓐ Ⓑ Ⓒ Ⓓ
2. Ⓙ Ⓚ Ⓛ Ⓜ
3. Ⓐ Ⓑ Ⓒ Ⓓ
4. Ⓙ Ⓚ Ⓛ Ⓜ
5. Ⓐ Ⓑ Ⓒ Ⓓ

6. Ⓙ Ⓚ Ⓛ Ⓜ
7. Ⓐ Ⓑ Ⓒ Ⓓ
8. Ⓙ Ⓚ Ⓛ Ⓜ
9. Ⓐ Ⓑ Ⓒ Ⓓ
10. Ⓙ Ⓚ Ⓛ Ⓜ

11. Ⓐ Ⓑ Ⓒ Ⓓ
12. Ⓙ Ⓚ Ⓛ Ⓜ
13. Ⓐ Ⓑ Ⓒ Ⓓ
14. Ⓙ Ⓚ Ⓛ Ⓜ
15. Ⓐ Ⓑ Ⓒ Ⓓ

16. Ⓙ Ⓚ Ⓛ Ⓜ
17. Ⓐ Ⓑ Ⓒ Ⓓ
18. Ⓙ Ⓚ Ⓛ Ⓜ
19. Ⓐ Ⓑ Ⓒ Ⓓ
20. Ⓙ Ⓚ Ⓛ Ⓜ

READING—PART 2

21. Ⓐ Ⓑ Ⓒ Ⓓ
22. Ⓙ Ⓚ Ⓛ Ⓜ
23. Ⓐ Ⓑ Ⓒ Ⓓ
24. Ⓙ Ⓚ Ⓛ Ⓜ
25. Ⓐ Ⓑ Ⓒ Ⓓ
26. Ⓙ Ⓚ Ⓛ Ⓜ
27. Ⓐ Ⓑ Ⓒ Ⓓ
28. Ⓙ Ⓚ Ⓛ Ⓜ

29. Ⓐ Ⓑ Ⓒ Ⓓ
30. Ⓙ Ⓚ Ⓛ Ⓜ
31. Ⓐ Ⓑ Ⓒ Ⓓ
32. Ⓙ Ⓚ Ⓛ Ⓜ
33. Ⓐ Ⓑ Ⓒ Ⓓ
34. Ⓙ Ⓚ Ⓛ Ⓜ
35. Ⓐ Ⓑ Ⓒ Ⓓ
36. Ⓙ Ⓚ Ⓛ Ⓜ

37. Ⓐ Ⓑ Ⓒ Ⓓ
38. Ⓙ Ⓚ Ⓛ Ⓜ
39. Ⓐ Ⓑ Ⓒ Ⓓ
40. Ⓙ Ⓚ Ⓛ Ⓜ
41. Ⓐ Ⓑ Ⓒ Ⓓ
42. Ⓙ Ⓚ Ⓛ Ⓜ
43. Ⓐ Ⓑ Ⓒ Ⓓ
44. Ⓙ Ⓚ Ⓛ Ⓜ

45. Ⓐ Ⓑ Ⓒ Ⓓ
46. Ⓙ Ⓚ Ⓛ Ⓜ
47. Ⓐ Ⓑ Ⓒ Ⓓ
48. Ⓙ Ⓚ Ⓛ Ⓜ
49. Ⓐ Ⓑ Ⓒ Ⓓ
50. Ⓙ Ⓚ Ⓛ Ⓜ

WRITTEN EXPRESSION—PART 1—ENGLISH

1. Ⓐ Ⓑ Ⓒ Ⓓ Ⓔ
2. Ⓙ Ⓚ Ⓛ Ⓜ Ⓝ
3. Ⓐ Ⓑ Ⓒ Ⓓ Ⓔ
4. Ⓙ Ⓚ Ⓛ Ⓜ Ⓝ
5. Ⓐ Ⓑ Ⓒ Ⓓ Ⓔ
6. Ⓙ Ⓚ Ⓛ Ⓜ Ⓝ
7. Ⓐ Ⓑ Ⓒ Ⓓ Ⓔ
8. Ⓙ Ⓚ Ⓛ Ⓜ Ⓝ
9. Ⓐ Ⓑ Ⓒ Ⓓ Ⓔ
10. Ⓙ Ⓚ Ⓛ Ⓜ Ⓝ

11. Ⓐ Ⓑ Ⓒ Ⓓ
12. Ⓙ Ⓚ Ⓛ Ⓜ
13. Ⓐ Ⓑ Ⓒ Ⓓ
14. Ⓙ Ⓚ Ⓛ Ⓜ
15. Ⓐ Ⓑ Ⓒ Ⓓ
16. Ⓙ Ⓚ Ⓛ Ⓜ
17. Ⓐ Ⓑ Ⓒ Ⓓ
18. Ⓙ Ⓚ Ⓛ Ⓜ
19. Ⓐ Ⓑ Ⓒ Ⓓ
20. Ⓙ Ⓚ Ⓛ Ⓜ

21. Ⓐ Ⓑ Ⓒ Ⓓ
22. Ⓙ Ⓚ Ⓛ Ⓜ
23. Ⓐ Ⓑ Ⓒ Ⓓ
24. Ⓙ Ⓚ Ⓛ Ⓜ
25. Ⓐ Ⓑ Ⓒ Ⓓ
26. Ⓙ Ⓚ Ⓛ Ⓜ
27. Ⓐ Ⓑ Ⓒ Ⓓ
28. Ⓙ Ⓚ Ⓛ Ⓜ
29. Ⓐ Ⓑ Ⓒ Ⓓ
30. Ⓙ Ⓚ Ⓛ Ⓜ

31. Ⓐ Ⓑ Ⓒ Ⓓ
32. Ⓙ Ⓚ Ⓛ Ⓜ
33. Ⓐ Ⓑ Ⓒ Ⓓ
34. Ⓙ Ⓚ Ⓛ Ⓜ
35. Ⓐ Ⓑ Ⓒ Ⓓ
36. Ⓙ Ⓚ Ⓛ Ⓜ
37. Ⓐ Ⓑ Ⓒ Ⓓ
38. Ⓙ Ⓚ Ⓛ Ⓜ
39. Ⓐ Ⓑ Ⓒ Ⓓ
40. Ⓙ Ⓚ Ⓛ Ⓜ

WRITTEN EXPRESSION—PART 2—PARAGRAPHS

41. Ⓐ Ⓑ Ⓒ Ⓓ   44. Ⓙ Ⓚ Ⓛ Ⓜ   47. Ⓐ Ⓑ Ⓒ Ⓓ   50. Ⓙ Ⓚ Ⓛ Ⓜ
42. Ⓙ Ⓚ Ⓛ Ⓜ   45. Ⓐ Ⓑ Ⓒ Ⓓ   48. Ⓙ Ⓚ Ⓛ Ⓜ
43. Ⓐ Ⓑ Ⓒ Ⓓ   46. Ⓙ Ⓚ Ⓛ Ⓜ   49. Ⓐ Ⓑ Ⓒ Ⓓ

MATH—PART 1

1. Ⓐ Ⓑ Ⓒ Ⓓ   9. Ⓐ Ⓑ Ⓒ Ⓓ   17. Ⓐ Ⓑ Ⓒ Ⓓ   25. Ⓐ Ⓑ Ⓒ Ⓓ
2. Ⓙ Ⓚ Ⓛ Ⓜ   10. Ⓙ Ⓚ Ⓛ Ⓜ   18. Ⓙ Ⓚ Ⓛ Ⓜ   26. Ⓙ Ⓚ Ⓛ Ⓜ
3. Ⓐ Ⓑ Ⓒ Ⓓ   11. Ⓐ Ⓑ Ⓒ Ⓓ   19. Ⓐ Ⓑ Ⓒ Ⓓ   27. Ⓐ Ⓑ Ⓒ Ⓓ
4. Ⓙ Ⓚ Ⓛ Ⓜ   12. Ⓙ Ⓚ Ⓛ Ⓜ   20. Ⓙ Ⓚ Ⓛ Ⓜ   28. Ⓙ Ⓚ Ⓛ Ⓜ
5. Ⓐ Ⓑ Ⓒ Ⓓ   13. Ⓐ Ⓑ Ⓒ Ⓓ   21. Ⓐ Ⓑ Ⓒ Ⓓ   29. Ⓐ Ⓑ Ⓒ Ⓓ
6. Ⓙ Ⓚ Ⓛ Ⓜ   14. Ⓙ Ⓚ Ⓛ Ⓜ   22. Ⓙ Ⓚ Ⓛ Ⓜ   30. Ⓙ Ⓚ Ⓛ Ⓜ
7. Ⓐ Ⓑ Ⓒ Ⓓ   15. Ⓐ Ⓑ Ⓒ Ⓓ   23. Ⓐ Ⓑ Ⓒ Ⓓ   31. Ⓐ Ⓑ Ⓒ Ⓓ
8. Ⓙ Ⓚ Ⓛ Ⓜ   16. Ⓙ Ⓚ Ⓛ Ⓜ   24. Ⓙ Ⓚ Ⓛ Ⓜ   32. Ⓙ Ⓚ Ⓛ Ⓜ

MATH—PART 2

33. Ⓐ Ⓑ Ⓒ Ⓓ   38. Ⓙ Ⓚ Ⓛ Ⓜ   43. Ⓐ Ⓑ Ⓒ Ⓓ   48. Ⓙ Ⓚ Ⓛ Ⓜ
34. Ⓙ Ⓚ Ⓛ Ⓜ   39. Ⓐ Ⓑ Ⓒ Ⓓ   44. Ⓙ Ⓚ Ⓛ Ⓜ   49. Ⓐ Ⓑ Ⓒ Ⓓ
35. Ⓐ Ⓑ Ⓒ Ⓓ   40. Ⓙ Ⓚ Ⓛ Ⓜ   45. Ⓐ Ⓑ Ⓒ Ⓓ   50. Ⓙ Ⓚ Ⓛ Ⓜ
36. Ⓙ Ⓚ Ⓛ Ⓜ   41. Ⓐ Ⓑ Ⓒ Ⓓ   46. Ⓙ Ⓚ Ⓛ Ⓜ
37. Ⓐ Ⓑ Ⓒ Ⓓ   42. Ⓙ Ⓚ Ⓛ Ⓜ   47. Ⓐ Ⓑ Ⓒ Ⓓ

ABILITY

1. Ⓐ Ⓑ Ⓒ Ⓓ Ⓔ   4. Ⓙ Ⓚ Ⓛ Ⓜ Ⓝ   7. Ⓐ Ⓑ Ⓒ Ⓓ Ⓔ   10. Ⓙ Ⓚ Ⓛ Ⓜ Ⓝ
2. Ⓙ Ⓚ Ⓛ Ⓜ Ⓝ   5. Ⓐ Ⓑ Ⓒ Ⓓ Ⓔ   8. Ⓙ Ⓚ Ⓛ Ⓜ Ⓝ
3. Ⓐ Ⓑ Ⓒ Ⓓ Ⓔ   6. Ⓙ Ⓚ Ⓛ Ⓜ Ⓝ   9. Ⓐ Ⓑ Ⓒ Ⓓ Ⓔ

*This TACHS test is a representative example of what you will find on the actual exam. Although it illustrates the types of problems you can expect, the number of questions may vary.

READING—PART 1

20 QUESTIONS   10 MINUTES

Directions: This is a test about words and their meanings.

- For each question, you are to decide which one of the four answers has most nearly the same meaning as the underlined word(s) above it.

1 an irrational decision

- **A** wise
- **B** fair
- **C** biased
- **D** unreasonable

2 be in a precarious position

- **J** safe and sound
- **K** high altitude
- **L** dangerously risky
- **M** first place

3 to assuage one's pain

- **A** massage
- **B** complain of
- **C** lessen
- **D** discuss

4 a bellicose personality

- **J** conniving
- **K** warlike
- **L** peaceful
- **M** methodical

5 waning strength

- **A** growing
- **B** new-found
- **C** physical
- **D** decreasing

6 to be distraught

- **J** upset
- **K** happy
- **L** patient
- **M** confused

7 a noisome chemical

- **A** foul smelling
- **B** bubbling
- **C** syrupy
- **D** acidic

8 a wily villain

- **J** angry
- **K** wicked
- **L** sympathetic
- **M** crafty

9 a meandering river

- **A** rapid
- **B** shallow
- **C** winding
- **D** subterranean

10 an obdurate nature

- **J** stubborn
- **K** sweet
- **L** impartial
- **M** awkward

GO TO NEXT PAGE ➡

11 <u>sage</u> advice

   A wise
   B unbidden
   C free
   D unreliable

12 a <u>paragon</u> of virtue

   J ideal model
   K song
   L advisor
   M story

13 <u>valorous</u> deeds

   A legal
   B brave
   C final
   D invisible

14 to provide <u>solace</u>

   J lend money
   K comfort
   L tell news
   M bring entertainment

15 our <u>intrepid</u> hero

   A clumsy
   B bold
   C cool
   D lost

16 to <u>ostracize</u> the outsider

   J welcome
   K understand
   L exclude
   M accuse

17 a <u>petty</u> bureaucrat

   A attractive
   B small-minded
   C wealthy
   D helpful

18 an <u>indelible</u> imprint

   J erasable
   K immovable
   L transient
   M permanent

19 to sound <u>precocious</u>

   A sarcastic
   B intelligent
   C tongue-tied
   D childish

20 to remain <u>cognizant</u>

   J aware
   K partners
   L useful
   M uninformed

GO TO NEXT PAGE ➡

READING—PART 2

30 QUESTIONS   25 MINUTES

Directions: This part has short reading passages, each one followed by questions. Choose the best answer to each question.

Correct marking of sample   Ⓐ ● Ⓒ Ⓓ

Example

The reading passages on the next part will be _____.

A   all on one page
B   followed by questions
C   easy to read
D   very long

PASSAGE FOR QUESTIONS 21–28

Chestnuts have got to be one of Nature's combinations of bane and boon. On the one hand, these mildly flavored nuts are quite versatile; they can be roasted over an open fire (just like in the Christmas carol) or ground into cake flour or incorporated into savory meat dishes. On the other hand, getting the nutmeats out of their tough shells can be quite a task.

A thick, spiny shell protects the chestnut as it undergoes its maturation cycle. Once pollinated, the chestnut develops a tender, lime-green casing that looks much like a sea urchin. The spines of the chestnut casing at this point in the chestnut's development are soft and flexible to the touch. However, at the point at which the chestnut has reached a ripened state, these spines have turned brown and have taken on a needle sharp edge, making it very difficult to pick up, much less open, the nut. This sharpening process functions as a protective measure, keeping the nuts out of the grasp of most hunting and gathering animals. One good way to get the nuts out of the casing is to roll the nuts underfoot while wearing heavy-soled shoes; ironically, however, despite the protective casing, most squirrels can abscond with the loot.

21   Based on the author's use of the words in this passage, which of the following would help the reader understand the words bane and boon?

    A   heavy load and burden
    B   burden and reward
    C   reward and happiness
    D   happiness and healthiness

22   Why do chestnuts form brown spines?

    J   to make it hard for people to get the nuts out
    K   to protect the nutmeat from all but the most persistent hunters
    L   to keep the nuts outside the casing until they ripen fully
    M   to facilitate the return of fertilized nuts to the earth for next year's crop

GO TO NEXT PAGE ➡

23 Why did the author write this article?

A to argue that chestnuts are the best nuts in the world

B to show how many recipes can include chestnuts

C to discuss the effect of chestnut production on the environment

D to give out information about the chestnut's maturation cycle

24 Based on the use of the word versatile in context of this passage, which of the following definitions works best?

J replaceable

K flexible

L interchangeable

M workable

25 What would the author's opinion be of cactus, based on this article's point of view?

A She or he would like them because they are prickly.

B She or he would not like them because they have spines.

C She or he would like them because they are all edible.

D We cannot tell from the information given.

26 What color is the chestnut casing when it is early in the maturation process?

J brown

K green

L blue

M red

27 Why do you think the author brings up squirrels and their attraction to chestnuts in the final paragraph?

A to point out just another cute thing that squirrels do

B to keep to the topic, since the entire piece is all about squirrels

C to emphasize the usefulness chestnuts bring to the world

D to point out the irony that squirrels can succeed at getting out the chestnut meat when most humans fail

28 What does the word abscond mean, based on its use in the passage?

J get away with

K run away from

L make an allusion to

M work its way around

GO TO NEXT PAGE ➡

Paris, France, is well known for virtually everything, but especially its food. Even a casual traveler associates Paris with wine, cheese, and (probably) snails. However, more important than eating in Paris is knowing where to go to get that food in the first place.

Parisians acquire their food in an entirely different manner than do Americans. While the French have supermarkets, for example, these markets are nowhere near as large as American supermarkets, nor do they stay open for as long periods of time as American markets. Food in France, moreover, comes in much smaller quantities at a time, with most liquids coming in liters (or less) and most solid foods coming in kilograms (or less). The average American attempting to buy a gallon of orange juice or a two-liter of Coca-Cola is sure to be disappointed. On the other hand, food displays in France are much more attractive, colorful, and fresh than those in America.

Americans accustomed to megastores and one-stop shopping will likely grow impatient with Parisian markets. The French shopper can get much of their food and cleaning supplies from the supermarket, but many things required several stops. Need pastries? Stop by the *patisserie*. Need fresh fruit? Hit the *fruitiere*. Need fresh meat or seafood? Run around the corner to the *butcherie* or the *poissonerie*.

While acquiring food in Paris is not an efficient pastime, it nevertheless is interesting and exciting and offers insight into fundamental differences into the way that these two very different cultural groups view life.

29 Based on your reading of Paragraph 3, what is the best meaning for *poissonerie*?

   A   fruit store
   B   meat shop
   C   candy store
   D   fish shop

30 Which of the following facts does *not* appear in the passage?

   J   Shoppers, generally speaking, in Paris will be disheartened by the price of everything.
   K   American shoppers in Paris will be disappointed by the small sizes of everything.
   L   Store displays in Paris are more attractive and more colorful than those in the states.
   M   Shopping in Paris is not an efficient activity.

31 What is the definition of a "megastore," according to this text?

   A   huge stores with everything from fresh food to clothing to car supplies
   B   medium stores with mainly fresh food and cleaning supplies
   C   small stores with mainly fresh food
   D   tiny stores with convenient, prewrapped food

32 What is the author's opinion on how the French go shopping?

   J   He or she approves with reservation.
   K   He or she approves wholeheartedly.
   L   He or she disapproves wholeheartedly.
   M   He or she disapproves with reservation.

GO TO NEXT PAGE ➡

33 Which of the following statements is true, based on this article?

   A   Food comes in much bigger packages in Paris.

   B   Food comes in much smaller packages in America.

   C   Food is an important part of any culture.

   D   Food is an important way to learn about different cultures.

34 Which of the following items can you likely get in Paris, according to this article?

   J   a gallon of orange juice

   K   a liter of milk

   L   a two-liter of Coca-Cola

   M   a 24-pack of bottled water

35 Which of the following titles would best fit this article?

   A   An American in Paris

   B   Bigger Is Better

   C   Shop Til You Drop

   D   Food: Insight into the Other

GO TO NEXT PAGE ➡

PASSAGE FOR QUESTIONS 36–43

Once there was a widow with two daughters; one was ugly, whom the mother loved, and the other was beautiful, whom the mother hated and forced to do all the work.

One day, the beautiful girl went to the well to gather water; while there, an old crone with a wart on her nose asked the girl for water, which the girl gladly gave. In gratitude, the old woman (who was really a fairy in disguise) cast a spell on the girl so that every time she spoke, either a flower or a jewel dropped out of her mouth.

Upon returning home, the mother quickly realized what had happened, and she sent her ugly daughter to the same well hoping that the miracle would repeat itself. The ugly girl did not come upon a crone, however, but a beautiful woman asking for water.

The ugly girl, angry and resentful, refused to give the water. The beautiful woman (again the fairy in disguise) cast a spell on the ugly girl so that every time she spoke either a snake or an insect dropped out of her mouth.

The mother, angry at what had happened to her favorite daughter, responded by throwing the beautiful daughter out of the house. However, the fates did not betray this girl, but instead led her straight into the path of a roaming prince. This prince immediately fell in love with her upon first sight and, spurred on by the treasure that escaped her lips with every word, married her.

—Paraphrased from tales compiled by Charles Perrault

36 Which of the following elements from the story are symbols of goodness?

- **J** the ugly daughter
- **K** the fairy
- **L** the beautiful daughter
- **M** the snake

37 Which of the following stories is this text most like?

- **A** *Aladdin and the Magic Lamp*
- **B** *Cinderella*
- **C** *Peter Pan*
- **D** *Alice in Wonderland*

38 What does the word gratitude mean as used in this passage?

- **J** happiness
- **K** thankfulness
- **L** being up high
- **M** a tip for doing good work

39 What is a synonym for crone?

- **A** a beautiful girl
- **B** a handsome man
- **C** a statuesque queen
- **D** a withered old woman

40 What does the water in the story symbolize?

- **J** compassion
- **K** water
- **L** fear
- **M** greed

41 What is the author's purpose in writing this story?

- **A** to encourage bad behavior in the reader
- **B** to encourage justice in the world
- **C** to encourage apathy in the world
- **D** to encourage manners in the world

GO TO NEXT PAGE ➡

42 How would you categorize the author's opinion of the mother's behavior in the story?

- **J** fair; a mother has the right to treat her children as she wishes
- **K** unfair; a mother needs to treat all of her children equally
- **L** neutral; it really doesn't matter. After all, it's only a story
- **M** None of the above are appropriate answers to the question.

43 What is an antonym for *widow*?

- **A** a married woman
- **B** a young, unmarried girl
- **C** a woman whose husband has died
- **D** a divorced woman

GO TO NEXT PAGE ➡

PASSAGE FOR QUESTIONS 44–50

We best know Marie Antoinette for her snide comment regarding her starving peasant subjects ("Let them eat cake!") and for her grisly demise (beheaded by the guillotine in 1793). However, Marie Antoinette should also command our attention for cultural innovations and challenges she made during her short lifetime.

Marie Antoinette, wife of King Louis XVI, became queen in 1769 at the tender age of fourteen. Fundamentally a young girl, with the headstrong behavior of youth and the authority (thanks to Louis) to back her up, Marie Antoinette chafed under the social and administrative rules that surrounded her. Traditionally, French queens had not enjoyed any freedoms in changing their surroundings (either physically or in terms of personal behavior) once accepting the role of ruler.

Marie Antoinette changed all that. By age nineteen, she imposed her own views and tastes on the Palace of Versailles and even commissioned a new construction: the Trianon estate bordering the Palace to which she could repair and escape the pressures and social constraints of court that she could not entirely bend to her will. At the Trianon estate, Marie Antoinette, inspired by Enlightenment thinking, dressed and behaved and organized her surroundings in a way that upset the traditional way of life and set a new standard for all who came later.

44 Where, according to the passage, did Marie Antoinette feel the most free?

- **J** the Palace of Versailles
- **K** the Trianon estate
- **L** the Tuilleries in Paris
- **M** The article does not specify.

45 How old was Marie Antoinette when she became queen?

- **A** fourteen
- **B** sixteen
- **C** nineteen
- **D** twenty-one

46 Which of the following is the best definition for the word repair as used in context of this passage?

- **J** fix
- **K** flee
- **L** forge
- **M** find

47 To which King of France was Marie Antoinette married, according to this article?

- **A** King Louis XIX
- **B** King Louis XVI
- **C** King Louis XIV
- **D** King Louis VIV

48 The reader can infer from Marie Antoinette's comment regarding her subjects' hunger that _____.

- **J** she cared deeply for herself
- **K** she worried little for the troubles of others
- **L** she wanted to institute major reforms for the poor
- **M** she liked cake quite a bit

GO TO NEXT PAGE →

49 Which of the following statements can we conclude, based on the comments of the passage?

A French queens never acquired social or behavioral freedom until monarchy died out.

B French queens always enjoyed a great deal of social and behavioral freedoms.

C French kings usually suffered more social and behavioral constraint than did the queens.

D French queens were almost never allowed social or behavioral freedoms while queen.

50 The reader can infer from Marie Antoinette's reference to cake that cake was _____.

J something highly valued and very nutritious

K something only poor people could afford

L something that primarily the wealthy people enjoyed

M something very new and innovative in French culture

STOP

If there is still time remaining, you may review your answers.

WRITTEN EXPRESSION

Part 1—English

40 QUESTIONS   23 MINUTES

> **Directions:** This is a test of how well you can find mistakes in writing. The directions below tell what type of mistake to look for.
>
> • On the questions with mistakes in spelling, capitalization, punctuation, and usage, choose the answer with the same letter as the line containing the mistake. When there is no mistake or no change needed, choose the last answer.
> • On the questions about expression, follow the specific directions for each question.

> **Directions:** Look for mistakes in **spelling**.

1 **A** coax
   B solace
   C ruminate
   D lucid
   E *(No mistakes)*

2 **J** torpid
   K veneer
   L cricket
   M dictionery
   N *(No mistakes)*

3 **A** extinct
   B abett
   C temperature
   D antique
   E *(No mistakes)*

4 **J** dilemna
   K column
   L enmity
   M mnemonic
   N *(No mistakes)*

5 **A** four
   B fourty
   C fourteen
   D forehead
   E *(No mistakes)*

6 **J** natural
   K calendar
   L computer
   M grammer
   N *(No mistakes)*

7 **A** preamble
   B predict
   C presede
   D preference
   E *(No mistakes)*

8 **J** lightning
   K lightening
   L thunder
   M whether
   N *(No mistakes)*

9 **A** finger
   B sculpture
   C populer
   D sculptor
   E *(No mistakes)*

10 **J** spearmint
   K necessary
   L terrain
   M villain
   N *(No mistakes)*

GO TO NEXT PAGE ➡

11
  A My cousin in Canada
  B lives in Quebec,
  C which is one of the French-Speaking cities.
  D *(No mistakes)*

12
  J Charles Dickens wrote
  K *A Tale of Two Cities,*
  L one of my favorite Novels.
  M *(No mistakes)*

13
  A After four years
  B of high school, I plan to
  C attend Oxford University.
  D *(No mistakes)*

14
  J Are you free on
  K Thursday, or should we
  L wait for the Weekend?
  M *(No mistakes)*

15
  A Many people don't understand
  B the veneration of the Virgin Mary,
  C an important part of Catholicism.
  D *(No mistakes)*

16
  J My mother is a lifelong democrat,
  K although in the last election
  L she voted for the Republican candidate.
  M *(No mistakes)*

17
  A My teacher said,
  B "if you memorize the multiplication tables,
  C you will be ahead of most people today."
  D *(No mistakes)*

18
  J "Everyone relies too much,"
  K she continued,
  L "On calculators and other machines."
  M *(No mistakes)*

19
  A I got into an argument with a man
  B from Scotland who said the constitution
  C of the United States is a naive document.
  D *(No mistakes)*

20
  J After four years of college,
  K my friend Sammye moved
  L to Washington and joined the cia.
  M *(No mistakes)*

Directions: Look for mistakes in **punctuation**.

21
  A That was, I think—
  B the worst movie I have
  C ever seen in my life.
  D *(No mistakes)*

22
  J Give the green pages
  K to the woman, who sits
  L behind the library counter.
  M *(No mistakes)*

23
  A Mr. Greenberg asked
  B if any of his students
  C had forgotten their homework?
  D *(No mistakes)*

24
  J I worked as hard
  K as I could; what more
  L can you ask?
  M *(No mistakes)*

25
  A My cousin Florian was born
  B on July 20, 1969
  C the same day as the first moon landing.
  D *(No mistakes)*

26
  J Mr. R.J. Speigelhalter earned
  K a B.A., M.A., M.S., and Ph.D.
  L before he decided to teach at P.S. 142
  M *(No mistakes)*

GO TO NEXT PAGE ➡

27
  A When the afternoon is
  B very hot, Bo enjoys a tall,
  C cool, glass of lemonade.
  D *(No mistakes)*

28
  J Even though, Uncle Jack
  K teases me, I know
  L he loves me very much.
  M *(No mistakes)*

29
  A "My favorite summertime
  B treat is a cool cup of lemon ice",
  C admitted Father Osborne.
  D *(No mistakes)*

30
  J Which is your favorite
  K Dickens novel: "A Tale of Two Cities"
  L or *Oliver Twist*?
  M *(No mistakes)*

Directions: Look for mistakes in **usage**.

31
  A Many recipes call,
  B for the following ingredients:
  C flour, butter, eggs, and water.
  D *(No mistakes)*

32
  J The play was
  K very good; the actors
  L performed good.
  M *(No mistakes)*

33
  A In the best hospitals,
  B a doctor learns to trust their nurses,
  C especially in an emergency.
  D *(No mistakes)*

34
  J My mother baked
  K a chocolate cake
  L for you're birthday.
  M *(No mistakes)*

35
  A Boris, Anastasia, and myself
  B ran the marathon,
  C which was a difficult course.
  D *(No mistakes)*

36
  J It was wrong to gossip
  K about one of our classmates.
  L We should of known better.
  M *(No mistakes)*

37
  A The directions are simple:
  B go past the mall, under the bridge,
  C over the tracks, and carefully.
  D *(No mistakes)*

38 Choose the <u>best</u> way of <u>expressing</u> the idea.

  J The document, easy to follow, was so
      even though the directions were vague.
  K Easy to follow document was so, even
      though the directions were vague.
  L Even though the directions were vague,
      the document was easy to follow.
  M The easy to follow document was vague
      in the directions, even so.

GO TO NEXT PAGE ➡

1 The symbol x stands for <u>a variety of so many things</u>, yet we don't seem to confuse them. **2** It's a letter in the alphabet, of course, but it's also a number: the number ten in Roman numerals. **3** In math, it means to multiply, but it also stands for an unknown quantity. **4** An x on a street sign warns of a railroad crossing, but an x on a pirate map can point to treasure. **5** And when is the last time you hunted for treasure? **6** People who don't write can even use x as an official signature. **7** The meaning of x depends on—you guessed it—the contex*t*.

39 What is the <u>best</u> way to write the underlined part of sentence 1?

  A a specific thing
  B a variety of things
  C far too many things
  D *(No mistakes)*

40 Which sentence should be left out of this paragraph?

  J sentence 1
  K sentence 2
  L sentence 5
  M sentence 6

GO TO NEXT PAGE ➡

10 QUESTIONS   7 MINUTES

PASSAGE FOR QUESTIONS 41–43

A Moment

As I was eating lunch one day, I noticed a man come into the diner. (1) He was a good-looking young man, but prematurely balding, and he had shaved his head, which is the fashion. (2) He wore baggy jeans and a jacket which identified him as a firefighter, and in one hand he held a camouflage hat. (3) In the other, he held the tiny hand of his little boy, as he guided him to their seats. (4)

The boy seemed around five years old, rosy-cheeked, wearing his own firefighter T-shirt and a small version of his father's camouflage hat. (5) I watched as the father lovingly inserted a straw into the boy's milk carton, poured out ketchup for the order of french fries that they were sharing, and wiped his son's mouth when necessary. (6) All of this was done out of habit, I'm sure, but I knew—and felt—that sense of loving obligation, that sacred duty, which the father carried out for his son. (7)

"How are your chicken strips? Hot?" the father asked. (8) "YUM!" the son replied. (9)

They ate quietly for the most part, but sometimes the man couldn't help himself and reached over and tickled his son. (10) The boy laughed, smiled at his dad, and then went back to the serious issue of eating. (11) I wondered who they were, where they lived, and what had brought them out to lunch on this dreary day. (12) But I was grateful to have witnessed this little bit of life with them (13). We could all use more exposure to unconditional love. (14)

41 How would you rewrite sentence 3?

   A He wore baggy jeans and a jacket that identified him as a firefighter, and in one hand he held a camouflage hat.

   B He wore baggy jeans and a jacket, that identified him as a firefighter, and in one hand he held a camouflage hat.

   C He wore baggy jeans, a jacket which identified him, as a firefighter, and in one hand he held a camouflage hat.

   D He wore baggy jeans and a jacket that said firefighter; his hand holding a camouflage hat.

42 How would you best improve the third paragraph?

   J italicize the word YUM
   K divide it into two paragraphs
   L change "the son replied" to "he said"
   M change the question mark to an exclamation point

43 What is the point of this vignette?

   A The writer is remembering his own father.
   B It's very cute when fathers and sons dress alike.
   C When the day is dreary, celebrate!
   D Love is shown in everyday behavior.

GO TO NEXT PAGE ➡

Beethoven's Secret

Ludwig van Beethoven was keeping a terrible secret. (1) Considering one of the greatest musical composers of his time, he was going deaf. (2) He began hearing ringing and buzzing in his ears during his 20s, and, soon after, he was unable to hear the high notes of singers and instruments. (3) He started to avoid talking to people because he couldn't hear them well enough to carry on a conversation. (4) Moreover, his music started to move into the lower registers so that he could hear well enough to compose with confidence. (5)

He continued to perform, but he could no longer gauge how loudly or softly he was playing a passage, so sometimes he'd bang on the piano with great force, while other times his notes could not be heard. (6) Beethoven's secret was out. (7) Sometimes he was loud, and other times he was soft. (8)

He tried many remedies, none of which brought him any relief or improvement. (9) He started carrying around conversation books so people could write to him instead of talking. (10) When he composed, he would sit at the piano with one end of a pencil in his teeth and the other end on the instrument, that way he could literally feel the vibrations of the notes he was playing. (11)

At some point, however, Beethoven had to except the fact that he could no longer hear and that he could no longer perform. (12) However, he would not except that he could no longer create music. (13) How would he go on? (14)

Like most composers, Beethoven understood the mathematical relationship between notes and how to compose harmonies. (15) He could see how the music worked. (16) While impressive, this is not impossible for a trained musician. (17) What made Beethoven a genius is that he understood the *feelings* evoked by these relationships—he could feel them himself in the music he heard in his mind. (18)

Moreover, he was free again to write high notes—very high notes, in fact—and to experiment with harmonies and forms. (19) Even today, listeners can hear Beethoven's heroic struggle and triumph over his physical limitations, stretching himself and his performers to their limits. (20)

GO TO NEXT PAGE ➡

44 How can you best improve sentence 2?

J No change is necessary.

K Considering was he one of the greatest musical composers of his time, he was going deaf.

L Considered one of the greatest musical composers of his time, he was going deaf.

M He was going deaf considering one of the greatest musical composers of his time.

45 What is the redundancy in the second paragraph?

A Sentence 6 should be removed.

B The second half of sentence 6 should be removed.

C Sentence 7 should be removed.

D Sentence 8 should be removed.

46 How can you best improve sentence 11?

J When he composed, he would sit at the piano with one end of a pencil in his teeth and the other end on the instrument; that way he could literally feel the vibrations of the notes he was playing.

K When he composed he would sit at the piano, with one end of a pencil in his teeth, and the other end on the instrument, so that way he could literally feel the vibrations of the notes he was playing.

L When he composed, he would sit at the piano with one end of a pencil in his teeth; and the other end on the instrument; that way he could literally feel the vibrations of the notes he was playing.

M When he composed, he would sit at the piano with one end of a pencil in his teeth and the other end on the instrument, that way he could literally feel it.

47 Which word is incorrect in sentences 12 and 13?

A could

B except

C hear

D perform

48 What is the best transitional word for the beginning of sentence 19, going into the final paragraph?

J Moreover

K However

L Anyway

M Nevertheless

GO TO NEXT PAGE ➡

Mr. Monopoly

You've probably seen the tuxedoed gentleman on the cover of Monopoly games but did you know he has a name? (1) In 1936, the mustachioed mascot of the Parker Brothers game was dubbed Rich Uncle Pennybags. (2) From the beginning, his top hat has been one of the tokens included in the game, and within the first couple of years, his car was racing around the board. (3) In the 1950s, he received a Scottie dog as his companion, which remains the most popular piece, according to player polls. (4)

In 1988, the Parker Brothers company revealed the character's full name; Milburn Pennybags. (5) However, in 1999, he was renamed Mr. Monopoly. (6) He regularly appears in *Forbes* magazine's list of fictional millionaires, usually competing with Bruce Wayne. (7) Scrooge McDuck is usually listed as the richest fictional character. (8)

49 What is the correct punctuation for sentence 5?

A No change is necessary.

B In 1988, the Parker Brother's company revealed the character's full name; Milburn Pennybags.

C In 1988, the Parker Brothers company revealed the character's full name: Milburn Pennybags.

D In 1988, the Parker Brothers company revealed the characters' full name: Milburn Pennybags.

50 Which sentence should be removed from the passage to retain focus?

J sentence 1

K sentence 3

L sentence 6

M sentence 8

STOP

If there is still time remaining, you may review your answers.

MATH—PART 1

32 QUESTIONS   30 MINUTES

> **Directions:** Select the best answer out of the four choices.

1 Simplify the following expression: $4(3+2)^2$.

  A   20
  B   80
  C   100
  D   125

2 Find the quotient of 25.8 and 4.3.

  J   6.1
  K   6
  L   60
  M   .6

3 Add $2\frac{3}{8}$ and $4\frac{3}{5}$.

  A $6\frac{39}{40}$

  B $6\frac{4}{5}$

  C $6\frac{7}{8}$

  D $6\frac{17}{20}$

4 What is the least common multiple of 3, 9, and 18?

  J   18
  K   9
  L   36
  M   27

5 Find the difference of 6.3 and $\frac{1}{2}$.

  A   6.1

  B $5\frac{1}{4}$

  C $5\frac{3}{4}$

  D   5.8

6 What is the equivalent of $(+4) + (-3) - (-1)$?

  J   8
  K   3
  L   4
  M   2

7 Select the smallest prime number.

  A   4
  B   6
  C   7
  D   11

8 What is the product of $3\frac{2}{3}$ and 9?

  J   33
  K   27
  L   30
  M   32

9 Change $4\frac{3}{8}$ to a decimal.

  A   4.380
  B   4.750
  C   4.375
  D   4.675

10 Express 7.002 as a fraction. *Reduce to lowest terms.*

  J $7\frac{2}{100}$

  K $7\frac{1}{500}$

  L $7\frac{2}{1,000}$

  M $7\frac{1}{50}$

GO TO NEXT PAGE ➡

11 Without stopping, Maxine drives from Danbury to San Sebastian, a distance of 348 miles. If she leaves at 8 A.M. and arrives at 2 P.M., what was her average rate of speed?

A 62 mph
B 61 mph
C 59 mph
D 58 mph

12 Carlos deposits $2,400 in a bank account at a simple annual interest rate of 2.5%. How much will he have at the end of three and a half years?

J $2,650
K $2,590
L $2,610
M $2,720

13 The temperature is 70° Celsius at 4 P.M. If it increases 10% by 10 P.M. and then decreases 20% by 8 A.M. the next morning, what is the temperature at 8 A.M.? Round off to the nearest degree.

A 68°
B 71.5°
C 62°
D 71°

14 Harry receives a salary of $700 per week. Hal gets 20% more. What is their total salary for six weeks?

J $9,280
K $9,240
L $9,360
M $9,410

15 Rusty, Henry, and Linda have recorded a hit song. If Rusty gets $\frac{2}{5}$ of the income and Henry gets $\frac{1}{3}$ and they earn $450,000, how much does Linda receive?

A $110,000
B $120,000
C $100,000
D $115,000

16 The height of a wall on a blueprint of an office building is 2 inches. If the actual wall is 15 feet high, what is the ratio of the blueprint diagram to the actual height of the wall?

J 1 : 90
K 2 : 75
L not given
M 4 : 71

17 Thirty-five history books were distributed to a social studies class at the beginning of the semester. Five books were lost and the rest were returned. In simplest terms, what is the ratio of returned books to lost books?

A 5 : 1
B 7 : 2
C 8 : 1
D 6 : 1

18 The Zebra Chemical Company is planning to repackage 1,134 ounces of one of their chemicals into 1-pound containers. How many ounces remain after all of the chemicals are repackaged? (Sixteen ounces equal 1 pound.)

J 12 ounces
K 13 ounces
L 14 ounces
M 11 ounces

GO TO NEXT PAGE ➡

19 Barbara receives a base salary of $600 per week plus a 9% commission on sales over $1,000 per week. If she sold $5,000 for the week, what was her total salary for the week?

A $930

B $860

C $960

D $890

20 Emily works for 48 hours at the rate of $22 per hour for the first 40 hours and time-and-a-half for any hours above 40. What is her total salary?

J $1,144

K $1,250

L $1,380

M $1,360

Directions: Use the graph below to answer questions 21 and 22.

Mayberry Student Population

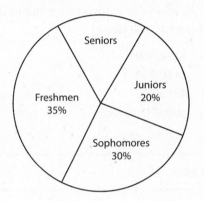

21 The circle graph shows the percentage of students in a particular year at Mayberry High School. If there are 2,800 students in the school, how many are seniors?

A   980

B   840

C   420

D   560

22 What is the ratio of juniors to sophomores? Simplify your answer.

J   2 : 3

K   not given

L   3 : 2

M   7 : 2

GO TO NEXT PAGE ➡

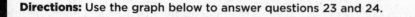

Directions: Use the graph below to answer questions 23 and 24.

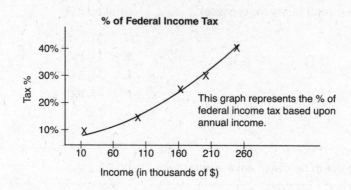

% of Federal Income Tax

This graph represents the % of federal income tax based upon annual income.

23 What is the best estimate of the income tax of someone earning $160,000 per year?

A $40,000
B $60,000
C $90,000
D $20,000

24 If someone paid $6,300 in federal income taxes, approximately how much did she or he earn for the year?

J $120,000
K $110,000
L $210,000
M $60,000

Directions: Use the chart below to answer questions 25 and 26.

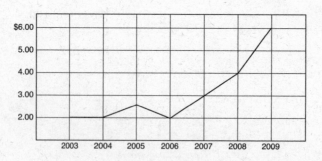

25 What is the approximate difference in the price of a gallon of gasoline between the years 2005 and 2009?

A $3.50
B $2.50
C $2.00
D $3.00

26 What was the average price for a gallon of gasoline in the years 2007 through and including 2009? Round off to the nearest cent.

J $2.00
K $3.00
L $2.50
M $4.33

GO TO NEXT PAGE ➡

TACHS PRACTICE EXAM 2

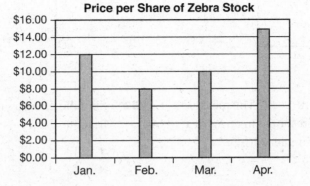

Price per Share of Zebra Stock

27 If an investor purchased 100 shares of Zebra stock in January and sold them in March, how much money did he or she make or lose?

A $200 gain
B $200 loss
C $150 gain
D $150 loss

28 Approximately, how much percent did the stock gain from February to April?

J 60%
K 120%
L 30%
M 90%

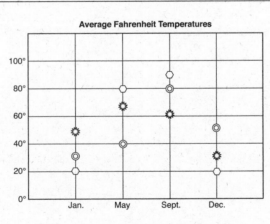

Average Fahrenheit Temperatures

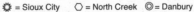

☀ = Sioux City   ⬡ = North Creek   ◎ = Danbury

29 Approximately, what is the difference in average temperatures between North Creek in January and North Creek in December?

A 0°
B 10°
C 15°
D 20°

30 What is the average 4-month temperature for Danbury?

J 40°
K 55°
L 50°
M 45°

GO TO NEXT PAGE ➡

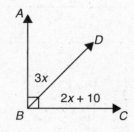

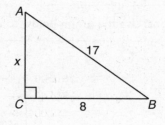

31 In the figure above, $AB \perp BC$. The measures of the angles are represented in terms of x. Find the measure of angle DBC.

A   36°

B   54°

C   42°

D   38°

32 Find the measure of side AC of the right triangle above.

J   13

K   12

L   15

M   14

MATH—PART 2

18 QUESTIONS   10 MINUTES

> **Directions:** Estimate the answer in your head. No writing is permitted. An exact answer is not expected.

33 Melissa is driving an average of 54 miles per hour. She leaves Morristown for Blue Ridge, a distance of 240 miles. Approximately how long should the drive take?

- **A** 5 hours
- **B** 4 hours
- **C** 3 hours
- **D** 6 hours

34 Groceries for the past four days cost $29, $18, $37, and $19. To the nearest whole dollar, what is the closest estimate of the average cost of food for these four days?

- **J** $29
- **K** $30
- **L** $26
- **M** $23

35 The cost of painting a square foot of the outside of a house is $2.10. Estimate the approximate cost of painting 354 square feet.

- **A** $500
- **B** $600
- **C** $800
- **D** $700

36 Carmen purchased $2\frac{3}{4}$ pounds of walnuts, $1\frac{7}{8}$ pounds of cashews, and $4\frac{5}{8}$ pounds of pecans. About how many pounds of nuts did Carmen purchase altogether?

- **J** 10 pounds
- **K** 7 pounds
- **L** 6 pounds
- **M** 11 pounds

37 Estimate $(.7)^3$.

- **A** .300
- **B** .350
- **C** .400
- **D** .450

38 A babysitter can earn $9.14 an hour or he can check out groceries for $11.87 per hour. What would the approximate difference in wages be for 10 hours of work?

- **J** $27
- **K** $34
- **L** $20
- **M** $18

39 Two dozen roses sell for $25.34. At the same cost per rose, how much would five roses cost?

- **A** $10
- **B** $9
- **C** $12
- **D** $5

40 About how much is the quotient of 6,512 and 813?

- **J** 6
- **K** 7
- **L** 9
- **M** 8

GO TO NEXT PAGE ➡

TACHS PRACTICE EXAM 2

41 Jessie deposited $822 into a bank account paying 3.25% simple annual interest. At this simple interest rate, about how much would the interest be after 4 years?

A $65

B $70

C $100

D $80

Number of Cars Manufactured by Year and Country, in millions

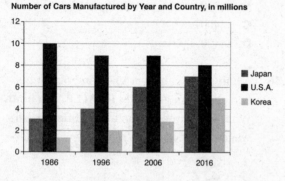

42 How many more cars were manufactured in the U.S.A. in 2006 than in Japan in 1986?

J 2.5 million

K 4 million

L 3 million

M 6 million

43 The area of a square is $4x^2$. Find its perimeter.

A $8x$

B $16x$

C $4x + 4$

D $4x$

44 Two hundred and ten dollars is to be divided equally into whole dollar amounts among a group of people. How many people are in the group?

J 16

K 15

L 17

M 13

45 Round 46.2476 to the nearest hundredth.

A 46.25

B 46.24

C 46.2

D 46.248

46 Malcolm earns $20 per hour and time-and-a-half for any time over 40 hours per week. If he worked for 46 hours last week, how much did he earn?

J $1,020

K $860

L $980

M $920

47 Hilda has $8,000 to save. If she saves part at a 3% simple annual interest and the remainder at 2% annual interest, she gets an annual return of $220. How much is she investing at 2%?

A $6,000

B $4,000

C $3,000

D $2,000

48 60 is what percent of 20?

J 200%

K 300%

L 250%

M 350%

GO TO NEXT PAGE ➡

49 The chart below shows the number of runs per game made by the Pittsburgh Mavericks. What was the mean for all five games?

Game	1	2	3	4	5
Number of Runs	8	4	4	10	8

A   8.3
B   6.9
C   8.1
D   6.8

50 If the price of a car is reduced by $800, and this represents a 20% reduction of the original price, what was the original price of the car?

J $5,000
K $5,500
L $4,000
M $6,000

If there is still time remaining, you may review your answers.

ABILITY

10 QUESTIONS   5 MINUTES

> **Directions:** For questions 1–3, the top three figures are similar in certain ways. Try to determine the similarity and then select the figure that continues the similarity.

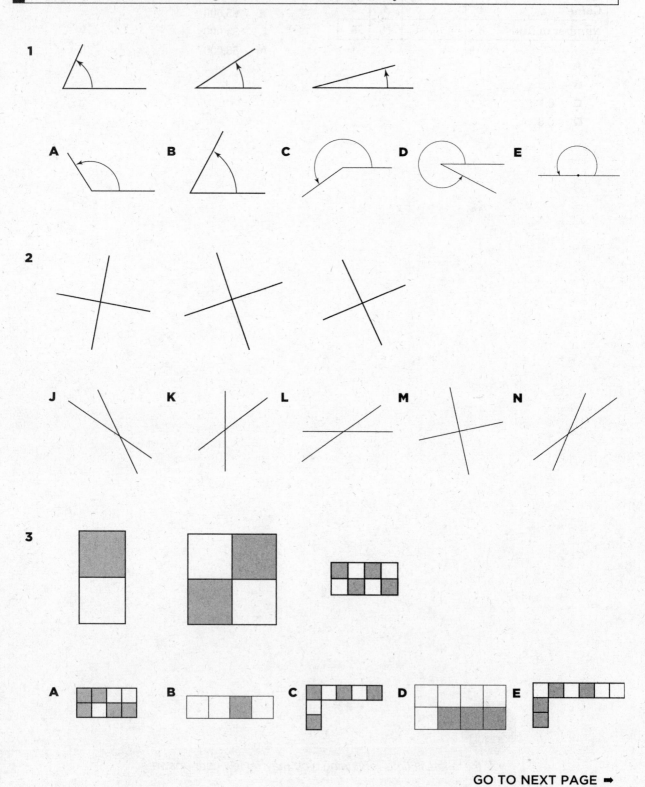

GO TO NEXT PAGE ➡

TACHS PRACTICE EXAM 2

Directions: For questions 4–7, in the illustrative example, the first figure is linked to the second figure. Using the same principle, select the form that is linked to the third figure.

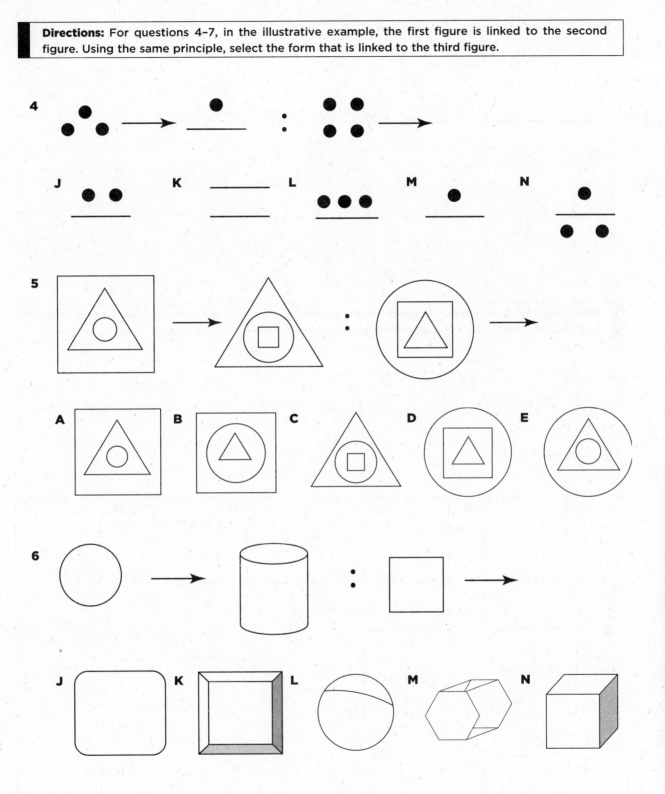

GO TO NEXT PAGE →

7

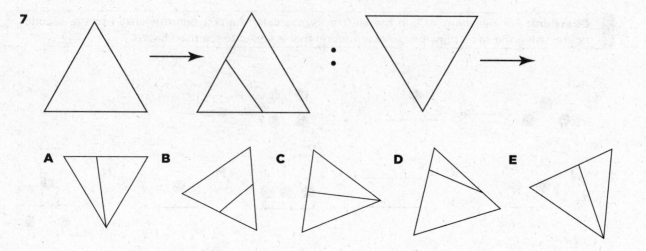

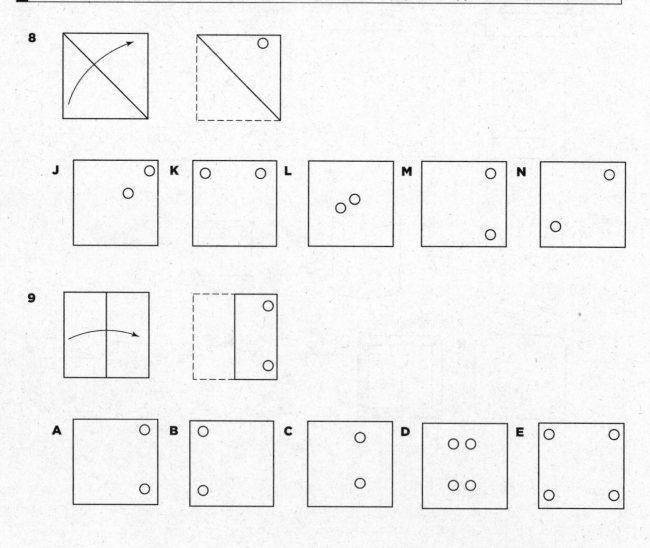

Directions: For questions 8–10, the diagrams on the first line indicate how a paper is to be folded and then punched. Select the diagram that indicates how the paper will appear after it is unfolded.

8

9

GO TO NEXT PAGE ➡

10

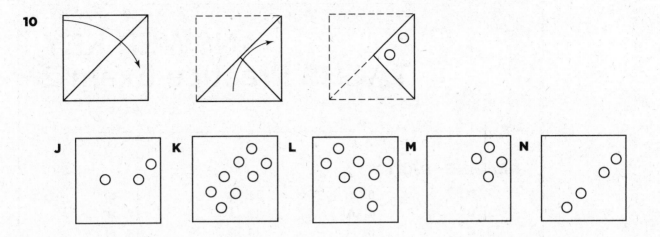

If there is still time remaining, you may review your answers.

TACHS PRACTICE EXAM 2   601

ANSWER KEY
TACHS Practice Exam 2

READING—PART 1

1. **D**	6. **J**	11. **A**	16. **L**
2. **L**	7. **A**	12. **J**	17. **B**
3. **C**	8. **M**	13. **B**	18. **M**
4. **K**	9. **C**	14. **K**	19. **B**
5. **D**	10. **J**	15. **B**	20. **J**

READING—PART 2

21. **B**	29. **D**	37. **B**	45. **A**
22. **K**	30. **J**	38. **K**	46. **K**
23. **D**	31. **A**	39. **D**	47. **B**
24. **K**	32. **J**	40. **J**	48. **K**
25. **D**	33. **D**	41. **D**	49. **D**
26. **K**	34. **K**	42. **K**	50. **L**
27. **D**	35. **D**	43. **A**	
28. **J**	36. **L**	44. **K**	

WRITTEN EXPRESSION—PART 1—ENGLISH

1. **E**	11. **C**	21. **A**	31. **A**
2. **M**	12. **L**	22. **K**	32. **L**
3. **B**	13. **D**	23. **C**	33. **B**
4. **J**	14. **L**	24. **M**	34. **L**
5. **B**	15. **D**	25. **B**	35. **A**
6. **M**	16. **J**	26. **L**	36. **L**
7. **C**	17. **B**	27. **C**	37. **C**
8. **N**	18. **L**	28. **J**	38. **L**
9. **C**	19. **B**	29. **B**	39. **B**
10. **N**	20. **L**	30. **K**	40. **L**

WRITTEN EXPRESSION—PART 2—PARAGRAPHS

41. **A**	44. **L**	47. **B**	50. **M**
42. **K**	45. **D**	48. **J**	
43. **D**	46. **J**	49. **C**	

ANSWER KEY
TACHS Practice Exam 2

MATH—PART 1

1. **C**	9. **C**	17. **D**	25. **A**
2. **K**	10. **K**	18. **L**	26. **M**
3. **A**	11. **D**	19. **C**	27. **B**
4. **J**	12. **L**	20. **J**	28. **M**
5. **D**	13. **C**	21. **C**	29. **A**
6. **M**	14. **K**	22. **J**	30. **L**
7. **C**	15. **B**	23. **A**	31. **C**
8. **J**	16. **J**	24. **M**	32. **L**

MATH—PART 2

33. **A**	38. **J**	43. **A**	48. **K**
34. **L**	39. **D**	44. **K**	49. **D**
35. **D**	40. **M**	45. **A**	50. **L**
36. **J**	41. **C**	46. **L**	
37. **B**	42. **M**	47. **D**	

ABILITY

1. **B**	4. **J**	7. **B**	10. **K**
2. **M**	5. **A**	8. **N**	
3. **E**	6. **N**	9. **E**	

Reading—Part 1

1. **(D)** *ir* (not) + *rational* = not rational, not reasonable

2. **(L)** *Precarious* is actually based on the root *prex* (pray). You might continue to pray when in a precarious position.

3. **(C)** *Assuage* means to comfort or make less severe.

4. **(K)** Bellona is the Roman goddess of war.

5. **(D)** To *wane* means to *decrease*; to wax means to increase. We usually see these words associated with phases of the moon.

6. **(J)** *Distraught* is related to the word *distract*. If you're *upset* or agitated, you're *really* distracted.

7. **(A)** Something *noisome* is offensive to the senses, especially smell. It's related to the word *annoy*.

8. **(M)** Wile E. Coyote is *crafty*, isn't he?

9. **(C)** Actually, the word *meander* (to wind) comes from a *winding* river named Menderes.

10. **(J)** *Durus* means hard, so *obdurate* means hard or *stubborn*.

11. **(A)** *Sage* is based on the word *sapere* (to know, to be *wise*).

12. **(J)** A *paragon* is a *model* of perfection or excellence.

13. **(B)** Valor is courage. It comes from a root meaning value, worth, or strength.

14. **(K)** *Solace* is *comfort*.

15. **(B)** Our hero is without trepidation.

16. **(L)** To *ostracize* is to banish. Voted off the island, the ostrich and the oyster were ostracized from the rest of the group.

17. **(B)** *Petty* is related to the French word *petit*, which means "small."

18. **(M)** Something *indelible* cannot be deleted.

19. **(B)** You'll always sound *precocious* now that you've studied.

20. **(J)** Remain *cognizant*. Remain *aware*.

Reading—Part 2

21. **(B)** First off, you should be able to tell that the words *bane* and *boon* are opposites, if not from your own rich vocabulary then from context clues. Rule out any choice that does not include opposites (A, C, or D). Only one choice remains—B.

22. **(K)** The article tells the reader that chestnuts undergo the formation of hard brown spines in order to keep people from getting the meat out, but this is said in jest; choice J is incorrect. Growing a protective casing in order to keep nuts *outside* this casing makes no sense; omit choice L. The return of unused nuts to the earth would probably happen equally well within or without the casing, and the article does not even mention this concept in any case; omit choice M. The only correct answer is K.

23. **(D)** While the author might think chestnuts are the best nuts around, the purpose of the article is not to make this point; indeed the passage hardly touches on that point. Rule out choice A. The author mentions that chestnuts can be used in many recipes, but the passage does not talk at any length about what those recipes might be; rule out choice B. The article at no point talks about the effect of chestnut production on the environment. Omit choice C. Therefore, the only true answer is choice D.

24. **(K)** A recipe based on a food substance must have at least traces of that substance in it or the recipe ceases to be a recipe based on that food substance; rule out choice J. For something to be interchangeable, one would have to know the original substance and the item being switched; rule out choice L. Workable is altogether too generic a term to give the sentence much meaning; rule out choice M. Choice K is the best choice.

25. **(D)** The author likes chestnuts *despite* the spines, and cactus are very different from chestnuts for a variety of reasons; one cannot, therefore, predict the author's opinion on another plant using this logic. Rule out both choices A and B. Not all cactus are edible, so choice C cannot work. Choice D is the only possible answer.

26. **(K)** Re-reading or memory proves that the correct answer is choice K.

27. **(D)** The author is not writing specifically about squirrels, so you can immediately rule out choice B. Discussing squirrels does not help make any points about the usefulness of chestnuts; omit choice C. Choice A is simply distracting you from the real answer, which is choice D.

28. **(J)** Context clues are your best weapon here. The sentence refers to squirrels being able to get through the chestnut's protective casing; furthermore, the sentence uses the word *loot*. Both of these facts should lead you to the conclusion that the squirrel is able to get the nuts open and steal the meats within—in other words, the squirrel is successful. The option that best matches up with the idea of success is choice J.

29. **(D)** If you re-read paragraph 3, you see the final two sentences read, "Need fresh meat or seafood? Go to X or Y." The structure of these two sentences are intended to be parallel, meaning, you can match meat with X and seafood with Y. Verifying that seafood equals Y reveals that a *poissonerie* is a fish shop.

30. **(J)** Re-reading the passage shows that choices K, L, and M all appear in the text. Choice J is the only sentence that does not appear.

31. **(A)** As the name implies, a megastore is likely to be big. Consider other words that use the prefix "mega." The option that best illustrates the concept of something really big is choice A.

32. **(J)** The author is describing the way the French shop for food; he or she is not happy with the inability to buy products in bulk; therefore, we cannot say he or she approves

of the French method of getting food. Rule out choice K. However, the author also seems fascinated by the differences in the way Americans and French people acquire food. Therefore, we cannot say that the author necessarily disapproves of the French ways; rule out choice L. The author generally seems intrigued by the situation, so we should not choose choice M. The best answer is choice J.

33. **(D)** The passage states that food generally, but not always, comes in small packages. Therefore, you can rule out choices A and B. Choice C is tempting, but choice D is best due to the author's statement in paragraph 4 that looking at the way food is distributed reveals cultural differences in an intriguing way.

34. **(K)** Since shoppers in France generally cannot get things in large sizes, rule out any choice that indicates a large scale purchase. That rules out choices J, L, and M. While the text does not specifically mention liters of milk, it does mention that shoppers can purchase liquids in liter sizes; buying milk in this size is therefore very likely. The best answer is choice K.

35. **(D)** The article is all about how we can use commonplace activities, like shopping, to learn about other cultures; the title that best describes this concept is choice D. Choice A is a nonsequitur, and B and C only address certain points the article makes rather than considering the global picture.

36. **(L)** As with any fairy tale, symbols abound. Good is often linked with beauty, evil with ugliness. So, too, here. The ugly daughter and the snake are symbols of evil; rule out choices J and M. Choice K is tempting because the fairy chooses to make herself beautiful at times. However, as she can take both good and evil forms, she is essentially a symbol for justice and balance, and takes neither side. The best answer is L. The beautiful girl is nothing but beautiful, which makes her a consistent representation of good.

37. **(B)** Since this story talks about a beautiful girl who is forced to do the family's work, the story of Cinderella should leap to mind rather than a boy suddenly given magic powers (A), or a boy who refuses to grow up (C), or a girl who has a wild dream on a sunny day (D).

38. **(K)** The crone appears to be tired and very thirsty; anyone in such a state when given water would feel thankful for the gift. Therefore, in context gratitude fits best with the idea of thankfulness.

39. **(D)** A synonym means something that means the same thing as something else; bad and evil are synonyms. A crone is an old woman; therefore, choice B cannot be right nor can A, for a crone is not a man, and a crone is not young. A crone could be a queen, but statuesque is a word that describes strength, which is inconsistent with the idea of crone. The best answer is choice D.

40. **(J)** Water in the story is depicted as something desired, needed, and somewhat difficult to get without aid (otherwise it would not be down in the well!). Look at your options and figure out which choices fit these parameters. Choices L and M do not work, as no one desires or needs fear or greed. K is incorrect because the question asks you what water symbolizes; water cannot symbolize water, since the concept of "symbol" requires something concrete to represent something abstract. In other words, a concrete object cannot represent itself. Choice J is the right answer.

41. **(D)** The story, as do most fairy tales, rewards the good and punishes the bad. Choice A, therefore, is clearly wrong, as it would be a strange fairy tale indeed that teaches the reader to do bad rather than good. Choice C is also wrong for a similar reason; apathy, while not as terrible as evil, is nevertheless a social problem of its own sort. Choice B is tempting, but justice in the story comes to the participants through the actions of the fairy; the fairy is not a character with whom we can feel kinship or sympathy. She is too cold and remote, as a symbol of justice should be. Therefore, the best answer is D; we are told through the story that we should emulate the beautiful girl, be kind, be generous, be patient—in short, have manners.

42. **(K)** The author is trying to teach a lesson about treating others well; this means the author has an opinion to share and that therefore choices L and M are inappropriate. The mother in this story does not treat her children equally well. The author, therefore, probably disagrees with this behavior; rule out choice J. The best answer is choice K.

43. **(A)** The idea of antonym is that of one thing being opposite another. A widow is a woman whose husband has died; therefore, the opposite of a widow would be a woman currently married. This rules out choices B, C, and D.

44. **(K)** According to the passage, Marie Antoinette felt most free on the Trianon estate.

45. **(A)** The passage supplies you with birth dates and coronation dates; simple subtraction reveals that Marie Antoinette was fourteen when she took the throne.

46. **(K)** To *repair* usually means to "fix," but not so here. The context of the passage talks about Marie Antoinette feeling pressured and desiring escape. The context, therefore, defines the phrase "to repair to" as fleeing, which is the correct contextual definition. The remaining two choices are included for camouflage purposes and do not apply to this context.

47. **(B)** Re-reading or memory tells you that the passage states that Marie Antoinette was married to King Louis XVI.

48. **(K)** Marie Antoinette's lack of concern for her subjects' hunger implies a callous, selfish attitude. Such a ruler would be highly unlikely to institute reform; rule out choice L. Marie Antoinette may have liked cake, but nothing about her statement necessarily makes it so; rule out choice M. We might infer that her lack of concern for others is balanced by a great concern for the self, but we cannot be certain; rule out choice J. The best answer is choice K; it is clear that whatever else Marie Antoinette may have thought, she worried little for the troubles of those surrounding her—neither the hunger of her subjects nor the diplomatic constraints of her husband and court. Choice K is the best answer.

49. **(D)** The passage suggests that Marie Antoinette was unique in that instead of putting up with the constraints on her behavior demanded by court she created a new way of life. This concept implies that most other French queens had forced themselves to put up with the constraints, which of course means that choices A and B cannot be true. Choice C is tempting, but the passage does not reveal specifically that this statement is true. Indeed, kings may have been the primary avenue through which queens lost their independence. The best answer is choice D, for it is both true and reasonably supportable based on the information in the passage.

50. **(L)** If Marie Antoinette was striving to be sarcastic, which she was, when she said the peasants should be eating cake rather than bread, then one can correctly conclude that cake is not something peasants typically have in their possession. Choice K is clearly wrong. What everyone knows about cake, moreover, is that while it generally tastes good, it is not healthy. Rule out choice J. The passage does not address choice M at all; omit it. The best answer is choice L.

Written Expression—Part 1—English

1. **(E)** *(No mistakes)*

2. **(M)** Change dictionery to dictionary.

3. **(B)** Abett should be abet.

4. **(J)** Dilemma has two m's and no n's.

5. **(B)** There is no u in forty.

6. **(M)** Grammar has an a, not an e.

7. **(C)** Precede contains a c, not an s.

8. **(N)** *(No mistakes)* This one is tricky. *Lightning* and *lightening* are two different words, both spelled correctly. *Whether* is also spelled correctly; it's a different word than *weather*, which is the category of thunder and lightning. Remember that you are looking for spelling here, not categories.

9. **(C)** Change populer to popular.

10. **(N)** *(No mistakes)*

11. **(C)** The word *speaking* is not a proper adjective: French-speaking cities.

12. **(L)** The word *novels* should not be capitalized.

13. **(D)** *(No mistakes)*

14. **(L)** Days of the week are capitalized, but the word *weekend* is not.

15. **(D)** *(No mistakes)*

16. **(J)** Capitalize the names of specific groups: Democrats and Republicans.

17. **(B)** Capitalize the first word in a sentence, even if it is a quote within another sentence.

18. **(L)** In this case, the first word of the quote is not the beginning of a sentence. Can you tell the difference between this example and the previous one?

19. **(B)** Official documents, such as the U.S. Constitution, are capitalized.

20. **(L)** Capitalize acronyms and initialisms, such as NASA and CIA.

21. **(A)** An interrupter, you know, should be separated by two commas, two dashes, or a pair of parentheses. However, don't mix the punctuation by using a comma and a dash.

22. **(K)** The comma here is unnecessary. It separates essential information from the sentence.

23. **(C)** This is an indirect question, so it does not require a question mark.

24. **(M)** *(No mistakes)*

25. **(B)** Use a comma after the year.

26. **(L)** Don't forget the period at the end of a sentence.

27. **(C)** The comma after the final adjective is unnecessary. Try replacing the commas with the word *and*, and you'll hear that it doesn't make sense: Bo enjoys a tall *and* cool *and* glass of lemonade.

28. **(J)** The comma here is not necessary; the introductory material is not completed.

29. **(B)** In a quote, commas should go inside the quotation marks.

30. **(K)** The titles of novels are italicized or underlined.

31. **(A)** The comma is not needed here.

32. **(L)** The actors performed *well*. *Well* is an adverb describing how they performed.

33. **(B)** The plural pronoun *their* does not agree with its singular antecedent *doctor*.

34. **(L)** The word *your* is possessive. The contraction *you're* stands for *you are*.

35. **(A)** The word *myself* cannot be used by itself as a subject or an object. Use the words *I* or *me*. (In this case it's a subject: *I*.)

36. **(L)** We should *have* known better. *Have* is a verb, while *of* is a preposition.

37. **(C)** Check for parallelism: the first three items in the series are prepositional phrases, but the last one is an adverb.

38. **(L)** Choice L is the clearest sentence.

39. **(B)** This choice simplifies the expression without changing its meaning.

40. **(L)** This sentence goes off on a tangent, so the paragraph loses focus here. Hunting for treasure is a fun game, though.

Written Expression—Part 2—Paragraphs

41. **(A)** In the original sentence, the word *which* requires a comma before it. (The word *that* does not require a comma.) Choices B and C contain additional comma errors, and choice D contains an awkward fragment.

42. **(K)** When a new speaker enters a conversation, each person's part of the dialogue should have a separate paragraph. In this case, it would allow the reader to easily differentiate between the two speakers.

43. **(D)** The other choices may have something to do with the story, but the overall theme is the love the writer witnessed.

44. **(L)** The correct word is *considered*, not *considering*.

45. **(D)** The information in sentence 8 was already stated earlier in the paragraph so this sentence is unnecessary.

46. **(J)** The original sentence includes a comma splice. The best solution is to use a semicolon (or a period) to separate the sentences. Choices K and L misuse commas and semicolons. Choice M leaves out necessary information.

47. **(B)** The word *accept* is mistakenly spelled as *except* twice.

48. **(J)** The word *moreover* tells us that additional material is to come.

49. **(C)** A colon is used to introduce material. The other choices misuse the semicolon and the apostrophe.

50. **(M)** The article focuses on the Monopoly mascot, not other fictional millionaires.

Math—Part 1

1. **(C)** Simplify the expression in the parentheses, square it, and then multiply by 4.

$$4(3 + 2)^2 = 4(5)^2 = 4(25) = 100$$

2. **(K)** First, move the decimal point one place to the right, then divide 258 by 43.

$$\begin{array}{r} 6 \\ 43\overline{)258} \\ -258 \\ \hline 0 \end{array}$$

3. **(A)** Find the least common denominator and add.

$$2\frac{3}{8} = \frac{15}{40}$$
$$+4\frac{3}{5} = \frac{24}{40}$$
$$\overline{6\frac{39}{40}}$$

4. **(J)** A multiple of a number is the product of the number and a positive integer. A common multiple of several numbers is a multiple of each of those numbers that they all share. Obviously, the least common multiple is the smallest such multiple.

$$3 \times 6 = 18$$
$$9 \times 2 = 18$$
$$18 \times 1 = 18$$

5. **(D)** Change $\frac{1}{2}$ to a decimal and subtract.

$$\begin{array}{r} 6.3 \\ -\frac{1}{2} = -.5 \\ \hline 5.8 \end{array}$$

6. **(M)** When you subtract, change the sign in the parentheses.

$$(+4) + (-3) - (-1) = +4 - 3 + 1 = +1 + 1 = +2$$

7. **(C)** A prime number has no other factors than 1 and itself.

   (A) $4 = 2 \times 2$ ✘
   (B) $6 = 3 \times 2$ ✘
   (C) $7 = 7 \times 1$ ✔
   (D) $11 = 11 \times 1$ ✘ (not the *smallest* prime)

8. **(J)** Change $3\frac{2}{3}$ to an improper fraction and multiply.

$$3\frac{2}{3} \times 9 = \frac{11}{\underset{1}{3}} \times \overset{3}{9} = 33$$

9. **(C)** Divide 8 into 3 and do not round off.

$$
\begin{array}{r}
.375 \\
8\overline{)3.000} \\
-2\,4 \\
\hline
60 \\
-56 \\
\hline
40 \\
-40 \\
\hline
0
\end{array}
\qquad
4\frac{3}{8} = 4.375
$$

10. **(K)** Three decimal places represent thousandths.

$$7.002 = 7\frac{2}{1000} = 7\frac{1}{500}$$

11. **(D)** Find the time between 8 A.M. and 2 P.M. and then divide that number into the distance.

$$
\begin{array}{cc}
2 \text{ P.M.} & 6\overline{)348} \\
-\ 8 \text{ A.M.} & -30\downarrow \\
\hline
6 \text{ hours} & 48 \\
& -48 \\
\cline{2-2}
& 0
\end{array}
$$

with quotient 58 above.

12. **(L)**

$$
\begin{array}{r}
.025 \times 3.5 \times \$2,400 = \quad \$210 \\
+ \ \$2,400 \\
\hline
\$2,610
\end{array}
$$

13. **(C)** By 10 P.M., the temperature increases by 10%, so we can multiply 70° by 110%. Then it drops by 20%, so at 8 A.M. in the morning the temperature is only 80% of what it was at 10 P.M. the previous evening.

   Ten percent increase in temperature by 10 P.M.:

$$110\% = 1.10$$

$$
\begin{array}{r}
70° \\
\times\ 1.10 \\
\hline
7\ 00 \\
70\ 00 \\
\hline
77.00
\end{array}
$$

If it drops 20% by 8 A.M., the temperature is only 80% of what it was the previous 10 P.M.:

$$80\% = .80$$

$$\begin{array}{r} 77 \\ \times\ .80 \\ \hline 61.60 \end{array}$$

$$61.6 \approx 62$$

14. **(K)** Hal's salary is 20% more than Harry's, so multiply Harry's salary by 120%. Then add their salaries for six weeks.

$$120\% = 1.20$$

Harry's weekly salary = $700

Hal's weekly salary = $700 × 1.20 = $840

Six weeks' salary for Harry: 6 × $700 = $4,200

+ Six weeks' salary for Hal: 6 × $840 = $5,040

$9,240

15. **(B)** Add $\frac{2}{5}$ and $\frac{1}{3}$ and then subtract from 1. To determine Linda's share, multiply the resultant fraction by the total earned; $450,000.

Rusty's share: $\frac{2}{5} = \frac{6}{15}$

+ Henry's share: $\frac{1}{3} = \frac{5}{15}$

$$\frac{11}{15}$$

Linda's share: $1 - \frac{11}{15} = \frac{15}{15} - \frac{11}{15} = \frac{4}{15}$

$$\frac{4}{\cancel{15}} \times \$\cancel{450,000}\,^{30,000} = \$120,000$$

16. **(J)** There are 12 inches in a foot, so to change 15 feet to inches, multiply 15 by 12. Then we can compare the same units (inches).

$$15 \text{ feet} = 15 \times 12 \text{ inches} = 180 \text{ inches}$$

$$\frac{\text{blueprint measure}}{\text{actual wall measure}} = \frac{2 \text{ inches}}{180 \text{ inches}} = \frac{1}{90}$$

17. **(D)** Determine the number of returned books and then show the ratio of returned books to lost books.

Lost books: 5

Returned books: 30

Total books distributed: 35

$$\frac{\text{returned books}}{\text{lost books}} = \frac{30}{5} = \frac{6}{1}$$

18. **(L)** One pound equals 16 ounces, so divide 1,134 by 16 and then determine the remainder.

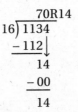

19. **(C)** Start with a base salary of $600 for the week. If Barbara sold $5,000, subtract $1,000 and multiply the result by 9%.

Commission based on: $5,000 – $1,000 = $4,000

$$\begin{aligned}
\text{Base salary:} &= \$600 \\
+ \text{ Commission: } .09 \times \$4,000 &= \$360 \\
\hline
&\quad\ \$960
\end{aligned}$$

20. **(J)** Multiply 40 hours by $22 per hour for the regular wages. She worked 8 hours overtime, which is paid at one-and-a-half times $22 per hour, so multiply 8 by 1.5 × $22. Then add the two figures.

$$\begin{aligned}
\$22 \times 40 &= \$880 \\
+8 \times 1.5 \times \$22 = 12 \times \$22 &= \$264 \\
\hline
\$1,&144
\end{aligned}$$

21. **(C)** To find the percentage of seniors, add the junior, freshmen, and sophomore percentages and subtract from 100%. Multiply the result by the total number of students in Mayberry High School.

$$\begin{aligned}
\text{Freshmen: } 35\% \qquad &\qquad \text{Seniors: } 100\% - 85\% = 15\% \\
\text{Juniors: } 20\% & \\
+ \text{ Sophomores: } 30\% & \\
\hline
85\% &
\end{aligned}$$

$$\begin{array}{r}
2800 \\
\times\ .15 \\
\hline
14000 \\
28000 \\
\hline
420.00
\end{array}$$

22. **(J)** The easiest way to find the ratio of juniors to sophomores is to just compare the percentages.

$$\frac{\text{juniors}}{\text{sophomores}} = \frac{20\%}{30\%} = \frac{2}{3}$$

23. **(A)** Find $160,000 on the horizontal axis, go up the solid line, and follow across to the vertical axis.

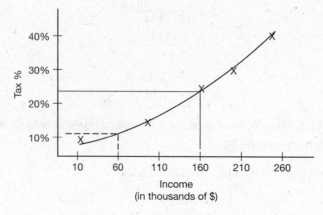

It looks as if the solid horizontal line intersects the vertical axis at 24%.

$$.24 \times \$160,000 = \$38,400$$

The closest choice we are given is $40,000.

24. **(M)** The best way of handling this problem is to check the taxes paid in each category.

As indicated by the broken line, the taxes paid on an income of $60,000 appear to be about 11%.

$$.11 \times \$60,000 = \$6,600$$

The taxes paid on the other incomes are much more than $6,600, so the best choice is $60,000.

25. **(A)** Approximate the price of 1 gallon of gasoline in 2005 and 2009 and subtract.

Approximate price of a gallon of gas in 2009: $6.00
−Approximate price of a gallon of gas in 2005: $2.50
_____
$3.50

26. **(M)** Add the prices of a gallon of gas in 2007, 2008, and 2009 and divide by 3. Round off to the nearest cent.

Price for one gallon of gas:

$$
\begin{array}{r}
2007:\ \ \$3.00 \\
2008:\ \ \$4.00 \\
+\ 2009:\ \ \$6.00 \\
\hline
\$13.00
\end{array}
$$

$$
\begin{array}{r}
4.333 \approx 4.33 \\
3\overline{)13.000} \\
-12\downarrow \\
\hline
1\,0 \\
-9\downarrow \\
\hline
10 \\
-9\downarrow \\
\hline
10 \\
-9 \\
\hline
1
\end{array}
$$

27. **(B)** Find the price of one share of Zebra stock in January and then in March. Find the difference, and since the investor purchased 100 shares, multiply by 100.

Price of one share of Zebra stock:

$$
\begin{array}{r}
\text{January: } \$12.00 \\
- \text{ March: } \$10.00 \\
\hline
\$\ 2.00 \ \ \times 100 = \$200 \text{ (loss)}
\end{array}
$$

28. **(M)** Determine the difference in the price of one share between February and April. Then, compare the difference to the price of the stock in February.

Price of one share of Zebra stock:

$$
\begin{array}{r}
\text{April: } \quad \$15 \\
- \text{ February: } \$8 \\
\hline
\$7
\end{array}
$$

$$\frac{7}{8} = .875 \approx .88 \approx .90$$

29. **(A)** Find the temperatures in North Creek in January and in December and subtract.

North Creek Temperatures:

$$
\begin{array}{r}
\text{January: } \quad 20° \\
- \text{ December: } 20° \\
\hline
0°
\end{array}
$$

30. **(L)** Determine the temperatures for all the months for Danbury and divide by 4.

Temperatures in Danbury:

$$
\begin{array}{r}
\text{January: } \quad 30° \\
\text{May: } \qquad 40° \\
\text{Sept: } \qquad 80° \\
+ \text{ Dec: } \qquad 50° \\
\hline
200°
\end{array}
\qquad
4\overline{)200}\,^{50}
$$

31. **(C)** Angles ABD and DBC are complementary.

$$3x + 2x + 10 = 90$$
$$5x + 10 = 90$$
$$5x = 80$$
$$x = 16$$

The measure of angle $DBC = 2x + 10 = 2(16) + 10 = 32 + 10 = 42°$

32. **(L)** Use the Pythagorean theorem.

$$a^2 + b^2 = c^2$$
$$8^2 + x^2 = 17^2$$
$$64 + x^2 = 289$$
$$x^2 = 225$$
$$x = 15$$

Math—Part 2

33. **(A)** Round off 54 to 50 and leave 240 alone.

$$\frac{240}{50} = 4\frac{4}{5} \approx 5$$

34. **(L)** Round up $29 to $30, $18 to $20, $19 to $20, and round down $37 to $35. Add all the dollars and divide by 4.

$$30 + 20 + 20 + 35 = 105$$

$$\frac{\$105}{4} \approx \$26$$

35. **(D)** Round off $2.10 to $2.00 and 354 to 350. Then multiply.

$$\$2 \times 350 = \$700$$

36. **(J)** Round $\frac{3}{4}$ up to 1 and $\frac{7}{8}$ up to 1. Round $\frac{5}{8}$ down to $\frac{1}{2}$.

Full pounds: $2 + 1 + 4 = 7$

Fractions: $1 + 1 + \frac{1}{2} = 2\frac{1}{2}$

$$7 + 2\frac{1}{2} = 9\frac{1}{2}$$

The closest choice is 10 pounds.

37. **(B)** Seven-tenths squared is easy. It's seven times seven, with two decimal places. Round off .49 to .50 and multiply once again by .7.

$$(.7)^2 = .49$$
$$.49 \approx .50$$
$$.7 \times .50 = .350 = .35$$

38. **(J)** The approximate difference of $11.87 and $9.14 is $2.70.

$$\$2.70 \times 10 = \$27$$

39. **(D)** Round off $25.34 to $25. Divide by 24 to get the cost of one rose and then multiply by 5 to determine the cost of five roses.

$$\frac{\$25}{24} \approx \$1 \text{ (approximate cost of 1 rose)}$$

$$5 \times \$1 = \$5 \text{ (approximate cost of 5 roses)}$$

40. **(M)** Round off 6,512 to 6,400 and 813 to 800.

$$\frac{6,400}{800} = 8$$

41. **(C)** Round off $822 to $800 and 3.25% to 3%. Then, find 3% of $800 and multiply the result by 4.

$$.03 \times \$800 = \$24$$
$$4 \times \$24 = \$96$$

The closest estimate is choice C, $100.

42. **(M)**

Number of Cars Manufactured by Year and Country, in millions

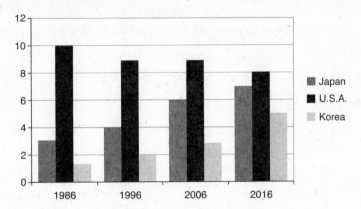

In 2006, the U.S.A. manufactured 9 million cars. In 1986, Japan manufactured 3 million cars.

$$9 \text{ million} - 3 \text{ million} = 6 \text{ million}$$

43. **(A)** If the area equals $4x^2$, and the area of a square equals side^2, then each side of the square equals $2x$ as shown in the figure below.

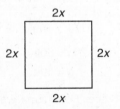

The perimeter equals $2x + 2x + 2x + 2x$, which equals $8x$.

44. **(K)** Test each answer choice to see which produces a whole number when it is divided into 210:

Choice J: $\dfrac{210}{16} = 13.125$ ✗

Choice K: $\dfrac{210}{15} = 14$ ✔

Choice L: $\dfrac{210}{17} = 12.35$ ✗

Choice M: $\dfrac{210}{13} = 16.15$ ✗

Therefore, choice K is the correct answer.

45. **(A)** Look at one place beyond the hundredth and round off.

$$\downarrow$$

$$46.2\ 4\ 7\ 6 \approx 46.25$$

46. **(L)**

40 hours:	$20 \times 40 = $800
+ 6 hours overtime:	$6 \times 1.5 \times $20 = $180
46 hours:	$980

47. **(D)** Let x equal the amount invested at 3% and let $8,000 - x$ represent the amount invested at 2%.

$$.03x + .02(8,000 - x) = 220$$

Multiply by 100:

$$100(.03x + .02(8,000 - x) = 220)$$
$$3x + 2(8,000 - x) = 22,000$$
$$3x + 16,000 - 2x = 22,000$$
$$x = $6,000$$

$$\text{Amount at 2\%} = $8,000 - x$$
$$= $8,000 - $6,000$$
$$= $2,000$$

48. **(K)** Let x equal the percentage.

$$\frac{is}{of} = \frac{percent}{100}$$

$$\frac{60}{20} = \frac{x}{100}$$

$$20x = 6000$$
$$x = 300$$

49. **(D)** Eight runs were scored twice. Four runs were scored twice and ten runs were scored once.

$$\frac{(2 \times 8) + (2 \times 4) + 10}{5} = \frac{16 + 8 + 10}{5} = \frac{34}{5} = 6.8$$

50. **(L)** Let x equal the original price of the car.

$$800 = .20x$$
$$4,000 = x$$